Gibbs, Giden, Locher, Turner & Senet LLP
CONSTRUCTION LAW SERIES

ACRET'S CALIFORNIA MECHANICS LIEN LAWS

2012 Edition

With foreword by Glenn E. Turner and annotations by Michael Wayne and Christopher Ng

MICHAEL I. WAYNE
CHRISTOPHER E. NG

BNi Building News

BNi® Building News

Construction Law Series

Other books by the attorneys at Gibbs, Giden, Locher, Turner & Senet LLP and Published by BNi Building News;

Acret's California Construction Laws Annotated – Volume I

Acret's California Construction Laws Annotated – Volume II, Public Contract Code

Acret's California Construction Law Digest

Acret's California Construction Law Manual, Contractor's Edition

Acret's California Public Contract Laws Annotated.

Acknowledgments. The authors would like to thank William. D. Locher, John Conrad, Luke N. Eaton and Angie Yoon for their contributions to this book. The authors would also like to thank the other attorneys and staff at Gibbs, Giden, Locher, Turner and Senet LLP for their assistances with this book.

This book is current with California Legislation enacted through November 1, 2011.

Los Angeles Office
1880 Century Park East
12th Floor
Los Angeles, California 90067
Telephone: 310-552-3400
Facsimile: 310-552-0805

Las Vegas Office
7450 Arroyo Crossing Parkway
Suite 270
Las Vegas, Nevada 89113-4059
Telephone: 702-836-9800
Facsimile: 702-836-9802

BNi® Building News

EDITOR-IN-CHIEF
William D. Mahoney, P.E.

TECHNICAL SERVICES
Ana Varela
Katherine Ritch

COVER DESIGN
Robert O. Wright

ANAHEIM
1612 S. Clementine St.
Anaheim, CA 92802

VISTA
990 Park Center Drive, Suite E
Vista, CA 92081

1-800-873-6397

ISBN 978-155701-754-3

Table of Contents

Author Biographies

Michael I. Wayne, Esq.
Partner
Gibbs, Giden, Locher, Turner & Senet LLP
1880 Century Park East, 12th Floor
Los Angeles, California 90067-1621
(310) 552-3400 – Phone
(310) 552-0805 – Fax
Email: mwayne@gglts.com

Professional Experience:

Mr. Wayne is a partner at the firm, where he is a member of the Commercial Litigation Department. His practice concentrates in the areas of commercial, construction and business litigation.

In construction-related litigation matters, Mr. Wayne has represented owners, contractors, subcontractors, suppliers and design professionals in connection with private and public and commercial and residential real estate developments. These developments have included commercial and industrial complexes, federal and state government projects, theaters, hospitals, and retail facilities.

In commercial litigation matters, Mr. Wayne regularly represents manufacturers and distributors in a variety of disputes including complex and class action litigation. He has co-authored manuals relating to statutory rights on California public and private construction projects Mr. Wayne frequently lectures on various topics related to construction and commercial litigation.

Practice Areas:
Commercial Litigation; Construction and Business Litigation

Education:
Southwestern University School of Law (J.D.), Los Angeles, CA, 1993

Loyola Marymount University (B.A., History), 1989

Professional Memberships and Associations:
State Bar of California
Los Angeles County Bar Association

Speaking Engagements:
Purchasing Law in California
Public and Private Construction Law in California
Statutory Remedies on Public and Private Projects

Bar Admissions:
California Bar No. 169840, 1994
U.S. District Court Central District of California, 1994

Publications:
Michael I. Wayne, *New California Law Alert*, eInsight (Construction Law Update), October 5, 2010.

Michael I. Wayne, *New California Mechanic's Lien Law Assembly Bill 457 Passes, Effective 1/1/2011*, eInsight (Construction Law Update), October 28, 2009.

Michael I. Wayne, California Construction Law – 2007 Edition, Chapter 15 - Public Works Claims Procedures (HLK Global Communications, Inc. 2007).

Michael I. Wayne, California Construction Law – 2007 Edition, Chapter 20 - Bankruptcy and Chapter Twenty-Two Procurement (HLK Global Communications, Inc. 2007).

Representative Clients and Experience:
Consolidated Electrical Distributors, Inc.
Porsche Design
Core-Mark International, Inc./Fleming Companies, Inc.
Penhall Company

Honors & Awards:
American Jurisprudence Award in Property

Community Activities:
John Wayne Cancer Institute

Author Biographies

Christopher E. Ng, Esq.
Partner
Gibbs, Giden, Locher, Turner & Senet LLP
1880 Century Park East, 12th Floor
Los Angeles, California 90067-1621
(310) 552-3400 – Phone
(310) 552-0805 – Fax
Email: cng@gglts.com

Professional Experience:
Christopher E. Ng is a partner with the firm where he has worked for over ten years. His areas of practice are commercial, construction and business litigation.

Mr. Ng represents business and governmental entities in a wide range of business and construction disputes. He focuses on successfully resolving such disputes in a cost-effective manner through prelitigation negotiation, mediation, arbitration and trial.

Mr. Ng is a member of the State Bar of California and is licensed to practice in all California state and federal courts. He is an active member of the American Bar and the Los Angeles County Bar Associations. Mr. Ng is an educator as an Associate Professor of Business Law at the School of Business and Economics at California State University, Northridge where he teaches subjects including Contracts, Intentional Torts, Negligence, Civil Procedure and Alternate Dispute Resolution. Mr. Ng is also an active speaker and a published author. He is a frequent contributor to several national publications on a wide variety of topics including legal, technology, financial, and health and wellness.

Mr. Ng earned his Juris Doctorate degree from Pepperdine University School of Law, *cum laude*, in 2001. He received a Bachelor of Science degree in Business Administration from California State University, Northridge, *magna cum laude*, in 1998.

Practice Areas:
Collections and Repossessions; Construction Contracts; Construction Liens; Contracts; Debtor/Creditor; Defects; Government Construction Contracts; Uniform Commercial Code

Education:
Pepperdine University School of Law (J.D., *cum laude*), Malibu, CA, 2001
Judicial Clerk for The Honorable Lawrence J. Mira, The Honorable James A. Albracht, The Honorable Terry J Adamson, Los Angeles County Superior Court, West District, 1999-2000
California State University, Northridge (B.S., Business Administration, *magna cum laude*), Northridge, CA, 1998

Professional Memberships and Associations:
State Bar of California
District of Columbia Bar
Los Angeles County Bar Association
American Bar Association

Speaking Engagements:
Purchasing Law in California

Surviving in the Construction Industry for Material Suppliers and Distributors

A Subcontractor's Guide to Surviving in the Construction Industry

Statutory Remedies on Public and Private Projects (Lorman Education Services)

Construction Liens and Other Construction Issues in California (Lorman Education Services)

Mechanic's Liens and Other Remedies in California

Construction Claims in California

Advanced Construction Law Seminar Series - Project Administration: Termination and Project Close-Out and Post Completion Issues

Bar Admissions:
California Bar No. 216969, 2001
District of Columbia 2011
U.S. District Courts Central, 2001
U.S. District Courts, Eastern, Northern and Southern Districts of California, 2002

Publications:
Christopher Ng, California Construction Law – 2007 Edition, Chapter 11 - Project Closeout (HLK Global Communications, Inc. 2007).

Christopher Ng, *Investigate the Payment Bond Surety - Or Else!* CASH Register, Volume XXI, July, 2000.

FOREWORD

By Glenn E. Turner III
and
John H. Conrad

I. INTRODUCTION

A. An Historical Perspective

The concept of the right to claim a lien against real property has been in existence since the second century, where under the Roman ruler, Marcus Aurelius, a lender of money for improvements had the right to claim a lien on the structure and land upon which the structure was built. The concept was simple and functional: instead of allowing tradesmen to physically remove the benefit provided by their work, labor and materials and thereby destroy the improvement, the owner's property was impressed with a lien and sold intact (hopefully for a greater value) if the debt was unpaid. This practical and utilitarian concept of lien rights was also adopted in the United States from its earliest origins. In 1791, Maryland enacted the country's first mechanics lien statute. Thus, by the time California was admitted into the United States in 1850, the principle of a mechanics lien had been well established throughout the country.

Originally, the mechanics lien rights in California were established by the California legislative Act of April 12, 1850. Subsequently, mechanics lien rights were incorporated into *California's Constitution* in 1879, where they remain today. Because of its origin in the state's constitution, persons furnishing labor or providing materials have a constitutional right to claim a lien against real property benefitted by that labor or materials. *Article XIV, Section 3 of California's Constitution.* It is of no small significance that a mechanics lien is the only creditor's remedy that is derived from the *California Constitution.* In deference to the constitutional origin of these special remedies, the courts tread carefully when weighing policy concerns and balancing the competing interests.

In 1872, the first comprehensive mechanics lien statutes were enacted in California, which were initially contained in the *Code of Civil Procedure* and the *Government Code.* Although these statutes underwent minor revisions on a continual basis, they lasted for more than 75 years before being substantially overhauled in 1951. This revision moved the mechanics lien statutes to Chapter 6 of the *Civil Code.* It should be noted, however, that much of the 1951 revisions still contained the arcane and outdated language from the original 1872 Act. After 1951, the legislature enacted minor modifications to these statutes on a piece-meal basis, until 1965 where it added certain *Business & Professions Code* sections providing bonding requirements for contractors and *Civil Code* sections which attempted to standardize certain notice requirements.

For the past 60 years, courts have used the constitutional right and the *Civil Code* sections to balance the interests of the owner, lender, contractor and material supplier and define the rights and obligations of the parties under the mechanics lien law. Due to the fundamentally practical underlying principles, construction industry professionals have generally understood their responsibilities and the actions required of them to protect their individual interests with regard to these statutory remedies. In other words, the system basically worked. It was not, however, without its flaws.

Now, the California legislature, with the assistance of key advisory groups from owners, contractors, subcontractors, and material suppliers, has enacted a revised statutory scheme that is meant to centralize all of the mechanics lien statutes and "provide a few substantive improvements designed to make it easier for owners to learn about the existence and validity of a recorded lien, and to challenge a clearly invalid lien.[1]" The following is an overview of the changes made to the "Mechanics Lien Law" by Senate Bill 189.

[1] Mechanics Lien Law, 37 Cal. L. Revision Comm'n Reports 527 (2007), p530.

II. SENATE BILL 189

A. Change is Coming

SB 189 was signed into law on September 30, 2010, and becomes effective July 1, 2012. This bill revises and recasts statutory provisions and makes both substantive and technical changes to the Mechanics Lien Law. To more easily understand the requirements and protections of the mechanics lien statutes, SB 189 moves all of the applicable mechanics lien statutes to *Sections* 8000 and 9000 of the *Civil Code*. In addition, the statutes have been divided based upon how they are to be utilizied between general requirements (Sections 8000 et seq.), private works (Sections 8200 et. seq.) and public works (Sections 9000 et seq.).

The hierarchy of the new sections is broken down as follows:

- Title 1 Works of Improvement Generally (*Sections* 8000 to 8154). These provisions apply to all aspects of the new statutes such as definitions, notice provisions, waiver and release provisions, bond provisions, and miscellaneous provisions;
- Title 2 Private Works of Improvement (*Sections* 8160 to 8848). These sections cover private work construction and certain provisions regarding completion and notice of completion, preliminary notices, design professional liens, mechanics liens, stop payment notices, payment bonds, owner security requirements, and prompt payment;
- and Title 3 Public Work of Improvement (*Sections* 9000 to 9566). These provisions cover completion, preliminary notices, stop payment notices, and payment bonds.

While the legislative committee did indicate that the revised statutes are not intended to propose radical changes to the operation of the existing construction law remedies, some substantive changes were intended.[2] In addition to the relocation and rearrangement of Code sections, SB 189 included substantive changes that are meant to facilitate the understanding of the requirements of the mechanics lien law, and avoid potential confusion in interpretation of the prior statutes. The main substantive changes involve standardizing notice requirements and forms and modifying key terminology to more accurately reflect the participants and documents involved.

Based on the significance of the changes, the legislature approved the revised statutes prior to their implementation to allow the construction industry some time to become familiar with the revised statutory scheme. Since the mechanics lien law is critical to all persons involved in the construction industry, this book has been prepared to identify the changes to the prior laws and facilitate the rapid understanding of this new law.

B. Standardized Notice Requirements and Procedures

The most sweeping changes of SB 189 are to the basic notice prerequisites to the enforcement of either a mechanics lien, stop payment notice, or payment bond remedy. These changes include: modification of the terms used for the forms themselves; the standardization of the notice forms utilized for all mechanics lien and stop payment notices; payment bond claims; the information required in each of these notices; the changes to the statutory release forms; and the modification of rules affecting stop payment notices.

---

[2] Mechanics Lien Law, 37 Cal. L. Revision Comm'n Reports 527 (2007), p530.

a. Changes in Terminology

Three key terminology changes are made by the new law. First, the term "original contactor' has been changed to "direct contractor." Second, the prior term of "20-Day Preliminary Notice" is now just the "Preliminary Notice". Third, the term "Stop Notice" has been changed to "Stop Payment Notice." The latter changes were made to more accurately define the documents themselves. In the case of the Stop Payment Notice the name change attempts to avoid confusion. With the prior name "Stop Notice," individuals in some instances interpreted the notice to require actual work to stop on the project, rather than the documents actual function which is to stop payments between the owner and the general contractor.

b. Standardization of Notice Requirements

Section 8100 et seq. of the new statutes comprise the standard notice requirements to be utilized for every aspect of the Mechanics Lien Law, with Section 8102 providing the basic required notice components. To show this uniformity of notice requirements, either *Section* 8102 or the entire 8100 series sections are referenced from *Sections* 8104, 8182, 8188, 8190, 8200, 8202, 8214, 8424, 8444, 8482, 8502, 8506, 8520, 8522, 8534, 8538, 8550, 8614, 8712, 8800, 8816, 8832, 8834, 8836, 8840, 9202, 9204, 9302, 9303, 9352, 9354, 9362, 9402, 9404, 9406, 9408, 9412, and 9562. In addition, several sections reference *Section* 8200 et seq., for additional notice requirements, which in turn reference *Section* 8100 et. seq. Also to make the use of lien waivers easier for contractors and material suppliers, *Section* 8108 clarifies where a notice must be sent, based on the intended recipient of that notice.

c. Methods of Service Permitted

SB 189, while providing many of the same delivery methods for service of notices and claims used in the past, modifies the allowable methods of service. For the first time, "overnight delivery by express service carrier" is allowed, but "first class mail" **has been eliminated** per *Section* 8110.

d. Changes to Statutory Releases

The most significant change to statutory waivers was the language of the waiver in the forms themselves. Starting July 1, 2012, parties **must** revise their existing lien waiver forms to comply with the new statutes. *Section* 8122 also now prevents a subcontractor from waiving or impairing the lien rights of others through contracts or other instruments unless and until a lien waiver is signed by that party.

e. Stop Payment Notice Changes

Two key changes were included in SB 189 which facilitate a party's ability to provide a stop payment release bond. Now **any** party may obtain a stop payment release bond, as compared to the previous statute which only allowed the owner, construction lender, prime contractor or subcontractor to post a bond. The language of the statutes has been revised to provide that a stop payment notice release bond must be issued by an "admitted surety insurer." The new statutes also eliminate the requirement of the old law that a contractor first dispute the validity of a stop payment notice prior to obtaining a release bond.

C. Summary of Other Substantive Changes

SB 189 itself states that the revisions made to the California statutes were mostly intended to be non-substantive. The bill, however, specifically indicates the following new *Civil Code* sections as having substantive changes to the former statutory scheme. A short description of these substantive changes is provided here, while a more complete identification of the changes is provided within the accompanying text.

Section	Comment
8014	Landscape Architects now entitled to a mechanics lien.
8064	Owner can execute documents on behalf of co-owner.
8122	Subcontractors cannot waive lien rights of others by contract.
8128	Clarifies stop payment notice release and reduction notice release.
8132	Revised lien waiver form.
8182	Notice of Completion now can be filed within 15 days of completion.
8186	Time limit to record notice of completion on multi-"direct" contracts is eliminated.
8190	Owner must provide a notice of the filing of a notice of completion to the direct contractor and claimants that provided a preliminary notice, pursuant to section 8100 et seq.
8200	Clarifies that the direct contractor must provide a preliminary notice to the construction lender.
8424	Penal sum of mechanics lien release bond now 125% of claim, not 150%.
8460	Combines previous sections 3144 and 3145 regarding time to foreclose and effect of not filing suit.
8482	Prior to bringing a petition to release property from a lien, an owner must now demand in writing that a claimant release the lien at least 10 days before filing the petition.
8486	Court to rule on petition to remove invalid lien within 60 days, notice required 15 days prior to hearing.
8488	Burden of proof on petitioner to prove compliance with service of petition, while claimant has burden of establishing the validity of lien amount. Prevailing party to recover reasonable attorney's fees.
8510	Any person may obtain release bond, from "admitted surety insurer"
8604	If lender accepts payment bond, it may not later object to validity.
8606	Bonds must be issued by an "admitted surety insurer."
8800	Notices demanding progress payments must meet the notice requirements of *Sections* 8100 et seq. If an owner fails to pay within 30 days of receipt of the notice it is liable for 2% interest per month, unless there is a good faith dispute.
8834	Notice of the intent to issue a stop work notice must comply with the notice requirements of Sections 8100 et seq.
8844	Owner may now seek expedited hearing for liability on stop payment notice.
9200	Defines completion for public project.
9204	Notice of completion may be recorded within 15 days of completion.
9362	Stop payment notice claimant fee changed from $2 to $10, to receive notices from the public entity, after completion of a public works contract and recordation of notice of cessation or completion.

Section	Comment
9408	Notice per *Section* 8100, deemed complete 5 days after mailed.
9550	While a direct contractor who is awarded a public contract in excess of $25,000 must provide a payment bond, the section clarifies that a design professional is not a direct contractor for the purposes of this section, thus is not required to provide a payment bond to the public entity when it contracts directly with the public entity.
9558	Suit on payment bond now only allowed by claimants, and not assigns.

The following former *Civil Code Sections* have been discontinued based upon the new statutory scheme.

3086(b)	The previous criteria for completion, acceptance by the owner, has been removed.
3105	The definition for the term "subdivision" has been removed.
3123(c)	The owner no longer has to notify the direct contractor or construction lender if the contract price is exceeded by 5 percent.
3131 – ¶2	The separate distinction of completion of a residential unit, containing multiple condo units, is no longer included in determining the time for filing an action on a single residential unit.
3149	Deleted former provision for separate claims on property to be joined and consolidated by the court.
3204	Deleted former provision precluding any code section from eliminating the California Constitution's right to a jury trial, or that party may waive that right.
3260(c) – ¶1	A public entity issuing a certificate of occupancy is no longer a criteria for establishing the date of completion, regarding the start of the 45 day period when retention payments are due.
3260(c) - ¶2	The date of completion on a notice of completion issued by a public entity is no longer a criteria for establishing the date of completion, regarding the start of the 45 day period when retention payments are due.

D. Conclusion

It is clear that SB 189, though meaning to simplify and clarify the requirements and protections regarding mechanics liens, stop payment notices, and payment bond issues, has significantly modified the previous California statutes. Even if the majority of these changes only involve notice requirements or relocation within the statutes, owners, contractors, and material suppliers need to become familiar with the new statutes to protect their individual interests. This publication will assist all parties in comparing the new statute language with the old language, provide key cross-references between the old and new statutes, and provide a short description of the most significant differences between the old and new language. Hopefully, this will increase the understanding of all parties in the construction industry and streamline the payment, release and remedial aspects of these constitutionally created protections.

Section I

SB 189

CIVIL CODE SECTIONS ("CC")
New Text (Operative July 1, 2012)

PART 6. WORKS OF IMPROVEMENT
TITLE 1. WORKS OF IMPROVEMENT GENERALLY

Chapter 1. General Provisions

Article 1. Definitions

§ 8000 Construction of Part

Unless the provision or context otherwise requires, the definitions in this article govern the construction of this part.

§ 8002 Admitted Surety Insurer Defined

"Admitted surety insurer" has the meaning provided in Section 995.120 of the Code of Civil Procedure.

§ 8004 Claimant Defined

"Claimant" means a person that has a right under this part to record a claim of lien, give a stop payment notice, or assert a claim against a payment bond, or do any combination of the foregoing.

§ 8006 Construction Lender Defined

"Construction lender" means either of the following:

(a) A mortgagee or beneficiary under a deed of trust lending funds with which the cost of all or part of a work of improvement is to be paid, or the assignee or successor in interest of the mortgagee or beneficiary.

(b) An escrow holder or other person holding funds provided by an owner, lender, or another person as a fund for with which the cost of all or part of a work of improvement is to be paid.

§ 8008 Contract Defined

"Contract" means an agreement that provides for all or part of a work of improvement.

§ 8010 Contract Price Defined

"Contract price" means the price agreed to in a direct contract for a work of improvement

§ 8012 Contractor Defined

"Contractor" includes a direct contractor, subcontractor, or both. This section does not apply to Sections 8018 and 8046.

§ 8014 Design Professional Defined

"Design professional" means a person licensed as an architect pursuant to Chapter 3 (commencing with Section 5500) of Division 3 of the Business and Professions Code, licensed as a landscape architect pursuant to Chapter 3.5 (commencing with Section 5615) of Division 3 of the Business and Professions Code, registered as a professional engineer pursuant to Chapter 7 (commencing with Section 6700) of Division 3 of the Business and Professions Code, or licensed as a land surveyor pursuant to Chapter 15 (commencing with Section 8700) of Division 3 of the Business and Professions Code.

§ 8016 Direct Contract Defined

"Direct contract" means a contract between an owner and a direct contractor that provides for all or part of a work of improvement.

§ 8018 Direct Contractor Defined

"Direct contractor" means a contractor that has a direct contractual relationship with an owner. A reference in another statute to a "prime contractor" in connection with the provisions in this part means a "direct contractor."

§ 8020 Funds Defined

For the purposes of Title 3 (commencing with Section 9000), "funds" means warrant, check, money, or bonds (if bonds are to be issued in payment of the public works contract).

§ 8022 Labor, Service, Equipment or Material Defined

"Labor, service, equipment, or material" includes, but is not limited to, labor, skills, services, material, supplies, equipment, appliances, power, and surveying, provided for a work of improvement.

§ 8024 Laborer Defined

(a) "Laborer" means a person who, acting as an employee, performs labor upon, or bestows skill or other necessary services on, a work of improvement.

(b) "Laborer" includes a person or entity to which a portion of a laborer's compensation for a work of improvement, including, but not limited to, employer payments described in Section 1773.1 of the Labor Code and implementing regulations, is paid by agreement with that laborer or the collective bargaining agent of that laborer.

(c) A person or entity described in subdivision (b) that has standing under applicable law to maintain a direct legal action, in its own name or as an assignee, to collect any portion of compensation owed for a laborer for a work of improvement, shall have standing to enforce any rights or claims of the laborer under this part, to the extent of the compensation agreed to be paid to the person or entity for labor on that improvement. This subdivision is intended to give effect to the longstanding public policy of this state to protect the entire compensation of a laborer on a work of improvement, regardless of the form in which that compensation is to be paid.

§ 8026 Lien Defined

"Lien" means a lien under Title 2 (commencing with Section 8160) and includes a lien of a design professional under Section 8302, a lien for a work of improvement under Section 8400, and a lien for a site improvement under Section 8402.

§ 8028 Material Supplier Defined

"Material supplier" means a person that provides material or supplies to be used or consumed in a work of improvement.

§ 8030 Payment Bond Defined

(a) For the purposes of Title 2 (commencing with Section 8160), "payment bond" means a bond given under Section 8600.

(b) For the purposes of Title 3 (commencing with Section 9000), "payment bond" means a bond required by Section 9550.

§ 8032 Person Defined

"Person" means an individual, corporation, public entity, business trust, estate, trust, partnership, limited liability company, association, or other entity.

§ 8034 Preliminary Notice Defined

(a) For the purposes of Title 2 (commencing with Section 8160), "preliminary notice" means the notice provided for in Chapter 2 (commencing with Section 8200) of Title 2.

(b) For the purposes of Title 3 (commencing with Section 9000), "preliminary notice" means the notice provided for in Chapter 3 (commencing with Section 9300) of Title 3.

§ 8036 Public Entity Defined

"Public entity" means the state, Regents of the University of California, a county, city, district, public authority, public agency, and any other political subdivision or public corporation in the state.

§ 8038 Public Works Contract Defined

"Public works contract" has the meaning provided in Section 1101 of the Public Contract Code.

§ 8040 Site Defined

"Site" means the real property on which a work of improvement is situated or planned.

§ 8042 Site Improvement Defined

"Site improvement" means any of the following work on real property:

(a) Demolition or removal of improvements, trees, or other vegetation.

(b) Drilling test holes.

(c) Grading, filling, or otherwise improving the real property or a street, highway, or sidewalk in front of or adjoining the real property.

(d) Construction or installation of sewers or other public utilities.

(e) Construction of areas, vaults, cellars, or rooms under sidewalks.

(f) Any other work or improvements in preparation of the site for a work of improvement.

§ 8044 Stop Payment Notice Defined

(a) (1) For the purposes of Title 2 (commencing with Section 8160), "stop payment notice" means the notice given by a claimant under Chapter 5 (commencing with Section 8500) of Title 2.

(2) A stop payment notice given under Title 2 (commencing with Section 8160) may be bonded or unbonded. A "bonded stop payment notice" is a notice given with a bond under Section 8532. An "unbonded stop payment notice" is a notice not given with a bond under Section 8532.

(3) Except to the extent Title 2 (commencing with Section 8160) distinguishes between a bonded and an unbonded stop payment notice, a reference in that title to a stop payment notice includes both a bonded and an unbonded notice.

(b) For the purposes of Title 3 (commencing with Section 9000), "stop payment notice" means the notice given by a claimant under Chapter 4 (commencing with Section 9350) of Title 3.

(c) A reference in another statute to a "stop notice" in connection with the remedies provided in this part means a stop payment notice.

§ 8046 Subcontractor Defined

"Subcontractor" means a contractor that does not have a direct contractual relationship with an owner. The term includes a contractor that has a contractual relationship with a direct contractor or with another subcontractor.

§ 8048 Work Defined

"Work" means labor, service, equipment, or material provided to a work of improvement.

§ 8050 Work of Improvement Defined

(a) "Work of improvement" includes, but is not limited to:

(1) Construction, alteration, repair, demolition, or removal, in whole or in part, of, or addition to, a building, wharf, bridge, ditch, flume, aqueduct, well, tunnel, fence, machinery, railroad, or road.

(2) Seeding, sodding, or planting of real property for landscaping purposes.

(3) Filling, leveling, or grading of real property.

(b) Except as otherwise provided in this part, "work of improvement" means the entire structure or scheme of improvement as a whole, and includes site improvement.

Article 2. Miscellaneous Provisions

§ 8052 Operative Date and Effect

(a) This part is operative on July 1, 2012.

(b) Notwithstanding subdivision (a), the effectiveness of a notice given or other action taken on a work of improvement before July 1, 2012, is governed by the applicable law in effect before July 1, 2012, and not by this part.

(c) A provision of this part, insofar as it is substantially the same as a previously existing provision relating to the same subject matter, shall be construed as a restatement and continuation thereof and not as a new enactment.

§ 8054 Transactions Excluded from Application of Part

(a) This part does not apply to a transaction governed by the Oil and Gas Lien Act (Chapter 2.5 (commencing with Section 1203.50) of Title 4 of Part 3 of the Code of Civil Procedure).

(b) This part does not apply to or change improvement security under the Subdivision Map Act (Division 2 (commencing with Section 66410) of Title 7 of the Government Code).

(c) This part does not apply to a transaction governed by Sections 20457 to 20464, inclusive, of the Public Contract Code.

§ 8056 Application of Code of Civil Procedure

Except as otherwise provided in this part, Part 2 (commencing with Section 307) of the Code of Civil Procedure provides the rules of practice in proceedings under this part.

§ 8058 Day Defined

For purposes of this part, "day" means a calendar day.

§ 8060 Filing or Recording with County Recorder; Satisfaction of Provisions; Procedure

(a) If this part provides for filing a contract, plan, or other paper with the county recorder, the provision is satisfied by filing the paper in the office of the county recorder of the county in which the work of improvement or part of it is situated.

(b) If this part provides for recording a notice, claim of lien, release of lien, payment bond, or other paper, the provision is satisfied by filing the paper for record in the office of the county recorder of the county in which the work of improvement or part of it is situated.

(c) The county recorder shall number, index, and preserve a contract, plan, or other paper presented for filing under this part, and shall number, index, and transcribe into the official records, in the same manner as a conveyance of real property, a notice, claim of lien, payment bond, or other paper recorded under this part.

(d) The county recorder shall charge and collect the fees provided in Article 5 (commencing with Section 27360) of Chapter 6 of Part 3 of Division 2 of Title 3 of the Government Code for performing duties under this section.

§ 8062 Construction of Good Faith and Compliant Acts

No act of an owner in good faith and in compliance with a provision of this part shall be construed to prevent a direct contractor's performance of the contract, or exonerate a surety on a performance or payment bond.

§ 8064 Acts on Behalf of Co-Owner

An owner may give a notice or execute or file a document under this part on behalf of a co-owner if the owner acts on the co-owner's behalf and includes in the notice or document the name and address of the co-owner on whose behalf the owner acts.

§ 8066 Acts by Agents

An act that may be done by or to a person under this part may be done by or to the person's agent to the extent the act is within the scope of the agent's authority.

Chapter 2. Notice

§ 8100 Written Notice

Notice under this part shall be in writing. Writing includes printing and typewriting.

§ 8102 Information to be Included in Notice

(a) Notice under this part shall, in addition to any other information required by statute for that type of notice, include all of the following information to the extent known to the person giving the notice:

(1) The name and address of the owner or reputed owner.

(2) The name and address of the direct contractor.

(3) The name and address of the construction lender, if any.

(4) A description of the site sufficient for identification, including the street address of the site, if any. If a sufficient legal description of the site is given, the effectiveness of the notice is not affected by the fact that the street address is erroneous or is omitted.

(5) The name, address, and relationship to the parties of the person giving the notice.

(6) If the person giving the notice is a claimant:

(A) A general statement of the work provided.

(B) The name of the person to or for whom the work is provided.

(C) A statement or estimate of the claimant's demand, if any, after deducting all just credits and offsets.

(b) Notice is not invalid by reason of any variance from the requirements of this section if the notice is sufficient to substantially inform the person given notice of the information required by this section and other information required in the notice.

§ 8104 Failure to Pay Laborer Full Compensation; Additional Information Required

(a) A direct contractor or subcontractor on a work of improvement governed by this part that employs a laborer and fails to pay the full compensation due the laborer, including any employer payments described in Section 1773.1 of the Labor Code and implementing regulations, shall not later than the date the compensation became delinquent, give the laborer, the laborer's bargaining representative, if any, the construction lender or reputed construction lender, if any, and the owner or reputed owner, notice that includes all of the following information, in addition to the information required by Section 8102:

(1) The name and address of the laborer, and of any person or entity described in subdivision (b) of Section 8024 to which employer payments are due.

(2) The total number of straight time and overtime hours worked by the laborer on each job.

(3) The amount then past due and owing.

(b) Failure to give the notice required by subdivision (a) constitutes grounds for disciplinary action under the Contractors' State License Law, Chapter 9 (commencing with Section 7000) of Division 3 of the Business and Professions Code.

§ 8106 Manner of Giving Notice

Except as otherwise provided by statute, notice under this part shall be given by any of the following means:

(a) Personal delivery.

(b) Mail in the manner provided in Section 8110.

(c) Leaving the notice and mailing a copy in the manner provided in Section 415.20 of the Code of Civil Procedure for service of summons and complaint in a civil action.

§ 8108 Location for Giving Notice

Except as otherwise provided by this part, notice under this part shall be given to the person to be notified at the person's residence, the person's place of business, or at any of the following addresses:

(a) If the person to be notified is an owner other than a public entity, the owner's address shown on the direct contract, the building permit, or a construction trust deed.

(b) If the person to be notified is a public entity, the office of the public entity or another address specified by the public entity in the contract or elsewhere for service of notices, papers, and other documents.

(c) If the person to be notified is a construction lender, the construction lender's address shown on the construction loan agreement or construction trust deed.

(d) If the person to be notified is a direct contractor or a subcontractor, the contractor's address shown on the building permit, on the contractor's contract, or on the records of the Contractors' State License Board.

(e) If the person to be notified is a claimant, the claimant's address shown on the claimant's contract, preliminary notice, claim of lien, stop payment notice, or claim against a payment bond, or on the records of the Contractors' State License Board.

(f) If the person to be notified is a surety on a bond, the surety's address shown on the bond for service of notices, papers, and other documents, or on the records of the Department of Insurance.

§ 8110 Notice by Mail

Except as otherwise provided by this part, notice by mail under this part shall be given by registered or certified mail, express mail, or overnight delivery by an express service carrier.

§ 8114 Posting of Notice; Conspicuous Location

A notice required by this part to be posted shall be displayed in a conspicuous location at the site.

§ 8116 Completion of Notice; Time Deemed Given

Notice under this part is complete and deemed to have been given at the following times:

(a) If given by personal delivery, when delivered.

(b) If given by mail, when deposited in the mail or with an express service carrier in the manner provided in Section 1013 of the Code of Civil Procedure.

(c) If given by leaving the notice and mailing a copy in the manner provided in Section 415.20 of the Code of Civil Procedure for service of summons in a civil action, five days after mailing.

(d) If given by posting, when displayed.

(e) If given by recording, when recorded in the office of the county recorder.

§ 8118 Proof of Notice; Declaration

(a) Proof that notice was given to a person in the manner required by this part shall be made by a proof of notice declaration that states all of the following:

(1) The type or description of the notice given.

(2) The date, place, and manner of notice, and facts showing that notice was given in the manner required by statute.

(3) The name and address of the person to which notice was given, and, if appropriate, the title or capacity in which the person was given notice.

(b) If the notice is given by mail, the declaration shall be accompanied by one of the following:

(1) Documentation provided by the United States Postal Service showing that payment was made to mail the notice using registered or certified mail, or express mail.

(2) Documentation provided by an express service carrier showing that payment was made to send the notice using an overnight delivery service.

(3) A return receipt, delivery confirmation, signature confirmation, tracking record, or other proof of delivery or attempted delivery provided by the United States Postal Service, or a photocopy of the record of delivery and receipt maintained by the United States Postal Service, showing the date of delivery and to whom delivered, or in the event of nondelivery, by the returned envelope itself.

(4) A tracking record or other documentation provided by an express service carrier showing delivery or attempted delivery of the notice.

Chapter 3. Waiver and Release

§ 8120 Application of Chapter

The provisions of this chapter apply to a work of improvement governed by this part.

§ 8122 Waiver or Impairment of Rights Prohibited; Exceptions

An owner, direct contractor, or subcontractor may not, by contract or otherwise, waive, affect, or impair any other claimant's rights under this part, whether with or without notice, and any term of a contract that purports to do so is void and unenforceable unless and until the claimant executes and delivers a waiver and release under this article.

§ 8124 Release from Lien or Claim; Conditions

A claimant's waiver and release does not release the owner, construction lender, or surety on a payment bond from a lien or claim unless both of the following conditions are satisfied:

(a) The waiver and release is in substantially the form provided in this article and is signed by the claimant.

(b) If the release is a conditional release, there is evidence of payment to the claimant. Evidence of payment may be either of the following:

(1) The claimant's endorsement on a single or joint payee check that has been paid by the financial institution on which it was drawn.

(2) Written acknowledgment of payment by the claimant.

§ 8126 Estoppel or Impairment of Lien or Claim; Conditions

An oral or written statement purporting to waive, release, impair or otherwise adversely affect a lien or claim is void and unenforceable and does not create an estoppel or impairment of the lien or claim unless either of the following conditions is satisfied:

(a) The statement is pursuant to a waiver and release under this article.

(b) The claimant has actually received payment in full for the claim.

§ 8128 Stop Payment Notice; Reduction or Release

(a) A claimant may reduce the amount of, or release in its entirety, a stop payment notice. The reduction or release shall be in writing and may be given in a form other than a waiver and release form provided in this article.

(b) The writing shall identify whether it is a reduction of the amount of the stop payment notice, or a release of the notice in its entirety. If the writing is a reduction, it shall state the amount of the reduction, and the amount to remain withheld after the reduction.

(c) A claimant's reduction or release of a stop payment notice has the following effect:

(1) The reduction or release releases the claimant's right to enforce payment of the claim stated in the notice to the extent of the reduction or release.

(2) The reduction or release releases the person given the notice from the obligation to withhold funds pursuant to the notice to the extent of the reduction or release.

(3) The reduction or release does not preclude the claimant from giving a subsequent stop payment notice that is timely and proper.

(4) The reduction or release does not release any right of the claimant other than the right to enforce payment of the claim stated in the stop payment notice to the extent of the reduction or release.

§ 8130 Accord and Satisfaction; Effect of Article

This article does not affect the enforceability of either an accord and satisfaction concerning a good faith dispute or an agreement made in settlement of an action pending in court if the accord and satisfaction or agreement and settlement make specific reference to the lien or claim.

§ 8132 Conditional Waiver and Release on Progress Payment; Form

If a claimant is required to execute a waiver and release in exchange for, or in order to induce payment of, a progress payment and the claimant is not, in fact, paid in exchange for the waiver and release or a single payee check or joint payee check is given in exchange for the waiver and release, the waiver and release shall be null, void, and unenforceable unless it is in substantially the following form:

CONDITIONAL WAIVER AND RELEASE ON PROGRESS PAYMENT

NOTICE: THIS DOCUMENT WAIVES THE CLAIMANT'S LIEN, STOP PAYMENT NOTICE, AND PAYMENT BOND RIGHTS EFFECTIVE ON RECEIPT OF PAYMENT. A PERSON SHOULD NOT RELY ON THIS DOCUMENT UNLESS SATISFIED THAT THE CLAIMANT HAS RECEIVED PAYMENT.

Identifying Information:

Name of Claimant:

____

Name of Customer:

____

Job Location:

____

Owner:

____

Through Date:

____

Conditional Waiver and Release

This document waives and releases lien, stop payment notice, and payment bond rights the claimant has for labor and service provided, and equipment and material delivered, to the customer on this job through the Through Date of this document. Rights based upon labor or service provided, or equipment or material delivered, pursuant to a written change order that has been fully executed by the parties prior to the date that this document is signed by the claimant, are waived and released by this document, unless listed as an Exception below. This document is effective only on the claimant's receipt of payment from the financial institution on which the following check is drawn:

Maker of Check:

____

Amount of Check: $ ____________________

Check Payable to:

____

Exceptions

This document does not affect any of the following:

(1) Retentions.

(2) Extras for which the claimant has not received payment.

(3) The following progress payments for which the claimant has previously given a conditional waiver and release but has not received payment:

Date(s) of waiver and release:

____

Amount(s) of unpaid progress payment(s): $______________________________

(4) Contract rights, including (A) a right based on rescission, abandonment, or breach of contract, and (B) the right to recover compensation for work not compensated by the payment.

Signature:

Claimant's Signature:

____

Claimant's Title:

____

Date of Signature:

____

§ 8134 Unconditional Waiver and Release on Progress Payment; Form

If the claimant is required to execute a waiver and release in exchange for, or in order to induce payment of, a progress payment and the claimant asserts in the waiver that the claimant has, in fact, been paid the progress payment, the waiver and release shall be null, void, and unenforceable unless it is in substantially the following form, with the text of the "Notice to Claimant" in at least as large a type as the largest type otherwise in the form:

UNCONDITIONAL WAIVER AND RELEASE ON PROGRESS PAYMENT

NOTICE TO CLAIMANT: THIS DOCUMENT WAIVES AND RELEASES LIEN, STOP PAYMENT NOTICE, AND PAYMENT BOND RIGHTS UNCONDITIONALLY AND STATES THAT YOU HAVE BEEN PAID FOR GIVING UP THOSE RIGHTS. THIS DOCUMENT IS ENFORCEABLE AGAINST YOU IF YOU SIGN IT, EVEN IF YOU HAVE NOT BEEN PAID. IF YOU HAVE NOT BEEN PAID, USE A CONDITIONAL WAIVER AND RELEASE FORM.

Identifying Information:

Name of Claimant:

____

Name of Customer:

____

Job Location:

____

Owner:

____

Through Date:

____

Unconditional Waiver and Release

This document waives and releases lien, stop payment notice, and payment bond rights the claimant has for labor and service provided, and equipment and material delivered, to the customer on this job through the Through Date of this document. Rights based upon labor or service provided, or equipment or material delivered, pursuant to a written change order that has been fully executed by the parties prior to the date that this document is signed by the claimant, are waived and released by this document, unless listed as an Exception below. The claimant has received the following progress payment:

$ ____

Exceptions

This document does not affect any of the following:

(1) Retentions.

(2) Extras for which the claimant has not received payment.

(3) Contract rights, including (A) a right based on rescission, abandonment, or breach of contract, and (B) the right to recover compensation for work not compensated by the payment.

Signature:

Claimant's Signature:

____

Claimant's Title:

____

Date of Signature:

____

§ 8136 Conditional Waiver and Release on Final Payment; Form

If the claimant is required to execute a waiver and release in exchange for, or in order to induce payment of, a final payment and the claimant is not, in fact, paid in exchange for the waiver and release or a single payee check or joint payee check is given in exchange for the waiver and release, the waiver and release shall be null, void, and unenforceable unless it is in substantially the following form:

CONDITIONAL WAIVER AND RELEASE ON FINAL PAYMENT

NOTICE: THIS DOCUMENT WAIVES THE CLAIMANT'S LIEN, STOP PAYMENT NOTICE, AND PAYMENT BOND RIGHTS EFFECTIVE ON RECEIPT OF PAYMENT. A PERSON SHOULD NOT RELY ON THIS DOCUMENT UNLESS SATISFIED THAT THE CLAIMANT HAS RECEIVED PAYMENT.

Identifying Information:

Name of Claimant:

____

Name of Customer:

____

Job Location:

____

Owner:

____

Conditional Waiver and Release

This document waives and releases lien, stop payment notice, and payment bond rights the claimant has for labor and service provided, and equipment and material delivered, to the customer on this job. Rights based upon labor or service provided, or equipment or material delivered, pursuant to a written change order that has been fully executed by the parties prior to the date that this document is signed by the claimant, are waived and released by this document, unless listed as an Exception below. This document is effective only on the claimant's receipt of payment from the financial institution on which the following check is drawn:

Maker of Check:

____

Amount of Check: $ ______________________

Check Payable to:

____

Exceptions

This document does not affect any of the following:

Disputed claims for extras in the amount of:

$ ___________________________________

Signature:

Claimant's Signature:

____

Claimant's Title:

____

Date of Signature:

____

§ 8138 Unconditional Waiver and Release on Final Payment; Form

If the claimant is required to execute a waiver and release in exchange for, or in order to induce payment of, a final payment and the claimant asserts in the waiver that the claimant has, in fact, been paid the final payment, the waiver and release shall be null, void, and unenforceable unless it is in substantially the following form, with the text of the "Notice to Claimant" in at least as large a type as the largest type otherwise in the form:

UNCONDITIONAL WAIVER AND RELEASE ON FINAL PAYMENT

NOTICE TO CLAIMANT: THIS DOCUMENT WAIVES AND RELEASES LIEN, STOP PAYMENT NOTICE, AND PAYMENT BOND RIGHTS UNCONDITIONALLY AND STATES THAT YOU HAVE BEEN PAID FOR GIVING UP THOSE RIGHTS. THIS DOCUMENT IS ENFORCEABLE AGAINST YOU IF YOU SIGN IT, EVEN IF YOU HAVE NOT BEEN PAID. IF YOU HAVE NOT BEEN PAID, USE A CONDITIONAL WAIVER AND RELEASE FORM.

Identifying Information:

Name of Claimant:

____

Name of Customer:

____

Job Location:

____

Owner:

____

Unconditional Waiver and Release

This document waives and releases lien, stop payment notice, and payment bond rights the claimant has for all labor and service provided, and equipment and material delivered, to the customer on this job. Rights based upon labor or service provided, or equipment or material delivered, pursuant to a written change order that has been fully executed by the parties prior to the date that this document is signed by the claimant, are waived and released by this document, unless listed as an Exception below. The claimant has been paid in full.

Exceptions

This document does not affect the following:

Disputed claims for extras in the amount of:

$ ______________________________

Signature:

Claimant's Signature:

____

Claimant's Title:

____

Date of Signature:

____

Chapter 4. Bonds

§ 8150 Application of Bond and Undertaking Law

The Bond and Undertaking Law (Chapter 2 (commencing with Section 995.010) of Title 14 of Part 2 of the Code of Civil Procedure) applies to a bond given under this part, except to the extent this part prescribes a different rule or is inconsistent.

§ 8152 Acts not Releasing Surety from Liability on Bond Given Under this Part

None of the following releases a surety from liability on a bond given under this part:

(a) A change, alteration, or modification to a contract, plan, specification, or agreement for a work of improvement or for work provided for a work of improvement.

(b) A change or modification to the terms of payment or an extension of the time for payment for a work of improvement.

(c) A rescission or attempted rescission of a contract, agreement, or bond.

(d) A condition precedent or subsequent in the bond purporting to limit the right of recovery of a claimant otherwise entitled to recover pursuant to a contract, agreement, or bond.

(e) In the case of a bond given for the benefit of claimants, the fraud of a person other than the claimant seeking to recover on the bond.

§ 8154 Construction of Bond; Liability of Surety; Condition for Recovery on Bond

(a) A bond given under this part shall be construed most strongly against the surety and in favor of all persons for whose benefit the bond is given.

(b) A surety is not released from liability to those for whose benefit the bond has been given by reason of a breach of the direct contract or on the part of any obligee named in the bond.

(c) Except as otherwise provided by statute, the sole conditions of recovery on the bond are that the claimant is a person described in Article 1 (commencing with Section 8400) of Chapter 4 of Title 2, or in Section 9100, and has not been paid the full amount of the claim.

TITLE 2. PRIVATE WORKS OF IMPROVEMENT

Chapter 1. General Provisions

Article 1. Application of Title

§ 8160 Title Governs Private Works of Improvement

This title applies to a work of improvement that is not governed by Title 3 (commencing with Section 9000) of this part.

Article 2. Construction Documents

§ 8170 Written Direct Contracts; Contents

(a) A written direct contract shall provide a space for the owner to enter the following information:

(1) The owner's name, address, and place of business, if any.

(2) The name and address of the construction lender, if any. This paragraph does not apply to a home improvement contract or swimming pool contract subject to Article 10 (commencing with Section 7150) of Chapter 9 of Division 3 of the Business and Professions Code.

(b) A written contract entered into between a direct contractor and subcontractor, or between subcontractors, shall provide a space for the name and address of the owner, direct contractor, and construction lender, if any.

§ 8172 Building Permits; Application Information Regarding Construction Lenders

(a) A public entity that issues building permits shall, in its application form for a building permit, provide space and a designation for the applicant to enter the name, branch designation, if any, and address of the construction lender and shall keep the information on file open for public inspection during the regular business hours of the public entity.

(b) If there is no known construction lender, the applicant shall note that fact in the designated space.

(c) Failure of the applicant to indicate the name and address of the construction lender on the application does not relieve a person required to give the construction lender preliminary notice from that duty.

§ 8174 Construction Trust Deed; Contents

(a) A mortgage, deed of trust, or other instrument securing a loan, any of the proceeds of which may be used for a work of improvement, shall bear the designation "Construction Trust Deed" prominently on its face and shall state all of the following:

(1) The name and address of the construction lender.

(2) The name and address of the owner of the real property described in the instrument.

(3) A legal description of the real property that secures the loan and, if known, the street address of the property.

(b) Failure to comply with subdivision (a) does not affect the validity of the mortgage, deed of trust, or other instrument.

(c) Failure to comply with subdivision (a) does not relieve a person required to give preliminary notice from that duty.

(d) The county recorder of the county in which the instrument is recorded shall indicate in the general index of the official records of the county that the instrument secures a construction loan.

Article 3. Completion

§ 8180 Acts Signifying Completion

(a) For the purpose of this title, completion of a work of improvement occurs upon the occurrence of any of the following events:

(1) Actual completion of the work of improvement.

(2) Occupation or use by the owner accompanied by cessation of labor.

(3) Cessation of labor for a continuous period of 60 days.

(4) Recordation of a notice of cessation after cessation of labor for a continuous period of 30 days.

(b) Notwithstanding subdivision (a), if a work of improvement is subject to acceptance by a public entity, completion occurs on acceptance.

§ 8182 Notice of Completion; Recording; Contents

(a) An owner may record a notice of completion on or within 15 days after the date of completion of a work of improvement.

(b) The notice of completion shall be signed and verified by the owner.

(c) The notice shall comply with the requirements of Chapter 2 (commencing with Section 8100) of Title 1, and shall also include all of the following information:

(1) If the notice is given only of completion of a contract for a particular portion of the work of improvement as provided in Section 8186, the name of the direct contractor under that contract and a general statement of the work provided pursuant to the contract.

(2) If signed by the owner's successor in interest, the name and address of the successor's transferor.

(3) The nature of the interest or estate of the owner.

(4) The date of completion. An erroneous statement of the date of completion does not affect the effectiveness of the notice if the true date of completion is 15 days or less before the date of recordation of the notice.

(d) A notice of completion that does not comply with the provisions of this section is not effective.

(e) For the purpose of this section, "owner" means the owner who causes a building, improvement, or structure to be constructed, altered, or repaired, or that person's successor in interest at the date a notice of completion is recorded, whether the interest or estate of the owner be in fee, as vendee under a contract of purchase, as lessee, or other interest or estate less than the fee. Where the interest or estate is held by two or more persons as joint tenants or tenants in common, any one or more of the cotenants may be deemed to be the "owner" within the meaning of this section.

§ 8184 Acceptance and Recording of Notice of Completion

A notice of completion in otherwise proper form, verified and containing the information required by this title, shall be accepted by the recorder for recording and is deemed duly recorded without acknowledgment.

§ 8186 Multiple Contracts; Notice of Completion for Portion of Work of Improvement

If a work of improvement is made pursuant to two or more direct contracts, each covering a portion of the work of improvement:

(a) The owner may record a notice of completion of a direct contract for a portion of the work of improvement. On recordation of the notice of completion, for the purpose of Sections 8412 and 8414, a direct contractor is deemed to have completed the contract for which the notice of completion is recorded and a claimant other than a direct contractor is deemed to have ceased providing work.

(b) If the owner does not record a notice of completion under this section, the period for recording a claim of lien is that provided in Sections 8412 and 8414.

§ 8188 Notice of Cessation; Recording; Contents

(a) An owner may record a notice of cessation if there has been a continuous cessation of labor on a work of improvement for at least 30 days prior to the recordation that continues through the date of the recordation.

(b) The notice shall be signed and verified by the owner.

(c) The notice shall comply with the requirements of Chapter 2 (commencing with Section 8100) of Title 1, and shall also include all of the following information:

(1) The date on or about which labor ceased.

(2) A statement that the cessation has continued until the recordation of the notice.

(d) For the purpose of this section, "owner" means the owner who causes a building, improvement, or structure to be constructed, altered, or repaired, or that person's successor in interest at the date a notice of cessation is recorded, whether the interest or estate of the owner be in fee, as vendee under a contract of purchase, as lessee, or other interest or estate less than the fee. Where the interest or estate is held by two or more persons as joint tenants or tenants in common, any one or more of the cotenants may be deemed to be the "owner" within the meaning of this section.

§ 8190 Notice of Completion or Cessation; Copies to be Provided

(a) An owner that records a notice of completion or cessation shall, within 10 days of the date the notice of completion or cessation is filed for record, give a copy of the notice to all of the following persons:

(1) A direct contractor.

(2) A claimant that has given the owner preliminary notice.

(b) The copy of the notice shall be given in compliance with the requirements of Chapter 2 (commencing with Section 8100) of Title 1.

(c) If the owner fails to give notice to a person as required by subdivision (a), the notice is ineffective to shorten the time within which that person may record a claim of lien under Sections 8412 and 8414. The ineffectiveness of the notice is the sole liability of the owner for failure to give notice to a person under subdivision (a).

(d) For the purpose of this section, "owner" means a person who has an interest in real property, or the person's successor in interest on the date a notice of completion or notice of cessation is recorded, who causes a building, improvement, or structure, to be constructed, altered, or repaired on the property. If the property is owned by two or more persons as joint tenants or tenants in common, any one or more of the cotenants may be deemed to be the "owner" within the meaning of this section. However, this section does not apply to any of the following owners:

(1) A person that occupies the real property as a personal residence, if the dwelling contains four or fewer residential units.

(2) A person that has a security interest in the property.

(3) A person that obtains an interest in the property pursuant to a transfer described in subdivision (b), (c), or (d) of Section 1102.2.

Chapter 2. Preliminary Notice

§ 8200 Preliminary Notice; Persons to Receive; Exceptions

(a) Except as otherwise provided by statute, before recording a lien claim, giving a stop payment notice, or asserting a claim against a payment bond, a claimant shall give preliminary notice to the following persons:

(1) The owner or reputed owner.

(2) The direct contractor or reputed direct contractor to which the claimant provides work, either directly or through one or more subcontractors.

(3) The construction lender or reputed construction lender, if any.

(b) The notice shall comply with the requirements of Chapter 2 (commencing with Section 8100) of Title 1.

(c) Compliance with this section is a necessary prerequisite to the validity of a lien claim or stop payment notice under this title.

(d) Compliance with this section or with Section 8612 is a necessary prerequisite to the validity of a claim against a payment bond under this title.

(e) Notwithstanding the foregoing subdivisions:

(1) A laborer is not required to give preliminary notice.

(2) A claimant with a direct contractual relationship with an owner or reputed owner is required to give preliminary notice only to the construction lender or reputed construction lender, if any.

§ 8202 Notice to Property Owner

(a) The preliminary notice shall comply with the requirements of Section 8102, and shall also include:

(1) A general description of the work to be provided.

(2) An estimate of the total price of the work provided and to be provided.

(3) The following statement in boldface type:

NOTICE TO PROPERTY OWNER

EVEN THOUGH YOU HAVE PAID YOUR CONTRACTOR IN FULL, if the person or firm that has given you this notice is not paid in full for labor, service, equipment, or material provided or to be provided to your construction project, a lien may be placed on your property. Foreclosure of the lien may lead to loss of all or part of your property. You may wish to protect yourself against this by (1) requiring your contractor to provide a signed release by the person or firm that has given you this notice before making payment to your contractor, or (2) any other method that is appropriate under the circumstances.

This notice is required by law to be served by the undersigned as a statement of your legal rights. This notice is not intended to reflect upon the financial condition of the contractor or the person employed by you on the construction project.

If you record a notice of cessation or completion of your construction project, you must within 10 days after recording, send a copy of the notice of completion to your contractor and the person or firm that has given you this notice. The notice must be sent by registered or certified mail. Failure to send the notice will extend the deadline to record a claim of lien. You are not required to send the notice if you are a residential homeowner of a dwelling containing four or fewer units.

(b) If preliminary notice is given by a subcontractor that has not paid all compensation due to a laborer, the notice shall include the name and address of the laborer and any person or entity described in subdivision (b) of Section 8024 to which payments are due.

(c) If an invoice for material or certified payroll contains the information required by this section and Section 8102, a copy of the invoice or payroll, given in compliance with the requirements of Chapter 2 (commencing with Section 8100) of Title 1, is sufficient.

§ 8204 Time for Giving Preliminary Notice

(a) A preliminary notice shall be given not later than 20 days after the claimant has first furnished work on the work of improvement. If work has been provided by a claimant who did not give a preliminary notice, that claimant shall not be precluded from giving a preliminary notice at any time thereafter. The claimant shall, however, be entitled to record a lien, give a stop payment notice, and assert a claim against a payment bond only for work performed within 20 days prior to the service of the preliminary notice, and at any time thereafter.

(b) A design professional who has furnished services for the design of the work of improvement and who gives a preliminary notice not later than 20 days after the work of improvement has commenced shall be deemed to have complied with Section 8200 with respect to the design services furnished, or to be furnished.

§ 8206 Single or Multiple Preliminary Notice

(a) Except as provided in subdivision (b), a claimant need give only one preliminary notice to each person to which notice must be given under this chapter with respect to all work provided by the claimant for a work of improvement.

(b) If a claimant provides work pursuant to contracts with more than one subcontractor, the claimant shall give a separate preliminary notice with respect to work provided pursuant to each contract.

(c) A preliminary notice that contains a general description of work provided by the claimant through the date of the notice also covers work provided by the claimant after the date of the notice whether or not they are within the scope of the general description contained in the notice.

§ 8208 Information to be Provided by Direct Contractor

A direct contractor shall make available to any person seeking to give preliminary notice the following information:

(a) The name and address of the owner.

(b) The name and address of the construction lender, if any.

§ 8210 Additional Construction Loan; Information to Persons Giving Preliminary Notice

If one or more construction loans are obtained after commencement of a work of improvement, the owner shall give notice of the name and address of the construction lender or lenders to each person that has given the owner preliminary notice.

§ 8212 Waiver of Rights Void and Unenforceable

An agreement made or entered into by an owner whereby the owner agrees to waive the rights conferred on the owner by this chapter is void and unenforceable.

§ 8214 Filing of Preliminary Notice; Purpose of Filing Pursuant to this Section

(a) Each person who has served a preliminary notice may file the preliminary notice with the county recorder. A preliminary notice filed pursuant to this section shall comply with the requirements of Section 8102.

(b) Upon the acceptance for recording of a notice of completion or notice of cessation the county recorder shall mail to those persons who have filed a preliminary notice, notification that a notice of completion or notice of cessation has been recorded on the property, and shall affix the date that the notice of completion or notice of cessation was recorded with the county recorder. The notification given by the county recorder under this section is not governed by the requirements of Chapter 2 (commencing with Section 8100) of Title 1.

(c) The failure of the county recorder to mail the notification to the person who filed a preliminary notice, or the failure of those persons to receive the notification or to receive complete notification, shall not affect the period within which a claim of lien is required to be recorded. However, the county recorder shall make a good faith effort to mail notification to those persons who have filed the preliminary notice under this section and to do so within five days after the recording of a notice of completion or notice of cessation.

(d) The county recorder may cause to be destroyed all documents filed pursuant to this section, two years after the date of filing.

(e) The preliminary notice that a person may file pursuant to this section is for the limited purpose of facilitating the mailing of notice by the county recorder of recorded notices of completion and notices of cessation. The notice that is filed is not a recordable document and shall not be entered into those official records of the county which by law impart constructive notice. Notwithstanding any other provision of law, the index maintained by the recorder of filed preliminary notices shall be separate and distinct from those indexes maintained by the county recorder of those official records of the county which by law impart constructive notice. The filing of a preliminary notice with the county recorder does not give rise to any actual or constructive notice with respect to any party of the existence or contents of a filed preliminary notice nor to any duty of inquiry on the part of any party as to the existence or contents of that notice.

§ 8216 Subcontractors; Failure to Give Notice as Grounds for Disciplinary Action

If the contract of any subcontractor on a particular work of improvement provides for payment to the subcontractor of more than four hundred dollars ($400), the failure of that subcontractor, licensed under the Contractors' State License Law (Chapter 9 (commencing with Section 7000) of Division 3 of the Business and Professions Code), to give the notice provided for in this chapter, constitutes grounds for disciplinary action under the Contractors' State License Law.

Chapter 3. Design Professionals Lien

§ 8300 Design Professional Defined

For purposes of this chapter, a "design professional" is a person described in Section 8014 who provides services pursuant to a written contract with a landowner for the design, engineering, or planning of a work of improvement.

§ 8302 Circumstances Giving Rise to Lien; Amount

(a) A design professional has, from the date of recordation of a claim of lien under this chapter, a lien on the site notwithstanding the absence of commencement of the planned work of improvement, if the landowner who contracted for the design professional's services is also the owner of the site at the time of recordation of the claim of lien.

(b) The lien of the design professional is for the amount of the design professional's fee for services provided under the contract or the reasonable value of those services, whichever is less. The amount of the lien is reduced by the amount of any deposit or prior payment under the contract.

(c) A design professional may not record a claim of lien, and a lien may not be created, under this chapter unless a building permit or other governmental approval in furtherance of the work of improvement has been obtained in connection with or utilizing the services provided by the design professional.

§ 8304 Entitlement to Lien; Conditions

A design professional is not entitled to a lien under this chapter unless all of the following conditions are satisfied:

(a) The work of improvement for which the design professional provided services has not commenced.

(b) The landowner defaults in a payment required under the contract or refuses to pay the demand of the design professional made under the contract.

(c) Not less than 10 days before recording a claim of lien, the design professional gives the landowner notice making a demand for payment, and stating that a default has occurred under the contract and the amount of the default.

(d) The design professional records a claim of lien. The claim of lien shall include all of the following information:

(1) The name of the design professional.

(2) The amount of the claim.

(3) The current owner of record of the site.

(4) A legal description of the site.

(5) Identification of the building permit or other governmental approval for the work of improvement.

§ 8306 Creation of Lien; Expiration; Satisfaction

(a) On recordation of the claim of lien, a lien is created in favor of the named design professional.

(b) The lien automatically expires and is null and void and of no further force or effect on the occurrence of either of the following events:

(1) The commencement of the work of improvement for which the design professional provided services.

(2) The expiration of 90 days after recording the claim of lien, unless the design professional commences an action to enforce the lien within that time.

(c) If the landowner partially or fully satisfies the lien, the design professional shall execute and record a document that evidences a partial or full satisfaction and release of the lien, as applicable.

§ 8308 Application of Part

(a) Except as provided in subdivision (b), no provision of this part applies to a lien created under this chapter.

(b) The following provisions of this part apply to a lien created under this chapter:

(1) This chapter.

(2) Article 1 (commencing with Section 8000) of Chapter 1 of Title 1.

(3) Section 8424.

(4) Article 6 (commencing with Section 8460) of Chapter 4.

(5) Article 7 (commencing with Section 8480) of Chapter 4.

(6) Article 8 (commencing with Section 8490) of Chapter 4.

§ 8310 Availability of Mechanics Lien

This chapter does not affect the ability of a design professional to obtain a lien for a work of improvement under Section 8400.

§ 8312 Time for Recording Claim of Lien

A design professional shall record a claim of lien under this chapter no later than 90 days after the design professional knows or has reason to know that the work of improvement will not be commenced.

§ 8314 Additional Remedies

The creation of a lien under this chapter does not affect the ability of the design professional to pursue other remedies.

§ 8316 Priority of Lien

(a) No lien created under this chapter affects or takes priority over the interest of record of a purchaser, lessee, or encumbrancer, if the interest of the purchaser, lessee, or encumbrancer in the real property was duly recorded before recordation of the claim of lien.

(b) No lien created under this chapter affects or takes priority over an encumbrance of a construction lender that funds the loan for the work of improvement for which the design professional provided services.

§ 8318 Exemptions

A design professional may not obtain a lien under this chapter for services provided for a work of improvement relating to a single-family, owner-occupied residence for which the expected construction cost is less than one hundred thousand dollars ($100,000).

§ 8319 Conversion of Design Professional Lien to Mechanics Lien

(a) A design professional may convert a recorded design professional lien to a mechanics lien if all of the following requirements are met:

(1) The design professional lien expires pursuant to paragraph (1) of subdivision (b) of Section 8306.

(2) The design professional lien remains fully or partially unpaid.

(3) Within 30 days of the expiration of the design professional lien pursuant to paragraph (1) of subdivision (b) of Section 8306, the design professional records a mechanics lien for the amount of the unpaid design professional lien.

(4) The recorded mechanics lien states that it is a converted design professional lien but shall be recorded and enforced as a mechanics lien, except the design professional need not provide a preliminary notice to enforce this mechanics lien. This mechanics lien shall be effective as of the date of recordation of this mechanics lien and shall be given priority pursuant to the provisions of Section 8450.

(b) This section shall not apply if a design professional lien expires pursuant to paragraph (2) of subdivision (b) of Section 8306.

Chapter 4. Mechanics Lien

Article 1. Who is Entitled to Lien

§ 8400 Persons Providing Work Authorized for Work of Improvement

A person that provides work authorized for a work of improvement, including, but not limited to, the following persons, has a lien right under this chapter:

(a) Direct contractor.

(b) Subcontractor.

(c) Material supplier.

(d) Equipment lessor.

(e) Laborer.

(f) Design professional.

§ 8402 Persons Providing Work Authorized for Site Improvement

A person that provides work authorized for a site improvement has a lien right under this chapter.

§ 8404 Work Authorized for Work of Improvement or Site Improvement

Work is authorized for a work of improvement or for a site improvement in any of the following circumstances:

(a) It is provided at the request of or agreed to by the owner.

(b) It is provided or authorized by a direct contractor, subcontractor, architect, project manager, or other person having charge of all or part of the work of improvement or site improvement.

Article 2. Conditions to Enforcing a Lien

§ 8410 Preliminary Notice; Proof of Notice

A claimant may enforce a lien only if the claimant has given preliminary notice to the extent required by Chapter 2 (commencing with Section 8200) and made proof of notice.

§ 8412 Multiple Contracts; Notice of Completion for Portion of Work of Improvement

A direct contractor may not enforce a lien unless the contractor records a claim of lien after the contractor completes the direct contract, and before the earlier of the following times:

(a) Ninety days after completion of the work of improvement.

(b) Sixty days after the owner records a notice of completion or cessation.

§ 8414 Persons other than Direct Contractors; Time for Recording Lien

A claimant other than a direct contractor may not enforce a lien unless the claimant records a claim of lien within the following times:

(a) After the claimant ceases to provide work.

(b) Before the earlier of the following times:

(1) Ninety days after completion of the work of improvement.

(2) Thirty days after the owner records a notice of completion or cessation.

§ 8416 Written Statement; Contents; Form; Recording; Service

(a) A claim of mechanics lien shall be a written statement, signed and verified by the claimant, containing all of the following:

(1) A statement of the claimant's demand after deducting all just credits and offsets.

(2) The name of the owner or reputed owner, if known.

(3) A general statement of the kind of work furnished by the claimant.

(4) The name of the person by whom the claimant was employed or to whom the claimant furnished work.

(5) A description of the site sufficient for identification.

(6) The claimant's address.

(7) A proof of service affidavit completed and signed by the person serving a copy of the claim of mechanics lien pursuant to subdivision (c). The affidavit shall show the date, place, and manner of service, and facts showing that the service was made in accordance with this section. The affidavit shall show the name and address of the owner or reputed owner upon whom the copy of the claim of mechanics lien was served pursuant to paragraphs (1) or (2) of subdivision (c), and the title or capacity in which the person or entity was served.

(8) The following statement, printed in at least 10-point boldface type. The letters of the last sentence shall be printed in uppercase type, excepting the Internet Web site address of the Contractors' State License Board, which shall be printed in lowercase type:

"NOTICE OF MECHANICS LIEN
ATTENTION!

Upon the recording of the enclosed MECHANICS LIEN with the county recorder's office of the county where the property is located, your property is subject to the filing of a legal action seeking a court-ordered foreclosure sale of the real property on which the lien has been recorded. That legal action must be filed with the court no later than 90 days after the date the mechanics lien is recorded.

The party identified in the enclosed mechanics lien may have provided labor or materials for improvements to your property and may not have been paid for these items. You are receiving this notice because it is a required step in filing a mechanics lien foreclosure action against your property. The foreclosure action will seek a sale of your property in order to pay for unpaid labor, materials, or improvements provided to your property. This may affect your ability to borrow against, refinance, or sell the property until the mechanics lien is released.

BECAUSE THE LIEN AFFECTS YOUR PROPERTY, YOU MAY WISH TO SPEAK WITH YOUR CONTRACTOR IMMEDIATELY, OR CONTACT AN ATTORNEY, OR FOR MORE INFORMATION ON MECHANICS LIENS GO TO THE CONTRACTORS' STATE LICENSE BOARD WEB SITE AT www.cslb.ca.gov."

(b) A claim of mechanics lien in otherwise proper form, verified and containing the information required in subdivision (a), shall be accepted by the recorder for recording and shall be deemed duly recorded without acknowledgment.

(c) A copy of the claim of mechanics lien, which includes the Notice of Mechanics Lien required by paragraph (8) of subdivision (a), shall be served on the owner or reputed owner. Service shall be made as follows:

(1) For an owner or reputed owner to be notified who resides in or outside this state, by registered mail, certified mail, or first-class mail, evidenced by a certificate of mailing, postage prepaid, addressed to the owner or reputed owner at the owner's or reputed owner's residence or place of business address or at the address shown by the building permit on file with the authority issuing a building permit for the work, or as otherwise provided in Section 8174.

(2) If the owner or reputed owner cannot be served by this method, then the copy of the claim of mechanics lien may be given by registered mail, certified mail, or first-class mail, evidenced by a certificate of mailing, postage prepaid, addressed to the construction lender or to the original contractor.

(d) Service of the copy of the claim of mechanics lien by registered mail, certified mail, or first-class mail, evidenced by a certificate of mailing, postage prepaid, is complete at the time of the deposit of that first-class, certified, or registered mail.

(e) Failure to serve the copy of the claim of mechanics lien as prescribed by this section, including the Notice of Mechanics Lien required by paragraph (8) of subdivision (a), shall cause the claim of mechanics lien to be unenforceable as a matter of law.

§ 8422 Erroneous Information

(a) Except as provided in subdivisions (b) and (c), erroneous information contained in a claim of lien relating to the claimant's demand, credits and offsets deducted, the work provided, or the description of the site, does not invalidate the claim of lien.

(b) Erroneous information contained in a claim of lien relating to the claimant's demand, credits and offsets deducted, or the work provided, invalidates the claim of lien if the court determines either of the following:

(1) The claim of lien was made with intent to defraud.

(2) An innocent third party, without notice, actual or constructive, became the bona fide owner of the property after recordation of the claim of lien, and the claim of lien was so deficient that it did not put the party on further inquiry in any manner.

(c) Any person who shall willfully include in a claim of lien labor, services, equipment, or materials not furnished for the property described in the claim, shall thereby forfeit the person's lien.

§ 8424 Lien Release Bond

(a) An owner of real property or an owner of any interest in real property subject to a recorded claim of lien, or a direct contractor or subcontractor affected by the claim of lien, that disputes the correctness or validity of the claim may obtain release of the real property from the claim of lien by recording a lien release bond. The principal on the bond may be the owner of the property, the direct contractor, or the subcontractor.

(b) The bond shall be conditioned on payment of any judgment and costs the claimant recovers on the lien. The bond shall be in an amount equal to 125 percent of the amount of the claim of lien or 125 percent of the amount allocated in the claim of lien to the real property to be released. The bond shall be executed by an admitted surety insurer.

(c) The bond may be recorded either before or after commencement of an action to enforce the lien. On recordation of the bond, the real property is released from the claim of lien and from any action to enforce the lien.

(d) A person that obtains and records a lien release bond shall give notice to the claimant. The notice shall comply with the requirements of Chapter 2 (commencing with Section 8100) of Title 1 and shall include a copy of the bond. Failure to give the notice required by this section does not affect the validity of the bond, but the statute of limitations for an action on the bond is tolled until notice is given. The claimant shall commence an action on the bond within six months after notice is given.

Article 3. Amount of Lien

§ 8430 Direct Liens; Amount

(a) The lien is a direct lien for the lesser of the following amounts:

(1) The reasonable value of the work provided by the claimant.

(2) The price agreed to by the claimant and the person that contracted for the work.

(b) The lien is not limited in amount by the contract price for the work of improvement except as provided in Section 8600.

(c) This section does not preclude the claimant from including in a claim of lien work performed based on a written modification of the contract, or as a result of rescission, abandonment, or breach of the contract. If there is a rescission, abandonment, or breach of the contract, the amount of the lien may not exceed the reasonable value of the work provided by the claimant.

§ 8432 Work Included in Claim; Constructive Notice

(a) A lien does not extend to work, whether or not the work is authorized by a direct contractor or subcontractor, if the work is not included in a direct contract or a modification of that contract, and the claimant had actual knowledge or constructive notice of the provisions of that contract or modification before providing the work.

(b) The filing of a contract or modification of that contract with the county recorder, before the commencement of a work of improvement, is constructive notice of the provisions of the contract or modification to a person providing work on that work of improvement.

§ 8434 Recovery by Direct Contractor or Subcontractor

A direct contractor or a subcontractor may enforce a lien only for the amount due pursuant to that contractor's contract after deducting all lien claims of other claimants for work provided and embraced within that contract.

Article 4. Property Subject to Lien

§ 8440 Attachment to Work and Real Property

Subject to Section 8442, a lien attaches to the work of improvement and to the real property on which the work of improvement is situated, including as much space about the work of improvement as is required for the convenient use and occupation of the work of improvement.

§ 8442 Interests in Real Property

The following interests in real property to which a lien attaches are subject to the lien:

(a) The interest of a person that contracted for the work of improvement.

(b) The interest of a person that did not contract for the work of improvement, if work for which the lien is claimed was provided with the knowledge of that person, unless that person gives notice of nonresponsibility under Section 8444.

§ 8444 Notice of Nonresponsibility

(a) An owner of real property or a person claiming an interest in real property on which a work of improvement is situated that did not contract for the work of improvement may give notice of nonresponsibility.

(b) A notice of nonresponsibility shall be signed and verified by the owner.

(c) The notice shall comply with the requirements of Chapter 2 (commencing with Section 8100) of Title 1.

(d) The notice shall also include all of the following information:

(1) The nature of the owner's title or interest.

(2) The name of a purchaser under contract, if any, or lessee, if known.

(3) A statement that the person giving the notice is not responsible for claims arising from the work of improvement.

(e) A notice of nonresponsibility is not effective unless, within 10 days after the person giving notice has knowledge of the work of improvement, the person both posts and records the notice.

§ 8446 One Claim on Two or More Works of Improvement; Conditions

A claimant may record one claim of lien on two or more works of improvement, subject to the following conditions:

(a) The works of improvement have or are reputed to have the same owner, or the work was contracted for by the same person for the works of improvement whether or not they have the same owner.

(b) The claimant in the claim of lien designates the amount due for each work of improvement. If the claimant contracted for a lump sum payment for work provided for the works of improvement and the contract does not segregate the amount due for each work of improvement separately, the claimant may estimate an equitable distribution of the amount due for each work of improvement based on the proportionate amount of work provided for each. If the claimant does not designate the amount due for each work of improvement, the lien is subordinate to other liens.

(c) If there is a single structure on real property of different owners, the claimant need not segregate the proportion of work provided for the portion of the structure situated on real property of each owner. In the lien enforcement action the court may, if it determines it equitable to do so, designate an equitable distribution of the lien among the real property of the owners.

(d) The lien does not extend beyond the amount designated as against other creditors having liens, by judgment, mortgage, or otherwise, on either the works of improvement or the real property on which the works of improvement are situated.

§ 8448 Separate Residential Units

(a) As used in this section, "separate residential unit" means one residential structure, including a residential structure containing multiple condominium units, together with any common area, garage, or other appurtenant improvements.

(b) If a work of improvement consists of the construction of two or more separate residential units:

(1) Each unit is deemed a separate work of improvement, and completion of each unit is determined separately for purposes of the time for recording a claim of lien on that unit. This paragraph does not affect any lien right under Section 8402 or 8446.

(2) Material provided for the work of improvement is deemed to be provided for use or consumption in each separate residential unit in which the material is actually used or consumed; but if the claimant is unable to segregate the amounts used or consumed in separate residential units, the claimant has the right to all the benefits of Section 8446.

Article 5. Priorities

§ 8450 Priority of Lien Under this Chapter

(a) A lien under this chapter, other than a lien provided for in Section 8402, has priority over a lien, mortgage, deed of trust, or other encumbrance on the work of improvement or the real property on which the work of improvement is situated, that (1) attaches after commencement of the work of improvement or (2) was unrecorded at the commencement of the work of improvement and of which the claimant had no notice.

(b) Subdivision (a) is subject to the exception provided for in Section 8452.

§ 8452 Mortgage or Deed of Trust; Recordation of Payment Bond; Requirements

A mortgage or deed of trust, otherwise subordinate to a lien under Section 8450, has priority over a lien for work provided after recordation of a payment bond that satisfies all of the following requirements:

(a) The bond refers to the mortgage or deed of trust.

(b) The bond is in an amount not less than 75 percent of the principal amount of the mortgage or deed of trust.

§ 8454 Site Improvements as Separate Direct Contract

If a site improvement is provided for in a direct contract separate from the direct contract for the remainder of the work of improvement, the site improvement is deemed a separate work of improvement and commencement of the site improvement is not commencement of the remainder of the work of improvement.

§ 8456 Loan Secured by Mortgage or Deed of Trust; Optional Advance of Funds

(a) This section applies to a construction loan secured by a mortgage or deed of trust that has priority over a lien under this chapter.

(b) An optional advance of funds by the construction lender that is used for construction costs has the same priority as a mandatory advance of funds by the construction lender, provided that the total of all advances does not exceed the amount of the original construction loan.

§ 8458 Liens for Site Improvement

(a) Except as provided in subdivision (b), a lien provided for in Section 8402 has priority over:

(1) A mortgage, deed of trust, or other encumbrance that attaches after commencement of the site improvement.

(2) A mortgage, deed of trust, or other encumbrance that was unrecorded at the commencement of the site improvement and of which the claimant had no notice.

(3) A mortgage, deed of trust, or other encumbrance that was recorded before commencement of the site improvement, if given for the sole or primary purpose of financing the site improvement. This subdivision does not apply if the loan proceeds are, in good faith, placed in the control of the lender pursuant to a binding agreement with the borrower to the effect that (A) the proceeds are to be applied to the payment of claimants and (B) no portion of the proceeds will be paid to the borrower in the absence of satisfactory evidence that all claims have been paid or that the time for recording a claim of lien has expired and no claim of lien has been recorded.

(b) A mortgage or deed of trust, otherwise subordinate under subdivision (a), has priority over a lien provided for in Section 8402 if a payment bond in an amount not less than 50 percent of the principal amount of the mortgage or deed of trust is recorded before completion of the work of improvement.

Article 6. Enforcement of Lien

§ 8460 Time for Commencement of Action; Exception for Extension of Credit

(a) The claimant shall commence an action to enforce a lien within 90 days after recordation of the claim of lien. If the claimant does not commence an action to enforce the lien within that time, the claim of lien expires and is unenforceable.

(b) Subdivision (a) does not apply if the claimant and owner agree to extend credit, and notice of the fact and terms of the extension of credit is recorded (1) within 90 days after recordation of the claim of lien or (2) more than 90 days after recordation of the claim of lien but before a purchaser or encumbrancer for value and in good faith acquires rights in the property. In that event the claimant shall commence an action to enforce the lien within 90 days after the expiration of the credit, but in no case later than one year after completion of the work of improvement. If the claimant does not commence an action to enforce the lien within that time, the claim of lien expires and is unenforceable.

§ 8461 Recording of Notice of Pendency of Action

After commencement of an action to enforce a lien, the plaintiff shall record in the office of the county recorder of the county, or of the several counties in which the property is situated, a notice of the pendency of the action, as provided in Title 4.5 (commencing with Section 405) of Part 2 of the Code of Civil Procedure, on or before 20 days after the commencement of the action. Only from the time of recording that notice shall a purchaser or encumbrancer of the property affected thereby be deemed to have constructive notice of the pendency of the action, and in that event only of its pendency against parties designated by their real names.

§ 8462 Dismissal

Notwithstanding Section 583.420 of the Code of Civil Procedure, if an action to enforce a lien is not brought to trial within two years after commencement of the action, the court may in its discretion dismiss the action for want of prosecution.

§ 8464 Costs

In addition to any other costs allowed by law, the court in an action to enforce a lien shall allow as costs to each claimant whose lien is established the amount paid to verify and record the claim of lien, whether the claimant is a plaintiff or defendant.

§ 8466 Deficiency Judgment

If there is a deficiency of proceeds from the sale of property on a judgment for enforcement of a lien, a deficiency judgment may be entered against a party personally liable for the deficiency in the same manner and with the same effect as in an action to foreclose a mortgage.

§ 8468 Personal Actions; Writ of Attachment; Judgment; Credit or Money Collected

(a) This chapter does not affect any of the following rights of a claimant:

(1) The right to maintain a personal action to recover a debt against the person liable, either in a separate action or in an action to enforce a lien.

(2) The right to a writ of attachment. In an application for a writ of attachment, the claimant shall refer to this section. The claimant's recording of a claim of lien does not affect the right to a writ of attachment.

(3) The right to enforce a judgment.

(b) A judgment obtained by the claimant in a personal action described in subdivision (a) does not impair or merge the claim of lien, but any amount collected on the judgment shall be credited on the amount of the lien.

§ 8470 Defense by Contractor

In an action to enforce a lien for work provided to a contractor:

(a) The contractor shall defend the action at the contractor's own expense. During the pendency of the action the owner may withhold from the direct contractor the amount of the lien claim.

(b) If the judgment in the action is against the owner or the owner's property, the owner may deduct the amount of the judgment and costs from any amount owed to the direct contractor. If the amount of the judgment and costs exceeds the amount owed to the direct contractor, or if the owner has settled with the direct contractor in full, the owner may recover from the direct contractor, or the sureties on a bond given by the direct contractor for faithful performance of the direct contract, the amount of the judgment and costs that exceed the contract price and for which the direct contractor was originally liable.

Article 7. Release Order

§ 8480 Release Order; Other Actions or Claims; Joinder of Claims

(a) The owner of property or the owner of any interest in property subject to a claim of lien may petition the court for an order to release the property from the claim of lien if the claimant has not commenced an action to enforce the lien within the time provided in Section 8460.

(b) This article does not bar any other cause of action or claim for relief by the owner of the property. A release order does not bar any other cause of action or claim for relief by the claimant, other than an action to enforce the claim of lien that is the subject of the release order.

(c) A petition for a release order under this article may be joined with a pending action to enforce the claim of lien that is the subject of the petition. No other action or claim for relief may be joined with a petition under this article.

(d) Notwithstanding Section 8056, Chapter 2.5 (commencing with Section 1141.10) of Title 3 of Part 3 of the Code of Civil Procedure does not apply to a proceeding under this article.

§ 8482 Time for Petition; Notice

An owner of property may not petition the court for a release order under this article unless at least 10 days before filing the petition the owner gives the claimant notice demanding that the claimant execute and record a release of the claim of lien. The notice shall comply with the requirements of Chapter 2 (commencing with Section 8100) of Title 1, and shall state the rounds for the demand.

§ 8484 Verified Petition; Contents

A petition for a release order shall be verified and shall allege all of the following:

(a) The date of recordation of the claim of lien. A certified copy of the claim of lien shall be attached to the petition.

(b) The county in which the claim of lien is recorded.

(c) The book and page or series number of the place in the official records where the claim of lien is recorded.

(d) The legal description of the property subject to the claim of lien.

(e) Whether an extension of credit has been granted under Section 8460, if so to what date, and that the time for commencement of an action to enforce the lien has expired.

(f) That the owner has given the claimant notice under Section 8482 demanding that the claimant execute and record a release of the lien and that the claimant is unable or unwilling to do so or cannot with reasonable diligence be found.

(g) Whether an action to enforce the lien is pending.

(h) Whether the owner of the property or interest in the property has filed for relief in bankruptcy or there is another restraint that prevents the claimant from commencing an action to enforce the lien.

§ 8486 Hearing Date; Service

(a) On the filing of a petition for a release order, the clerk shall set a hearing date. The date shall be not more than 30 days after the filing of the petition. The court may continue the hearing only on a showing of good cause, but in any event the court shall rule and make any necessary orders on the petition not later than 60 days after the filing of the petition.

(b) The petitioner shall serve a copy of the petition and a notice of hearing on the claimant at least 15 days before the hearing. Service shall be made in the same manner as service of summons, or by certified or registered mail, postage prepaid, return receipt requested, addressed to the claimant as provided in Section 8108.

(c) Notwithstanding Section 8116, when service is made by mail, service is complete on the fifth day following deposit of the petition and notice in the mail.

§ 8488 Hearing; Burden of Production; Burden of Proof; Judgment, Attorney Fees

(a) At the hearing both (1) the petition and (2) the issue of compliance with the service and date for hearing requirements of this article are deemed controverted by the claimant. The petitioner has the initial burden of producing evidence on those matters. The petitioner has the burden of proof as to the issue of compliance with the service and date for hearing requirements of this article. The claimant has the burden of proof as to the validity of the lien.

(b) If judgment is in favor of the petitioner, the court shall order the property released from the claim of lien.

(c) The prevailing party is entitled to reasonable attorney's fees.

Article 8. Removal of Claim of Lien from Record

§ 8490 Order Dismissing Cause of Action or Judgment that no Lien Exists

(a) A court order dismissing a cause of action to enforce a lien or releasing property from a claim of lien, or a judgment that no lien exists, shall include all of the following information:

(1) The date of recordation of the claim of lien.

(2) The county in which the claim of lien is recorded.

(3) The book and page or series number of the place in the official records where the claim of lien is recorded.

(4) The legal description of the property.

(b) A court order or judgment under this section is equivalent to cancellation of the claim of lien and its removal from the record.

(c) A court order or judgment under this section is a recordable instrument. On recordation of a certified copy of the court order or judgment, the property described in the order or judgment is released from the claim of lien.

(d) This section does not apply to a court order dismissing an action to enforce a lien that is expressly stated to be without prejudice.

§ 8494 Expiration or Recordation of Order or Judgment; Notice

If a claim of lien expires and is unenforceable under Section 8460, or if a court order or judgment is recorded under Section 8490, the claim of lien does not constitute actual or constructive notice of any of the matters contained, claimed, alleged, or contended in the claim of lien, or create a duty of inquiry in any person thereafter dealing with the affected property.

Chapter 5. Stop Payment Notice

Article 1. General Provisions

§ 8500 Exclusive Remedy

The rights of all persons furnishing work for any work of improvement, with respect to any fund for payment of construction costs, are governed exclusively by this chapter, and no person may assert any legal or equitable right with respect to the fund, other than a right created by a written contract between that person and the person holding the fund, except pursuant to the provisions of this chapter.

§ 8502 Requirements; Contents; Amount Claimed

(a) A stop payment notice shall comply with the requirements of Chapter 2 (commencing with Section 8100) of Title 1, and shall be signed and verified by the claimant.

(b) The notice shall include a general description of work to be provided, and an estimate of the total amount in value of the work to be provided.

(c) The amount claimed in the notice may include only the amount due the claimant for work provided through the date of the notice.

§ 8504 False Stop Payment Notice

A claimant that willfully gives a false stop payment notice or that willfully includes in the notice a demand to withhold for work that has not been provided forfeits all right to participate in the distribution of the funds withheld and all right to a lien under Chapter 4 (commencing with Section 8400).

§ 8506 Notice

(a) A stop payment notice to an owner shall be given to the owner or to the owner's architect, if any.

(b) A stop payment notice to a construction lender holding construction funds shall not be effective unless given to the manager or other responsible officer or person at the office or branch of the lender administering or holding the construction funds.

(c) A stop payment notice shall comply with the requirements of Chapter 2 (commencing with Section 8100) of Title 1.

§ 8508 Validity of Notice; Conditions

A stop payment notice is not valid unless both of the following conditions are satisfied:

(a) The claimant gave preliminary notice to the extent required by Chapter 2 (commencing with Section 8200).

(b) The claimant gave the stop payment notice before expiration of the time within which a claim of lien must be recorded under Chapter 4 (commencing with Section 8400).

§ 8510 Release Bond

(a) A person may obtain release of funds withheld pursuant to a stop payment notice by giving the person withholding the funds a release bond.

(b) A release bond shall be given by an admitted surety insurer and shall be conditioned for payment of any amount not exceeding the penal obligation of the bond that the claimant recovers on the claim, together with costs of suit awarded in the action. The bond shall be in an amount equal to 125 percent of the amount claimed in the stop payment notice.

(c) On receipt of a release bond, the person withholding funds pursuant to the stop payment notice shall release them.

Article 2. Stop Payment Notice to Owner

§ 8520 Persons Who May Give Notice

(a) A person that has a lien right under Chapter 4 (commencing with Section 8400), other than a direct contractor, may give the owner a stop payment notice.

(b) The owner may give notice, in compliance with the requirements of Chapter 2 (commencing with Section 8100) of Title 1, demanding that a person that has a lien right under Chapter 4 (commencing with Section 8400) give the owner a stop payment notice. If the person fails to give the owner a bonded or unbonded stop payment notice, the person forfeits the right to a lien under Chapter 4 (commencing with Section 8400).

§ 8522 Withholding of Sufficient Amount to Pay Claim; Exception

(a) Except as provided in subdivision (b), on receipt of a stop payment notice an owner shall withhold from the direct contractor or from any person acting under authority of a direct contractor a sufficient amount due or to become due to the direct contractor to pay the claim stated in the notice.

(b) The owner may, but is not required to, withhold funds if the owner has previously recorded a payment bond under Section 8600. If the owner does not withhold funds, the owner shall, within 30 days after receipt of the stop payment notice, give notice to the claimant that a payment bond has been recorded and provide the claimant a copy of the bond. The notice shall comply with the requirements of Chapter 2 (commencing with Section 8100) of Title 1.

Article 3. Stop Payment Notice to Construction Lender

§ 8530 Person Who May Give Notice

A person that has a lien right under Chapter 4 (commencing with Section 8400) may give a construction lender a stop payment notice.

§ 8532 Bond

A claimant may give a construction lender a stop payment notice accompanied by a bond in an amount equal to 125 percent of the amount of the claim. The bond shall be conditioned that if the defendant recovers judgment in an action to enforce payment of the claim stated in the stop payment notice or to enforce a claim of lien recorded by the claimant, the claimant will pay all costs that are awarded the owner, direct contractor, or construction lender, and all damages to the owner, direct contractor, or construction lender that result from the stop payment notice or recordation of the claim of lien, not exceeding the amount of the bond.

§ 8534 Notice of Objection to Sufficiency of Sureties; Substitution

(a) A construction lender that objects to the sufficiency of sureties on the bond given with a bonded stop payment notice shall give notice to the claimant of the objection, within 20 days after the bonded stop payment notice is given. The notice shall comply with the requirements of Chapter 2 (commencing with Section 8100) of Title 1.

(b) The claimant may within 10 days after notice of the objection is given substitute for the initial bond a bond executed by an admitted surety insurer. If the claimant does not substitute a bond executed by an admitted surety insurer, the construction lender may disregard the bonded stop payment notice and release all funds withheld in response to that notice.

§ 8536 Withholding of Sufficient Funds; Exception

(a) Except as provided in subdivision (b), on receipt of a stop payment notice a construction lender shall withhold from the borrower or other person to whom the lender or the owner is obligated to make payments or advancement out of the construction fund sufficient funds to pay the claim stated in the notice.

(b) The construction lender may, at its option, elect not to withhold funds in any of the following circumstances:

(1) The stop payment notice is unbonded.

(2) The stop payment notice is given by a claimant other than a direct contractor, and a payment bond is recorded before the lender is given any stop payment notice.

§ 8538 Request for Notice of Election

(a) The claimant may make a written request for notice of an election by the construction lender under Section 8536 not to withhold funds. The request shall be made at the time the claimant gives the construction lender the stop payment notice and shall be accompanied by a preaddressed, stamped envelope.

(b) If the construction lender elects not to withhold funds under Section 8536, the lender shall, within 30 days after making the election, give notice of that fact to a claimant who has requested notice of the election under subdivision (a). The notice shall comply with the requirements of Chapter 2 (commencing with Section 8100) of Title 1. If the basis of the election is the recordation of a payment bond under Section 8600, the construction lender shall include a copy of the bond with the notice.

(c) A construction lender is not liable for failure to include a copy of the bond with the notice under this section if all of the following conditions are satisfied:

(1) The failure was not intentional and resulted from a bona fide error.

(2) The lender maintains reasonable procedures to avoid an error of that type.

(3) The lender corrected the error not later than 20 days after the date the lender discovered the violation.

Article 4. Priorities

§ 8540 Order of Priority; Pro Rata Distribution

(a) Funds withheld pursuant to a stop payment notice shall be distributed in the following order of priority:

(1) First, to pay claims of persons that have given a bonded stop payment notice. If funds are insufficient to pay the claims of those persons in full, the funds shall be distributed pro rata among the claimants in the ratio that the claim of each bears to the aggregate of all claims for which a bonded stop payment notice is given.

(2) Second, to pay claims of persons that have given an unbonded stop payment notice. If funds are insufficient to pay the claims of those persons in full, the funds shall be distributed among the claimants in the ratio that the claim of each bears to the aggregate of all claims for which an unbonded stop payment notice is given.

(b) Pro rata distribution under this section shall be made among the persons entitled to share in the distribution without regard to the order in which the person has given a stop payment notice or commenced an enforcement action.

§ 8542 Recovery of Net Amount Due Only; Maximum Amount to be Withheld

Notwithstanding Section 8540:

(a) If funds are withheld pursuant to a stop payment notice given to a construction lender by a direct contractor or subcontractor, the direct contractor or subcontractor may recover only the net amount due the direct contractor or subcontractor after deducting any funds that are withheld by the construction lender pursuant to the claims of subcontractors and material suppliers that have given a stop payment notice for work done on behalf of the direct contractor or subcontractor.

(b) In no event is the construction lender required to withhold, pursuant to a stop payment notice, more than the net amount provided in subdivision (a). Notwithstanding any other provision of this chapter, a construction lender is not liable for failure to withhold more than that net amount on receipt of a stop payment notice.

§ 8544 Assignment of Construction Loan Funds; Rights of Claimant Not Affected

The rights of a claimant who gives a construction lender a stop payment notice are not affected by an assignment of construction loan funds made by the owner or direct contractor, and the stop payment notice has priority over the assignment, whether the assignment is made before or after the stop payment notice is given.

Article 5. Enforcement of Claim Stated in Stop Payment Notice

§ 8550 Time for Commencement of Action; Notice

(a) A claimant shall commence an action to enforce payment of the claim stated in a stop payment notice at any time after 10 days from the date the claimant gives the stop payment notice.

(b) A claimant shall commence an action to enforce payment of the claim stated in a stop payment notice not later than 90 days after expiration of the time within which a stop payment notice must be given.

(c) An action under this section may not be brought to trial or judgment entered before expiration of the time provided in subdivision (b).

(d) If a claimant does not commence an action to enforce payment of the claim stated in a stop payment notice within the time prescribed in subdivision (b), the notice ceases to be effective and the person withholding funds pursuant to the notice shall release them.

(e) Within five days after commencement of an action to enforce payment of the claim stated in a stop payment notice, the claimant shall give notice of commencement of the action to the persons to whom the stop payment notice was given. The notice shall comply with the requirements of Chapter 2 (commencing with Section 8100) of Title 1.

§ 8552 Multiple Claimants

If more than one claimant has given a stop payment notice:

(a) Any number of claimants may join in the same enforcement action.

(b) If claimants commence separate actions, the court first acquiring jurisdiction may order the actions consolidated.

(c) On motion of the owner or construction lender the court shall require all claimants to be impleaded in one action, to the end that the rights of all parties may be adjudicated in the action.

§ 8554 Dismissal for Want of Prosecution

Notwithstanding Section 583.420 of the Code of Civil Procedure, if an action to enforce payment of the claim stated in a stop payment notice is not brought to trial within two years after commencement of the action, the court may in its discretion dismiss the action for want of prosecution.

§ 8556 Dismissal or Judgment; Effect

A stop payment notice ceases to be effective, and a person withholding funds pursuant to the notice shall release them, in either of the following circumstances:

(a) An action to enforce payment of the claim stated in the stop payment notice is dismissed, unless expressly stated to be without prejudice.

(b) Judgment in an action to enforce payment of the claim stated in the stop payment notice is against the claimant.

§ 8558 Attorney Fees; Prevailing Party

(a) In an action to enforce payment of the claim stated in a bonded stop payment notice, the prevailing party is entitled to a reasonable attorney's fee in addition to costs and damages.

(b) The court, on notice and motion by a party, shall determine who is the prevailing party or that there is no prevailing party for the purpose of this section, regardless of whether the action proceeds to final judgment. The prevailing party is the party that recovers greater relief in the action, subject to the following limitations:

(1) If the action is voluntarily dismissed or dismissed pursuant to a settlement, there is no prevailing party.

(2) If the defendant tenders to the claimant the full amount to which the claimant is entitled, and deposits in court for the claimant the amount so tendered, and alleges those facts in the answer and the allegation is determined to be true, the defendant is deemed to be the prevailing party.

§ 8560 Interest

If the claimant is the prevailing party in an action to enforce payment of the claim stated in a bonded stop payment notice, any amount awarded on the claim shall include interest at the legal rate calculated from the date the stop payment notice is given.

Chapter 6. Payment Bond

§ 8600 Application; Restriction of Lien Enforcement

(a) This section applies if, before the commencement of work, the owner in good faith files a direct contract with the county recorder, and records a payment bond of the direct contractor in an amount not less than 50 percent of the price stated in the direct contract.

(b) If the conditions of subdivision (a) are satisfied, the court shall, where equitable to do so, restrict lien enforcement under this title to the aggregate amount due from the owner to the direct contractor and shall enter judgment against the direct contractor and surety on the bond for any deficiency that remains between the amount due to the direct contractor and the whole amount due to claimants.

§ 8602 Bond or Other Security

Section 8600 does not preclude an owner from requiring a performance bond, payment bond, or other security as protection against a direct contractor's failure to perform the direct contract or to make full payment for all work provided pursuant to the contract.

§ 8604 Lending Institutions; Objections to Bond

(a) If a lending institution requires that a payment bond be given as a condition of lending money to finance a work of improvement, and accepts in writing as sufficient a bond given in fulfillment of the requirement, the lending institution may not thereafter object to the borrower as to the validity of the bond or refuse to make the loan based on an objection to the bond if the bond is given by an admitted surety insurer.

(b) For purposes of this section, a "lending institution" includes a commercial bank, savings and loan institution, credit union, or other organization or person engaged in the business of financing loans.

§ 8606 Nature of Bond; Principal; Enforcement

(a) A payment bond under this title shall be conditioned for the payment in full of the claims of all claimants and shall by its terms inure to the benefit of all claimants so as to give a claimant a right of action to enforce the liability on the bond. The bond shall be given by an admitted surety insurer.

(b) An owner, direct contractor, or subcontractor may be the principal on the bond.

(c) A claimant may enforce the liability on the bond in an action to enforce a lien under this part or in a separate action on the bond.

§ 8608 Work Done for Direct Contractor on Bond; Claim

(a) This title does not give a claimant a right to recover on a direct contractor's payment bond given under this chapter unless the claimant provided work to the direct contractor either directly or through one or more subcontractors, pursuant to a direct contract.

(b) Nothing in this section affects the stop payment notice right of, and relative priorities among, design professionals and holders of secured interests in the real property.

§ 8609 Invalidity of Provisions Limiting Actions

Any provision in a payment bond attempting by contract to shorten the period prescribed in Section 337 of the Code of Civil Procedure for the commencement of an action on the bond shall not be valid under either of the following circumstances:

(a) If the provision attempts to limit the time for commencement of an action on the bond to a shorter period than six months from the completion of any work of improvement.

(b) As applied to any action brought by a claimant, unless the bond is recorded before the work of improvement is commenced.

§ 8610 Bonds Recorded Before Improvements Completed; Actions Against Sureties

Notwithstanding Section 8609, if a payment bond under this title is recorded before completion of a work of improvement, an action to enforce the liability on the bond may not be commenced later than six months after completion of the work of improvement.

§ 8612 Preliminary Notice Required; Exceptions

(a) In order to enforce a claim against a payment bond under this title, a claimant shall give the preliminary notice provided in Chapter 2 (commencing with Section 8200).

(b) If preliminary notice was not given as provided in Chapter 2 (commencing with Section 8200), a claimant may enforce a claim by giving written notice to the surety and the bond principal within 15 days after recordation of a notice of completion. If no notice of completion has been recorded, the time for giving written notice to the surety and the bond principal is extended to 75 days after completion of the work of improvement.

(c) Commencing July 1, 2012, and except as provided in subdivision (b), if the preliminary notice was required to be given by a person who has no direct contractual relationship with the contractor, and who has not given notice as provided in Chapter 2 (commencing with Section 8200), that person may enforce a claim by giving written notice to the surety and the bond principal, as provided in Section 8614, within 15 days after recordation of a notice of completion. If no notice of completion has been recorded, the time for giving written notice to the surety and the bond principal is extended to 75 days after completion of the work of improvement.

(d) Subdivision (c) shall not apply in either of the following circumstances:

(1) All progress payments, except for those disputed in good faith, have been made to a subcontractor who has a direct contractual relationship with the general contractor to whom the claimant has provided materials or services.

(2) The subcontractor who has a direct contractual relationship with the general contractor to whom the claimant has provided materials or services has been terminated from the project pursuant to the contract, and all progress payments, except those disputed in good faith, have been made as of the termination date.

(e) Pursuant to Section 8200, this section shall not apply to a laborer, as defined under Section 8024.

(f) This section shall become operative on July 1, 2012.

§ 8614 Notice Requirements

Notice to the principal and surety under Section 8612 shall comply with the requirements of Chapter 2 (commencing with Section 8100) of Title 1.

Chapter 7. Security for Large Project

Article 1. Application of Chapter

§ 8700 Conditions for Application of Chapter

(a) This chapter applies if any of the following conditions is satisfied:

(1) The owner of the fee interest in property contracts for a work of improvement on the property with a contract price greater than five million dollars ($5,000,000).

(2) The owner of a less than fee interest in property, including a leasehold interest, contracts for a work of improvement on the property with a contract price greater than one million dollars ($1,000,000).

(b) For the purpose of this section:

(1) The owner of the fee interest in property is not deemed to be the owner of a less than fee interest by reason of a mortgage, deed of trust, ground lease, or other lien or encumbrance or right of occupancy that encumbers the fee interest.

(2) A lessee of real property is deemed to be the owner of a fee interest in the real property if all of the following conditions are satisfied:

(A) The initial term of the lease is at least 35 years.

(B) The lease covers one or more lawful parcels under the Subdivision Map Act, Division 2 (commencing with Section 66410) of Title 7 of the Government Code, and any applicable local ordinance adopted under that act, in their entirety, including, but not limited to, a parcel approved pursuant to a certificate of compliance proceeding.

§ 8702 Chapter Not Applicable to Specified Works of Improvement

This chapter does not apply to any of the following works of improvement:

(a) A single-family residence, including a single-family residence located within a subdivision, and any associated fixed work that requires the services of a general engineering contractor as defined in Section 7056 of the Business and Professions Code. As used in this subdivision, "single-family residence" means a real property improvement used or intended to be used as a dwelling unit for one family.

(b) A housing development eligible for a density bonus under Section 65915 of the Government Code.

§ 8704 Chapter Not Applicable to Specified Owners

This chapter does not apply to any of the following owners:

(a) A qualified publicly traded company or a wholly owned subsidiary of a qualified publicly traded company, if the obligations of the subsidiary pursuant to the contract for the work of improvement are guaranteed by the parent. As used in this subdivision, "qualified publicly traded company" means a company having a class of equity securities listed for trading on the New York Stock Exchange, the American Stock Exchange, or the NASDAQ stock market, and the nonsubordinated debt securities of which are rated as "investment grade" by either Fitch ICBA, Inc., Moody's Investor Services, Inc., Standard & Poor's Ratings Services, or a similar statistical rating organization that is nationally recognized for rating the creditworthiness of a publicly traded company. If at any time before final payment of all amounts due pursuant to the contract the nonsubordinated debt securities of the qualified publicly traded company are downgraded to below " investment grade" by any of those rating organizations, the owner is no longer exempt from this chapter.

(b) A qualified private company or a wholly owned subsidiary of a qualified private company, if the obligations of the subsidiary pursuant to the contract for the work of improvement are guaranteed by the parent. As used in this subdivision, "qualified private company" means a company that has no equity securities listed for trading on the New York Stock Exchange, the American Stock Exchange, or the NASDAQ stock market, and that has a net worth determined in accordance with generally accepted accounting principles in excess of fifty million dollars ($50,000,000). If at any time before final payment of all amounts due pursuant to the contract the net worth of the qualified private company is reduced below that level, the owner is no longer exempt from this chapter.

Article 2. Security Requirement

§ 8710 Security and Disclosure of Amount of Construction Loan

An owner described in subdivision (a) of Section 8700 shall provide the direct contractor all of the following:

(a) Security for the owner's payment obligation pursuant to the contract. The security shall be used only if the owner defaults on the payment obligation to the direct contractor. This subdivision does not apply to an owner that is the majority owner of the direct contractor.

(b) A copy, certified by the county recorder, of any recorded mortgage or deed of trust that secures the construction loan of a lending institution for the work of improvement, disclosing the amount of the loan.

§ 8712 Failure to Provide or Maintain Security

If an owner fails to provide or maintain the security required by this chapter, the direct contractor may give the owner notice demanding security. The notice shall comply with the requirements of Chapter 2 (commencing with Section 8100) of Title 1. If the owner does not provide or maintain the security within 10 days after notice demanding security is given, the direct contractor may suspend work until the owner provides or maintains the security.

§ 8714 Waiver Against Public Policy

It is against public policy to waive the provisions of this chapter by contract.

§ 8716 Effect on Rights of Subcontractor

This chapter does not affect any statute providing for mechanics liens, stop payment notices, bond remedies, or prompt payment rights of a subcontractor, including the direct contractor's payment responsibilities under Section 7108.5 of the Business and Professions Code.

Article 3. Form of Security

§ 8720 Means of Providing Security

An owner shall provide security by any of the following means:

(a) A bond that satisfies Section 8722.

(b) An irrevocable letter of credit that satisfies Section 8724.

(c) An escrow account that satisfies Section 8726.

§ 8722 Bond; Requirements

A bond under this chapter shall satisfy all of the following requirements:

(a) The bond shall be executed by an admitted surety insurer that is either listed in the Department of the Treasury's Listing of Approved Sureties (Department Circular 570) or that has an A.M. Best rating of A or better and has an underwriting limitation, under Section 12090 of the Insurance Code, greater than the amount of the bond.

(b) The bond shall be in an amount not less than 15 percent of the contract price for the work of improvement or, if the work of improvement is to be substantially completed within six months after the commencement of work, not less than 25 percent of the contract price.

(c) The bond shall be conditioned for payment on default by the owner of any undisputed amount pursuant to the contract that is due and payable for more than 30 days.

§ 8724 Irrevocable Letter of Credit; Requirements

An irrevocable letter of credit under this chapter shall satisfy all of the following requirements:

(a) The letter of credit shall be issued by a financial institution, as defined in Section 5107 of the Financial Code, inuring to the benefit of the direct contractor.

(b) The letter of credit shall be in an amount not less than 15 percent of the contract price for the work of improvement or, if the work of improvement is to be substantially completed within six months after the commencement of work, not less than 25 percent of the contract price.

(c) The maturity date and other terms of the letter of credit shall be determined by agreement between the owner, the direct contractor, and the financial institution, except that the owner shall maintain the letter of credit in effect until the owner has satisfied its payment obligation to the direct contractor.

§ 8726 Escrow Account; Requirements

An escrow account under this chapter shall satisfy all of the following requirements:

(a) The account shall be designated as a "construction security escrow account."

(b) The account shall be located in this state and maintained with an escrow agent licensed under the Escrow Law, Division 6 (commencing with Section 17000) of the Financial Code, or with any person exempt from the Escrow Law under paragraph (1) or (3) of subdivision (a) of Section 17006 of the Financial Code.

(c) The owner shall deposit funds in the account in the amount provided in Section 8728. This chapter does not require a construction lender to agree to deposit proceeds of a construction loan in the account.

(d) The owner shall grant the direct contractor a perfected, first priority security interest in the account and in all funds deposited by the owner in the account and in their proceeds, established to the reasonable satisfaction of the direct contractor, which may be by a written opinion of legal counsel for the owner.

(e) The funds on deposit in the account shall be the sole property of the owner, subject to the security interest of the direct contractor. The owner and the direct contractor shall instruct the escrow holder to hold the funds on deposit in the account for the purpose of perfecting the direct contractor's security interest in the account and to disburse those funds only on joint authorization of the owner and the direct contractor, or pursuant to a court order that is binding on both of them.

§ 8728 Construction Security Escrow Account; Deposit or Disbursement

The following provisions govern a deposit to or disbursement from a construction security escrow account under this chapter:

(a) Before the commencement of work the owner shall make an initial deposit to the account in an amount not less than 15 percent of the contract price for the work of improvement or, if the work of improvement is to be substantially completed within six months after the commencement of work, not less than 25 percent of the contract price.

(b) If the contract provides for a retention to be withheld from a periodic payment to the direct contractor, the owner shall deposit to the account the amount withheld as retention at the time the owner makes the corresponding payment to the direct contractor from which the retention is withheld.

(c) The amount required to be maintained on deposit shall not exceed the total amount remaining to be paid to the direct contractor pursuant to the contract or as adjusted by agreement between the owner and the direct contractor. If the amount on deposit equals or exceeds the total amount remaining to be paid to the direct contractor, the owner and the direct contractor shall authorize disbursement to the direct contractor for progress payments then due the direct contractor, but a party is not obligated to authorize disbursement that would cause the amount remaining on deposit following the disbursement to be less than the total amount remaining to be paid to the direct contractor.

(d) The owner and the direct contractor shall authorize the disbursement to the owner of any funds remaining on deposit after the direct contractor has been paid all amounts due pursuant to the contract. The owner and the direct contractor shall authorize the disbursement of funds on deposit pursuant to a court order that is binding on both of them. The owner and the direct contractor may agree in the contract to additional conditions for the disbursement of funds on deposit, except that the conditions may not cause the amount remaining on deposit to be less than the amount required under this section.

§ 8730 Contract Price Not Fixed Price; Amount of Security

If the contract price for a work of improvement is not a fixed price, the amount of security provided under this chapter shall be the guaranteed maximum price or, if there is no guaranteed maximum price, the owner's and direct contractor's good faith estimate of the reasonable value of the work to be provided pursuant to the contract.

Chapter 8. Prompt Payment

Article 1. Progress Payment

§ 8800 Progress Payments; Good Faith Disputes; Liability of Owner

(a) Except as otherwise agreed in writing by the owner and direct contractor, the owner shall pay the direct contractor, within 30 days after notice demanding payment pursuant to the contract is given, any progress payment due as to which there is no good faith dispute between them. The notice given shall comply with the requirements of Chapter 2 (commencing with Section 8100) of Title 1.

(b) If there is a good faith dispute between the owner and direct contractor as to a progress payment due, the owner may withhold from the progress payment an amount not in excess of 150 percent of the disputed amount.

(c) An owner that violates this section is liable to the direct contractor for a penalty of 2 percent per month on the amount wrongfully withheld, in place of any interest otherwise due. In an action for collection of the amount wrongfully withheld, the prevailing party is entitled to costs and a reasonable attorney's fee.

(d) This section does not supersede any requirement of Article 2 (commencing with Section 8810) relating to the withholding of a retention.

§ 8802 Payments to Subcontractors; Liability of Direct Contractor; Remedies

(a) This section applies to a contract between a public utility and a direct contractor for all or part of a work of improvement.

(b) Unless the direct contractor and a subcontractor otherwise agree in writing, within 21 days after receipt of a progress payment from the public utility the direct contractor shall pay the subcontractor the amount allowed the direct contractor on account of the work performed by the subcontractor to the extent of the subcontractor's interest in the work. If there is a good faith dispute over all or part of the amount due on a progress payment from the direct contractor to a subcontractor, the direct contractor may withhold an amount not in excess of 150 percent of the disputed amount.

(c) A direct contractor that violates this section is liable to the subcontractor for a penalty of 2 percent of the disputed amount due per month for every month that payment is not made. In an action for collection of the amount wrongfully withheld, the prevailing party is entitled to costs and a reasonable attorney's fee.

(d) This section does not limit or impair a contractual, administrative, or judicial remedy otherwise available to a contractor or subcontractor in a dispute involving late payment or nonpayment by the contractor or deficient performance or nonperformance by the subcontractor.

Article 2. Retention Payment

§ 8810 Scope of Article

This article governs a retention payment withheld by an owner from a direct contractor or by a direct contractor from a subcontractor.

§ 8812 Time for Payment of Retention to Direct Contractor

(a) If an owner withholds a retention from a direct contractor, the owner shall, within 45 days after completion of the work of improvement, pay the retention to the contractor.

(b) If part of a work of improvement ultimately will become the property of a public entity, the owner may condition payment of a retention allocable to that part on acceptance of the part by the public entity.

(c) If there is a good faith dispute between the owner and direct contractor as to a retention payment due, the owner may withhold from final payment an amount not in excess of 150 percent of the disputed amount.

§ 8814 Time for Payment of Retention to Subcontractor

(a) If a direct contractor has withheld a retention from one or more subcontractors, the direct contractor shall, within 10 days after receiving all or part of a retention payment, pay to each subcontractor from whom retention has been withheld that subcontractor's share of the payment.

(b) If a retention received by the direct contractor is specifically designated for a particular subcontractor, the direct contractor shall pay the retention payment to the designated subcontractor, if consistent with the terms of the subcontract.

(c) If a good faith dispute exists between the direct contractor and a subcontractor, the direct contractor may withhold from the retention to the subcontractor an amount not in excess of 150 percent of the estimated value of the disputed amount.

§ 8816 Notice that Disputed Work has been Completed in Accordance with Contract

(a) If the direct contractor gives the owner, or a subcontractor gives the direct contractor, notice that work in dispute has been completed in accordance with the contract, the owner or direct contractor shall within 10 days give notice advising the notifying party of the acceptance or rejection of the disputed work. Both notices shall comply with the requirements of Chapter 2 (commencing with Section 8100) of Title 1.

(b) Within 10 days after acceptance of disputed work, the owner or direct contractor shall pay the portion of the retention relating to the disputed work.

§ 8818 Failure to Make Payment within Required Time; Liability

If an owner or direct contractor does not make a retention payment within the time required by this article:

(a) The owner or direct contractor is liable to the person to which payment is owed for a penalty of 2 percent per month on the amount wrongfully withheld, in place of any interest otherwise due.

(b) In an action for collection of the amount wrongfully withheld, the prevailing party is entitled to costs and reasonable attorney's fees.

§ 8820 Waiver Against Public Policy

It is against public policy to waive the provisions of this article by contract.

§ 8822 Retention Payments Withheld by Lender Pursuant to Loan Agreement

This article does not apply to a retention payment withheld by a lender pursuant to a construction loan agreement.

Article 3. Stop Work Notice

§ 8830 Stop Work Notice Defined

"Stop work notice" means notice given under this article by a direct contractor to an owner that the contractor will stop work if the amount owed the contractor is not paid within 10 days after notice is given.

§ 8832 Conditions for Stop Payment Notice

If a direct contractor is not paid the amount due pursuant to a written contract within 35 days after the date payment is due under the contract, and there is no dispute as to the satisfactory performance of the contractor, the contractor may give the owner a stop work notice. The notice shall comply with the requirements of Chapter 2 (commencing with Section 8100) of Title 1.

§ 8834 Additional Notice with Stop Work Notice

A direct contractor that gives an owner a stop work notice shall give the following additional notice:

(a) At least five days before giving the stop work notice, the contractor shall post notice of intent to give a stop work notice. The notice shall comply with the requirements of Chapter 2 (commencing with Section 8100) of Title 1. In addition to posting the notice pursuant to Section 8114, the notice shall also be posted at the main office of the site, if one exists.

(b) At the same time the contractor gives the stop work notice, the contractor shall give a copy of the stop work notice to all subcontractors with whom the contractor has a direct contractual relationship on the work of improvement.

§ 8836 Copy of Notice to be Given to Construction Lender

Within five days after receipt of a stop work notice from a direct contractor, the owner shall give a copy of the notice to the construction lender, if any. The copy of the notice shall be given in compliance with the requirements of Chapter 2 (commencing with Section 8100) of Title 1.

§ 8838 Liability for Delay or Damage; Limitations on Liability

(a) The direct contractor or the direct contractor's surety, or a subcontractor or a subcontractor's surety, is not liable for delay or damage that the owner or a contractor of a subcontractor may suffer as a result of the direct contractor giving a stop work notice and subsequently stopping work for nonpayment, if the notice and posting requirements of this article are satisfied.

(b) A direct contractor's or original subcontractor's liability to a subcontractor or material supplier after the direct contractor stops work under this article is limited to the amount the subcontractor or material supplier could otherwise recover under this title for work provided up to the date the subcontractor or material supplier ceases work, subject to the following exceptions:

(1) The direct contractor's or original subcontractor's liability continues for work provided up to and including the 10-day notice period and not beyond.

(2) This subdivision does not limit liability for custom work, including materials that have been fabricated, manufactured, or ordered to specifications that are unique to the job.

§ 8840 Resolution of Claim or Cancellation of Stop Work Notice

On resolution of the claim in the stop work notice or the direct contractor's cancellation of the stop work notice, the contractor shall post, and give subcontractors with whom the contractor has a direct contractual relationship on the work of improvement, notice of the resolution or cancellation. The notice shall comply with the requirements of Chapter 2 (commencing with Section 8100) of Title 1. In addition to posting the notice pursuant to Section 8114, the notice shall also be posted at the main office of the site, if one exists.

§ 8842 Other Remedies

A direct contractor's right to stop work under this article is in addition to other rights the direct contractor may have under the law.

§ 8844 Expedited Proceeding

(a) If payment of the amount claimed is not made within 10 days after a stop work notice is given, the direct contractor, the direct contractor's surety, or an owner may in an expedited proceeding in the superior court in the county in which the private work of improvement is located, seek a judicial determination of liability for the amount due.

(b) The expedited proceeding shall be set for hearing or trial at the earliest possible date in order that it shall be quickly heard and determined, and shall take precedence over all other cases except older matter of the same character and other matters to which special precedence has been given.

§ 8846 Waiver Against Public Policy

It is against public policy to waive the provisions of this article by contract.

§ 8848 Application of Article

(a) This article applies to a contract entered into on or after January 1, 1999.

(b) This article does not apply to a retention withheld by a lender pursuant to a construction loan agreement.

TITLE 3. PUBLIC WORK OF IMPROVEMENT

Chapter 1. General Provisions

Article 1. Application of Title

§ 9000 Title Application to Public Works of Improvement

This title applies to a work of improvement contracted for by a public entity.

Article 2. Claimants

§ 9100 Persons Who may Give Stop Payment Notice or Assert Claim

(a) Except as provided in subdivision (b), any of the following persons that have not been paid in full may give a stop payment notice to the public entity or assert a claim against a payment bond:

(1) A person that provides work for a public works contract, if the work is authorized by a direct contractor, subcontractor, architect, project manager, or other person having charge of all or part of the public works contract.

(2) A laborer.

(3) A person described in Section 4107.7 of the Public Contract Code.

(b) A direct contractor may not give a stop payment notice or assert a claim against a payment bond under this title.

Chapter 2. Completion

§ 9200 Time of Completion

For the purpose of this title, completion of a work of improvement occurs at the earliest of the following times:

(a) Acceptance of the work of improvement by the public entity.

(b) Cessation of labor on the work of improvement for a continuous period of 60 days. This subdivision does not apply to a contract awarded under the State Contract Act, Part 2 (commencing with Section 10100) of Division 2 of the Public Contract Code.

§ 9202 Notice of Cessation; Recording; Requirements and Contents

(a) A public entity may record a notice of cessation if there has been a continuous cessation of labor for at least 30 days prior to the recordation that continues through the date of the recordation.

(b) The notice shall be signed and verified by the public entity or its agent.

(c) The notice shall comply with the requirements of Chapter 2 (commencing with Section 8100) of Title 1, and shall also include all of the following information:

(1) The date on or about which the labor ceased.

(2) A statement that the cessation has continued until the recordation of the notice.

§ 9204 Notice of Completion; Recording; Requirements and Contents

(a) A public entity may record a notice of completion on or within 15 days after the date of completion of a work of improvement.

(b) The notice shall be signed and verified by the public entity or its agent.

(c) The notice shall comply with the requirements of Chapter 2 (commencing with Section 8100) of Title 1, and shall also include the date of completion. An erroneous statement of the date of completion does not affect the effectiveness of the notice if the true date of completion is 15 days or less before the date of recordation of the notice.

§ 9208 Acceptance of Notice by Completion by Recorder

A notice of completion in otherwise proper form, verified and containing the information required by this title shall be accepted by the recorder for recording and is deemed duly recorded without acknowledgment.

Chapter 3. Preliminary Notice

§ 9300 Persons Who Should Receive Notice

(a) Except as otherwise provided by statute, before giving a stop payment notice or asserting a claim against a payment bond, a claimant shall give preliminary notice to the following persons:

(1) The public entity.

(2) The direct contractor to which the claimant provides work.

(b) Notwithstanding subdivision (a):

(1) A laborer is not required to give preliminary notice.

(2) A claimant that has a direct contractual relationship with a direct contractor is not required to give preliminary notice.

(c) Compliance with this section is a necessary prerequisite to the validity of a stop payment notice under this title.

(d) Compliance with this section or with Section 9562 is a necessary prerequisite to the validity of a claim against a payment bond under this title.

§ 9302 Notice

(a) Except as provided in subdivision (b), preliminary notice shall be given in compliance with the requirements of Chapter 2 (commencing with Section 8100) of Title 1.

(b) If the public works contract is for work constructed by the Department of Public Works or the Department of General Services of the state, preliminary notice to the public entity shall be given to the disbursing officer of the department constructing the work.

§ 9303 Additional Compliance Requirements and Contents

The preliminary notice shall comply with the requirements of Section 8102, and shall also include:

(a) A general description of the work to be provided.

(b) An estimate of the total price of the work provided and to be provided.

§ 9304 Limitations on Stop Payment Notice or Assertion of Claim

A claimant may give a stop payment notice or assert a claim against a payment bond only for work provided within 20 days before giving preliminary notice and at any time thereafter.

§ 9306 Failure of Subcontractor to Give Notice; Grounds for Discipline

If the contract of any subcontractor on a particular work of improvement provides for payment to the subcontractor of more than four hundred dollars ($400), the failure of that subcontractor, licensed under the Contractors' State License Law (Chapter 9 (commencing with Section 7000) of Division 3 of the Business and Professions Code), to give the notice provided for in this chapter, constitutes grounds for disciplinary action under the Contractors' State License Law.

Chapter 4. Stop Payment Notice

Article 1. General Provisions

§ 9350 Right of Persons Furnishing Work Pursuant to Public Works Contract

The rights of all persons furnishing work pursuant to a public works contract, with respect to any fund for payment of construction costs, are governed exclusively by this chapter, and no person may assert any legal or equitable right with respect to that fund, other than a right created by direct written contract between the person and the person holding the fund, except pursuant to the provisions of this chapter.

§ 9352 Stop Payment Notice; Requirements; Contents; Amount Claimed

(a) A stop payment notice shall comply with the requirements of Chapter 2 (commencing with Section 8100) of Title 1, and shall be signed and verified by the claimant.

(b) The notice shall include a general description of work to be provided, and an estimate of the total amount in value of the work to be provided.

(c) The amount claimed in the notice may include only the amount due the claimant for work provided through the date of the notice.

§ 9354 Notice to Public Entity

(a) Except as provided in subdivision (b), a stop payment notice shall be given in compliance with the requirements of Chapter 2 (commencing with Section 8100) of Title 1.

(b) A stop payment notice shall be given to the public entity by giving the notice to the following person:

(1) In the case of a public works contract of the state, the director of the department that awarded the contract.

(2) In the case of a public works contract of a public entity other than the state, the office of the controller, auditor, or other public disbursing officer whose duty it is to make payment pursuant to the contract, or the commissioners, managers, trustees, officers, board of supervisors, board of trustees, common council, or other body by which the contract was awarded.

§ 9356 Time for Giving Stop Payment Notice

A stop payment notice is not effective unless given before the expiration of whichever of the following time periods is applicable:

(a) If a notice of completion, acceptance, or cessation is recorded, 30 days after that recordation.

(b) If a notice of completion, acceptance, or cessation is not recorded, 90 days after cessation or completion.

§ 9358 Withholding of Sufficient Funds

(a) The public entity shall, on receipt of a stop payment notice, withhold from the direct contractor sufficient funds due or to become due to the direct contractor to pay the claim stated in the stop payment notice and to provide for the public entity's reasonable cost of any litigation pursuant to the stop payment notice.

(b) The public entity may satisfy its duty under this section by refusing to release funds held in escrow under Section 10263 or 22300 of the Public Contract Code.

§ 9360 Payment of Funds When Stop Payment Notice Received

(a) This chapter does not prohibit payment of funds to a direct contractor or a direct contractor's assignee if a stop payment notice is not received before the disbursing officer actually surrenders possession of the funds.

(b) This chapter does not prohibit payment of any amount due to a direct contractor or a direct contractor's assignee in excess of the amount necessary to pay the total amount of all claims stated in stop payment notices received by the public entity at the time of payment plus any interest and court costs that might reasonably be anticipated in connection with the claims.

§ 9362 Notice of Time for Commencing Action to Enforce Payment of Claim

(a) Not later than 10 days after each of the following events, the public entity shall give notice to a claimant that has given a stop payment notice of the time within which an action to enforce payment of the claim stated in the stop payment notice must be commenced:

(1) Completion of a public works contract, whether by acceptance or cessation.

(2) Recordation of a notice of cessation or completion.

(b) The notice shall comply with the requirements of Chapter 2 (commencing with Section 8100) of Title 1.

(c) A public entity need not give notice under this section unless the claimant has paid the public entity ten dollars ($10) at the time of giving the stop payment notice.

§ 9364 Release Bond; Procedure

(a) A public entity may, in its discretion, permit the direct contractor to give the public entity a release bond. The bond shall be executed by an admitted surety insurer, in an amount equal to 125 percent of the claim stated in the stop payment notice, conditioned for the payment of any amount the claimant recovers in an action on the claim, together with court costs if the claimant prevails.

(b) On receipt of a release bond, the public entity shall not withhold funds from the direct contractor pursuant to the stop payment notice.

(c) The surety on a release bond is jointly and severally liable to the claimant with the sureties on any payment bond given under Chapter 5 (commencing with Section 9550).

Article 2. Summary Proceeding for Release of Funds

§ 9400 Release of Funds; Grounds

A direct contractor may obtain release of funds withheld pursuant to a stop payment notice under the summary proceeding provided in this article on any of the following grounds:

(a) The claim on which the notice is based is not a type for which a stop payment notice is authorized under this chapter.

(b) The claimant is not a person authorized under Section 9100 to give a stop payment notice.

(c) The amount of the claim stated in the stop payment notice is excessive.

(d) There is no basis for the claim stated in the stop payment notice.

§ 9402 Affidavit; Service on Public Entity; Contents

The direct contractor shall serve on the public entity an affidavit, together with a copy of the affidavit, in compliance with the requirements of Chapter 2 (commencing with Section 8100) of Title 1, that includes all of the following information:

(a) An allegation of the grounds for release of the funds and a statement of the facts supporting the allegation.

(b) A demand for the release of all or the portion of the funds that are alleged to be withheld improperly or in an excessive amount.

(c) A statement of the address of the contractor within the state for the purpose of permitting service by mail on the contractor of any notice or document.

§ 9404 Affidavit; Service of Copy on Claimant

The public entity shall serve on the claimant a copy of the direct contractor's affidavit, together with a notice stating that the public entity will release the funds withheld, or the portion of the funds demanded, unless the claimant serves on the public entity a counteraffidavit on or before the time stated in the notice. The time stated in the notice shall be not less than 10 days nor more than 20 days after service on the claimant of the copy of the affidavit. The notice shall comply with the requirements of Chapter 2 (commencing with Section 8100) of Title 1.

§ 9406 Counteraffidavit; Service on Public Entity

(a) A claimant that contests the direct contractor's affidavit shall serve on the public entity a counteraffidavit alleging the details of the claim and describing the specific basis on which the claimant contests or rebuts the allegations of the contractor's affidavit. The counteraffidavit shall be served within the time stated in the public entity's notice, together with proof of service of a copy of the counteraffidavit on the direct contractor. The service of the counteraffidavit on the public entity and the copy of the affidavit on the direct contractor shall comply with the requirements of Chapter 2 (commencing with Section 8100) of Title 1.

(b) If no counteraffidavit with proof of service is served on the public entity within the time stated in the public entity's notice, the public entity shall immediately release the funds, or the portion of the funds demanded by the affidavit, without further notice to the claimant, and the public entity is not liable in any manner for their release.

(c) The public entity is not responsible for the validity of an affidavit or counteraffidavit under this article.

§ 9408 Action for Declaration of Rights of Parties

(a) If a counteraffidavit, together with proof of service, is served under Section 9406, either the direct contractor or the claimant may commence an action for a declaration of the rights of the parties.

(b) After commencement of the action, either the direct contractor or the claimant may move the court for a determination of rights under the affidavit and counteraffidavit. The party making the motion shall give not less than five days' notice of the hearing to the public entity and to the other party.

(c) The notice of hearing shall comply with the requirements of Chapter 2 (commencing with Section 8100) of Title 1. Notwithstanding Section 8116, when notice of the hearing is made by mail, the notice is complete on the fifth day following deposit of the notice in the mail.

(d) The court shall hear the motion within 15 days after the date of the motion, unless the court continues the hearing for good cause.

§ 9410 Affidavit and Counteraffidavit to Constitute Pleadings; Burden of Proof

(a) The affidavit and counteraffidavit shall be filed with the court by the public entity and shall constitute the pleadings, subject to the power of the court to permit an amendment in the interest of justice. The affidavit of the direct contractor shall be deemed controverted by the counteraffidavit of the claimant, and both shall be received in evidence.

(b) At the hearing, the direct contractor has the burden of proof.

§ 9412 Findings Not Required; Order at Conclusion of Hearing

(a) No findings are required in a summary proceeding under this article.

(b) If at the hearing no evidence other than the affidavit and counteraffidavit is offered, the court may, if satisfied that sufficient facts are shown, make a determination on the basis of the affidavit and counteraffidavit. If the court is not satisfied that sufficient facts are shown, the court shall order the hearing continued for production of other evidence, oral or documentary, or the filing of other affidavits and counteraffidavits.

(c) At the conclusion of the hearing, the court shall make an order determining whether the demand for release is allowed. The court's order is determinative of the right of the claimant to have funds further withheld by the public entity.

(d) The direct contractor shall serve a copy of the court's order on the public entity in compliance with the requirements of Chapter 2 (commencing with Section 8100) of Title 1.

§ 9414 Determination Not Res Judicata

A determination in a summary proceeding under this article is not res judicata with respect to a right of action by the claimant against either the principal or surety on a payment bond or with respect to a right of action against a party personally liable to the claimant.

Article 3. Distribution of Funds Withheld

§ 9450 Insufficient Funds to Pay all Claims; Pro Rata Distribution

If funds withheld pursuant to a stop payment notice are insufficient to pay in full the claims of all persons who have given a stop payment notice, the funds shall be distributed among the claimants in the ratio that the claim of each bears to the aggregate of all claims for which a stop payment notice is given, without regard to the order in which the notices were given or enforcement actions were commenced.

§ 9452 Unpaid Deficit; Recovery on Payment Bond

Nothing in this chapter impairs the right of a claimant to recover from the direct contractor or the contractor's sureties in an action on a payment bond under Chapter 5 (commencing with Section 9550) any deficit that remains unpaid after the distribution under Section 9450.

§ 9454 False Stop Payment Notice or Inclusion of Work Not Provided for in Contract

A person that willfully gives a false stop payment notice to the public entity or that willfully includes in the notice work not provided for the public works contract for which the stop payment notice is given forfeits all right to participate in the distribution under Section 9450.

§ 9456 Priority of Stop Payment Notice

(a) A stop payment notice takes priority over an assignment by a direct contractor of any amount due or to become due pursuant to a public works contract, including contract changes, whether made before or after the giving of a stop payment notice, and the assignment has no effect on the rights of the claimant.

(b) Any garnishment of an amount due or to become due pursuant to a public works contract by a creditor of a direct contractor under Article 8 (commencing with Section 708.710) of Chapter 6 of Division 2 of Title 9 of Part 2 of the Code of Civil Procedure and any statutory lien on that amount is subordinate to the rights of a claimant.

Article 4. Enforcement of Payment of Claim Stated in Stop Payment Notice

§ 9500 Claim Filing Procedures for Actions Against Public Entities

(a) A claimant may not enforce payment of the claim stated in a stop payment notice unless the claimant has complied with all of the following conditions:

(1) The claimant has given preliminary notice to the extent required by Chapter 3 (commencing with Section 9300).

(2) The claimant has given the stop payment notice within the time provided in Section 9356.

(b) The claim filing procedures of Part 3 (commencing with Section 900) of Division 3.6 of Title 1 of the Government Code do not apply to an action under this article.

§ 9502 Commencement of Action

(a) The claimant shall commence an action against the public entity and the direct contractor to enforce payment of the claim stated in a stop payment notice at any time after 10 days from the date the claimant gives the stop payment notice.

(b) The claimant shall commence an action against the public entity and the direct contractor to enforce payment of the claim stated in a stop payment notice not later than 90 days after expiration of the time within which a stop payment notice must be given.

(c) An action under this section may not be brought to trial or judgment entered before expiration of the time provided in subdivision (b).

(d) If a claimant does not commence an action to enforce payment of the claim stated in a stop payment notice within the time provided in subdivision (b), the notice ceases to be effective and the public entity shall release funds withheld pursuant to the notice.

§ 9504 Notice of Commencement of Action

Within five days after commencement of an action to enforce payment of the claim stated in a stop payment notice, the claimant shall give notice of commencement of the action to the public entity in the same manner that a stop payment notice is given.

§ 9506 Multiple Claimants

If more than one claimant has given a stop payment notice:

(a) Any number of claimants may join in the same enforcement action.

(b) If claimants commence separate actions, the court that first acquires jurisdiction may order the actions consolidated.

(c) On request of the public entity, the court shall require that all claimants be impleaded in one action and shall adjudicate the rights of all parties in the action.

§ 9508 Dismissal

Notwithstanding Section 583.420 of the Code of Civil Procedure, if an action to enforce payment of the claim stated in a stop payment notice is not brought to trial within two years after commencement of the action, the court may in its discretion dismiss the action for want of prosecution.

§ 9510 Effect of Dismissal or Judgment

A stop payment notice ceases to be effective, and the public entity shall release funds withheld, in either of the following circumstances:

(a) An action to enforce payment of the claim stated in the stop payment notice is dismissed, unless expressly stated to be without prejudice.

(b) Judgment in an action to enforce payment of the claim stated in the stop payment notice is against the claimant.

Chapter 5. Payment Bond

§ 9550 Necessity of Bond; Inclusion in Call for Bids

(a) A direct contractor that is awarded a public works contract involving an expenditure in excess of twenty-five thousand dollars ($25,000) shall, before commencement of work, give a payment bond to and approved by the officer or public entity by whom the contract was awarded.

(b) A public entity shall state in its call for bids that a payment bond is required for a public works contract involving an expenditure in excess of twenty-five thousand dollars ($25,000).

(c) A payment bond given and approved under this section will permit performance of and provide coverage for work pursuant to a public works contract that supplements the contract for which the bond is given, if the requirement of a new bond is waived by the public entity.

(d) For the purpose of this section, a design professional is not deemed a direct contractor and is not required to give a payment bond.

(e) This section does not apply to a public works contract with a "state entity" as defined in subdivision (d) of Section 7103 of the Public Contract Code.

§ 9552 Payment Bond Not Given and Approved

If a payment bond is not given and approved as required by Section 9550:

(a) Neither the public entity awarding the public works contract nor any officer of the public entity shall audit, allow, or pay a claim of the direct contractor pursuant to the contract.

(b) A claimant shall receive payment of a claim pursuant to a stop payment notice in the manner provided by Chapter 4 (commencing with Section 9350).

§ 9554 Amount of Bond

(a) A payment bond shall be in an amount not less than 100 percent of the total amount payable pursuant to the public works contract. The bond shall be in the form of a bond and not a deposit in lieu of a bond. The bond shall be executed by an admitted surety insurer.

(b) The payment bond shall provide that if the direct contractor or a subcontractor fails to pay any of the following, the surety will pay the obligation and, if an action is brought to enforce the liability on the bond, a reasonable attorney's fee, to be fixed by the court:

(1) A person authorized under Section 9100 to assert a claim against a payment bond.

(2) Amounts due under the Unemployment Insurance Code with respect to work or labor performed pursuant to the public works contract.

(3) Amounts required to be deducted, withheld, and paid over to the Employment Development Department from the wages of employees of the contractor and subcontractors under Section 13020 of the Unemployment Insurance Code with respect to the work and labor.

(c) The payment bond shall be conditioned for the payment in full of the claims of all claimants and by its terms inure to the benefit of any person authorized under Section 9100 to assert a claim against a payment bond so as to give a right of action to that person or that person's assigns in an action to enforce the liability on the bond.

(d) The direct contractor may require that a subcontractor give a bond to indemnify the direct contractor for any loss sustained by the direct contractor because of any default of the subcontractor under this section.

§ 9558 Commencement of Action to Enforce Liability on Bond' Limitations

A claimant may commence an action to enforce the liability on the bond at any time after the claimant ceases to provide work, but not later than six months after the period in which a stop payment notice may be given under Section 9356.

§ 9560 Claim Against Payment Bond; Preliminary Notice Required

(a) In order to enforce a claim against a payment bond, a claimant shall give the preliminary notice provided in Chapter 3 (commencing with Section 9300).

(b) If preliminary notice was not given as provided in Chapter 3 (commencing with Section 9300), a claimant may enforce a claim by giving written notice to the surety and the bond principal within 15 days after recordation of a notice of completion. If no notice of completion has been recorded, the time for giving written notice to the surety and the bond principal is extended to 75 days after completion of the work of improvement.

(c) Commencing July 1, 2012, and except as provided in subdivision (b), if the preliminary notice was required to be given by a person who has no direct contractual relationship with the contractor, and who has not given notice as provided in Chapter 3 (commencing with Section 9300), that person may enforce a claim by giving written notice to the surety and the bond principal, as provided in Section 9562, within 15 days after recordation of a notice of completion. If no notice of completion has been recorded, the time for giving written notice to the surety and the bond principal is extended to 75 days after completion of the work of improvement.

(d) Subdivision (c) shall not apply in either of the following circumstances:

(1) All progress payments, except for those disputed in good faith, have been made to a subcontractor who has a direct contractual relationship with the general contractor to whom the claimant has provided materials or services.

(2) The subcontractor who has a direct contractual relationship with the general contractor to whom the claimant has provided materials or services has been terminated from the project pursuant to the contract, and all progress payments, except those disputed in good faith, have been made as of the termination date.

(e) Pursuant to Section 9300, this section shall not apply to a laborer, as defined under Section 8024.

(f) This section shall become operative on July 1, 2012.

§ 9562 Notice to Principal and Surety; Requirements

Notice to the principal and surety under Section 9560 shall comply with the requirements of Chapter 2 (commencing with Section 8100) of Title 1.

§ 9564 Maintenance of Action Without Filing Stop Notice or Suing Public Entity

(a) A claimant may maintain an action to enforce the liability of a surety on a payment bond whether or not the claimant has given the public entity a stop payment notice.

(b) A claimant may maintain an action to enforce the liability on the bond separately from and without commencement of an action against the public entity by whom the contract was awarded or against any officer of the public entity.

(c) In an action to enforce the liability on the bond, the court shall award the prevailing party a reasonable attorney's fee.

§ 9566 Work Done for Direct Contractor on Bond; Claim

(a) A claimant does not have a right to recover on a payment bond unless the claimant provided work to the direct contractor either directly or through one or more subcontractors pursuant to a public works contract.

(b) Nothing in this section affects the stop payment notice rights of, and relative priorities among, design professionals

MISCELLANEOUS CIVIL CODE SECTIONS

Appreciation Loans

§1917.166 Lien of Shared Appreciation Loan; Time of Attachment; Priority

The lien of a shared appreciation loan, including the principal amount and all interest, whether accrued or to be accrued, and all amounts of contingent deferred interest, shall attach from the time of the recordation of the deed of trust securing the loan, and the lien, including the lien of the interest accrued or to be accrued and of the contingent deferred interest, shall have priority over any other lien or encumbrance affecting the property secured by the shared appreciation instrument, recorded after the time of recordation of the shared appreciation instrument. However, nothing in this section or Section 1917.165 shall preclude a junior lien or encumbrance subordinate to the obligation of the shared appreciation loan. In no case may a junior lien achieve priority over the lien securing the obligation of the shared appreciation loan, provided that nothing in this section shall be construed to supersede Section 8450.

§1917.615 Lien of Shared Appreciation Loan for Seniors; Attachment; Priority

The lien of a shared appreciation loan for seniors, including the total loan obligation, shall attach from the time of the recordation of the deed of trust securing the loan, and the lien, including the lien of the total loan obligation accrued or to be accrued, shall have priority over any other lien or encumbrance affecting the property secured by the shared appreciation instrument and recorded after the time of recordation of the shared appreciation instrument. However, nothing in this section or Section 1917.614 shall preclude a junior lien or encumbrance subordinate to the total loan obligation of the shared appreciation loan for seniors. In no case may a junior lien achieve priority over the lien securing the total loan obligation of the shared appreciation loan, provided that nothing in this section shall be construed to supersede Section 8450.

§3059 Mechanic's Lien

The liens of mechanics, for materials and services upon real property, are regulated by Chapter 4 (commencing with Section 8400) of Title 2 of Part 6 of Division 4.

§3060 Liens Against Mining Claims and Mining Property

(a) As used in this section, "mine" means a mining claim or real property worked on as a mine.

(b) Any person who performs labor in a mine, either in its development or in working on it by the subtractive process, or furnishes materials to be used or consumed in it, has a lien upon the mine and the works owned and used by the owners for milling or reducing the ores from the mine, for the value of the work or labor done or materials furnished by each, whether done or furnished at the instance of the owner of the mine, or the owner's agent, and every contractor, subcontractor, superintendent, or other person having charge of any mining or work or labor performed in and about the mine, either as lessee or under a working bond or contract thereon shall be held to be the agent of the owner for the purposes of this section. The liens provided for by this section shall be enforced in the same manner as those provided for by Part 6 (commencing with Section 8000) of Division 4.

Design Professionals

§3319 Private Works Contracts; Late Payment Penalty

(a) In each written contract for private works of improvement entered into on or after January 1, 1996, the contracting party and the design professional may agree to contractual provisions that include a late payment penalty, in lieu of any interest otherwise due. The terms of the late payment penalty shall be specifically set forth in the written contract.

(b) The penalty authorized pursuant to subdivision (a) shall be separate from, and in addition to, the design professionals liens provided by Chapter 3 (commencing with Section 8300) of Title 2 of Part 6 of Division 4, mechanics liens provided by Chapter 4 (commencing with Section 8400) of Title 2 of Part 6 of Division 4, and stop payment notices provided by Chapter 5 (commencing with Section 8500) of Title 2 of Part 6 of Division 4.

(c) None of the rights or obligations created or permitted by this section between design professionals and contracting parties shall apply to construction loan funds held by a lender pursuant to a construction loan agreement.

(d) For purposes of this section, the following definitions apply:

(1) "Contracting party" means any person or entity entering into a written contract with a design professional for professional design services for a private work of improvement.

(2) "Design professional" means a person licensed as an architect pursuant to Chapter 3 (commencing with Section 5500) of Division 3 of the Business and Professions Code, registered as a professional engineer pursuant to Chapter 7 (commencing with Section 6700) of Division 3 of the Business and Professions Code, or licensed as a land surveyor pursuant to Chapter 15 (commencing with Section 8700) of Division 3 of the Business and Professions Code.

§3320 Public Works Contracts; Progress and Final Retention Payments

(a) In each contract for public works of improvement, entered into on or after January 1, 1996, the public agency shall pay to the prime design professional any progress payment within 30 days of receipt of a written demand for payment in accordance with the contract, and the final retention payment within 45 days of receipt of a written demand for payment in accordance with the contract. If the public agency disputes in good faith any portion of the amount due, it may withhold from the payment an amount not to exceed 150 percent of the disputed amount. The disputed amount withheld is not subject to any penalty authorized by this section.

(b) If any amount is wrongfully withheld or is not timely paid in violation of this section, the prime design professional shall be entitled to a penalty of 1 1/2 percent for the improperly withheld amount, in lieu of any interest otherwise due, per month for every month that payment is not made. In any action for the collection of amounts withheld in violation of this section, the prevailing party is entitled to his or her reasonable attorney's fees and costs.

(c) The penalty described in subdivision (b) is separate from, and in addition to, the design professionals liens provided by Chapter 3 (commencing with Section 8300) of Title 2 of Part 6 of Division 4, mechanics liens provided by Chapter 4 (commencing with Section 8400) of Title 2 of Part 6 of Division 4, and stop payment notices on public works provided by Chapter 4 (commencing with Section 9350) of Title 3 of Part 6 of Division 4.

(d) This section does not apply to state agency contracts subject to Section 927.6 of the Government Code.

(e) None of the rights or obligations created by this section between prime design professionals and public agencies apply to construction loan funds held by a lender pursuant to a construction loan agreement.

(f) For purposes of this section:

(1) "Public agency" means the state, any county, any city, any city and county, any district, any public authority, any public agency, any municipal corporation, or other political subdivision or political corporation of the state.

(2) "Design professional" means a person licensed as an architect pursuant to Chapter 3 (commencing with Section 5500) of Division 3 of the Business and Professions Code, registered as a professional engineer pursuant to Chapter 7 (commencing with Section 6700) of Division 3 of the Business and Professions Code, or licensed as a land surveyor pursuant to Chapter 15 (commencing with Section 8700) of Division 3 of the Business and Professions Code.

(3) "Prime design professional" means a design professional with a written contract directly with the public agency.

§3321 Public Works Contracts; Payment to Subconsultant Design Professional

(a) In each contract for public works of improvement, a prime design professional shall pay to each subconsultant design professional the amount due him or her from the payment received, not later than 15 days after receipt of each progress payment or final retention payment. If the prime design professional disputes in good faith any portion of the amount due, he or she may withhold from the payment an amount not to exceed 150 percent of the disputed amount. The disputed amount withheld shall not be subject to any penalty authorized by this section.

(b) If any amount is wrongfully withheld or is not timely paid in violation of this section, the subconsultant design professional shall be entitled to a penalty of 1 1/2 percent of the improperly withheld amount, in lieu of any interest otherwise due, per month, for each month that payment is not made. In any action for the collection of amounts withheld in violation of this section, the prevailing party shall be entitled to his or her reasonable attorney' s fees and costs.

(c) The penalty described in subdivision (b) shall be separate from, and in addition to, the design professionals liens provided by Chapter 3 (commencing with Section 8300) of Title 2 of Part 6 of Division 4, mechanics liens provided by Chapter 4 (commencing with Section 8400) of Title 2 of Part 6 of Division 4, and stop payment notices on public works provided by Chapter 4 (commencing with Section 9350) of Title 3 of Part 6 of Division 4.

(d) None of the rights or obligations created by this section between prime design professionals and subconsultant design professionals shall apply to construction loan funds held by a lender pursuant to a construction loan agreement.

(e) For purposes of this section:

(1) "Public agency" means the state, any county, any city, any city and county, any district, any public authority, any public agency, any municipal corporation, or other political subdivision or political corporation of the state.

(2) "Design professional" means a person licensed as an architect pursuant to Chapter 3 (commencing with Section 5500) of Division 3 of the Business and Professions Code, registered as a professional engineer pursuant to Chapter 7 (commencing with Section 6700) of Division 3 of the Business and Professions Code, or licensed as a land surveyor pursuant to Chapter 15 (commencing with Section 8700) of Division 3 of the Business and Professions Code.

(3) "Prime design professional" means a design professional having a written contract directly with the public agency.

(4) "Subconsultant design professional" means a design professional having a written contract with a prime design professional.

BUSINESS AND PROFESSIONS CODE SECTIONS ("B&P")
New Text (Operative July 1, 2012)

§7034 Prohibited Clauses

(a) No contractor that is required to be licensed under this chapter shall insert in any contract, or be a party, with a subcontractor that is licensed under this chapter to any contract which contains a provision, clause, covenant, or agreement which is void or unenforceable under Section 2782 of the Civil Code.

(b) No contractor that is required to be licensed under this chapter shall require a waiver of lien rights from any subcontractor, employee, or supplier in violation of Section 8122 of the Civil Code.

§7071.5 Contractor's Bond

The contractor's bond required by this article shall be executed by an admitted surety in favor of the State of California, in a form acceptable to the registrar and filed with the registrar by the licensee or applicant. The contractor's bond shall be for the benefit of the following:

(a) A homeowner contracting for home improvement upon the homeowner's personal family residence damaged as a result of a violation of this chapter by the licensee.

(b) A property owner contracting for the construction of a single-family dwelling who is damaged as a result of a violation of this chapter by the licensee. That property owner shall only recover under this subdivision if the single-family dwelling is not intended for sale or offered for sale at the time the damages were incurred.

(c) A person damaged as a result of a willful and deliberate violation of this chapter by the licensee, or by the fraud of the licensee in the execution or performance of a construction contract.

(d) An employee of the licensee damaged by the licensee's failure to pay wages.

(e) A person or entity, including a laborer described in subdivision (b) of Section 8024 of the Civil Code, to which a portion of the compensation of an employee of a licensee is paid by agreement with that employee or the collective bargaining agent of that employee, damaged as the result of the licensee's failure to pay fringe benefits for its employees, including, but not limited to, employer payments described in Section 1773.1 of the Labor Code and regulations thereunder (without regard to whether the work was performed on a private or public work). Damage to a person or entity under this subdivision is limited to actual employer payments required to be made on behalf of employees of the licensee, as part of the overall compensation of those employees, which the licensee fails to pay.

§7071.10 Qualifying Individual's Bond; Standards

The qualifying individual's bond required by this article shall be executed by an admitted surety insurer in favor of the State of California, in a form acceptable to the registrar and filed with the registrar by the qualifying individual. The qualifying individual's bond shall not be required in addition to the contractor's bond when, as set forth under paragraph (1) of subdivision (b) of Section 7068, the individual proprietor has qualified for the license by his or her personal appearance, or the qualifier is a general partner as set forth under paragraph (2) of subdivision (b) of Section 7068. The qualifying individual's bond shall be for the benefit of the following persons:

(a) A homeowner contracting for home improvement upon the homeowner's personal family residence damaged as a result of a violation of this chapter by the licensee.

(b) A property owner contracting for the construction of a single-family dwelling who is damaged as a result of a violation of this chapter by the licensee. That property owner shall only recover under this subdivision if the single-family dwelling is not intended for sale or offered for sale at the time the damages were incurred.

(c) A person damaged as a result of a willful and deliberate violation of this chapter by the licensee, or by the fraud of the licensee in the execution or performance of a construction contract.

(d) An employee of the licensee damaged by the licensee's failure to pay wages.

(e) A person or entity, including a laborer described in subdivision (b) of Section 8024 of the Civil Code, to which a portion of the compensation of an employee of a licensee is paid by agreement with that employee or the collective bargaining agent of that employee, that is damaged as the result of the licensee's failure to pay fringe benefits for its employees including, but not limited to, employer payments described in Section 1773.1 of the Labor Code and regulations adopted thereunder (without regard to whether the work was performed on a public or private work). Damage to a person or entity under this subdivision is limited to employer payments required to be made on behalf of employees of the licensee, as part of the overall compensation of those employees, which the licensee fails to pay.

§7159 Requirements for Home Improvement Contracts; Discipline

(a) (1) This section identifies the projects for which a home improvement contract is required, outlines the contract requirements, and lists the items that shall be included in the contract, or may be provided as an attachment.

(2) This section does not apply to service and repair contracts that are subject to Section 7159.10, if the contract for the applicable services complies with Sections 7159.10 to 7159.14, inclusive.

(3) This section does not apply to the sale, installation, and servicing of a fire alarm sold in conjunction with an alarm system, as defined in subdivision (n) of Section 7590.1, if all costs attributable to making the fire alarm system operable, including sale and installation costs, do not exceed five hundred dollars ($500), and the licensee complies with the requirements set forth in Section 7159.9.

(4) This section does not apply to any costs associated with monitoring a burglar or fire alarm system.

(5) Failure by the licensee, his or her agent or salesperson, or by a person subject to be licensed under this chapter, to provide the specified information, notices, and disclosures in the contract, or to otherwise fail to comply with any provision of this section, is cause for discipline.

(b) For purposes of this section, "home improvement contract" means an agreement, whether oral or written, or contained in one or more documents, between a contractor and an owner or between a contractor and a tenant, regardless of the number of residence or dwelling units contained in the building in which the tenant resides, if the work is to be performed in, to, or upon the residence or dwelling unit of the tenant, for the performance of a home improvement, as defined in Section 7151, and includes all labor, services, and materials to be furnished and performed thereunder, if the aggregate contract price specified in one or more improvement contracts, including all labor, services, and materials to be furnished by the contractor, exceeds five hundred dollars ($500). "Home improvement contract" also means an agreement, whether oral or written, or contained in one or more documents, between a salesperson, whether or not he or she is a home improvement salesperson, and an owner or a tenant, regardless of the number of residence or dwelling units contained in the building in which the tenant resides, which provides for the sale, installation, or furnishing of home improvement goods or services.

(c) In addition to the specific requirements listed under this section, every home improvement contract and any person subject to licensure under this chapter or his or her agent or salesperson shall comply with all of the following:

(1) The writing shall be legible.

(2) Any printed form shall be readable. Unless a larger typeface is specified in this article, text in any printed form shall be in at least 10-point typeface and the headings shall be in at least 10-point boldface type.

(3) (A) Before any work is started, the contractor shall give the buyer a copy of the contract signed and dated by both the contractor and the buyer. The buyer's receipt of the copy of the contract initiates the buyer's rights to cancel the contract pursuant to Sections 1689.5 to 1689.14, inclusive, of the Civil Code.

(B) The contract shall contain on the first page, in a typeface no smaller than that generally used in the body of the document, both of the following:

(i) The date the buyer signed the contract.

(ii) The name and address of the contractor to which the applicable "Notice of Cancellation" is to be mailed, immediately preceded by a statement advising the buyer that the "Notice of Cancellation" may be sent to the contractor at the address noted on the contract.

(4) The contract shall include a statement that, upon satisfactory payment being made for any portion of the work performed, the contractor, prior to any further payment being made, shall furnish to the person contracting for the home improvement or swimming pool work a full and unconditional release from any potential lien claimant claim or mechanics lien authorized pursuant to Sections 8400 and 8404 of the Civil Code for that portion of the work for which payment has been made.

(5) A change-order form for changes or extra work shall be incorporated into the contract and shall become part of the contract only if it is in writing and signed by the parties prior to the commencement of any work covered by a change order.

(6) The contract shall contain, in close proximity to the signatures of the owner and contractor, a notice stating that the owner or tenant has the right to require the contractor to have a performance and payment bond.

(7) If the contract provides for a contractor to furnish joint control, the contractor shall not have any financial or other interest in the joint control.

(8) The provisions of this section are not exclusive and do not relieve the contractor from compliance with any other applicable provision of law.

(d) A home improvement contract and any changes to the contract shall be in writing and signed by the parties to the contract prior to the commencement of work covered by the contract or an applicable change order and, except as provided in paragraph (8) of subdivision (a) of Section 7159.5, shall include or comply with all of the following:

(1) The name, business address, and license number of the contractor.

(2) If applicable, the name and registration number of the home improvement salesperson that solicited or negotiated the contract.

(3) The following heading on the contract form that identifies the type of contract in at least 10-point boldface type: "Home Improvement."

(4) The following statement in at least 12-point boldface type: "You are entitled to a completely filled in copy of this agreement, signed by both you and the contractor, before any work may be started."

(5) The heading: "Contract Price," followed by the amount of the contract in dollars and cents.

(6) If a finance charge will be charged, the heading: "Finance Charge," followed by the amount in dollars and cents. The finance charge is to be set out separately from the contract amount.

(7) The heading: "Description of the Project and Description of the Significant Materials to be Used and Equipment to be Installed," followed by a description of the project and a description of the significant materials to be used and equipment to be installed. For swimming pools, the project description required under this paragraph also shall include a plan and scale drawing showing the shape, size, dimensions, and the construction and equipment specifications.

(8) If a downpayment will be charged, the details of the downpayment shall be expressed in substantially the following form, and shall include the text of the notice as specified in subparagraph (C):

(A) The heading: "Downpayment."

(B) A space where the actual downpayment appears.

(C) The following statement in at least 12-point boldface type:

"THE DOWNPAYMENT MAY NOT EXCEED $1,000 OR 10 PERCENT OF THE CONTRACT PRICE, WHICHEVER IS LESS."

(9) If payments, other than the downpayment, are to be made before the project is completed, the details of these payments, known as progress payments, shall be expressed in substantially the following form, and shall include the text of the statement as specified in subparagraph (C):

(A) A schedule of progress payments shall be preceded by the heading: "Schedule of Progress Payments."

(B) Each progress payment shall be stated in dollars and cents and specifically reference the amount of work or services to be performed and materials and equipment to be supplied.

(C) The section of the contract reserved for the progress payments shall include the following statement in at least 12-point boldface type:

"The schedule of progress payments must specifically describe each phase of work, including the type and amount of work or services scheduled to be supplied in each phase, along with the amount of each proposed progress payment. IT IS AGAINST THE LAW FOR A CONTRACTOR TO COLLECT PAYMENT FOR WORK NOT YET COMPLETED, OR FOR MATERIALS NOT YET DELIVERED. HOWEVER, A CONTRACTOR MAY REQUIRE A DOWNPAYMENT."

(10) The contract shall address the commencement of work to be performed in substantially the following form:

(A) A statement that describes what constitutes substantial commencement of work under the contract.

(B) The heading: "Approximate Start Date."

(C) The approximate date on which work will be commenced.

(11) The estimated completion date of the work shall be referenced in the contract in substantially the following form:

(A) The heading: "Approximate Completion Date."

(B) The approximate date of completion.

(12) If applicable, the heading: "List of Documents to be Incorporated into the Contract," followed by the list of documents incorporated into the contract.

(13) The heading: "Note About Extra Work and Change Orders," followed by the following statement:

"Extra Work and Change Orders become part of the contract once the order is prepared in writing and signed by the parties prior to the commencement of work covered by the new change order. The order must describe the scope of the extra work or change, the cost to be added or subtracted from the contract, and the effect the order will have on the schedule of progress payments."

(e) Except as provided in paragraph (8) of subdivision (a) of Section 7159.5, all of the following notices shall be provided to the owner as part of the contract form as specified or, if otherwise authorized under this subdivision, may be provided as an attachment to the contract:

(1) A notice concerning commercial general liability insurance. This notice may be provided as an attachment to the contract if the contract includes the following statement: "A notice concerning commercial general liability insurance is attached to this contract." The notice shall include the heading "Commercial General Liability Insurance (CGL)," followed by whichever of the following statements is both relevant and correct:

(A) "(The name on the license or "This contractor') does not carry commercial general liability insurance."

(B) "(The name on the license or "This contractor') carries commercial general liability insurance written by (the insurance company). You may call (the insurance company) at ________________________________ to check the contractor's insurance coverage."

(C) "(The name on the license or "This contractor') is self-insured."

(D) "(The name on the license or 'This contractor') is a limited liability company that carries liability insurance or maintains other security as required by law. You may call (the insurance company or trust company or bank) at ____ to check on the contractor's insurance coverage or security."

(2) A notice concerning workers' compensation insurance. This notice may be provided as an attachment to the contract if the contract includes the statement: "A notice concerning workers' compensation insurance is attached to this contract." The notice shall include the heading "Workers' Compensation Insurance" followed by whichever of the following statements is correct:

(A) "(The name on the license or "This contractor') has no employees and is exempt from workers' compensation requirements."

(B) "(The name on the license or "This contractor') carries workers' compensation insurance for all employees."

(3) A notice that provides the buyer with the following information about the performance of extra or change-order work:

(A) A statement that the buyer may not require a contractor to perform extra or change-order work without providing written authorization prior to the commencement of work covered by the new change order.

(B) A statement informing the buyer that extra work or a change order is not enforceable against a buyer unless the change order also identifies all of the following in writing prior to the commencement of work covered by the new change order:

(i) The scope of work encompassed by the order.

(ii) The amount to be added or subtracted from the contract.

(iii) The effect the order will make in the progress payments or the completion date.

(C) A statement informing the buyer that the contractor's failure to comply with the requirements of this paragraph does not preclude the recovery of compensation for work performed based upon legal or equitable remedies designed to prevent unjust enrichment.

(4) A notice with the heading "Mechanics Lien Warning" written as follows:

"MECHANICS LIEN WARNING:

Anyone who helps improve your property, but who is not paid, may record what is called mechanics lien on your property. A mechanics lien is a claim, like a mortgage or home equity loan, made against your property and recorded with the county recorder.

Even if you pay your contractor in full, unpaid subcontractors, suppliers, and laborers who helped to improve your property may record mechanics liens and sue you in court to foreclose the lien. If a court finds the lien is valid, you could be forced to pay twice or have a court officer sell your home to pay the lien. Liens can also affect your credit.

To preserve their right to record a lien, each subcontractor and material supplier must provide you with a document called a 'Preliminary Notice.' This notice is not a lien. The purpose of the notice is to let you know that the person who sends you the notice has the right to record a lien on your property if he or she is not paid.

BE CAREFUL. The Preliminary Notice can be sent up to 20 days after the subcontractor starts work or the supplier provides material. This can be a big problem if you pay your contractor before you have received the Preliminary Notices.

You will not get Preliminary Notices from your prime contractor or from laborers who work on your project. The law assumes that you already know they are improving your property.

PROTECT YOURSELF FROM LIENS. You can protect yourself from liens by getting a list from your contractor of all the subcontractors and material suppliers that work on your project. Find out from your contractor when these subcontractors started work and when these suppliers delivered goods or materials. Then wait 20 days, paying attention to the Preliminary Notices you receive.

PAY WITH JOINT CHECKS. One way to protect yourself is to pay with a joint check. When your contractor tells you it is time to pay for the work of a subcontractor or supplier who has provided you with a Preliminary Notice, write a joint check payable to both the contractor and the subcontractor or material supplier.

For other ways to prevent liens, visit CSLB's Internet Web site at www.cslb.ca.gov or call CSLB at 800-321-CSLB (2752).

REMEMBER, IF YOU DO NOTHING, YOU RISK HAVING A LIEN PLACED ON YOUR HOME. This can mean that you may have to pay twice, or face the forced sale of your home to pay what you owe."

(5) The following notice shall be provided in at least 12-point typeface:

"Information about the Contractors' State License Board (CSLB):

CSLB is the state consumer protection agency that licenses and regulates construction contractors.

Contact CSLB for information about the licensed contractor you are considering, including information about disclosable complaints, disciplinary actions, and civil judgments that are reported to CSLB.

Use only licensed contractors. If you file a complaint against a licensed contractor within the legal deadline (usually four years), CSLB has authority to investigate the complaint. If you use an unlicensed contractor, CSLB may not be able to help you resolve your complaint. Your only remedy may be in civil court, and you may be liable for damages arising out of any injuries to the unlicensed contractor or the unlicensed contractor's employees.

For more information:

Visit CSLB's Internet Web site at www.cslb.ca.gov

Call CSLB at 800-321-CSLB (2752)

Write CSLB at P.O. Box 26000, Sacramento, CA 95826."

(6) (A) The notice set forth in subparagraph (B) and entitled "Three-Day Right to Cancel," shall be provided to the buyer unless the contract is:

(i) Negotiated at the contractor's place of business.

(ii) Subject to the "Seven-Day Right to Cancel," as set forth in paragraph (7).

(iii) Subject to licensure under the Alarm Company Act (Chapter 11.6 (commencing with Section 7590)), provided the alarm company licensee complies with Sections 1689.5, 1689.6, and 1689.7 of the Civil Code, as applicable.

(B) "Three-Day Right to Cancel

You, the buyer, have the right to cancel this contract within three business days. You may cancel by e-mailing, mailing, faxing, or delivering a written notice to the contractor at the contractor's place of business by midnight of the third business day after you received a signed and dated copy of the contract that includes this notice. Include your name, your address, and the date you received the signed copy of the contract and this notice.

If you cancel, the contractor must return to you anything you paid within 10 days of receiving the notice of cancellation. For your part, you must make available to the contractor at your residence, in substantially as good condition as you received them, goods delivered to you under this contract or sale. Or, you may, if you wish, comply with the contractor's instructions on how to return the goods at the contractor's expense and risk. If you do make the goods available to the contractor and the contractor does not pick them up within 20 days of the date of your notice of cancellation, you may keep them without any further obligation. If you fail to make the goods available to the contractor, or if you agree to return the goods to the contractor and fail to do so, then you remain liable for performance of all obligations under the contract."

(C) The "Three-Day Right to Cancel" notice required by this paragraph shall comply with all of the following:

(i) The text of the notice is at least 12-point boldface type.

(ii) The notice is in immediate proximity to a space reserved for the owner's signature.

(iii) The owner acknowledges receipt of the notice by signing and dating the notice form in the signature space.

(iv) The notice is written in the same language, e.g., Spanish, as that principally used in any oral sales presentation.

(v) The notice may be attached to the contract if the contract includes, in at least 12-point boldface type, a checkbox with the following statement: "The law requires that the contractor give you a notice explaining your right to cancel. Initial the checkbox if the contractor has given you a "Notice of the Three-Day Right to Cancel.' "

(vi) The notice shall be accompanied by a completed form in duplicate, captioned "Notice of Cancellation," which also shall be attached to the agreement or offer to purchase and be easily detachable, and which shall contain the following statement written in the same language, e.g., Spanish, as used in the contract:

"“Notice of Cancellation”

/enter date of transaction/

____

(Date)

You may cancel this transaction, without any penalty or obligation, within three business days from the above date.

If you cancel, any property traded in, any payments made by you under the contract or sale, and any negotiable instrument executed by you will be returned within 10 days following receipt by the seller of your cancellation notice, and any security interest arising out of the transaction will be canceled.

If you cancel, you must make available to the seller at your residence, in substantially as good condition as when received, any goods delivered to you under this contract or sale, or you may, if you wish, comply with the instructions of the seller regarding the return shipment of the goods at the seller's expense and risk.

If you do make the goods available to the seller and the seller does not pick them up within 20 days of the date of your notice of cancellation, you may retain or dispose of the goods without any further obligation. If you fail to make the goods available to the seller, or if you agree to return the goods to the seller and fail to do so, then you remain liable for performance of all obligations under the contract."

To cancel this transaction, mail or deliver a signed and dated copy of this cancellation notice, or any other written notice, or send a telegram

to ____,

/name of seller/

at ____

/address of seller's place of business/

not later than midnight of _________________________________.

(Date)

I hereby cancel this transaction. ______________________________

(Date)

____

(Buyer's signature)

(7)(A) The following notice entitled "Seven-Day Right to Cancel" shall be provided to the buyer for any contract that is written for the repair or restoration of residential premises damaged by any sudden or catastrophic event for which a state of emergency has been declared by the President of the United States or the Governor, or for which a local emergency has been declared by the executive officer or governing body of any city, county, or city and county:

"Seven-Day Right to Cancel

You, the buyer, have the right to cancel this contract within seven business days. You may cancel by e-mailing, mailing, faxing, or delivering a written notice to the contractor at the contractor's place of business by midnight of the seventh business day after you received a signed and dated copy of the contract that includes this notice. Include your name, your address, and the date you received the signed copy of the contract and this notice.

If you cancel, the contractor must return to you anything you paid within 10 days of receiving the notice of cancellation. For your part, you must make available to the contractor at your residence, in substantially as good condition as you received them, goods delivered to you under this contract or sale. Or, you may, if you wish, comply with the contractor's instructions on how to return the goods at the contractor's expense and risk. If you do make the goods available to the contractor and the contractor does not pick them up within 20 days of the date of your notice of cancellation, you may keep them without any further obligation. If you fail to make the goods available to the contractor, or if you agree to return the goods to the contractor and fail to do so, then you remain liable for performance of all obligations under the contract."

(B) The "Seven-Day Right to Cancel" notice required by this subdivision shall comply with all of the following:

(i) The text of the notice is at least 12-point boldface type.

(ii) The notice is in immediate proximity to a space reserved for the owner's signature.

(iii) The owner acknowledges receipt of the notice by signing and dating the notice form in the signature space.

(iv) The notice is written in the same language, e.g., Spanish, as that principally used in any oral sales presentation.

(v) The notice may be attached to the contract if the contract includes, in at least 12-point boldface type, a checkbox with the following statement: "The law requires that the contractor give you a notice explaining your right to cancel. Initial the checkbox if the contractor has given you a "Notice of the Seven-Day Right to Cancel."

(vi) The notice shall be accompanied by a completed form in duplicate, captioned "Notice of Cancellation," which shall also be attached to the agreement or offer to purchase and be easily detachable, and which shall contain the following statement written in the same language, e.g., Spanish, as used in the contract:

"Notice of Cancellation"

/enter date of transaction/

____

(Date)

"You may cancel this transaction, without any penalty or obligation, within seven business days from the above date.

If you cancel, any property traded in, any payments made by you under the contract or sale, and any negotiable instrument executed by you will be returned within 10 days following receipt by the seller of your cancellation notice, and any security interest arising out of the transaction will be canceled.

If you cancel, you must make available to the seller at your residence, in substantially as good condition as when received, any goods delivered to you under this contract or sale, or you may, if you wish, comply with the instructions of the seller regarding the return shipment of the goods at the seller's expense and risk.

If you do make the goods available to the seller and the seller does not pick them up within 20 days of the date of your notice of cancellation, you may retain or dispose of the goods without any further obligation. If you fail to make the goods available to the seller, or if you agree to return the goods to the seller and fail to do so, then you remain liable for performance of all obligations under the contract."

To cancel this transaction, mail or deliver a signed and dated copy of this cancellation notice, or any other written notice, or send a telegram

to ____,

/name of seller/

at ____

/address of seller's place of business/

not later than midnight of ___________________________________.

(Date)

I hereby cancel this transaction. __________________________________

(Date)

____

(Buyer's signature)

§7159.1 Required Contract Provision: Door to Door Sales

(a) In any contract for the sale of home improvement goods or services offered by door-to-door sale that contains or is secured by a lien on real property, the contract shall be accompanied by the following notice in 18-point boldfaced type:

"WARNING TO BUYER: IF YOU SIGN THE CONTRACT WHICH ACCOMPANIES THIS NOTICE, YOU WILL BE PUTTING UP YOUR HOME AS SECURITY. THIS MEANSTHAT YOUR HOME COULD BE SOLD WITHOUT YOUR PERMISSION AND WITHOUT ANY COURT ACTION IF YOU MISS ANY PAYMENT REQUIRED BY THIS CONTRACT."

This notice shall be written in the same language as the rest of the contract. It shall be on a separate piece of paper from the rest of the contract and shall be signed and dated by the buyer. The home improvement contractor or home improvement salesperson shall deliver to the buyer at the time of the buyer's signing and dating of the notice a legible copy of the signed and dated notice. A security interest created in any contract described in this section that does not provide the notice as required by this section shall be void and unenforceable.

(b) This section shall not apply to any of the following:

(1) Any contract that is subject to Chapter 1 (commencing with Section 1801) of Title 2 of Part 4 of Division 3 of the Civil Code.

(2) A mechanics lien established pursuant to Chapter 4 (commencing with Section 8400) of Title 2 of Part 6 of Division 4 of the Civil Code.

(3) Any contract that is subject to subdivision (a) of Section 7159.2.

§7159.5 Home Improvement Contracts – Further Requirements – Crimes

This section applies to all home improvement contracts, as defined in Section 7151.2, between an owner or tenant and a contractor, whether a general contractor or a specialty contractor, that is licensed or subject to be licensed pursuant to this chapter with regard to the transaction.

(a) Failure by the licensee or a person subject to be licensed under this chapter, or by his or her agent or salesperson, to comply with the following provisions is cause for discipline:

(1) The contract shall be in writing and shall include the agreed contract amount in dollars and cents. The contract amount shall include the entire cost of the contract, including profit, labor, and materials, but excluding finance charges.

(2) If there is a separate finance charge between the contractor and the person contracting for home improvement, the finance charge shall be set out separately from the contract amount.

(3) If a downpayment will be charged, the downpayment may not exceed one thousand dollars ($1,000) or 10 percent of the contract amount, whichever is less.

(4) If, in addition to a downpayment, the contract provides for payments to be made prior to completion of the work, the contract shall include a schedule of payments in dollars and cents specifically referencing the amount of work or services to be performed and any materials and equipment to be supplied.

(5) Except for a downpayment, the contractor may neither request nor accept payment that exceeds the value of the work performed or material delivered.

(6) Upon any payment by the person contracting for home improvement, and prior to any further payment being made, the contractor shall, if requested, obtain and furnish to the person a full and unconditional release from any potential lien claimant claim or mechanics lien authorized pursuant to Sections 8400 and 8404 of the Civil Code for any portion of the work for which payment has been made. The person contracting for home improvement may withhold all further payments until these releases are furnished.

(7) If the contract provides for a payment of a salesperson's commission out of the contract price, that payment shall be made on a pro rata basis in proportion to the schedule of payments made to the contractor by the disbursing party in accordance with paragraph (4).

(8) A contractor furnishing a performance and payment bond, lien and completion bond, or a bond equivalent or joint control approved by the registrar covering full performance and payment is exempt from paragraphs (3), (4), and (5), and need not include, as part of the contract, the statement regarding the down payment specified in subparagraph (C) of paragraph (8) of subdivision (d) of Section 7159, the details and statement regarding progress payments specified in paragraph (9) of subdivision (d) of Section 7159, or the Mechanics Lien Warning specified in paragraph (4) of subdivision (e) of Section 7159. A contractor furnishing these bonds, bond equivalents, or a joint control approved by the registrar may accept payment prior to completion. If the contract provides for a contractor to furnish joint control, the contractor shall not have any financial or other interest in the joint control.

(b) A violation of paragraph (1), (3), or (5) of subdivision (a) by a licensee or a person subject to be licensed under this chapter, or by his or her agent or salesperson, is a misdemeanor punishable by a fine of not less than one hundred dollars ($100) nor more than five thousand dollars ($5,000), or by imprisonment in a county jail not exceeding one year, or by both that fine and imprisonment.

(1) An indictment or information against a person who is not licensed but who is required to be licensed under this chapter shall be brought, or a criminal complaint filed, for a violation of this section, in accordance with paragraph (4) of subdivision (d) of Section 802 of the Penal Code, within four years from the date of the contract or, if the contract is not reduced to writing, from the date the buyer makes the first payment to the contractor.

(2) An indictment or information against a person who is licensed under this chapter shall be brought, or a criminal complaint filed, for a violation of this section, in accordance with paragraph (2) of subdivision (d) of Section 802 of the Penal Code, within two years from the date of the contract or, if the contract is not reduced to writing, from the date the buyer makes the first payment to the contractor.

(3) The limitations on actions in this subdivision shall not apply to any administrative action filed against a licensed contractor.

(c) Any person who violates this section as part of a plan or scheme to defraud an owner or tenant of a residential or nonresidential structure, including a mobile home or manufactured home, in connection with the offer or performance of repairs to the structure for damage caused by a natural disaster, shall be ordered by the court to make full restitution to the victim based on the person's ability to pay, as defined in subdivision (e) of Section 1203.1b of the Penal Code. In addition to full restitution, and imprisonment authorized by this section, the court may impose a fine of not less than five hundred dollars ($500) nor more than twenty-five thousand dollars ($25,000), based upon the defendant's ability to pay. This subdivision applies to natural disasters for which a state of emergency is proclaimed by the Governor pursuant to Section 8625 of the Government Code, or for which an emergency or major disaster is declared by the President of the United States.

§7159.14 Service and Repair Contracts – Further Requirements – Crimes

(a) This section applies to a service and repair contract as defined in Section 7159.10. A violation of this section by a licensee or a person subject to be licensed under this chapter, or by his or her agent or salesperson, is cause for discipline.

(1) The contract may not exceed seven hundred fifty dollars ($750).

(2) The contract shall be in writing and shall state the agreed contract amount, which may be stated as either a fixed contract amount in dollars and cents or, if a time and materials formula is used, as an estimated contract amount in dollars and cents.

(3) The contract amount shall include the entire cost of the contract including profit, labor, and materials, but excluding finance charges.

(4) The actual contract amount of a time and materials contract may not exceed the estimated contract amount without written authorization from the buyer.

(5) The prospective buyer must have initiated contact with the contractor to request work.

(6) The contractor may not sell the buyer goods or services beyond those reasonably necessary to take care of the particular problem that caused the buyer to contact the contractor.

(7) No payment may be due before the project is completed.

(8) A service and repair contractor may charge only one service charge. For purposes of this chapter, a service charge includes such charges as a service or trip charge, or an inspection fee.

(9) A service and repair contractor charging a service charge must disclose in all advertisements that there is a service charge and, when the customer initiates the call for service, must disclose the amount of the service charge.

(10) The service and repair contractor must offer to the customer any parts that were replaced.

(11) Upon any payment by the buyer, the contractor shall, if requested, obtain and furnish to the buyer a full and unconditional release from any potential lien claimant claim or mechanics lien authorized pursuant to Sections 8400 and 8404 of the Civil Code for any portion of the work for which payment has been made.

(b) A violation of paragraph (1), (2), (3), (4), (5), (6), or (8) of subdivision (a) by a licensee or a person subject to be licensed under this chapter, or by his or her agent or salesperson, is a misdemeanor punishable by a fine of not less than one hundred dollars ($100) nor more than five thousand dollars ($5,000), or by imprisonment in a county jail not exceeding one year, or by both that fine and imprisonment.

(1) An indictment or information against a person who is not licensed but who is required to be licensed under this chapter shall be brought, or a criminal complaint filed, for a violation of this section, in accordance with paragraph (4) of subdivision (d) of Section 802 of the Penal Code, within four years from the date of the contract or, if the contract is not reduced to writing, from the date the buyer makes the first payment to the contractor.

(2) An indictment or information against a person who is licensed under this chapter shall be brought, or a criminal complaint filed, for a violation of this section, in accordance with paragraph (2) of subdivision (d) of Section 802 of the Penal Code, within two years from the date of the contract or, if the contract is not reduced to writing, from the date the buyer makes the first payment to the contractor.

(3) The limitations on actions in this subdivision shall not apply to any administrative action filed against a licensed contractor. (c) Any person who violates this section as part of a plan or scheme to defraud an owner or tenant of a residential or nonresidential structure, including a mobile home or manufactured home, in connection with the offer or performance of repairs to the structure for damage caused by a natural disaster, shall be ordered by the court to make full restitution to the victim based on the person's ability to pay, as defined in subdivision (e) of Section 1203.1b of the Penal Code. In addition to full restitution, and imprisonment authorized by this section, the court may impose a fine of not less than five hundred dollars ($500) nor more than twenty-five thousand dollars ($25,000), based upon the defendant's ability to pay. This subdivision applies to natural disasters for which a state of emergency is proclaimed by the Governor pursuant to Section 8625 of the Government Code, or for which an emergency or major disaster is declared by the President of the United States.

§7164 Contracts Between Owner and Contractor: Writing and Notice Requirement

(a) Notwithstanding Section 7044, every contract and any changes in a contract, between an owner and a contractor, for the construction of a single-family dwelling to be retained by the owner for at least one year shall be evidenced in writing signed by both parties.

(b) The writing shall contain the following:

(1) The name, address, and license number of the contractor.

(2) The approximate dates when the work will begin and be substantially completed.

(3) A legal description of the location where the work will be done.

(4) A statement with the heading "Mechanics Lien Warning" as follows:

"MECHANICS LIEN WARNING:

Anyone who helps improve your property, but who is not paid, may record what is called a mechanics lien on your property. A mechanics lien is a claim, like a mortgage or home equity loan, made against your property and recorded with the county recorder.

Even if you pay your contractor in full, unpaid subcontractors, suppliers, and laborers who helped to improve your property may record mechanics liens and sue you in court to foreclose the lien. If a court finds the lien is valid, you could be forced to pay twice or have a court officer sell your home to pay the lien. Liens can also affect your credit.

To preserve their right to record a lien, each subcontractor and material supplier must provide you with a document called a 'Preliminary Notice.' This notice is not a lien. The purpose of the notice is to let you know that the person who sends you the notice has the right to record a lien on your property if he or she is not paid.

BE CAREFUL. The Preliminary Notice can be sent up to 20 days after the subcontractor starts work or the supplier provides material. This can be a big problem if you pay your contractor before you have received the Preliminary Notices.

You will not get Preliminary Notices from your prime contractor or other persons you contract with directly or from laborers who work on your project. The law assumes that you already know they are improving your property.

PROTECT YOURSELF FROM LIENS. You can protect yourself from liens by getting a list from your contractor of all the subcontractors and material suppliers that work on your project. Find out from your contractor when these subcontractors started work and when these suppliers delivered goods or materials. Then wait 20 days, paying attention to the Preliminary Notices you receive.

PAY WITH JOINT CHECKS. One way to protect yourself is to pay with a joint check. When your contractor tells you it is time to pay for the work of a subcontractor or supplier who has provided you with a Preliminary Notice, write a joint check payable to both the contractor and the subcontractor or material supplier.

For other ways to prevent liens, visit CSLB's Web site at www.cslb.ca.gov or call CSLB at 800-321-CSLB (2752).

REMEMBER, IF YOU DO NOTHING, YOU RISK HAVING A LIEN PLACED ON YOUR HOME. This can mean that you may have to pay twice, or face the forced sale of your home to pay what you owe."

(5)(A) A statement prepared by the board through regulation that emphasizes the value of commercial general liability insurance and encourages the owner to verify the contractor's insurance coverage and status.

(B) A check box indicating whether or not the contractor carries commercial general liability insurance, and if that is the case, the name and the telephone number of the insurer.

(c) The writing may also contain other matters agreed to by the parties to the contract. The writing shall be legible and shall clearly describe any other document which is to be incorporated into the contract. Prior to commencement of any work, the owner shall be furnished a copy of the written agreement, signed by the contractor. The provisions of this section are not exclusive and do not relieve the contractor from compliance with all other applicable provisions of law.

(d) Every contract subject to the provisions of this section shall contain, in close proximity to the signatures of the owner and contractor, a notice in at least 10-point boldface type or in all capital letters, stating that the owner has the right to require the contractor to have a performance and payment bond and that the expense of the bond may be borne by the owner.

(e) The requirements in paragraph (5) of subdivision (b) shall become operative three months after the board adopts the regulations referenced in subparagraph (A) of paragraph (5) of subdivision (b).

(f) This section shall become operative on January 1, 2006.

§8513 Registered Pest Control Companies; Notice to Owners

(a) The board shall prescribe a form entitled "Notice to Owner" that shall describe, in nontechnical language and in a clear and coherent manner using words with common and everyday meaning, the pertinent provisions of this state's mechanics lien laws and the rights and responsibilities of an owner of property and a registered pest control company thereunder. Each company registered under this chapter, prior to entering into a contract with an owner for work for which a company registration is required, shall give a copy of this "Notice to Owner" to the owner, his or her agent, or the payer.

(b) No company that is required to be registered under this chapter shall require or request a waiver of lien rights from any subcontractor, employee, or supplier.

(c) Each company registered under this chapter that acts as a subcontractor for another company registered under this chapter shall, within 20 days of commencement of any work for which a company registration is required, give the preliminary notice in accordance with Chapter 2 (commencing with Section 8200) of Title 2 of Part 6 of Division 4 of the Civil Code, to the owner, his or her agent, or the payer.

(d) Each company registered under this chapter that acts as a prime contractor for work for which a company registration is required shall, prior to accepting payment for the work, furnish to the owner, his or her agent, or the payer a full and unconditional release from any claim of mechanics lien by any subcontractor entitled to enforce a mechanics lien pursuant to Section 8410 of the Civil Code.

(e) Each company registered under this chapter that subcontracts to another company registered under this chapter work for which a company registration is required shall furnish to the subcontractor the name of the owner, his or her agent, or the payer.

(f) The provisions of this section shall be applicable only to those registered companies, as defined in Section 8506.1, operating pursuant to a Branch 1 or Branch 3 registration.

(g) A violation of the provisions of this section is a ground for disciplinary action.

§17577.5 Home Water Treatment Device; Lien

(a) No contract or offer for the sale, lease, or rental of a home water treatment device and no purchase money loan, as defined in subdivision (b), shall provide for a lien on real property. Any lien taken in violation of this section is void and unenforceable.

(b) For the purpose of this section, "purchase money loan" means a loan or an advance under an open-end credit account if both of the following occur:

(1) The primary purpose of the loan or the primary purpose of establishing the open-end credit account is to finance all or a portion of the purchase price or any of the lease or rental payments for a water treatment device.

(2) The creditor knows the primary purpose of the loan or the primary purpose of establishing the open-end credit account when the loan is initially made or the open-end credit account is established.

(c) The creditor shall be deemed to know that the primary purpose of the loan or the primary purpose of establishing the open-end credit account is the primary purpose described in paragraph (1) of subdivision (b) if any of the following occur:

(1) The consumer's application for credit or any other document in the creditor's possession before the loan is made or the open-end account is established indicates the primary purpose of the loan or the open-end credit account.

(2) The seller, lessor, or renter arranges or guarantees the loan or open-end account, or participates in the preparation of the consumer's application for credit or other loan documents, or receives from the creditor a loan commission, brokerage, or referral fee.

(d) For the purpose of this section, "open-end credit" has the same meaning as used in Section 226.2 of Title 12 of the Code of Federal Regulations.

(e) This section does not apply to mechanics liens established pursuant to Chapter 4 (commencing with Section 8400) of Title 2 of Part 6 of Division 4 of the Civil Code.

CODE OF CIVIL PROCEDURE SECTIONS ("CCP")

New Text (Operative July 1, 2012)

§86 Limited Jurisdiction

(a) The following civil cases and proceedings are limited civil cases:

(1) A case at law in which the demand, exclusive of interest, or the value of the property in controversy amounts to twenty-five thousand dollars ($25,000) or less. This paragraph does not apply to a case that involves the legality of any tax, impost, assessment, toll, or municipal fine, except an action to enforce payment of delinquent unsecured personal property taxes if the legality of the tax is not contested by the defendant.

(2) An action for dissolution of partnership where the total assets of the partnership do not exceed twenty-five thousand dollars ($25,000); an action of interpleader where the amount of money or the value of the property involved does not exceed twenty-five thousand dollars ($25,000).

(3) An action to cancel or rescind a contract when the relief is sought in connection with an action to recover money not exceeding twenty-five thousand dollars ($25,000) or property of a value not exceeding twenty-five thousand dollars ($25,000), paid or delivered under, or in consideration of, the contract; an action to revise a contract where the relief is sought in an action upon the contract if the action otherwise is a limited civil case.

(4) A proceeding in forcible entry or forcible or unlawful detainer where the whole amount of damages claimed is twenty-five thousand dollars ($25,000) or less.

(5) An action to enforce and foreclose a lien on personal property where the amount of the lien is twenty-five thousand dollars ($25,000) or less.

(6) An action to enforce and foreclose, or a petition to release, a lien arising under the provisions of Chapter 4 (commencing with Section 8400) of Title 2 of Part 6 of Division 4 of the Civil Code, or to enforce and foreclose an assessment lien on a common interest development as defined in Section 1351 of the Civil Code, where the amount of the liens is twenty-five thousand dollars ($25,000) or less. However, if an action to enforce the lien affects property that is also affected by a similar pending action that is not a limited civil case, or if the total amount of liens sought to be foreclosed against the same property aggregates an amount in excess of twenty-five thousand dollars ($25,000), the action is not a limited civil case.

(7) An action for declaratory relief when brought pursuant to either of the following:

(A) By way of cross-complaint as to a right of indemnity with respect to the relief demanded in the complaint or a cross-complaint in an action or proceeding that is otherwise a limited civil case.

(B) To conduct a trial after a nonbinding fee arbitration between an attorney and client, pursuant to Article 13 (commencing with Section 6200) of Chapter 4 of Division 3 of the Business and Professions Code, where the amount in controversy is twenty-five thousand dollars ($25,000) or less.

(8) An action to issue a temporary restraining order or preliminary injunction; to take an account, where necessary to preserve the property or rights of any party to a limited civil case; to make any order or perform any act, pursuant to Title 9 (commencing with Section 680.010) of Part 2 (enforcement of judgments) in a limited civil case; to appoint a receiver pursuant to Section 564 in a limited civil case; to determine title to personal property seized in a limited civil case.

(9) An action under Article 3 (commencing with Section 708.210) of Chapter 6 of Division 2 of Title 9 of Part 2 for the recovery of an interest in personal property or to enforce the liability of the debtor of a judgment debtor where the interest claimed adversely is of a value not exceeding twenty-five thousand dollars ($25,000) or the debt denied does not exceed twenty-five thousand dollars ($25,000).

(10) An arbitration-related petition filed pursuant to either of the following:

(A) Article 2 (commencing with Section 1292) of Chapter 5 of Title 9 of Part 3, except for uninsured motorist arbitration proceedings in accordance with Section 11580.2 of the Insurance Code, if the petition is filed before the arbitration award becomes final and the matter to be resolved by arbitration is a limited civil case under paragraphs (1) to (9), inclusive, of subdivision (a) or if the petition is filed after the arbitration award becomes final and the amount of the award and all other rulings, pronouncements, and decisions made in the award are within paragraphs (1) to (9), inclusive, of subdivision (a).

(B) To confirm, correct, or vacate a fee arbitration award between an attorney and client that is binding or has become binding, pursuant to Article 13 (commencing with Section 6200) of Chapter 4 of Division 3 of the Business and Professions Code, where the arbitration award is twenty-five thousand dollars ($25,000) or less.

(b) The following cases in equity are limited civil cases:

(1) A case to try title to personal property when the amount involved is not more than twenty-five thousand dollars ($25,000).

(2) A case when equity is pleaded as a defensive matter in any case that is otherwise a limited civil case.

(3) A case to vacate a judgment or order of the court obtained in a limited civil case through extrinsic fraud, mistake, inadvertence, or excusable neglect.

§410.42 Construction Subcontracts; Provisions Requiring Dispute Resolution Outside State Unenforceable

(a) The following provisions of a contract between the contractor and a subcontractor with principal offices in this state, for the construction of a public or private work of improvement in this state, shall be void and unenforceable:

(1) A provision which purports to require any dispute between the parties to be litigated, arbitrated, or otherwise determined outside this state.

(2) A provision which purports to preclude a party from commencing such a proceeding or obtaining a judgment or other resolution in this state or the courts of this state.

(b) For purposes of this section, "construction" means any work or services performed on, or materials provided for, a work of improvement, as defined in Section 8050 of the Civil Code, and for which a lien may be claimed pursuant to Section 8400 of the Civil Code (whether or not a lien is in fact claimed) or for which such a lien could be claimed but for Section 8160 of the Civil Code.

§708.760 Procedure Where Judgment Debtor is Contractor upon a Public Work

(a) If the judgment debtor named in the abstract or certified copy of the judgment filed pursuant to this article is a contractor upon a public work, the cost of which is to be paid out of public moneys voted, appropriated, or otherwise set apart for such purpose, only so much of the contract price shall be deemed owing and unpaid within the meaning of Section 708.740 or 708.750 as may remain payable under the terms of the contractor's contract, upon the completion thereof, after deducting sums due and to become due to persons described in Section 9100 of the Civil Code. In ascertaining the sums due or to become due to such persons, only claims which are filed against the moneys due or to become due to the judgment debtor in accordance with Chapter 4 (commencing with Section 9350) of Title 3 of Part 6 of Division 4 of the Civil Code shall be considered.

(b) The Controller, auditor, or other public disbursing officer whose duty it is to make payments under the provisions of the contract may not deposit an amount with the court pursuant to this article until the contract is completed, but may deposit an amount with the court to satisfy the claim of the judgment debtor before the payments specified in subdivision (a) are made so long as a sufficient amount is retained for the satisfaction of the claims of persons described in Section 9100 of the Civil Code.

§1203.61 Enforcement of Lien

(a) Any lien provided for by this chapter shall be enforced in the same manner as provided in Chapter 4 (commencing with Section 8400) of Title 2 of Part 6 of Division 4 of the Civil Code. The action shall be filed within 180 days from the time of the recording of the lien. If a credit is given and notice of the fact and terms of the credit is filed in the office of the county recorder subsequent to the filing of the lien and prior to the expiration of the 180-day period, then the lien continues in force until 180 days after the expiration of the credit, but no lien continues in force by reason of any agreement to give credit for a longer time than one year from the time the work is completed. If the proceedings to enforce the lien are not prosecuted to trial within two years after commencement, the court may in its discretion dismiss the action for want of prosecution, and in all cases the dismissal of the action (unless it is expressly stated that it is without prejudice) or a judgment in the action that no lien exists is equivalent to the cancellation and removal from the record of the lien.

(b) As against any purchaser or encumbrancer for value and in good faith whose rights are acquired subsequent to the expiration of the 180-day period following the filing of the lien, no giving of credit or extension of the lien or time to enforce the lien shall be effective unless evidenced by a notice or agreement filed for record in the office of the county recorder prior to the acquisition of the rights of the purchaser or encumbrancer.

§1281.5 Waiver of Right to Arbitration; Actions to Enforce Lien

(a) Any person who proceeds to record and enforce a claim of lien by commencement of an action pursuant to Chapter 4 (commencing with Section 8400) of Title 2 of Part 6 of Division 4 of the Civil Code, does not thereby waive any right of arbitration the person may have pursuant to a written agreement to arbitrate, if, in filing an action to enforce the claim of lien, the claimant does either of the following:

(1) Includes an allegation in the complaint that the claimant does not intend to waive any right of arbitration, and intends to move the court, within 30 days after service of the summons and complaint, for an order to stay further proceedings in the action.

(2) At the same time that the complaint is filed, the claimant files an application that the action be stayed pending the arbitration of any issue, question, or dispute that is claimed to be arbitrable under the agreement and that is relevant to the action to enforce the claim of lien.

(b) Within 30 days after service of the summons and complaint, the claimant shall file and serve a motion and notice of motion pursuant to Section 1281.4 to stay the action pending the arbitration of any issue, question, or dispute that is claimed to be arbitrable under the agreement and that is relevant to the action to enforce the claim of lien. The failure of a claimant to comply with this subdivision is a waiver of the claimant's right to compel arbitration.

(c) The failure of a defendant to file a petition pursuant to Section 1281.2 at or before the time the defendant answers the complaint filed pursuant to subdivision (a) is a waiver of the defendant's right to compel arbitration.

§1800 Recovery of Preferences

(a) As used in this section, the following terms have the following meanings:

(1) "Insolvent" means:

(A) With reference to a person other than a partnership, a financial condition such that the sum of the person's debts is greater than all of the person's property, at a fair valuation, exclusive of both of the following:

(i) Property transferred, concealed, or removed with intent to hinder, delay, or defraud the person's creditors.

(ii) Property that is exempt from property of the estate pursuant to the election of the person made pursuant to Section 1801.

(B) With reference to a partnership, financial condition such that the sum of the partnership's debts are greater than the aggregate of, at a fair valuation, both of the following:

(i) All of the partnership's property, exclusive of property of the kind specified in clause (i) of subparagraph (A).

(ii) The sum of the excess of the value of each general partner's separate property, exclusive of property of the kind specified in clause (ii) of subparagraph (A), over the partner's separate debts.

(2) "Inventory" means personal property leased or furnished, held for sale or lease, or to be furnished under a contract for service, raw materials, work in process, or materials used or consumed in a business, including farm products such as crops or livestock, held for sale or lease.

(3) "Insider" means:

(A) If the assignor is an individual, any of the following:

(i) A relative of the assignor or of a general partner of the assignor.

(ii) A partnership in which the assignor is a general partner.

(iii) A general partner of the assignor.

(iv) A corporation of which the assignor is a director, officer, or person in control.

(B) If the assignor is a corporation, any of the following:

(i) A director of the assignor.

(ii) An officer of the assignor.

(iii) A person in control of the assignor.

(iv) A partnership in which the assignor is a general partner.

(v) A general partner of the assignor.

(vi) A relative of a general partner, director, officer, or person in control of the assignor.

(C) If the assignor is a partnership, any of the following:

(i) A general partner in the assignor.

(ii) A relative of a general partner in, general partner of, or person in control of the assignor.

(iii) A partnership in which the assignor is a general partner.

(iv) A general partner of the assignor.

(v) A person in control of the assignor.

(D) An affiliate of the assignor or an insider of an affiliate as if the affiliate were the assignor.

(E) A managing agent of the assignor.

As used in this paragraph, the following terms have the following meanings:

"Relative" means an individual related by affinity or consanguinity within the third degree as determined by the common law, or an individual in a step or adoptive relationship within the third degree.

An "affiliate" means a person that directly or indirectly owns, controls, or holds, with power to vote, 20 percent or more of the outstanding voting securities of the assignor, or 20 percent or more of whose outstanding voting securities are directly or indirectly owned, controlled, or held with power to vote by the assignor, excluding securities held in a fiduciary or agency capacity without sole discretionary power to vote, or held solely to secure a debt if the holder has not in fact exercised the power to vote, or a person who operates the business of the assignor under a lease or operating agreement or whose business is operated by the assignor under a lease or operating agreement.

(4) "Judicial lien" means a lien obtained by judgment, levy, sequestration, or other legal or equitable process or proceeding.

(5) "New value" means money or money's worth in goods, services, or new credit, or release by a transferee of property previously transferred to the transferee in a transaction that is neither void nor voidable by the assignor or the assignee under any applicable law, but does not include an obligation substituted for an existing obligation.

(6) "Receivable" means a right to payment, whether or not the right has been earned by performance.

(7) "Security agreement" means an agreement that creates or provides for a security interest.

(8) "Security interest" means a lien created by an agreement.

(9) "Statutory lien" means a lien arising solely by force of a statute on specified circumstances or conditions, or lien of distress for rent, whether or not statutory, but does not include a security interest or judicial lien, whether or not the interest or lien is provided by or is dependent on a statute and whether or not the interest or lien is made fully effective by statute.

(10) "Transfer" means every mode, direct or indirect, absolute or conditional, voluntary or involuntary, or disposing of or parting with property or with an interest in property, including retention of title as a security interest.

(b) Except as provided in subdivision (c), the assignee of any general assignment for the benefit of creditors, as defined in Section 493.010, may recover any transfer of property of the assignor that is all of the following:

(1) To or for the benefit of a creditor.

(2) For or on account of an antecedent debt owed by the assignor before the transfer was made.

(3) Made while the assignor was insolvent.

(4) Made on or within 90 days before the date of the making of the assignment or made between 90 days and one year before the date of making the assignment if the creditor, at the time of the transfer, was an insider and had reasonable cause to believe the debtor was insolvent at the time of the transfer.

(5) Enables the creditor to receive more than another creditor of the same class.

(c) The assignee may not recover under this section a transfer as follows:

(1) To the extent that the transfer was both of the following:

(A) Intended by the assignor and the creditor to or for whose benefit the transfer was made to be a contemporaneous exchange for new value given to the assignor.

(B) In fact a substantially contemporaneous exchange.

(2) To the extent that the transfer was all of the following:

(A) In payment of a debt incurred in the ordinary course of business or financial affairs of the assignor and the transferee.

(B) Made in the ordinary course of business or financial affairs of the assignor and the transferee.

(C) Made according to ordinary business terms.

(3) Of a security interest in property acquired by the assignor that meets both of the following:

(A) To the extent the security interest secures new value that was all of the following:

(i) Given at or after the signing of a security agreement that contains a description of the property as collateral.

(ii) Given by or on behalf of the secured party under the agreement.

(iii) Given to enable the assignor to acquire the property.

(iv) In fact used by the assignor to acquire the property.

(B) That is perfected within 20 days after the security interest attaches.

(4) To or for the benefit of a creditor, to the extent that, after the transfer, the creditor gave new value to or for the benefit of the assignor that meets both of the following:

(A) Not secured by an otherwise unavoidable security interest.

(B) On account of which new value the assignor did not make an otherwise unavoidable transfer to or for the benefit of the creditor.

(5) Of a perfected security interest in inventory or a receivable or the proceeds of either, except to the extent that the aggregate of all the transfers to the transferee caused a reduction, as of the date of the making of the assignment and to the prejudice of other creditors holding unsecured claims, of any amount by which the debt secured by the security interest exceeded the value of all security interest for the debt on the later of the following:

(A) Ninety days before the date of the making of the assignment.

(B) The date on which new value was first given under the security agreement creating the security interest.

(6) That is the fixing of a statutory lien.

(7) That is payment to a claimant, as defined in Section 8004 of the Civil Code, in exchange for the claimant's waiver or release of any potential or asserted claim of lien, stop payment notice, or right to recover on a payment bond, or any combination thereof.

(8) To the extent that the transfer was a bona fide payment of a debt to a spouse, former spouse, or child of the debtor, for alimony to, maintenance for, or support of, the spouse or child, in connection with a separation agreement, divorce decree, or other order of a court of record, or a determination made in accordance with state or territorial law by a governmental unit, or property settlement agreement; but not to the extent that either of the following occurs:

(A) The debt is assigned to another entity voluntarily, by operation of law or otherwise, in which case the assignee may not recover that portion of the transfer that is assigned to the state or any political subdivision of the state pursuant to Part D of Title IV of the Social Security Act (42 U.S.C. Sec. 601 et seq.) and passed on to the spouse, former spouse, or child of the debtor.

(B) The debt includes a liability designated as alimony, maintenance, or support, unless the liability is actually in the nature of alimony, maintenance, or support.

(d) An assignee of any general assignment for the benefit of creditors, as defined in Section 493.010, may avoid a transfer of property of the assignor transferred to secure reimbursement of a surety that furnished a bond or other obligation to dissolve a judicial lien that would have been avoidable by the assignee under subdivision (b). The liability of the surety under the bond or obligation shall be discharged to the extent of the value of the property recovered by the assignee or the amount paid to the assignee.

(e) (1) For the purposes of this section:

(A) A transfer of real property other than fixtures, but including the interest of a seller or purchaser under a contract for the sale of real property, is perfected when a bona fide purchaser of the property from the debtor, against whom applicable law permits the transfer to be perfected, cannot acquire an interest that is superior to the interest of the transferee.

(B) A transfer of a fixture or property other than real property is perfected when a creditor on a simple contract cannot acquire a judicial lien that is superior to the interest of the transferee.

(2) For the purposes of this section, except as provided in paragraph (3), a transfer is made at any of the following times:

(A) At the time the transfer takes effect between the transferor and the transferee, if the transfer is perfected at, or within 10 days after, the time, except as provided in subparagraph (B) of paragraph (3) of subdivision (c).

(B) At the time the transfer is perfected, if the transfer is perfected after the 10 days.

(C) Immediately before the date of making the assignment if the transfer is not perfected at the later of:

(i) The making of the assignment.

(ii) Ten days after the transfer takes effect between the transferor and the transferee.

(3) For the purposes of this section, a transfer is not made until the assignor has acquired rights in the property transferred.

(f) For the purposes of this section, the assignor is presumed to have been insolvent on and during the 90 days immediately preceding the date of making the assignment.

(g) An action by an assignee under this section must be commenced within one year after making the assignment.

EDUCATION CODE SECTIONS ("EC")
New Text (Operative July 1, 2012)

§17307.5 Construction Work on Public Schools; Stop Work Orders

(a) Notwithstanding any provision of law to the contrary, including, but not limited to, Title 3 (commencing with Section 9000) of Part 6 of Division 4 of the Civil Code, the Department of General Services may issue a stop work order when construction work on a public school is not being performed in accordance with existing law and would compromise the structural integrity of the building, thereby endangering the public safety. The Department of General Services shall allow construction of incidental and minor nonstructural additions or nonstructural alterations without invoking its stop work authority.

(b) A school district, county superintendent of schools, county board of education, or other public board, body, or officer whose construction work on a public school is subject to a stop work order issued pursuant to subdivision (a) shall not be held liable in any action filed against the public board, body, or officer for stopping work as required by the stop work order, or for any delays caused by compliance with the stop work order, except to the extent that an error or omission by the public board, body, or officer is the basis for the issuance of the stop work order.

§81133.5 Construction Work on Community Colleges; Stop Work Orders

(a) Notwithstanding any provision of law to the contrary, including, but not limited to, Title 3 (commencing with Section 9000) of Part 6 of Division 4 of the Civil Code, the Department of General Services may issue a stop work order when construction work on a community college is not being performed in accordance with existing law and would compromise the structural integrity of the building, thereby endangering the public safety. The Department of General Services shall allow construction of incidental and minor nonstructural additions or nonstructural alterations without invoking its stop work authority.

(b) A community college district or other public board, body, or officer whose construction work on a community college is subject to a stop work order issued pursuant to subdivision (a) shall not be held liable in any action filed against the public board, body, or officer for stopping work as required by the stop work order, or for any delays caused by compliance with the stop work order, except to the extent that an error or omission by the public board, body, or officer is that basis for the issuance of the stop work order.

GOVERNMENT CODE SECTIONS ("GC")
New Text (Operative July 1, 2012)

§ 7480 Authorized Acts

Nothing in this chapter shall prohibit any of the following:

(a) The dissemination of any financial information that is not identified with, or identifiable as being derived from, the financial records of a particular customer.

(b) When any police or sheriff's department or district attorney in this state certifies to a bank, credit union, or savings association in writing that a crime report has been filed that involves the alleged fraudulent use of drafts, checks, access cards, or other orders drawn upon any bank, credit union, or savings association in this state, the police or sheriff's department or district attorney, a county adult protective services office when investigating the financial abuse of an elder or dependent adult, or a long-term care ombudsman when investigating the financial abuse of an elder or dependent adult, may request a bank, credit union, or savings association to furnish, and a bank, credit union, or savings association shall furnish, a statement setting forth the following information with respect to a customer account specified by the requesting party for a period 30 days prior to, and up to 30 days following, the date of occurrence of the alleged illegal act involving the account:

(1) The number of items dishonored.

(2) The number of items paid that created overdrafts.

(3) The dollar volume of the dishonored items and items paid which created overdrafts and a statement explaining any credit arrangement between the bank, credit union, or savings association and customer to pay overdrafts.

(4) The dates and amounts of deposits and debits and the account balance on these dates.

(5) A copy of the signature card, including the signature and any addresses appearing on a customer's signature card.

(6) The date the account opened and, if applicable, the date the account closed.

(7) Surveillance photographs and video recordings of persons accessing the crime victim's financial account via an automated teller machine (ATM) or from within the financial institution for dates on which illegal acts involving the account were alleged to have occurred. Nothing in this paragraph does any of the following:

(A) Requires a financial institution to produce a photograph or video recording if it does not possess the photograph or video recording.

(B) Affects any existing civil immunities as provided in Section 47 of the Civil Code or any other provision of law.

(8) A bank, credit union, or savings association that provides the requesting party with copies of one or more complete account statements prepared in the regular course of business shall be deemed to be in compliance with paragraphs (1), (2), (3), and (4).

(c) When any police or sheriff's department or district attorney in this state certifies to a bank, credit union, or savings association in writing that a crime report has been filed that involves the alleged fraudulent use of drafts, checks, access cards, or other orders drawn upon any bank, credit union, or savings association doing business in this state, the police or sheriff's department or district attorney, a county adult protective services office when investigating the financial abuse of an elder or dependent adult, or a long-term care ombudsman when investigating the financial abuse of an elder or dependent adult, may request, with the consent of the accountholder, the bank, credit union, or savings association to furnish, and the bank, credit union, or savings association shall furnish, a statement setting forth the following information with respect to a customer account specified by the requesting party for a period 30 days prior to, and up to 30 days following, the date of occurrence of the alleged illegal act involving the account:

(1) The number of items dishonored.

(2) The number of items paid that created overdrafts.

(3) The dollar volume of the dishonored items and items paid which created overdrafts and a statement explaining any credit arrangement between the bank, credit union, or savings association and customer to pay overdrafts.

(4) The dates and amounts of deposits and debits and the account balance on these dates.

(5) A copy of the signature card, including the signature and any addresses appearing on a customer's signature card.

(6) The date the account opened and, if applicable, the date the account closed.

(7) Surveillance photographs and video recordings of persons accessing the crime victim's financial account via an automated teller machine (ATM) or from within the financial institution for dates on which illegal acts involving this account were alleged to have occurred. Nothing in this paragraph does any of the following:

(A) Requires a financial institution to produce a photograph or video recording if it does not possess the photograph or video recording.

(B) Affects any existing civil immunities as provided in Section 47 of the Civil Code or any other provision of law.

(8) A bank, credit union, or savings association doing business in this state that provides the requesting party with copies of one or more complete account statements prepared in the regular course of business shall be deemed to be in compliance with paragraphs (1), (2), (3), and (4).

(d) For purposes of subdivision (c), consent of the accountholder shall be satisfied if an accountholder provides to the financial institution and the person or entity seeking disclosure, a signed and dated statement containing all of the following:

(1) Authorization of the disclosure for the period specified in subdivision (c).

(2) The name of the agency or department to which disclosure is authorized and, if applicable, the statutory purpose for which the information is to be obtained.

(3) A description of the financial records that are authorized to be disclosed.

(e) (1) The Attorney General, a supervisory agency, the Franchise Tax Board, the State Board of Equalization, the Employment Development Department, the Controller or an inheritance tax referee when administering the Prohibition of Gift and Death Taxes (Part 8 (commencing with Section 13301) of Division 2 of the Revenue and Taxation Code), a police or sheriff's department or district attorney, a county adult protective services office when investigating the financial abuse of an elder or dependent adult, a long-term care ombudsman when investigating the financial abuse of an elder or dependent adult, a county welfare department when investigating welfare fraud, a county auditor-controller or director of finance when investigating fraud against the county, or the Department of Corporations when conducting investigations in connection with the enforcement of laws administered by the Commissioner of Corporations, from requesting of an office or branch of a financial institution, and the office or branch from responding to a request, as to whether a person has an account or accounts at that office or branch and, if so, any identifying numbers of the account or accounts.

(2) No additional information beyond that specified in this section shall be released to a county welfare department without either the accountholder's written consent or a judicial writ, search warrant, subpoena, or other judicial order.

(3) A county auditor-controller or director of finance who unlawfully discloses information he or she is authorized to request under this subdivision is guilty of the unlawful disclosure of confidential data, a misdemeanor, which shall be punishable as set forth in Section 7485.

(f) The examination by, or disclosure to, any supervisory agency of financial records that relate solely to the exercise of its supervisory function. The scope of an agency's supervisory function shall be determined by reference to statutes that grant authority to examine, audit, or require reports of financial records or financial institutions as follows:

(1) With respect to the Commissioner of Financial Institutions by reference to Division 1 (commencing with Section 99), Division 1.5 (commencing with Section 4800), Division 2 (commencing with Section 5000), Division 5 (commencing with Section 14000), Division 7 (commencing with Section 18000), Division 15 (commencing with Section 31000), and Division 16 (commencing with Section 33000), of the Financial Code.

(2) With respect to the Controller by reference to Title 10 (commencing with Section 1300) of Part 3 of the Code of Civil Procedure.

(3) With respect to the Administrator of Local Agency Security by reference to Article 2 (commencing with Section 53630) of Chapter 4 of Part 1 of Division 2 of Title 5 of the Government Code.

(g) The disclosure to the Franchise Tax Board of (1) the amount of any security interest that a financial institution has in a specified asset of a customer or (2) financial records in connection with the filing or audit of a tax return or tax information return that are required to be filed by the financial institution pursuant to Part 10 (commencing with Section 17001), Part 11 (commencing with Section 23001), or Part 18 (commencing with Section 38001), of the Revenue and Taxation Code.

(h) The disclosure to the State Board of Equalization of any of the following:

(1) The information required by Sections 6702, 6703, 8954, 8957, 30313, 30315, 32383, 32387, 38502, 38503, 40153, 40155, 41122, 41123.5, 43443, 43444.2, 44144, 45603, 45605, 46404, 46406, 50134, 50136, 55203, 55205, 60404, and 60407 of the Revenue and Taxation Code.

(2) The financial records in connection with the filing or audit of a tax return required to be filed by the financial institution pursuant to Part 1 (commencing with Section 6001), Part 2 (commencing with Section 7301), Part 3 (commencing with Section 8601), Part 13 (commencing with Section 30001), Part 14 (commencing with Section 32001), and Part 17 (commencing with Section 37001), of Division 2 of the Revenue and Taxation Code.

(3) The amount of any security interest a financial institution has in a specified asset of a customer, if the inquiry is directed to the branch or office where the interest is held.

(i) The disclosure to the Controller of the information required by Section 7853 of the Revenue and Taxation Code.

(j) The disclosure to the Employment Development Department of the amount of any security interest a financial institution has in a specified asset of a customer, if the inquiry is directed to the branch or office where the interest is held.

(k) The disclosure by a construction lender, as defined in Section 8006 of the Civil Code, to the Registrar of Contractors, of information concerning the making of progress payments to a prime contractor requested by the registrar in connection with an investigation under Section 7108.5 of the Business and Professions Code.

(l) Upon receipt of a written request from a local child support agency referring to a support order pursuant to Section 17400 of the Family Code, a financial institution shall disclose the following information concerning the account or the person named in the request, whom the local child support agency shall identify, whenever possible, by social security number:

(1) If the request states the identifying number of an account at a financial institution, the name of each owner of the account.

(2) Each account maintained by the person at the branch to which the request is delivered, and, if the branch is able to make a computerized search, each account maintained by the person at any other branch of the financial institution located in this state.

(3) For each account disclosed pursuant to paragraphs (1) and (2), the account number, current balance, street address of the branch where the account is maintained, and, to the extent available through the branch's computerized search, the name and address of any other person listed as an owner.

(4) Whenever the request prohibits the disclosure, a financial institution shall not disclose either the request or its response, to an owner of the account or to any other person, except the officers and employees of the financial institution who are involved in responding to the request and to attorneys, employees of the local child support agencies, auditors, and regulatory authorities who have a need to know in order to perform their duties, and except as disclosure may be required by legal process.

(5) No financial institution, or any officer, employee, or agent thereof, shall be liable to any person for (A) disclosing information in response to a request pursuant to this subdivision, (B) failing to notify the owner of an account, or complying with a request under this paragraph not to disclose to the owner, the request or disclosure under this subdivision, or (C) failing to discover any account owned by the person named in the request pursuant to a computerized search of the records of the financial institution.

(6) The local child support agency may request information pursuant to this subdivision only when the local child support agency has received at least one of the following types of physical evidence:

(A) Any of the following, dated within the last three years:

(i) Form 599.

(ii) Form 1099.

(iii) A bank statement.

(iv) A check.

(v) A bank passbook.

(vi) A deposit slip.

(vii) A copy of a federal or state income tax return.

(viii) A debit or credit advice.

(ix) Correspondence that identifies the child support obligor by name, the bank, and the account number.

(x) Correspondence that identifies the child support obligor by name, the bank, and the banking services related to the account of the obligor.

(xi) An asset identification report from a federal agency.

(B) A sworn declaration of the custodial parent during the 12 months immediately preceding the request that the person named in the request has had or may have had an account at an office or branch of the financial institution to which the request is made.

(7) Information obtained by a local child support agency pursuant to this subdivision shall be used only for purposes that are directly connected with the administration of the duties of the local child support agency pursuant to Section 17400 of the Family Code.

(m) (1) As provided in paragraph (1) of subdivision (c) of Section 666 of Title 42 of the United States Code, upon receipt of an administrative subpoena on the current federally approved interstate child support enforcement form, as approved by the federal Office of Management and Budget, a financial institution shall provide the information or documents requested by the administrative subpoena.

(2) The administrative subpoena shall refer to the current federal Office of Management and Budget control number and be signed by a person who states that he or she is an authorized agent of a state or county agency responsible for implementing the child support enforcement program set forth in Part D (commencing with Section 651) of Subchapter IV of Chapter 7 of Title 42 of the United States Code. A financial institution may rely on the statements made in the subpoena and has no duty to inquire into the truth of any statement in the subpoena.

(3) If the person who signs the administrative subpoena directs a financial institution in writing not to disclose either the subpoena or its response to any owner of an account covered by the subpoena, the financial institution shall not disclose the subpoena or its response to the owner.

(4) No financial institution, or any officer, employee, or agent thereof, shall be liable to any person for (A) disclosing information or providing documents in response to a subpoena pursuant to this subdivision, (B) failing to notify any owner of an account covered by the subpoena or complying with a request not to disclose to the owner, the subpoena or disclosure under this subdivision, or (C) failing to discover any account owned by the person named in the subpoena pursuant to a computerized search of the records of the financial institution.

(n) The dissemination of financial information and records pursuant to any of the following:

(1) Compliance by a financial institution with the requirements of Section 2892 of the Probate Code.

(2) Compliance by a financial institution with the requirements of Section 2893 of the Probate Code.

(3) An order by a judge upon a written ex parte application by a peace officer showing specific and articulable facts that there are reasonable grounds to believe that the records or information sought are relevant and material to an ongoing investigation of a felony violation of Section 186.10 or of any felony subject to the enhancement set forth in Section 186.11.

(A) The ex parte application shall specify with particularity the records to be produced, which shall be only those of the individual or individuals who are the subject of the criminal investigation.

(B) The ex parte application and any subsequent judicial order shall be open to the public as a judicial record unless ordered sealed by the court, for a period of 60 days. The sealing of these records may be extended for 60-day periods upon a showing to the court that it is necessary for the continuance of the investigation. Sixty-day extensions may continue for up to one year or until termination of the investigation of the individual or individuals, whichever is sooner.

(C) The records ordered to be produced shall be returned to the peace officer applicant or his or her designee within a reasonable time period after service of the order upon the financial institution.

(D) Nothing in this subdivision shall preclude the financial institution from notifying a customer of the receipt of the order for production of records unless a court orders the financial institution to withhold notification to the customer upon a finding that the notice would impede the investigation.

(E) Where a court has made an order pursuant to this paragraph to withhold notification to the customer under this paragraph, the peace officer or law enforcement agency who obtained the financial information shall notify the customer by delivering a copy of the ex parte order to the customer within 10 days of the termination of the investigation.

(4) No financial institution, or any officer, employee, or agent thereof, shall be liable to any person for any of the following:

(A) Disclosing information to a probate court pursuant to Sections 2892 and 2893.

(B) Disclosing information in response to a court order pursuant to paragraph (3).

(C) Complying with a court order under this subdivision not to disclose to the customer, the order, or the dissemination of information pursuant to the court order.

(o) Disclosure by a financial institution to a peace officer, as defined in Section 830.1 of the Penal Code, pursuant to the following:

(1) Paragraph (1) of subdivision (a) of Section 1748.95 of the Civil Code, provided that the financial institution has first complied with the requirements of paragraph (2) of subdivision (a) and subdivision (b) of Section 1748.95 of the Civil Code.

(2) Paragraph (1) of subdivision (a) of Section 4002 of the Financial Code, provided that the financial institution has first complied with the requirements of paragraph (2) of subdivision (a) and subdivision (b) of Section 4002 of the Financial Code.

(3) Paragraph (1) of subdivision (a) of Section 22470 of the Financial Code, provided that any financial institution that is a finance lender has first complied with the requirements of paragraph (2) of subdivision (a) and subdivision (b) of Section 22470 of the Financial Code.

(p) When the governing board of the Public Employees' Retirement System or the State Teachers' Retirement System certifies in writing to a financial institution that a benefit recipient has died and that transfers to the benefit recipient's account at the financial institution from the retirement system occurred after the benefit recipient's date of death, the financial institution shall furnish the retirement system with the name and address of any co-owner, cosigner, or any other person who had access to the funds in the account following the date of the benefit recipient's death, or if the account has been closed, the name and address of the person who closed the account.

(q) When the retirement board of a retirement system established under the County Employees Retirement Law of 1937 certifies in writing to a financial institution that a retired member or the beneficiary of a retired member has died and that transfers to the account of the retired member or beneficiary of a retired member at the financial institution from the retirement system occurred after the date of death of the retired member or beneficiary of a retired member, the financial institution shall furnish the retirement system with the name and address of any co-owner, cosigner, or any other person who had access to the funds in the account following the date of death of the retired member or beneficiary of a retired member, or if the account has been closed, the name and address of the person who closed the account.

(r) When the Franchise Tax Board certifies in writing to a financial institution that (1) a taxpayer filed a tax return that authorized a direct deposit refund with an incorrect financial institution account or routing number that resulted in all or a portion of the refund not being received, directly or indirectly, by the taxpayer; (2) the direct deposit refund was not returned to the Franchise Tax Board; and (3) the refund was deposited directly on a specified date into the account of an accountholder of the financial institution who was not entitled to receive the refund, then the financial institution shall furnish to the Franchise Tax Board the name and address of any co-owner, cosigner, or any other person who had access to the funds in the account following the date of direct deposit refund, or if the account has been closed, the name and address of the person who closed the account.

§14975 Payment Bond

Notwithstanding the provisions of Section 9550 of the Civil Code, the contractor under any contract made under this chapter need not provide a payment bond before the commencement of the work but must provide a payment bond as otherwise required by law prior to payment under the contract.

§15820.105 Public Works; Compliance with Building Codes

(a) Plans and specifications for the project shall comply with applicable building codes.

(b) The project is hereby deemed to be governed by Title 3 (commencing with Section 9000) of Part 6 of Division 4 of the Civil Code.

(c) The provisions of Chapter 1 (commencing with Section 1720) of Part 7 of Division 2 of the Labor Code shall apply to all public works contracts entered into for the project.

(d) Other than as provided in this section and Sections 15820.101 to 15820.104, inclusive, private sector methods may be used to deliver the project. Specifically, the procurement and contracting for the delivery of the project is not subject to the State Contract Act (Part 2 (commencing with Section 10100) of Division 2 of the Public Contract Code) or any other provision of California law governing public procurement or public works projects.

§27287 Recorded Instrument must be Acknowledged

Unless it belongs to the class provided for in either Sections 27282 to 27286, inclusive, or Section 1202 or 1203, of the Civil Code, or is a fictitious mortgage or deed of trust as provided in Section 2952 or 2963 of the Civil Code, or is a fictitious oil and gas lease as provided in Section 1219 of the Civil Code, or is a claim of lien under Section 8416 of the Civil Code or a notice of completion under Section 8182 or 9204 of the Civil Code, before an instrument can be recorded its execution shall be acknowledged by the person executing it, or if executed by a corporation, by its president or secretary or other person executing it on behalf of the corporation, or, except for any quitclaim deed or grant deed other than a trustee's deed or a deed of reconveyance, mortgage, deed of trust, or security agreement, proved by subscribing witness or as provided in Sections 1198 and 1199 of the Civil Code, and the acknowledgment or proof certified as prescribed by law.

§27361.9 Additional Fee; Preliminary 20-Day Notice

The board of supervisors of any county may provide for an additional fee for filing every preliminary notice pursuant to subdivision (a) of Section 8214 of the Civil Code for the exclusive purpose of defraying the cost of implementing and maintaining a system to facilitate compliance with subdivision (b) of Section 8214 of the Civil Code.

§66499.2 Bond for Security of Laborers and Materialmen

A bond or bonds by one or more duly authorized corporate sureties for the security of laborers and material suppliers shall be in substantially the following form:

> Whereas, The Board of Supervisors of the County of ________________________ (or City Council of the City of ___________________), State of California, and ___________________ (hereinafter designated as "the principal") have entered into an agreement whereby the principal agrees to install and complete certain designated public improvements, which agreement, dated ___________, 20______, and identified as project ____, is hereby referred to and made a part hereof; and
>
> Whereas, Under the terms of the agreement, the principal is required before entering upon the performance of the work, to file a good and sufficient payment bond with the County of ________________________ (or the City of _________________) to secure the claims to which reference is made in Title 3 (commencing with Section 9000) of Part 6 of Division 4 of the Civil Code.
>
> Now, therefore, the principal and the undersigned as corporate surety, are held firmly bound unto the County of ____________________ (or the City of ___________) and all contractors, subcontractors, laborers, material suppliers, and other persons employed in the performance of the agreement and referred to in Title 3 (commencing with Section 9000) of Part 6 of Division 4 of the Civil Code in the sum of ________________________ dollars ($________), for materials furnished or labor thereon of any kind, or for amounts due under the Unemployment Insurance Act with respect to this work or labor, that the surety will pay the same in an amount not exceeding the amount hereinabove set forth, and also in case suit is brought upon

this bond, will pay, in addition to the face amount thereof, costs and reasonable expenses and fees, including reasonable attorney's fees, incurred by county (or city) in successfully enforcing this obligation, to be awarded and fixed by the court, and to be taxed as costs and to be included in the judgment therein rendered.

It is hereby expressly stipulated and agreed that this bond shall inure to the benefit of any and all persons, companies, and corporations entitled to file claims under Title 3 (commencing with Section 9000) of Part 6 of Division 4 of the Civil Code, so as to give a right of action to them or their assigns in any suit brought upon this bond.

Should the condition of this bond be fully performed, then this obligation shall become null and void, otherwise it shall be and remain in full force and effect.

The surety hereby stipulates and agrees that no change, extension of time, alteration, or addition to the terms of the agreement or the specifications accompanying the same shall in any manner affect its obligations on this bond, and it does hereby waive notice of any such change, extension, alteration, or addition.

In witness whereof, this instrument has been duly executed by the principal and surety above named, on ______________________, 20________.

§66499.7 Release of Security

The security furnished by the subdivider shall be released in whole or in part in the following manner:

(a) Security given for faithful performance of any act or agreement shall be released upon the performance of the act or final completion and acceptance of the required work. The legislative body may provide for the partial release of the security upon the partial performance of the act or the acceptance of the work as it progresses, consistent with the provisions of this section. The security may be a surety bond, a cash deposit, a letter of credit, escrow account, or other form of performance guarantee required as security by the legislative body that meets the requirements as acceptable security pursuant to law. If the security furnished by the subdivider is a documentary evidence of security such as a surety bond or a letter of credit, the legislative body shall release the documentary evidence and return the original to the issuer upon performance of the act or final completion and acceptance of the required work. In the event that the legislative body is unable to return the original documentary evidence to the issuer, the security shall be released by written notice sent by certified mail to the subdivider and issuer of the documentary evidence within 30 days of the acceptance of the work. The written notice shall contain a statement that the work for which the security was furnished has been performed or completed and accepted by the legislative body, a description of the project subject to the documentary evidence and the notarized signature of the authorized representative of the legislative body.

(b) At the time that the subdivider believes that the obligation to perform the work for which security was required is complete, the subdivider may notify the local agency in writing of the completed work, including a list of work completed. Upon receipt of the written notice, the local agency shall have 45 days to review and comment or approve the completion of the required work. If the local agency does not agree that all work has been completed in accordance with the plans and specifications for the improvements, it shall supply a list of all remaining work to be completed.

(c) Within 45 days of receipt of the list of remaining work from the local agency, the subdivider may then provide cost estimates for all remaining work for review and approval by the local agency. Upon receipt of the cost estimates, the local agency shall then have 45 days to review, comment, and approve, modify, or disapprove those cost estimates. No local agency shall be required to engage in this process of partial release more than once between the start of work and completion and acceptance of all work; however, nothing in this section prohibits a local agency from allowing for a partial release as it otherwise deems appropriate.

(d) If the local agency approves the cost estimate, the local agency shall release all performance security except for security in an amount up to 200 percent of the cost estimate of the remaining work. The process allowing for a partial release of performance security shall occur when the cost estimate of the remaining work does not exceed 20 percent of the total original performance security unless the local agency allows for a release at an earlier time. Substitute bonds or other security may be used as a replacement for the performance security, subject to the approval of the local agency. If substitute bonds or other security is used as a replacement for the performance security released, the release shall not be effective unless and until the local agency receives and approves that form of replacement security. A reduction in the performance security, authorized under this section, is not, and shall not be deemed to be, an acceptance by the local agency of the completed improvements, and the risk of loss or damage to the improvements and the obligation to maintain the improvements shall remain the sole responsibility of the subdivider until all required public improvements have been accepted by the local agency and all other required improvements have been fully completed in accordance with the plans and specifications for the improvements.

(e) The subdivider shall complete the works of improvement until all remaining items are accepted by the local agency.

(f) Upon the completion of the improvements, the subdivider, or his or her assigns, shall be notified in writing by the local agency within 45 days.

(g) Within 45 days of the issuance of the notification by the local agency, the release of any remaining performance security shall be placed upon the agenda of the legislative body of the local agency for approval of the release of any remaining performance security. If the local agency delegates authority for the release of performance security to a public official or other employee, any remaining performance security shall be released within 60 days of the issuance of the written statement of completion.

(h) Security securing the payment to the contractor, his or her subcontractors and to persons furnishing labor, materials or equipment shall, after passage of the time within which claims of lien are required to be recorded pursuant to Article 2 (commencing with Section 8410) of Chapter 4 of Title 2 of Part 6 of Division 4 of the Civil Code and after acceptance of the work, be reduced to an amount equal to the total claimed by all claimants for whom claims of lien have been recorded and notice thereof given in writing to the legislative body, and if no claims have been recorded, the security shall be released in full.

(i) The release shall not apply to any required guarantee and warranty period required by Section 66499.9 for the guarantee or warranty nor to the amount of the security deemed necessary by the local agency for the guarantee and warranty period nor to costs and reasonable expenses and fees, including reasonable attorney's fees.

(j) The legislative body may authorize any of its public officers or employees to authorize release or reduction of the security in accordance with the conditions hereinabove set forth and in accordance with any rules that it may prescribe.

(k) This section shall remain in effect only until January 1, 2016, and as of that date is repealed, unless a later enacted statute, that is enacted before January 1, 2016, deletes or extends that date.

HEALTH AND SAFETY CODE SECTIONS ("H&S")
New Text (Operative July 1, 2012)

§5463 Refusal to Connect Dwelling with Sewer

Any health officer or governing board of any city, county, sanitary district, or other district having the power to operate and maintain a sewerage system, having served written notice upon the owner or reputed owner of land upon which there is a dwelling house, and the owner or reputed owner, after 30 days, having refused, neglected, or failed to connect the dwelling house, together with all toilets, sinks, and other plumbing therein, properly vented, and in a sanitary manner, with the adjoining street sewer, may construct the same at a reasonable cost, and the person doing that work at the request of the health officer or governing board has a lien upon that real estate for his or her work done and materials furnished, and the work done and materials furnished shall be held to have been done and furnished at the instance of the owner or reputed owner, or person claiming or having any interest therein. The governing board may pay all or any part of the cost or price of such connection to the person or persons who furnished labor, materials, or equipment for the same, and, to the extent the governing board pays the cost or price of the connection, it shall succeed to and have all the rights, including the lien provided for above, of the person or persons against the real estate and against the owner or reputed owner thereof.

As an alternative power to the enforcement of the lien provided for in this section, the governing body of the public agency performing the work of connection to the public sewer may, by order entered upon its minutes, declare that the amount of the costs of the work and the administrative expenses incurred by the governing body incident to the proceedings, together with other charges uniformly applicable within the jurisdiction of the governing body for the connection of the premises to the public sewer, shall be transmitted to the assessor and tax collector of the public agency, whereupon it shall be the duty of those officers to add the amount of the assessment to the next regular bill for taxes levied against the lot or parcel of land.

The liens provided for by this section shall be enforced in the same manner as those provided for by Part 6 (commencing with Section 8000) of Division 4, of the Civil Code.

The governing board may also use the procedures in Section 5474 for levying the costs incurred for the construction of the improvements for the connection of the premises to the public sewer.

§16017.5 Construction Work on Essential Services Facilities

(a) Notwithstanding any provision of law to the contrary, including, but not limited to, Part 6 (commencing with Section 8000) of Division 4 of the Civil Code, the Department of General Services may issue a stop work order when construction work on an essential services facility is not being performed in accordance with existing law and would compromise the structural integrity of the building, thereby endangering the public safety. The Department of General Services shall allow construction of incidental and minor nonstructural additions or nonstructural alterations without invoking its stop work authority.

(b) A public board, body, or officer whose construction work on an essential services facility is subject to a stop work order issued pursuant to subdivision (a) shall not be held liable in any action filed against the public board, body, or officer for stopping work as required by the stop work order, or for any delays caused by compliance with the stop work order, except to the extent that an error or omission by the public board, body, or officer is the basis for the issuance of the stop work order.

§19825 Permit Application; Notice to Property Owner

(a) Every city, county, or city and county, whether general law or chartered, that requires the issuance of a permit as a condition precedent to the construction, alteration, improvement, demolition, or repair of any building or structure, shall require the execution of a permit application, in substantially the same form set forth under this subdivision, and require any individual who executes the Owner-Builder Declaration to present documentation sufficient to identify the property owner and, as necessary, verify the signature of the property owner. A city, county, or city and county may require additional information on the permit application.

PERMIT APPLICATION
BUILDING PROJECT IDENTIFICATION

Applicant's Mailing Address:

____

____

____

Property Location or Address:

____

____

Property Owner's Name:

____

Property Owner's Telephone No.: ___________________________________

Licensed Design Professional (Architect or Engineer) in charge of the project:

____

Mailing Address of Licensed Design Professional:

____

____

____

License No.: ____

LICENSED CONTRACTOR'S DECLARATION

I hereby affirm under penalty of perjury that I am licensed under provisions of Chapter 9 (commencing with Section 7000) of Division 3 of the Business and Professions Code, and my license is in full force and effect.

License Class: ______________________________

License No.: ______________________________

Date ______________________________

Contractor Signature ______________________________

OWNER-BUILDER DECLARATION

I hereby affirm under penalty of perjury that I am exempt from the Contractors' State License Law for the reason(s) indicated below by the checkmark(s) I have placed next to the applicable item(s) (Section 7031.5, Business and Professions Code: Any city or county that requires a permit to construct, alter, improve, demolish, or repair any structure, prior to its issuance, also requires the applicant for the permit to file a signed statement that he or she is licensed pursuant to the provisions of the Contractors' State License Law (Chapter 9 (commencing with Section 7000) of Division 3 of the Business and Professions Code) or that he or she is exempt from licensure and the basis for the alleged exemption. Any violation of Section 7031.5 by any applicant for a permit subjects the applicant to a civil penalty of not more than five hundred dollars ($500).):

(__) I, as owner of the property, or my employees with wages as their sole compensation, will do (_) all of or (_) portions of the work, and the structure is not intended or offered for sale (Section 7044, Business and Professions Code: The Contractors' State License Law does not apply to an owner of property who, through employees' or personal effort, builds or improves the property, provided that the improvements are not intended or offered for sale. If, however, the building or improvement is sold within one year of completion, the Owner-Builder will have the burden of proving that it was not built or improved for the purpose of sale.).

(__) I, as owner of the property, am exclusively contracting with licensed Contractors to construct the project (Section 7044, Business and Professions Code: The Contractors' State License Law does not apply to an owner of property who builds or improves thereon, and who contracts for the projects with a licensed Contractor pursuant to the Contractors' State License Law.).

(__) I am exempt from licensure under the Contractors' State License Law for the following reason:

____

____

____

By my signature below I acknowledge that, except for my personal residence in which I must have resided for at least one year prior to completion of the improvements covered by this permit, I cannot legally sell a structure that I have built as an owner-builder if it has not been constructed in its entirety by licensed contractors. I understand that a copy of the applicable law, Section 7044 of the Business and Professions Code, is available upon request when this application is submitted or at the following Web site: http://www.leginfo.ca.gov/calaw.html.

Date: ______________________________

Signature of Property Owner or Authorized Agent:

____

WORKERS' COMPENSATION DECLARATION

WARNING: FAILURE TO SECURE WORKERS' COMPENSATION COVERAGE IS UNLAWFUL, AND SHALL SUBJECT AN EMPLOYER TO CRIMINAL PENALTIES AND CIVIL FINES UP TO ONE HUNDRED THOUSAND DOLLARS ($100,000), IN ADDITION TO THE COST OF COMPENSATION, DAMAGES AS PROVIDED FOR IN SECTION 3706 OF THE LABOR CODE, INTEREST, AND ATTORNEY'S FEES.

I hereby affirm under penalty of perjury one of the following declarations:

(__) I have and will maintain a certificate of consent to self-insure for workers' compensation, issued by the Director of Industrial Relations as provided for by Section 3700 of the Labor Code, for the performance of the work for which this permit is issued.

Policy No. ____________________________

(__) I have and will maintain workers' compensation insurance, as required by Section 3700 of the Labor Code, for the performance of the work for which this permit is issued. My workers' compensation insurance carrier and policy number are:

Carrier: ____________________________

Policy Number: ____________________________

Expiration Date: ____________________________

Name of Agent: ____________________________

Phone #: ____________________________

(__) I certify that, in the performance of the work for which this permit is issued, I shall not employ any person in any manner so as to become subject to the workers' compensation laws of California, and agree that, if I should become subject to the workers' compensation provisions of Section 3700 of the Labor Code, I shall forthwith comply with those provisions.

____

Signature of Applicant

____

Date

DECLARATION REGARDING CONSTRUCTION LENDING AGENCY

I hereby affirm under penalty of perjury that there is a construction lending agency for the performance of the work for which this permit is issued (Section 8172, Civil Code).

Lender's Name: ______________________________

Branch Designation: ______________________________

Lender's Address: ______________________________

By my signature below, I certify to each of the following:

- I am the property owner or authorized to act on the property owner's behalf.
- I have read this application and the information I have provided is correct.
- I agree to comply with all applicable city and county ordinances and state laws relating to building construction.
- I authorize representatives of this city or county to enter the above-identified property for inspection purposes.

Signature of Property Owner or Authorized Agent:

____

Date: ______________________________

(b) When the Permit Application and the Owner-Builder Declaration have been executed by a person other than the property owner, prior to issuing the permit, the following shall be completed by the property owner and returned to the agency responsible for issuing the permit:

AUTHORIZATION OF AGENT TO ACT ON PROPERTY OWNER'S BEHALF

Excluding the Notice to Property Owner, the execution of which I understand is my personal responsibility, I hereby authorize the following person(s) to act as my agent(s) to apply for, sign, and file the documents necessary to obtain an Owner-Builder Permit for my project.

Scope of Construction Project (or Description of Work):

____

____

Project Location or Address:

____

____

____

Name of Authorized Agent:

____

Address of Authorized Agent:

____

____

____

Phone Number of Authorized Agent:

____

I declare under penalty of perjury that I am the property owner for the address listed above and I personally filled out the above information and certify its accuracy.

Property Owner's Signature:

____

Date: ____

Note: A copy of the owner's driver's license, form notarization, or other verification acceptable to the agency is required to be presented when the permit is issued to verify the property owner's signature.

(c) When the Owner-Builder Declaration required under subdivision (a) is executed, a Notice to Property Owner also shall be executed by the property owner in substantially the same form set forth under this section. The Notice to Property Owner shall appear on the official letterhead of the issuer and shall be provided to the applicant by one of the following methods chosen by the permitting authority: regular mail, electronic format, or given directly to the applicant at the time the application for the permit is made. Except as otherwise provided, the Notice to Property Owner pursuant to this section shall be completed and signed by the property owner and returned prior to issuance of the permit. An agent of the owner shall not execute this notice unless the property owner obtains the prior approval of the permitting authority. A permit shall not be issued unless the property owner complies with this section.

NOTICE TO PROPERTY OWNER

Dear Property Owner:

An application for a building permit has been submitted in your name listing yourself as the builder of the property improvements specified at ______________. We are providing you with an Owner-Builder Acknowledgment and Information Verification Form to make you aware of your responsibilities and possible risk you may incur by having this permit issued in your name as the Owner-Builder. We will not issue a building permit until you have read, initialed your understanding of each provision, signed, and returned this form to us at our official address indicated. An agent of the owner cannot execute this notice unless you, the property owner, obtain the prior approval of the permitting authority.

OWNER'S ACKNOWLEDGMENT
AND VERIFICATION OF INFORMATION

DIRECTIONS: Read and initial each statement below to signify you understand or verify this information.

____1. I understand a frequent practice of unlicensed persons is to have the property owner obtain an "Owner-Builder" building permit that erroneously implies that the property owner is providing his or her own labor and material personally. I, as an Owner-Builder, may be held liable and subject to serious financial risk for any injuries sustained by an unlicensed person and his or her employees while working on my property. My homeowner's insurance may not provide coverage for those injuries. I am willfully acting as an Owner-Builder and am aware of the limits of my insurance coverage for injuries to workers on my property.

____2. I understand building permits are not required to be signed by property owners unless they are responsible for the construction and are not hiring a licensed Contractor to assume this responsibility.

____3. I understand as an "Owner-Builder" I am the responsible party of record on the permit. I understand that I may protect myself from potential financial risk by hiring a licensed Contractor and having the permit filed in his or her name instead of my own.

____4. I understand Contractors are required by law to be licensed and bonded in California and to list their license numbers on permits and contracts.

____5. I understand if I employ or otherwise engage any persons, other than California licensed Contractors, and the total value of my construction is at least five hundred dollars ($500), including labor and materials, I may be considered an "employer" under state and federal law.

____6. I understand if I am considered an "employer" under state and federal law, I must register with the state and federal government, withhold payroll taxes, provide workers' compensation disability insurance, and contribute to unemployment compensation for each "employee." I also understand my failure to abide by these laws may subject me to serious financial risk.

____7. I understand under California Contractors' State License Law, an Owner- Builder who builds single-family residential structures cannot legally build them with the intent to offer them for sale, unless all work is performed by licensed subcontractors and the number of structures does not exceed four within any calendar year, or all of the work is performed under contract with a licensed general building Contractor.

____8. I understand as an Owner-Builder if I sell the property for which this permit is issued, I may be held liable for any financial or personal injuries sustained by any subsequent owner(s) that result from any latent construction defects in the workmanship or materials.

____9. I understand I may obtain more information regarding my obligations as an "employer" from the Internal Revenue Service, the United States Small Business Administration, the California Department of Benefit Payments, and the California Division of Industrial Accidents. I also understand I may contact the California Contractors' State License Board (CSLB) at 1-800-321-CSLB (2752) or www.cslb.ca.gov for more information about licensed contractors.

____10. I am aware of and consent to an Owner-Builder building permit applied for in my name, and understand that I am the party legally and financially responsible for proposed construction activity at the following address:

____

____

____

____11. I agree that, as the party legally and financially responsible for this proposed construction activity, I will abide by all applicable laws and requirements that govern Owner-Builders as well as employers.

____ 12. I agree to notify the issuer of this form immediately of any additions, deletions, or changes to any of the information I have provided on this form.

Licensed contractors are regulated by laws designed to protect the public. If you contract with someone who does not have a license, the Contractors' State License Board may be unable to assist you with any financial loss you may sustain as a result of a complaint. Your only remedy against unlicensed Contractors may be in civil court. It is also important for you to understand that if an unlicensed Contractor or employee of that individual or firm is injured while working on your property, you may be held liable for damages. If you obtain a permit as Owner- Builder and wish to hire Contractors, you will be responsible for verifying whether or not those Contractors are properly licensed and the status of their workers' compensation insurance coverage.

Before a building permit can be issued, this form must be completed and signed by the property owner and returned to the agency responsible for issuing the permit.

Note: A copy of the property owner's driver's license, form notarization, or other verification acceptable to the agency is required to be presented when the permit is issued to verify the property owner's signature.

Signature of Property Owner: ____

Date: ____

§34218 Applicability of Civil Code

Chapter 5 (commencing with Section 9550) of Title 3 of Part 6 of Division 4 of the Civil Code applies to any housing project constructed under this chapter. Notwithstanding the provisions of this section, a housing authority may require a 20 percent cash escrow or a 25 percent irrevocable letter of credit or the payment bond required by this section if the contract is for work undertaken pursuant to the Comprehensive Improvement Assistance Program established by Section 14 of the United States Housing Act of 1937, as amended (42 U.S.C.A. Secs. 1437d and 1437l), or the Public Housing Modernization Act established by Section 5(c)(3)(C) of the United States Housing Act of 1937, as amended (42 U.S.C.A. Secs. 1437d and 1437l).

INSURANCE CODE SECTIONS ("INS")
New Text (Operative July 1, 2012)

§11751.82 Wrap-Up Insurance Policies; Report

(a) An insurer under a wrap-up insurance policy shall report workers' compensation losses and payroll information for each contractor and subcontractor to its rating organization on a timely basis and in accordance with the uniform statistical plan. Within 10 days, upon request, the insurer shall provide to each contractor and subcontractor copies of the report covering workers' compensation losses and payroll information for that contractor or subcontractor.

(b) For the purposes of this section, a "wrap-up insurance policy" is an insurance policy, or series of policies, written to cover risks associated with a work of improvement, as defined in Section 8050 of the Civil Code, and covering two or more of the contractors or subcontractors that work on that work of improvement.

LABOR CODE SECTION ("LABOR")
New Text (Operative July 1, 2012)

§218.5 Action for Nonpayment of Wages, Fringe Benefits or Pension Fund Contributions

In any action brought for the nonpayment of wages, fringe benefits, or health and welfare or pension fund contributions, the court shall award reasonable attorney's fees and costs to the prevailing party if any party to the action requests attorney's fees and costs upon the initiation of the action. This section shall not apply to an action brought by the Labor Commissioner. This section shall not apply to a surety issuing a bond pursuant to Chapter 9 (commencing with Section 7000) of Division 3 of the Business and Professions Code or to an action to enforce a mechanics lien brought under Chapter 4 (commencing with Section 8400) of Title 2 of Part 6 of Division 2 of the Civil Code. This section does not apply to any action for which attorney's fees are recoverable under Section 1194.

PUBLIC CONTRACT CODE SECTION ("PCC")
New Text (Operative July 1, 2012)

§4107.7 Nonpayment of Subcontractor Registered as Hazardous Waste Hauler

If a contractor who enters into a contract with a public entity for investigation, removal or remedial action, or disposal relative to the release or presence of a hazardous material or hazardous waste fails to pay a subcontractor registered as a hazardous waste hauler pursuant to Section 25163 of the Health and Safety Code within 10 days after the investigation, removal or remedial action, or disposal is completed, the subcontractor may serve a stop notice upon the public entity in accordance with Chapter 4 (commencing with Section 9350) of Title 3 of Part 6 of Division 4 of the Civil Code.

§7103 Payment Bonds

(a) (1) Every original contractor that is awarded a contract by a state entity, as defined in subdivision (d), involving an expenditure in excess of twenty-five thousand dollars ($25,000) for any public work shall, before entering upon the performance of the work, file a payment bond with and approved by the officer or state entity that awarded the contract. The bond shall be in a sum not less than 100 percent of the total amount payable by the terms of the contract.

(2) The state entity shall state in its call for bids for any contract that a payment bond is required in the case of such an expenditure.

(b) A payment bond filed and approved in accordance with this section shall be sufficient to enter upon the performance of work under a duly authorized contract that supplements the contract for which the payment bond was filed if the requirement of a new bond is waived by the state entity.

(c) For purposes of this section, providers of architectural, engineering, and land surveying services pursuant to a contract with a state entity for a public work shall not be deemed an original contractor and shall not be required to post or file the payment bond required in subdivisions (a) and (b).

(d) For purposes of this section, "state entity" means every state office, department, division, bureau, board, or commission, but does not include the Legislature, the courts, any agency in the judicial branch of government, or the University of California. All other public entities shall be governed by Section 9550 of the Civil Code.

(e) For purposes of this section, "public work" includes the erection, construction, alteration, repair, or improvement of any state structure, building, road, or other state improvement of any kind.

§7201 Public Works; Limits on Retention Proceeds

(a) (1) This section shall apply with respect to all contracts entered into on or after January 1, 2012, between a public entity and an original contractor, between an original contractor and a subcontractor, and between all subcontractors thereunder, relating to the construction of any public work of improvement.

(2) Under no circumstances shall any provision of this section be construed to limit the ability of any public entity to withhold 150 percent of the value of any disputed amount of work from the final payment, as provided for in subdivision (c) of Section 7107. In the event of a good faith dispute, nothing in this section shall be construed to require a public entity to pay for work that is not approved or accepted in accordance with the proper plans or specifications.

(3) For purposes of this section, "public entity" means the state, including every state agency, office, department, division, bureau, board, or commission, the California State University, the University of California, a city, county, city and county, including charter cities and charter counties, district, special district, public authority, political subdivision, public corporation, or nonprofit transit corporation wholly owned by a public agency and formed to carry out the purposes of the public agency.

(b) (1) The retention proceeds withheld from any payment by a public entity from the original contractor, by the original contractor from any subcontractor, and by a subcontractor from any subcontractor thereunder shall not exceed 5 percent of the payment. In no event shall the total retention proceeds withheld exceed 5 percent of the contract price.

In a contract between the original contractor and a subcontractor, and in a contract between a subcontractor and any subcontractor thereunder, the percentage of the retention proceeds withheld shall not exceed the percentage specified in the contract between the public entity and the original contractor.

(2) This subdivision shall not apply if the contractor provides written notice to the subcontractor, pursuant to subdivision (c) of Section 4108, prior to, or at, the time that the bid is requested, that bonds shall be required, and the subcontractor subsequently is unable or refuses to furnish to the contractor a performance and payment bond issued by an admitted surety insurer.

(3) Notwithstanding any other provision of this subdivision, the retention proceeds withheld from any payment by an awarding entity set forth in paragraphs (1) to (5), inclusive, of subdivision (a) of Section 10106, from the original contractor, by the original contractor from any subcontractor, and by a subcontractor from any subcontractor thereunder, may exceed 5 percent on specific projects where the director of the department has made a finding prior to the bid that the project is substantially complex and therefore requires a higher retention amount than 5 percent and the department includes both this finding and the actual retention amount in the bid documents. In a contract between the original contractor and a subcontractor, and in a contract between a subcontractor and any subcontractor thereunder, the percentage of the retention proceeds withheld shall not exceed the percentage specified in the contract between the department and the original contractor.

(4) Notwithstanding any other provision of this subdivision, the retention proceeds withheld from any payment by the awarding entity of a city, county, city and county, including charter cities and charter counties, district, special district, public authority, political subdivision, public corporation, or nonprofit transit corporation wholly owned by a public agency and formed to carry out the purposes of the public agency, from the original contractor, by the original contractor from any subcontractor, and by a subcontractor from any subcontractor thereunder, may exceed 5 percent on specific projects where the governing body of the public entity or designee, including, but not limited to, a general manager or other director of an appropriate department, has approved a finding during a properly noticed and normally scheduled public hearing and prior to bid that the project is substantially complex and therefore requires a higher retention amount than 5 percent and the awarding entity includes both this finding and the actual retention amount in the bid documents. In a contract between the original contractor and a subcontractor, and in a contract between a subcontractor and any subcontractor thereunder, the percentage of the retention proceeds withheld shall not exceed the percentage specified in the contract between the department and the original contractor.

(c) A party identified in subdivision (a) shall not require any other party to waive any provision of this section.

(d) This section shall remain in effect only until January 1, 2016, and as of that date is repealed, unless a later enacted statute, that is enacted before January 1, 2016, deletes or extends that date.

§10222 Amount of Bonds

(a) Each bond shall equal at least one-half of the contract price, except as otherwise provided in Section 9554 of the Civil Code, in the California Toll Bridge Authority Act (Chapter 1 (commencing with Section 30000) of Division 7 of the Streets and Highways Code), or in subdivision (b).

(b) Notwithstanding subdivision (a), for projects with a contract price greater than two hundred fifty million dollars ($250,000,000), the Department of Transportation shall have the discretion to specify that the payment bond shall equal not less than one-half of the contract price or five hundred million dollars ($500,000,000), whichever is less.

§10822 Amount of Performance and Payment Bonds

Each bond shall be in a sum equal to at least one-half of the contract price, except as otherwise provided in Section 9554 of the Civil Code.

§20104 Applicability of Article

(a) (1) This article applies to all public works claims of three hundred seventy-five thousand dollars ($375,000) or less which arise between a contractor and a local agency.

(2) This article shall not apply to any claims resulting from a contract between a contractor and a public agency when the public agency has elected to resolve any disputes pursuant to Article 7.1 (commencing with Section 10240) of Chapter 1 of Part 2.

(b) (1) "Public work" means "public works contract" as defined in Section 1101 but does not include any work or improvement contracted for by the state or the Regents of the University of California.

(2) "Claim" means a separate demand by the contractor for (A) a time extension, (B) payment of money or damages arising from work done by, or on behalf of, the contractor pursuant to the contract for a public work and payment of which is not otherwise expressly provided for or the claimant is not otherwise entitled to, or (C) an amount the payment of which is disputed by the local agency.

(c) The provisions of this article or a summary thereof shall be set forth in the plans or specifications for any work which may give rise to a claim under this article.

(d) This article applies only to contracts entered into on or after January 1, 1991.

§ 20134 County Procedures for Relief of Great Emergencies; Overcrowded Corrections Facilities, or Inadequate Courtrooms

(a) In cases of emergency, when repair or replacements are necessary to permit the continued conduct of county operations or services, the board of supervisors, by majority consent, may proceed at once to replace or repair any and all structures without adopting the plans, specifications, strain sheets, or working details or, subject to Chapter 2.5 (commencing with Section 22050), giving notice for bids to let contracts. If notice for bids to let contracts will not be given, the board shall comply with Chapter 2.5 (commencing with Section 22050). The work may be done by day labor under the direction of the board, by contract, or by a combination of the two. If the work is done wholly or in part by contract, the contractor shall be paid the actual cost of the use of machinery and tools and of material, and labor and of workers' compensation insurance expended by him or her in doing the work, plus not more than 15 percent to cover all profits and administration. No more than the lowest current market prices shall be paid for materials whenever possible.

(b) In a county of the first, second, third, or fourth class, which is under court order to relieve jail overcrowding or in which the sheriff certifies that the inmate capacity of the county jail system is exceeded by more than 20 percent and that the overpopulation is likely to continue and poses a threat to public safety, health, and welfare, the board of supervisors may contract for the construction or expansion of jail facilities without the formality of obtaining bids, adopting plans and specifications, or complying with other requirements of this article, except as required by this subdivision. The person to whom the contract is awarded shall execute a bond for faithful performance in accordance with Section 20129. Any plans and specifications adopted by the board may only be altered or changed in accordance with Section 20135 and all contracts awarded pursuant to this subdivision may only be altered or changed in accordance with Sections 20136, 20137, and 20138. The award of the contract shall be made after a public hearing on the basis of a request for proposals advertised in accordance with Section 6062 or 6062a of the Government Code. The contract may be awarded only to a contractor who has responded to the request for proposals and who is licensed to do the work in accordance with Chapter 9 (commencing with Section 7000) of Division 3 of the Business and Professions Code. The contract shall be upon terms which the board determines are necessary for the expeditious completion of the work. A contract shall not be entered into unless at least three proposals to do the work have been evaluated by a competitive process established by the board. If the board does not select the lowest bid, it shall make a finding stating the reasons that the lowest bid was not selected.

(c) In any county that has agreed to permit the transfer of prisoners or parole violators under Section 2910 or 2910.5 of the Penal Code or of wards under Section 1753.3 of the Welfare and Institutions Code, the board of supervisors may contract for the construction or expansion of the facilities to be used for that purpose without the formality of obtaining bids, adopting plans and specifications, or complying with other requirements of this article, except as required by this subdivision. The person to whom the contract is awarded shall execute a bond for faithful performance in accordance with Section 20129. Any plans and specifications adopted by the board may only be altered or changed in accordance with Section 20135 and all contracts awarded pursuant to this subdivision may only be altered or changed in accordance with Sections 20136, 20137, and 20138. The award of the contract shall be made after a public hearing on the basis of a request for proposals advertised in accordance with Section 6062 or 6062a of the

Government Code. The contract may be awarded only to a contractor who has responded to the request for proposals and who is licensed to do the work in accordance with Chapter 9 (commencing with Section 7000) of Division 3 of the Business and Professions Code. The contract shall be upon terms which the board determines are necessary for the expeditious completion of the work. A contract shall not be entered into unless at least three proposals to do the work have been evaluated by a competitive process established by the board and the lowest bid is selected.

(d) Proposed construction or expansion of jail or return-to-custody facilities as authorized under subdivision (b) or (c) shall not commence in a county of the third class without the affirmative vote of a majority of the city council of the incorporated city within which the construction or expansion is proposed.

(e) The board of supervisors may waive the requirements of Title 3 (commencing with Section 9000) of Part 6 of Division 4 of the Civil Code for work performed pursuant to subdivision (b) or (c).

(f) If any county that is under court order to relieve overcrowding in a county juvenile facility, as defined by subdivision (c) of Section 4481 of the Penal Code or in which the chief probation officer certifies that the juvenile detention capacity of the county juvenile facilities is exceeded by more than 20 percent and that the overpopulation is likely to continue and poses a threat to public safety, health, and welfare, the board of supervisors may contract for the construction or expansion of county juvenile facilities without the formality of obtaining bids, adopting plans and specifications, or complying with other requirements of this article, except as required by this subdivision. The person to whom the contract is awarded shall execute a bond for faithful performance in accordance with Section 20129. Any plans and specifications adopted by the board may only be altered or changed in accordance with Section 20135 and all contracts awarded pursuant to this subdivision may only be altered or changed in accordance with Sections 20136, 20137, and 20138. The award of the contract shall be made after a public hearing on the basis of a request for proposals advertised in accordance with Section 6062 or 6062a of the Government Code. The contract may be awarded only to a contractor who has responded to the request for proposals and who is licensed to do the work in accordance with Chapter 9 (commencing with Section 7000) of Division 3 of the Business and Professions Code. The contract shall be upon terms which the board determines are necessary for the expeditious completion of the work. A contract shall not be entered into unless at least three proposals to do the work have been evaluated by a competitive process established by the board. If the board does not select the lowest bidder, it shall make a finding stating the reasons that the lowest bidder was not selected.

(g) In a county of the third class in which there are no available courtrooms to accommodate all authorized judicial positions or in which the board of supervisors certifies that there is a significant need to expeditiously construct new court and court support facilities, the board of supervisors may contract for the construction or expansion of court and court support facilities without the formality of obtaining bids, adopting plans and specifications, or complying with other requirements of this article, except as required by this subdivision. The person to whom the contract is awarded shall execute a bond for faithful performance in accordance with Section 20129. Any plans and specifications adopted by the board may only be altered or changed in accordance with Section 20135 and all contracts awarded pursuant to this subdivision may only be altered or changed in accordance with Sections 20136, 20137, and 20138. The award of the contract shall be made after a public hearing on the basis of a request for proposals advertised in accordance with Section 6062 or 6062a of the Government Code. The contract may be awarded only to a contractor who has responded to the request for proposals and who is licensed to do the work in accordance with Chapter 9 (commencing with Section 7000) of Division 3 of the Business and Professions Code. The contract shall be upon terms which the board determines are necessary for the expeditious completion of the work. A contract shall not be entered into unless at least three proposals to do the work have been evaluated by a competitive process established by the board and the lowest bid is selected. This subdivision shall remain in effect until December 31, 1994.

§20461 Priority of Claims Over Assignments

No assignment by the contractor of the whole or any part of the money, assessment, partial assessment, any reassessment and any bonds which may be issued to represent any assessment or reassessment, due or to be due under the contract, or for "extras" in connection therewith, whether made before or after a verified claim is filed pursuant to this chapter, shall take priority over the claims, and the assignment shall have no binding force insofar as the rights of the claimants, or their assigns, are concerned. None of the provisions of Title 3 (commencing with Section 9000) of Part 6 of Division 4 of the Civil Code shall be applicable to any assessment, partial assessment, reassessment, bonds, moneys or funds payable to the contractor or assignee under this division or to any matter contained in this chapter.

§20496 Claims for Work and Materials

The provisions of Title 3 (commencing with Section 9000) of Part 6 of Division 4 of the Civil Code are hereby expressly made applicable to the construction of works and improvements under this article.

§20682.5 Force Account Work; Competitive Bidding

(a) A district may construct or complete any building, structure, or improvement with its own forces or by contract without bidding when the cost does not exceed twenty-five thousand dollars ($25,000).

(b) All contracts for the construction or completion of any building, structure, or improvement, when the cost exceeds twenty-five thousand dollars ($25,000), shall be contracted for and let to the lowest responsible bidder after notice. If two or more bids are the same and the lowest, the district board may accept the one it chooses.

(c) The district shall publish a notice inviting bids for any contract for which competitive bidding is required at least one time in a newspaper of general circulation in the district at least 10 days before the time specified for receiving bids. The notice inviting bids shall set a date for opening the bids and distinctly state the work to be done.

(d) If the general manager recommends and the board of directors determines that the publication of advertisements of the notice in trade journals and papers in lieu of publication pursuant to subdivision (c) will increase the number of business enterprises receiving that notice, the board of directors may by resolution declare that those notices shall be published in trade journals and papers at least 10 days prior to the time specified for receiving bids.

(e) If plans and specifications are prepared describing the work, all bidders shall be afforded an opportunity to examine the plans and specifications, and the plans and specifications shall be attached to and become part of the contract, if one is awarded.

(f) At its discretion, the board of directors may reject any bids presented and readvertise.

(g) In the case of an emergency, the board of directors may act pursuant to Chapter 2.5 (commencing with Section 22050).

(h) The board of directors may, subject to Chapter 5 (commencing with Section 9550) of Title 3 of Part 6 of Division 4 of the Civil Code, require the posting of those bonds it deems desirable as a condition to the filing of a bid or the letting of a contract."

(i) The district shall keep cost records of the work in the manner provided in Chapter 1 (commencing with Section 4000) of Division 5 of Title 1 of the Government Code.

(j) As an alternate to the procedures required by this section, a district may rely on the Uniform Public Construction Cost Accounting Act, Chapter 2 (commencing with Section 22000) of Part 3 of Division 2.

§20688.4 Performance Bonds

An agency shall require each successful bidder to file with it good and sufficient bonds, to be approved by it. The bonds shall be conditioned upon the faithful performance of the contract and upon the payment of all claims for labor and material in connection with the contract. The bonds shall contain the terms and conditions set forth in Chapter 5 (commencing with Section 9550) of Title 3 of Part 6 of Division 4 of the Civil Code and are subject to the provisions of that chapter.

The only change to the following statutes was to update the cross reference from the old section numbers to the new section numbers. These changes are effective July 1, 2012.

§20813 Construction Contracts; Competitive Bidding by Fire Protection Districts
§20815.3 Notice by Recreation and Park Districts, Rejection, Readvertising, Emergencies
§20991 Competitive Bidding by Los Angeles County Flood Control District, Bonds, Rejection of Bids
§21061 Competitive Bidding by San Bernardino County Flood Control District, Bonds, Rejection of Bids
§21071 Competitive Bidding by Ventura County Flood Control District, Purchases in Open Market
§21081 Competitive Bidding by Humbolt County Flood Control District
§21091 Competitive Bidding by Riverside County Flood Control District
§21101 Competitive Bidding by San Luis Obispo County Flood Control and Water Conservation District

§21111 Competitive Bidding by Santa Barbara County Water Agency
§21121 Competitive Bidding by Monterey County Flood Control and Water Conservation District
§21131 Competitive Bidding by Sonoma County Flood Control and Water Conservation District
§21141 Competitive Bidding by Mendocino County Flood Control and Water Conservation District
§21151 Competitive Bidding by Alameda County Flood Control and Water Conservation District
§21161 Competitive Bidding by Santa Clara Valley Water District
§21171 Competitive Bidding by Napa County Flood Control and Water Conservation District
§21181 Competitive Bidding by Lake County Flood Control and Water Conservation District
§21196 Competitive Bidding by Solano County Water Agency
§21212 Competitive Bidding by Sacramento County Water Agency
§21231 Competitive Bidding by Marin County Flood Control and Water Conservation District
§21241 Competitive Bidding by Contra Costa County Storm Drainage District
§21251 Competitive Bidding by San Benito County Water Conservation and Flood Control District
§21261 Competitive Bidding by Del Norte County Flood Control District
§21271 Competitive Bidding by Santa Barbara Flood Control and Water Conservation District, Emergencies, Maintenance and Alteration, Payment and Performance Bonds, Open Market
§21311 Competitive Bidding by San Joaquin County Flood Control and Water Conservation District
§21321 Competitive Bidding by Placer County Water Agency
§21331 Competitive Bidding by Tehama County Flood Control and Water Conservation District
§21341 Competitive Bidding by Shasta County Water Agency
§21351 Competitive Bidding by Yuba County Water Agency
§21361 Competitive Bidding by Mariposa County Water Agency
§21371 Competitive Bidding by Sutter County Water Agency
§21381 Competitive Bidding by San Mateo County Flood Control District
§21391 Competitive Bidding by Plumas County Flood Control and Water Conservation District
§21401 Competitive Bidding by Siskiyou County Flood Control and Water Conservation District
§21411 Competitive Bidding by Nevada County Water Agency
§21421 Competitive Bidding by Sierra County Flood Control and Water Conservation District
§21431 Competitive Bidding by Lassen-Modoc County Flood Control and Water Conservation District
§21441 Competitive Bidding by Yuba-Bear River Basin Authority
§21451 Competitive Bidding by Amador County Water Agency
§21461 Competitive Bidding by El Dorado County Water Agency
§21491 Competitive Bidding by Kern County Water Agency
§21501 Competitive Bidding by Desert Water Agency, Informal Bidding Procedures
§21511 Competitive Bidding by San Gorgonio Pass Water Agency
§21521 Competitive Bidding by Alpine County Water Agency
§21531 Competitive Bidding by Castaic Lake Water Agency
§21541 Competitive Bidding by Crestline-Lake Arrowhead Water Agency
§21572 Competitive Bidding by Madera County Flood Control and Water Conservation Agency
§21581 Competitive Bidding by Tulare County Flood Control District
§21591 Competitive Bidding by Bighorn Mountains Water Agency
§21601 Competitive Bidding by Tuolumne County Water Agency
§21622 Payment and Performance Bonds Required by Monterey Peninsula Water Management District
§21631 Competitive Bidding by Merced County Flood Control District

STREETS AND HIGHWAYS CODE SECTIONS ("S&H")

New Text (Operative July 1, 2012)

§136.5 Applicability of State Contract Act; Competitive Bidding

(a) The contracts referred to in Sections 135, 136, and 136.1 are not subject to the State Contract Act (Part 2 (commencing with Section 10100) of Division 2 of the Public Contract Code). Except for emergency work of the type described in subdivision (b), whenever the estimated amount of a contract exceeds two thousand five hundred dollars ($2,500), it shall be awarded to the lowest responsible bidder, after competitive bidding on any reasonable notice that the department may prescribe. Posting of notice for five days in a public place in the district office within which the work is to be done, or the equipment used, is sufficient. Those contracts shall be subject to the applicable payment bond provisions of Chapter 5 (commencing with Section 9550) of Title 3 of Part 6 of Division 4 of the Civil Code. The department may require faithful performance bonds when considered necessary. The advertisement for each contract shall state whether or not a bond shall be required.

(b) In cases of emergency work necessitated by the imminence or occurrence of a landslide, flood, storm damage, accident, or other casualty, tools or equipment may be rented for a period of not to exceed 60 days without competitive bidding, and the department may waive the requirements of Chapter 5 (commencing with Section 9550) of Title 3 of Part 6 of Division 4 of the Civil Code to the extent that a contractor may commence performance of the work under the contract for the rental of tools or equipment prior to filing a payment bond with the department. In that case, no payment shall be made to the contractor until a payment bond covering all work of the contract is filed with the department.

Section II

SB 189

Comparisons,
Old Code to New Code

How To Use This Section

New Text (Operative July 1, 2012) | **Old Text**

Section II presents a side-by-side comparison of the new law from SB 189, as amended with annotations to explain what has been deleted, changed, or added. The section follows the format below:

New Section Number* *(In Italics)

Old Section Number

The left-hand column presents the new text of SB 189, effective July 1, 2012.

The right-hand column presents the text of existing law.

The bottom row contains annotations explaining the changes, additions, and deletions to the section directly above.

New Text (Operative July 1, 2012) **Old Text**

CIVIL CODE SECTIONS ("CC")

PART 6. WORKS OF IMPROVEMENT

TITLE 1. WORKS OF IMPROVEMENT GENERALLY

Chapter 1. General Provisions

Article 1. Definitions

CC 8000

Unless the provision or context otherwise requires, the definitions in this article govern the construction of this part.

CC 3082

Unless the context otherwise requires, the provisions in this chapter govern the construction of this title.

•••

CC 8002

"Admitted surety insurer" has the meaning provided in Section 995.120 of the Code of Civil Procedure.

No previous text

Adds requirement that sureties on bonds issued pursuant to this part be an "admitted surety insurer" (See CCP Section 995.120)

•••

CC 8004

"Claimant" means a person that has a right under this part to record a claim of lien, give a stop payment notice, or assert a claim against a payment bond, or do any combination of the foregoing.

CC 3085

"Claimant" means any person entitled under this title to record a claim of lien, to give a stop notice in connection with any work of improvement, or to recover on any payment bond, or any combination of the foregoing.

•••

CC 8006

"Construction lender" means either of the following:

(a) A mortgagee or beneficiary under a deed of trust lending funds with which the cost of all or part of a work of improvement is to be paid, or the assignee or successor in interest of the mortgagee or beneficiary.

(b) An escrow holder or other person holding funds provided by an owner, lender, or another person as a fund for with which the cost of all or part of a work of improvement is to be paid.

CC 3087

"Construction lender" means any mortgagee or beneficiary under a deed of trust lending funds with which the cost of the work of improvement is, wholly or in part, to be defrayed, or any assignee or successor in interest of either, or any escrow holder or other party holding any funds furnished or to be furnished by the owner or lender or any other person as a fund from which to pay construction costs.

Adds phrase to address works of improvement with multiple lenders.

•••

New Text (Operative July 1, 2012)	Old Text

CC 8008

"Contract" means an agreement that provides for all or part of a work of improvement.

CC 3088

"Contract" means an agreement between an owner and any original contractor providing for the work of improvement or any part thereof.

••

CC 8010

"Contract price" means the price agreed to in a direct contract for a work of improvement

No previous text

Defines the concept mentioned in prior law (see former Civil Code §3123)

••

CC 8012

"Contractor" includes a direct contractor, subcontractor, or both. This section does not apply to Sections 8018 and 8046.

No previous text

••

CC 8014

"Design professional" means a person licensed as an architect pursuant to Chapter 3 (commencing with Section 5500) of Division 3 of the Business and Professions Code, licensed as a landscape architect pursuant to Chapter 3.5 (commencing with Section 5615) of Division 3 of the Business and Professions Code, registered as a professional engineer pursuant to Chapter 7 (commencing with Section 6700) of Division 3 of the Business and Professions Code, or licensed as a land surveyor pursuant to Chapter 15 (commencing with Section 8700) of Division 3 of the Business and Professions Code.

CC 3081.1

For purposes of this chapter, "design professional" means any certificated architect, registered professional engineer, or licensed land surveyor who furnishes services pursuant to a written contract with a landowner for the design, engineering, or planning of a work of improvement.

Adds "licensed landscape architects," per B&P Code 5615, to list of Design Professionals entitled to assert a design professional's lien and a mechanics lien.

••

New Text (Operative July 1, 2012) | **Old Text**

CC 8016

"Direct contract" means a contract between an owner and a direct contractor that provides for all or part of a work of improvement.

CC 3088

"Contract" means an agreement between an owner and any original contractor providing for the work of improvement or any part thereof.

Clarifies the term "contract" by replacing it with the term "direct contract."

CC 8018

"Direct contractor" means a contractor that has a direct contractual relationship with an owner. A reference in another statute to a "prime contractor" in connection with the provisions in this part means a "direct contractor."

CC 3095

"Original contractor" means any contractor who has a direct contractual relationship with the owner.

Replaces the term "original contractor" with the new term "direct contractor."

CC 8020

For the purposes of Title 3 (commencing with Section 9000), "funds" means warrant, check, money, or bonds (if bonds are to be issued in payment of the public works contract).

No previous text

Adds new definition.

CC 8022

"Labor, service, equipment, or material" includes, but is not limited to, labor, skills, services, material, supplies, equipment, appliances, power, and surveying, provided for a work of improvement.

No previous text

Adds new definition.

New Text (Operative July 1, 2012) | **Old Text**

CC 8024

(a) "Laborer" means a person who, acting as an employee, performs labor upon, or bestows skill or other necessary services on, a work of improvement.

(b) "Laborer" includes a person or entity to which a portion of a laborer's compensation for a work of improvement, including, but not limited to, employer payments described in Section 1773.1 of the Labor Code and implementing regulations, is paid by agreement with that laborer or the collective bargaining agent of that laborer.

(c) A person or entity described in subdivision (b) that has standing under applicable law to maintain a direct legal action, in its own name or as an assignee, to collect any portion of compensation owed for a laborer for a work of improvement, shall have standing to enforce any rights or claims of the laborer under this part, to the extent of the compensation agreed to be paid to the person or entity for labor on that improvement. This subdivision is intended to give effect to the longstanding public policy of this state to protect the entire compensation of a laborer on a work of improvement, regardless of the form in which that compensation is to be paid.

CC 3089 and CC 3111

CC 3089

(a) "Laborer" means any person who, acting as an employee, performs labor upon or bestows skill or other necessary services on any work of improvement.

(b) "Laborer" also includes any person or entity, including an express trust fund described in Section 3111, to whom a portion of the compensation of a laborer as defined in subdivision (a) is paid by agreement with that laborer or the collective bargaining agent of that laborer. To the extent that a person or entity defined in this subdivision has standing under applicable law to maintain a direct legal action, in their own name or as an assignee, to collect any portion of compensation owed for a laborer, that person or entity shall have standing to enforce any rights under this title to the same extent as the laborer. This section is intended to give effect to the long-standing public policy of this state to protect the entire compensation of laborers on works of improvement, regardless of the form in which that compensation is to be paid.

CC 3111

For the purposes of this chapter, an express trust fund to which a portion of a laborer's total compensation is to be paid pursuant to an applicable employment agreement or a collective bargaining agreement for the provision of benefits, including, but not limited to, employer payments described in Section 1773.1 of the Labor Code and regulations thereunder, shall be entitled to assert the same rights and claims as laborers performing labor upon, or bestowing skill or other necessary services on, a work of improvement, to the extent of the compensation agreed to be paid to that express trust fund for labor on that improvement only.

Simplifies current law by combining prior Civil Code §§3089 and 3111 into a single Section. Maintains cross reference to Labor Code §1773.1. (See Labor Code §1773.1.)

New Text (Operative July 1, 2012)	Old Text

CC 8026

"Lien" means a lien under Title 2 (commencing with Section 8160) and includes a lien of a design professional under Section 8302, a lien for a work of improvement under Section 8400, and a lien for a site improvement under Section 8402.

No previous text

Adds new definition.

CC 8028

"Material supplier" means a person that provides material or supplies to be used or consumed in a work of improvement.

CC 3090

"Materialman" means any person who furnishes materials or supplies to be used or consumed in any work of improvement.

Modernizes term and makes it gender neutral.

CC 8030

(a) For the purposes of Title 2 (commencing with Section 8160), "payment bond" means a bond given under Section 8600.

(b) For the purposes of Title 3 (commencing with Section 9000), "payment bond" means a bond required by Section 9550.

No previous text

Adds new definition.

Definition distinguishes between public and private.

CC 8032

"Person" means an individual, corporation, public entity, business trust, estate, trust, partnership, limited liability company, association, or other entity.

No previous text

Adds new definition.

New Text (Operative July 1, 2012) | **Old Text**

CC 8034

(a) For the purposes of Title 2 (commencing with Section 8160), "preliminary notice" means the notice provided for in Chapter 2 (commencing with Section 8200) of Title 2.

(b) For the purposes of Title 3 (commencing with Section 9000), "preliminary notice" means the notice provided for in Chapter 3 (commencing with Section 9300) of Title 3.

CC 3097 and CC 3098

CC 3097

"Preliminary 20-day notice (private work)" means a written notice from a claimant that is given prior to the recording of a Mechanic's lien, prior to the filing of a stop notice, and prior to asserting a claim against a payment bond, and is required to be given under the following circumstances:

(a) Except one under direct contract with the owner or one performing actual labor for wages as described in subdivision (a) of Section 3089, or a person or entity to whom a portion of a laborer's compensation is paid as described in subdivision (b) of Section 3089, every person who furnishes labor, service, equipment, or material for which a lien or payment bond otherwise can be claimed under this title, or for which a notice to withhold can otherwise be given under this title, shall, as a necessary prerequisite to the validity of any claim of lien, payment bond, and of a notice to withhold, cause to be given to the owner or reputed owner, to the original contractor, or reputed contractor, and to the construction lender, if any, or to the reputed construction lender, if any, a written preliminary notice as prescribed by this section.

(b) Except the contractor, or one performing actual labor for wages as described in subdivision (a) of Section 3089, or a person or entity to whom a portion of a laborer's compensation is paid as described in subdivision (b) of Section 3089, all persons who have a direct contract with the owner and who furnish labor, service, equipment, or material for which a lien or payment bond otherwise can be claimed under this title, or for which a notice to withhold can otherwise be given under this title, shall, as a necessary prerequisite to the validity of any claim of lien, claim on a payment bond, and of a notice to withhold, cause to be given to the construction lender, if any, or to the reputed construction lender, if any, a written preliminary notice as prescribed by this section.

(c) The preliminary notice referred to in subdivisions (a) and (b) shall contain the following information:

(1) A general description of the labor, service, equipment, or materials furnished, or to be furnished, and an estimate of the total price thereof.

(2) The name and address of the person furnishing that labor, service, equipment, or materials.

(3) The name of the person who contracted for purchase of that labor, service, equipment, or materials.

(4) A description of the jobsite sufficient for identification.

(5) The following statement in boldface type:

New Text (Operative July 1, 2012) | **Old Text**

NOTICE TO PROPERTY OWNER

If bills are not paid in full for the labor, services, equipment, or materials furnished or to be furnished, a Mechanic's lien leading to the loss, through court foreclosure proceedings, of all or part of your property being so improved may be placed against the property even though you have paid your contractor in full. You may wish to protect yourself against this consequence by (1) requiring your contractor to furnish a signed release by the person or firm giving you this notice before making payment to your contractor, or (2) any other method or device that is appropriate under the circumstances. Other than residential homeowners of dwellings containing fewer than five units, private project owners must notify the original contractor and any lien claimant who has provided the owner with a preliminary 20-day lien notice in accordance with Section 3097 of the Civil Code that a notice of completion or notice of cessation has been recorded within 10 days of its recordation. Notice shall be by registered mail, certified mail, or first-class mail, evidenced by a certificate of mailing. Failure to notify will extend the deadlines to record a lien.

(6) If the notice is given by a subcontractor who has failed to pay all compensation due to his or her laborers on the job, the notice shall also contain the identity and address of any laborer and any express trust fund to whom employer payments are due. If an invoice for materials or certified payroll contains the information required by this section, a copy of the invoice, transmitted in the manner prescribed by this section shall be sufficient notice.

A certificated architect, registered engineer, or licensed land surveyor who has furnished services for the design of the work of improvement and who gives a preliminary notice as provided in this section not later than 20 days after the work of improvement has commenced shall be deemed to have complied with subdivisions (a) and (b) with respect to architectural, engineering, or surveying services furnished, or to be furnished.

(d) The preliminary notice referred to in subdivisions (a) and (b) shall be given not later than 20 days after the claimant has first furnished labor, service, equipment, or materials to the jobsite. If labor, service, equipment, or materials have been furnished to a jobsite by a claimant who did not give a preliminary notice, that claimant shall not be precluded from giving a preliminary notice at any time thereafter. The claimant shall, however, be entitled to record a lien, file a stop notice, and assert a claim against a payment bond only for labor, service, equipment, or

New Text (Operative July 1, 2012)	Old Text

material furnished within 20 days prior to the service of the preliminary notice, and at any time thereafter.

(e) Any agreement made or entered into by an owner, whereby the owner agrees to waive the rights or privileges conferred upon the owner by this section shall be void and of no effect.

(f) The notice required under this section may be served as follows:

(1) If the person to be notified resides in this state, by delivering the notice personally, or by leaving it at his or her address of residence or place of business with some person in charge, or by first-class registered or certified mail, postage prepaid, addressed to the person to whom notice is to be given at his or her residence or place of business address or at the address shown by the building permit on file with the authority issuing a building permit for the work, or at an address recorded pursuant to subdivision (j).

(2) If the person to be notified does not reside in this state, by any method enumerated in paragraph (1) of this subdivision. If the person cannot be served by any of these methods, then notice may be given by first-class certified or registered mail, addressed to the construction lender or to the original contractor.

(3) If service is made by first-class certified or registered mail, service is complete at the time of the deposit of that registered or certified mail.

(g) A person required by this section to give notice to the owner, to an original contractor, and to a person to whom a notice to withhold may be given, need give only one notice to the owner, to the original contractor, and to the person to whom a notice to withhold may be given with respect to all materials, services, labor, or equipment he or she furnishes for a work of improvement, that means the entire structure or scheme of improvements as a whole, unless the same is furnished under contracts with more than one subcontractor, in which event, the notice requirements shall be met with respect to materials, services, labor, or equipment furnished to each contractor.

If a notice contains a general description required by subdivision (a) or (b) of the materials, services, labor, or equipment furnished to the date of notice, it is not defective because, after that date, the person giving notice furnishes materials, services, labor, or equipment not within the scope of this general description.

(h) If the contract price to be paid to any subcontractor on a particular work of improvement exceeds four hundred dollars ($400), the failure of that contractor, licensed under

New Text (Operative July 1, 2012) | **Old Text**

Chapter 9 (commencing with Section 7000) of Division 3 of the Business and Professions Code, to give the notice provided for in this section, constitutes grounds for disciplinary action by the Registrar of Contractors.

If the notice is required to contain the information set forth in paragraph (6) of subdivision (c), a failure to give the notice, including that information, that results in the filing of a lien, claim on a payment bond, or the delivery of a stop notice by the express trust fund to which the obligation is owing constitutes grounds for disciplinary action by the Registrar of Contractors against the subcontractor if the amount due the trust fund is not paid.

(i) Every city, county, city and county, or other governmental authority issuing building permits shall, in its application form for a building permit, provide space and a designation for the applicant to enter the name, branch, designation, if any, and address of the construction lender and shall keep the information on file open for public inspection during the regular business hours of the authority.

If there is no known construction lender, that fact shall be noted in the designated space. Any failure to indicate the name and address of the construction lender on the application, however, shall not relieve any person from the obligation to give to the construction lender the notice required by this section.

(j) A mortgage, deed of trust, or other instrument securing a loan, any of the proceeds of which may be used for the purpose of constructing improvements on real property, shall bear the designation "Construction Trust Deed" prominently on its face and shall state all of the following: (1) the name and address of the lender, and the name and address of the owner of the real property described in the instrument, and (2) a legal description of the real property that secures the loan and, if known, the street address of the property. The failure to be so designated or to state any of the information required by this subdivision shall not affect the validity of the mortgage, deed of trust, or other instrument.

Failure to provide this information on this instrument when recorded shall not relieve persons required to give preliminary notice under this section from that duty.

The county recorder of the county in which the instrument is recorded shall indicate in the general index of the official records of the county that the instrument secures a construction loan.

(k) Every contractor and subcontractor employing laborers as described in subdivision (a) of Section 3089 who has failed to pay those laborers their full compensation when it

New Text (Operative July 1, 2012)	Old Text

became due, including any employer payments described in Section 1773.1 of the Labor Code and regulations adopted thereunder shall, without regard to whether the work was performed on a public or private work, cause to be given to those laborers, their bargaining representatives, if any, and to the construction lender, if any, or to the reputed construction lender, if any, not later than the date the compensation became delinquent, a written notice containing all of the following:

(1) The name of the owner and the contractor.

(2) A description of the jobsite sufficient for identification.

(3) The identity and address of any express trust fund described in Section 3111 to which employer payments are due.

(4) The total number of straight time and overtime hours on each job.

(5) The amount then past due and owing.

Failure to give this notice shall constitute grounds for disciplinary action by the Registrar of Contractors.

(l) Every written contract entered into between a property owner and an original contractor shall provide space for the owner to enter his or her name, residence address, and place of business if any. The original contractor shall make available the name and address of residence of the owner to any person seeking to serve the notice specified in subdivision (c).

(m) Every written contract entered into between a property owner and an original contractor, except home improvement contracts and swimming pool contracts subject to Article 10 (commencing with Section 7150) of Chapter 9 of Division 3 of the Business and Professions Code, shall provide space for the owner to enter the name and address of the construction lender or lenders. The original contractor shall make available the name and address of the construction lender or lenders to any person seeking to serve the notice specified in subdivision (c). Every contract entered into between an original contractor and subcontractor, and between subcontractors, shall provide a space for the name and address of the owner, original contractor, and any construction lender.

(n) If one or more construction loans are obtained after commencement of construction, the property owner shall provide the name and address of the construction lender or lenders to each person who has given the property owner the notice specified in subdivision (c).

(o)(1) Each person who has served a preliminary 20-day notice pursuant to subdivision (f) may file the preliminary 20-day notice with the county recorder in the county in which any portion of the property is located. A

New Text (Operative July 1, 2012)	Old Text

preliminary 20-day notice filed pursuant to this section shall contain all of the following:

(A) The name and address of the person furnishing the labor, service, equipment, or materials.

(B) The name of the person who contracted for purchase of the labor, services, equipment, or materials.

(C) The common street address of the jobsite.

(2) Upon the acceptance for recording of a notice of completion or notice of cessation the county recorder shall mail to those persons who have filed a preliminary 20-day notice, notification that a notice of completion or notice of cessation has been recorded on the property, and shall affix the date that the notice of completion or notice of cessation was recorded with the county recorder.

(3) The failure of the county recorder to mail the notification to the person who filed a preliminary 20-day notice, or the failure of those persons to receive the notification or to receive complete notification, shall not affect the period within which a claim of lien is required to be recorded. However, the county recorder shall make a good faith effort to mail notification to those persons who have filed the preliminary 20-day notice under this section and to do so within five days after the recording of a notice of completion or notice of cessation.

(4) This new function of the county recorder shall not become operative until July 1, 1988. The county recorder may cause to be destroyed all documents filed pursuant to this section, two years after the date of filing.

(5) The preliminary 20-day notice that a person may file pursuant to this subdivision is for the limited purpose of facilitating the mailing of notice by the county recorder of recorded notices of completion and notices of cessation. The notice that is filed is not a recordable document and shall not be entered into those official records of the county which by law impart constructive notice.

Notwithstanding any other provision of law, the index maintained by the recorder of filed preliminary 20-day notices shall be separate and distinct from those indexes maintained by the county recorder of those official records of the county which by law impart constructive notice. The filing of a preliminary 20-day notice with the county recorder does not give rise to any actual or constructive notice with respect to any party of the existence or contents of a filed preliminary 20-day notice nor to any duty of inquiry on the part of any party as to the existence or contents of that notice.

New Text (Operative July 1, 2012)	Old Text

(p)(1) The change made to the statement described in subdivision (c) by Chapter 974 of the Statutes of 1994 shall have no effect upon the validity of any notice that otherwise meets the requirements of this section. The failure to provide, pursuant to Chapter 974 of the Statutes of 1994, a written preliminary notice to a subcontractor with whom the claimant has contracted shall not affect the validity of any preliminary notice provided pursuant to this section.

(2)(A) The inclusion of the language added to paragraph (5) of subdivision (c) by Chapter 795 of the Statutes of 1999, shall not affect the validity of any preliminary notice given on or after January 1, 2000, and prior to the operative date of the amendments to this section enacted at the 2000 portion of the 1999-2000 Regular Session, that otherwise meets the requirements of that subdivision.

(B) A preliminary notice given on or after January 1, 2000, and prior to the operative date of the amendments to this section enacted at the 2000 portion of the 1999-2000 Regular Session, shall not be invalid because of the failure to include the language added to paragraph (5) of subdivision (c) by Chapter 795 of the Statutes of 1999, if the notice otherwise complies with that subdivision.

(C) The failure to provide an affidavit form or notice of rights, or both, pursuant to the requirements of Chapter 795 of the Statutes of 1999, shall not affect the validity of any preliminary notice pursuant to this section.

CC 3098

"Preliminary 20-day notice (public work)" means a written notice from a claimant that was given prior to the assertion of a claim against a payment bond, or the filing of a stop notice on public work, and is required to be given under the following circumstances:

(a) In any case in which the law of this state affords a right to a person furnishing labor or materials for a public work who has not been paid therefor to assert a claim against a payment bond, or to file a stop notice with the public agency concerned, and thereby cause the withholding of payment from the contractor for the public work, any person that has no direct contractual relationship with the contractor, other than a person who performed actual labor for wages or an express trust fund described in Section 3111, may file the preliminary notice, but no payment shall be withheld from the contractor pursuant to that notice unless the person has caused written notice to be given to the contractor, and the public agency concerned,

New Text (Operative July 1, 2012) | **Old Text**

not later than 20 days after the claimant has first furnished labor, services, equipment, or materials to the jobsite, stating with substantial accuracy a general description of labor, service, equipment, or materials furnished or to be furnished, and the name of the party to whom the same was furnished. This notice shall be served by mailing the same by first-class mail, registered mail, or certified mail, postage prepaid, in an envelope addressed to the contractor at any place the contractor maintains an office or conducts business, or his or her residence, or by personal service. In case of any public works constructed by the Department of Public Works or the Department of General Services of the state, such notice shall be served by mailing in the same manner as above, addressed to the office of the disbursing officer of the department constructing the work, or by personal service upon the officer. When service is by registered or certified mail, service is complete at the time of the deposit of the registered or certified mail.

(b) Where the contract price to be paid to any subcontractor on a particular work of improvement exceeds four hundred dollars ($400), the failure of that contractor, licensed under Chapter 9, (commencing with Section 7000) of Division 3 of the Business and Professions Code, to give the notice provided for in this section, constitutes grounds for disciplinary action by the Registrar of Contractors.

(c) The notice requirements of this section shall not apply to a laborer described in Section 3089 or to an express trust fund described in Section 3111.

(d) If labor, service, equipment, or materials have been furnished to a jobsite by a claimant who did not give a preliminary notice pursuant to subdivision (a), that claimant shall not be precluded from giving a preliminary notice at any time thereafter. The claimant shall, however, be entitled to assert a claim against a payment bond and file a stop notice only for labor, service, equipment, or material furnished within 20 days prior to the service of the preliminary notice, and at any time thereafter.

(e) The failure to provide, pursuant to Chapter 974 of the Statutes of 1994, a written preliminary notice to a subcontractor with whom the claimant has contracted shall not affect the validity of any preliminary notice provided pursuant to this section.

Definition distinguishes between private and public work of improvement.

New Text (Operative July 1, 2012) | **Old Text**

CC 8036

"Public entity" means the state, Regents of the University of California, a county, city, district, public authority, public agency, and any other political subdivision or public corporation in the state.

CC 3099

"Public entity" means the state, Regents of the University of California, a county, city, district, public authority, public agency, and any other political subdivision or public corporation in the state.

••

CC 8038

"Public works contract" has the meaning provided in Section 1101 of the Public Contract Code.

CC 3100

"Public work" means any work of improvement contracted for by a public entity.

Incorporates definition found in Section 1101 of Public Contract Code which provides: PCC 1101. "Public works contract," as used in this part, means an agreement for the erection, construction, alteration, repair, or improvement of any public structure, building, road, or other public improvement of any kind.

••

CC 8040

"Site" means the real property on which a work of improvement is situated or planned.

CC 3101

"Site" means the real property upon which the work of improvement is being constructed or performed.

Expands the concept of "site" to include real property on which a work of improvement is planned.

••

CC 8042

"Site improvement" means any of the following work on real property:
(a) Demolition or removal of improvements, trees, or other vegetation.
(b) Drilling test holes.
(c) Grading, filling, or otherwise improving the real property or a street, highway, or sidewalk in front of or adjoining the real property.
(d) Construction or installation of sewers or other public utilities.
(e) Construction of areas, vaults, cellars, or rooms under sidewalks.
(f) Any other work or improvements in preparation of the site for a work of improvement.

CC 3102

"Site improvement" means the demolishing or removing of improvements, trees, or other vegetation located thereon, or drilling test holes or the grading, filling, or otherwise improving of any lot or tract of land or the street, highway, or sidewalk in front of or adjoining any lot or tract of land, or constructing or installing sewers or other public utilities therein, or constructing any areas, vaults, cellars, or rooms under said sidewalks or making any improvements thereon.

Broadens the definition of site improvement by adding following generalized phrase at Subsection (f) "Any other work or improvements in preparation of the site for a work of improvement."

••

New Text (Operative July 1, 2012) **Old Text**

CC 8044

(a)(1) For the purposes of Title 2 (commencing with Section 8160), "stop payment notice" means the notice given by a claimant under Chapter 5 (commencing with Section 8500) of Title 2.

(2) A stop payment notice given under Title 2 (commencing with Section 8160) may be bonded or unbonded. A "bonded stop payment notice" is a notice given with a bond under Section 8532. An "unbonded stop payment notice" is a notice not given with a bond under Section 8532.

(3) Except to the extent Title 2 (commencing with Section 8160) distinguishes between a bonded and an unbonded stop payment notice, a reference in that title to a stop payment notice includes both a bonded and an unbonded notice.

(b) For the purposes of Title 3 (commencing with Section 9000), "stop payment notice" means the notice given by a claimant under Chapter 4 (commencing with Section 9350) of Title 3.

(c) A reference in another statute to a "stop notice" in connection with the remedies provided in this part means a stop payment notice.

CC 3103

"Stop notice" means a written notice, signed and verified by the claimant or his or her agent, stating in general terms all of the following:

(a) The kind of labor, services, equipment, or materials furnished or agreed to be furnished by such claimant.

(b) The name of the person to or for whom the same was done or furnished.

(c) The amount in value, as near as may be, of that already done or furnished and of the whole agreed to be done or furnished.

(d) The name and address of the claimant.

The notice, in the case of any work of improvement other than a public work, shall be delivered to the owner personally or left at his or her residence or place of business with some person in charge, or delivered to his or her architect, if any, if the notice is served upon a construction lender, holding construction funds and maintaining branch offices, it shall not be effective as against the construction lender unless given to or served upon the manager or other responsible officer or person at the office or branch thereof administering or holding the construction funds. The notice, in the case of any public work for the state, shall be filed with the director of the department which let the contract and, in the case of any other public work, shall be filed in the office of the controller, auditor, or other public disbursing officer whose duty it is to make payments under the provisions of the contract, or with the commissioners, managers, trustees, officers, board of supervisors, board of trustees, common council, or other body by whom the contract was awarded. No stop notice shall be invalid by reason of any defect in form if it is sufficient to substantially inform the owner of the information required.

Any stop notice may be served by registered or certified mail with the same effect as by personal service.

Redefines the term "Stop Notice" as "Stop Payment Notice."
Recognizes both "bonded" and "un-bonded" stop payment notices on private works.
Moves the requirements for a "Stop Payment Notice" from the definition and references other sections (Civil Code §8532 – private work; and §9350 – public work).

••

CC 8046

"Subcontractor" means a contractor that does not have a direct contractual relationship with an owner. The term includes a contractor that has a contractual relationship with a direct contractor or with another subcontractor.

CC 3104

"Subcontractor" means any contractor who has no direct contractual relationship with the owner.

Clarifies that the term "subcontractor" includes lower tier contractors (i.e., sub-subcontractors, a contractor that takes a portion of the work from a subcontractor).

••

New Text (Operative July 1, 2012)	Old Text

CC 8048

"Work" means labor, service, equipment, or material provided to a work of improvement.

No previous text

Adds new definition.
Incorporates the phrase "labor, service, equipment or material" which is now defined in Civil Code §8022.

••

CC 8050

(a) "Work of improvement" includes, but is not limited to:
(1) Construction, alteration, repair, demolition, or removal, in whole or in part, of, or addition to, a building, wharf, bridge, ditch, flume, aqueduct, well, tunnel, fence, machinery, railroad, or road.
(2) Seeding, sodding, or planting of real property for landscaping purposes.
(3) Filling, leveling, or grading of real property.
(b) Except as otherwise provided in this part, "work of improvement" means the entire structure or scheme of improvement as a whole, and includes site improvement.

CC 3106

"Work of improvement" includes but is not restricted to the construction, alteration, addition to, or repair, in whole or in part, of any building, wharf, bridge, ditch, flume, aqueduct, well, tunnel, fence, machinery, railroad, or road, the seeding, sodding, or planting of any lot or tract of land for landscaping purposes, the filling, leveling, or grading of any lot or tract of land, the demolition of buildings, and the removal of buildings. Except as otherwise provided in this title, "work of improvement" means the entire structure or scheme of improvement as a whole.

Adds "site improvement " to the definition, which term is now defined in Civil Code §8042.

••

PART 6. WORKS OF IMPROVEMENT

TITLE 1. WORKS OF IMPROVEMENT GENERALLY

Chapter 1. General Provisions

Article 2. Miscellaneous Provisions

CC 8052

(a) This part is operative on July 1, 2012.
(b) Notwithstanding subdivision (a), the effectiveness of a notice given or other action taken on a work of improvement before July 1, 2012, is governed by the applicable law in effect before July 1, 2012, and not by this part.
(c) A provision of this part, insofar as it is substantially the same as a previously existing provision relating to the same subject matter, shall be construed as a restatement and continuation thereof and not as a new enactment.

No previous text

Confirms three critical items:
(1) effective date of new law is July 1, 2012;
(2) actions taken prior to July 1, 2012 shall be governed by prior law; and
(3) provisions that are "substantially the same as a previously existing provision . . . shall be construed as a restatement . . . and not as a new enactment."

••

New Text (Operative July 1, 2012) | **Old Text**

CC 8054

(a) This part does not apply to a transaction governed by the Oil and Gas Lien Act (Chapter 2.5 (commencing with Section 1203.50) of Title 4 of Part 3 of the Code of Civil Procedure).

(b) This part does not apply to or change improvement security under the Subdivision Map Act (Division 2 (commencing with Section 66410) of Title 7 of the Government Code).

(c) This part does not apply to a transaction governed by Sections 20457 to 20464, inclusive, of the Public Contract Code.

CC 3266

(a) This title does not supersede the Oil and Gas Lien Act, Chapter 2.5 (commencing with Section 1203.50), Title 4, Part 3, of the Code of Civil Procedure, and the provisions of that act shall govern those transactions to which it applies rather than the provisions of this title.

(b) This title does not supersede Chapter 12 (commencing with Section 5290), Part 3, Division 7, of the Streets and Highways Code, and the provisions of that chapter shall govern those transactions to which it applies rather than the provisions of this title.

Confirms that the Title-Works of Improvement, does not apply to the following: (1) transactions under Oil and Gas Lien Act; (2) improvement security under the Subdivision Map Act, or (3) transactions governed by Sections 20457 to 20464 of the Public Contract Code.

•••

CC 8056

Except as otherwise provided in this part, Part 2 (commencing with Section 307) of the Code of Civil Procedure provides the rules of practice in proceedings under this part.

CC 3259

Except as otherwise provided in this title, the provisions of Part 2 (commencing with Section 307) of the Code of Civil Procedure are applicable to, and constitute the rules of practice in, the proceedings mentioned in this title. The provisions of Part 2 (commencing with Section 307) of the Code of Civil Procedure, relative to new trials and appeals, except insofar as they are inconsistent with the provisions of this title or with rules adopted by the Judicial Council, apply to the proceedings mentioned in this title.

•••

CC 8058

For purposes of this part, "day" means a calendar day.

No previous text

Adds new definition.

•••

New Text (Operative July 1, 2012) | **Old Text**

__CC 8060__

(a) If this part provides for filing a contract, plan, or other paper with the county recorder, the provision is satisfied by filing the paper in the office of the county recorder of the county in which the work of improvement or part of it is situated.

(b) If this part provides for recording a notice, claim of lien, release of lien, payment bond, or other paper, the provision is satisfied by filing the paper for record in the office of the county recorder of the county in which the work of improvement or part of it is situated.

(c) The county recorder shall number, index, and preserve a contract, plan, or other paper presented for filing under this part, and shall number, index, and transcribe into the official records, in the same manner as a conveyance of real property, a notice, claim of lien, payment bond, or other paper recorded under this part.

(d) The county recorder shall charge and collect the fees provided in Article 5 (commencing with Section 27360) of Chapter 6 of Part 3 of Division 2 of Title 3 of the Government Code for performing duties under this section.

CC 3258

The county recorder shall number, index, and preserve all contracts, plans, and other papers presented to him for filing pursuant to this title, and shall number, index, and transcribe into the official records in his office in the same manner as a conveyance of land, all notices, claims of lien, payment bonds, and other papers recorded pursuant to this title. He shall receive therefor the fees prescribed in Article 5 (commencing with Section 27360), Chapter 6, Part 3, Division 2, Title 3 of the Government Code.

Maintains the distinction between "filing" and "recording" documents with the County Recorder.

••

__CC 8062__

No act of an owner in good faith and in compliance with a provision of this part shall be construed to prevent a direct contractor's performance of the contract, or exonerate a surety on a performance or payment bond.

CC 3263

No act done by an owner in good faith and in compliance with any of the provisions of this title shall be held to be a prevention of the performance of any contract between the owner and an original contractor by an original contractor, or to exonerate the sureties on any bond given for faithful performance or for the payment of claimants.

••

__CC 8064__

An owner may give a notice or execute or file a document under this part on behalf of a co-owner if the owner acts on the co-owner's behalf and includes in the notice or document the name and address of the co-owner on whose behalf the owner acts.

No previous text

Adds new definition. Co-owner may give a notice or execute or file a document on behalf of co-owner, but must include the name and address of co-owner therein.

••

New Text (Operative July 1, 2012) | **Old Text**

CC 8066

An act that may be done by or to a person under this part may be done by or to the person's agent to the extent the act is within the scope of the agent's authority.

No previous text

Adds new definition.

Recognizes the concept of "agency".

••

PART 6. WORKS OF IMPROVEMENT

TITLE 1. WORKS OF IMPROVEMENT GENERALLY

Chapter 2. Notice

CC 8100

Notice under this part shall be in writing. Writing includes printing and typewriting.

No previous text

Adds new definition.

••

CC 8102

(a) Notice under this part shall, in addition to any other information required by statute for that type of notice, include all of the following information to the extent known to the person giving the notice:

(1) The name and address of the owner or reputed owner.

(2) The name and address of the direct contractor.

(3) The name and address of the construction lender, if any.

(4) A description of the site sufficient for identification, including the street address of the site, if any. If a sufficient legal description of the site is given, the effectiveness of the notice is not affected by the fact that the street address is erroneous or is omitted.

(5) The name, address, and relationship to the parties of the person giving the notice.

(6) If the person giving the notice is a claimant:

(A) A general statement of the work provided.

(B) The name of the person to or for whom the work is provided.

(C) A statement or estimate of the claimant's demand, if any, after deducting all just credits and offsets.

(b) Notice is not invalid by reason of any variance

CC 3097(c)

(c) The preliminary notice referred to in subdivisions (a) and (b) shall contain the following information:

(1) A general description of the labor, service, equipment, or materials furnished, or to be furnished, and an estimate of the total price thereof.

(2) The name and address of the person furnishing that labor, service, equipment, or materials.

(3) The name of the person who contracted for purchase of that labor, service, equipment, or materials.

(4) A description of the jobsite sufficient for identification.

(5) The following statement in boldface type:

NOTICE TO PROPERTY OWNER

If bills are not paid in full for the labor, services, equipment, or materials furnished or to be furnished, a Mechanic's lien leading to the loss, through court foreclosure proceedings, of all or part of your property being so improved may be placed against the property even though you have paid your contractor in full. You may wish to protect yourself against this consequence by (1) requiring your contractor to furnish a signed release by the person or firm giving you this notice before making payment to your contractor, or (2) any other method or device that is appropriate under the circumstances. Other than residential homeowners of

New Text (Operative July 1, 2012) | **Old Text**

from the requirements of this section if the notice is sufficient to substantially inform the person given notice of the information required by this section and other information required in the notice.

dwellings containing fewer than five units, private project owners must notify the original contractor and any lien claimant who has provided the owner with a preliminary 20-day lien notice in accordance with Section 3097 of the Civil Code that a notice of completion or notice of cessation has been recorded within 10 days of its recordation. Notice shall be by registered mail, certified mail, or first-class mail, evidenced by a certificate of mailing. Failure to notify will extend the deadlines to record a lien.

(6) If the notice is given by a subcontractor who has failed to pay all compensation due to his or her laborers on the job, the notice shall also contain the identity and address of any laborer and any express trust fund to whom employer payments are due. If an invoice for materials or certified payroll contains the information required by this section, a copy of the invoice, transmitted in the manner prescribed by this section shall be sufficient notice.

A certificated architect, registered engineer, or licensed land surveyor who has furnished services for the design of the work of improvement and who gives a preliminary notice as provided in this section not later than 20 days after the work of improvement has commenced shall be deemed to have complied with subdivisions (a) and (b) with respect to architectural, engineering, or surveying services furnished, or to be furnished.

New standardizes requirement for notices. The minimum content includes: (1) identification of the project owner; (2) identification of the direct contractor; (3) identification of the construction lender; (4) a description of the project site; and (5) identification of the party giving notice.

Also standardizes procedural requirements for giving notice.

Adds a "substantial compliance" provision to the statute.

<u>CC 8104</u>

(a) A direct contractor or subcontractor on a work of improvement governed by this part that employs a laborer and fails to pay the full compensation due the laborer, including any employer payments described in Section 1773.1 of the Labor Code and implementing regulations, shall not later than the date the compensation became delinquent, give the laborer, the laborer's bargaining representative, if any, the construction lender or reputed construction lender, if any, and the owner or reputed owner, notice that includes all of the following information, in addition to the information required by Section 8102:

CC 3097(k)

(k) Every contractor and subcontractor employing laborers as described in subdivision (a) of Section 3089 who has failed to pay those laborers their full compensation when it became due, including any employer payments described in Section 1773.1 of the Labor Code and regulations adopted thereunder shall, without regard to whether the work was performed on a public or private work, cause to be given to those laborers, their bargaining representatives, if any, and to the construction lender, if any, or to the reputed construction lender, if any, not later than the date the compensation became delinquent, a written notice containing all of the following:

New Text (Operative July 1, 2012) | **Old Text**

(1) The name and address of the laborer, and of any person or entity described in subdivision (b) of Section 8024 to which employer payments are due.

(2) The total number of straight time and overtime hours worked by the laborer on each job.

(3) The amount then past due and owing.

(b) Failure to give the notice required by subdivision (a) constitutes grounds for disciplinary action under the Contractors' State License Law, Chapter 9 (commencing with Section 7000) of Division 3 of the Business and Professions Code.

(1) The name of the owner and the contractor.

(2) A description of the jobsite sufficient for identification.

(3) The identity and address of any express trust fund described in Section 3111 to which employer payments are due.

(4) The total number of straight time and overtime hours on each job.

(5) The amount then past due and owing.

Failure to give this notice shall constitute grounds for disciplinary action by the Registrar of Contractors.

Adds the obligation provide the owner with the Notice required by the prior Civil Code §3097 (k).

••

CC 8106

Except as otherwise provided by statute, notice under this part shall be given by any of the following means:

(a) Personal delivery.

(b) Mail in the manner provided in Section 8110.

(c) Leaving the notice and mailing a copy in the manner provided in Section 415.20 of the Code of Civil Procedure for service of summons and complaint in a civil action.

No previous text

Defines required methods of delivery, which, by incorporation of Section 8110, now includes "express mail and overnight delivery by an express service carrier."

••

CC 8108

Except as otherwise provided by this part, notice under this part shall be given to the person to be notified at the person's residence, the person's place of business, or at any of the following addresses:

(a) If the person to be notified is an owner other than a public entity, the owner's address shown on the direct contract, the building permit, or a construction trust deed.

(b) If the person to be notified is a public entity, the office of the public entity or another address specified by the public entity in the contract or elsewhere for service of notices, papers, and other documents.

(c) If the person to be notified is a construction lender, the construction lender's address shown on the construction loan agreement or construction trust deed.

No previous text

New Text (Operative July 1, 2012) | **Old Text**

(d) If the person to be notified is a direct contractor or a subcontractor, the contractor's address shown on the building permit, on the contractor's contract, or on the records of the Contractors' State License Board.

(e) If the person to be notified is a claimant, the claimant's address shown on the claimant's contract, preliminary notice, claim of lien, stop payment notice, or claim against a payment bond, or on the records of the Contractors' State License Board.

(f) If the person to be notified is a surety on a bond, the surety's address shown on the bond for service of notices, papers, and other documents, or on the records of the Department of Insurance.

Defines the proper address for service of notices.

••

CC 8110

Except as otherwise provided by this part, notice by mail under this part shall be given by registered or certified mail, express mail, or overnight delivery by an express service carrier.

No previous text

Expands prior law and authorizes service of notices by express mail and overnight delivery by an express service carrier.

••

CC 8114

A notice required by this part to be posted shall be displayed in a conspicuous location at the site.

No previous text

••

CC 8116

Notice under this part is complete and deemed to have been given at the following times:

(a) If given by personal delivery, when delivered.

(b) If given by mail, when deposited in the mail or with an express service carrier in the manner provided in Section 1013 of the Code of Civil Procedure.

(c) If given by leaving the notice and mailing a copy in the manner provided in Section 415.20 of the Code of Civil Procedure for service of summons in a civil action, five days after mailing.

(d) If given by posting, when displayed.

CC 3097(f)

(f) The notice required under this section may be served as follows:

(1) If the person to be notified resides in this state, by delivering the notice personally, or by leaving it at his or her address of residence or place of business with some person in charge, or by first-class registered or certified mail, postage prepaid, addressed to the person to whom notice is to be given at his or her residence or place of business address or at the address shown by the building permit on file with the authority issuing a building permit for the work, or at an address recorded pursuant to subdivision (j).

New Text (Operative July 1, 2012)

(e) If given by recording, when recorded in the office of the county recorder.

Old Text

(2) If the person to be notified does not reside in this state, by any method enumerated in paragraph (1) of this subdivision. If the person cannot be served by any of these methods, then notice may be given by first-class certified or registered mail, addressed to the construction lender or to the original contractor.

(3) If service is made by first-class certified or registered mail, service is complete at the time of the deposit of that registered or certified mail.

Provides specific guidance as to when notice is complete. Please note that when the notice provided by mail, notice is deemed complete five (5) days after mailing.

••

CC 8118

(a) Proof that notice was given to a person in the manner required by this part shall be made by a proof of notice declaration that states all of the following:

(1) The type or description of the notice given.

(2) The date, place, and manner of notice, and facts showing that notice was given in the manner required by statute.

(3) The name and address of the person to which notice was given, and, if appropriate, the title or capacity in which the person was given notice.

(b) If the notice is given by mail, the declaration shall be accompanied by one of the following:

(1) Documentation provided by the United States Postal Service showing that payment was made to mail the notice using registered or certified mail, or express mail.

(2) Documentation provided by an express service carrier showing that payment was made to send the notice using an overnight delivery service.

(3) A return receipt, delivery confirmation, signature confirmation, tracking record, or other proof of delivery or attempted delivery provided by the United States Postal Service, or a photocopy of the record of delivery and receipt maintained by the United States Postal Service, showing the date of delivery and to whom delivered, or in the event of nondelivery, by the returned envelope itself.

(4) A tracking record or other documentation provided by an express service carrier showing delivery or attempted delivery of the notice.

CC 3097.1

Proof that the preliminary 20-day notice required by Section 3097 was served in accordance with subdivision (f) of Section 3097 shall be made as follows:

(a) If served by mail, by the proof of service affidavit described in subdivision (c) of this section accompanied either by the return receipt of certified or registered mail, or by a photocopy of the record of delivery and receipt maintained by the post office, showing the date of delivery and to whom delivered, or, in the event of nondelivery, by the returned envelope itself.

(b) If served by personally delivering the notice to the person to be notified, or by leaving it at his address or place of business with some person in charge, by the proof of service affidavit described in subdivision (c).

(c) A "proof of service affidavit" is an affidavit of the person making the service, showing the time, place and manner of service and facts showing that such service was made in accordance with Section 3097. Such affidavit shall show the name and address of the person upon whom a copy of the preliminary 20-day notice was served, and, if appropriate, the title or capacity in which he was served.

Establishes new requirements for proof of service for notices, which requirements have two components if service is by mail, express mail or overnight delivery service:

(1) Proof of Notice Declaration; and (2) documentation regarding (a) payment and (b) delivery on attempted delivery.

••

New Text (Operative July 1, 2012) | **Old Text**

PART 6. WORKS OF IMPROVEMENT
TITLE 1. WORKS OF IMPROVEMENT GENERALLY
Chapter 3. Waiver and Release

CC 8120
The provisions of this chapter apply to a work of improvement governed by this part.

No previous text

••

CC 8122
An owner, direct contractor, or subcontractor may not, by contract or otherwise, waive, affect, or impair any other claimant's rights under this part, whether with or without notice, and any term of a contract that purports to do so is void and unenforceable unless and until the claimant executes and delivers a waiver and release under this article.

CC 3262(a)
(a) Neither the owner nor original contractor by any term of their contract, or otherwise, shall waive, affect, or impair the claims and liens of other persons whether with or without notice except by their written consent, and any term of the contract to that effect shall be null and void. Any written consent given by any claimant pursuant to this subdivision shall be null, void, and unenforceable unless and until the claimant executes and delivers a waiver and release. That waiver and release shall be binding and effective to release the owner, construction lender, and surety on a payment bond from claims and liens only if the waiver and release follows substantially one of the forms set forth in this section and is signed by the claimant or his or her authorized agent, and, in the case of a conditional release, there is evidence of payment to the claimant. Evidence of payment may be by the claimant's endorsement on a single or joint payee check which has been paid by the bank upon which it was drawn or by written acknowledgment of payment given by the claimant.

Subcontractors added to list of parties that cannot waive or impair lien rights of others by contract terms, unless and until a proper lien waiver is provided by that other party.

••

CC 8124
A claimant's waiver and release does not release the owner, construction lender, or surety on a payment bond from a lien or claim unless both of the following conditions are satisfied:

(a) The waiver and release is in substantially the form provided in this article and is signed by the claimant.

(b) If the release is a conditional release, there is evidence of payment to the claimant. Evidence of payment may be either of the following:

(1) The claimant's endorsement on a single or joint payee check that has been paid by the financial institution on which it was drawn.

CC 3262(a)
(a) Neither the owner nor original contractor by any term of their contract, or otherwise, shall waive, affect, or impair the claims and liens of other persons whether with or without notice except by their written consent, and any term of the contract to that effect shall be null and void. Any written consent given by any claimant pursuant to this subdivision shall be null, void, and unenforceable unless and until the claimant executes and delivers a waiver and release. That waiver and release shall be binding and effective to release the owner, construction lender, and surety on a payment bond from claims and liens only if the waiver and release follows substantially

New Text (Operative July 1, 2012) | **Old Text**

(2) Written acknowledgment of payment by the claimant.

one of the forms set forth in this section and is signed by the claimant or his or her authorized agent, and, in the case of a conditional release, there is evidence of payment to the claimant. Evidence of payment may be by the claimant's endorsement on a single or joint payee check which has been paid by the bank upon which it was drawn or by written acknowledgment of payment given by the claimant.

•••

CC 8126

An oral or written statement purporting to waive, release, impair or otherwise adversely affect a lien or claim is void and unenforceable and does not create an estoppel or impairment of the lien or claim unless either of the following conditions is satisfied:

(a) The statement is pursuant to a waiver and release under this article.

(b) The claimant has actually received payment in full for the claim.

CC 3262(b)(1)

(b) No oral or written statement purporting to waive, release, impair or otherwise adversely affect a claim is enforceable or creates any estoppel or impairment of a claim unless (1) it is pursuant to a waiver and release prescribed herein, or (2) the claimant had actually received payment in full for the claim. Nothing in this section precludes a stop notice claimant from reducing the amount of, or releasing in its entirety, a stop notice that has been served upon an owner. The reduction or release of a stop notice, which shall be in writing, may be served in a form other than the forms of release set forth in this section. Any reduction or release of a stop notice: (1) shall not preclude the service of a subsequent stop notice that is timely and proper.

•••

CC 8128

(a) A claimant may reduce the amount of, or release in its entirety, a stop payment notice. The reduction or release shall be in writing and may be given in a form other than a waiver and release form provided in this article.

(b) The writing shall identify whether it is a reduction of the amount of the stop payment notice, or a release of the notice in its entirety. If the writing is a reduction, it shall state the amount of the reduction, and the amount to remain withheld after the reduction.

(c) A claimant's reduction or release of a stop payment notice has the following effect:

(1) The reduction or release releases the claimant's right to enforce payment of the claim stated in the notice to the extent of the reduction or release.

(2) The reduction or release releases the person given the notice from the obligation to withhold funds pursuant to the notice to the extent of the

CC 3262(b)(2)

(b) No oral or written statement purporting to waive, release, impair or otherwise adversely affect a claim is enforceable or creates any estoppel or impairment of a claim unless (1) it is pursuant to a waiver and release prescribed herein, or (2) the claimant had actually received payment in full for the claim. Nothing in this section precludes a stop notice claimant from reducing the amount of, or releasing in its entirety, a stop notice that has been served upon an owner. The reduction or release of a stop notice, which shall be in writing, may be served in a form other than the forms of release set forth in this section. Any reduction or release of a stop notice: (2) shall release the owner from any obligation to withhold money on account of the stop notice, to the extent of the reduction or release;

New Text (Operative July 1, 2012) | **Old Text**

reduction or release.
(3) The reduction or release does not preclude the claimant from giving a subsequent stop payment notice that is timely and proper.
(4) The reduction or release does not release any right of the claimant other than the right to enforce payment of the claim stated in the stop payment notice to the extent of the reduction or release.

Clarifies requirements for stop notice release or reduction notice.

•••

CC 8130

This article does not affect the enforceability of either an accord and satisfaction concerning a good faith dispute or an agreement made in settlement of an action pending in court if the accord and satisfaction or agreement and settlement make specific reference to the lien or claim.

CC 3262(c)

(c) This section does not affect the enforceability of either an accord and satisfaction regarding a bona fide dispute or any agreement made in settlement of an action pending in any court provided the accord and satisfaction or agreement and settlement make specific reference to the Mechanic's lien, stop notice, or bond claims.

•••

New Text (Operative July 1, 2012)

CC 8132

If a claimant is required to execute a waiver and release in exchange for, or in order to induce payment of, a progress payment and the claimant is not, in fact, paid in exchange for the waiver and release or a single payee check or joint payee check is given in exchange for the waiver and release, the waiver and release shall be null, void, and unenforceable unless it is in substantially the following form:

CONDITIONAL WAIVER AND RELEASE ON PROGRESS PAYMENT

NOTICE: THIS DOCUMENT WAIVES THE CLAIMANT'S LIEN, STOP PAYMENT NOTICE, AND PAYMENT BOND RIGHTS EFFECTIVE ON RECEIPT OF PAYMENT. A PERSON SHOULD NOT RELY ON THIS DOCUMENT UNLESS SATISFIED THAT THE CLAIMANT HAS RECEIVED PAYMENT.

Identifying Information

Name of Claimant: ____________________
Name of Customer: ____________________
Job Location: ____________________
Owner: ____________________
Through Date: ____________________

Conditional Waiver and Release

This document waives and releases lien, stop payment notice, and payment bond rights the claimant has for labor and service provided, and equipment and material delivered, to the customer on this job through the Through Date of this document. Rights based upon labor or service provided, or equipment or material delivered, pursuant to a written change order that has been fully executed by the parties prior to the date that this document is signed by the claimant, are waived and released by this document, unless listed as an Exception below. This document is effective only on the claimant's receipt of payment from the financial institution on which the following check is drawn:

Maker of Check: ____________________
Amount of Check: $ ____________________
Check Payable to:

____

Old Text

CC 3262(d)(1)

(d) The waiver and release given by any claimant hereunder shall be null, void, and unenforceable unless it follows substantially the following forms in the following circumstances:

(1) If the claimant is required to execute a waiver and release in exchange for, or in order to induce the payment of, a progress payment and the claimant is not, in fact, paid in exchange for the waiver and release or a single payee check or joint payee check is given in exchange for the waiver and release, the waiver and release shall follow substantially the following form:

CONDITIONAL WAIVER AND RELEASE UPON PROGRESS PAYMENT

Upon receipt by the undersigned of a check from

____
(Maker of Check)

in the sum of $_________ (Amount of Check) payable to

____
(Payee or Payees of Check)

and when the check has been properly endorsed and has been paid by the bank upon which it is drawn, this document shall become effective to release any Mechanic's lien, stop notice, or bond right the undersigned has on the job of ________ located at ___________________
(Owner) (Job Description)

to the following extent. This release covers a progress payment for labor, services, equipment, or material furnished to

____
(Your Customer)

through ________________________________
(Date)

only and does not cover any retentions retained before or after the release date; extras furnished before the release date for which payment has not been received; extras or items furnished after the release date. Rights based upon work performed or items furnished under a written change order which has been fully executed by the parties prior to the release date are covered by this release unless specifically reserved by the claimant in this release. This release of any Mechanic's lien, stop notice, or bond right shall not otherwise affect the contract rights, including rights between parties to the contract based upon a rescission, abandonment, or breach of the contract, or the right of the undersigned to recover compensation for furnished labor, services, equipment, or

New Text (Operative July 1, 2012)	Old Text

Exceptions
This document does not affect any of the following:
(1) Retentions.
(2) Extras for which the claimant has not received payment.
(3) The following progress payments for which the claimant has previously given a conditional waiver and release but has not received payment:
Date(s) of waiver and release:
____
Amount(s) of unpaid progress payment(s):
*$*____________________________
(4) Contract rights, including (A) a right based on rescission, abandonment, or breach of contract, and (B) the right to recover compensation for work not compensated by the payment.

Signature:
*Claimant's Signature:*____________________
Claimant's Title: ____________________
Date of Signature: ____________________

material covered by this release if that furnished labor, services, equipment, or material was not compensated by the progress payment. Before any recipient of this document relies on it, said party should verify evidence of payment to the undersigned.
Dated: ________________________________

____
(Company Name)

By__________________________________
(Title)

Creates new Conditional Waiver Upon Progress Payment.
Clarifies the limitations found in prior Civil Code §3262(d)(1) regarding scope of waiver.
Highlights notification to recipient that waiver is conditional on receipt of payment.

New Text (Operative July 1, 2012)

CC 8134

If the claimant is required to execute a waiver and release in exchange for, or in order to induce payment of, a progress payment and the claimant asserts in the waiver that the claimant has, in fact, been paid the progress payment, the waiver and release shall be null, void, and unenforceable unless it is in substantially the following form, with the text of the "Notice to Claimant" in at least as large a type as the largest type otherwise in the form:

UNCONDITIONAL WAIVER AND RELEASE ON PROGRESS PAYMENT

NOTICE TO CLAIMANT: THIS DOCUMENT WAIVES AND RELEASES LIEN, STOP PAYMENT NOTICE, AND PAYMENT BOND RIGHTS UNCONDITIONALLY AND STATES THAT YOU HAVE BEEN PAID FOR GIVING UP THOSE RIGHTS. THIS DOCUMENT IS ENFORCEABLE AGAINST YOU IF YOU SIGN IT, EVEN IF YOU HAVE NOT BEEN PAID. IF YOU HAVE NOT BEEN PAID, USE A CONDITIONAL WAIVER AND RELEASE FORM.

Identifying Information

Name of Claimant: ____________________
Name of Customer: ____________________
Job Location: ____________________
Owner: ____________________
Through Date: ____________________

Unconditional Waiver and Release

*This document waives and releases lien, stop payment notice, and payment bond rights the claimant has for labor and service provided, and equipment and material delivered, to the customer on this job through the Through Date of this document. Rights based upon labor or service provided, or equipment or material delivered, pursuant to a written change order that has been fully executed by the parties prior to the date that this document is signed by the claimant, are waived and released by this document, unless listed as an Exception below. The claimant has received the following progress payment: $*____________________

Exceptions

This document does not affect any of the following:

(1) Retentions.

Old Text

CC 3262(d)(2)

(d) The waiver and release given by any claimant hereunder shall be null, void, and unenforceable unless it follows substantially the following forms in the following circumstances:

(2) If the claimant is required to execute a waiver and release in exchange for, or in order to induce payment of, a progress payment and the claimant asserts in the waiver it has, in fact, been paid the progress payment, the waiver and release shall follow substantially the following form:

UNCONDITIONAL WAIVER AND RELEASE UPON PROGRESS PAYMENT

The undersigned has been paid and has received a progress payment in the sum of $_________ for labor, services, equipment, or material furnished to

____
(Your Customer)

on the job of

____
(Owner)

located at ______________________________
(Job Description)

and does hereby release any Mechanic's lien, stop notice, or bond right that the undersigned has on the above referenced job to the following extent. This release covers a progress payment for labor, services, equipment, or materials furnished to______________________________
(Your Customer)

through ____________________________ only
(Date)

and does not cover any retentions retained before or after the release date; extras furnished before the release date for which payment has not been received; extras or items furnished after the release date. Rights based upon work performed or items furnished under a written change order which has been fully executed by the parties prior to the release date are covered by this release unless specifically reserved by the claimant in this release. This release of any Mechanic's lien, stop notice, or bond right shall not otherwise affect the contract rights, including rights between parties to the contract based upon a rescission, abandonment, or breach of the contract, or the right of the undersigned to recover compensation for furnished labor, services, equipment, or material covered by this release if that furnished labor, services, equipment, or material was not

New Text (Operative July 1, 2012)

(2) Extras for which the claimant has not received payment.
(3) Contract rights, including (A) a right based on rescission, abandonment, or breach of contract, and (B) the right to recover compensation for work not compensated by the payment.

Signature:
Claimant's Signature: ____________________
Claimant's Title: ____________________
Date of Signature: ____________________

Old Text

compensated by the progress payment.
Dated: ______________________________

____
(Company Name)
By ______________________________
(Title)

Each unconditional waiver in this provision shall contain the following language, in at least as large a type as the largest type otherwise on the document: "NOTICE: THIS DOCUMENT WAIVES RIGHTS UNCONDITIONALLY AND STATES THAT YOU HAVE BEEN PAID FOR GIVING UP THOSE RIGHTS. THIS DOCUMENT IS ENFORCEABLE AGAINST YOU IF YOU SIGN IT, EVEN IF YOU HAVE NOT BEEN PAID. IF YOU HAVE NOT BEEN PAID, USE A CONDITIONAL RELEASE FORM."

Creates new Unconditional Waiver upon Progress Payment.
Requires that "Notice to Claimant" be in at least as large as the largest type in the form.
Maintains exclusions from scope of release.

••

CC 8136

If the claimant is required to execute a waiver and release in exchange for, or in order to induce payment of, a final payment and the claimant is not, in fact, paid in exchange for the waiver and release or a single payee check or joint payee check is given in exchange for the waiver and release, the waiver and release shall be null, void, and unenforceable unless it is in substantially the following form:

CC 3262(d)(3)

(d) The waiver and release given by any claimant hereunder shall be null, void, and unenforceable unless it follows substantially the following forms in the following circumstances:

(3) If the claimant is required to execute a waiver and release in exchange for, or in order to induce the payment of, a final payment and the claimant is not, in fact, paid in exchange for the waiver and release or a single payee check or joint payee check is given in exchange for the waiver and release, the waiver and release shall follow substantially the following form:

New Text (Operative July 1, 2012)

CONDITIONAL WAIVER AND RELEASE ON FINAL PAYMENT

NOTICE: THIS DOCUMENT WAIVES THE CLAIMANT'S LIEN, STOP PAYMENT NOTICE, AND PAYMENT BOND RIGHTS EFFECTIVE ON RECEIPT OF PAYMENT. A PERSON SHOULD NOT RELY ON THIS DOCUMENT UNLESS SATISFIED THAT THE CLAIMANT HAS RECEIVED PAYMENT.

Identifying Information
Name of Claimant: ____________________
Name of Customer: ____________________
Job Location: ____________________
Owner: ____________________

Conditional Waiver and Release

This document waives and releases lien, stop payment notice, and payment bond rights the claimant has for labor and service provided, and equipment and material delivered, to the customer on this job. Rights based upon labor or service provided, or equipment or material delivered, pursuant to a written change order that has been fully executed by the parties prior to the date that this document is signed by the claimant, are waived and released by this document, unless listed as an Exception below. This document is effective only on the claimant's receipt of payment from the financial institution on which the following check is drawn:

Maker of Check: ____________________
Amount of Check: $ ____________________
Check Payable to: ____________________
Exceptions
This document does not affect any of the following:
Disputed claims for extras in the amount of:
$ ______________________________
Signature
Claimant's Signature: ____________________
Claimant's Title: ____________________
Date of Signature: ____________________

Old Text

CONDITIONAL WAIVER AND RELEASE UPON FINAL PAYMENT

Upon receipt by the undersigned of a check from ______________________________ in the sum of $________ payable to ____________ and when the check has been properly endorsed and has been paid by the bank upon which it is drawn, this document shall become effective to release any Mechanic's lien, stop notice, or bond right the undersigned has on the job of:

____
(Owner)

located at: ______________________________
(Job Description)

This release covers the final payment to the undersigned for all labor, services, equipment, or material furnished on the job, except for disputed claims for additional work in the amount of $_________. Before any recipient of this document relies on it, the party should verify evidence of payment to the undersigned.

Dated: ______________________________

____
(Company Name)

By ______________________________
(Title)

Creates new Conditional Waiver upon Final Payment.
Highlights notification to recipient that Waiver is "conditional" on receipt of payment.
Maintains exclusion for "disputed claims for extras" and provides that the disputed amount must be listed.

New Text (Operative July 1, 2012)

CC 8138

If the claimant is required to execute a waiver and release in exchange for, or in order to induce payment of, a final payment and the claimant asserts in the waiver that the claimant has, in fact, been paid the final payment, the waiver and release shall be null, void, and unenforceable unless it is in substantially the following form, with the text of the "Notice to Claimant" in at least as large a type as the largest type otherwise in the form:

UNCONDITIONAL WAIVER AND RELEASE ON FINAL PAYMENT

NOTICE TO CLAIMANT: THIS DOCUMENT WAIVES AND RELEASES LIEN, STOP PAYMENT NOTICE, AND PAYMENT BOND RIGHTS UNCONDITIONALLY AND STATES THAT YOU HAVE BEEN PAID FOR GIVING UP THOSE RIGHTS. THIS DOCUMENT IS ENFORCEABLE AGAINST YOU IF YOU SIGN IT, EVEN IF YOU HAVE NOT BEEN PAID. IF YOU HAVE NOT BEEN PAID, USE A CONDITIONAL WAIVER AND RELEASE FORM.

Identifying Information

Name of Claimant: ____________________
Name of Customer: ____________________
Job Location: ____________________
Owner: ____________________

Unconditional Waiver and Release

This document waives and releases lien, stop payment notice, and payment bond rights the claimant has for all labor and service provided, and equipment and material delivered, to the customer on this job. Rights based upon labor or service provided, or equipment or material delivered, pursuant to a written change order that has been fully executed by the parties prior to the date that this document is signed by the claimant, are waived and released by this document, unless listed as an Exception below. The claimant has been paid in full.

Exceptions
This document does not affect the following:
Disputed claims for extras in the amount of:
*$*____________________________

Signature
Claimant's Signature: ____________________
Claimant's Title: ____________________
Date of Signature: ____________________

Old Text

CC 3262(d)(4)

d) The waiver and release given by any claimant hereunder shall be null, void, and unenforceable unless it follows substantially the following forms in the following circumstances:

(4) If the claimant is required to execute a waiver and release in exchange for, or in order to induce payment of, a final payment and the claimant asserts in the waiver it has, in fact, been paid the final payment, the waiver and release shall follow substantially the following form:

UNCONDITIONAL WAIVER AND RELEASE UPON FINAL PAYMENT

The undersigned has been paid in full for all labor, services, equipment or material furnished to

____
(Your Customer)

on the job of

____
(Owner)

located at

____
(Job Description)

and does hereby waive and release any right to a Mechanic's lien, stop notice, or any right against a labor and material bond on the job, except for disputed claims for extra work in the amount of
$________.

Dated: ______________________________

____
(Company Name)

By ______________________________
(Title)

Each unconditional waiver in this provision shall contain the following language, in at least as large a type as the largest type otherwise on the document: "NOTICE: THIS DOCUMENT WAIVES RIGHTS UNCONDITIONALLY AND STATES THAT YOU HAVE BEEN PAID FOR GIVING UP THOSE RIGHTS. THIS DOCUMENT IS ENFORCEABLE AGAINST YOU IF YOU SIGN IT, EVEN IF YOU HAVE NOT BEEN PAID. IF YOU HAVE NOT BEEN PAID, USE A CONDITIONAL RELEASE FORM."

Creates new Unconditional Waiver upon Final Payment.
Requires that "Notice to Claimant" be in at least as large as the largest type in the form.
Maintains exclusion for "disputed claims for extras" and provides that disputed amount must be listed.

New Text (Operative July 1, 2012) | **Old Text**

PART 6. WORKS OF IMPROVEMENT
TITLE 1. WORKS OF IMPROVEMENT GENERALLY
Chapter 4. Bonds

CC 8150

The Bond and Undertaking Law (Chapter 2 (commencing with Section 995.010) of Title 14 of Part 2 of the Code of Civil Procedure) applies to a bond given under this part, except to the extent this part prescribes a different rule or is inconsistent.

No previous text

Confirms that the Bond and Undertaking Law found in the Code of Civil Procedure applies to bonds issued under this part.

CC 8152

None of the following releases a surety from liability on a bond given under this part:

(a) A change, alteration, or modification to a contract, plan, specification, or agreement for a work of improvement or for work provided for a work of improvement.

(b) A change or modification to the terms of payment or an extension of the time for payment for a work of improvement.

(c) A rescission or attempted rescission of a contract, agreement, or bond.

(d) A condition precedent or subsequent in the bond purporting to limit the right of recovery of a claimant otherwise entitled to recover pursuant to a contract, agreement, or bond.

(e) In the case of a bond given for the benefit of claimants, the fraud of a person other than the claimant seeking to recover on the bond.

CC 3225

The surety or sureties on any bond given pursuant to any of the provisions of this title shall not be exonerated or released from the obligation of the bond by any change, alteration, or modification in or of any contract, plans, specifications, or agreement pertaining or relating to any scheme or work of improvement or pertaining or relating to the furnishing of labor, materials, or equipment therefor, nor by any change or modification of any terms of payment or extension of the time for any payment pertaining or relating to any scheme or work of improvement, nor by any rescission or attempted rescission of the contract, agreement or bond, nor by any conditions precedent or subsequent in the bond attempting to limit the right of recovery of claimants otherwise entitled to recover under any such contract or agreement or under the bond, nor, where the bond is given for the benefit of claimants, by any fraud practiced by any person other than the claimant seeking to recover on the bond.

CC 8154

(a) A bond given under this part shall be construed most strongly against the surety and in favor of all persons for whose benefit the bond is given.

(b) A surety is not released from liability to those for whose benefit the bond has been given by reason of a breach of the direct contract or on the part of any obligee named in the bond.

(c) Except as otherwise provided by statute, the sole conditions of recovery on the bond are that the claimant is a person described in Article 1 (commencing with Section 8400) of Chapter 4 of Title 2, or in Section 9100, and has not been paid the full amount of the claim.

CC 3226

Any bond given pursuant to the provisions of this title will be construed most strongly against the surety and in favor of all persons for whose benefit such bond is given, and under no circumstances shall a surety be released from liability to those for whose benefit such bond has been given, by reason of any breach of contract between the owner and original contractor or on the part of any obligee named in such bond, but the sole conditions of recovery shall be that claimant is a person described in Section 3110, 3111, or 3112, and has not been paid the full amount of his claim.

PART 6. WORKS OF IMPROVEMENT
TITLE 2. PRIVATE WORKS OF IMPROVEMENT
Chapter 1. General Provisions
Article 1. Application of Title

New Text (Operative July 1, 2012) | **Old Text**

CC 8160

This title applies to a work of improvement that is not governed by Title 3 (commencing with Section 9000) of this part.

CC 3109

This chapter does not apply to any public work.

••

CC 8160

This title applies to a work of improvement that is not governed by Title 3 (commencing with Section 9000) of this part.

CC 3156

The provisions of this chapter do not apply to any public work.

••

PART 6. WORKS OF IMPROVEMENT
TITLE 2. PRIVATE WORKS OF IMPROVEMENT
Chapter 1. General Provisions
Article 2. Construction Documents

CC 8170

(a) A written direct contract shall provide a space for the owner to enter the following information:

(1) The owner's name, address, and place of business, if any.

(2) The name and address of the construction lender, if any. This paragraph does not apply to a home improvement contract or swimming pool contract subject to Article 10 (commencing with Section 7150) of Chapter 9 of Division 3 of the Business and Professions Code.

(b) A written contract entered into between a direct contractor and subcontractor, or between subcontractors, shall provide a space for the name and address of the owner, direct contractor, and construction lender, if any.

CC 3097(l) and CC3097(m)

CC 3097(l):

(l) Every written contract entered into between a property owner and an original contractor shall provide space for the owner to enter his or her name, residence address, and place of business if any. The original contractor shall make available the name and address of residence of the owner to any person seeking to serve the notice specified in subdivision (c).

CC 3097(m):

(m) Every written contract entered into between a property owner and an original contractor, except home improvement contracts and swimming pool contracts subject to Article 10 (commencing with Section 7150) of Chapter 9 of Division 3 of the Business and Professions Code, shall provide space for the owner to enter the name and address of the construction lender or lenders. The original contractor shall make available the name and address of the construction lender or lenders to any person seeking to serve the notice specified in subdivision (c). Every contract entered into between an original contractor and subcontractor, and between subcontractors, shall provide a space for the name and address of the owner, original contractor, and any construction lender.

Combines prior Civil Code §§3097(l) and 3097(m) into a single Section. Clarifies that all subcontracts must provide a space for the name and address of the owner, direct contractor and the construction lender, if any.

••

New Text (Operative July 1, 2012) | **Old Text**

CC 8172

(a) A public entity that issues building permits shall, in its application form for a building permit, provide space and a designation for the applicant to enter the name, branch designation, if any, and address of the construction lender and shall keep the information on file open for public inspection during the regular business hours of the public entity.

(b) If there is no known construction lender, the applicant shall note that fact in the designated space.

(c) Failure of the applicant to indicate the name and address of the construction lender on the application does not relieve a person required to give the construction lender preliminary notice from that duty.

CC 3097(i)

(i) Every city, county, city and county, or other governmental authority issuing building permits shall, in its application form for a building permit, provide space and a designation for the applicant to enter the name, branch, designation, if any, and address of the construction lender and shall keep the information on file open for public inspection during the regular business hours of the authority.

If there is no known construction lender, that fact shall be noted in the designated space. Any failure to indicate the name and address of the construction lender on the application, however, shall not relieve any person from the obligation to give to the construction lender the notice required by this section.

Confirms that the building permit application shall provide space for the name, branch designation and address of construction lender.

Obligates applicant to fill in the construction lender information or note "no known lender" in the space provided for the lender's name.

Confirms that applicant's failure to provide construction lender information does not relieve person of the duty to provide the required preliminary notice.

••

CC 8174

(a) A mortgage, deed of trust, or other instrument securing a loan, any of the proceeds of which may be used for a work of improvement, shall bear the designation "Construction Trust Deed" prominently on its face and shall state all of the following:

(1) The name and address of the construction lender.

(2) The name and address of the owner of the real property described in the instrument.

(3) A legal description of the real property that secures the loan and, if known, the street address of the property.

(b) Failure to comply with subdivision (a) does not affect the validity of the mortgage, deed of trust, or other instrument.

(c) Failure to comply with subdivision (a) does not relieve a person required to give preliminary notice from that duty.

(d) The county recorder of the county in which the

CC 3097(j)

(j) A mortgage, deed of trust, or other instrument securing a loan, any of the proceeds of which may be used for the purpose of constructing improvements on real property, shall bear the designation "Construction Trust Deed" prominently on its face and shall state all of the following: (1) the name and address of the lender, and the name and address of the owner of the real property described in the instrument, and (2) a legal description of the real property that secures the loan and, if known, the street address of the property. The failure to be so designated or to state any of the information required by this subdivision shall not affect the validity of the mortgage, deed of trust, or other instrument.

Failure to provide this information on this instrument when recorded shall not relieve persons required to give preliminary notice under this section from that duty.

The county recorder of the county in which the

New Text (Operative July 1, 2012)	Old Text

instrument is recorded shall indicate in the general index of the official records of the county that the instrument secures a construction loan.

instrument is recorded shall indicate in the general index of the official records of the county that the instrument secures a construction loan.

Reaffirms requirements for construction deed of trust.
Confirms that the failure to include required information does not: (1) invalidate the deed of trust; or (2) relieve a person of the duty to provide the required preliminary notice.

••

PART 6. WORKS OF IMPROVEMENT
TITLE 2. PRIVATE WORKS OF IMPROVEMENT
Chapter 1. General Provisions
Article 3. Completion

CC 8180

(a) For the purpose of this title, completion of a work of improvement occurs upon the occurrence of any of the following events:
(1) Actual completion of the work of improvement.
(2) Occupation or use by the owner accompanied by cessation of labor.
(3) Cessation of labor for a continuous period of 60 days.
(4) Recordation of a notice of cessation after cessation of labor for a continuous period of 30 days.

(b) Notwithstanding subdivision (a), if a work of improvement is subject to acceptance by a public entity, completion occurs on acceptance.

CC 3086 (except subd (b))

"Completion" means, in the case of any work of improvement other than a public work, actual completion of the work of improvement. Any of the following shall be deemed equivalent to a completion:

(a) The occupation or use of a work of improvement by the owner, or his agent, accompanied by cessation of labor thereon.

(c) After the commencement of a work of improvement, a cessation of labor thereon for a continuous period of 60 days, or a cessation of labor thereon for a continuous period of 30 days or more if the owner files for record a notice of cessation.

If the work of improvement is subject to acceptance by any public entity, the completion of such work of improvement shall be deemed to be the date of such acceptance; provided, however, that, except as to contracts awarded under the State Contract Act, Chapter 3 (commencing with Section 14250), Part 5, Division 3, Title 2 of the Government Code, a cessation of labor on any public work for a continuous period of 30 days shall be a completion thereof.

Maintains indicia of completion.
Acceptance by the owner is no longer criteria for "completion".

••

New Text (Operative July 1, 2012)

CC 8182

(a) An owner may record a notice of completion on or within 15 days after the date of completion of a work of improvement.

(b) The notice of completion shall be signed and verified by the owner.

(c) The notice shall comply with the requirements of Chapter 2 (commencing with Section 8100) of Title 1, and shall also include all of the following information:

(1) If the notice is given only of completion of a contract for a particular portion of the work of improvement as provided in Section 8186, the name of the direct contractor under that contract and a general statement of the work provided pursuant to the contract.

(2) If signed by the owner's successor in interest, the name and address of the successor's transferor.

(3) The nature of the interest or estate of the owner.

(4) The date of completion. An erroneous statement of the date of completion does not affect the effectiveness of the notice if the true date of completion is 15 days or less before the date of recordation of the notice.

(d) A notice of completion that does not comply with the provisions of this section is not effective.

(e) For the purpose of this section, "owner" means the owner who causes a building, improvement, or structure to be constructed, altered, or repaired, or that person's successor in interest at the date a notice of completion is recorded, whether the interest or estate of the owner be in fee, as vendee under a contract of purchase, as lessee, or other interest or estate less than the fee. Where the interest or estate is held by two or more persons as joint tenants or tenants in common, any one or more of the cotenants may be deemed to be the "owner" within the meaning of this section.

Old Text

CC 3093

"Notice of completion" means a written notice, signed and verified by the owner or his agent, containing all of the following:

(a) The date of completion (other than a cessation of labor). The recital of an erroneous date of completion shall not, however, affect the validity of the notice if the true date of completion is within 10 days preceding the date of recording of such notice.

(b) The name and address of the owner.

(c) The nature of the interest or estate of the owner.

(d) A description of the site sufficient for identification, containing the street address of the site, if any. If a sufficient legal description of the site is given, the validity of the notice shall not, however, be affected by the fact that the street address recited is erroneous or that such street address is omitted.

(e) The name of the original contractor, if any, or if the notice is given only of completion of a contract for a particular portion of such work of improvement, as provided in Section 3117, then the name of the original contractor under such contract, and a general statement of the kind of work done or materials furnished pursuant to such contract.

The notice of completion shall be recorded in the office of the county recorder of the county in which the site is located, within 10 days after such completion. A notice of completion in otherwise proper form, verified and containing the information required by this section shall be accepted by the recorder for recording and shall be deemed duly recorded without acknowledgment.

If there is more than one owner, any notice of completion signed by less than all of such co-owners shall recite the names and addresses of all of such co-owners; and provided further, that any notice of completion signed by a successor in interest shall recite the names and addresses of his transferor or transferors.

For the purpose of this section, owner is defined as set forth in subdivision (g) of Section 3092.

Expands time period from 10 to 15 days. (see Section 8186).
Incorporates notice requirements found in Section 8100.
Allows for recordation of a Notice of Completion on specific direct contracts.
Defines owner; recognizes that the owner signing the notice of completion may be different than the owner that caused the improvement to be constructed (i.e., successor in interest).
Authorizes the owner to sign notice of completion on behalf of joint or co-owners.

New Text (Operative July 1, 2012)

CC 8184

A notice of completion in otherwise proper form, verified and containing the information required by this title, shall be accepted by the recorder for recording and is deemed duly recorded without acknowledgment.

Old Text

CC 3093

"Notice of completion" means a written notice, signed and verified by the owner or his agent, containing all of the following:

(a) The date of completion (other than a cessation of labor). The recital of an erroneous date of completion shall not, however, affect the validity of the notice if the true date of completion is within 10 days preceding the date of recording of such notice.

(b) The name and address of the owner.

(c) The nature of the interest or estate of the owner.

(d) A description of the site sufficient for identification, containing the street address of the site, if any. If a sufficient legal description of the site is given, the validity of the notice shall not, however, be affected by the fact that the street address recited is erroneous or that such street address is omitted.

(e) The name of the original contractor, if any, or if the notice is given only of completion of a contract for a particular portion of such work of improvement, as provided in Section 3117, then the name of the original contractor under such contract, and a general statement of the kind of work done or materials furnished pursuant to such contract.

The notice of completion shall be recorded in the office of the county recorder of the county in which the site is located, within 10 days after such completion. A notice of completion in otherwise proper form, verified and containing the information required by this section shall be accepted by the recorder for recording and shall be deemed duly recorded without acknowledgment.

If there is more than one owner, any notice of completion signed by less than all of such co-owners shall recite the names and addresses of all of such co-owners; and provided further, that any notice of completion signed by a successor in interest shall recite the names and addresses of his transferor or transferors.

For the purpose of this section, owner is defined as set forth in subdivision (g) of Section 3092.

Restates the recording protocol found in prior Civil Code §3093.

New Text (Operative July 1, 2012) | **Old Text**

CC 8186

If a work of improvement is made pursuant to two or more direct contracts, each covering a portion of the work of improvement:

(a) The owner may record a notice of completion of a direct contract for a portion of the work of improvement. On recordation of the notice of completion, for the purpose of Sections 8412 and 8414, a direct contractor is deemed to have completed the contract for which the notice of completion is recorded and a claimant other than a direct contractor is deemed to have ceased providing work.

(b) If the owner does not record a notice of completion under this section, the period for recording a claim of lien is that provided in Sections 8412 and 8414.

CC 3117

Where the work of improvement is not made pursuant to one original contract for the work of improvement but is made in whole or in part pursuant to two or more original contracts, each covering a particular portion of the work of improvement, the owner may, within 10 days after completion of any such contract for a particular portion of the work of improvement, record a notice of completion. If such notice of completion be recorded, notwithstanding the provisions of Sections 3115 and 3116, the original contractor under the contract covered by such notice must, within 60 days after recording of such notice, and any claimant under such contract other than the original contractor must, within 30 days after the recording of such notice of completion, record his claim of lien. If such notice is not recorded, then the period for recording claims of lien shall be as provided for in Sections 3115 and 3116.

Confirms owner's right to record separate notices of completion for each direct contract.
Time limit to record notice of completion on multi-"direct" contracts is eliminated.
References Sections 8412 and 8414 for time period to record lien or serve stop payment notice.

CC 8188

(a) An owner may record a notice of cessation if there has been a continuous cessation of labor on a work of improvement for at least 30 days prior to the recordation that continues through the date of the recordation.

(b) The notice shall be signed and verified by the owner.

(c) The notice shall comply with the requirements of Chapter 2 (commencing with Section 8100) of Title 1, and shall also include all of the following information:

(1) The date on or about which labor ceased.

(2) A statement that the cessation has continued until the recordation of the notice.

(d) For the purpose of this section, "owner" means the owner who causes a building, improvement, or structure to be constructed, altered, or repaired, or that person's successor in interest at the date a notice of cessation is recorded, whether the interest or estate of the owner be in fee, as vendee under a contract of purchase, as lessee, or other interest or estate less than the fee. Where the interest or estate is held by two or more persons as joint tenants or tenants in common, any one or more of the cotenants may be deemed to be

CC 3092

"Notice of cessation" means a written notice, signed and verified by the owner or his agent, containing all of the following:

(a) The date on or about when the cessation of labor commenced.

(b) A statement that such cessation has continued until the recording of the notice of cessation.

(c) The name and address of the owner.

(d) The nature of the interest or estate of the owner.

(e) A description of the site sufficient for identification, containing the street address of the site, if any. If a sufficient legal description of the site is given, the validity of the notice shall not, however, be affected by the fact that the street address is erroneous or is omitted.

(f) The name of the original contractor, if any, for the work of improvement as a whole.

(g) For the purpose of this section, "owner" means the owner who causes a building, improvement, or structure, to be constructed, altered, or repaired (or his successor in interest at the date of a notice of cessation from labor is filed for record) whether the interest or estate of such owner be in

New Text (Operative July 1, 2012) | **Old Text**

the "owner" within the meaning of this section.

fee, as vendee under a contract of purchase, as lessee, or other interest or estate less than the fee. Where such interest or estate is held by two or more persons as joint tenants or tenants in common, any one or more of the co-tenants may be deemed to be the "owner" within the meaning of this section. Any notice of cessation signed by less than all of such co-tenants shall recite the names and addresses of all such co-tenants.

The notice of cessation shall be recorded in the office of the county recorder of the county in which the site is located and shall be effective only if there has been a continuous cessation of labor for at least 30 days prior to such recording.

Requires continuous cessation of labor for at least 30 days.
Incorporates notice requirements from Section 8100 et seq.
Restates definition of owner (see Section 8182).

••

CC 8190

(a) An owner that records a notice of completion or cessation shall, within 10 days of the date the notice of completion or cessation is filed for record, give a copy of the notice to all of the following persons:

(1) A direct contractor.

(2) A claimant that has given the owner preliminary notice.

(b) The copy of the notice shall be given in compliance with the requirements of Chapter 2 (commencing with Section 8100) of Title 1.

(c) If the owner fails to give notice to a person as required by subdivision (a), the notice is ineffective to shorten the time within which that person may record a claim of lien under Sections 8412 and 8414. The ineffectiveness of the notice is the sole liability of the owner for failure to give notice to a person under subdivision (a).

(d) For the purpose of this section, "owner" means a person who has an interest in real property, or the person's successor in interest on the date a notice of completion or notice of cessation is recorded, who causes a building, improvement, or structure, to be constructed, altered, or repaired on the property. If the property is owned by two or more persons as joint tenants or tenants in common, any one or more of the

CC 3259.5

(a) The owner of a private work of improvement shall notify the original contractor, and any claimant other than the original contractor who has provided a preliminary 20-day notice in accordance with Section 3097, that a notice of completion or notice of cessation has been recorded. The notice shall be sent within 10 days after recordation of the notice of completion or notice of cessation. Notification shall be sent by registered or certified mail, or by first-class mail, evidenced by a certificate of mailing. Failure to give notice to a contractor or claimant within 10 days of recording the notice of completion or notice of cessation shall extend the period of time in which that contractor or claimant may file a Mechanic's lien or stop notice to 90 days beyond the date that a notice of completion or notice of cessation has been recorded. The sole liability for failing to give notice shall be the extension of the period of time in which that contractor or claimant may file a Mechanic's lien or stop notice.

(b) For purposes of this section, "owner" means a person who has an interest in real property, or the person's successor in interest on the date a notice of completion or notice of cessation from labor is filed for record, who causes a building, improvement, or structure, to be constructed, altered, or repaired on the property. If the property is owned by two or more persons as joint

New Text (Operative July 1, 2012)	Old Text
cotenants may be deemed to be the "owner" within the meaning of this section. However, this section does not apply to any of the following owners: *(1) A person that occupies the real property as a personal residence, if the dwelling contains four or fewer residential units.* *(2) A person that has a security interest in the property.* *(3) A person that obtains an interest in the property pursuant to a transfer described in subdivision (b), (c), or (d) of Section 1102.2.*	tenants or tenants in common, any one or more of the cotenants may be deemed to be the "owner" within the meaning of this section. However, "owner" does not include a person who occupies the real property as a personal residence and the dwelling contains not more than four residential units, nor does it include a person who has a security interest in the property or obtains an interest pursuant to a transfer described in subdivision (b), (c), or (d) of Section 1102.2.

Mandates that owner provide notice of recording notice of completion to: (1) direct contractor; and (2) claimants that provided preliminary notice.

Notice to comply with Section 8100 et seq.

Failure to provide notice renders notice of completion ineffective to shorten time for recording lien.

Restates definition of owner (see Section 8182), but includes three exceptions: (1) person that occupies real property as personal residence; (2) person that has security interest in the property; and (3) person that obtains interest in property pursuant to transfer described in Section 1102.2(b), (c) or (d).

New Text (Operative July 1, 2012) | Old Text

PART 6. WORKS OF IMPROVEMENT
TITLE 2. PRIVATE WORKS OF IMPROVEMENT
Chapter 2. Preliminary Notice

CC 8200

(a) Except as otherwise provided by statute, before recording a lien claim, giving a stop payment notice, or asserting a claim against a payment bond, a claimant shall give preliminary notice to the following persons:

(1) The owner or reputed owner.

(2) The direct contractor or reputed direct contractor to which the claimant provides work, either directly or through one or more subcontractors.

(3) The construction lender or reputed construction lender, if any.

(b) The notice shall comply with the requirements of Chapter 2 (commencing with Section 8100) of Title 1.

(c) Compliance with this section is a necessary prerequisite to the validity of a lien claim or stop payment notice under this title.

(d) Compliance with this section or with Section 8612 is a necessary prerequisite to the validity of a claim against a payment bond under this title.

(e) Notwithstanding the foregoing subdivisions:

(1) A laborer is not required to give preliminary notice.

(2) A claimant with a direct contractual relationship with an owner or reputed owner is required to give preliminary notice only to the construction lender or reputed construction lender, if any.

CC 3097, CC 3097(a) and CC 3097(b)

CC 3097

"Preliminary 20-day notice (private work)" means a written notice from a claimant that is given prior to the recording of a Mechanic's lien, prior to the filing of a stop notice, and prior to asserting a claim against a payment bond, and is required to be given under the following circumstances:

(a) Except one under direct contract with the owner or one performing actual labor for wages as described in subdivision (a) of Section 3089, or a person or entity to whom a portion of a laborer's compensation is paid as described in subdivision (b) of Section 3089, every person who furnishes labor, service, equipment, or material for which a lien or payment bond otherwise can be claimed under this title, or for which a notice to withhold can otherwise be given under this title, shall, as a necessary prerequisite to the validity of any claim of lien, payment bond, and of a notice to withhold, cause to be given to the owner or reputed owner, to the original contractor, or reputed contractor, and to the construction lender, if any, or to the reputed construction lender, if any, a written preliminary notice as prescribed by this section.

(b) Except the contractor, or one performing actual labor for wages as described in subdivision (a) of Section 3089, or a person or entity to whom a portion of a laborer's compensation is paid as described in subdivision (b) of Section 3089, all persons who have a direct contract with the owner and who furnish labor, service, equipment, or material for which a lien or payment bond otherwise can be claimed under this title, or for which a notice to withhold can otherwise be given under this title, shall, as a necessary prerequisite to the validity of any claim of lien, claim on a payment bond, and of a notice to withhold, cause to be given to the construction lender, if any, or to the reputed construction lender, if any, a written preliminary notice as prescribed by this section.

(c) The preliminary notice referred to in subdivisions (a) and (b) shall contain the following information:

(1) A general description of the labor, service, equipment, or materials furnished, or to be furnished, and an estimate of the total price thereof.

New Text (Operative July 1, 2012)	Old Text

(2) The name and address of the person furnishing that labor, service, equipment, or materials.

(3) The name of the person who contracted for purchase of that labor, service, equipment, or materials.

(4) A description of the jobsite sufficient for identification.

(5) The following statement in boldface type:

NOTICE TO PROPERTY OWNER

If bills are not paid in full for the labor, services, equipment, or materials furnished or to be furnished, a Mechanic's lien leading to the loss, through court foreclosure proceedings, of all or part of your property being so improved may be placed against the property even though you have paid your contractor in full. You may wish to protect yourself against this consequence by (1) requiring your contractor to furnish a signed release by the person or firm giving you this notice before making payment to your contractor, or (2) any other method or device that is appropriate under the circumstances. Other than residential homeowners of dwellings containing fewer than five units, private project owners must notify the original contractor and any lien claimant who has provided the owner with a preliminary 20-day lien notice in accordance with Section 3097 of the Civil Code that a notice of completion or notice of cessation has been recorded within 10 days of its recordation. Notice shall be by registered mail, certified mail, or first-class mail, evidenced by a certificate of mailing. Failure to notify will extend the deadlines to record a lien.

(6) If the notice is given by a subcontractor who has failed to pay all compensation due to his or her laborers on the job, the notice shall also contain the identity and address of any laborer and any express trust fund to whom employer payments are due. If an invoice for materials or certified payroll contains the information required by this section, a copy of the invoice, transmitted in the manner prescribed by this section shall be sufficient notice.

A certificated architect, registered engineer, or licensed land surveyor who has furnished services for the design of the work of improvement and who gives a preliminary notice as provided in this section not later than 20 days after the work of improvement

New Text (Operative July 1, 2012)	Old Text

has commenced shall be deemed to have complied with subdivisions (a) and (b) with respect to architectural, engineering, or surveying services furnished, or to be furnished.

(d) The preliminary notice referred to in subdivisions (a) and (b) shall be given not later than 20 days after the claimant has first furnished labor, service, equipment, or materials to the jobsite. If labor, service, equipment, or materials have been furnished to a jobsite by a claimant who did not give a preliminary notice, that claimant shall not be precluded from giving a preliminary notice at any time thereafter. The claimant shall, however, be entitled to record a lien, file a stop notice, and assert a claim against a payment bond only for labor, service, equipment, or material furnished within 20 days prior to the service of the preliminary notice, and at any time thereafter.

(e) Any agreement made or entered into by an owner, whereby the owner agrees to waive the rights or privileges conferred upon the owner by this section shall be void and of no effect.

(f) The notice required under this section may be served as follows:

(1) If the person to be notified resides in this state, by delivering the notice personally, or by leaving it at his or her address of residence or place of business with some person in charge, or by first-class registered or certified mail, postage prepaid, addressed to the person to whom notice is to be given at his or her residence or place of business address or at the address shown by the building permit on file with the authority issuing a building permit for the work, or at an address recorded pursuant to subdivision (j).

(2) If the person to be notified does not reside in this state, by any method enumerated in paragraph (1) of this subdivision. If the person cannot be served by any of these methods, then notice may be given by first-class certified or registered mail, addressed to the construction lender or to the original contractor.

(3) If service is made by first-class certified or registered mail, service is complete at the time of the deposit of that registered or certified mail.

(g) A person required by this section to give notice to the owner, to an original contractor, and to a person to whom a notice to withhold may be given, need give only one notice to the owner, to the original contractor,

New Text (Operative July 1, 2012)	Old Text

and to the person to whom a notice to withhold may be given with respect to all materials, services, labor, or equipment he or she furnishes for a work of improvement, that means the entire structure or scheme of improvements as a whole, unless the same is furnished under contracts with more than one subcontractor, in which event, the notice requirements shall be met with respect to materials, services, labor, or equipment furnished to each contractor.

If a notice contains a general description required by subdivision (a) or (b) of the materials, services, labor, or equipment furnished to the date of notice, it is not defective because, after that date, the person giving notice furnishes materials, services, labor, or equipment not within the scope of this general description.

(h) If the contract price to be paid to any subcontractor on a particular work of improvement exceeds four hundred dollars ($400), the failure of that contractor, licensed under Chapter 9 (commencing with Section 7000) of Division 3 of the Business and Professions Code, to give the notice provided for in this section, constitutes grounds for disciplinary action by the Registrar of Contractors.

If the notice is required to contain the information set forth in paragraph (6) of subdivision (c), a failure to give the notice, including that information, that results in the filing of a lien, claim on a payment bond, or the delivery of a stop notice by the express trust fund to which the obligation is owing constitutes grounds for disciplinary action by the Registrar of Contractors against the subcontractor if the amount due the trust fund is not paid.

(i) Every city, county, city and county, or other governmental authority issuing building permits shall, in its application form for a building permit, provide space and a designation for the applicant to enter the name, branch, designation, if any, and address of the construction lender and shall keep the information on file open for public inspection during the regular business hours of the authority.

If there is no known construction lender, that fact shall be noted in the designated space. Any failure to indicate the name and address of the construction lender on the application, however, shall not relieve any person from the obligation to give to the construction lender the notice required by this section.

(j) A mortgage, deed of trust, or other instrument securing a loan, any of the proceeds of which may be used for the

New Text (Operative July 1, 2012)	Old Text

purpose of constructing improvements on real property, shall bear the designation "Construction Trust Deed" prominently on its face and shall state all of the following: (1) the name and address of the lender, and the name and address of the owner of the real property described in the instrument, and (2) a legal description of the real property that secures the loan and, if known, the street address of the property. The failure to be so designated or to state any of the information required by this subdivision shall not affect the validity of the mortgage, deed of trust, or other instrument.

Failure to provide this information on this instrument when recorded shall not relieve persons required to give preliminary notice under this section from that duty.

The county recorder of the county in which the instrument is recorded shall indicate in the general index of the official records of the county that the instrument secures a construction loan.

(k) Every contractor and subcontractor employing laborers as described in subdivision (a) of Section 3089 who has failed to pay those laborers their full compensation when it became due, including any employer payments described in Section 1773.1 of the Labor Code and regulations adopted thereunder shall, without regard to whether the work was performed on a public or private work, cause to be given to those laborers, their bargaining representatives, if any, and to the construction lender, if any, or to the reputed construction lender, if any, not later than the date the compensation became delinquent, a written notice containing all of the following:

(1) The name of the owner and the contractor.

(2) A description of the jobsite sufficient for identification.

(3) The identity and address of any express trust fund described in Section 3111 to which employer payments are due.

(4) The total number of straight time and overtime hours on each job.

(5) The amount then past due and owing.

Failure to give this notice shall constitute grounds for disciplinary action by the Registrar of Contractors.

(l) Every written contract entered into between a property owner and an original contractor shall provide space for the owner to enter his or her name, residence address, and place of business if any. The original

New Text (Operative July 1, 2012)	Old Text

contractor shall make available the name and address of residence of the owner to any person seeking to serve the notice specified in subdivision (c).

(m) Every written contract entered into between a property owner and an original contractor, except home improvement contracts and swimming pool contracts subject to Article 10 (commencing with Section 7150) of Chapter 9 of Division 3 of the Business and Professions Code, shall provide space for the owner to enter the name and address of the construction lender or lenders. The original contractor shall make available the name and address of the construction lender or lenders to any person seeking to serve the notice specified in subdivision (c). Every contract entered into between an original contractor and subcontractor, and between subcontractors, shall provide a space for the name and address of the owner, original contractor, and any construction lender.

(n) If one or more construction loans are obtained after commencement of construction, the property owner shall provide the name and address of the construction lender or lenders to each person who has given the property owner the notice specified in subdivision (c).

(o)(1) Each person who has served a preliminary 20-day notice pursuant to subdivision (f) may file the preliminary 20-day notice with the county recorder in the county in which any portion of the property is located. A preliminary 20-day notice filed pursuant to this section shall contain all of the following:

(A) The name and address of the person furnishing the labor, service, equipment, or materials.

(B) The name of the person who contracted for purchase of the labor, services, equipment, or materials.

(C) The common street address of the jobsite.

(2) Upon the acceptance for recording of a notice of completion or notice of cessation the county recorder shall mail to those persons who have filed a preliminary 20-day notice, notification that a notice of completion or notice of cessation has been recorded on the property, and shall affix the date that the notice of completion or notice of cessation was recorded with the county recorder.

(3) The failure of the county recorder to mail the notification to the person who filed a preliminary 20-day notice, or the failure of those persons to receive the notification or to receive complete notification,

New Text (Operative July 1, 2012)	Old Text

shall not affect the period within which a claim of lien is required to be recorded. However, the county recorder shall make a good faith effort to mail notification to those persons who have filed the preliminary 20-day notice under this section and to do so within five days after the recording of a notice of completion or notice of cessation.

(4) This new function of the county recorder shall not become operative until July 1, 1988. The county recorder may cause to be destroyed all documents filed pursuant to this section, two years after the date of filing.

(5) The preliminary 20-day notice that a person may file pursuant to this subdivision is for the limited purpose of facilitating the mailing of notice by the county recorder of recorded notices of completion and notices of cessation. The notice that is filed is not a recordable document and shall not be entered into those official records of the county which by law impart constructive notice.

Notwithstanding any other provision of law, the index maintained by the recorder of filed preliminary 20-day notices shall be separate and distinct from those indexes maintained by the county recorder of those official records of the county which by law impart constructive notice. The filing of a preliminary 20-day notice with the county recorder does not give rise to any actual or constructive notice with respect to any party of the existence or contents of a filed preliminary 20-day notice nor to any duty of inquiry on the part of any party as to the existence or contents of that notice.

(p)(1) The change made to the statement described in subdivision (c) by Chapter 974 of the Statutes of 1994 shall have no effect upon the validity of any notice that otherwise meets the requirements of this section. The failure to provide, pursuant to Chapter 974 of the Statutes of 1994, a written preliminary notice to a subcontractor with whom the claimant has contracted shall not affect the validity of any preliminary notice provided pursuant to this section.

(2)(A) The inclusion of the language added to paragraph (5) of subdivision (c) by Chapter 795 of the Statutes of 1999, shall not affect the validity of any preliminary notice given on or after January 1, 2000, and prior to the operative date of the amendments to this section enacted at the 2000 portion of the 1999-

New Text (Operative July 1, 2012)	Old Text

2000 Regular Session, that otherwise meets the requirements of that subdivision.

(B) A preliminary notice given on or after January 1, 2000, and prior to the operative date of the amendments to this section enacted at the 2000 portion of the 1999-2000 Regular Session, shall not be invalid because of the failure to include the language added to paragraph (5) of subdivision (c) by Chapter 795 of the Statutes of 1999, if the notice otherwise complies with that subdivision.

(C) The failure to provide an affidavit form or notice of rights, or both, pursuant to the requirements of Chapter 795 of the Statutes of 1999, shall not affect the validity of any preliminary notice pursuant to this section.

CC 3097(a):

(a) Except one under direct contract with the owner or one performing actual labor for wages as described in subdivision (a) of Section 3089, or a person or entity to whom a portion of a laborer's compensation is paid as described in subdivision (b) of Section 3089, every person who furnishes labor, service, equipment, or material for which a lien or payment bond otherwise can be claimed under this title, or for which a notice to withhold can otherwise be given under this title, shall, as a necessary prerequisite to the validity of any claim of lien, payment bond, and of a notice to withhold, cause to be given to the owner or reputed owner, to the original contractor, or reputed contractor, and to the construction lender, if any, or to the reputed construction lender, if any, a written preliminary notice as prescribed by this section.

New Text (Operative July 1, 2012)	Old Text
	CC 3097(b): (b) Except the contractor, or one performing actual labor for wages as described in subdivision (a) of Section 3089, or a person or entity to whom a portion of a laborer's compensation is paid as described in subdivision (b) of Section 3089, all persons who have a direct contract with the owner and who furnish labor, service, equipment, or material for which a lien or payment bond otherwise can be claimed under this title, or for which a notice to withhold can otherwise be given under this title, shall, as a necessary prerequisite to the validity of any claim of lien, claim on a payment bond, and of a notice to withhold, cause to be given to the construction lender, if any, or to the reputed construction lender, if any, a written preliminary notice as prescribed by this section.

Affirms that preliminary notice is a statutory prerequisite to recording a lien, giving a stop payment notice, or asserting a payment bond claim (unless claimant complies with Civil Code §8612).
Incorporates notice requirements from Section 8100, et seq.
Clarifies that: Direct Contractor must provide preliminary notice to construction lender or reputed construction lender; and that a laborer (see Definition, Civil Code §8024) needs not serve a preliminary notice.

New Text (Operative July 1, 2012)

CC 8202

(a) The preliminary notice shall comply with the requirements of Section 8102, and shall also include:

(1) A general description of the work to be provided.

(2) An estimate of the total price of the work provided and to be provided.

(3) The following statement in boldface type:

NOTICE TO PROPERTY OWNER

EVEN THOUGH YOU HAVE PAID YOUR CONTRACTOR IN FULL, if the person or firm that has given you this notice is not paid in full for labor, service, equipment, or material provided or to be provided to your construction project, a lien may be placed on your property. Foreclosure of the lien may lead to loss of all or part of your property. You may wish to protect yourself against this by (1) requiring your contractor to provide a signed release by the person or firm that has given you this notice before making payment to your contractor, or (2) any other method that is appropriate under the circumstances.

This notice is required by law to be served by the undersigned as a statement of your legal rights. This notice is not intended to reflect upon the financial condition of the contractor or the person employed by you on the construction project.

If you record a notice of cessation or completion of your construction project, you must within 10 days after recording, send a copy of the notice of completion to your contractor and the person or firm that has given you this notice. The notice must be sent by registered or certified mail. Failure to send the notice will extend the deadline to record a claim of lien. You are not required to send the notice if you are a residential homeowner of a dwelling containing four or fewer units.

(b) If preliminary notice is given by a subcontractor that has not paid all compensation due to a laborer, the notice shall include the name and address of the laborer and any person or entity described in subdivision (b) of Section 8024 to which payments are due.

(c) If an invoice for material or certified payroll contains the information required by this section and Section 8102, a copy of the invoice or payroll, given in compliance with the requirements of Chapter 2 (commencing with Section 8100) of Title 1, is sufficient.

Old Text

CC 3097(c)

(c) The preliminary notice referred to in subdivisions (a) and (b) shall contain the following information:

(1) A general description of the labor, service, equipment, or materials furnished, or to be furnished, and an estimate of the total price thereof.

(2) The name and address of the person furnishing that labor, service, equipment, or materials.

(3) The name of the person who contracted for purchase of that labor, service, equipment, or materials.

(4) A description of the jobsite sufficient for identification.

(5) The following statement in boldface type:

NOTICE TO PROPERTY OWNER

If bills are not paid in full for the labor, services, equipment, or materials furnished or to be furnished, a Mechanic's lien leading to the loss, through court foreclosure proceedings, of all or part of your property being so improved may be placed against the property even though you have paid your contractor in full. You may wish to protect yourself against this consequence by (1) requiring your contractor to furnish a signed release by the person or firm giving you this notice before making payment to your contractor, or (2) any other method or device that is appropriate under the circumstances. Other than residential homeowners of dwellings containing fewer than five units, private project owners must notify the original contractor and any lien claimant who has provided the owner with a preliminary 20-day lien notice in accordance with Section 3097 of the Civil Code that a notice of completion or notice of cessation has been recorded within 10 days of its recordation. Notice shall be by registered mail, certified mail, or first-class mail, evidenced by a certificate of mailing. Failure to notify will extend the deadlines to record a lien.

(6) If the notice is given by a subcontractor who has failed to pay all compensation due to his or her laborers on the job, the notice shall also contain the identity and address of any laborer and any express trust fund to whom employer payments are due. If an invoice for materials or certified payroll contains the information required by this section, a copy of the invoice, transmitted in the manner prescribed by this section shall be sufficient notice.

A certificated architect, registered engineer, or licensed land surveyor who has furnished services for the design of the work of improvement and who

New Text (Operative July 1, 2012) | **Old Text**

gives a preliminary notice as provided in this section not later than 20 days after the work of improvement has commenced shall be deemed to have complied with subdivisions (a) and (b) with respect to architectural, engineering, or surveying services furnished, or to be furnished.

Incorporates the requirements from Section 8100 et seq. and specifically Section 8102.
Establishes requirements for preliminary notice.
Expands "notice to property owner" found in prior law (see former Civil Code § 3097(c)).
References the requirement that an owner must send a copy of any notice of completion or notice of cessation to the person providing the preliminary notice.

••

CC 8204

(a) A preliminary notice shall be given not later than 20 days after the claimant has first furnished work on the work of improvement. If work has been provided by a claimant who did not give a preliminary notice, that claimant shall not be precluded from giving a preliminary notice at any time thereafter. The claimant shall, however, be entitled to record a lien, give a stop payment notice, and assert a claim against a payment bond only for work performed within 20 days prior to the service of the preliminary notice, and at any time thereafter.

(b) A design professional who has furnished services for the design of the work of improvement and who gives a preliminary notice not later than 20 days after the work of improvement has commenced shall be deemed to have complied with Section 8200 with respect to the design services furnished, or to be furnished.

CC 3097(d)

(d) The preliminary notice referred to in subdivisions (a) and (b) shall be given not later than 20 days after the claimant has first furnished labor, service, equipment, or materials to the jobsite. If labor, service, equipment, or materials have been furnished to a jobsite by a claimant who did not give a preliminary notice, that claimant shall not be precluded from giving a preliminary notice at any time thereafter. The claimant shall, however, be entitled to record a lien, file a stop notice, and assert a claim against a payment bond only for labor, service, equipment, or material furnished within 20 days prior to the service of the preliminary notice, and at any time thereafter.

Reaffirms the time for giving the preliminary notice.
Preserves the "late notice" curative provision.
Establishes the time period for design professionals to give a preliminary notice.

••

New Text (Operative July 1, 2012) | **Old Text**

CC 8206

(a) Except as provided in subdivision (b), a claimant need give only one preliminary notice to each person to which notice must be given under this chapter with respect to all work provided by the claimant for a work of improvement.

(b) If a claimant provides work pursuant to contracts with more than one subcontractor, the claimant shall give a separate preliminary notice with respect to work provided pursuant to each contract.

(c) A preliminary notice that contains a general description of work provided by the claimant through the date of the notice also covers work provided by the claimant after the date of the notice whether or not they are within the scope of the general description contained in the notice.

CC 3097(g)

(g) A person required by this section to give notice to the owner, to an original contractor, and to a person to whom a notice to withhold may be given, need give only one notice to the owner, to the original contractor, and to the person to whom a notice to withhold may be given with respect to all materials, services, labor, or equipment he or she furnishes for a work of improvement, that means the entire structure or scheme of improvements as a whole, unless the same is furnished under contracts with more than one subcontractor, in which event, the notice requirements shall be met with respect to materials, services, labor, or equipment furnished to each contractor.

If a notice contains a general description required by subdivision (a) or (b) of the materials, services, labor, or equipment furnished to the date of notice, it is not defective because, after that date, the person giving notice furnishes materials, services, labor, or equipment not within the scope of this general description.

Maintains the separate notice requirement if claimant is providing work to more than one subcontractor.

•••

CC 8208

A direct contractor shall make available to any person seeking to give preliminary notice the following information:

(a) The name and address of the owner.

(b) The name and address of the construction lender, if any.

CC 3097(l) and CC3097(m)

CC 3097(l):

(l) Every written contract entered into between a property owner and an original contractor shall provide space for the owner to enter his or her name, residence address, and place of business if any. The original contractor shall make available the name and address of residence of the owner to any person seeking to serve the notice specified in subdivision (c).

CC 3097(m):

(m) Every written contract entered into between a property owner and an original contractor, except home improvement contracts and swimming pool contracts subject to Article 10 (commencing with Section 7150) of Chapter 9 of Division 3 of the Business and Professions Code, shall provide space for the owner to enter the name and address of the construction lender or lenders. The original contractor shall make available the name and address of the construction lender or lenders to any person seeking to serve the notice specified in subdivision (c). Every contract entered into between an original contractor and subcontractor, and between subcontractors, shall provide a space for the name and address of the owner, original contractor, and any construction lender

Confirms direct contractor's obligation to make available to any person the name and address of the owner and construction lender.

•••

New Text (Operative July 1, 2012) | **Old Text**

CC 8210

If one or more construction loans are obtained after commencement of a work of improvement, the owner shall give notice of the name and address of the construction lender or lenders to each person that has given the owner preliminary notice.

CC 3097(n)

(n) If one or more construction loans are obtained after commencement of construction, the property owner shall provide the name and address of the construction lender or lenders to each person who has given the property owner the notice specified in subdivision (c).

Confirms owner's obligation to give notice to all persons that provided a preliminary notice of the name and address of construction lender(s) obtained after the commencement of the work.

••

CC 8212

An agreement made or entered into by an owner whereby the owner agrees to waive the rights conferred on the owner by this chapter is void and unenforceable.

CC 3097(e)

(e) Any agreement made or entered into by an owner, whereby the owner agrees to waive the rights or privileges conferred upon the owner by this section shall be void and of no effect.

••

CC 8214

(a) Each person who has served a preliminary notice may file the preliminary notice with the county recorder. A preliminary notice filed pursuant to this section shall comply with the requirements of Section 8102.

(b) Upon the acceptance for recording of a notice of completion or notice of cessation the county recorder shall mail to those persons who have filed a preliminary notice, notification that a notice of completion or notice of cessation has been recorded on the property, and shall affix the date that the notice of completion or notice of cessation was recorded with the county recorder. The notification given by the county recorder under this section is not governed by the requirements of Chapter 2 (commencing with Section 8100) of Title 1.

(c) The failure of the county recorder to mail the notification to the person who filed a preliminary notice, or the failure of those persons to receive the notification or to receive complete notification, shall not affect the period within which a claim of lien is required to be recorded. However, the

CC 3097(o)

(o)(1) Each person who has served a preliminary 20-day notice pursuant to subdivision (f) may file the preliminary 20-day notice with the county recorder in the county in which any portion of the property is located. A preliminary 20-day notice filed pursuant to this section shall contain all of the following:

(A) The name and address of the person furnishing the labor, service, equipment, or materials.

(B) The name of the person who contracted for purchase of the labor, services, equipment, or materials.

(C) The common street address of the jobsite.

(2) Upon the acceptance for recording of a notice of completion or notice of cessation the county recorder shall mail to those persons who have filed a preliminary 20-day notice, notification that a notice of completion or notice of cessation has been recorded on the property, and shall affix the date that the notice of completion or notice of cessation was recorded with the county recorder.

(3) The failure of the county recorder to mail the notification to the person who filed a preliminary 20-

New Text (Operative July 1, 2012)

county recorder shall make a good faith effort to mail notification to those persons who have filed the preliminary notice under this section and to do so within five days after the recording of a notice of completion or notice of cessation.

(d) The county recorder may cause to be destroyed all documents filed pursuant to this section, two years after the date of filing.

(e) The preliminary notice that a person may file pursuant to this section is for the limited purpose of facilitating the mailing of notice by the county recorder of recorded notices of completion and notices of cessation. The notice that is filed is not a recordable document and shall not be entered into those official records of the county which by law impart constructive notice. Notwithstanding any other provision of law, the index maintained by the recorder of filed preliminary notices shall be separate and distinct from those indexes maintained by the county recorder of those official records of the county which by law impart constructive notice. The filing of a preliminary notice with the county recorder does not give rise to any actual or constructive notice with respect to any party of the existence or contents of a filed preliminary notice nor to any duty of inquiry on the part of any party as to the existence or contents of that notice.

Old Text

day notice, or the failure of those persons to receive the notification or to receive complete notification, shall not affect the period within which a claim of lien is required to be recorded. However, the county recorder shall make a good faith effort to mail notification to those persons who have filed the preliminary 20-day notice under this section and to do so within five days after the recording of a notice of completion or notice of cessation.

(4) This new function of the county recorder shall not become operative until July 1, 1988. The county recorder may cause to be destroyed all documents filed pursuant to this section, two years after the date of filing.

(5) The preliminary 20-day notice that a person may file pursuant to this subdivision is for the limited purpose of facilitating the mailing of notice by the county recorder of recorded notices of completion and notices of cessation. The notice that is filed is not a recordable document and shall not be entered into those official records of the county which by law impart constructive notice.

Notwithstanding any other provision of law, the index maintained by the recorder of filed preliminary 20-day notices shall be separate and distinct from those indexes maintained by the county recorder of those official records of the county which by law impart constructive notice. The filing of a preliminary 20-day notice with the county recorder does not give rise to any actual or constructive notice with respect to any party of the existence or contents of a filed preliminary 20-day notice nor to any duty of inquiry on the part of any party as to the existence or contents of that notice.

Preserves the practice of filing the preliminary notice with the County Recorder and the County Recorder's duty to notify persons that filed a preliminary notice of the recording of a notice of completion or notice of cessation

New Text (Operative July 1, 2012)

CC 8216

If the contract of any subcontractor on a particular work of improvement provides for payment to the subcontractor of more than four hundred dollars ($400), the failure of that subcontractor, licensed under the Contractors' State License Law (Chapter 9 (commencing with Section 7000) of Division 3 of the Business and Professions Code), to give the notice provided for in this chapter, constitutes grounds for disciplinary action under the Contractors' State License Law.

Old Text

CC 3097(h)

(h) If the contract price to be paid to any subcontractor on a particular work of improvement exceeds four hundred dollars ($400), the failure of that contractor, licensed under Chapter 9 (commencing with Section 7000) of Division 3 of the Business and Professions Code, to give the notice provided for in this section, constitutes grounds for disciplinary action by the Registrar of Contractors.

If the notice is required to contain the information set forth in paragraph (6) of subdivision (c), a failure to give the notice, including that information, that results in the filing of a lien, claim on a payment bond, or the delivery of a stop notice by the express trust fund to which the obligation is owing constitutes grounds for disciplinary action by the Registrar of Contractors against the subcontractor if the amount due the trust fund is not paid.

Mandates that subcontractors serve a preliminary notice if subcontract price exceeds $400.00.

New Text (Operative July 1, 2012) | **Old Text**

PART 6. WORKS OF IMPROVEMENT
TITLE 2. PRIVATE WORKS OF IMPROVEMENT
Chapter 3. Design Professionals Lien

CC 8300

For purposes of this chapter, a "design professional" is a person described in Section 8014 who provides services pursuant to a written contract with a landowner for the design, engineering, or planning of a work of improvement.

CC 3081.1

For purposes of this chapter, "design professional" means any certificated architect, registered professional engineer, or licensed land surveyor who furnishes services pursuant to a written contract with a landowner for the design, engineering, or planning of a work of improvement.

Except as otherwise expressly provided, the definition in this section does not apply to, or limit or expand the meaning of, provisions of law other than this chapter.

Incorporates definition from Section 8014.
Adds "licensed landscape architects," under Business & Profession Code §5615, to list of Design Professionals.

•••

CC 8302

(a) A design professional has, from the date of recordation of a claim of lien under this chapter, a lien on the site notwithstanding the absence of commencement of the planned work of improvement, if the landowner who contracted for the design professional's services is also the owner of the site at the time of recordation of the claim of lien.

(b) The lien of the design professional is for the amount of the design professional's fee for services provided under the contract or the reasonable value of those services, whichever is less. The amount of the lien is reduced by the amount of any deposit or prior payment under the contract.

(c) A design professional may not record a claim of lien, and a lien may not be created, under this chapter unless a building permit or other governmental approval in furtherance of the work of improvement has been obtained in connection with or utilizing the services provided by the design professional.

CC 3081.2

A design professional shall, from the date of recordation pursuant to Section 3081.3, have a lien upon the real property for which the work of improvement is planned to be constructed, notwithstanding the absence of commencement of actual construction of the planned work of improvement, if the landowner contracted for the design professional's services and is also the owner of the real property at the time of recordation of the lien. The lien of the design professional shall be for the amount of the design professional's fee for any services rendered prior to commencement of the work of improvement or the reasonable value of those services, whichever is less. The amount of the lien shall be reduced by the amount of any deposit or prior payments, as specified by a written contract entered into by the design professional and by the landowner or his or her agent. However, no lien shall arise pursuant to this chapter, and a design professional may not record a notice of lien pursuant to subdivision (c) of Section 3081.3, unless a building permit or other governmental approval in furtherance of the work of improvement has been obtained in connection with or utilizing the services rendered by the design professional.

Maintains requirement that a building permit or other governmental approval in furtherance of the work of improvement is a condition precedent to the right to record of the lien.

•••

New Text (Operative July 1, 2012) | **Old Text**

<u>CC 8304</u>

A design professional is not entitled to a lien under this chapter unless all of the following conditions are satisfied:

(a) The work of improvement for which the design professional provided services has not commenced.

(b) The landowner defaults in a payment required under the contract or refuses to pay the demand of the design professional made under the contract.

(c) Not less than 10 days before recording a claim of lien, the design professional gives the landowner notice making a demand for payment, and stating that a default has occurred under the contract and the amount of the default.

(d) The design professional records a claim of lien. The claim of lien shall include all of the following information:

(1) The name of the design professional.

(2) The amount of the claim.

(3) The current owner of record of the site.

(4) A legal description of the site.

(5) Identification of the building permit or other governmental approval for the work of improvement.

CC 3081.3

In order for the design professional to be entitled to a lien pursuant to Section 3081.2, all of the following shall occur:

(a) The landowner defaults in any payment required pursuant to the terms of the written contract or refuses to pay upon the demand of the design professional made in accordance with the written contract.

(b) Not less than 10 days prior to recordation pursuant to subdivision (c), the design professional mails by first-class registered or certified mail, postage prepaid, addressed to the landowner, a written demand for payment specifying that a default has occurred pursuant to the contract or agreement and the amount of the default.

(c) The design professional records, in the office of the county recorder in the county in which the real property or some portion thereof is located, a notice of lien which specifies that a lien is created in favor of the named design professional, specifies the amount thereof, identifies the current owner of record of the real property, provides a legal description of the real property to be improved, and specifies the building permit or other governmental approval for the work of improvement required as a condition of recording the notice of lien by Section 3081.2.

Adds requirement that work of improvement has not commenced.
Establishes requirements for design professional's lien.

<u>CC 8306</u>

(a) On recordation of the claim of lien, a lien is created in favor of the named design professional.

(b) The lien automatically expires and is null and void and of no further force or effect on the occurrence of either of the following events:

(1) The commencement of the work of improvement for which the design professional provided services.

(2) The expiration of 90 days after recording the claim of lien, unless the design professional commences an action to enforce the lien within that time.

(c) If the landowner partially or fully satisfies the lien, the design professional shall execute and record a document that evidences a partial or full satisfaction and release of the lien, as applicable.

CC 3081.4

(a) Upon recordation of the notice of lien pursuant to subdivision (c) of Section 3081.3, a lien is created in favor of the named design professional.

(b) The lien created pursuant to subdivision (a) shall automatically expire and be null and void and of no further force or effect on the occurrence of either of the following:

(1) The commencement of the work of improvement for which the design professional furnished services at the request of the landowner.

(2) The expiration of 90 days after recording the notice of lien, unless the design professional files suit to enforce the lien within 90 days of recordation.

(c) In the event the landowner partially or fully satisfies the lien of the design professional, the design professional shall execute and record a document which evidences a partial or full satisfaction and release of the lien, as the case may be.

New Text (Operative July 1, 2012) | **Old Text**

CC 8308
(a) Except as provided in subdivision (b), no provision of this part applies to a lien created under this chapter.
(b) The following provisions of this part apply to a lien created under this chapter:
(1) This chapter.
(2) Article 1 (commencing with Section 8000) of Chapter 1 of Title 1.
(3) Section 8424.
(4) Article 6 (commencing with Section 8460) of Chapter 4.
(5) Article 7 (commencing with Section 8480) of Chapter 4.
(6) Article 8 (commencing with Section 8490) of Chapter 4.

CC 3081.5
Any design professionals' lien perfected pursuant to this chapter shall be enforced pursuant to the provisions contained in Article 7 (commencing with Section 3143) of Chapter 2 of Title 15.

Identifies provisions from this part which apply to design professional's lien.

CC 8310
This chapter does not affect the ability of a design professional to obtain a lien for a work of improvement under Section 8400.

CC 3081.6
This chapter does not affect the ability of a design professional to obtain a Mechanic's lien pursuant to Title 15 (commencing with Section 3082) of this part.

Reiterates that design professionals are entitled to claim lien under Section 8400.

CC 8312
A design professional shall record a claim of lien under this chapter no later than 90 days after the design professional knows or has reason to know that the work of improvement will not be commenced.

CC 3081.7
A design professional shall record a notice of lien pursuant to subdivision (c) of Section 3081.3 no later than 90 days after the design professional knows or has reason to know that the landowner is not commencing the work of improvement.

Sets time limit for recording design professional's lien.

CC 8314
The creation of a lien under this chapter does not affect the ability of the design professional to pursue other remedies.

CC 3081.8
The lien of a design professional perfected pursuant to this chapter shall not affect the ability of the design professional to pursue other remedies.

New Text (Operative July 1, 2012)

CC 8316

(a) No lien created under this chapter affects or takes priority over the interest of record of a purchaser, lessee, or encumbrancer, if the interest of the purchaser, lessee, or encumbrancer in the real property was duly recorded before recordation of the claim of lien.

(b) No lien created under this chapter affects or takes priority over an encumbrance of a construction lender that funds the loan for the work of improvement for which the design professional provided services.

Old Text

CC 3081.9

(a) No lien created by this chapter shall affect or take priority over the interest of record of a purchaser, lessee, or encumbrancer, if the interest of the purchaser, lessee, or encumbrancer in the real property was duly recorded before recordation of the design professionals' lien.

(b) No lien created by this chapter shall affect or take priority over an encumbrance of a construction lender which funds the loan to commence the work of improvement for which the design professional furnished services at the request of the landowner.

Establishes rules for determining priority of design professional's lien.

CC 8318

A design professional may not obtain a lien under this chapter for services provided for a work of improvement relating to a single-family, owner-occupied residence for which the expected construction cost is less than one hundred thousand dollars ($100,000).

CC 3081.10

The design professionals' lien provided in this chapter shall not apply to a work of improvement relating to a single-family owner occupied residence where the construction costs are less than one hundred thousand dollars ($100,000) in value.

CC 8319

(a) A design professional may convert a recorded design professional lien to a mechanics lien if all of the following requirements are met:

(1) The design professional lien expires pursuant to paragraph (1) of subdivision (b) of Section 8306.

(2) The design professional lien remains fully or partially unpaid.

(3) Within 30 days of the expiration of the design professional lien pursuant to paragraph (1) of subdivision (b) of Section 8306, the design professional records a mechanics lien for the amount of the unpaid design professional lien.

(4) The recorded mechanics lien states that it is a converted design professional lien but shall be recorded and enforced as a mechanics lien, except the design professional need not provide a preliminary

No previous text

New Text (Operative July 1, 2012) | **Old Text**

notice to enforce this mechanics lien. This mechanics lien shall be effective as of the date of recordation of this mechanics lien and shall be given priority pursuant to the provisions of Section 8450.

(b) This section shall not apply if a design professional lien expires pursuant to paragraph (2) of subdivision (b) of Section 8306.

NOTE: Added by Senate Bill 424 [Approved by Governor July 26, 2011 and filed with Secretary of State July 26, 2011]. This new section specifically authorizes a design professional to convert a recorded design professional lien to a mechanics lien if certain requirements are satisfied.

Defines requirements for converting design professional's lien to a mechanic's lien.

Requires that the design professional record its mechanic's lien within 30 days after commencement of the work of improvement.

Provides that the mechanic's lien (i.e, the "converted" design professional's lien) shall state that it is a converted design professional's lien.

PART 6. WORKS OF IMPROVEMENT

TITLE 2. PRIVATE WORKS OF IMPROVEMENT

Chapter 4. Mechanics Lien

Article 1. Who is Entitled to Lien

CC 8400

A person that provides work authorized for a work of improvement, including, but not limited to, the following persons, has a lien right under this chapter:

(a) Direct contractor.
(b) Subcontractor.
(c) Material supplier.
(d) Equipment lessor.
(e) Laborer.
(f) Design professional.

CC 3110

Mechanics, materialmen, contractors, subcontractors, lessors of equipment, artisans, architects, registered engineers, licensed land surveyors, machinists, builders, teamsters, and draymen, and all persons and laborers of every class performing labor upon or bestowing skill or other necessary services on, or furnishing materials or leasing equipment to be used or consumed in or furnishing appliances, teams, or power contributing to a work of improvement shall have a lien upon the property upon which they have bestowed labor or furnished materials or appliances or leased equipment for the value of such labor done or materials furnished and for the value of the use of such appliances, equipment, teams, or power whether done or furnished at the instance of the owner or of any person acting by his authority or under him as contractor or otherwise. For the purposes of this chapter, every contractor, subcontractor, sub-subcontractor, architect, builder, or other person having charge of a work of improvement or portion thereof shall be held to be the agent of the owner.

Identifies persons that have a lien right, but list is not exclusive.

Provides that work must be "authorized" in order for claimant to have lien right. (See Civil Code §8404.)

New Text (Operative July 1, 2012) | **Old Text**

CC 8402
A person that provides work authorized for a site improvement has a lien right under this chapter.

CC 3112
Any claimant who, at the instance or request of the owner (or any other person acting by his authority or under him, as contractor or otherwise) of any lot or tract of land, has made any site improvement has a lien upon such lot or tract of land for work done or materials furnished.

Defines persons that have a lien right based on definition of "work" (see Civil Code §8048) and limits the class of persons with the term "authorized". (See Civil Code § 8404)

••

CC 8404
Work is authorized for a work of improvement or for a site improvement in any of the following circumstances:
- *(a) It is provided at the request of or agreed to by the owner.*
- *(b) It is provided or authorized by a direct contractor, subcontractor, architect, project manager, or other person having charge of all or part of the work of improvement or site improvement.*

CC 3110 and CC 3112

CC 3110
Mechanics, materialmen, contractors, subcontractors, lessors of equipment, artisans, architects, registered engineers, licensed land surveyors, machinists, builders, teamsters, and draymen, and all persons and laborers of every class performing labor upon or bestowing skill or other necessary services on, or furnishing materials or leasing equipment to be used or consumed in or furnishing appliances, teams, or power contributing to a work of improvement shall have a lien upon the property upon which they have bestowed labor or furnished materials or appliances or leased equipment for the value of such labor done or materials furnished and for the value of the use of such appliances, equipment, teams, or power whether done or furnished at the instance of the owner or of any person acting by his authority or under him as contractor or otherwise. For the purposes of this chapter, every contractor, subcontractor, sub-subcontractor, architect, builder, or other person having charge of a work of improvement or portion thereof shall be held to be the agent of the owner.

CC 3112
Any claimant who, at the instance or request of the owner (or any other person acting by his authority or under him, as contractor or otherwise) of any lot or tract of land, has made any site improvement has a lien upon such lot or tract of land for work done or materials furnished.

Defines "authorized" as for the purposes §§ 8400 and 8402.

••

New Text (Operative July 1, 2012) | **Old Text**

PART 6. WORKS OF IMPROVEMENT
TITLE 2. PRIVATE WORKS OF IMPROVEMENT
Chapter 4. Mechanics Lien
Article 2. Conditions to Enforcing a Lien

CC 8410

A claimant may enforce a lien only if the claimant has given preliminary notice to the extent required by Chapter 2 (commencing with Section 8200) and made proof of notice.

CC 3114

A claimant shall be entitled to enforce a lien only if he has given the preliminary 20-day notice (private work) in accordance with the provisions of Section 3097, if required by that section, and has made proof of service in accordance with the provisions of Section 3097.1.

Maintains the preliminary notice requirement set forth in prior law (See former Civil Code §3097.)

••

CC 8412

A direct contractor may not enforce a lien unless the contractor records a claim of lien after the contractor completes the direct contract, and before the earlier of the following times:

(a) Ninety days after completion of the work of improvement.

(b) Sixty days after the owner records a notice of completion or cessation.

CC 3115

Each original contractor, in order to enforce a lien, must record his claim of lien after he completes his contract and before the expiration of (a) 90 days after the completion of the work of improvement as defined in Section 3106 if no notice of completion or notice of cessation has been recorded, or (b) 60 days after recordation of a notice of completion or notice of cessation.

Preserves the time limits found in prior law (see former Civil Code §3115.)

••

CC 8414

A claimant other than a direct contractor may not enforce a lien unless the claimant records a claim of lien within the following times:

(a) After the claimant ceases to provide work.

(b) Before the earlier of the following times:

(1) Ninety days after completion of the work of improvement.

(2) Thirty days after the owner records a notice of completion or cessation.

CC 3116

Each claimant other than an original contractor, in order to enforce a lien, must record his claim of lien after he has ceased furnishing labor, services, equipment, or materials, and before the expiration of (a) 90 days after completion of the work of improvement if no notice of completion or cessation has been recorded, or (b) 30 days after recordation of a notice of completion or notice of cessation.

Maintains the time limits found in prior law (see former Civil Code § 3116.)

••

New Text (Operative July 1, 2012)	Old Text

CC 8416

(a) A claim of mechanics lien shall be a written statement, signed and verified by the claimant, containing all of the following:

(1) A statement of the claimant's demand after deducting all just credits and offsets.

(2) The name of the owner or reputed owner, if known.

(3) A general statement of the kind of work furnished by the claimant.

(4) The name of the person by whom the claimant was employed or to whom the claimant furnished work.

(5) A description of the site sufficient for identification.

(6) The claimant's address.

(7) A proof of service affidavit completed and signed by the person serving a copy of the claim of mechanics lien pursuant to subdivision (c). The affidavit shall show the date, place, and manner of service, and facts showing that the service was made in accordance with this section. The affidavit shall show the name and address of the owner or reputed owner upon whom the copy of the claim of mechanics lien was served pursuant to paragraphs (1) or (2) of subdivision (c), and the title or capacity in which the person or entity was served.

(8) The following statement, printed in at least 10-point boldface type. The letters of the last sentence shall be printed in uppercase type, excepting the Internet Web site address of the Contractors' State License Board, which shall be printed in lowercase type:

NOTICE OF MECHANICS LIEN

ATTENTION!

Upon the recording of the enclosed MECHANICS LIEN with the county recorder's office of the county where the property is located, your property is subject to the filing of a legal action seeking a court-ordered foreclosure sale of the real property on which the lien has been recorded. That legal action must be filed with the court no later than 90 days after the date the mechanics lien is recorded.

The party identified in the enclosed mechanics lien may have provided labor or materials for improvements to your property and may not have been paid for these items. You are receiving this notice because it is a required step in filing a mechanics lien foreclosure action against your property. The foreclosure action will seek a sale of your property in order to pay for unpaid labor, materials, or improvements provided to your property. This may affect your ability to borrow against, refinance, or sell the property until the mechanics lien is released.

CC 3084

(a) "Claim of lien" or "Mechanic's lien" means a written statement, signed and verified by the claimant or by the claimant's agent, containing all of the following:

(1) A statement of the claimant's demand after deducting all just credits and offsets.

(2) The name of the owner or reputed owner, if known.

(3) A general statement of the kind of labor, services, equipment, or materials furnished by the claimant.

(4) The name of the person by whom the claimant was employed or to whom the claimant furnished the labor, services, equipment, or materials.

(5) A description of the site sufficient for identification.

(6) A proof of service affidavit completed and signed by the person serving the Notice of Mechanic's Lien pursuant to subdivision (c). A "proof of service affidavit" is an affidavit of the person making the service, showing the date, place, and manner of service and facts showing that the service was made in accordance with this section. The affidavit shall show the name and address of the person or persons upon whom a copy of the Mechanic's lien and the Notice of Mechanic's Lien was served, and, if appropriate, the title or capacity in which he or she was served.

(7) The following statement, printed in at least 10-point boldface type. The letters of the last sentence shall be printed in uppercase type, excepting the Internet Web site address of the Contractors' State License Board, which shall be printed in lowercase type:

NOTICE OF MECHANIC'S LIEN

ATTENTION!

Upon the recording of the enclosed MECHANIC'S LIEN with the county recorder's office of the county where the property is located, your property is subject to the filing of a legal action seeking a court-ordered foreclosure sale of the real property on which the lien has been recorded. That legal action must be filed with the court no later than 90 days after the date the Mechanic's lien is recorded.

The party identified in the Mechanic's lien may have provided labor or materials for improvements to your property and may not have been paid for these items. You are receiving this notice because it is a required step in filing a Mechanic's lien foreclosure action against your property. The foreclosure action will seek a sale of your property in order to pay for unpaid labor, materials, or improvements provided to your property. This may affect your ability to borrow against, refinance, or sell the property until the Mechanic's lien is released.

New Text (Operative July 1, 2012)

BECAUSE THE LIEN AFFECTS YOUR PROPERTY, YOU MAY WISH TO SPEAK WITH YOUR CONTRACTOR IMMEDIATELY, OR CONTACT AN ATTORNEY, OR FOR MORE INFORMATION ON MECHANICS LIENS GO TO THE CONTRACTORS' STATE LICENSE BOARD WEB SITE AT www.cslb.ca.gov."

(b) A claim of mechanics lien in otherwise proper form, verified and containing the information required in subdivision (a), shall be accepted by the recorder for recording and shall be deemed duly recorded without acknowledgment.

(c) A copy of the claim of mechanics lien, which includes the Notice of Mechanics Lien required by paragraph (8) of subdivision (a), shall be served on the owner or reputed owner. Service shall be made as follows:

(1) For an owner or reputed owner to be notified who resides in or outside this state, by registered mail, certified mail, or first-class mail, evidenced by a certificate of mailing, postage prepaid, addressed to the owner or reputed owner at the owner's or reputed owner's residence or place of business address or at the address shown by the building permit on file with the authority issuing a building permit for the work, or as otherwise provided in Section 8174.

(2) If the owner or reputed owner cannot be served by this method, then the copy of the claim of mechanics lien may be given by registered mail, certified mail, or first-class mail, evidenced by a certificate of mailing, postage prepaid, addressed to the construction lender or to the original contractor.

(d) Service of the copy of the claim of mechanics lien by registered mail, certified mail, or first-class mail, evidenced by a certificate of mailing, postage prepaid, is complete at the time of the deposit of that first-class, certified, or registered mail.

(e) Failure to serve the copy of the claim of mechanics lien as prescribed by this section, including the Notice of Mechanics Lien required by paragraph (8) of subdivision (a), shall cause the claim of mechanics lien to be unenforceable as a matter of law.

Old Text

BECAUSE THE LIEN AFFECTS YOUR PROPERTY, YOU MAY WISH TO SPEAK WITH YOUR CONTRACTOR IMMEDIATELY, OR CONTACT AN ATTORNEY, OR FOR MORE INFORMATION ON MECHANIC'S LIENS GO TO THE CONTRACTORS' STATE LICENSE BOARD WEB SITE AT www.cslb.ca.gov.

(b) A Mechanic's lien or claim of lien in otherwise proper form, verified and containing the information required by this section shall be accepted by the recorder for recording and shall be deemed duly recorded without acknowledgment.

(c) (1) The Mechanic's lien and the Notice of Mechanic's Lien described in this section shall be served on the owner or reputed owner. Service shall be made as follows:

(A) For an owner or reputed owner to be notified who resides in or outside this state, by registered mail, certified mail, or first-class mail, evidenced by a certificate of mailing, postage prepaid, addressed to the owner or reputed owner at the owner's or reputed owner's residence or place of business address or at the address shown by the building permit on file with the authority issuing a building permit for the work, or as otherwise provided in subdivision (j) of Section 3097.

(B) If the owner or reputed owner cannot be served by this method, then the notice may be given by registered mail, certified mail, or first-class mail, evidenced by a certificate of mailing, postage prepaid, addressed to the construction lender or to the original contractor.

(2) Service by registered mail, certified mail, or first-class mail, evidenced by a certificate of mailing, postage prepaid, is complete at the time of the deposit of that first-class certified or registered mail.

(d) Failure to serve the Mechanic's lien, including the Notice of Mechanic's Lien, as prescribed by this section, shall cause the Mechanic's lien to be unenforceable as a matter of law.

NOTE: updated through Assembly Bill 456 (Approved by Governor on October 9, 2011). Requires claimant to include claimant's address on claim of lien. Preserves service and notice of mechanic's lien provisions which became effective January 1, 2011. Does not incorporate all of the service methods authorized by Section 8106. Service by registered mail, certified mail or first class mail evidenced by certificate of mailing.

New Text (Operative July 1, 2012) | **Old Text**

CC 8422

(a) *Except as provided in subdivisions (b) and (c), erroneous information contained in a claim of lien relating to the claimant's demand, credits and offsets deducted, the work provided, or the description of the site, does not invalidate the claim of lien.*

(b) *Erroneous information contained in a claim of lien relating to the claimant's demand, credits and offsets deducted, or the work provided, invalidates the claim of lien if the court determines either of the following:*

(1) The claim of lien was made with intent to defraud.

(2) An innocent third party, without notice, actual or constructive, became the bona fide owner of the property after recordation of the claim of lien, and the claim of lien was so deficient that it did not put the party on further inquiry in any manner.

(c) *Any person who shall willfully include in a claim of lien labor, services, equipment, or materials not furnished for the property described in the claim, shall thereby forfeit the person's lien.*

CC 3118 and CC 3261

CC 3118

Any person who shall willfully include in his claim of lien labor, services, equipment, or materials not furnished for the property described in such claim shall thereby forfeit his lien.

CC 3261

No mistake or errors in the statement of the demand, or of the amount of credits and offsets allowed, or of the balance asserted to be due the claimant, or in the description of the property against which the lien is recorded, shall invalidate the lien, unless the court finds that such mistake or error in the statement of the demand, credits and offsets, or of the balance due, was made with the intent to defraud, or that an innocent third party, without notice, direct or constructive, has since the claim was recorded become the bona fide owner of the property, and that the notice of claim was so deficient that it did not put the party on further inquiry in any manner.

NOTE: Amended by Senate Bill 190 (Approved by Governor June 29, 2011 and filed with Secretary of State July 1, 2011).
Clarifies that erroneous information in a claim of lien does not invalidate a lien claim.
Maintains circumstances that will invalidate lien (intends to defraud; innocent third party purchaser without notice of lien; and willful overstatement).

New Text (Operative July 1, 2012) | **Old Text**

CC 8424

(a) An owner of real property or an owner of any interest in real property subject to a recorded claim of lien, or a direct contractor or subcontractor affected by the claim of lien, that disputes the correctness or validity of the claim may obtain release of the real property from the claim of lien by recording a lien release bond. The principal on the bond may be the owner of the property, the direct contractor, or the subcontractor.

(b) The bond shall be conditioned on payment of any judgment and costs the claimant recovers on the lien. The bond shall be in an amount equal to 125 percent of the amount of the claim of lien or 125 percent of the amount allocated in the claim of lien to the real property to be released. The bond shall be executed by an admitted surety insurer.

(c) The bond may be recorded either before or after commencement of an action to enforce the lien. On recordation of the bond, the real property is released from the claim of lien and from any action to enforce the lien.

(d) A person that obtains and records a lien release bond shall give notice to the claimant. The notice shall comply with the requirements of Chapter 2 (commencing with Section 8100) of Title 1 and shall include a copy of the bond. Failure to give the notice required by this section does not affect the validity of the bond, but the statute of limitations for an action on the bond is tolled until notice is given. The claimant shall commence an action on the bond within six months after notice is given.

CC 3143 and CC 3144.5

CC 3143

If the owner of property, or the owner of any interest therein, sought to be charged with a claim of lien, or any original contractor or subcontractor disputes the correctness or validity of any claim of lien, he may record in the office of the county recorder in which such claim of lien was recorded, either before or after the commencement of an action to enforce such claim of lien, a bond executed by a corporation authorized to issue surety bonds in the State of California, in a penal sum equal to 11/2 times the amount of the claim or 11/2 times the amount allocated in the claim of lien to the parcel or parcels of real property sought to be released, which bond shall be conditioned for the payment of any sum which the claimant may recover on the claim together with his cost of suit in the action, if he recovers therein. Upon the recording of such bond the real property described in such bond is released from the lien and from any action brought to foreclose such lien. The principal upon such bond may be either the owner of the property or the owner of any interest therein, or any original contractor, subcontractor, or sub-subcontractor affected by such claim of lien.

CC 3144.5

Any person who obtains a lien release bond which is recorded pursuant to Section 3143 shall give notice of the recording to the lienholder by mailing a copy of the bond to the lienholder at the address appearing on the lien. Service of the notice shall be by certified or registered mail, return receipt requested. Failure to give the notice provided by this section shall not affect the validity of the lien release bond, but the statute of limitations on any action on the bond shall be tolled until the notice is given. Any action on the lien release bond shall be commenced by the claimant within six months of the recording of the lien release bond.

Reduces penal sum for certain lien release bonds from 150% to 125% of the lien amount.
Requires that surety on release bond must be admitted surety insurer (see Civil Code § 8002).
Mandates that notice of release bond must comply with the requirements of Section 8100, et seq.

New Text (Operative July 1, 2012) **Old Text**

PART 6. WORKS OF IMPROVEMENT
TITLE 2. PRIVATE WORKS OF IMPROVEMENT
Chapter 4. Mechanics Lien
Article 4. Amount of Lien

CC 8430

(a) The lien is a direct lien for the lesser of the following amounts:
(1) The reasonable value of the work provided by the claimant.
(2) The price agreed to by the claimant and the person that contracted for the work.

(b) The lien is not limited in amount by the contract price for the work of improvement except as provided in Section 8600.

(c) This section does not preclude the claimant from including in a claim of lien work performed based on a written modification of the contract, or as a result of rescission, abandonment, or breach of the contract. If there is a rescission, abandonment, or breach of the contract, the amount of the lien may not exceed the reasonable value of the work provided by the claimant.

CC 3123(a) and CC 3123(b)

CC 3123(a)

(a) The liens provided for in this chapter shall be direct liens, and shall be for the reasonable value of the labor, services, equipment, or materials furnished or for the price agreed upon by the claimant and the person with whom he or she contracted, whichever is less. The lien shall not be limited in amount by the price stated in the contract as defined in Section 3088, except as provided in Sections 3235 and 3236 and in subdivision (c) of this section.

CC 3123(b):

(b) This section does not preclude the claimant from including in the lien any amount due for labor, services, equipment, or materials furnished based on a written modification of the contract or as a result of the rescission, abandonment, or breach of the contract. However, in the event of rescission, abandonment, or breach of the contract, the amount of the lien may not exceed the reasonable value of the labor, services, equipment, and materials furnished by the claimant.

Preserves the "lesser of" limit on amount of lien found in Section 3123 and the exceptions related to abandonment and breach of contract.
Deletes requirement found in prior law that an owner provide notice when any change order increases the contract price by 5% or more has been eliminated (see former Civil Code §3123(c)).

••

CC 8432

(a) A lien does not extend to work, whether or not the work is authorized by a direct contractor or subcontractor, if the work is not included in a direct contract or a modification of that contract, and the claimant had actual knowledge or constructive notice of the provisions of that contract or modification before providing the work.

(b) The filing of a contract or modification of that contract with the county recorder, before the commencement of a work of improvement, is constructive notice of the provisions of the contract or modification to a person providing work on that work of improvement.

CC 3124

In any case where the claimant was employed by a contractor or subcontractor, his claim of lien shall not extend to any labor, services, equipment, or materials not included in the contract between the owner and original contractor or any modification thereof, if the claimant had actual knowledge or constructive notice of the contract as defined in Section 3088 or any such modification before he furnished such labor, service, equipment, or materials. The filing of a contract for a work of improvement or of a modification of such contract with the county recorder of the county where the property is situated, before the commencement of work, shall be equivalent to the giving of actual notice of the provisions thereof by the owner to all persons performing work or furnishing materials thereunder.

Maintains limitation under prior law on extent of lien (see former Civil Code §3124.)

••

New Text (Operative July 1, 2012)	Old Text
CC 8434 *A direct contractor or a subcontractor may enforce a lien only for the amount due pursuant to that contractor's contract after deducting all lien claims of other claimants for work provided and embraced within that contract.*	**CC 3140** Any original contractor or subcontractor shall be entitled to recover, upon a claim of lien recorded by him, only such amount as may be due him according to the terms of his contract after deducting all claims of other claimants for labor, services, equipment, or materials furnished and embraced within his contract.

Preserves limitation under prior law on amount of recovery of lien (see former Civil Code §3140)

New Text (Operative July 1, 2012) **Old Text**

PART 6. WORKS OF IMPROVEMENT
TITLE 2. PRIVATE WORKS OF IMPROVEMENT
Chapter 4. Mechanics Lien
Article 4. Property Subject to Lien

CC 8440

Subject to Section 8442, a lien attaches to the work of improvement and to the real property on which the work of improvement is situated, including as much space about the work of improvement as is required for the convenient use and occupation of the work of improvement.

CC 3112 and CC 3128

CC 3112

Any claimant who, at the instance or request of the owner (or any other person acting by his authority or under him, as contractor or otherwise) of any lot or tract of land, has made any site improvement has a lien upon such lot or tract of land for work done or materials furnished.

CC 3128

The liens provided for in this chapter shall attach to the work of improvement and the land on which it is situated together with a convenient space about the same or so much as may be required for the convenient use and occupation thereof, if at the commencement of the work or of the furnishing of the materials for the same, the land belonged to the person who caused such work of improvement to be constructed, but if such person owned less than a fee simple estate in such land then only his interest therein is subject to such lien, except as provided in Section 3129.

Clarifies that the lien attaches to the real property as well as "as much space about the work of improvement as is required for the convenient use and occupation of the work of improvement."

New Text (Operative July 1, 2012) | **Old Text**

CC 8442

The following interests in real property to which a lien attaches are subject to the lien:

(a) The interest of a person that contracted for the work of improvement.

(b) The interest of a person that did not contract for the work of improvement, if work for which the lien is claimed was provided with the knowledge of that person, unless that person gives notice of nonresponsibility under Section 8444.

CC 3128 and CC 3129

CC 3128

The liens provided for in this chapter shall attach to the work of improvement and the land on which it is situated together with a convenient space about the same or so much as may be required for the convenient use and occupation thereof, if at the commencement of the work or of the furnishing of the materials for the same, the land belonged to the person who caused such work of improvement to be constructed, but if such person owned less than a fee simple estate in such land then only his interest therein is subject to such lien, except as provided in Section 3129.

CC 3129

Every work of improvement constructed upon any land and all work or labor performed or materials furnished in connection therewith with the knowledge of the owner or of any person having or claiming any estate therein shall be held to have been constructed, performed, or furnished at the instance of such owner or person having or claiming any estate therein and such interest shall be subject to any lien recorded under this chapter unless such owner or person having or claiming any estate therein shall give a notice of non-responsibility pursuant to Section 3094.

•••

CC 8444

(a) An owner of real property or a person claiming an interest in real property on which a work of improvement is situated that did not contract for the work of improvement may give notice of nonresponsibility.

(b) A notice of nonresponsibility shall be signed and verified by the owner.

(c) The notice shall comply with the requirements of Chapter 2 (commencing with Section 8100) of Title 1.

(d) The notice shall also include all of the following information:

(1) The nature of the owner's title or interest.

(2) The name of a purchaser under contract, if any, or lessee, if known.

(3) A statement that the person giving the notice is not responsible for claims arising from the work of improvement.

(e) A notice of nonresponsibility is not effective unless, within 10 days after the person giving notice has knowledge of the work of improvement, the person both posts and records the notice.

CC 3094

"Notice of non-responsibility" means a written notice, signed and verified by a person owning or claiming an interest in the site who has not caused the work of improvement to be performed, or his agent, containing all of the following:

(a) A description of the site sufficient for identification.

(b) The name and nature of the title or interest of the person giving the notice.

(c) The name of the purchaser under contract, if any, or lessee, if known.

(d) A statement that the person giving the notice will not be responsible for any claims arising from the work of improvement.

Within 10 days after the person claiming the benefits of non-responsibility has obtained knowledge of the work of improvement, the notice provided for in this section shall be posted in some conspicuous place on the site. Within the same 10-day period provided for the posting of the notice, the notice shall be recorded in the office of the county recorder of the county in which the site or some part thereof is located.

Incorporates requirements of Section 8100.
Defines content and protocol for effective notice of responsibility.

•••

New Text (Operative July 1, 2012) | **Old Text**

CC 8446

A claimant may record one claim of lien on two or more works of improvement, subject to the following conditions:

(a) The works of improvement have or are reputed to have the same owner, or the work was contracted for by the same person for the works of improvement whether or not they have the same owner.

(b) The claimant in the claim of lien designates the amount due for each work of improvement. If the claimant contracted for a lump sum payment for work provided for the works of improvement and the contract does not segregate the amount due for each work of improvement separately, the claimant may estimate an equitable distribution of the amount due for each work of improvement based on the proportionate amount of work provided for each. If the claimant does not designate the amount due for each work of improvement, the lien is subordinate to other liens.

(c) If there is a single structure on real property of different owners, the claimant need not segregate the proportion of work provided for the portion of the structure situated on real property of each owner. In the lien enforcement action the court may, if it determines it equitable to do so, designate an equitable distribution of the lien among the real property of the owners.

(d) The lien does not extend beyond the amount designated as against other creditors having liens, by judgment, mortgage, or otherwise, on either the works of improvement or the real property on which the works of improvement are situated.

CC 3130

In every case in which one claim is filed against two or more buildings or other works of improvement owned or reputed to be owned by the same person or on which the claimant has been employed by the same person to do his work or furnish his materials, whether such works of improvement are owned by one or more owners, the person filing such claim must at the same time designate the amount due to him on each of such works of improvement; otherwise the lien of such claim is postponed to other liens. If such claimant has been employed to furnish labor or materials under a contract providing for a lump sum to be paid to him for his work or materials on such works of improvement as a whole, and such contract does not segregate the amount due for the work done and materials furnished on such works of improvement separately, then such claimant, for the purposes of this section, may estimate an equitable distribution of the sum due him over all of such works of improvement based upon the proportionate amount of work done or materials furnished upon such respective works of improvement. The lien of such claimant does not extend beyond the amount designated as against other creditors having liens, by judgment, mortgage, or otherwise, upon either such works of improvement or upon the land upon which the same are situated.

For all purposes of this section, if there is a single structure on more than one parcel of land owned by one or more different owners, it shall not be the duty of the claimant to segregate the proportion of material or labor entering into the structure on any one of such parcels; but upon the trial thereof the court may, when it deems it equitable so to do, distribute the lien equitably as between the several parcels involved.

Defines when claimant may record one claim of lien on two or more works of improvement.
Adds limitation on extent of lien vis-à-vis other creditors having liens.

New Text (Operative July 1, 2012)	Old Text

CC 8448

(a) As used in this section, "separate residential unit" means one residential structure, including a residential structure containing multiple condominium units, together with any common area, garage, or other appurtenant improvements.

(b) If a work of improvement consists of the construction of two or more separate residential units:

(1) Each unit is deemed a separate work of improvement, and completion of each unit is determined separately for purposes of the time for recording a claim of lien on that unit. This paragraph does not affect any lien right under Section 8402 or 8446.

(2) Material provided for the work of improvement is deemed to be provided for use or consumption in each separate residential unit in which the material is actually used or consumed; but if the claimant is unable to segregate the amounts used or consumed in separate residential units, the claimant has the right to all the benefits of Section 8446.

CC 3131 (first paragraph)

If a work of improvement consists in the construction of two or more separate residential units, each such unit shall be considered a separate "work of improvement," and the time for filing claims of lien against each such residential unit shall commence to run upon the completion of each such residential unit. A separate residential unit means one residential structure, including a residential structure containing multiple condominium units, together with any common area, or any garage or other improvements appurtenant thereto. The provisions of this qualification shall not impair any rights conferred under the provisions of Section 3112 and 3130. Materials delivered to or upon any portion of such entire work of improvement or furnished to be used in such entire work of improvement and ultimately used or consumed in one of such separate residential units shall, for all the purposes of this title, be deemed to have been furnished to be used or consumed in the separate residential unit in which the same shall have been actually used or consumed; provided, however, that if the claimant is unable to segregate the amounts used on or consumed in such separate units, he shall be entitled to all the benefits of Section 3130.

New Text (Operative July 1, 2012) **Old Text**

PART 6. WORKS OF IMPROVEMENT
TITLE 2. PRIVATE WORKS OF IMPROVEMENT
Chapter 4. Mechanics Lien
Article 5. Priorities

CC 8450

(a) A lien under this chapter, other than a lien provided for in Section 8402, has priority over a lien, mortgage, deed of trust, or other encumbrance on the work of improvement or the real property on which the work of improvement is situated, that (1) attaches after commencement of the work of improvement or (2) was unrecorded at the commencement of the work of improvement and of which the claimant had no notice.

(b) Subdivision (a) is subject to the exception provided for in Section 8452.

CC 3134

The liens provided for in this chapter (other than with respect to site improvements) are, subject to the exception in Section 3138, preferred to any lien, mortgage, deed of trust, or other encumbrance upon the work of improvement and the site, which attaches subsequent to the commencement of the work of improvement, and also to any lien, mortgage, deed of trust, or other encumbrance of which the claimant had no notice and which was unrecorded at the time of commencement of the work of improvement.

Maintains "relation back" principle for priority and exception to priority rule if payment bond recorded (see Civil Code §8452).

••

CC 8452

A mortgage or deed of trust, otherwise subordinate to a lien under Section 8450, has priority over a lien for work provided after recordation of a payment bond that satisfies all of the following requirements:

(a) The bond refers to the mortgage or deed of trust.

(b) The bond is in an amount not less than 75 percent of the principal amount of the mortgage or deed of trust.

CC 3138

If the holder of any mortgage or deed of trust which is subordinate pursuant to Section 3134 to any lien, shall procure a payment bond as defined in Section 3096 in an amount not less than 75 percent of the principal amount of such mortgage or deed of trust, which bond refers to such mortgage or deed of trust, and shall record such payment bond in the office of the county recorder in the county where the site is located, then such mortgage or deed of trust shall be preferred to all liens for labor, services, equipment, or materials furnished after such recording.

Confirms requirements for payment bond used to defeat "relation back" priority.

••

CC 8454

If a site improvement is provided for in a direct contract separate from the direct contract for the remainder of the work of improvement, the site improvement is deemed a separate work of improvement and commencement of the site improvement is not commencement of the remainder of the work of improvement.

CC 3135

If any site improvement is provided for in a separate contract from any contract with respect to the erection of residential units or other structures, then the site improvement shall be considered a separate work of improvement and the commencement thereof shall not constitute a commencement of the work of improvement consisting of the erection of any residential unit or other structure.

••

New Text (Operative July 1, 2012) | **Old Text**

CC 8456

(a) This section applies to a construction loan secured by a mortgage or deed of trust that has priority over a lien under this chapter.

(b) An optional advance of funds by the construction lender that is used for construction costs has the same priority as a mandatory advance of funds by the construction lender, provided that the total of all advances does not exceed the amount of the original construction loan.

CC 3136

A mortgage or deed of trust which would be prior to the liens provided for in this chapter to the extent of obligatory advances made thereunder in accordance with the commitment of the lender shall also be prior to the liens provided for in this chapter as to any other advances, secured by such mortgage or deed of trust, which are used in payment of any claim of lien which is recorded at the date or dates of such other advances and thereafter in payment of costs of the work of improvement. Such priority shall not, however, exceed the original obligatory commitment of the lender as shown in such mortgage or deed of trust.

Clarifies the rule governing priority of optional advances.

CC 8458

(a) Except as provided in subdivision (b), a lien provided for in Section 8402 has priority over:

(1) A mortgage, deed of trust, or other encumbrance that attaches after commencement of the site improvement.

(2) A mortgage, deed of trust, or other encumbrance that was unrecorded at the commencement of the site improvement and of which the claimant had no notice.

(3) A mortgage, deed of trust, or other encumbrance that was recorded before commencement of the site improvement, if given for the sole or primary purpose of financing the site improvement. This subdivision does not apply if the loan proceeds are, in good faith, placed in the control of the lender pursuant to a binding agreement with the borrower to the effect that (A) the proceeds are to be applied to the payment of claimants and (B) no portion of the proceeds will be paid to the borrower in the absence of satisfactory evidence that all claims have been paid or that the time for recording a claim of lien has expired and no claim of lien has been recorded.

(b) A mortgage or deed of trust, otherwise subordinate under subdivision (a), has priority over a lien provided for in Section 8402 if a payment bond in an amount not less than 50 percent of the principal amount of the mortgage or deed of trust is recorded before completion of the work of improvement.

CC 3137 and CC 3139

CC 3137

The liens provided for in Section 3112 with respect to site improvements are, subject to the exception in Section 3139, preferred to (a) any mortgage, deed of trust, or other encumbrance which attaches subsequent to the commencement of the site improvement work; and (b) any mortgage, deed of trust, or other encumbrance of which the claimant had no notice and which was unrecorded at the time of the commencement of such site improvement; and (c) any mortgage, deed of trust, or other encumbrance recorded before the commencement of the site improvement work which was given for the sole or primary purpose of financing such site improvements, unless the loan proceeds are, in good faith, placed in the control of the lender under a binding agreement with the borrower to the effect that such proceeds are to be applied to the payment of claims of claimants and that no portion of such proceeds will be paid to the borrower in the absence of satisfactory evidence that all such claims have been paid or that the time for recording claims of liens has expired and no such claims have been recorded.

CC 3139

If the owner of the land or holder of any mortgage or deed of trust, which is subordinate pursuant to Section 3137 to any lien, shall procure a payment bond in an amount not less than 50 percent of the principal amount of such mortgage or deed of trust and shall record such payment bond in the office of the county recorder in the county where the site is located before completion of the work of improvement, then such mortgage or deed of trust shall be preferred to all such liens provided in Section 3112.

New Text (Operative July 1, 2012) **Old Text**

PART 6. WORKS OF IMPROVEMENT
TITLE 2. PRIVATE WORKS OF IMPROVEMENT
Chapter 4. Mechanics Lien
Article 6. Enforcement of Lien

CC 8460

(a) The claimant shall commence an action to enforce a lien within 90 days after recordation of the claim of lien. If the claimant does not commence an action to enforce the lien within that time, the claim of lien expires and is unenforceable.

(b) Subdivision (a) does not apply if the claimant and owner agree to extend credit, and notice of the fact and terms of the extension of credit is recorded (1) within 90 days after recordation of the claim of lien or (2) more than 90 days after recordation of the claim of lien but before a purchaser or encumbrancer for value and in good faith acquires rights in the property. In that event the claimant shall commence an action to enforce the lien within 90 days after the expiration of the credit, but in no case later than one year after completion of the work of improvement. If the claimant does not commence an action to enforce the lien within that time, the claim of lien expires and is unenforceable.

CC 3144 and CC 3145

CC 3144

(a) No lien provided for in this chapter binds any property for a longer period of time than 90 days after the recording of the claim of lien, unless within that time an action to foreclose the lien is commenced in a proper court, except that, if credit is given and notice of the fact and terms of such credit is recorded in the office of the county recorder subsequent to the recording of such claim of lien and prior to the expiration of such 90-day period, then such lien continues in force until 90 days after the expiration of such credit, but in no case longer than one year from the time of completion of the work of improvement.

(b) If the claimant fails to commence an action to foreclose the lien within the time limitation provided in this section, the lien automatically shall be null and void and of no further force and effect.

CC 3145

As against any purchaser or encumbrancer for value and in good faith whose rights are acquired subsequent to the expiration of the 90-day period following the recording of the claim of lien, no giving of credit or extension of the lien or of the time to enforce the same shall be effective unless evidenced by a notice or agreement recorded in the office of the county recorder prior to the acquisition of the rights of such purchaser or encumbrancer.

Maintains the ninety (90) day limitations period found in prior law (see former Civil Code §3144).
Allows extensions of time for filing an action on a lien, beyond the time periods set forth in prior law, but in no event more than one (1) year from completion of the work of improvement.
Authorizes extension of credit after expiration of initial ninety (90) day limitation period provided that extension of credit is recorded prior to a purchaser or encumbrancer acquires rights in property.

New Text (Operative July 1, 2012) | **Old Text**

CC 8461

After commencement of an action to enforce a lien, the plaintiff shall record in the office of the county recorder of the county, or of the several counties in which the property is situated, a notice of the pendency of the action, as provided in Title 4.5 (commencing with Section 405) of Part 2 of the Code of Civil Procedure, on or before 20 days after the commencement of the action. Only from the time of recording that notice shall a purchaser or encumbrancer of the property affected thereby be deemed to have constructive notice of the pendency of the action, and in that event only of its pendency against parties designated by their real names.

CC 3146

After the filing of the complaint in the proper court to foreclose on the Mechanic's lien, the plaintiff shall record in the office of the county recorder of the county, or of the several counties in which the property is situated, a notice of the pendency of the proceedings, as provided in Title 4.5 (commencing with Section 405) of Part 2 of the Code of Civil Procedure on or before 20 days after the filing of the Mechanic's lien foreclosure action. Only from the time of recording that notice shall a purchaser or encumbrancer of the property affected thereby be deemed to have constructive notice of the pendency of the action, and in that event only of its pendency against parties designated by their real names.

Maintains the requirement that plaintiff record a notice of pendency of action within twenty (20) days of filing an action to foreclose, a lien, which requirement became effective January 1, 2011.

••

CC 8462

Notwithstanding Section 583.420 of the Code of Civil Procedure, if an action to enforce a lien is not brought to trial within two years after commencement of the action, the court may in its discretion dismiss the action for want of prosecution.

CC 3147

If the action to foreclose the lien is not brought to trial within two years after the commencement thereof, the court may in its discretion dismiss the same for want of prosecution.

••

CC 8464

In addition to any other costs allowed by law, the court in an action to enforce a lien shall allow as costs to each claimant whose lien is established the amount paid to verify and record the claim of lien, whether the claimant is a plaintiff or defendant.

CC 3150

In addition to any other costs allowed by law, the court in an action to foreclose a lien must also allow as costs the money paid for verifying and recording the lien, such costs to be allowed each claimant whose lien is established, whether he be plaintiff or defendant.

••

CC 8466

If there is a deficiency of proceeds from the sale of property on a judgment for enforcement of a lien, a deficiency judgment may be entered against a party personally liable for the deficiency in the same manner and with the same effect as in an action to foreclose a mortgage.

CC 3151

Whenever on the sale of the property subject to any liens provided for in this chapter, under a judgment of foreclosure of such lien, there is a deficiency of proceeds, judgment for the deficiency may be entered against any party personally liable therefor in like manner and with like effect as in an action for the foreclosure of a mortgage.

••

New Text (Operative July 1, 2012) | **Old Text**

CC 8468

(a) This chapter does not affect any of the following rights of a claimant:

(1) The right to maintain a personal action to recover a debt against the person liable, either in a separate action or in an action to enforce a lien.

(2) The right to a writ of attachment. In an application for a writ of attachment, the claimant shall refer to this section. The claimant's recording of a claim of lien does not affect the right to a writ of attachment.

(3) The right to enforce a judgment.

(b) A judgment obtained by the claimant in a personal action described in subdivision (a) does not impair or merge the claim of lien, but any amount collected on the judgment shall be credited on the amount of the lien.

CC 3152

Nothing contained in this title affects the right of a claimant to maintain a personal action to recover a debt against the person liable therefor either in a separate action or in the action to foreclose the lien, nor any right the claimant may have to the issuance of a writ of attachment or execution or to enforce a judgment by other means. In an application for a writ of attachment, the claimant shall refer to this section. A lien held by the claimant under this chapter does not affect the right to procure a writ of attachment. The judgment, if any, obtained by the claimant in a personal action, or personal judgment obtained in a Mechanic's lien action, does not impair or merge a lien held by the claimant under this chapter, but any money collected on the judgment shall be credited on the amount of the lien.

Preserves right to maintain a personal (contract) action separate from the lien action and the right to a writ of attachment.

••

CC 8470

In an action to enforce a lien for work provided to a contractor:

(a) The contractor shall defend the action at the contractor's own expense. During the pendency of the action the owner may withhold from the direct contractor the amount of the lien claim.

(b) If the judgment in the action is against the owner or the owner's property, the owner may deduct the amount of the judgment and costs from any amount owed to the direct contractor. If the amount of the judgment and costs exceeds the amount owed to the direct contractor, or if the owner has settled with the direct contractor in full, the owner may recover from the direct contractor, or the sureties on a bond given by the direct contractor for faithful performance of the direct contract, the amount of the judgment and costs that exceed the contract price and for which the direct contractor was originally liable.

CC 3153

In all cases where a claim of lien is recorded for labor, services, equipment, or materials furnished to any contractor, he shall defend any action brought thereon at his own expense, and during the pendency of such action the owner may withhold from the original contractor the amount of money for which the claim of lien is recorded. In case of judgment in such action against the owner or his property upon the lien, the owner shall be entitled to deduct from any amount then or thereafter due from him to the original contractor the amount of such judgment and costs. If the amount of such judgment and costs exceeds the amount due from him to the original contractor, or if he has settled with the original contractor in full, he shall be entitled to recover back from the original contractor, or the sureties on any bond given by him for the faithful performance of his contract, any amount of such judgment and costs in excess of the contract price, and for which the original contractor was originally the party liable.

••

New Text (Operative July 1, 2012) | **Old Text**

PART 6. WORKS OF IMPROVEMENT
TITLE 2. PRIVATE WORKS OF IMPROVEMENT
Chapter 4. Mechanics Lien
Article 7. Release Order

CC 8480

(a) The owner of property or the owner of any interest in property subject to a claim of lien may petition the court for an order to release the property from the claim of lien if the claimant has not commenced an action to enforce the lien within the time provided in Section 8460.

(b) This article does not bar any other cause of action or claim for relief by the owner of the property. A release order does not bar any other cause of action or claim for relief by the claimant, other than an action to enforce the claim of lien that is the subject of the release order.

(c) A petition for a release order under this article may be joined with a pending action to enforce the claim of lien that is the subject of the petition. No other action or claim for relief may be joined with a petition under this article.

(d) Notwithstanding Section 8056, Chapter 2.5 (commencing with Section 1141.10) of Title 3 of Part 3 of the Code of Civil Procedure does not apply to a proceeding under this article.

CC 3154(a), CC 3154(h), and CC 3154(i)

CC 3154(a)

(a) At any time after the expiration of the time period specified by Section 3144 with regard to the period during which property is bound by a lien after recordation of a claim of lien, where no action has been brought to enforce that lien, the owner of the property or the owner of any interest therein may petition the proper court for a decree to release the property from the lien.

CC 3154(h)

(h) Nothing in this section shall be construed to bar any other cause of action or claim for relief by the owner of the property or an interest in the property, nor shall a decree canceling a claimant's lien bar the lien claimant from bringing any other cause of action or claim for relief, other than an action foreclosing the lien. However, no other action or claim shall be joined with the claim for relief established by this section.

CC 3154(i)

(i) Chapter 2.5 (commencing with Section 1141.10) of Title 3 of Part 3 of the Code of Civil Procedure does not apply to causes commenced pursuant to this section.

Allows for filing a petition to release a "stale" lien even though the claimant commenced an action, whereas the prior Civil Code §3154(a) only allowed a petition where no action had been filed.
Bars the joinder of owner's other actions or claims for relief with petition.

CC 8482

An owner of property may not petition the court for a release order under this article unless at least 10 days before filing the petition the owner gives the claimant notice demanding that the claimant execute and record a release of the claim of lien. The notice shall comply with the requirements of Chapter 2 (commencing with Section 8100) of Title 1, and shall state the rounds for the demand.

No previous text

Adds requirement that owner give the claimant notice demanding the release of the claim of lien at least ten (10) before filing the petition.
Incorporates notice requirements in Civil Code §8100 et seq.

New Text (Operative July 1, 2012) | **Old Text**

CC 8484

A petition for a release order shall be verified and shall allege all of the following:

(a) The date of recordation of the claim of lien. A certified copy of the claim of lien shall be attached to the petition.

(b) The county in which the claim of lien is recorded.

(c) The book and page or series number of the place in the official records where the claim of lien is recorded.

(d) The legal description of the property subject to the claim of lien.

(e) Whether an extension of credit has been granted under Section 8460, if so to what date, and that the time for commencement of an action to enforce the lien has expired.

(f) That the owner has given the claimant notice under Section 8482 demanding that the claimant execute and record a release of the lien and that the claimant is unable or unwilling to do so or cannot with reasonable diligence be found.

(g) Whether an action to enforce the lien is pending.

(h) Whether the owner of the property or interest in the property has filed for relief in bankruptcy or there is another restraint that prevents the claimant from commencing an action to enforce the lien.

CC 3154(b)

(b) The petition shall be verified and shall allege all of the following:

(1) The date of recordation of the claim of lien.

(2) The legal description of the property affected by the claim of lien.

(3) That no action to foreclose the lien is pending, or that no extension of credit has been recorded, and that the time period during which suit can be brought to foreclose the lien has expired.

(4) That the lien claimant is unable or unwilling to execute a release of the lien or cannot with reasonable diligence be found.

(5) That the owner of the property or interest in the property has not filed for relief under any law governing bankruptcy, and that there exists no other restraint to prevent the lien claimant from filing to foreclose the lien. A certified copy of the claim of lien shall be attached to the petition. The petition shall be deemed controverted by the lien claimant.

Adds several new requirements to the petition release a lien including the county the lien was recorded, the book and page or series number where the claim of lien was recorded, whether an extension of credit was given and verification that proper notice was provided to the claimant. The petition must also include a certified copy of the claim of lien.

••

CC 8486

(a) On the filing of a petition for a release order, the clerk shall set a hearing date. The date shall be not more than 30 days after the filing of the petition. The court may continue the hearing only on a showing of good cause, but in any event the court shall rule and make any necessary orders on the petition not later than 60 days after the filing of the petition.

(b) The petitioner shall serve a copy of the petition and a notice of hearing on the claimant at least 15 days before the hearing. Service shall be made in the same manner as service of summons, or by certified or registered mail, postage prepaid, return receipt requested, addressed to the claimant as provided in Section 8108.

(c) Notwithstanding Section 8116, when service is

CC 3154(c), CC 3154(d) and CC3154(e)

CC 3154(c)

(c) Upon the filing of the petition, and before any further proceedings are had, the clerk shall set a date for the hearing not more than 30 days following the filing of the petition. The court may continue the hearing beyond the 30-day period, but good cause shall be shown for any continuance.

CC 3154(d)

(d) A copy of the petition and the notice setting the date for the hearing shall be served upon the lien claimant at least 10 days prior to the date set for hearing, in the manner in which a summons is required to be served, or by certified or registered mail, postage prepaid, return receipt requested, addressed to the lien claimant at the claimant's address as shown in any of the following:

New Text (Operative July 1, 2012) | **Old Text**

made by mail, service is complete on the fifth day following deposit of the petition and notice in the mail.

(1) The preliminary 20-day notice served by the claimant pursuant to Section 3097.

(2) The records of the registrar of contractors.

(3) The contract on which the lien is based.

(4) The claim of lien itself.

CC3154(e)

(e) When service is made by mail as provided in this section, service is complete on the fifth day following the day of the deposit of the mail. No decree shall issue in favor of the petitioner unless the petitioner proves that service of the petition and the order fixing the date for hearing was made in compliance with this subdivision. The issue of compliance with this subdivision shall be deemed controverted by the lien claimant.

Establishes an outside time limit of sixty (60) days for a ruling on a petition to release a lien.
Requires that the petition now be served on the claimant at least fifteen (15) days prior to the hearing.
Incorporates the service requirements found in Section 8108.
Provides exception to Section 8116, if service by mail, service complete on the fifth day following deposit in the mail.

__CC 8488__

(a) At the hearing both (1) the petition and (2) the issue of compliance with the service and date for hearing requirements of this article are deemed controverted by the claimant. The petitioner has the initial burden of producing evidence on those matters. The petitioner has the burden of proof as to the issue of compliance with the service and date for hearing requirements of this article. The claimant has the burden of proof as to the validity of the lien.

(b) If judgment is in favor of the petitioner, the court shall order the property released from the claim of lien.

(c) The prevailing party is entitled to reasonable attorney's fees.

CC 3154(b), CC 3154 (e), CC 3154 (f), and CC 3154 (g)

CC 3154(b)

(b) The petition shall be verified and shall allege all of the following:

(1) The date of recordation of the claim of lien.

(2) The legal description of the property affected by the claim of lien.

(3) That no action to foreclose the lien is pending, or that no extension of credit has been recorded, and that the time period during which suit can be brought to foreclose the lien has expired.

(4) That the lien claimant is unable or unwilling to execute a release of the lien or cannot with reasonable diligence be found.

(5) That the owner of the property or interest in the property has not filed for relief under any law governing bankruptcy, and that there exists no other restraint to prevent the lien claimant from filing to foreclose the lien. A certified copy of the claim of lien shall be attached to the petition. The petition shall be deemed controverted by the lien claimant.

New Text (Operative July 1, 2012)	Old Text
	CC 3154(e) (e) When service is made by mail as provided in this section, service is complete on the fifth day following the day of the deposit of the mail. No decree shall issue in favor of the petitioner unless the petitioner proves that service of the petition and the order fixing the date for hearing was made in compliance with this subdivision. The issue of compliance with this subdivision shall be deemed controverted by the lien claimant. **CC 3154(f)** (f) In the event judgment is rendered in favor of the petitioner, the decree shall indicate all of the following: (1) The date the lien was recorded. (2) The county and city, if any, in which the lien was recorded. (3) The book and page of the place in the official records where the lien is recorded. (4) The legal description of the property affected. Upon the recordation of a certified copy of the decree, the property described in the decree shall be released from the lien. **CC 3154(g)** (g) The prevailing party shall be entitled to attorneys' fees not to exceed two thousand dollars ($2,000).

Expands "controverted" statement in prior Civil Code §3154(b).
Clarifies the burden of producing evidence including proper service. The claimant has the burden of establishing validity of lien.
Eliminates the requirements for decree releasing claim of lien found in prior Civil Code §3154(f). Requirements now found in Section 8490.
Allows "reasonable" attorneys fees as opposed to the limit of $2,000 found in prior Civil Code §3154(g).

New Text (Operative July 1, 2012) | **Old Text**

PART 6. WORKS OF IMPROVEMENT
TITLE 2. PRIVATE WORKS OF IMPROVEMENT
Chapter 4. Mechanics Lien
Article 8. Removal of Claim of Lien from Record

CC 8490

(a) A court order dismissing a cause of action to enforce a lien or releasing property from a claim of lien, or a judgment that no lien exists, shall include all of the following information:
(1) The date of recordation of the claim of lien.
(2) The county in which the claim of lien is recorded.
(3) The book and page or series number of the place in the official records where the claim of lien is recorded.
(4) The legal description of the property.

(b) A court order or judgment under this section is equivalent to cancellation of the claim of lien and its removal from the record.

(c) A court order or judgment under this section is a recordable instrument. On recordation of a certified copy of the court order or judgment, the property described in the order or judgment is released from the claim of lien.

(d) This section does not apply to a court order dismissing an action to enforce a lien that is expressly stated to be without prejudice.

CC 3148

In all cases the dismissal of an action to foreclose the lien (unless it is expressly stated that the same is without prejudice) or a judgment rendered therein that no lien exists shall be equivalent to the cancellation and removal from the record of such lien.

Restates the requirements found in prior Civil Code §3154(f).
Clarifies that judgment or order is a recordable instrument and that the recordation of a certified copy releases the property described therein from the lien.
Preserves the "dismissal" without prejudice exception.

CC 8494

If a claim of lien expires and is unenforceable under Section 8460, or if a court order or judgment is recorded under Section 8490, the claim of lien does not constitute actual or constructive notice of any of the matters contained, claimed, alleged, or contended in the claim of lien, or create a duty of inquiry in any person thereafter dealing with the affected property.

No previous text

Provides that an expired lien which is unenforceable (re no action filed or extension of credit issued) or a lien that is subject to a judgment or order recorded under Section 8490, does not constitute notice of any matters contained in the lien.

New Text (Operative July 1, 2012) | **Old Text**

PART 6. WORKS OF IMPROVEMENT
TITLE 2. PRIVATE WORKS OF IMPROVEMENT
Chapter 5. Stop Payment Notice
Article 1. General Provisions

CC 8500

The rights of all persons furnishing work for any work of improvement, with respect to any fund for payment of construction costs, are governed exclusively by this chapter, and no person may assert any legal or equitable right with respect to the fund, other than a right created by a written contract between that person and the person holding the fund, except pursuant to the provisions of this chapter.

CC 3264

The rights of all persons furnishing labor, services, equipment, or materials for any work of improvement, with respect to any fund for payment of construction costs, are governed exclusively by Chapters 3 (commencing with Section 3156) and 4 (commencing with Section 3179) of this title, and no person may assert any legal or equitable right with respect to such fund, other than a right created by direct written contract between such person and the person holding the fund, except pursuant to the provisions of such chapters.

Uses broad definition of "all persons furnishing work for any work of improvement" to define persons entitled to assert the remedy.

Preserves "exclusive remedy" provision.

CC 8502

(a) A stop payment notice shall comply with the requirements of Chapter 2 (commencing with Section 8100) of Title 1, and shall be signed and verified by the claimant.

(b) The notice shall include a general description of work to be provided, and an estimate of the total amount in value of the work to be provided.

(c) The amount claimed in the notice may include only the amount due the claimant for work provided through the date of the notice.

CC 3103

"Stop notice" means a written notice, signed and verified by the claimant or his or her agent, stating in general terms all of the following:

(a) The kind of labor, services, equipment, or materials furnished or agreed to be furnished by such claimant.

(b) The name of the person to or for whom the same was done or furnished.

(c) The amount in value, as near as may be, of that already done or furnished and of the whole agreed to be done or furnished.

(d) The name and address of the claimant.

The notice, in the case of any work of improvement other than a public work, shall be delivered to the owner personally or left at his or her residence or place of business with some person in charge, or delivered to his or her architect, if any, if the notice is served upon a construction lender, holding construction funds and maintaining branch offices, it shall not be effective as against the construction lender unless given to or served upon the manager or other responsible officer or person at the office or branch thereof administering or holding the construction funds. The notice, in the case of any public work for the state, shall be filed with the director of the department which let the contract and, in the case of any other public work, shall be filed in the office of the controller, auditor, or other public disbursing officer whose duty it is to make payments under the provisions of the contract, or with the commissioners, managers, trustees, officers, board of supervisors, board of trustees, common council, or other body by whom the contract was awarded. No stop notice shall be invalid by reason of any defect in form if it is sufficient to substantially inform the owner of the information required.

Any stop notice may be served by registered or certified mail with the same effect as by personal service.

Changes name of the stop notice to stop payment notice.
Incorporates requirements of Section 8100 et seq.
Clarifies that the amount of the stop payment notice may include only the amount due claimant as of the date of the notice.

•••

CC 8504

A claimant that willfully gives a false stop payment notice or that willfully includes in the notice a demand to withhold for work that has not been provided forfeits all right to participate in the distribution of the funds withheld and all right to a lien under Chapter 4 (commencing with Section 8400).

CC 3168

Any person who willfully gives a false stop notice or bonded stop notice or who willfully includes in his notice labor, services, equipment, or materials not furnished for the property described in such notice forfeits all right to participate in the pro rata distribution of such money and all right to any lien under Chapter 2 (commencing with Section 3109).

Maintains "penalty" for false or willfully overstated stop notice.

•••

CC 8506

(a) A stop payment notice to an owner shall be given to the owner or to the owner's architect, if any.

(b) A stop payment notice to a construction lender holding construction funds shall not be effective unless given to the manager or other responsible officer or person at the office or branch of the lender administering or holding the construction funds.

(c) A stop payment notice shall comply with the requirements of Chapter 2 (commencing with Section 8100) of Title 1.

CC 3083 and CC 3103

CC 3083

"Bonded stop notice" means a stop notice, given to any construction lender, accompanied by a bond with good and sufficient sureties in a penal sum equal to 11/4 times the amount of such claim conditioned that if the defendant recovers judgment in an action brought on such verified claim or on the lien filed by the claimant, the claimant will pay all costs that may be awarded against the owner, original contractor, construction lender, or any of them, and all damages that such owner, original contractor, or construction lender may sustain by reason of the equitable garnishment effected by the claim or by reason of the lien, not exceeding the sum specified in the bond. To be effective such bonded stop notice shall be delivered to the manager or other responsible officer or person at the office of the construction

New Text (Operative July 1, 2012)	Old Text

lender or must be sent to such office by registered or certified mail. If such notice is delivered or sent to any institution or organization maintaining branch offices, it shall not be effective unless delivered or sent to the office or branch administering or holding such construction funds.

CC 3103

"Stop notice" means a written notice, signed and verified by the claimant or his or her agent, stating in general terms all of the following:

(a) The kind of labor, services, equipment, or materials furnished or agreed to be furnished by such claimant.

(b) The name of the person to or for whom the same was done or furnished.

(c) The amount in value, as near as may be, of that already done or furnished and of the whole agreed to be done or furnished.

(d) The name and address of the claimant.

The notice, in the case of any work of improvement other than a public work, shall be delivered to the owner personally or left at his or her residence or place of business with some person in charge, or delivered to his or her architect, if any, if the notice is served upon a construction lender, holding construction funds and maintaining branch offices, it shall not be effective as against the construction lender unless given to or served upon the manager or other responsible officer or person at the office or branch thereof administering or holding the construction funds. The notice, in the case of any public work for the state, shall be filed with the director of the department which let the contract and, in the case of any other public work, shall be filed in the office of the controller, auditor, or other public disbursing officer whose duty it is to make payments under the provisions of the contract, or with the commissioners, managers, trustees, officers, board of supervisors, board of trustees, common council, or other body by whom the contract was awarded. No stop notice shall be invalid by reason of any defect in form if it is sufficient to substantially inform the owner of the information required.

Any stop notice may be served by registered or certified mail with the same effect as by personal service.

Incorporates requirements of Section 8100 et seq.

New Text (Operative July 1, 2012) | **Old Text**

<u>*CC 8508*</u>

A stop payment notice is not valid unless both of the following conditions are satisfied:

(a) The claimant gave preliminary notice to the extent required by Chapter 2 (commencing with Section 8200).

(b) The claimant gave the stop payment notice before expiration of the time within which a claim of lien must be recorded under Chapter 4 (commencing with Section 8400).

CC 3160

Service of a stop notice or a bonded stop notice shall be effective only if the claimant:

(a) Gave the preliminary 20-day notice (private work) in accordance with the provisions of Section 3097 if required by that section; and

(b) Served his stop notice as defined in Section 3103 or his bonded stop notice as defined in Section 3083 prior to the expiration of the period within which his claim of lien must be recorded under Section 3115, 3116, or 3117.

Establishes two prerequisites for valid stop payment notice: (1) preliminary notice, if required by Section 8400 et seq.; and (2) timely giving of the stop payment notice pursuant to Section 8400 et seq.

<u>*CC 8510*</u>

(a) A person may obtain release of funds withheld pursuant to a stop payment notice by giving the person withholding the funds a release bond.

(b) A release bond shall be given by an admitted surety insurer and shall be conditioned for payment of any amount not exceeding the penal obligation of the bond that the claimant recovers on the claim, together with costs of suit awarded in the action. The bond shall be in an amount equal to 125 percent of the amount claimed in the stop payment notice.

(c) On receipt of a release bond, the person withholding funds pursuant to the stop payment notice shall release them.

CC 3171

If the owner, construction lender or any original contractor or subcontractor disputes the correctness or validity of any stop notice or bonded stop notice, he may file with the person upon whom such notice was served a bond executed by good and sufficient sureties in a penal sum equal to 11/4 times the amount stated in such notice, conditioned for the payment of any sum not exceeding the penal obligation of the bond which the claimant may recover on the claim, together with his costs of suit in the action, if he recovers therein. Upon the filing of such bond, the funds withheld to respond to the stop notice or bonded stop notice shall forthwith be released.

Removes the "disputes" term found in prior law (See former Civil Code §3171.)
Expands the class of persons that may obtain a stop notice release bond.
Requires that any release bond be provided by an "admitted surety insurer". (Eliminates "good and sufficient surety" language.)

New Text (Operative July 1, 2012) | **Old Text**

PART 6. WORKS OF IMPROVEMENT
TITLE 2. PRIVATE WORKS OF IMPROVEMENT
Chapter 5. Stop Payment Notice
Article 2. Stop Payment Notice to Owner

CC 8520

(a) A person that has a lien right under Chapter 4 (commencing with Section 8400), other than a direct contractor, may give the owner a stop payment notice.

(b) The owner may give notice, in compliance with the requirements of Chapter 2 (commencing with Section 8100) of Title 1, demanding that a person that has a lien right under Chapter 4 (commencing with Section 8400) give the owner a stop payment notice. If the person fails to give the owner a bonded or unbonded stop payment notice, the person forfeits the right to a lien under Chapter 4 (commencing with Section 8400).

CC 3158

Any of the persons named in Sections 3110, 3111, and 3112, other than the original contractor, may give to the owner a stop notice. Any person who shall fail to serve such a stop notice after a written demand therefor from the owner shall forfeit his right to a Mechanic's lien.

Distinguishes stop payment notice to owner from stop payment notice to construction lender (see Section 8530).
Defines class of persons entitled to serve stop notice by incorporation of Section 8400 et seq.
Incorporates notice requirements of Section 8100 et seq.
Preserves owners right to demand stop payment notice as well as forfeiture of lien rights if claimant fails to give the notice.

••

CC 8522

(a) Except as provided in subdivision (b), on receipt of a stop payment notice an owner shall withhold from the direct contractor or from any person acting under authority of a direct contractor a sufficient amount due or to become due to the direct contractor to pay the claim stated in the notice.

(b) The owner may, but is not required to, withhold funds if the owner has previously recorded a payment bond under Section 8600. If the owner does not withhold funds, the owner shall, within 30 days after receipt of the stop payment notice, give notice to the claimant that a payment bond has been recorded and provide the claimant a copy of the bond. The notice shall comply with the requirements of Chapter 2 (commencing with Section 8100) of Title 1.

CC 3161

It shall be the duty of the owner upon receipt of a stop notice pursuant to Section 3158 to withhold from the original contractor or from any person acting under his or her authority and to whom labor or materials, or both, have been furnished, or agreed to be furnished, sufficient money due or to become due to such contractor to answer such claim and any claim of lien that may be recorded therefor, unless a payment bond has been recorded pursuant to the provisions of Section 3235, in which case the owner may, but is not obligated to, withhold such money.

If the owner elects not to withhold pursuant to a stop notice by reason of a payment bond having been previously recorded, then the owner shall, within 30 days after receipt of the stop notice, give a written notice to the claimant at the address shown in the stop notice that the bond has been recorded and furnish to the claimant a copy of that bond.

Incorporates notice requirements of Section 8100 et seq.

••

New Text (Operative July 1, 2012) | Old Text

PART 6. WORKS OF IMPROVEMENT
TITLE 2. PRIVATE WORKS OF IMPROVEMENT
Chapter 5. Stop Payment Notice
Article 3. Stop Payment Notice to Construction Lender

CC 8530

A person that has a lien right under Chapter 4 (commencing with Section 8400) may give a construction lender a stop payment notice.

CC 3159

(a) Any of the persons named in Sections 3110, 3111, and 3112 may, prior to the expiration of the period within which his or her claim of lien must be recorded under Chapter 2 (commencing with Section 3109), give to a construction lender a stop notice or a bonded stop notice. The construction lender shall be subject to the following:

(1) The construction lender shall withhold funds pursuant to a bonded stop notice filed by an original contractor, regardless of whether a payment bond has previously been recorded in the office of the county recorder where the site is located in accordance with Section 3235.

(2) The construction lender shall withhold funds pursuant to a bonded stop notice filed by any other person named in Sections 3110, 3111, and 3112, unless a payment bond has previously been recorded in the office of the county recorder where the site is located in accordance with Section 3235. If a payment bond has previously been recorded, the construction lender may, at its option, withhold funds pursuant to the bonded stop notice or stop notice, or may elect not to withhold pursuant to the bonded stop notice or stop notice given by anyone other than an original contractor.

(3) If, when giving the construction lender the stop notice or bonded stop notice, the claimant makes a written request for notice of the election, accompanied by a preaddressed, stamped envelope, the construction lender shall furnish the claimant a copy of the bond within 30 days after making the election. A lender shall not be liable for a failure to furnish a copy of the bond if the failure was not intentional and resulted from a bona fide error, if the lender maintains reasonable procedures to avoid such an error, and if the error was corrected not later than 20 days from the date on which the violation was discovered. The payment bond may be recorded at any time prior to the serving of the first stop notice. The notice may only be given for materials, equipment, or services furnished, or labor performed.

(b) In the case of a stop notice or bonded stop notice filed by the original contractor or by a subcontractor, the original contractor or subcontractor shall only be entitled to recover on his or her stop notice or bonded stop notice the

New Text (Operative July 1, 2012) | **Old Text**

net amount due the original contractor or subcontractor after deducting the stop notice claims of all subcontractors or material suppliers who have filed bonded stop notices on account of work done on behalf of the original contractor or the subcontractor.

(c) In no event shall the construction lender be required to withhold, pursuant to a bonded stop notice, more than the net amount identified in subdivision (b). Notwithstanding any other provision, no construction lender shall have any liability for the failure to withhold more than this net amount upon receipt of a bonded stop notice.

Distinguishes stop payment notice to construction lender from stop payment notice to owner (See Section 8520). Defines class of persons entitled to serve stop payment notice by incorporation of Section 8400 et seq.

••

CC 8532

A claimant may give a construction lender a stop payment notice accompanied by a bond in an amount equal to 125 percent of the amount of the claim. The bond shall be conditioned that if the defendant recovers judgment in an action to enforce payment of the claim stated in the stop payment notice or to enforce a claim of lien recorded by the claimant, the claimant will pay all costs that are awarded the owner, direct contractor, or construction lender, and all damages to the owner, direct contractor, or construction lender that result from the stop payment notice or recordation of the claim of lien, not exceeding the amount of the bond.

CC 3083

"Bonded stop notice" means a stop notice, given to any construction lender, accompanied by a bond with good and sufficient sureties in a penal sum equal to 11/4 times the amount of such claim conditioned that if the defendant recovers judgment in an action brought on such verified claim or on the lien filed by the claimant, the claimant will pay all costs that may be awarded against the owner, original contractor, construction lender, or any of them, and all damages that such owner, original contractor, or construction lender may sustain by reason of the equitable garnishment effected by the claim or by reason of the lien, not exceeding the sum specified in the bond. To be effective such bonded stop notice shall be delivered to the manager or other responsible officer or person at the office of the construction lender or must be sent to such office by registered or certified mail. If such notice is delivered or sent to any institution or organization maintaining branch offices, it shall not be effective unless delivered or sent to the office or branch administering or holding such construction funds.

Does not mention bond from admitted surety insurer.

••

New Text (Operative July 1, 2012) | **Old Text**

CC 8534

(a) A construction lender that objects to the sufficiency of sureties on the bond given with a bonded stop payment notice shall give notice to the claimant of the objection, within 20 days after the bonded stop payment notice is given. The notice shall comply with the requirements of Chapter 2 (commencing with Section 8100) of Title 1.

(b) The claimant may within 10 days after notice of the objection is given substitute for the initial bond a bond executed by an admitted surety insurer. If the claimant does not substitute a bond executed by an admitted surety insurer, the construction lender may disregard the bonded stop payment notice and release all funds withheld in response to that notice.

CC 3163

If the construction lender objects to the sufficiency of the sureties on the bond accompanying the bonded stop notice, he must give notice in writing of such objection to the claimant within 20 days after the service of the bonded stop notice. The claimant may within 10 days after the receipt of such written objection substitute for the initial bond a bond in like amount executed by a corporate surety licensed to write such bonds in the State of California. If the claimant fails to do so, the construction lender may disregard the bonded stop notice and release all funds withheld in response thereto.

Preserves construction lender's right to object surety on stop payment notice bond.
Incorporates notice requirement from Section 8100.
Requires that replacement bond be issued by admitted surety insurer, or construction lender may ignore the stop payment notice.

CC 8536

(a) Except as provided in subdivision (b), on receipt of a stop payment notice a construction lender shall withhold from the borrower or other person to whom the lender or the owner is obligated to make payments or advancement out of the construction fund sufficient funds to pay the claim stated in the notice.

(b) The construction lender may, at its option, elect not to withhold funds in any of the following circumstances:

(1) The stop payment notice is unbonded.

(2) The stop payment notice is given by a claimant other than a direct contractor, and a payment bond is recorded before the lender is given any stop payment notice.

CC 3159(a) and CC 3162(a)

CC 3159(a)

(a) Any of the persons named in Sections 3110, 3111, and 3112 may, prior to the expiration of the period within which his or her claim of lien must be recorded under Chapter 2 (commencing with Section 3109), give to a construction lender a stop notice or a bonded stop notice. The construction lender shall be subject to the following:

(1) The construction lender shall withhold funds pursuant to a bonded stop notice filed by an original contractor, regardless of whether a payment bond has previously been recorded in the office of the county recorder where the site is located in accordance with Section 3235.

(2) The construction lender shall withhold funds pursuant to a bonded stop notice filed by any other person named in Sections 3110, 3111, and 3112, unless a payment bond has previously been recorded in the office of the county recorder where the site is located in accordance with Section 3235. If a payment bond has previously been recorded, the construction lender may, at its option, withhold funds pursuant to the bonded stop notice or stop notice, or may elect not to withhold pursuant to the bonded stop notice or stop notice given by anyone other than an original contractor.

New Text (Operative July 1, 2012) | **Old Text**

(3) If, when giving the construction lender the stop notice or bonded stop notice, the claimant makes a written request for notice of the election, accompanied by a preaddressed, stamped envelope, the construction lender shall furnish the claimant a copy of the bond within 30 days after making the election. A lender shall not be liable for a failure to furnish a copy of the bond if the failure was not intentional and resulted from a bona fide error, if the lender maintains reasonable procedures to avoid such an error, and if the error was corrected not later than 20 days from the date on which the violation was discovered. The payment bond may be recorded at any time prior to the serving of the first stop notice. The notice may only be given for materials, equipment, or services furnished, or labor performed.

CC 3162(a)

(a) Upon receipt of a stop notice pursuant to Section 3159, the construction lender may, and upon receipt of a bonded stop notice the construction lender shall, except as provided in this section, withhold from the borrower or other person to whom it or the owner may be obligated to make payments or advancement out of the construction fund, sufficient money to answer the claim and any claim of lien that may be recorded therefor. The construction lender shall be subject to the following:

(1) The construction lender shall withhold funds pursuant to a bonded stop notice filed by an original contractor, regardless of whether a payment bond has previously been recorded in the office of the county recorder where the site is located in accordance with Section 3235.

(2) The construction lender shall withhold funds pursuant to a bonded stop notice filed by any other person named in Sections 3110, 3111, and 3112, unless a payment bond has previously been recorded in the office of the county recorder where the site is located in accordance with Section 3235. If a payment bond has previously been recorded, the construction lender may, at its option, withhold funds pursuant to the bonded stop notice or stop notice, or may elect not to withhold pursuant to the bonded stop notice or stop notice given by anyone other than an original contractor.

(3) If, when giving the construction lender the stop notice or bonded stop notice, the claimant makes a written request for notice of the election, accompanied by a preaddressed, stamped envelope, the construction lender shall furnish the claimant a copy of the bond within 30 days after making the election. A lender shall not be liable for a failure to furnish a copy of the bond if the failure was not intentional and resulted from a bona fide error, if the

New Text (Operative July 1, 2012) | **Old Text**

lender maintains reasonable procedures to avoid such an error, and if the error was corrected not later than 20 days from the date on which the violation was discovered. The payment bond may be recorded at any time prior to the serving of the first stop notice.

Mandates that construction lender withhold funds, unless: (1) stop payment notice is not bonded; or (2) claimant is a person other than a direct contractor AND a payment bond was recorded before the first stop payment notice. Simplifies terminology in former Section 3162.

••

CC 8538

(a) The claimant may make a written request for notice of an election by the construction lender under Section 8536 not to withhold funds. The request shall be made at the time the claimant gives the construction lender the stop payment notice and shall be accompanied by a preaddressed, stamped envelope.

(b) If the construction lender elects not to withhold funds under Section 8536, the lender shall, within 30 days after making the election, give notice of that fact to a claimant who has requested notice of the election under subdivision (a). The notice shall comply with the requirements of Chapter 2 (commencing with Section 8100) of Title 1. If the basis of the election is the recordation of a payment bond under Section 8600, the construction lender shall include a copy of the bond with the notice.

(c) A construction lender is not liable for failure to include a copy of the bond with the notice under this section if all of the following conditions are satisfied:

(1) The failure was not intentional and resulted from a bona fide error.

(2) The lender maintains reasonable procedures to avoid an error of that type.

(3) The lender corrected the error not later than 20 days after the date the lender discovered the violation.

CC 3159(a) and CC 3162(a)

CC 3159(a)

(a) Any of the persons named in Sections 3110, 3111, and 3112 may, prior to the expiration of the period within which his or her claim of lien must be recorded under Chapter 2 (commencing with Section 3109), give to a construction lender a stop notice or a bonded stop notice. The construction lender shall be subject to the following:

(1) The construction lender shall withhold funds pursuant to a bonded stop notice filed by an original contractor, regardless of whether a payment bond has previously been recorded in the office of the county recorder where the site is located in accordance with Section 3235.

(2) The construction lender shall withhold funds pursuant to a bonded stop notice filed by any other person named in Sections 3110, 3111, and 3112, unless a payment bond has previously been recorded in the office of the county recorder where the site is located in accordance with Section 3235. If a payment bond has previously been recorded, the construction lender may, at its option, withhold funds pursuant to the bonded stop notice or stop notice, or may elect not to withhold pursuant to the bonded stop notice or stop notice given by anyone other than an original contractor.

(3) If, when giving the construction lender the stop notice or bonded stop notice, the claimant makes a written request for notice of the election, accompanied by a preaddressed, stamped envelope, the construction lender shall furnish the claimant a copy of the bond within 30 days after making the election. A lender shall not be liable for a failure to furnish a copy of the bond if the failure was not intentional and resulted from a bona fide error, if the lender maintains reasonable procedures to avoid such an error, and if the error was corrected not later than 20 days from the date on which the violation was discovered. The payment bond may be recorded at any time prior to the serving of the first stop notice. The notice may only be given for materials, equipment, or services furnished, or labor performed.

New Text (Operative July 1, 2012) | **Old Text**

CC 3162(a)

(a) Upon receipt of a stop notice pursuant to Section 3159, the construction lender may, and upon receipt of a bonded stop notice the construction lender shall, except as provided in this section, withhold from the borrower or other person to whom it or the owner may be obligated to make payments or advancement out of the construction fund, sufficient money to answer the claim and any claim of lien that may be recorded therefor. The construction lender shall be subject to the following:

(1) The construction lender shall withhold funds pursuant to a bonded stop notice filed by an original contractor, regardless of whether a payment bond has previously been recorded in the office of the county recorder where the site is located in accordance with Section 3235.

(2) The construction lender shall withhold funds pursuant to a bonded stop notice filed by any other person named in Sections 3110, 3111, and 3112, unless a payment bond has previously been recorded in the office of the county recorder where the site is located in accordance with Section 3235. If a payment bond has previously been recorded, the construction lender may, at its option, withhold funds pursuant to the bonded stop notice or stop notice, or may elect not to withhold pursuant to the bonded stop notice or stop notice given by anyone other than an original contractor.

(3) If, when giving the construction lender the stop notice or bonded stop notice, the claimant makes a written request for notice of the election, accompanied by a preaddressed, stamped envelope, the construction lender shall furnish the claimant a copy of the bond within 30 days after making the election. A lender shall not be liable for a failure to furnish a copy of the bond if the failure was not intentional and resulted from a bona fide error, if the lender maintains reasonable procedures to avoid such an error, and if the error was corrected not later than 20 days from the date on which the violation was discovered. The payment bond may be recorded at any time prior to the serving of the first stop notice.

Preserves claimant's right to request that construction lender make an election.
Incorporates notice requirements of Section 8100 should lender elect "not to withhold funds".
Incorporates exceptions to liability if construction lender fails to include copy of payment bond with notice.
Eliminates repetition found in former Sections 3159(a) and 3162.

New Text (Operative July 1, 2012) | **Old Text**

PART 6. WORKS OF IMPROVEMENT
TITLE 2. PRIVATE WORKS OF IMPROVEMENT
Chapter 5. Stop Payment Notice
Article 4. Priorities

CC 8540

(a) Funds withheld pursuant to a stop payment notice shall be distributed in the following order of priority:

(1) First, to pay claims of persons that have given a bonded stop payment notice. If funds are insufficient to pay the claims of those persons in full, the funds shall be distributed pro rata among the claimants in the ratio that the claim of each bears to the aggregate of all claims for which a bonded stop payment notice is given.

(2) Second, to pay claims of persons that have given an unbonded stop payment notice. If funds are insufficient to pay the claims of those persons in full, the funds shall be distributed among the claimants in the ratio that the claim of each bears to the aggregate of all claims for which an unbonded stop payment notice is given.

(b) Pro rata distribution under this section shall be made among the persons entitled to share in the distribution without regard to the order in which the person has given a stop payment notice or commenced an enforcement action.

CC 3167

(a) If the money withheld or required to be withheld pursuant to any bonded stop notice shall be insufficient to pay in full the valid claims of all persons by whom such notices were given, the same shall be distributed among such persons in the same ratio that their respective claims bear to the aggregate of all such valid claims. Such pro rata distribution shall be made among the persons entitled to share therein without regard to the order of time in which their respective notices may have been given or their respective actions, if any, commenced.

(b) If the money withheld or required to be withheld pursuant to any stop notice shall be insufficient to pay in full the valid claims of all persons by whom such notices were given, the same shall be distributed among such persons in the same ratio that their respective claims bear to the aggregate of all such valid claims. Such pro rata distribution shall be made among the persons entitled to share therein without regard to the order of time in which their respective notices may have been given or their respective actions, if any, commenced.

Clarifies priority afforded persons that filed bonded stop payment notice (i.e. Bonded stop payment notices are to be paid before stop payment notices).

Preserves pro rata distribution rules if funds insufficient to pay all claims.

New Text (Operative July 1, 2012) | **Old Text**

CC 8542

Notwithstanding Section 8540:

(a) If funds are withheld pursuant to a stop payment notice given to a construction lender by a direct contractor or subcontractor, the direct contractor or subcontractor may recover only the net amount due the direct contractor or subcontractor after deducting any funds that are withheld by the construction lender pursuant to the claims of subcontractors and material suppliers that have given a stop payment notice for work done on behalf of the direct contractor or subcontractor.

(b) In no event is the construction lender required to withhold, pursuant to a stop payment notice, more than the net amount provided in subdivision (a). Notwithstanding any other provision of this chapter, a construction lender is not liable for failure to withhold more than that net amount on receipt of a stop payment notice.

CC 3159(b), CC 3159 (c), CC 3162(b), and CC 3162 (c)

CC 3159(b)

(b) In the case of a stop notice or bonded stop notice filed by the original contractor or by a subcontractor, the original contractor or subcontractor shall only be entitled to recover on his or her stop notice or bonded stop notice the net amount due the original contractor or subcontractor after deducting the stop notice claims of all subcontractors or material suppliers who have filed bonded stop notices on account of work done on behalf of the original contractor or the subcontractor.

CC 3159(c)

(c) In no event shall the construction lender be required to withhold, pursuant to a bonded stop notice, more than the net amount identified in subdivision (b). Notwithstanding any other provision, no construction lender shall have any liability for the failure to withhold more than this net amount upon receipt of a bonded stop notice.

CC 3162(b)

(b) In the case of a stop notice or bonded stop notice filed by the original contractor or by a subcontractor, the original contractor or subcontractor shall only be entitled to recover on his or her stop notice or bonded stop notice the net amount due the original contractor or subcontractor after deducting the stop notice claims of all subcontractors or material suppliers who have filed bonded stop notices on account of work done on behalf of the original contractor or the subcontractor.

CC 3162(c)

(c) In no event shall the construction lender be required to withhold, pursuant to a bonded stop notice, more than the net amount identified in subdivision (b). Notwithstanding any other provision, no construction lender shall have any liability for the failure to withhold more than this net amount upon receipt of a bonded stop notice.

Eliminates repetition found in former Sections 3159 and 3162.

CC 8544

The rights of a claimant who gives a construction lender a stop payment notice are not affected by an assignment of construction loan funds made by the owner or direct contractor, and the stop payment notice has priority over the assignment, whether the assignment is made before or after the stop payment notice is given.

CC 3166

No assignment by the owner or contractor of construction loan funds, whether made before or after a stop notice or bonded stop notice is given to a construction lender, shall be held to take priority over the stop notice or bonded stop notice, and such assignment shall have no effect insofar as the rights of claimants who give the stop notice or bonded stop notice are concerned.

Preserves priority of stop payment notice over assignment of construction loan funds.

New Text (Operative July 1, 2012) **Old Text**

PART 6. WORKS OF IMPROVEMENT
TITLE 2. PRIVATE WORKS OF IMPROVEMENT
Chapter 5. Stop Payment Notice
Article 5. Enforcement of Claim Stated in Stop Payment Notice

CC 8550

(a) A claimant shall commence an action to enforce payment of the claim stated in a stop payment notice at any time after 10 days from the date the claimant gives the stop payment notice.

(b) A claimant shall commence an action to enforce payment of the claim stated in a stop payment notice not later than 90 days after expiration of the time within which a stop payment notice must be given.

(c) An action under this section may not be brought to trial or judgment entered before expiration of the time provided in subdivision (b).

(d) If a claimant does not commence an action to enforce payment of the claim stated in a stop payment notice within the time prescribed in subdivision (b), the notice ceases to be effective and the person withholding funds pursuant to the notice shall release them.

(e) Within five days after commencement of an action to enforce payment of the claim stated in a stop payment notice, the claimant shall give notice of commencement of the action to the persons to whom the stop payment notice was given. The notice shall comply with the requirements of Chapter 2 (commencing with Section 8100) of Title 1.

CC 3172

An action against the owner or construction lender to enforce payment of the claim stated in the stop notice or bonded stop notice may be commenced at any time after 10 days from the date of the service of the stop notice upon either the owner or construction lender and shall be commenced not later than 90 days following the expiration of the period within which claims of lien must be recorded as prescribed in Chapter 2 (commencing with Section 3109). No such action shall be brought to trial or judgment entered until the expiration of said 90-day period. No money shall be withheld by reason of any such notice longer than the expiration of such 90-day period unless such action is commenced. If no such action is commenced, such notice shall cease to be effective and such moneys shall be paid or delivered to the contractor or other person to whom they are due. Notice of commencement of any such action shall be given within five days after commencement thereof to the same persons and in the same manner as provided for service of a stop notice or bonded stop notice.

Maintains the "window" for filing an action to enforce stop payment notice and the restriction on bringing action to trial. Incorporates notice requirements of Section 8100 for notice of commencement of an action to enforce a stop payment notice.

••

CC 8552

If more than one claimant has given a stop payment notice:

(a) Any number of claimants may join in the same enforcement action.

(b) If claimants commence separate actions, the court first acquiring jurisdiction may order the actions consolidated.

(c) On motion of the owner or construction lender the court shall require all claimants to be impleaded in one action, to the end that the rights of all parties may be adjudicated in the action.

CC 3175

Any number of persons who have given stop notices or bonded stop notices may join in the same action and when separate actions are commenced the court first acquiring jurisdiction may consolidate them. Upon the motion of the owner or construction lender the court shall require all claimants to the moneys withheld pursuant to stop notices and bonded stop notices to be impleaded in one action, to the end that the respective rights of all parties may be adjudicated therein.

••

New Text (Operative July 1, 2012) | **Old Text**

CC 8554

Notwithstanding Section 583.420 of the Code of Civil Procedure, if an action to enforce payment of the claim stated in a stop payment notice is not brought to trial within two years after commencement of the action, the court may in its discretion dismiss the action for want of prosecution.

CC 3173

In case such action is commenced as provided in Section 3172 but is not brought to trial within two years after the commencement thereof, the court may in its discretion dismiss the action for want of prosecution.

••

CC 8556

A stop payment notice ceases to be effective, and a person withholding funds pursuant to the notice shall release them, in either of the following circumstances:

(a) An action to enforce payment of the claim stated in the stop payment notice is dismissed, unless expressly stated to be without prejudice.

(b) Judgment in an action to enforce payment of the claim stated in the stop payment notice is against the claimant.

CC 3174

Upon the dismissal of an action to enforce a stop notice or bonded stop notice, unless expressly stated to be without prejudice, or upon a judgment rendered therein against the claimant, the stop notice or bonded stop notice shall cease to be effective and the moneys withheld shall be paid or delivered to the person to whom they are due.

Removes the reference to "the person to whom they are due".

••

CC 8558

(a) In an action to enforce payment of the claim stated in a bonded stop payment notice, the prevailing party is entitled to a reasonable attorney's fee in addition to costs and damages.

(b) The court, on notice and motion by a party, shall determine who is the prevailing party or that there is no prevailing party for the purpose of this section, regardless of whether the action proceeds to final judgment. The prevailing party is the party that recovers greater relief in the action, subject to the following limitations:

(1) If the action is voluntarily dismissed or dismissed pursuant to a settlement, there is no prevailing party.

(2) If the defendant tenders to the claimant the full amount to which the claimant is entitled, and deposits in court for the claimant the amount so tendered, and alleges those facts in the answer and the allegation is determined to be true, the defendant is deemed to be the prevailing party.

CC 3176

In any action against an owner or construction lender to enforce payment of a claim stated in a bonded stop notice, the prevailing party shall be entitled to collect from the party held liable by the court for payment of the claim, reasonable attorney's fees in addition to other costs and in addition to any liability for damages.

The court, upon notice and motion by a party, shall determine who is the prevailing party for purposes of this section, whether or not the suit proceeds to final judgment. Except as otherwise provided by this section, the prevailing party shall be the party who recovered a greater relief in the action. The court may also determine that there is no prevailing party. Where an action has been voluntarily dismissed or dismissed pursuant to a settlement of the case, there shall be no prevailing party for purposes of this section.

Where the defendant alleges in his or her answer that he or she tendered to the plaintiff the full amount to which he or she was entitled, and thereupon deposits in court for the plaintiff, the amount so tendered, and the allegation is found to be true, then the defendant is deemed to be a prevailing party.

Preserves the prevailing party's right to attorney's fees in an action on a bonded stop notice.

••

New Text (Operative July 1, 2012) | **Old Text**

CC 8560

If the claimant is the prevailing party in an action to enforce payment of the claim stated in a bonded stop payment notice, any amount awarded on the claim shall include interest at the legal rate calculated from the date the stop payment notice is given.

CC 3176.5

If the plaintiff is the prevailing party in any action against an owner or construction lender to enforce payment of a claim stated in a bonded stop notice, any amount awarded on the claim shall include interest at the legal rate calculated from the date the bonded stop notice is served upon the owner or construction lender pursuant to Section 3172.

Maintains claimant's right to recover interest from the date the stop payment notice is given.

PART 6. WORKS OF IMPROVEMENT

TITLE 2. PRIVATE WORKS OF IMPROVEMENT

Chapter 6. Payment Bond

CC 8600

(a) This section applies if, before the commencement of work, the owner in good faith files a direct contract with the county recorder, and records a payment bond of the direct contractor in an amount not less than 50 percent of the price stated in the direct contract.

(b) If the conditions of subdivision (a) are satisfied, the court shall, where equitable to do so, restrict lien enforcement under this title to the aggregate amount due from the owner to the direct contractor and shall enter judgment against the direct contractor and surety on the bond for any deficiency that remains between the amount due to the direct contractor and the whole amount due to claimants.

CC 3235 and CC 3236

CC 3235

In case the original contract for a private work of improvement is filed in the office of the county recorder of the county where the property is situated before the work is commenced, and the payment bond of the original contractor in an amount not less than 50 percent of the contract price named in such contract is recorded in such office, then the court must, where it would be equitable so to do, restrict the recovery under lien claims to an aggregate amount equal to the amount found to be due from the owner to the original contractor and render judgment against the original contractor and his sureties on such bond for any deficiency or difference there may remain between such amount so found to be due to the original contractor and the whole amount found to be due to claimants.

CC 3236

It is the intent and purpose of Section 3235 to limit the owner's liability, in all cases, to the measure of the contract price where he shall have filed or caused to be filed in good faith his original contract and recorded a payment bond as therein provided. It shall be lawful for the owner to protect himself against any failure of the original contractor to perform his contract and make full payment for all work done and materials furnished thereunder by exacting such bond or other security as he may deem necessary.

Combines former Section 3235 ad 3236 into a single Section.
Removes reference to legislative intent found in prior law (see former Civil Code §3236.)

New Text (Operative July 1, 2012) | **Old Text**

CC 8602

Section 8600 does not preclude an owner from requiring a performance bond, payment bond, or other security as protection against a direct contractor's failure to perform the direct contract or to make full payment for all work provided pursuant to the contract.

CC 3236

It is the intent and purpose of Section 3235 to limit the owner's liability, in all cases, to the measure of the contract price where he shall have filed or caused to be filed in good faith his original contract and recorded a payment bond as therein provided. It shall be lawful for the owner to protect himself against any failure of the original contractor to perform his contract and make full payment for all work done and materials furnished thereunder by exacting such bond or other security as he may deem necessary.

••

CC 8604

(a) If a lending institution requires that a payment bond be given as a condition of lending money to finance a work of improvement, and accepts in writing as sufficient a bond given in fulfillment of the requirement, the lending institution may not thereafter object to the borrower as to the validity of the bond or refuse to make the loan based on an objection to the bond if the bond is given by an admitted surety insurer.

(b) For purposes of this section, a "lending institution" includes a commercial bank, savings and loan institution, credit union, or other organization or person engaged in the business of financing loans.

CC 3237

When a lending institution requires that a payment bond be furnished as a condition of lending money to finance a private work of improvement, and accepts in writing as sufficient a payment bond posted in fulfillment of this requirement, it may thereafter object to the borrower as to the validity of that payment bond or refuse to make the loan based upon any objection to the payment bond only if the bond underwriter was licensed by the Department of Insurance.

As used in this section, "lending institution" includes commercial banks, savings and loan institutions, credit unions, and any other organizations or persons that are engaged in the business of financing loans.

If a lending institution accepts a payment bond as a condition to making a loan and the bond is issued by an admitted surety insurer, the lender may not later object to the validity of that payment bond.

••

CC 8606

(a) A payment bond under this title shall be conditioned for the payment in full of the claims of all claimants and shall by its terms inure to the benefit of all claimants so as to give a claimant a right of action to enforce the liability on the bond. The bond shall be given by an admitted surety insurer.

(b) An owner, direct contractor, or subcontractor may be the principal on the bond.

(c) A claimant may enforce the liability on the bond in an action to enforce a lien under this part or in a separate action on the bond.

CC 3096

"Payment bond" means a bond with good and sufficient sureties that is conditioned for the payment in full of the claims of all claimants and that also by its terms is made to inure to the benefit of all claimants so as to give these persons a right of action to recover upon this bond in any suit brought to foreclose the liens provided for in this title or in a separate suit brought on the bond. An owner, original contractor, or a subcontractor may be the principal upon any payment bond.

Replaces "good and sufficient" surety requirement with admitted surety insurer.
Replaces the term "original contractor" with "direct contractor" as a principal on the bond.

••

New Text (Operative July 1, 2012)	Old Text

CC 8608

(a) This title does not give a claimant a right to recover on a direct contractor's payment bond given under this chapter unless the claimant provided work to the direct contractor either directly or through one or more subcontractors, pursuant to a direct contract.

(b) Nothing in this section affects the stop payment notice right of, and relative priorities among, design professionals and holders of secured interests in the real property.

CC 3267

Nothing contained in this title shall be construed to give to any person any right of action on any original contractor's private or public work payment bond described in Chapter 6 (commencing with Section 3235) or Chapter 7 (commencing with Section 3247), unless the work forming the basis for his claim was performed by such person for the principal on such payment bond, or one of his subcontractors, pursuant to the contract between the original contractor and the owner.

Nothing in this section shall affect the stop notice rights of, and relative priorities among, architects, registered engineers, or licensed land surveyors and holders of secured interests on the land.

Clarifies that claimant must have provided work to direct contractor or ANY subcontractors.

•••

CC 8609

Any provision in a payment bond attempting by contract to shorten the period prescribed in Section 337 of the Code of Civil Procedure for the commencement of an action on the bond shall not be valid under either of the following circumstances:

(a) If the provision attempts to limit the time for commencement of an action on the bond to a shorter period than six months from the completion of any work of improvement.

(b) As applied to any action brought by a claimant, unless the bond is recorded before the work of improvement is commenced.

CC 3239

No provision in any payment bond given pursuant to any of the provisions of this chapter attempting by contract to shorten the period prescribed in Section 337 of the Code of Civil Procedure for the commencement of an action thereon shall be valid if such provision attempts to limit the time for commencement of action thereon to a shorter period than six months from the completion of any work of improvement, nor shall any provision in any of such bonds attempting to limit the period for the commencement of actions thereon be valid insofar as actions brought by claimants are concerned, unless such bond is recorded, before the work of improvement is commenced, with the county recorder of the county in which the property referred to therein is situated.

Maintains minimum limitation period of six months.

•••

CC 8610

Notwithstanding Section 8609, if a payment bond under this title is recorded before completion of a work of improvement, an action to enforce the liability on the bond may not be commenced later than six months after completion of the work of improvement.

CC 3240

Notwithstanding Section 3239, if a surety on any payment bond given pursuant to this chapter records the payment bond in the office of the county recorder of the county in which the property is situated before the work of improvement is completed, then any action against the surety or sureties shall be commenced not later than six months after the completion of the work of improvement.

Preserves six month statute of limitations.

•••

New Text (Operative July 1, 2012)

__CC 8612__

(a) In order to enforce a claim against a payment bond under this title, a claimant shall give the preliminary notice provided in Chapter 2 (commencing with Section 8200).

(b) If preliminary notice was not given as provided in Chapter 2 (commencing with Section 8200), a claimant may enforce a claim by giving written notice to the surety and the bond principal within 15 days after recordation of a notice of completion. If no notice of completion has been recorded, the time for giving written notice to the surety and the bond principal is extended to 75 days after completion of the work of improvement.

(c) Commencing July 1, 2012, and except as provided in subdivision (b), if the preliminary notice was required to be given by a person who has no direct contractual relationship with the contractor, and who has not given notice as provided in Chapter 2 (commencing with Section 8200), that person may enforce a claim by giving written notice to the surety and the bond principal, as provided in Section 8614, within 15 days after recordation of a notice of completion. If no notice of completion has been recorded, the time for giving written notice to the surety and the bond principal is extended to 75 days after completion of the work of improvement.

(d) Subdivision (c) shall not apply in either of the following circumstances:

(1) All progress payments, except for those disputed in good faith, have been made to a subcontractor who has a direct contractual relationship with the general contractor to whom the claimant has provided materials or services.

(2) The subcontractor who has a direct contractual relationship with the general contractor to whom the claimant has provided materials or services has been terminated from the project pursuant to the contract, and all progress payments, except those disputed in good faith, have been made as of the termination date.

(e) Pursuant to Section 8200, this section shall not apply to a laborer, as defined under Section 8024.

(f) This section shall become operative on July 1, 2012.

Old Text

CC 3242

(a) With regard to a contract entered into on or after January 1, 1995, in order to enforce a claim upon any payment bond given in connection with a private work, a claimant shall give the 20-day private work preliminary notice provided in Section 3097.

(b) If the 20-day private work preliminary notice was not given as provided in Section 3097, a claimant may enforce a claim by giving written notice to the surety and the bond principal as provided in Section 3227 within 15 days after recordation of a notice of completion. If no notice of completion has been recorded, the time for giving written notice to the surety and the bond principal is extended to 75 days after completion of the work of improvement.

NOTE: Updated through Senate Bill 293 (Approved by Governor on October 9, 2011). Maintains statutory prerequisites of: (1) preliminary notice; or (2) 15/75 day bond notice to surety and bond principal. Limits the use of the 15/75 day notice by second tier subcontractors and suppliers to circumstances where the party to whom the claimant furnished materials and/or services has not yet been paid for its work. This curative notice is no longer available if the subcontractor who has a direct contractual relationship has been paid or has been terminated.

New Text (Operative July 1, 2012)

CC 8614

Notice to the principal and surety under Section 8612 shall comply with the requirements of Chapter 2 (commencing with Section 8100) of Title 1.

Old Text

CC 3227

(a) The written notice to be given to the surety and the bond principal may be given by personal delivery, or by depositing the notice in the mail, postage prepaid, certified or registered, and addressed in accordance with any of the following that may be applicable:

(1) If to an individual surety, at his or her residence or place of business, if known. If to an individual surety whose residence is unknown, then in care of the clerk of the county in which the bond has been recorded.

(2) If to a corporate surety, at the office of or in care of the agent designated by the surety in the bond as the address to which notice shall be sent.

(3) At the office of or in care of any officer of the surety in this state.

(4) At the office of or in care of the statutory agent of the surety in this state.

(5) To the bond principal at the last known address.

(6) By service in the manner provided by law for the service of a summons in a civil action.

(b) The written notice described in subdivision (a) shall contain all of the following:

(1) The kind of labor, services, equipment, or materials furnished or agreed to be furnished by the claimant.

(2) The name of the person to or for whom the labor, services, equipment, or materials were furnished.

(3) The amount in value, as near as may be determined, of any labor, services, equipment, or materials already furnished or to be furnished.

Makes notice requirement found in Section 8100 et seq. applicable to the 15/75 day bond notice.

PART 6. WORKS OF IMPROVEMENT
TITLE 2. PRIVATE WORKS OF IMPROVEMENT
Chapter 7. Security for Large Project
Article 1. Application of Chapter

CC 8700

(a) This chapter applies if any of the following conditions is satisfied:

(1) The owner of the fee interest in property contracts for a work of improvement on the property with a contract price greater than five million dollars ($5,000,000).

(2) The owner of a less than fee interest in property, including a leasehold interest, contracts for a work of improvement on the property with a contract price greater than one million dollars ($1,000,000).

(b) For the purpose of this section:

(1) The owner of the fee interest in property is not deemed to be the owner of a less than fee interest by reason of a mortgage, deed of trust, ground lease, or other lien or encumbrance or right of occupancy that encumbers the fee interest.

(2) A lessee of real property is deemed to be the owner of a fee interest in the real property if all of the following conditions are satisfied:

(A) The initial term of the lease is at least 35 years.

(B) The lease covers one or more lawful parcels under the Subdivision Map Act, Division 2 (commencing with Section 66410) of Title 7 of the Government Code, and any applicable local ordinance adopted under that act, in their entirety, including, but not limited to, a parcel approved pursuant to a certificate of compliance proceeding.

CC 3110.5(a)(1) and CC 3110.5(a)(2)

CC 3110.5(a)(1)

(a)(1) This section shall apply only to an owner who contracts for a work of improvement for construction, alteration, addition to, or repair upon, property, whether the contracting owner is the owner of a fee simple absolute interest in the property or the owner of any lesser interest in the property. For purposes of this section, a lessee of real property shall be considered to be the owner of a fee simple absolute interest in that real property if and only if: (A) the initial term of the lease is at least 35 years and (B) the lease covers one or more lawful parcels under the Subdivision Map Act (Division 2 (commencing with Section 66410) of Title 7 of the Government Code) and any applicable local ordinances adopted pursuant thereto, in their entirety, including, but not limited to, parcels approved pursuant to certificate of compliance proceedings. For purposes of this section, the owner of a fee simple absolute interest shall not be deemed to be the owner of less than a fee simple absolute interest by reason of any mortgages, deeds of trust, ground leases, or other liens or encumbrances or rights to occupancy that may encumber the fee simple absolute interest. If the owner contracting for the work of improvement is an owner of an interest in the property which is less than a fee simple absolute interest, this section does not require the owner of the fee simple absolute interest who does not contract for the work of improvement to provide any security pursuant to this section or to comply with any of the other obligations of an owner under this section. If the owner contracting for the work of improvement is an owner of the fee simple absolute interest in the property, this section does not require the owner of an interest in the property which is less than a fee simple absolute interest who does not contract for the work of improvement to provide any security pursuant to this section or to comply with any of the other obligations of an owner under this section.

CC 3110.5(a)(2)

(a)(2) An owner contracting for a work of improvement is subject to this section only if one of the following conditions is satisfied:

(A) The owner contracting for the work of improvement is the owner of a fee simple absolute interest in the property upon which the

New Text (Operative July 1, 2012) | **Old Text**

work of improvement is to be made, and the value of the contract for the work of improvement is more than five million dollars ($5,000,000).

(B) The owner contracting for the work of improvement is the owner of an interest which is less than a fee simple absolute interest, including a leasehold interest, in the property upon which the work of improvement is to be made, and the value of the contract for the work of improvement is more than one million dollars ($1,000,000).

••

CC 8702

This chapter does not apply to any of the following works of improvement:

(a) A single-family residence, including a single-family residence located within a subdivision, and any associated fixed work that requires the services of a general engineering contractor as defined in Section 7056 of the Business and Professions Code. As used in this subdivision, "single-family residence" means a real property improvement used or intended to be used as a dwelling unit for one family.

(b) A housing development eligible for a density bonus under Section 65915 of the Government Code.

CC 3110.5(e)

(e) This section does not apply to the construction of single-family residences, including single-family residences located within a subdivision, and any associated fixed works that require the services of a general engineering contractor, as defined in Section 7056 of the Business and Professions Code, any public works projects, or housing developments eligible for a density bonus pursuant to Section 65915 of the Government Code. As used in this section, the term "single-family residence" means a real property improvement used or intended to be used as a dwelling unit for one family.

••

CC 8704

This chapter does not apply to any of the following owners:

(a) A qualified publicly traded company or a wholly owned subsidiary of a qualified publicly traded company, if the obligations of the subsidiary pursuant to the contract for the work of improvement are guaranteed by the parent. As used in this subdivision, "qualified publicly traded company" means a company having a class of equity securities listed for trading on the New York Stock Exchange, the American Stock Exchange, or the NASDAQ stock market, and the nonsubordinated debt securities of which are rated as "investment grade" by either Fitch ICBA, Inc., Moody's Investor Services, Inc., Standard & Poor's Ratings Services, or a similar statistical rating organization that is nationally recognized for rating

CC 3110.5(f)

(f) This section does not apply to either of the following:

(1) Any contract where the contracting owner is either a qualified publicly traded company or a wholly owned subsidiary of a qualified publicly traded company, provided that the obligations of the subsidiary under the construction contract are guaranteed by the parent which is a qualified publicly traded company. As used in this section, the term "qualified publicly traded company" means any company having a class of equity securities listed for trading on the New York Stock Exchange, the American Stock Exchange or the NASDAQ stock market and the nonsubordinated debt securities thereof which are rated as "investment grade" by either Fitch ICBA, Inc., Moody's Investor Services, Inc., Standard & Poor's Ratings Services or a similar

New Text (Operative July 1, 2012)

the creditworthiness of a publicly traded company. If at any time before final payment of all amounts due pursuant to the contract the nonsubordinated debt securities of the qualified publicly traded company are downgraded to below " investment grade" by any of those rating organizations, the owner is no longer exempt from this chapter.

(b) A qualified private company or a wholly owned subsidiary of a qualified private company, if the obligations of the subsidiary pursuant to the contract for the work of improvement are guaranteed by the parent. As used in this subdivision, "qualified private company" means a company that has no equity securities listed for trading on the New York Stock Exchange, the American Stock Exchange, or the NASDAQ stock market, and that has a net worth determined in accordance with generally accepted accounting principles in excess of fifty million dollars ($50,000,000). If at any time before final payment of all amounts due pursuant to the contract the net worth of the qualified private company is reduced below that level, the owner is no longer exempt from this chapter.

Old Text

statistical rating organization which is nationally recognized for rating the creditworthiness of publicly traded companies. If at any time prior to final payment of all sums due under the construction contract the nonsubordinated debt securities of the qualified publicly traded company are downgraded to below "investment grade" by one of the referenced rating agencies, the contracting owner of the property will no longer be exempt from the provisions of this section.

(2) Any contract where the contracting owner is either a qualified private company or a wholly owned subsidiary of a qualified private company, provided that the obligations of the subsidiary under the construction contract are guaranteed by the parent which is a qualified private company. As used in this section, the term "qualified private company" means any company that has no equity securities listed for trading on the New York Stock Exchange, the American Stock Exchange or the NASDAQ stock market, and that has a net worth determined in accordance with generally accepted accounting principles in excess of fifty million dollars ($50,000,000). If at any time prior to final payment of all sums due under the construction contract the net worth of the qualified private company is reduced below the level referenced in this section, the owner of the property will no longer be exempt from the provisions of this section.

New Text (Operative July 1, 2012) | **Old Text**

PART 6. WORKS OF IMPROVEMENT
TITLE 2. PRIVATE WORKS OF IMPROVEMENT
Chapter 7. Security for Large Project
Article 2. Security Requirement

CC 8710

An owner described in subdivision (a) of Section 8700 shall provide the direct contractor all of the following:

(a) Security for the owner's payment obligation pursuant to the contract. The security shall be used only if the owner defaults on the payment obligation to the direct contractor. This subdivision does not apply to an owner that is the majority owner of the direct contractor.

(b) A copy, certified by the county recorder, of any recorded mortgage or deed of trust that secures the construction loan of a lending institution for the work of improvement, disclosing the amount of the loan.

CC 3110.5(b)

(b) If an owner of property, whether an owner of a fee simple absolute interest or any lesser interest therein, contracts for any work of improvement for construction, alteration, addition to, or repair upon, the property, and the contracting owner is subject to the requirements of this section, as determined by subdivision (a), the contracting owner shall supply to the original contractor, if a lending institution is providing a construction loan, a copy certified by the county recorder of the recorded construction mortgage or deed of trust that shall disclose the amount of the construction loan. In addition, if the contracting owner is not the majority owner of the original contractor, the contracting owner shall provide security for the contracting owner's payment obligations under the construction contract. The security shall be used only when the contracting owner defaults on his or her contractual obligations to the original contractor. The security for the contracting owner's payment obligations under the construction contract shall be provided by one of the following means:

(1) A payment bond, as defined in Section 3096, in the amount of either (A) not less than 25 percent of the total amount of any construction contract that is subject to this section where the construction contract provides that the work of improvement is scheduled to be substantially completed within six months following the commencement thereof, or (B) not less than 15 percent of the total amount of any other construction contract that is subject to this section, which payment bond shall be payable upon default by the contracting owner of any undisputed amount under the contract that has been due and payable for more than 30 days. The payment bond shall be from a California admitted surety which is either listed in the Department of the Treasury's Listing of Approved Sureties (Department Circular 570) or

New Text (Operative July 1, 2012)	Old Text

that has an A.M. Best rating of A or better and has an underwriting limitation, pursuant to Section 12090 of the Insurance Code, greater than the value of the contract amount of the bond.

(2) An irrevocable letter of credit from a financial institution, as defined in Section 5107 of the Financial Code, inuring to the benefit of the original contractor in the amount of either (A) not less than 25 percent of the total amount of any construction contract that is subject to this section where the construction contract provides that the work of improvement is scheduled to be substantially completed within six months following the commencement thereof, or (B) not less than 15 percent of the total amount of any other construction contract that is subject to this section. The maturity date of the letter of credit and other terms of the letter of credit shall be determined by agreement between the contracting owner, the original contractor, and the issuer of the letter of credit provided that the contracting owner shall be required to maintain the letter of credit in effect until the contracting owner has satisfied all of its payment obligations to the original contractor.

(3)(A) An escrow account, designated as a "construction security escrow account," maintained with an escrow agent licensed under the Escrow Law, as set forth in Division 6 (commencing with Section 17000) of the Financial Code, or with any person exempt from the Escrow Law pursuant to paragraph (1) or (3) of subdivision (a) of Section 17006 of the Financial Code, which construction security escrow account shall be located in California and in which the contracting owner shall deposit funds in the amount provided in subparagraph (B); provided that the original contractor shall not be obligated to accept a construction security escrow account as security unless the contracting owner establishes to the reasonable satisfaction of the original contractor (which may be established by a written opinion of legal counsel for the contracting owner), that the contracting owner has granted the original contractor a perfected, first priority security interest in the construction security escrow account and all funds deposited by the contracting owner therein and the proceeds thereof. The funds on

New Text (Operative July 1, 2012)	Old Text

deposit in the construction security escrow account shall be the sole property of the contracting owner, subject to the security interest in favor of the original contractor. The escrow holder shall be instructed by the contracting owner and the original contractor to hold the funds on deposit in the construction security escrow account for the purpose of perfecting the original contractor's security interest therein and to disburse those funds only upon the joint authorization of the contracting owner and the original contractor, or in accordance with an order of any court which is binding on both the owner and the original contractor. This section does not require any construction lender to agree to deposit proceeds of a construction loan in a construction security escrow account.

(B) Prior to commencement of the work under the construction contract, the contracting owner shall make an initial deposit to the construction security escrow account in the amount of either (i) not less than 25 percent of the total amount of any construction contract which is subject to this section where the construction contract provides that the work of improvement is scheduled to be substantially completed within six months following the commencement thereof, or (ii) not less than 15 percent of the total amount of any other construction contract which is subject to this section. In addition, if the construction contract provides for a so-called retainage or retention to be withheld from periodic payments to the original contractor, the contracting owner shall deposit all amounts withheld as retainage or retention in the construction security escrow account at the same time the contracting owner makes the corresponding payment to the original contractor from which the retainage or retention is withheld provided, however, that in no event shall the amount required to be maintained on deposit in the construction security escrow account exceed the total amount of future payments remaining to be due the original contractor under its construction contract (as the same may be adjusted by agreement between the contracting owner and the original contractor). If the amount of funds on deposit in the construction security escrow account equals or exceeds the total amount of

New Text (Operative July 1, 2012) | **Old Text**

future payments remaining to be due the original contractor, the contracting owner and the original contractor shall authorize the disbursement to the original contractor of funds on deposit in the construction security escrow account to pay progress payments then due the original contractor under its construction contract (in whole or in part), but in no event shall either party be obligated to authorize the disbursement of any funds that would cause the amount remaining on deposit in the construction security escrow account following that disbursement to be less than the total amount of future payments remaining to be due the original contractor after application of any funds disbursed to the original contractor. The contracting owner and the original contractor shall authorize the disbursement to the contracting owner of any funds remaining on deposit in the construction security escrow account after the original contractor has been paid all amounts due under its construction contract. The contracting owner and the original contractor shall authorize the disbursement of funds on deposit in the construction security escrow account in accordance with the order of any court which is binding on both of them. The contracting owner and the original contractor may agree in the construction contract upon additional conditions for the disbursement of funds on deposit in the construction security escrow account provided that the conditions shall not cause the amount remaining on deposit in the construction security escrow account to be less than the amount required pursuant to this subparagraph.

••

CC 8712

If an owner fails to provide or maintain the security required by this chapter, the direct contractor may give the owner notice demanding security. The notice shall comply with the requirements of Chapter 2 (commencing with Section 8100) of Title 1. If the owner does not provide or maintain the security within 10 days after notice

CC 3110.5(c)

(c) For the purposes of subdivision (b), if the price under the construction contract is not a fixed price, the amount of security to be provided shall be determined with reference to the guaranteed maximum price, if there is one, or if there is no guaranteed maximum price, the amount of security shall be determined with reference to

New Text (Operative July 1, 2012)

demanding security is given, the direct contractor may suspend work until the owner provides or maintains the security.

Old Text

the contracting owner's and original contractor's good faith estimate as to the total cost anticipated to be incurred under the construction contract. If any contracting owner that is required to provide security under this section with respect to a construction contract fails to provide that security or fails to maintain that security as required, the original contractor may make written demand on the contracting owner to do so, and if the contracting owner fails to provide and maintain that security within 10 days after the original contractor makes written demand on the owner, the original contractor may suspend work until the required security is provided and maintained in accordance with this section.

Preserves direct contractor's right to suspend work if owner fails to provide required security within ten (10) days of demand. Incorporates notice requirement of Section 8100.

<u>CC 8714</u>
It is against public policy to waive the provisions of this chapter by contract.

CC 3110.5(g)

(g) It is against public policy to waive the provisions of this section in any contract for any private work of improvement to which this section applies.

<u>CC 8716</u>
This chapter does not affect any statute providing for mechanics liens, stop payment notices, bond remedies, or prompt payment rights of a subcontractor, including the direct contractor's payment responsibilities under Section 7108.5 of the Business and Professions Code.

CC 3110.5(d)

(d) This section does not affect provisions in this code providing for Mechanic's liens, stop notices, bond remedies, or prompt payment rights of a subcontractor, including the original contractor's payment responsibilities as set forth in Section 7108.5 of the Business and Professions Code and Section 10262 of the Public Contract Code.

Deletes reference to Public Contract Code §10262.

PART 6. WORKS OF IMPROVEMENT
TITLE 2. PRIVATE WORKS OF IMPROVEMENT
Chapter 7. Security for Large Project
Article 3. Form of Security

CC 8720

An owner shall provide security by any of the following means:

(a) A bond that satisfies Section 8722.

(b) An irrevocable letter of credit that satisfies Section 8724.

(c) An escrow account that satisfies Section 8726.

CC 3110.5(b)

(b) If an owner of property, whether an owner of a fee simple absolute interest or any lesser interest therein, contracts for any work of improvement for construction, alteration, addition to, or repair upon, the property, and the contracting owner is subject to the requirements of this section, as determined by subdivision (a), the contracting owner shall supply to the original contractor, if a lending institution is providing a construction loan, a copy certified by the county recorder of the recorded construction mortgage or deed of trust that shall disclose the amount of the construction loan. In addition, if the contracting owner is not the majority owner of the original contractor, the contracting owner shall provide security for the contracting owner's payment obligations under the construction contract. The security shall be used only when the contracting owner defaults on his or her contractual obligations to the original contractor. The security for the contracting owner's payment obligations under the construction contract shall be provided by one of the following means:

(1) A payment bond, as defined in Section 3096, in the amount of either (A) not less than 25 percent of the total amount of any construction contract that is subject to this section where the construction contract provides that the work of improvement is scheduled to be substantially completed within six months following the commencement thereof, or (B) not less than 15 percent of the total amount of any other construction contract that is subject to this section, which payment bond shall be payable upon default by the contracting owner of any undisputed amount under the contract that has been due and payable for more than 30 days. The payment bond shall be from a California admitted surety which is either listed in the Department of the Treasury's Listing of Approved Sureties (Department Circular 570) or that has an A.M. Best rating of A or better and has an underwriting limitation, pursuant to Section 12090 of the Insurance Code, greater than the value of the contract amount of the bond.

(2) An irrevocable letter of credit from a financial institution, as defined in Section 5107 of the Financial

New Text (Operative July 1, 2012) | **Old Text**

Code, inuring to the benefit of the original contractor in the amount of either (A) not less than 25 percent of the total amount of any construction contract that is subject to this section where the construction contract provides that the work of improvement is scheduled to be substantially completed within six months following the commencement thereof, or (B) not less than 15 percent of the total amount of any other construction contract that is subject to this section. The maturity date of the letter of credit and other terms of the letter of credit shall be determined by agreement between the contracting owner, the original contractor, and the issuer of the letter of credit provided that the contracting owner shall be required to maintain the letter of credit in effect until the contracting owner has satisfied all of its payment obligations to the original contractor.

(3)(A) An escrow account, designated as a "construction security escrow account," maintained with an escrow agent licensed under the Escrow Law, as set forth in Division 6 (commencing with Section 17000) of the Financial Code, or with any person exempt from the Escrow Law pursuant to paragraph (1) or (3) of subdivision (a) of Section 17006 of the Financial Code, which construction security escrow account shall be located in California and in which the contracting owner shall deposit funds in the amount provided in subparagraph (B); provided that the original contractor shall not be obligated to accept a construction security escrow account as security unless the contracting owner establishes to the reasonable satisfaction of the original contractor (which may be established by a written opinion of legal counsel for the contracting owner), that the contracting owner has granted the original contractor a perfected, first priority security interest in the construction security escrow account and all funds deposited by the contracting owner therein and the proceeds thereof. The funds on deposit in the construction security escrow account shall be the sole property of the contracting owner, subject to the security interest in favor of the original contractor. The escrow holder shall be instructed by the contracting owner and the original contractor to hold the funds on deposit in the construction security escrow account for the purpose of perfecting the original contractor's security interest therein and to disburse those funds only upon the joint authorization of the contracting owner and the original contractor, or in accordance with an order of any court which is binding on both the owner and the original contractor.

New Text (Operative July 1, 2012)	Old Text

This section does not require any construction lender to agree to deposit proceeds of a construction loan in a construction security escrow account.

(B) Prior to commencement of the work under the construction contract, the contracting owner shall make an initial deposit to the construction security escrow account in the amount of either (i) not less than 25 percent of the total amount of any construction contract which is subject to this section where the construction contract provides that the work of improvement is scheduled to be substantially completed within six months following the commencement thereof, or (ii) not less than 15 percent of the total amount of any other construction contract which is subject to this section. In addition, if the construction contract provides for a so-called retainage or retention to be withheld from periodic payments to the original contractor, the contracting owner shall deposit all amounts withheld as retainage or retention in the construction security escrow account at the same time the contracting owner makes the corresponding payment to the original contractor from which the retainage or retention is withheld provided, however, that in no event shall the amount required to be maintained on deposit in the construction security escrow account exceed the total amount of future payments remaining to be due the original contractor under its construction contract (as the same may be adjusted by agreement between the contracting owner and the original contractor). If the amount of funds on deposit in the construction security escrow account equals or exceeds the total amount of future payments remaining to be due the original contractor, the contracting owner and the original contractor shall authorize the disbursement to the original contractor of funds on deposit in the construction security escrow account to pay progress payments then due the original contractor under its construction contract (in whole or in part), but in no event shall either party be obligated to authorize the disbursement of any funds that would cause the amount remaining on deposit in the construction security escrow account following that disbursement to be less than the total amount of future payments remaining to be due the original contractor after application of any funds disbursed to the original contractor. The contracting owner and the original contractor shall authorize the disbursement to the contracting owner of any funds remaining on deposit in the construction security escrow account after the original contractor has been paid all amounts due under its construction contract. The contracting

New Text (Operative July 1, 2012) | **Old Text**

owner and the original contractor shall authorize the disbursement of funds on deposit in the construction security escrow account in accordance with the order of any court which is binding on both of them. The contracting owner and the original contractor may agree in the construction contract upon additional conditions for the disbursement of funds on deposit in the construction security escrow account provided that the conditions shall not cause the amount remaining on deposit in the construction security escrow account to be less than the amount required pursuant to this subparagraph.

Lists forms of acceptable security:
(a) bond
(b) irrevocable letter of credit; or
(c) escrow account.

••

CC 8722

A bond under this chapter shall satisfy all of the following requirements:

(a) The bond shall be executed by an admitted surety insurer that is either listed in the Department of the Treasury's Listing of Approved Sureties (Department Circular 570) or that has an A.M. Best rating of A or better and has an underwriting limitation, under Section 12090 of the Insurance Code, greater than the amount of the bond.

(b) The bond shall be in an amount not less than 15 percent of the contract price for the work of improvement or, if the work of improvement is to be substantially completed within six months after the commencement of work, not less than 25 percent of the contract price.

(c) The bond shall be conditioned for payment on default by the owner of any undisputed amount pursuant to the contract that is due and payable for more than 30 days.

CC 3110.5(b)(1)

(1) A payment bond, as defined in Section 3096, in the amount of either (A) not less than 25 percent of the total amount of any construction contract that is subject to this section where the construction contract provides that the work of improvement is scheduled to be substantially completed within six months following the commencement thereof, or (B) not less than 15 percent of the total amount of any other construction contract that is subject to this section, which payment bond shall be payable upon default by the contracting owner of any undisputed amount under the contract that has been due and payable for more than 30 days. The payment bond shall be from a California admitted surety which is either listed in the Department of the Treasury's Listing of Approved Sureties (Department Circular 570) or that has an A.M. Best rating of A or better and has an underwriting limitation, pursuant to Section 12090 of the Insurance Code, greater than the value of the contract amount of the bond.

Establishes requirements for owner's "security bond".
Maintains rating and underwriting requirements and adds admitted surety requirement.

••

New Text (Operative July 1, 2012) | **Old Text**

__CC 8724__

An irrevocable letter of credit under this chapter shall satisfy all of the following requirements:

(a) The letter of credit shall be issued by a financial institution, as defined in Section 5107 of the Financial Code, inuring to the benefit of the direct contractor.

(b) The letter of credit shall be in an amount not less than 15 percent of the contract price for the work of improvement or, if the work of improvement is to be substantially completed within six months after the commencement of work, not less than 25 percent of the contract price.

(c) The maturity date and other terms of the letter of credit shall be determined by agreement between the owner, the direct contractor, and the financial institution, except that the owner shall maintain the letter of credit in effect until the owner has satisfied its payment obligation to the direct contractor.

CC 3110.5(b)(2)

(2) An irrevocable letter of credit from a financial institution, as defined in Section 5107 of the Financial Code, inuring to the benefit of the original contractor in the amount of either (A) not less than 25 percent of the total amount of any construction contract that is subject to this section where the construction contract provides that the work of improvement is scheduled to be substantially completed within six months following the commencement thereof, or (B) not less than 15 percent of the total amount of any other construction contract that is subject to this section. The maturity date of the letter of credit and other terms of the letter of credit shall be determined by agreement between the contracting owner, the original contractor, and the issuer of the letter of credit provided that the contracting owner shall be required to maintain the letter of credit in effect until the contracting owner has satisfied all of its payment obligations to the original contractor.

Confirms requirements for irrevocable letter of credit.
Maintains minimum percentage amounts found in prior law (see former Civil Code §3110.5(b)(2)).

••

__CC 8726__

An escrow account under this chapter shall satisfy all of the following requirements:

(a) The account shall be designated as a "construction security escrow account."

(b) The account shall be located in this state and maintained with an escrow agent licensed under the Escrow Law, Division 6 (commencing with Section 17000) of the Financial Code, or with any person exempt from the Escrow Law under paragraph (1) or (3) of subdivision (a) of Section 17006 of the Financial Code.

(c) The owner shall deposit funds in the account in the amount provided in Section 8728. This chapter does not require a construction lender to agree to deposit proceeds of a construction loan in the account.

(d) The owner shall grant the direct contractor a perfected, first priority security interest in the account and in all funds deposited by the owner in the account and in their proceeds, established to the reasonable satisfaction of the direct

CC 3110.5(b)(3)

(3)(A) An escrow account, designated as a "construction security escrow account," maintained with an escrow agent licensed under the Escrow Law, as set forth in Division 6 (commencing with Section 17000) of the Financial Code, or with any person exempt from the Escrow Law pursuant to paragraph (1) or (3) of subdivision (a) of Section 17006 of the Financial Code, which construction security escrow account shall be located in California and in which the contracting owner shall deposit funds in the amount provided in subparagraph (B); provided that the original contractor shall not be obligated to accept a construction security escrow account as security unless the contracting owner establishes to the reasonable satisfaction of the original contractor (which may be established by a written opinion of legal counsel for the contracting owner), that the contracting owner has granted the original contractor a perfected, first priority security interest in the construction security escrow account and all funds deposited by the contracting owner therein and the

New Text (Operative July 1, 2012)

contractor, which may be by a written opinion of legal counsel for the owner.

(e) The funds on deposit in the account shall be the sole property of the owner, subject to the security interest of the direct contractor. The owner and the direct contractor shall instruct the escrow holder to hold the funds on deposit in the account for the purpose of perfecting the direct contractor's security interest in the account and to disburse those funds only on joint authorization of the owner and the direct contractor, or pursuant to a court order that is binding on both of them.

Old Text

proceeds thereof. The funds on deposit in the construction security escrow account shall be the sole property of the contracting owner, subject to the security interest in favor of the original contractor. The escrow holder shall be instructed by the contracting owner and the original contractor to hold the funds on deposit in the construction security escrow account for the purpose of perfecting the original contractor's security interest therein and to disburse those funds only upon the joint authorization of the contracting owner and the original contractor, or in accordance with an order of any court which is binding on both the owner and the original contractor. This section does not require any construction lender to agree to deposit proceeds of a construction loan in a construction security escrow account.

(B) Prior to commencement of the work under the construction contract, the contracting owner shall make an initial deposit to the construction security escrow account in the amount of either (i) not less than 25 percent of the total amount of any construction contract which is subject to this section where the construction contract provides that the work of improvement is scheduled to be substantially completed within six months following the commencement thereof, or (ii) not less than 15 percent of the total amount of any other construction contract which is subject to this section. In addition, if the construction contract provides for a so-called retainage or retention to be withheld from periodic payments to the original contractor, the contracting owner shall deposit all amounts withheld as retainage or retention in the construction security escrow account at the same time the contracting owner makes the corresponding payment to the original contractor from which the retainage or retention is withheld provided, however, that in no event shall the amount required to be maintained on deposit in the construction security escrow account exceed the total amount of future payments remaining to be due the original contractor under its construction contract (as the same may be adjusted by agreement between the contracting owner and the original contractor). If the amount of funds on deposit in the construction security escrow account equals or exceeds the total amount of future payments

New Text (Operative July 1, 2012) | **Old Text**

remaining to be due the original contractor, the contracting owner and the original contractor shall authorize the disbursement to the original contractor of funds on deposit in the construction security escrow account to pay progress payments then due the original contractor under its construction contract (in whole or in part), but in no event shall either party be obligated to authorize the disbursement of any funds that would cause the amount remaining on deposit in the construction security escrow account following that disbursement to be less than the total amount of future payments remaining to be due the original contractor after application of any funds disbursed to the original contractor. The contracting owner and the original contractor shall authorize the disbursement to the contracting owner of any funds remaining on deposit in the construction security escrow account after the original contractor has been paid all amounts due under its construction contract. The contracting owner and the original contractor shall authorize the disbursement of funds on deposit in the construction security escrow account in accordance with the order of any court which is binding on both of them. The contracting owner and the original contractor may agree in the construction contract upon additional conditions for the disbursement of funds on deposit in the construction security escrow account provided that the conditions shall not cause the amount remaining on deposit in the construction security escrow account to be less than the amount required pursuant to this subparagraph.

Reaffirms the requirements for a "construction security escrow account". Maintains the first priority security interest in favor of direct contractor.

New Text (Operative July 1, 2012)

__CC 8728__

The following provisions govern a deposit to or disbursement from a construction security escrow account under this chapter:

(a) Before the commencement of work the owner shall make an initial deposit to the account in an amount not less than 15 percent of the contract price for the work of improvement or, if the work of improvement is to be substantially completed within six months after the commencement of work, not less than 25 percent of the contract price.

(b) If the contract provides for a retention to be withheld from a periodic payment to the direct contractor, the owner shall deposit to the account the amount withheld as retention at the time the owner makes the corresponding payment to the direct contractor from which the retention is withheld.

(c) The amount required to be maintained on deposit shall not exceed the total amount remaining to be paid to the direct contractor pursuant to the contract or as adjusted by agreement between the owner and the direct contractor. If the amount on deposit equals or exceeds the total amount remaining to be paid to the direct contractor, the owner and the direct contractor shall authorize disbursement to the direct contractor for progress payments then due the direct contractor, but a party is not obligated to authorize disbursement that would cause the amount remaining on deposit following the disbursement to be less than the total amount remaining to be paid to the direct contractor.

(d) The owner and the direct contractor shall authorize the disbursement to the owner of any funds remaining on deposit after the direct contractor has been paid all amounts due pursuant to the contract. The owner and the direct contractor shall authorize the disbursement of funds on deposit pursuant to a court order that is binding on both of them. The owner and the direct contractor may agree in the contract to additional conditions for the disbursement of funds on deposit, except that the conditions may not cause the amount remaining on deposit to be less than the amount required under this section.

Old Text

CC 3110.5(b)(3)

(3)(A) An escrow account, designated as a "construction security escrow account," maintained with an escrow agent licensed under the Escrow Law, as set forth in Division 6 (commencing with Section 17000) of the Financial Code, or with any person exempt from the Escrow Law pursuant to paragraph (1) or (3) of subdivision (a) of Section 17006 of the Financial Code, which construction security escrow account shall be located in California and in which the contracting owner shall deposit funds in the amount provided in subparagraph (B); provided that the original contractor shall not be obligated to accept a construction security escrow account as security unless the contracting owner establishes to the reasonable satisfaction of the original contractor (which may be established by a written opinion of legal counsel for the contracting owner), that the contracting owner has granted the original contractor a perfected, first priority security interest in the construction security escrow account and all funds deposited by the contracting owner therein and the proceeds thereof. The funds on deposit in the construction security escrow account shall be the sole property of the contracting owner, subject to the security interest in favor of the original contractor. The escrow holder shall be instructed by the contracting owner and the original contractor to hold the funds on deposit in the construction security escrow account for the purpose of perfecting the original contractor's security interest therein and to disburse those funds only upon the joint authorization of the contracting owner and the original contractor, or in accordance with an order of any court which is binding on both the owner and the original contractor. This section does not require any construction lender to agree to deposit proceeds of a construction loan in a construction security escrow account.

(B) Prior to commencement of the work under the construction contract, the contracting owner shall make an initial deposit to the construction security escrow account in the amount of either (i) not less than 25 percent of the total amount of any construction contract which is subject to this section where the construction contract provides that the work of improvement is scheduled to be substantially completed within six months following the commencement thereof, or (ii) not less than 15 percent of the total amount of any other construction contract which is subject to this section. In addition, if the construction contract provides for a so-called retainage or retention to be withheld from periodic payments to the original contractor, the contracting owner shall deposit all amounts withheld as retainage or retention in the construction security escrow account at the same time the contracting owner makes the corresponding payment to the original contractor from which the retainage or retention is withheld provided, however, that in no event shall the amount required to be maintained on deposit in the construction security escrow account exceed the total amount of future payments remaining to be due the original contractor under its construction contract (as the same may be adjusted by agreement between the contracting owner and the original contractor). If the amount of funds on deposit in the construction security escrow account equals or exceeds the total amount of future payments remaining to be due the original contractor, the contracting owner and the original contractor shall authorize the disbursement to the original contractor of funds on deposit in the construction security escrow account to pay progress payments then due the original contractor under its construction contract (in whole or in part), but in no event shall either party be obligated to authorize the disbursement of any funds that would cause the amount remaining on deposit in the construction security escrow account following that disbursement to be less than the total amount of future payments remaining to be due the original contractor after application of any funds disbursed to the original contractor. The contracting owner and the original contractor shall authorize the disbursement to the contracting owner of any funds remaining on deposit in the construction security escrow account after the original contractor has been paid all amounts due under its construction contract. The contracting owner and the original contractor shall authorize the disbursement of funds on deposit in the construction security escrow account in accordance with the order of any court which is binding on both of them. The contracting owner and the original contractor may agree in the construction contract upon additional conditions for the disbursement of funds on deposit in the construction security escrow account provided that the conditions shall not cause the amount remaining on deposit in the construction security escrow account to be less than the amount required pursuant to this subparagraph.

Maintains the minimum percentage amounts found in prior law (see former Civil Code §3110.5(b)(3)) and the requirement that the owner deposit into the escrow account all amounts withheld from the direct contractor as retention.

New Text (Operative July 1, 2012) | **Old Text**

CC 8730

If the contract price for a work of improvement is not a fixed price, the amount of security provided under this chapter shall be the guaranteed maximum price or, if there is no guaranteed maximum price, the owner's and direct contractor's good faith estimate of the reasonable value of the work to be provided pursuant to the contract.

CC 3110.5(c)

(c) For the purposes of subdivision (b), if the price under the construction contract is not a fixed price, the amount of security to be provided shall be determined with reference to the guaranteed maximum price, if there is one, or if there is no guaranteed maximum price, the amount of security shall be determined with reference to the contracting owner's and original contractor's good faith estimate as to the total cost anticipated to be incurred under the construction contract. If any contracting owner that is required to provide security under this section with respect to a construction contract fails to provide that security or fails to maintain that security as required, the original contractor may make written demand on the contracting owner to do so, and if the contracting owner fails to provide and maintain that security within 10 days after the original contractor makes written demand on the owner, the original contractor may suspend work until the required security is provided and maintained in accordance with this section.

Preserves "rules" for determining contract price found in prior law (see former Civil Code § 3110.5(c)).

New Text (Operative July 1, 2012)	Old Text

PART 6. WORKS OF IMPROVEMENT
TITLE 2. PRIVATE WORKS OF IMPROVEMENT
Chapter 8. Prompt Payment
Article 1. Progress Payment

CC 8800

(a) Except as otherwise agreed in writing by the owner and direct contractor, the owner shall pay the direct contractor, within 30 days after notice demanding payment pursuant to the contract is given, any progress payment due as to which there is no good faith dispute between them. The notice given shall comply with the requirements of Chapter 2 (commencing with Section 8100) of Title 1.

(b) If there is a good faith dispute between the owner and direct contractor as to a progress payment due, the owner may withhold from the progress payment an amount not in excess of 150 percent of the disputed amount.

(c) An owner that violates this section is liable to the direct contractor for a penalty of 2 percent per month on the amount wrongfully withheld, in place of any interest otherwise due. In an action for collection of the amount wrongfully withheld, the prevailing party is entitled to costs and a reasonable attorney's fee.

(d) This section does not supersede any requirement of Article 2 (commencing with Section 8810) relating to the withholding of a retention.

CC 3260.1

(a) This section is applicable with respect to all contracts entered into on or after January 1, 1992, relating to the construction of any private work of improvement.

(b) Except as otherwise agreed in writing, the owner shall pay to the contractor, within 30 days following receipt of a demand for payment in accordance with the contract, any progress payment due thereunder as to which there is no good faith dispute between the parties. In the event of a dispute between the owner and the contractor, the owner may withhold from the progress payment an amount not to exceed 150 percent of the disputed amount. If any amount is wrongfully withheld in violation of this subdivision, the contractor shall be entitled to the penalty specified in subdivision (g) of Section 3260.

(c) Nothing in this section shall be deemed to supersede any requirement of Section 3260 respecting the withholding of retention proceeds.

Incorporates notice requirements of Section 8100.
Maintains requirement to pay undisputed amounts within thirty (30) days of notice demanding payment; owner's right to withhold 150 percent of any disputed amount; and right to recover interest at two percent (2%) per month and attorney's fees if owner violates the provisions of this section.

New Text (Operative July 1, 2012) | **Old Text**

<u>*CC 8802*</u>

(a) This section applies to a contract between a public utility and a direct contractor for all or part of a work of improvement.

(b) Unless the direct contractor and a subcontractor otherwise agree in writing, within 21 days after receipt of a progress payment from the public utility the direct contractor shall pay the subcontractor the amount allowed the direct contractor on account of the work performed by the subcontractor to the extent of the subcontractor's interest in the work. If there is a good faith dispute over all or part of the amount due on a progress payment from the direct contractor to a subcontractor, the direct contractor may withhold an amount not in excess of 150 percent of the disputed amount.

(c) A direct contractor that violates this section is liable to the subcontractor for a penalty of 2 percent of the disputed amount due per month for every month that payment is not made. In an action for collection of the amount wrongfully withheld, the prevailing party is entitled to costs and a reasonable attorney's fee.

(d) This section does not limit or impair a contractual, administrative, or judicial remedy otherwise available to a contractor or subcontractor in a dispute involving late payment or nonpayment by the contractor or deficient performance or nonperformance by the subcontractor.

CC 3262.5

(a) Any person or corporation which has contracted to do business with a public utility, hereafter referred to in this section as a contractor, shall pay any subcontractors within 15 working days of receipt of each progress payment from the public utility, unless otherwise agreed in writing by the parties, the respective amounts allowed the contractor on account of the work performed by the subcontractors, to the extent of each of the Subcontractor's interest in that work. In the event that there is a good faith dispute over all or any portion of the amount due on a progress payment from a contractor to a subcontractor, then the contractor may withhold no more than 150 percent of the disputed amount.

(b) Any contractor who violates this section shall pay to the subcontractor a penalty of 2 percent of the disputed amount due per month for every month that payment is not made. In any action for the collection of funds wrongfully withheld, the prevailing party shall be entitled to his or her attorney's fees and costs.

(c) This section shall not be construed to limit or impair any contractual, administrative, or judicial remedies otherwise available to a contractor or a subcontractor in the event of a dispute involving late payment or nonpayment by a contractor, or deficient performance or nonperformance by a subcontractor.

Changes the time period for direct contractor's payment to subcontractors from 15 working days to 21 days following receipt of payment from a public utility.

Maintains right to withhold for disputed amounts and penalties for violating section.

New Text (Operative July 1, 2012) — **Old Text**

PART 6. WORKS OF IMPROVEMENT
TITLE 2. PRIVATE WORKS OF IMPROVEMENT
Chapter 8. Prompt Payment

CC 8810

This article governs a retention payment withheld by an owner from a direct contractor or by a direct contractor from a subcontractor.

CC 3260(b)

(b) The retention proceeds withheld from any payment by the owner from the original contractor, or by the original contractor from any subcontractor, shall be subject to this section

••

CC 8812

(a) If an owner withholds a retention from a direct contractor, the owner shall, within 45 days after completion of the work of improvement, pay the retention to the contractor.

(b) If part of a work of improvement ultimately will become the property of a public entity, the owner may condition payment of a retention allocable to that part on acceptance of the part by the public entity.

(c) If there is a good faith dispute between the owner and direct contractor as to a retention payment due, the owner may withhold from final payment an amount not in excess of 150 percent of the disputed amount.

CC 3260(c)

(c) Within 45 days after the date of completion, the retention withheld by the owner shall be released. "Date of completion," for purposes of this section, means any of the following:

(1) The date of issuance of any certificate of occupancy covering the work by the public agency issuing the building permit.

(2) The date of completion indicated on a valid notice of completion recorded pursuant to Section 3093.

(3) The date of completion as defined in Section 3086.

However, release of retentions withheld for any portion of the work of improvement which ultimately will become the property of a public agency, may be conditioned upon the acceptance of the work by the public agency. In the event of a dispute between the owner and the original contractor, the owner may withhold from the final payment an amount not to exceed 150 percent of the disputed amount

••

CC 8814

(a) If a direct contractor has withheld a retention from one or more subcontractors, the direct contractor shall, within 10 days after receiving all or part of a retention payment, pay to each subcontractor from whom retention has been withheld that subcontractor's share of the payment.

(b) If a retention received by the direct contractor is specifically designated for a particular subcontractor, the direct contractor shall pay the retention payment to the designated subcontractor, if consistent with the terms of the subcontract.

(c) If a good faith dispute exists between the direct contractor and a subcontractor, the direct contractor may withhold from the retention to the subcontractor an amount not in excess of 150 percent of the estimated value of the disputed amount.

CC 3260(d) and CC 3260(e)

CC 3260(d)

(d) Subject to subdivision (e), within 10 days from the time that all or any portion of the retention proceeds are received by the original contractor, the original contractor shall pay each of its subcontractors from whom retention has been withheld, each subcontractor's share of the retention received. However, if a retention payment received by the original contractor is specifically designated for a particular subcontractor, payment of the retention shall be made to the designated subcontractor, if the payment is consistent with the terms of the subcontract.

CC 3260(e)

(e) If a bona fide dispute exists between a subcontractor and the original contractor, the original contractor may withhold from that subcontractor with whom the dispute exists its portion of the retention proceeds. The amount withheld from the retention payment shall not exceed 150 percent of the estimated value of the disputed amount

••

New Text (Operative July 1, 2012) | **Old Text**

<u>CC 8814</u>

(a) If a direct contractor has withheld a retention from one or more subcontractors, the direct contractor shall, within 10 days after receiving all or part of a retention payment, pay to each subcontractor from whom retention has been withheld that subcontractor's share of the payment.

(b) If a retention received by the direct contractor is specifically designated for a particular subcontractor, the direct contractor shall pay the retention payment to the designated subcontractor, if consistent with the terms of the subcontract.

(c) If a good faith dispute exists between the direct contractor and a subcontractor, the direct contractor may withhold from the retention to the subcontractor an amount not in excess of 150 percent of the estimated value of the disputed amount.

CC 3260(e)

(e) If a bona fide dispute exists between a subcontractor and the original contractor, the original contractor may withhold from that subcontractor with whom the dispute exists its portion of the retention proceeds. The amount withheld from the retention payment shall not exceed 150 percent of the estimated value of the disputed amount.

••

<u>CC 8816</u>

(a) If the direct contractor gives the owner, or a subcontractor gives the direct contractor, notice that work in dispute has been completed in accordance with the contract, the owner or direct contractor shall within 10 days give notice advising the notifying party of the acceptance or rejection of the disputed work. Both notices shall comply with the requirements of Chapter 2 (commencing with Section 8100) of Title 1.

(b) Within 10 days after acceptance of disputed work, the owner or direct contractor shall pay the portion of the retention relating to the disputed work.

CC 3260(f)

(f) Within 10 days of receipt of written notice by the owner from the original contractor or by the original contractor from the subcontractor, as the case may be, that any work in dispute has been completed in accordance with the terms of the contract, the owner or original contractor shall advise the notifying party of the acceptance or rejection of the disputed work. Within 10 days of acceptance of the disputed work, the owner or original contractor, as the case may be, shall release the retained portion of the retention proceeds.

Maintains protocol for notification regarding correction/ completion of disputed work.
Incorporates notice requirements found in Section 8100.
Maintains 10 day time period for payment.

••

New Text (Operative July 1, 2012) | **Old Text**

CC 8818

If an owner or direct contractor does not make a retention payment within the time required by this article:

(a) The owner or direct contractor is liable to the person to which payment is owed for a penalty of 2 percent per month on the amount wrongfully withheld, in place of any interest otherwise due.

(b) In an action for collection of the amount wrongfully withheld, the prevailing party is entitled to costs and reasonable attorney's fees.

CC 3260(g)

(g) In the event that retention payments are not made within the time periods required by this section, the owner or original contractor withholding the unpaid amounts shall be subject to a charge of 2 percent per month on the improperly withheld amount, in lieu of any interest otherwise due. Additionally, in any action for the collection of funds wrongfully withheld, the prevailing party shall be entitled to his or her attorney's fees and costs.

Maintains interest penalty of two percent (2%) on wrongfully withheld amounts and the prevailing party's right to recover attorney's fees.

••

CC 8820

It is against public policy to waive the provisions of this article by contract.

No previous text

Confirms that any waiver of the provisions of this article is against public policy.

••

CC 8822

This article does not apply to a retention payment withheld by a lender pursuant to a construction loan agreement

No previous text

Confirms that this article does not apply to retention held by a lender.

••

PART 6. WORKS OF IMPROVEMENT
TITLE 2. PRIVATE WORKS OF IMPROVEMENT
Chapter 8. Prompt Payment
Article 3. Stop Work Notice

CC 8830

"Stop work notice" means notice given under this article by a direct contractor to an owner that the contractor will stop work if the amount owed the contractor is not paid within 10 days after notice is given.

CC 3260.2(a)

"Stop work notice" means notice given under this article by a direct contractor to an owner that the contractor will stop work if the amount owed the contractor is not paid within 10 days after notice is given.

Simplifies prior law by dividing Section 3260.2(a) into several sections.

•••

CC 8832

If a direct contractor is not paid the amount due pursuant to a written contract within 35 days after the date payment is due under the contract, and there is no dispute as to the satisfactory performance of the contractor, the contractor may give the owner a stop work notice. The notice shall comply with the requirements of Chapter 2 (commencing with Section 8100) of Title 1.

CC 3260.2(a)

(a) If an original contractor is not paid all moneys which are owed pursuant to a written contract for a private work of improvement within 35 days from the date payment is due pursuant to the written contract, and there is no dispute as to the satisfactory performance of that original contractor, the original contractor shall have a right to serve upon the owner a "10-day stop work order" that states that unless all amounts then due the original contractor are paid within 10 days from the date notice is provided under this section, the original contractor will stop work on the project. At least five days before service upon the owner of a "10-day stop work order," the contractor shall post, in a conspicuous location at the job site and at the main office, if one exists, of the job site, a notice that the original contractor intends to file a 10-day stop work order pursuant to this section. A copy of the written notice shall also be served upon all subcontractors with whom the original contractor has a direct contractual relationship on the project at the same time the notice is served upon the owner. Within five days of receipt of written notice by an original contractor pursuant to this section, the owner shall forward to the construction lender, if any, at the address provided in the construction loan agreement, a copy of the notice by first-class mail.

Upon resolution of the dispute or cancellation of the 10-day notice by the original contractor, the original contractor shall post, in a conspicuous location at the job site and at the main office, and serve a notice to inform the subcontractors with whom the original contractor has a direct contractual relationship of this resolution or cancellation.

Incorporates notice requirements found in Section 8800.

•••

New Text (Operative July 1, 2012) | **Old Text**

CC 8834

A direct contractor that gives an owner a stop work notice shall give the following additional notice:

(a) At least five days before giving the stop work notice, the contractor shall post notice of intent to give a stop work notice. The notice shall comply with the requirements of Chapter 2 (commencing with Section 8100) of Title 1. In addition to posting the notice pursuant to Section 8114, the notice shall also be posted at the main office of the site, if one exists.

(b) At the same time the contractor gives the stop work notice, the contractor shall give a copy of the stop work notice to all subcontractors with whom the contractor has a direct contractual relationship on the work of improvement.

CC 3260.2(a)

(a) If an original contractor is not paid all moneys which are owed pursuant to a written contract for a private work of improvement within 35 days from the date payment is due pursuant to the written contract, and there is no dispute as to the satisfactory performance of that original contractor, the original contractor shall have a right to serve upon the owner a "10-day stop work order" that states that unless all amounts then due the original contractor are paid within 10 days from the date notice is provided under this section, the original contractor will stop work on the project. At least five days before service upon the owner of a "10-day stop work order," the contractor shall post, in a conspicuous location at the job site and at the main office, if one exists, of the job site, a notice that the original contractor intends to file a 10-day stop work order pursuant to this section. A copy of the written notice shall also be served upon all subcontractors with whom the original contractor has a direct contractual relationship on the project at the same time the notice is served upon the owner. Within five days of receipt of written notice by an original contractor pursuant to this section, the owner shall forward to the construction lender, if any, at the address provided in the construction loan agreement, a copy of the notice by first-class mail.

Upon resolution of the dispute or cancellation of the 10-day notice by the original contractor, the original contractor shall post, in a conspicuous location at the job site and at the main office, and serve a notice to inform the subcontractors with whom the original contractor has a direct contractual relationship of this resolution or cancellation.

Maintains the "posting" requirements.
Maintains requirement that direct contractor send a copy of the stop work notice on all subcontractors with in contractual privity with the direct contractor.
Incorporates notice requirements found in Section 8100 and the posting requirements found in Section 8114.

••

CC 8836

Within five days after receipt of a stop work notice from a direct contractor, the owner shall give a copy of the notice to the construction lender, if any. The copy of the notice shall be given in compliance with the requirements of Chapter 2 (commencing with Section 8100) of Title 1.

CC 3260.2(a)

(a) If an original contractor is not paid all moneys which are owed pursuant to a written contract for a private work of improvement within 35 days from the date payment is due pursuant to the written contract, and there is no dispute as to the satisfactory performance of that original contractor, the original contractor shall have a right to serve upon the owner a "10-day stop work order" that states that unless all amounts then due the original contractor are paid within

10 days from the date notice is provided under this section, the original contractor will stop work on the project. At least five days before service upon the owner of a "10-day stop work order," the contractor shall post, in a conspicuous location at the job site and at the main office, if one exists, of the job site, a notice that the original contractor intends to file a 10-day stop work order pursuant to this section. A copy of the written notice shall also be served upon all subcontractors with whom the original contractor has a direct contractual relationship on the project at the same time the notice is served upon the owner. Within five days of receipt of written notice by an original contractor pursuant to this section, the owner shall forward to the construction lender, if any, at the address provided in the construction loan agreement, a copy of the notice by first-class mail.

Upon resolution of the dispute or cancellation of the 10-day notice by the original contractor, the original contractor shall post, in a conspicuous location at the job site and at the main office, and serve a notice to inform the subcontractors with whom the original contractor has a direct contractual relationship of this resolution or cancellation.

Incorporates notice requirements found in Section 8100.

CC 8838

(a) The direct contractor or the direct contractor's surety, or a subcontractor or a subcontractor's surety, is not liable for delay or damage that the owner or a contractor of a subcontractor may suffer as a result of the direct contractor giving a stop work notice and subsequently stopping work for nonpayment, if the notice and posting requirements of this article are satisfied.

(b) A direct contractor's or original subcontractor's liability to a subcontractor or material supplier after the direct contractor stops work under this article is limited to the amount the subcontractor or material supplier could otherwise recover under this title for work provided up to the date the subcontractor or material supplier ceases work, subject to the following exceptions:

(1) The direct contractor's or original subcontractor's liability continues for work provided up to and including the 10-day notice period and not beyond.

CC 3260.2(c)

(c) Notwithstanding any other provision, the original contractor or his or her surety, or subcontractor or his or her surety, shall not be liable for any delays or damages that the owner or contractor of a subcontractor may suffer as a result of the original contractor serving the owner with a 10-day stop work order, and subsequently stopping work for nonpayment if all of the posting and notice requirements described in subdivision (a) are met. An original contractor's or original subcontractor's liability to a subcontractor or material supplier resulting from the cessation of work under this section shall be limited to the amount of monetary damages the subcontractor or material supplier could recover under the Mechanic's lien law for goods and services provided up to the date the subcontractor ceases work, provided that (1) liability shall continue for work performed and materials supplied up to and including the 10-day notice period and not beyond, and (2) this provision does not apply to limit monetary damages for custom work, including materials which have been fabricated, manufactured, or ordered to specifications that are unique to the job.

New Text (Operative July 1, 2012) | **Old Text**

(2) This subdivision does not limit liability for custom work, including materials that have been fabricated, manufactured, or ordered to specifications that are unique to the job.

Preserves exception from liability and limitation on liability found in prior law (see former Civil Code §3260.2(c)).

••

CC 8840

On resolution of the claim in the stop work notice or the direct contractor's cancellation of the stop work notice, the contractor shall post, and give subcontractors with whom the contractor has a direct contractual relationship on the work of improvement, notice of the resolution or cancellation. The notice shall comply with the requirements of Chapter 2 (commencing with Section 8100) of Title 1. In addition to posting the notice pursuant to Section 8114, the notice shall also be posted at the main office of the site, if one exists.

CC 3260.2(a)

(a) If an original contractor is not paid all moneys which are owed pursuant to a written contract for a private work of improvement within 35 days from the date payment is due pursuant to the written contract, and there is no dispute as to the satisfactory performance of that original contractor, the original contractor shall have a right to serve upon the owner a "10-day stop work order" that states that unless all amounts then due the original contractor are paid within 10 days from the date notice is provided under this section, the original contractor will stop work on the project. At least five days before service upon the owner of a "10-day stop work order," the contractor shall post, in a conspicuous location at the job site and at the main office, if one exists, of the job site, a notice that the original contractor intends to file a 10-day stop work order pursuant to this section. A copy of the written notice shall also be served upon all subcontractors with whom the original contractor has a direct contractual relationship on the project at the same time the notice is served upon the owner. Within five days of receipt of written notice by an original contractor pursuant to this section, the owner shall forward to the construction lender, if any, at the address provided in the construction loan agreement, a copy of the notice by first-class mail.

Upon resolution of the dispute or cancellation of the 10-day notice by the original contractor, the original contractor shall post, in a conspicuous location at the job site and at the main office, and serve a notice to inform the subcontractors with whom the original contractor has a direct contractual relationship of this resolution or cancellation.

Incorporates notice requirements of Section 8100 and posting requirements of Section 8114.

••

New Text (Operative July 1, 2012) | **Old Text**

__CC 8842__

A direct contractor's right to stop work under this article is in addition to other rights the direct contractor may have under the law.

CC 3260.2(b)

(b) The original contractor's right to stop work pursuant to this section is in addition to any and all other rights the original contractor may have under the law.

••

__CC 8844__

(a) If payment of the amount claimed is not made within 10 days after a stop work notice is given, the direct contractor, the direct contractor's surety, or an owner may in an expedited proceeding in the superior court in the county in which the private work of improvement is located, seek a judicial determination of liability for the amount due.

(b) The expedited proceeding shall be set for hearing or trial at the earliest possible date in order that it shall be quickly heard and determined, and shall take precedence over all other cases except older matter of the same character and other matters to which special precedence has been given.

CC 3260.2(d)

(d) If the payment is not made within 10 days from the date the notice was served, the original contractor or his or her surety, may seek a judicial determination of liability for the amount not paid for work performed in an expedited proceeding in the superior court in the county in which the private work improvement is located.

Adds the owner to the persons that may now seek an expedited proceeding to determine the liability for the amount due on a stop work notice.

Confirms that the expedited proceeding shall be afforded precedence.

••

__CC 8846__

It is against public policy to waive the provisions of this article by contract.

CC 3260.2(e)

(e) It shall be against public policy to waive the provisions of this section in any written contract for private work of improvement.

Reiterates that any waiver of this article is against public policy.

••

__CC 8848__

(a) This article applies to a contract entered into on or after January 1, 1999.

(b) This article does not apply to a retention withheld by a lender pursuant to a construction loan agreement.

CC 3260.2(f)

(f) This section shall apply to any contract entered into on or after January 1, 1999. However, nothing in this section shall be construed to apply to retentions withheld by a lender in accordance with the construction loan agreement.

Maintains reference to contracts after January 1, 1999 and inapplicability to retention held by a construction lender.

••

New Text (Operative July 1, 2012) | **Old Text**

PART 6. WORKS OF IMPROVEMENT
TITLE 3. PUBLIC WORK OF IMPROVEMENT
Chapter 1. General Provisions
Article 1. Application of Title

CC 9000

This title applies to a work of improvement contracted for by a public entity.

CC 3179

The provisions of this chapter apply only to a public work.

Changes reference from "public work" to improvements contracted

PART 6. WORKS OF IMPROVEMENT
TITLE 3. PUBLIC WORK OF IMPROVEMENT
Chapter 1. General Provisions
Article 2. Claimants

CC 9100

(a) Except as provided in subdivision (b), any of the following persons that have not been paid in full may give a stop payment notice to the public entity or assert a claim against a payment bond:

(1) A person that provides work for a public works contract, if the work is authorized by a direct contractor, subcontractor, architect, project manager, or other person having charge of all or part of the public works contract.

(2) A laborer.

(3) A person described in Section 4107.7 of the Public Contract Code.

(b) A direct contractor may not give a stop payment notice or assert a claim against a payment bond under this title.

CC 3110, CC 3111, CC 3112 and CC 3181

CC 3110

Mechanics, materialmen, contractors, subcontractors, lessors of equipment, artisans, architects, registered engineers, licensed land surveyors, machinists, builders, teamsters, and draymen, and all persons and laborers of every class performing labor upon or bestowing skill or other necessary services on, or furnishing materials or leasing equipment to be used or consumed in or furnishing appliances, teams, or power contributing to a work of improvement shall have a lien upon the property upon which they have bestowed labor or furnished materials or appliances or leased equipment for the value of such labor done or materials furnished and for the value of the use of such appliances, equipment, teams, or power whether done or furnished at the instance of the owner or of any person acting by his authority or under him as contractor or otherwise. For the purposes of this chapter, every contractor, subcontractor, sub-subcontractor, architect, builder, or other person having charge of a work of improvement or portion thereof shall be held to be the agent of the owner.

CC 3111

For the purposes of this chapter, an express trust fund to which a portion of a laborer's total compensation is to be paid pursuant to an applicable employment agreement or a collective bargaining agreement for the provision of benefits, including, but not limited to, employer payments described in Section 1773.1 of the Labor Code and regulations thereunder, shall be entitled to assert the same rights and claims as laborers performing labor upon, or bestowing skill or other necessary services on, a work of improvement, to the extent of the compensation agreed to be paid to that express trust fund for labor on that improvement only.

CC 3112

Any claimant who, at the instance or request of the owner (or any other person acting by his authority or under him, as contractor or otherwise) of any lot or tract of land, has made

New Text (Operative July 1, 2012) | **Old Text**

any site improvement has a lien upon such lot or tract of land for work done or materials furnished.

CC 3181

Except for an original contractor, any person mentioned in Section 3110, 3111, or 3112, or in Section 4107.7 of the Public Contract Code, or furnishing provisions, provender, or other supplies, may serve a stop notice upon the public entity responsible for the public work in accordance with this chapter.

Changes name from "stop notice" to "stop payment notice".
Identifies class of persons that may serve a stop payment notice or make a claim on a payment bond on a public work of improvement.
Classifies persons by contractual relationship rather than by type of work or service.
Confirms that a direct contractor is not entitled to serve a stop payment notice or assert a claim against a payment bond.
Uses term "laborer" which includes a person or entity to which a portion of the laborers' compensation is paid (See Civil Code §8024).
Maintains reference to persons described in Public Contract Code §4107.7.

••

CC 9200

For the purpose of this title, completion of a work of improvement occurs at the earliest of the following times:

(a) Acceptance of the work of improvement by the public entity.

(b) Cessation of labor on the work of improvement for a continuous period of 60 days. This subdivision does not apply to a contract awarded under the State Contract Act, Part 2 (commencing with Section 10100) of Division 2 of the Public Contract Code.

CC 3086 (except subd (b))

"Completion" means, in the case of any work of improvement other than a public work, actual completion of the work of improvement. Any of the following shall be deemed equivalent to a completion:

(a) The occupation or use of a work of improvement by the owner, or his agent, accompanied by cessation of labor thereon.

(c) After the commencement of a work of improvement, a cessation of labor thereon for a continuous period of 60 days, or a cessation of labor thereon for a continuous period of 30 days or more if the owner files for record a notice of cessation.

If the work of improvement is subject to acceptance by any public entity, the completion of such work of improvement shall be deemed to be the date of such acceptance; provided, however, that, except as to contracts awarded under the State Contract Act, Chapter 3 (commencing with Section 14250), Part 5, Division 3, Title 2 of the Government Code, a cessation of labor on any public work for a continuous period of 30 days shall be a completion thereof.

Defines "completion" on public works of improvement.
Maintains time period for cessation of labor from thirty (30) to (60) days.
Eliminates "notice of cessation" language and moves it to Civil Code §9202.
Maintains exception for contracts awarded under State Contact Act, Public Contract Code Section 10100.

••

New Text (Operative July 1, 2012)

CC 9202

(a) A public entity may record a notice of cessation if there has been a continuous cessation of labor for at least 30 days prior to the recordation that continues through the date of the recordation.

(b) The notice shall be signed and verified by the public entity or its agent.

(c) The notice shall comply with the requirements of Chapter 2 (commencing with Section 8100) of Title 1, and shall also include all of the following information:

(1) The date on or about which the labor ceased.

(2) A statement that the cessation has continued until the recordation of the notice.

Old Text

C 3092

"Notice of cessation" means a written notice, signed and verified by the owner or his agent, containing all of the following:

(a) The date on or about when the cessation of labor commenced.

(b) A statement that such cessation has continued until the recording of the notice of cessation.

(c) The name and address of the owner.

(d) The nature of the interest or estate of the owner.

(e) A description of the site sufficient for identification, containing the street address of the site, if any. If a sufficient legal description of the site is given, the validity of the notice shall not, however, be affected by the fact that the street address is erroneous or is omitted.

(f) The name of the original contractor, if any, for the work of improvement as a whole.

(g) For the purpose of this section, "owner" means the owner who causes a building, improvement, or structure, to be constructed, altered, or repaired (or his successor in interest at the date of a notice of cessation from labor is filed for record) whether the interest or estate of such owner be in fee, as vendee under a contract of purchase, as lessee, or other interest or estate less than the fee. Where such interest or estate is held by two or more persons as joint tenants or tenants in common, any one or more of the co-tenants may be deemed to be the "owner" within the meaning of this section. Any notice of cessation signed by less than all of such co-tenants shall recite the names and addresses of all such co-tenants.

The notice of cessation shall be recorded in the office of the county recorder of the county in which the site is located and shall be effective only if there has been a continuous cessation of labor for at least 30 days prior to such recording.

Authorizes recording of notice of cessation on public works.
Incorporates requirements found in Section 8100.
Defines other requirements for notice of cessation.

New Text (Operative July 1, 2012)

<u>*CC 9204*</u>

(a) A public entity may record a notice of completion on or within 15 days after the date of completion of a work of improvement.

(b) The notice shall be signed and verified by the public entity or its agent.

(c) The notice shall comply with the requirements of Chapter 2 (commencing with Section 8100) of Title 1, and shall also include the date of completion. An erroneous statement of the date of completion does not affect the effectiveness of the notice if the true date of completion is 15 days or less before the date of recordation of the notice.

Old Text

CC 3093

"Notice of completion" means a written notice, signed and verified by the owner or his agent, containing all of the following:

(a) The date of completion (other than a cessation of labor). The recital of an erroneous date of completion shall not, however, affect the validity of the notice if the true date of completion is within 10 days preceding the date of recording of such notice.

(b) The name and address of the owner.

(c) The nature of the interest or estate of the owner.

(d) A description of the site sufficient for identification, containing the street address of the site, if any. If a sufficient legal description of the site is given, the validity of the notice shall not, however, be affected by the fact that the street address recited is erroneous or that such street address is omitted.

(e) The name of the original contractor, if any, or if the notice is given only of completion of a contract for a particular portion of such work of improvement, as provided in Section 3117, then the name of the original contractor under such contract, and a general statement of the kind of work done or materials furnished pursuant to such contract.

The notice of completion shall be recorded in the office of the county recorder of the county in which the site is located, within 10 days after such completion. A notice of completion in otherwise proper form, verified and containing the information required by this section shall be accepted by the recorder for recording and shall be deemed duly recorded without acknowledgment.

If there is more than one owner, any notice of completion signed by less than all of such co-owners shall recite the names and addresses of all of such co-owners; and provided further, that any notice of completion signed by a successor in interest shall recite the names and addresses of his transferor or transferors.

For the purpose of this section, owner is defined as set forth in subdivision (g) of Section 3092.

Expands the time period for recording notice of completion from ten (10) days to fifteen (15) days after completion of work.
Incorporates notice requirements found in Section 8100.
Confirms requirements for notice of completion on public works and that the inclusion of an erroneous date will not invalidate the notice so long as the true date of completion is within fifteen (15) days of the recording of the notice.

New Text (Operative July 1, 2012)	Old Text

<u>CC 9208</u>

A notice of completion in otherwise proper form, verified and containing the information required by this title shall be accepted by the recorder for recording and is deemed duly recorded without acknowledgment.

CC 3093

"Notice of completion" means a written notice, signed and verified by the owner or his agent, containing all of the following:

(a) The date of completion (other than a cessation of labor). The recital of an erroneous date of completion shall not, however, affect the validity of the notice if the true date of completion is within 10 days preceding the date of recording of such notice.

(b) The name and address of the owner.

(c) The nature of the interest or estate of the owner.

(d) A description of the site sufficient for identification, containing the street address of the site, if any. If a sufficient legal description of the site is given, the validity of the notice shall not, however, be affected by the fact that the street address recited is erroneous or that such street address is omitted.

(e) The name of the original contractor, if any, or if the notice is given only of completion of a contract for a particular portion of such work of improvement, as provided in Section 3117, then the name of the original contractor under such contract, and a general statement of the kind of work done or materials furnished pursuant to such contract.

The notice of completion shall be recorded in the office of the county recorder of the county in which the site is located, within 10 days after such completion. A notice of completion in otherwise proper form, verified and containing the information required by this section shall be accepted by the recorder for recording and shall be deemed duly recorded without acknowledgment.

If there is more than one owner, any notice of completion signed by less than all of such co-owners shall recite the names and addresses of all of such co-owners; and provided further, that any notice of completion signed by a successor in interest shall recite the names and addresses of his transferor or transferors.

For the purpose of this section, owner is defined as set forth in subdivision (g) of Section 3092.

PART 6. WORKS OF IMPROVEMENT

TITLE 3. PUBLIC WORK OF IMPROVEMENT

Chapter 3. Preliminary Notice

CC 9300

(a) Except as otherwise provided by statute, before giving a stop payment notice or asserting a claim against a payment bond, a claimant shall give preliminary notice to the following persons:

(1) The public entity.

(2) The direct contractor to which the claimant provides work.

(b) Notwithstanding subdivision (a):

(1) A laborer is not required to give preliminary notice.

(2) A claimant that has a direct contractual relationship with a direct contractor is not required to give preliminary notice.

(c) Compliance with this section is a necessary prerequisite to the validity of a stop payment notice under this title.

(d) Compliance with this section or with Section 9562 is a necessary prerequisite to the validity of a claim against a payment bond under this title.

CC 3098, CC 3098(a) and CC 3098(c)

CC 3098

"Preliminary 20-day notice (public work)" means a written notice from a claimant that was given prior to the assertion of a claim against a payment bond, or the filing of a stop notice on public work, and is required to be given under the following circumstances:

(a) In any case in which the law of this state affords a right to a person furnishing labor or materials for a public work who has not been paid therefor to assert a claim against a payment bond, or to file a stop notice with the public agency concerned, and thereby cause the withholding of payment from the contractor for the public work, any person that has no direct contractual relationship with the contractor, other than a person who performed actual labor for wages or an express trust fund described in Section 3111, may file the preliminary notice, but no payment shall be withheld from the contractor pursuant to that notice unless the person has caused written notice to be given to the contractor, and the public agency concerned, not later than 20 days after the claimant has first furnished labor, services, equipment, or materials to the jobsite, stating with substantial accuracy a general description of labor, service, equipment, or materials furnished or to be furnished, and the name of the party to whom the same was furnished. This notice shall be served by mailing the same by first-class mail, registered mail, or certified mail, postage prepaid, in an envelope addressed to the contractor at any place the contractor maintains an office or conducts business, or his or her residence, or by personal service. In case of any public works constructed by the Department of Public Works or the Department of General Services of the state, such notice shall be served by mailing in the same manner as above, addressed to the office of the disbursing officer of the department constructing the work, or by personal service upon the officer. When service is by registered or certified mail, service is complete at the time of the deposit of the registered or certified mail.

(b) Where the contract price to be paid to any subcontractor on a particular work of improvement exceeds four hundred dollars ($400), the failure of that contractor, licensed under Chapter 9, (commencing with Section 7000) of Division 3 of the Business and Professions Code, to give the notice provided for in this section, constitutes grounds for disciplinary action by the Registrar of Contractors.

New Text (Operative July 1, 2012)	Old Text

(c) The notice requirements of this section shall not apply to a laborer described in Section 3089 or to an express trust fund described in Section 3111.

(d) If labor, service, equipment, or materials have been furnished to a jobsite by a claimant who did not give a preliminary notice pursuant to subdivision (a), that claimant shall not be precluded from giving a preliminary notice at any time thereafter. The claimant shall, however, be entitled to assert a claim against a payment bond and file a stop notice only for labor, service, equipment, or material furnished within 20 days prior to the service of the preliminary notice, and at any time thereafter.

(e) The failure to provide, pursuant to Chapter 974 of the Statutes of 1994, a written preliminary notice to a subcontractor with whom the claimant has contracted shall not affect the validity of any preliminary notice provided pursuant to this section.

CC 3098(a)

(a) In any case in which the law of this state affords a right to a person furnishing labor or materials for a public work who has not been paid therefor to assert a claim against a payment bond, or to file a stop notice with the public agency concerned, and thereby cause the withholding of payment from the contractor for the public work, any person that has no direct contractual relationship with the contractor, other than a person who performed actual labor for wages or an express trust fund described in Section 3111, may file the preliminary notice, but no payment shall be withheld from the contractor pursuant to that notice unless the person has caused written notice to be given to the contractor, and the public agency concerned, not later than 20 days after the claimant has first furnished labor, services, equipment, or materials to the jobsite, stating with substantial accuracy a general description of labor, service, equipment, or materials furnished or to be furnished, and the name of the party to whom the same was furnished. This notice shall be served by mailing the same by first-class mail, registered mail, or certified mail, postage prepaid, in an envelope addressed to the contractor at any place the contractor maintains an office or conducts business, or his or her residence, or by personal service. In case of any public works constructed by the Department of Public Works or the Department of General Services of the state, such notice shall be served by mailing in the same manner as above, addressed to the office of the disbursing officer of the department constructing the work, or by personal service upon the officer. When service is by registered or certified mail, service is complete at the time of the deposit of the registered or certified mail.

New Text (Operative July 1, 2012) | **Old Text**

CC 3098(c)

(c) The notice requirements of this section shall not apply to a laborer described in Section 3089 or to an express trust fund described in Section 3111.

Confirms that certain persons must serve a preliminary notice as a prerequisite to the giving of a stop payment notice or asserting a payment bond claim.
Maintains exception for persons in contractual privity with the direct contractor and laborer (see Civil Code §8024).
Preserves right to assert a payment bond claim if notice provided in compliance with Section 9562.

••

__CC 9302__

(a) Except as provided in subdivision (b), preliminary notice shall be given in compliance with the requirements of Chapter 2 (commencing with Section 8100) of Title 1.

(b) If the public works contract is for work constructed by the Department of Public Works or the Department of General Services of the state, preliminary notice to the public entity shall be given to the disbursing officer of the department constructing the work.

CC 3098(a)

(a) In any case in which the law of this state affords a right to a person furnishing labor or materials for a public work who has not been paid therefor to assert a claim against a payment bond, or to file a stop notice with the public agency concerned, and thereby cause the withholding of payment from the contractor for the public work, any person that has no direct contractual relationship with the contractor, other than a person who performed actual labor for wages or an express trust fund described in Section 3111, may file the preliminary notice, but no payment shall be withheld from the contractor pursuant to that notice unless the person has caused written notice to be given to the contractor, and the public agency concerned, not later than 20 days after the claimant has first furnished labor, services, equipment, or materials to the jobsite, stating with substantial accuracy a general description of labor, service, equipment, or materials furnished or to be furnished, and the name of the party to whom the same was furnished. This notice shall be served by mailing the same by first-class mail, registered mail, or certified mail, postage prepaid, in an envelope addressed to the contractor at any place the contractor maintains an office or conducts business, or his or her residence, or by personal service. In case of any public works constructed by the Department of Public Works or the Department of General Services of the state, such notice shall be served by mailing in the same manner as above, addressed to the office of the disbursing officer of the department constructing the work, or by personal service upon the officer. When service is by registered or certified mail, service is complete at the time of the deposit of the registered or certified mail.

Incorporates requirements found in Section 8100.
Maintains requirement that preliminary notice be served on the disbursing officer of the department constructing the work if the work of improvement is being constructed by the Department of Public Works or the Department of General Services of the State.

••

New Text (Operative July 1, 2012) | **Old Text**

CC 9303
The preliminary notice shall comply with the requirements of Section 8102, and shall also include:
(a) A general description of the work to be provided.
(b) An estimate of the total price of the work provided and to be provided.

CC 3098(a)
(a) In any case in which the law of this state affords a right to a person furnishing labor or materials for a public work who has not been paid therefor to assert a claim against a payment bond, or to file a stop notice with the public agency concerned, and thereby cause the withholding of payment from the contractor for the public work, any person that has no direct contractual relationship with the contractor, other than a person who performed actual labor for wages or an express trust fund described in Section 3111, may file the preliminary notice, but no payment shall be withheld from the contractor pursuant to that notice unless the person has caused written notice to be given to the contractor, and the public agency concerned, not later than 20 days after the claimant has first furnished labor, services, equipment, or materials to the jobsite, stating with substantial accuracy a general description of labor, service, equipment, or materials furnished or to be furnished, and the name of the party to whom the same was furnished. This notice shall be served by mailing the same by first-class mail, registered mail, or certified mail, postage prepaid, in an envelope addressed to the contractor at any place the contractor maintains an office or conducts business, or his or her residence, or by personal service. In case of any public works constructed by the Department of Public Works or the Department of General Services of the state, such notice shall be served by mailing in the same manner as above, addressed to the office of the disbursing officer of the department constructing the work, or by personal service upon the officer. When service is by registered or certified mail, service is complete at the time of the deposit of the registered or certified mail.

Incorporates the requirements of Section 8102 and adds: (1) description of the work to be provided; and (2) estimate of the total price of work provided and to be provided.

•••

CC 9304
A claimant may give a stop payment notice or assert a claim against a payment bond only for work provided within 20 days before giving preliminary notice and at any time thereafter.

CC 3098(a) and CC 3098(d)
CC 3098(a)
(a) In any case in which the law of this state affords a right to a person furnishing labor or materials for a public work who has not been paid therefor to assert a claim against a payment bond, or to file a stop notice with the public agency concerned, and thereby cause the withholding of payment from the contractor for the public work, any person that has no direct contractual relationship with the contractor, other than a person who performed actual labor for wages or an express trust fund described in Section 3111, may file the preliminary notice, but no payment shall be withheld from the contractor pursuant to that

New Text (Operative July 1, 2012) | **Old Text**

notice unless the person has caused written notice to be given to the contractor, and the public agency concerned, not later than 20 days after the claimant has first furnished labor, services, equipment, or materials to the jobsite, stating with substantial accuracy a general description of labor, service, equipment, or materials furnished or to be furnished, and the name of the party to whom the same was furnished. This notice shall be served by mailing the same by first-class mail, registered mail, or certified mail, postage prepaid, in an envelope addressed to the contractor at any place the contractor maintains an office or conducts business, or his or her residence, or by personal service. In case of any public works constructed by the Department of Public Works or the Department of General Services of the state, such notice shall be served by mailing in the same manner as above, addressed to the office of the disbursing officer of the department constructing the work, or by personal service upon the officer. When service is by registered or certified mail, service is complete at the time of the deposit of the registered or certified mail.

CC 3098(d)

(d) If labor, service, equipment, or materials have been furnished to a jobsite by a claimant who did not give a preliminary notice pursuant to subdivision (a), that claimant shall not be precluded from giving a preliminary notice at any time thereafter. The claimant shall, however, be entitled to assert a claim against a payment bond and file a stop notice only for labor, service, equipment, or material furnished within 20 days prior to the service of the preliminary notice, and at any time thereafter.

Maintains the twenty (20) day "look back" period for work "covered by" the preliminary notice.

••

<u>CC 9306</u>

If the contract of any subcontractor on a particular work of improvement provides for payment to the subcontractor of more than four hundred dollars ($400), the failure of that subcontractor, licensed under the Contractors' State License Law (Chapter 9 (commencing with Section 7000) of Division 3 of the Business and Professions Code), to give the notice provided for in this chapter, constitutes grounds for disciplinary action under the Contractors' State License Law.

CC 3098(b)

(b) Where the contract price to be paid to any subcontractor on a particular work of improvement exceeds four hundred dollars ($400), the failure of that contractor, licensed under Chapter 9, (commencing with Section 7000) of Division 3 of the Business and Professions Code, to give the notice provided for in this section, constitutes grounds for disciplinary action by the Registrar of Contractors.

Maintains $400 threshold for mandatory Preliminary Notice or sublet to CSLB disciplinary action.

••

PART 6. WORKS OF IMPROVEMENT
TITLE 3. PUBLIC WORK OF IMPROVEMENT
Chapter 4. Stop Payment Notice
Article 1. General Provisions

CC 9350

The rights of all persons furnishing work pursuant to a public works contract, with respect to any fund for payment of construction costs, are governed exclusively by this chapter, and no person may assert any legal or equitable right with respect to that fund, other than a right created by direct written contract between the person and the person holding the fund, except pursuant to the provisions of this chapter.

CC 3264

The rights of all persons furnishing labor, services, equipment, or materials for any work of improvement, with respect to any fund for payment of construction costs, are governed exclusively by Chapters 3 (commencing with Section 3156) and 4 (commencing with Section 3179) of this title, and no person may assert any legal or equitable right with respect to such fund, other than a right created by direct written contract between such person and the person holding the fund, except pursuant to the provisions of such chapters.

Confirms that rights with respect to fund for public work of improvement are exclusive.

•••

CC 9352

(a) A stop payment notice shall comply with the requirements of Chapter 2 (commencing with Section 8100) of Title 1, and shall be signed and verified by the claimant.

(b) The notice shall include a general description of work to be provided, and an estimate of the total amount in value of the work to be provided.

(c) The amount claimed in the notice may include only the amount due the claimant for work provided through the date of the notice.

CC 3103

"Stop notice" means a written notice, signed and verified by the claimant or his or her agent, stating in general terms all of the following:

(a) The kind of labor, services, equipment, or materials furnished or agreed to be furnished by such claimant.

(b) The name of the person to or for whom the same was done or furnished.

(c) The amount in value, as near as may be, of that already done or furnished and of the whole agreed to be done or furnished.

(d) The name and address of the claimant.

The notice, in the case of any work of improvement other than a public work, shall be delivered to the owner personally or left at his or her residence or place of business with some person in charge, or delivered to his or her architect, if any, if the notice is served upon a construction lender, holding construction funds and maintaining branch offices, it shall not be effective as against the construction lender unless given to or served upon the manager or other responsible officer or person at the office or branch thereof administering or holding the construction funds. The notice, in the case of any public work for the state, shall be filed with the director of the department which let the contract and, in the case of any other public work, shall be filed in the office of the controller, auditor, or other public disbursing officer whose duty it is to make payments under the provisions of the contract, or with the commissioners, managers, trustees, officers, board of

New Text (Operative July 1, 2012) | **Old Text**

supervisors, board of trustees, common council, or other body by whom the contract was awarded. No stop notice shall be invalid by reason of any defect in form if it is sufficient to substantially inform the owner of the information required.

Any stop notice may be served by registered or certified mail with the same effect as by personal service.

Incorporates requirements found in Section 8100.
Provides that notice shall include a general description of work and an estimate of the total amount in value provided and the amount claimed due.

•••

CC 9354

(a) Except as provided in subdivision (b), a stop payment notice shall be given in compliance with the requirements of Chapter 2 (commencing with Section 8100) of Title 1.

(b) A stop payment notice shall be given to the public entity by giving the notice to the following person:
(1) In the case of a public works contract of the state, the director of the department that awarded the contract.
(2) In the case of a public works contract of a public entity other than the state, the office of the controller, auditor, or other public disbursing officer whose duty it is to make payment pursuant to the contract, or the commissioners, managers, trustees, officers, board of supervisors, board of trustees, common council, or other body by which the contract was awarded.

CC 3103

"Stop notice" means a written notice, signed and verified by the claimant or his or her agent, stating in general terms all of the following:

(a) The kind of labor, services, equipment, or materials furnished or agreed to be furnished by such claimant.
(b) The name of the person to or for whom the same was done or furnished.
(c) The amount in value, as near as may be, of that already done or furnished and of the whole agreed to be done or furnished.
(d) The name and address of the claimant.

The notice, in the case of any work of improvement other than a public work, shall be delivered to the owner personally or left at his or her residence or place of business with some person in charge, or delivered to his or her architect, if any, if the notice is served upon a construction lender, holding construction funds and maintaining branch offices, it shall not be effective as against the construction lender unless given to or served upon the manager or other responsible officer or person at the office or branch thereof administering or holding the construction funds. The notice, in the case of any public work for the state, shall be filed with the director of the department which let the contract and, in the case of any other public work, shall be filed in the office of the controller, auditor, or other public disbursing officer whose duty it is to make payments under the provisions of the contract, or with the commissioners, managers, trustees, officers, board of supervisors, board of trustees, common council, or other body by whom the contract was awarded. No stop notice shall be invalid by reason of any defect in form if it is sufficient to substantially inform the owner of the information required.

Any stop notice may be served by registered or certified mail with the same effect as by personal service.

Incorporates requirements found in Section 8100.
Specifies the persons to whom the stop payment notice shall be given.
Eliminates "substantial compliance" exception listed in prior law (see former Civil Code §3103).

•••

New Text (Operative July 1, 2012) | **Old Text**

<u>*CC 9356*</u>

A stop payment notice is not effective unless given before the expiration of whichever of the following time periods is applicable:

(a) If a notice of completion, acceptance, or cessation is recorded, 30 days after that recordation.

(b) If a notice of completion, acceptance, or cessation is not recorded, 90 days after cessation or completion.

CC 3184

To be effective, any stop notice pursuant to this chapter must be served before the expiration of:

(a) Thirty days after the recording of a notice of completion (sometimes referred to in public works as a notice of acceptance) or notice of cessation, if such notice is recorded.

(b) If no notice of completion or notice of cessation is recorded, 90 days after completion or cessation.

••

<u>*CC 9358*</u>

(a) The public entity shall, on receipt of a stop payment notice, withhold from the direct contractor sufficient funds due or to become due to the direct contractor to pay the claim stated in the stop payment notice and to provide for the public entity's reasonable cost of any litigation pursuant to the stop payment notice.

(b) The public entity may satisfy its duty under this section by refusing to release funds held in escrow under Section 10263 or 22300 of the Public Contract Code.

CC 3186

It shall be the duty of the public entity, upon receipt of a stop notice pursuant to this chapter, to withhold from the original contractor, or from any person acting under his or her authority, money or bonds (where bonds are to be issued in payment for the work of improvement) due or to become due to that contractor in an amount sufficient to answer the claim stated in the stop notice and to provide for the public entity's reasonable cost of any litigation thereunder. The public entity may satisfy this duty by refusing to release money held in escrow pursuant to Section 10263 or 22300 of the Public Contract Code.

••

<u>*CC 9360*</u>

(a) This chapter does not prohibit payment of funds to a direct contractor or a direct contractor's assignee if a stop payment notice is not received before the disbursing officer actually surrenders possession of the funds.

(b) This chapter does not prohibit payment of any amount due to a direct contractor or a direct contractor's assignee in excess of the amount necessary to pay the total amount of all claims stated in stop payment notices received by the public entity at the time of payment plus any interest and court costs that might reasonably be anticipated in connection with the claims.

CC 3187

This chapter does not prohibit (a) the payment of any money or bonds to the original contractor or his assignee unless a stop notice is on file before the disbursing officer has actually surrendered possession of either the warrant, check, bonds, or money, or (b) the payment to the original contractor or his assignee of any money due him in excess of an amount sufficient to answer the total amount of the claims stated in stop notices on file at the time of such payment plus such interest and court costs as might be reasonably anticipated in connection with the claims.

Restates requirement that stop notice be received before disbursing officer surrenders possession of the funds.

••

New Text (Operative July 1, 2012) | **Old Text**

CC 9362

(a) Not later than 10 days after each of the following events, the public entity shall give notice to a claimant that has given a stop payment notice of the time within which an action to enforce payment of the claim stated in the stop payment notice must be commenced:

(1) Completion of a public works contract, whether by acceptance or cessation.

(2) Recordation of a notice of cessation or completion.

(b) The notice shall comply with the requirements of Chapter 2 (commencing with Section 8100) of Title 1.

(c) A public entity need not give notice under this section unless the claimant has paid the public entity ten dollars ($10) at the time of giving the stop payment notice.

CC 3185

No later than 10 days after the filing of a notice of completion or after the cessation of labor has been deemed a completion of the public work or after the acceptance of completion, whichever is later, the public entity shall give notice of the expiration of such period to each stop notice claimant by personal service, or registered or certified mail. When service is by registered or certified mail, service is complete at the time of the deposit of the registered or certified mail in a United States post office, addressed to the claimant at the address shown upon his stop notice claim. No such notice need be given unless the claimant shall have paid to the public entity the sum of two dollars ($2) at the time of filing his stop notice.

Preserves the public entity's duty to provide notice to all stop payment notice claimants, of the time within which an action must be commenced to enforce payment of a claim.

Increases the amount which stop payment notice claimant must pay to the public entity from $2 to $10.

Incorporates notice requirements found in Section 8100.

••

CC 9364

(a) A public entity may, in its discretion, permit the direct contractor to give the public entity a release bond. The bond shall be executed by an admitted surety insurer, in an amount equal to 125 percent of the claim stated in the stop payment notice, conditioned for the payment of any amount the claimant recovers in an action on the claim, together with court costs if the claimant prevails.

(b) On receipt of a release bond, the public entity shall not withhold funds from the direct contractor pursuant to the stop payment notice.

(c) The surety on a release bond is jointly and severally liable to the claimant with the sureties on any payment bond given under Chapter 5 (commencing with Section 9550).

CC 3196

If the original contractor or subcontractor disputes the correctness or validity or enforceability of any stop notice, the public entity may, in its discretion, permit the original contractor to file with the public entity a bond executed by a corporate surety, in an amount equal to 125 percent of the claim stated in the stop notice conditioned for the payment of any sum which the stop notice claimant may recover on the claim together with his costs of suit in the action, if he recovers therein. Upon the filing of such bond with the public entity, the public entity shall not withhold any money or bonds (where bonds are to be issued in payment for the work of improvement) from the original contractor on account of the stop notice. The surety or sureties upon such bond shall be jointly and severally liable to the stop notice claimant with the surety or sureties upon any payment bond furnished pursuant to Chapter 7 (commencing with Section 3247).

Eliminates the "disputes the correctness or validity or enforceability" of any stop payment notice.

Resumes bond from "admitted surety insurer".

Maintains bond amount at 125% of the claim.

••

New Text (Operative July 1, 2012) **Old Text**

PART 6. WORKS OF IMPROVEMENT
TITLE 3. PUBLIC WORK OF IMPROVEMENT
Chapter 4. Stop Payment Notice

<u>CC 9400</u>

A direct contractor may obtain release of funds withheld pursuant to a stop payment notice under the summary proceeding provided in this article on any of the following grounds:

(a) The claim on which the notice is based is not a type for which a stop payment notice is authorized under this chapter.

(b) The claimant is not a person authorized under Section 9100 to give a stop payment notice.

(c) The amount of the claim stated in the stop payment notice is excessive.

(d) There is no basis for the claim stated in the stop payment notice.

CC 3197

If the original contractor asserts (1) that the claim upon which the stop notice is based is not included within the types or classifications of claims referred to in this article, or (2) that the claimant is not one of the persons named in Section 3181, or (3) that the amount of the claim as specified in the stop notice is excessive, or (4) that there is no basis in law for the claim as referred to and set out in the stop notice, he may have the question determined in a summary proceedings in accordance with the provisions of Sections 3198 to 3205, inclusive.

Maintains the summary proceeding remedy.
Eliminates the "in law" requirement found in prior law (see former Civil Code §3197).

•••

<u>CC 9402</u>

The direct contractor shall serve on the public entity an affidavit, together with a copy of the affidavit, in compliance with the requirements of Chapter 2 (commencing with Section 8100) of Title 1, that includes all of the following information:

(a) An allegation of the grounds for release of the funds and a statement of the facts supporting the allegation.

(b) A demand for the release of all or the portion of the funds that are alleged to be withheld improperly or in an excessive amount.

(c) A statement of the address of the contractor within the state for the purpose of permitting service by mail on the contractor of any notice or document.

CC 3198

The original contractor shall serve upon the public entity an affidavit and a copy thereof alleging the legal grounds upon which he bases his claim and the facts in support thereof, and demanding the release of all or such portion of such money or bonds as is alleged to be withheld improperly or in an excessive amount. Such affidavit shall also state the address of the original contractor within this state for the purpose of permitting service by mail upon him of any notice or legal document.

Incorporates requirements found in Civil Code §8100.
Specifies the requirements for the affidavit.

•••

New Text (Operative July 1, 2012) | **Old Text**

CC 9404

The public entity shall serve on the claimant a copy of the direct contractor's affidavit, together with a notice stating that the public entity will release the funds withheld, or the portion of the funds demanded, unless the claimant serves on the public entity a counteraffidavit on or before the time stated in the notice. The time stated in the notice shall be not less than 10 days nor more than 20 days after service on the claimant of the copy of the affidavit. The notice shall comply with the requirements of Chapter 2 (commencing with Section 8100) of Title 1.

CC 3199

The public entity shall serve upon the claimant, either personally or by registered or certified mail, addressed to the last known address of the claimant, a copy of the affidavit and the demand for release together with a written notice stating that the public entity will release such money or bonds, or such portion of either as has been demanded, unless the claimant files with the public entity a counter affidavit on or before a time designated in the notice, which shall not be less than 10, nor more than 20 days, after service upon the claimant of the copy of such affidavit. Proof of service shall be made by an affidavit.

Restates public entity's obligation.
Maintains time period for claimant's response (counter affidavit).
Incorporates notice requirement found in Section 8100.

CC 9406

(a) A claimant that contests the direct contractor's affidavit shall serve on the public entity a counteraffidavit alleging the details of the claim and describing the specific basis on which the claimant contests or rebuts the allegations of the contractor's affidavit. The counteraffidavit shall be served within the time stated in the public entity's notice, together with proof of service of a copy of the counteraffidavit on the direct contractor. The service of the counteraffidavit on the public entity and the copy of the affidavit on the direct contractor shall comply with the requirements of Chapter 2 (commencing with Section 8100) of Title 1.

(b) If no counteraffidavit with proof of service is served on the public entity within the time stated in the public entity's notice, the public entity shall immediately release the funds, or the portion of the funds demanded by the affidavit, without further notice to the claimant, and the public entity is not liable in any manner for their release.

(c) The public entity is not responsible for the validity of an affidavit or counteraffidavit under this article.

CC 3200

If the claimant desires to contest the original contractor's affidavit and demand for release, he shall, within the time allowed, serve upon the public entity a counter affidavit alleging the details of his claim and shall also set forth in detail the specific basis upon which he contests or rebuts the allegations of the original contractor's affidavit, together with proof of service of a copy of such counter affidavit upon the original contractor. If no such counter affidavit with proof of service is served upon the public entity within the time allowed, then the public entity shall forthwith release the money or bonds, or such portion thereof as has been demanded by such affidavit, without further notice to the claimant, and the public entity shall not be liable in any manner for making such release. The public entity shall not be responsible for the validity of the affidavit or counter affidavit.

Confirms the requirements for claimant's counter-affidavit.
Incorporates notice requirements found in Section 8100.

New Text (Operative July 1, 2012) | **Old Text**

CC 9408

(a) If a counteraffidavit, together with proof of service, is served under Section 9406, either the direct contractor or the claimant may commence an action for a declaration of the rights of the parties.

(b) After commencement of the action, either the direct contractor or the claimant may move the court for a determination of rights under the affidavit and counteraffidavit. The party making the motion shall give not less than five days' notice of the hearing to the public entity and to the other party.

(c) The notice of hearing shall comply with the requirements of Chapter 2 (commencing with Section 8100) of Title 1. Notwithstanding Section 8116, when notice of the hearing is made by mail, the notice is complete on the fifth day following deposit of the notice in the mail.

(d) The court shall hear the motion within 15 days after the date of the motion, unless the court continues the hearing for good cause.

CC 3201

If such counter affidavit, together with proof of service, is so filed, either the original contractor or the claimant may file an action in the appropriate superior court for a declaration of the respective rights of the parties. After the filing of such action, either the original contractor or the claimant shall be entitled to a hearing by the court for the purpose of determining his rights under the affidavit and demand for release and the counter affidavit. Such hearing must be granted by the court within 15 days from the date of making of such motion, unless continued by the court for good cause. The party making the motion for hearing must give not less than five days' notice in writing of such hearing to the public entity and to the other party.

Incorporates the notice requirements found in Section 8100.
Establishes minimum of five (5) days prior to notice for hearing or motion for determination.
Maintains fifteen (15) day time period for hearing on motion.

CC 9410

(a) The affidavit and counteraffidavit shall be filed with the court by the public entity and shall constitute the pleadings, subject to the power of the court to permit an amendment in the interest of justice. The affidavit of the direct contractor shall be deemed controverted by the counteraffidavit of the claimant, and both shall be received in evidence.

(b) At the hearing, the direct contractor has the burden of proof.

CC 3202

At such hearing, the original contractor shall have the burden of proof. The affidavit and counter affidavit shall be filed with the court by the public entity and they shall constitute the pleadings, subject to the power of the court to permit an amendment in the interest of justice. The affidavit of the original contractor shall be deemed controverted by the counter affidavit, and both shall be received in evidence.

New Text (Operative July 1, 2012) | **Old Text**

CC 9412

(a) No findings are required in a summary proceeding under this article.

(b) If at the hearing no evidence other than the affidavit and counteraffidavit is offered, the court may, if satisfied that sufficient facts are shown, make a determination on the basis of the affidavit and counteraffidavit. If the court is not satisfied that sufficient facts are shown, the court shall order the hearing continued for production of other evidence, oral or documentary, or the filing of other affidavits and counteraffidavits.

(c) At the conclusion of the hearing, the court shall make an order determining whether the demand for release is allowed. The court's order is determinative of the right of the claimant to have funds further withheld by the public entity.

(d) The direct contractor shall serve a copy of the court's order on the public entity in compliance with the requirements of Chapter 2 (commencing with Section 8100) of Title 1.

CC 3203

No findings shall be required in a summary proceeding under this article. When the hearing is before the court sitting without a jury and no evidence other than the affidavit and counter affidavit is offered, if the court is satisfied that sufficient facts are shown thereby, it may make its determination thereon; otherwise, it shall order the hearing continued for the production of other evidence, oral or documentary, or the filing of other affidavits and counter affidavits. At the conclusion of the hearing, the court shall make and enter its order determining whether the demand for release shall be allowed or not, which order shall be determinative as to the right of the claimant to have the money or bonds further withheld by the public entity. The original contractor shall serve a copy of such order on the public entity.

Maintains process found in prior law (see former Civil Code §3203).
Restates that the court's order is determinative of the right of the claimant to have funds held.
Incorporates notice requirements found in Section 8100.

CC 9414

A determination in a summary proceeding under this article is not res judicata with respect to a right of action by the claimant against either the principal or surety on a payment bond or with respect to a right of action against a party personally liable to the claimant.

CC 3205

No determination in the summary proceedings under this article shall be res judicata with respect to any right of action by the claimant against either principal or surety on any labor and material bond or with respect to any right of action against any party personally liable to the claimant.

Confirms that order in summary proceeding is not res judicata of claimant's other right.

New Text (Operative July 1, 2012) **Old Text**

PART 6. WORKS OF IMPROVEMENT
TITLE 4. PUBLIC WORK OF IMPROVEMENT
Chapter 4. Stop Payment Notice
Article 3. Distribution of Funds Withheld

CC 9450

If funds withheld pursuant to a stop payment notice are insufficient to pay in full the claims of all persons who have given a stop payment notice, the funds shall be distributed among the claimants in the ratio that the claim of each bears to the aggregate of all claims for which a stop payment notice is given, without regard to the order in which the notices were given or enforcement actions were commenced.

CC 3190

If the money withheld pursuant to stop notices shall be insufficient to pay in full all of the valid claims stated in such notices, the same shall be distributed among the stop notice claimants in the same ratio that their respective claims bear to the aggregate of such valid claims, without regard to the order of time in which their respective notices may have been served or their respective actions, if any, commenced.

Confirms pro rata distribution if the case of insufficient funds.

••

CC 9452

Nothing in this chapter impairs the right of a claimant to recover from the direct contractor or the contractor's sureties in an action on a payment bond under Chapter 5 (commencing with Section 9550) any deficit that remains unpaid after the distribution under Section 9450.

CC 3191

Nothing in this article shall impair the right of any stop notice claimant to recover from the contractor or his sureties any deficit that may remain unpaid after such pro rata distribution in an action upon the bond provided for by Chapter 7 (commencing with Section 3247).

Preserves claimant's right to recover any deficit from contractor and surety on payment bond.

••

CC 9454

A person that willfully gives a false stop payment notice to the public entity or that willfully includes in the notice work not provided for the public works contract for which the stop payment notice is given forfeits all right to participate in the distribution under Section 9450.

CC 3192

Any person who willfully gives a false stop notice to the public entity or who willfully includes in his notice labor, services, equipment, or materials not furnished for the work of improvement with respect to which such notice is given, forfeits all right to participate in the pro rata distribution of money or bonds withheld.

••

CC 9456

(a) A stop payment notice takes priority over an assignment by a direct contractor of any amount due or to become due pursuant to a public works contract, including contract changes, whether made before or after the giving of a stop payment notice, and the assignment has no effect on the rights of the claimant.

(b) Any garnishment of an amount due or to become due pursuant to a public works contract by a creditor of a direct contractor under Article 8 (commencing with Section 708.710) of Chapter 6 of Division 2 of Title 9 of Part 2 of the Code of Civil Procedure and any statutory lien on that amount is subordinate to the rights of a claimant.

CC 3193

No assignment by the original contractor of any of the money due or to become due to the original contractor under the contract, or for "extras" in connection therewith whether made before or after the service of a stop notice, takes priority over a stop notice under this chapter and such assignment has no effect on the rights of the stop notice claimants. Any garnishment of such money by any creditor of the original contractor pursuant to Article 8 (commencing with Section 708.710) of Chapter 6 of Division 2 of Title 9 of Part 2 of the Code of Civil Procedure and any statutory lien thereon are subordinate to the rights of all stop notice claimants.

Maintains priority of stop payment notice claim over assignment of funds and creditor claims.

••

PART 6. WORKS OF IMPROVEMENT
TITLE 3. PUBLIC WORK OF IMPROVEMENT
Chapter 4. Stop Payment Notice
Article 4. Enforcement of Payment of Claim Stated in Stop Payment Notice

CC 9500

(a) A claimant may not enforce payment of the claim stated in a stop payment notice unless the claimant has complied with all of the following conditions:

(1) The claimant has given preliminary notice to the extent required by Chapter 3 (commencing with Section 9300).

(2) The claimant has given the stop payment notice within the time provided in Section 9356.

(b) The claim filing procedures of Part 3 (commencing with Section 900) of Division 3.6 of Title 1 of the Government Code do not apply to an action under this article.

CC 3183 and CC 3265

CC 3183

A claimant shall be entitled to enforce a stop notice only if he has complied with each of the following conditions:

(a) He shall have given the preliminary 20-day notice (public work) in accordance with Section 3098 if required by that section.

(b) He shall have filed his stop notice as defined in Section 3103 and in accordance with Section 3184.

CC 3265

The claim filing procedures set forth in Part 3 (commencing with Section 900) of Division 3.6 of Title 1 of the Government Code do not apply to actions commenced pursuant to Section 3210 of this code.

Establishes conditions precedent to enforcement of stop payment notice: (1) preliminary notice to extent required; and (2) timely giving of stop payment notice.

•••

CC 9502

(a) The claimant shall commence an action against the public entity and the direct contractor to enforce payment of the claim stated in a stop payment notice at any time after 10 days from the date the claimant gives the stop payment notice.

(b) The claimant shall commence an action against the public entity and the direct contractor to enforce payment of the claim stated in a stop payment notice not later than 90 days after expiration of the time within which a stop payment notice must be given.

(c) An action under this section may not be brought to trial or judgment entered before expiration of the time provided in subdivision (b).

(d) If a claimant does not commence an action to enforce payment of the claim stated in a stop payment notice within the time provided in subdivision (b), the notice ceases to be effective and the public entity shall release funds withheld pursuant to the notice.

CC 3210

An action against the original contractor and the public entity to enforce payment of the claim stated in the stop notice may be commenced at any time after 10 days from the date of the service of the stop notice upon the public entity and shall be commenced not later than 90 days following the expiration of the period within which stop notices must be filed as provided in Section 3184. No such action shall be brought to trial or judgment entered until the expiration of said 90-day period. No money or bond shall be withheld by reason of any such notice longer than the expiration of such 90-day period unless proceedings be commenced in a proper court within that time by the claimant to enforce his claim, and if such proceedings have not been commenced such notice shall cease to be effective and the moneys or bonds withheld shall be paid or delivered to the contractor or other person to whom they are due.

Maintains the prohibition on trial before the expiration of the stated time period.

•••

New Text (Operative July 1, 2012) | **Old Text**

<u>CC 9504</u>

Within five days after commencement of an action to enforce payment of the claim stated in a stop payment notice, the claimant shall give notice of commencement of the action to the public entity in the same manner that a stop payment notice is given.

CC 3211

Notice of the commencement of any such action shall be given to the public entity within five days after commencement of the action described in Section 3210 in the same manner as provided in Section 3103.

•••

<u>CC 9506</u>

If more than one claimant has given a stop payment notice:

(a) Any number of claimants may join in the same enforcement action.

(b) If claimants commence separate actions, the court that first acquires jurisdiction may order the actions consolidated.

(c) On request of the public entity, the court shall require that all claimants be impleaded in one action and shall adjudicate the rights of all parties in the action.

CC 3214

Any number of persons who have given stop notices may join the same action and when separate actions are commenced the court first acquiring jurisdiction may consolidate them. Upon the request of the public entity the court shall require all claimants to the moneys withheld pursuant to stop notices to be impleaded in one action, to the end that the respective rights of all parties may be adjudicated therein.

Preserves right to request consolidation in the event of multiple stop payment notices.

•••

<u>CC 9508</u>

Notwithstanding Section 583.420 of the Code of Civil Procedure, if an action to enforce payment of the claim stated in a stop payment notice is not brought to trial within two years after commencement of the action, the court may in its discretion dismiss the action for want of prosecution.

CC 3212

In case such action is commenced as provided in Section 3210 but is not brought to trial within two years after the commencement thereof, the court may in its discretion dismiss the same for want of prosecution.

•••

<u>CC 9510</u>

A stop payment notice ceases to be effective, and the public entity shall release funds withheld, in either of the following circumstances:

(a) An action to enforce payment of the claim stated in the stop payment notice is dismissed, unless expressly stated to be without prejudice.

(b) Judgment in an action to enforce payment of the claim stated in the stop payment notice is against the claimant.

CC 3213

In all cases upon the dismissal of an action commenced as provided in Section 3210, unless expressly stated to be without prejudice, or upon a judgment rendered therein against the claimant, the stop notice shall cease to be effective and the moneys or bonds withheld shall be paid or delivered to the person to whom they are due.

•••

New Text (Operative July 1, 2012) | **Old Text**

PART 6. WORKS OF IMPROVEMENT
TITLE 3. PUBLIC WORK OF IMPROVEMENT
Chapter 5. Payment Bond

CC 9550

(a) A direct contractor that is awarded a public works contract involving an expenditure in excess of twenty-five thousand dollars ($25,000) shall, before commencement of work, give a payment bond to and approved by the officer or public entity by whom the contract was awarded.

(b) A public entity shall state in its call for bids that a payment bond is required for a public works contract involving an expenditure in excess of twenty-five thousand dollars ($25,000).

(c) A payment bond given and approved under this section will permit performance of and provide coverage for work pursuant to a public works contract that supplements the contract for which the bond is given, if the requirement of a new bond is waived by the public entity.

(d) For the purpose of this section, a design professional is not deemed a direct contractor and is not required to give a payment bond.

(e) This section does not apply to a public works contract with a "state entity" as defined in subdivision (d) of Section 7103 of the Public Contract Code.

CC 3247

(a) Every original contractor to whom is awarded a contract by a public entity, except as provided in subdivision (d) of Section 7103 of the Public Contract Code, involving an expenditure in excess of twenty-five thousand dollars ($25,000) for any public work shall, before entering upon the performance of the work, file a payment bond with and approved by the officer or public entity by whom the contract was awarded.

A public entity shall state in its call for bids for any such contract that a payment bond is required in the case of such an expenditure.

(b) A payment bond filed and approved in accordance with this section shall be sufficient to enter upon the performance of work under a duly authorized contract which supplements the contract for which such payment bond was filed, if the requirement of a new bond is waived by the public entity.

(c) For purposes of this section, providers of architectural, engineering, and land surveying services pursuant to a contract with a public entity for any public work shall not be deemed an original contractor and shall not be required to post or file the payment bond required in subdivisions (a) and (b). This subdivision shall apply to all contracts entered into subsequent to January 1, 1971.

The amendment to this section made during the 1980 portion of the 1979-80 Regular Session of the Legislature by Chapter 293 of the Statutes of 1980, does not constitute a change in, but is declaratory of, existing law.

Maintains payment bond requirement on all public works contracts involving an expenditure in excess of $25,000. Includes in reference to "design professionals" exception to the requirement to post a payment bond. Preserves exception for public works contract with state entity (see Public Contract Code Section 7103).

CC 9552

If a payment bond is not given and approved as required by Section 9550:

(a) Neither the public entity awarding the public works contract nor any officer of the public entity shall audit, allow, or pay a claim of the direct contractor pursuant to the contract.

(b) A claimant shall receive payment of a claim pursuant to a stop payment notice in the manner provided by Chapter 4 (commencing with Section 9350).

CC 3251

Unless a payment bond is filed and approved as provided in this chapter, no claim in favor of the original contractor arising under the contract shall be audited, allowed or paid by the public entity awarding the contract or any officer thereof. Claimants shall receive payment of their respective claims in the manner provided by Chapter 4 (commencing with Section 3179) upon complying with the provisions thereof.

This section shall become operative on the 181st day after it becomes effective.

Maintains prohibition on processing of payments to direct contractor until payment bond is approved.

New Text (Operative July 1, 2012) | **Old Text**

CC 9554

(a) A payment bond shall be in an amount not less than 100 percent of the total amount payable pursuant to the public works contract. The bond shall be in the form of a bond and not a deposit in lieu of a bond. The bond shall be executed by an admitted surety insurer.

(b) The payment bond shall provide that if the direct contractor or a subcontractor fails to pay any of the following, the surety will pay the obligation and, if an action is brought to enforce the liability on the bond, a reasonable attorney's fee, to be fixed by the court:

(1) A person authorized under Section 9100 to assert a claim against a payment bond.

(2) Amounts due under the Unemployment Insurance Code with respect to work or labor performed pursuant to the public works contract.

(3) Amounts required to be deducted, withheld, and paid over to the Employment Development Department from the wages of employees of the contractor and subcontractors under Section 13020 of the Unemployment Insurance Code with respect to the work and labor.

(c) The payment bond shall be conditioned for the payment in full of the claims of all claimants and by its terms inure to the benefit of any person authorized under Section 9100 to assert a claim against a payment bond so as to give a right of action to that person or that person's assigns in an action to enforce the liability on the bond.

(d) The direct contractor may require that a subcontractor give a bond to indemnify the direct contractor for any loss sustained by the direct contractor because of any default of the subcontractor under this section.

CC 3096 and CC 3248

CC 3096

"Payment bond" means a bond with good and sufficient sureties that is conditioned for the payment in full of the claims of all claimants and that also by its terms is made to inure to the benefit of all claimants so as to give these persons a right of action to recover upon this bond in any suit brought to foreclose the liens provided for in this title or in a separate suit brought on the bond. An owner, original contractor, or a subcontractor may be the principal upon any payment bond.

CC 3248

In order to be approved, the payment bond shall satisfy all of the following requirements:

(a) The bond shall be in a sum not less than one hundred percent of the total amount payable by the terms of the contract.

(b) The bond shall provide that if the original contractor or a subcontractor fails to pay (1) any of the persons named in Section 3181, (2) amounts due under the Unemployment Insurance Code with respect to work or labor performed under the contract, or (3) for any amounts required to be deducted, withheld, and paid over to the Employment Development Department from the wages of employees of the contractor and subcontractors pursuant to Section 13020 of the Unemployment Insurance Code with respect to the work and labor, that the sureties will pay for the same, and also, in case suit is brought upon the bond, a reasonable attorney's fee, to be fixed by the court. The original contractor may require of the subcontractors a bond to indemnify the original contractor for any loss sustained by the original contractor because of any default by the subcontractors under this section.

(c) The bond shall, by its terms, inure to the benefit of any of the persons named in Section 3181 so as to give a right of action to those persons or their assigns in any suit brought upon the bond.

(d) The bond shall be in the form of a bond and not a deposit in lieu of a bond.

Sets forth the requirements for a public works payment bond substitutes "admitted surety insurer" in place of "good and sufficient sureties".

Confirms that Section 9100 identifies persons that may assert a claim.

Authorizes direct contractor to require bond from subcontractor.

••

New Text (Operative July 1, 2012) | **Old Text**

CC 9558

A claimant may commence an action to enforce the liability on the bond at any time after the claimant ceases to provide work, but not later than six months after the period in which a stop payment notice may be given under Section 9356.

CC 3249

Suit against the surety or sureties on the payment bond may be brought by any claimant, or his assigns, at any time after the claimant has furnished the last of the labor or materials, or both, but must be commenced before the expiration of six months after the period in which stop notices may be filed as provided in Section 3184.

Eliminates reference to "assigns".
Sets the time for filing action on payment bond.

CC 9560

(a) In order to enforce a claim against a payment bond, a claimant shall give the preliminary notice provided in Chapter 3 (commencing with Section 9300).

(b) If preliminary notice was not given as provided in Chapter 3 (commencing with Section 9300), a claimant may enforce a claim by giving written notice to the surety and the bond principal within 15 days after recordation of a notice of completion. If no notice of completion has been recorded, the time for giving written notice to the surety and the bond principal is extended to 75 days after completion of the work of improvement.

(c) Commencing July 1, 2012, and except as provided in subdivision (b), if the preliminary notice was required to be given by a person who has no direct contractual relationship with the contractor, and who has not given notice as provided in Chapter 3 (commencing with Section 9300), that person may enforce a claim by giving written notice to the surety and the bond principal, as provided in Section 9562, within 15 days after recordation of a notice of completion. If no notice of completion has been recorded, the time for giving written notice to the surety and the bond principal is extended to 75 days after completion of the work of improvement.

(d) Subdivision (c) shall not apply in either of the following circumstances:

(1) All progress payments, except for those disputed in good faith, have been made to a subcontractor who has a direct contractual relationship with the general contractor to whom the claimant has provided materials or services.

(2) The subcontractor who has a direct contractual relationship with the general contractor to whom the claimant has provided

CC 3252

(a) With regard to a contract entered into on or after January 1, 1995, in order to enforce a claim upon any payment bond given in connection with a public work, a claimant shall give the 20-day public works preliminary bond notice as provided in Section 3098.

(b) If the 20-day public work preliminary bond notice was not given as provided in Section 3098, a claimant may enforce a claim by giving written notice to the surety and the bond principal as provided in Section 3227 within 15 days after recordation of a notice of completion. If no notice of completion has been recorded, the time for giving written notice to the surety and the bond principal is extended to 75 days after completion of the work of improvement.

New Text (Operative July 1, 2012) | **Old Text**

materials or services has been terminated from the project pursuant to the contract, and all progress payments, except those disputed in good faith, have been made as of the termination date.

(e) Pursuant to Section 9300, this section shall not apply to a laborer, as defined under Section 8024.

(f) This section shall become operative on July 1, 2012.

NOTE: Updated through Senate Bill 293 (Approved by Governor on October 9, 2011).
Reiterates the requirement of a preliminary notice.
Maintains the 15 or 75 day notice to surety and bond principal.
Limits the use of the 15/75 day notice to circumstances where the party to whom the claimant furnished materials and/or services has not yet been paid for its work (i.e., curative notice not available if the subcontractor who has a direct contractual relationship has been paid or has been terminated).

•••

CC 9562

Notice to the principal and surety under Section 9560 shall comply with the requirements of Chapter 2 (commencing with Section 8100) of Title 1.

CC 3227

(a) The written notice to be given to the surety and the bond principal may be given by personal delivery, or by depositing the notice in the mail, postage prepaid, certified or registered, and addressed in accordance with any of the following that may be applicable:

(1) If to an individual surety, at his or her residence or place of business, if known. If to an individual surety whose residence is unknown, then in care of the clerk of the county in which the bond has been recorded.

(2) If to a corporate surety, at the office of or in care of the agent designated by the surety in the bond as the address to which notice shall be sent.

(3) At the office of or in care of any officer of the surety in this state.

(4) At the office of or in care of the statutory agent of the surety in this state.

(5) To the bond principal at the last known address.

(6) By service in the manner provided by law for the service of a summons in a civil action.

(b) The written notice described in subdivision (a) shall contain all of the following:

(1) The kind of labor, services, equipment, or materials furnished or agreed to be furnished by the claimant.

(2) The name of the person to or for whom the labor, services, equipment, or materials were furnished.

(3) The amount in value, as near as may be determined, of any labor, services, equipment, or materials already furnished or to be furnished.

Incorporates the notice requirements found in Section 8100 for notice to surety and principal.

•••

New Text (Operative July 1, 2012) | **Old Text**

CC 9564

(a) A claimant may maintain an action to enforce the liability of a surety on a payment bond whether or not the claimant has given the public entity a stop payment notice.

(b) A claimant may maintain an action to enforce the liability on the bond separately from and without commencement of an action against the public entity by whom the contract was awarded or against any officer of the public entity.

(c) In an action to enforce the liability on the bond, the court shall award the prevailing party a reasonable attorney's fee.

CC 3250

The filing of a stop notice is not a condition precedent to the maintenance of an action against the surety or sureties on the payment bond. An action on the payment bond may be maintained separately from and without the filing of an action against the public entity by whom the contract was awarded or any officer thereof. In any action, the court shall award to the prevailing party a reasonable attorney's fee, to be taxed as costs.

Preserves the prevailing party's right to recover attorney's fees.

••

CC 9566

(a) A claimant does not have a right to recover on a payment bond unless the claimant provided work to the direct contractor either directly or through one or more subcontractors pursuant to a public works contract.

(b) Nothing in this section affects the stop payment notice rights of, and relative priorities among, design professionals

CC 3267

Nothing contained in this title shall be construed to give to any person any right of action on any original contractor's private or public work payment bond described in Chapter 6 (commencing with Section 3235) or Chapter 7 (commencing with Section 3247), unless the work forming the basis for his claim was performed by such person for the principal on such payment bond, or one of his subcontractors, pursuant to the contract between the original contractor and the owner.

Nothing in this section shall affect the stop notice rights of, and relative priorities among, architects, registered engineers, or licensed land surveyors and holders of secured interests on the land.

Maintains requirement that claimant provide work to direct contractor either directly or through one or more subcontractors.

••

The Following Sections are repealed effective July 1, 2012 and Not Replaced

§3086(b)- repealed effective July 1, 2012

Acceptance by the owner is no longer a criteria for "completion of the work."

••

§3097(p) - repealed effective July 1, 2012

••

§3098(e) - repealed effective July 1, 2012

••

§3105 - repealed effective July 1, 2012

The term "subdivision" is no longer defined within the code.

••

§3123(c) - repealed effective July 1, 2012

Removes requirement that the owner had to notify the prime contractor and construction lender if the contract price is increased by 5 percent.

••

§3131 (second paragraph) - repealed effective July 1, 2012

Eliminates distinction of completion of a residential structure, containing multiple condominium units and common areas, is for filing an action on a single residential unit.

••

§3149 - repealed effective July 1, 2012

Deletes provision for separate claims on property to be joined to the same action, and consolidated by the court.

••

§3204 - repealed effective July 1, 2012

Deletes provision that precluded the elimination of right to a jury trial, as well as the provision that the party may waive that right.

••

§3260(a) - repealed effective July 1, 2012

••

§3260(c)(1) - repealed effective July 1, 2012

Deletes the issuance of a certificate of occupancy by a public entity as one criteria for establishing the date of completion.

§3260(c)(2) - repealed effective July 1, 2012

••

§3260.2(g) - repealed effective July 1, 2012

••

New Text (Operative July 1, 2012) | **Old Text**

Appreciation Loans

CC 1917.166

The lien of a shared appreciation loan, including the principal amount and all interest, whether accrued or to be accrued, and all amounts of contingent deferred interest, shall attach from the time of the recordation of the deed of trust securing the loan, and the lien, including the lien of the interest accrued or to be accrued and of the contingent deferred interest, shall have priority over any other lien or encumbrance affecting the property secured by the shared appreciation instrument, recorded after the time of recordation of the shared appreciation instrument. However, nothing in this section or Section 1917.165 shall preclude a junior lien or encumbrance subordinate to the obligation of the shared appreciation loan. In no case may a junior lien achieve priority over the lien securing the obligation of the shared appreciation loan, provided that nothing in this section shall be construed to supersede Section 8450.

CC 1917.166

The lien of a shared appreciation loan, including the principal amount and all interest, whether accrued or to be accrued, and all amounts of contingent deferred interest, shall attach from the time of the recordation of the deed of trust securing the loan, and the lien, including the lien of the interest accrued or to be accrued and of the contingent deferred interest, shall have priority over any other lien or encumbrance affecting the property secured by the shared appreciation instrument, recorded after the time of recordation of the shared appreciation instrument. However, nothing in this section or Section 1917.165 shall preclude a junior lien or encumbrance subordinate to the obligation of the shared appreciation loan. In no case may a junior lien achieve priority over the lien securing the obligation of the shared appreciation loan, provided that nothing in this section shall be construed to supersede Section 3134 of the Civil Code.

Revised to include reference to new Section 8000 et seq.

CC 1917.615

The lien of a shared appreciation loan for seniors, including the total loan obligation, shall attach from the time of the recordation of the deed of trust securing the loan, and the lien, including the lien of the total loan obligation accrued or to be accrued, shall have priority over any other lien or encumbrance affecting the property secured by the shared appreciation instrument and recorded after the time of recordation of the shared appreciation instrument. However, nothing in this section or Section 1917.614 shall preclude a junior lien or encumbrance subordinate to the total loan obligation of the shared appreciation loan for seniors. In no case may a junior lien achieve priority over the lien securing the total loan obligation of the shared appreciation loan, provided that nothing in this section shall be construed to supersede Section 8450.

CC 1917.615

The lien of a shared appreciation loan for seniors, including the total loan obligation, shall attach from the time of the recordation of the deed of trust securing the loan, and the lien, including the lien of the total loan obligation accrued or to be accrued, shall have priority over any other lien or encumbrance affecting the property secured by the shared appreciation instrument and recorded after the time of recordation of the shared appreciation instrument. However, nothing in this section or Section 1917.614 shall preclude a junior lien or encumbrance subordinate to the total loan obligation of the shared appreciation loan for seniors. In no case may a junior lien achieve priority over the lien securing the total loan obligation of the shared appreciation loan, provided that nothing in this section shall be construed to supersede Section 3134.

Revised to include reference to new Section 8000 et seq.

CC 3059

The liens of mechanics, for materials and services upon real property, are regulated by Chapter 4 (commencing with Section 8400) of Title 2 of Part 6 of Division 4.

CC 3059

The liens of mechanics, for materials and services upon real property, are regulated by Chapter 2 (commencing with Section 3109) of Title 15 of this part.

New Text (Operative July 1, 2012)

__CC 3060__

(a) As used in this section, "mine" means a mining claim or real property worked on as a mine.

(b) Any person who performs labor in a mine, either in its development or in working on it by the subtractive process, or furnishes materials to be used or consumed in it, has a lien upon the mine and the works owned and used by the owners for milling or reducing the ores from the mine, for the value of the work or labor done or materials furnished by each, whether done or furnished at the instance of the owner of the mine, or the owner's agent, and every contractor, subcontractor, superintendent, or other person having charge of any mining or work or labor performed in and about the mine, either as lessee or under a working bond or contract thereon shall be held to be the agent of the owner for the purposes of this section. The liens provided for by this section shall be enforced in the same manner as those provided for by Part 6 (commencing with Section 8000) of Division 4.

Old Text

CC 3060

Any person who performs labor in any mining claim or claims, or in or upon any real property worked as a mine, either in the development thereof or in working thereon by the subtractive process, or furnishes materials to be used or consumed therein, has a lien upon the same and the works owned and used by the owners for milling or reducing the ores from the same, for the value of the work or labor done or materials furnished by each respectively, whether done or furnished at the instance of the owner of such mining claim or claims or real property worked as a mine, or his agent, and every contractor, subcontractor, superintendent, or other person having charge of any mining or work or labor performed in and about such mining claim or claims or real property worked as a mine, either as lessee or under a working bond or contract thereon shall be held to be the agent of the owner for the purposes of this section. The liens provided for by this section shall be enforced in the same manner as those provided for by Title 15 (commencing with Section 3082), Part 4, Division 3.

Clarified and revised to include new Section 8000 et seq. reference.

Design Professionals

__CC 3319__

(a) In each written contract for private works of improvement entered into on or after January 1, 1996, the contracting party and the design professional may agree to contractual provisions that include a late payment penalty, in lieu of any interest otherwise due. The terms of the late payment penalty shall be specifically set forth in the written contract.

(b) The penalty authorized pursuant to subdivision (a) shall be separate from, and in addition to, the design professionals liens provided by Chapter 3 (commencing with Section 8300) of Title 2 of Part 6 of Division 4, mechanics liens provided by Chapter 4 (commencing with Section 8400) of Title 2 of Part 6 of Division 4, and stop payment notices provided by Chapter 5 (commencing with Section 8500) of Title 2 of Part 6 of Division 4.

(c) None of the rights or obligations created or permitted by this section between design

CC 3319

(a) In each written contract for private works of improvement entered into on or after January 1, 1996, the contracting party and the design professional may agree to contractual provisions that include a late payment penalty, in lieu of any interest otherwise due. The terms of the late payment penalty shall be specifically set forth in the written contract.

(b) The penalty authorized pursuant to subdivision (a) shall be separate from, and in addition to, the design professional's liens provided by Chapter 8 (commencing with Section 3081.1) of Title 14 of Part 4 of Division 3, mechanics liens provided by Chapter 2 (commencing with Section 3109) of Title 15 of Part 4 of Division 3, and stop notices for private works provided in Chapter 3 (commencing with Section 3156) of Title 15 of Part 4 of Division 3.

(c) None of the rights or obligations created or permitted

New Text (Operative July 1, 2012)

professionals and contracting parties shall apply to construction loan funds held by a lender pursuant to a construction loan agreement.

(d) For purposes of this section, the following definitions apply:

(1) "Contracting party" means any person or entity entering into a written contract with a design professional for professional design services for a private work of improvement.

(2) "Design professional" means a person licensed as an architect pursuant to Chapter 3 (commencing with Section 5500) of Division 3 of the Business and Professions Code, registered as a professional engineer pursuant to Chapter 7 (commencing with Section 6700) of Division 3 of the Business and Professions Code, or licensed as a land surveyor pursuant to Chapter 15 (commencing with Section 8700) of Division 3 of the Business and Professions Code.

Old Text

by this section between design professionals and contracting parties shall apply to construction loan funds held by a lender pursuant to a construction loan agreement.

(d) For purposes of this section:

(1) "Contracting party" means any person or entity entering into a written contract with a design professional for professional design services for a private work of improvement.

(2) "Design professional" means a person licensed as an architect pursuant to Chapter 3 (commencing with Section 5500) of Division 3 of the Business and Professions Code, registered as a professional engineer pursuant to Chapter 7 (commencing with Section 6700) of Division 3 of the Business and Professions Code, or licensed as a land surveyor pursuant to Chapter 15 (commencing with Section 8700) of Division 3 of the Business and Professions Code.

Revised to include new terminology and reference to new Section 8000 et seq.

●●

CC 3320

(a) In each contract for public works of improvement, entered into on or after January 1, 1996, the public agency shall pay to the prime design professional any progress payment within 30 days of receipt of a written demand for payment in accordance with the contract, and the final retention payment within 45 days of receipt of a written demand for payment in accordance with the contract. If the public agency disputes in good faith any portion of the amount due, it may withhold from the payment an amount not to exceed 150 percent of the disputed amount. The disputed amount withheld is not subject to any penalty authorized by this section.

(b) If any amount is wrongfully withheld or is not timely paid in violation of this section, the prime design professional shall be entitled to a penalty of 1 1/2 percent for the improperly withheld amount, in lieu of any interest otherwise due, per month for every month that payment is not made. In any action for the collection of amounts withheld in violation of this section, the prevailing party is entitled to his or her reasonable attorney's fees and costs.

(c) The penalty described in subdivision (b) is separate from, and in addition to, the design professionals

CC 3320

(a) In each contract for public works of improvement, entered into on or after January 1, 1996, the public agency shall pay to the prime design professional any progress payment within 30 days of receipt of a written demand for payment in accordance with the contract, and the final retention payment within 45 days of receipt of a written demand for payment in accordance with the contract. If the public agency disputes in good faith any portion of the amount due, it may withhold from the payment an amount not to exceed 150 percent of the disputed amount. The disputed amount withheld is not subject to any penalty authorized by this section.

(b) If any amount is wrongfully withheld or is not timely paid in violation of this section, the prime design professional shall be entitled to a penalty of 1 1/2 percent for the improperly withheld amount, in lieu of any interest otherwise due, per month for every month that payment is not made. In any action for the collection of amounts withheld in violation of this section, the prevailing party is entitled to his or her reasonable attorney's fees and costs.

(c) The penalty described in subdivision (b) is separate from, and in addition to, the design professionals'

New Text (Operative July 1, 2012)

liens provided by Chapter 3 (commencing with Section 8300) of Title 2 of Part 6 of Division 4, mechanics liens provided by Chapter 4 (commencing with Section 8400) of Title 2 of Part 6 of Division 4, and stop payment notices on public works provided by Chapter 4 (commencing with Section 9350) of Title 3 of Part 6 of Division 4.

(d) This section does not apply to state agency contracts subject to Section 927.6 of the Government Code.

(e) None of the rights or obligations created by this section between prime design professionals and public agencies apply to construction loan funds held by a lender pursuant to a construction loan agreement.

(f) For purposes of this section:

(1) "Public agency" means the state, any county, any city, any city and county, any district, any public authority, any public agency, any municipal corporation, or other political subdivision or political corporation of the state.

(2) "Design professional" means a person licensed as an architect pursuant to Chapter 3 (commencing with Section 5500) of Division 3 of the Business and Professions Code, registered as a professional engineer pursuant to Chapter 7 (commencing with Section 6700) of Division 3 of the Business and Professions Code, or licensed as a land surveyor pursuant to Chapter 15 (commencing with Section 8700) of Division 3 of the Business and Professions Code.

(3) "Prime design professional" means a design professional with a written contract directly with the public agency.

Old Text

liens provided by Chapter 8 (commencing with Section 3081.1) of Title 14 of Part 4 of Division 3, mechanics' liens provided by Chapter 2 (commencing with Section 3109) of Title 15 of Part 4 of Division 3, and stop notices for public works provided in Chapter 3 (commencing with Section 3156) of Title 15 of Part 4 of Division 3.

(d) This section does not apply to state agency contracts subject to Section 927.6 of the Government Code.

(e) None of the rights or obligations created by this section between prime design professionals and public agencies apply to construction loan funds held by a lender pursuant to a construction loan agreement.

(f) For purposes of this section:

(1) "Public agency" means the state, any county, any city, any city and county, any district, any public authority, any public agency, any municipal corporation or other political subdivision or political corporation of the state.

(2) "Design professional" means a person licensed as an architect pursuant to Chapter 3 (commencing with Section 5500) of Division 3 of the Business and Professions Code, registered as a professional engineer pursuant to Chapter 7 (commencing with Section 6700) of Division 3 of the Business and Professions Code, or licensed as a land surveyor pursuant to Chapter 15 (commencing with Section 8700) of Division 3 of the Business and Professions Code.

(3) "Prime design professional" means a design professional with a written contract directly with the public agency.

Revised to include new terminology and reference to new Section 8000 et seq.

••

CC 3321

(a) In each contract for public works of improvement, a prime design professional shall pay to each subconsultant design professional the amount due him or her from the payment received, not later than 15 days after receipt of each progress payment or final retention payment. If the prime design professional disputes in good faith any portion of the amount due, he or she may withhold from the payment an amount not to exceed 150 percent of the disputed amount. The disputed amount withheld shall not be subject to any penalty authorized by this section.

(b) If any amount is wrongfully withheld or is not timely

CC 3321

(a) In each contract for public works of improvement, a prime design professional shall pay to each subconsultant design professional the amount due him or her from the payment received, not later than 15 days after receipt of each progress payment or final retention payment. If the prime design professional disputes in good faith any portion of the amount due, he or she may withhold from the payment an amount not to exceed 150 percent of the disputed amount. The disputed amount withheld shall not be subject to any penalties authorized by this section.

(b) If any amount is wrongfully withheld or is not timely paid in violation of this section, the subconsultant design

New Text (Operative July 1, 2012)

paid in violation of this section, the subconsultant design professional shall be entitled to a penalty of 1 1/2 percent of the improperly withheld amount, in lieu of any interest otherwise due, per month, for each month that payment is not made. In any action for the collection of amounts withheld in violation of this section, the prevailing party shall be entitled to his or her reasonable attorney' s fees and costs.

(c) The penalty described in subdivision (b) shall be separate from, and in addition to, the design professionals liens provided by Chapter 3 (commencing with Section 8300) of Title 2 of Part 6 of Division 4, mechanics liens provided by Chapter 4 (commencing with Section 8400) of Title 2 of Part 6 of Division 4, and stop payment notices on public works provided by Chapter 4 (commencing with Section 9350) of Title 3 of Part 6 of Division 4.

(d) None of the rights or obligations created by this section between prime design professionals and subconsultant design professionals shall apply to construction loan funds held by a lender pursuant to a construction loan agreement.

(e) For purposes of this section:

(1) "Public agency" means the state, any county, any city, any city and county, any district, any public authority, any public agency, any municipal corporation, or other political subdivision or political corporation of the state.

(2) "Design professional" means a person licensed as an architect pursuant to Chapter 3 (commencing with Section 5500) of Division 3 of the Business and Professions Code, registered as a professional engineer pursuant to Chapter 7 (commencing with Section 6700) of Division 3 of the Business and Professions Code, or licensed as a land surveyor pursuant to Chapter 15 (commencing with Section 8700) of Division 3 of the Business and Professions Code.

(3) "Prime design professional" means a design professional having a written contract directly with the public agency.

(4) "Subconsultant design professional" means a design professional having a written contract with a prime design professional.

Old Text

professional shall be entitled to a penalty of 11/2 percent of the improperly withheld amount, in lieu of any interest otherwise due, per month, for each month that payment is not made. In any action for the collection of amounts withheld in violation of this section, the prevailing party shall be entitled to his or her reasonable attorney's fees and costs.

(c) The penalty described in subdivision (b) shall be separate from, and in addition to, the design professional's liens provided by Chapter 8 (commencing with Section 3081.1) of Title 14 of Part 4 of Division 3, mechanics liens provided by Chapter 2 (commencing with Section 3109) of Title 15 of Part 4 of Division 3, and stop notices for public works provided in Chapter 3 (commencing with Section 3156) of Title 15 of Part 4 of Division 3.

(d) None of the rights or obligations created by this section between prime design professionals and subconsultant design professionals shall apply to construction loan funds held by a lender pursuant to a construction loan agreement.

(e) For purposes of this section:

(1) "Public agency" means the state, any county, any city, any city and county, any district, any public authority, any public agency, any municipal corporation or other political subdivision or political corporation of the state.

(2) "Design professional" means a person licensed as an architect pursuant to Chapter 3 (commencing with Section 5500) of Division 3 of the Business and Professions Code, registered as a professional engineer pursuant to Chapter 7 (commencing with Section 6700) of Division 3 of the Business and Professions Code, or licensed as a land surveyor pursuant to Chapter 15 (commencing with Section 8700) of Division 3 of the Business and Professions Code.

(3) "Prime design professional" means a design professional with a written contract directly with the public agency.

(4) "Subconsultant design professional" means a design professional having a written contract with a prime design professional.

Revised to include new terminology and reference to new Section 8000 et seq.

New Text (Operative July 1, 2012) | **Old Text**

BUSINESS AND PROFESSIONS CODE SECTIONS ("B&P")

B&P 7034

(a) No contractor that is required to be licensed under this chapter shall insert in any contract, or be a party, with a subcontractor that is licensed under this chapter to any contract which contains a provision, clause, covenant, or agreement which is void or unenforceable under Section 2782 of the Civil Code.

(b) No contractor that is required to be licensed under this chapter shall require a waiver of lien rights from any subcontractor, employee, or supplier in violation of Section 8122 of the Civil Code.

B&P 7034

(a) No contractor who is required to be licensed under this chapter shall insert in any contract, or be a party, with a subcontractor who is licensed under this chapter to any contract which contains, a provision, clause, covenant, or agreement which is void or unenforceable under Section 2782 of the Civil Code.

(b) No contractor who is required to be licensed under this chapter shall require a waiver of lien rights from any subcontractor, employee, or supplier in violation of Section 3262 of the Civil Code.

Clarified and revised to reference to new Section 8000 et seq.

•••

B&P 7071.5

The contractor's bond required by this article shall be executed by an admitted surety in favor of the State of California, in a form acceptable to the registrar and filed with the registrar by the licensee or applicant. The contractor's bond shall be for the benefit of the following:

(a) A homeowner contracting for home improvement upon the homeowner's personal family residence damaged as a result of a violation of this chapter by the licensee.

(b) A property owner contracting for the construction of a single-family dwelling who is damaged as a result of a violation of this chapter by the licensee. That property owner shall only recover under this subdivision if the single-family dwelling is not intended for sale or offered for sale at the time the damages were incurred.

(c) A person damaged as a result of a willful and deliberate violation of this chapter by the licensee, or by the fraud of the licensee in the execution or performance of a construction contract.

(d) An employee of the licensee damaged by the licensee's failure to pay wages.

(e) A person or entity, including a laborer described in subdivision (b) of Section 8024 of the Civil Code, to which a portion of the compensation of an employee of a licensee is paid by agreement with that employee or the collective bargaining agent of that employee, damaged as the result of the licensee's failure to pay fringe benefits for its employees, including, but not limited to, employer payments described in Section 1773.1 of the Labor Code and regulations thereunder (without regard to whether the work was performed on a private or public work). Damage to a person or entity under this subdivision is limited to actual employer payments required to be made on behalf of employees of the licensee, as part of the overall compensation of those employees, which the licensee fails to pay.

B&P 7071.5

The contractor's bond required by this article shall be executed by an admitted surety in favor of the State of California, in a form acceptable to the registrar and filed with the registrar by the licensee or applicant. The contractor's bond shall be for the benefit of the following:

(a) A homeowner contracting for home improvement upon the homeowner's personal family residence damaged as a result of a violation of this chapter by the licensee.

(b) A property owner contracting for the construction of a single-family dwelling who is damaged as a result of a violation of this chapter by the licensee. That property owner shall only recover under this subdivision if the single-family dwelling is not intended for sale or offered for sale at the time the damages were incurred.

(c) A person damaged as a result of a willful and deliberate violation of this chapter by the licensee, or by the fraud of the licensee in the execution or performance of a construction contract.

(d) An employee of the licensee damaged by the licensee's failure to pay wages.

(e) A person or entity, including an express trust fund described in Section 3111 of the Civil Code, to whom a portion of the compensation of an employee of a licensee is paid by agreement with that employee or the collective bargaining agent of that employee, damaged as the result of the licensee's failure to pay fringe benefits for its employees, including, but not limited to, employer payments described in Section 1773.1 of the Labor Code and regulations thereunder (without regard to whether the work was performed on a private or public work). Damage to an express trust fund is limited to actual employer payments required to be made on behalf of employees of the licensee, as part of the overall compensation of those employees, which the licensee fails to pay.

Revised to include new terminology and reference to new Section 8000 et seq.

•••

New Text (Operative July 1, 2012)

B&P 7071.10

The qualifying individual's bond required by this article shall be executed by an admitted surety insurer in favor of the State of California, in a form acceptable to the registrar and filed with the registrar by the qualifying individual. The qualifying individual's bond shall not be required in addition to the contractor's bond when, as set forth under paragraph (1) of subdivision (b) of Section 7068, the individual proprietor has qualified for the license by his or her personal appearance, or the qualifier is a general partner as set forth under paragraph (2) of subdivision (b) of Section 7068. The qualifying individual's bond shall be for the benefit of the following persons:

(a) A homeowner contracting for home improvement upon the homeowner's personal family residence damaged as a result of a violation of this chapter by the licensee.

(b) A property owner contracting for the construction of a single-family dwelling who is damaged as a result of a violation of this chapter by the licensee. That property owner shall only recover under this subdivision if the single-family dwelling is not intended for sale or offered for sale at the time the damages were incurred.

(c) A person damaged as a result of a willful and deliberate violation of this chapter by the licensee, or by the fraud of the licensee in the execution or performance of a construction contract.

(d) An employee of the licensee damaged by the licensee's failure to pay wages.

(e) A person or entity, including a laborer described in subdivision (b) of Section 8024 of the Civil Code, to which a portion of the compensation of an employee of a licensee is paid by agreement with that employee or the collective bargaining agent of that employee, that is damaged as the result of the licensee's failure to pay fringe benefits for its employees including, but not limited to, employer payments described in Section 1773.1 of the Labor Code and regulations adopted thereunder (without regard to whether the work was performed on a public or private work). Damage to a person or entity under this subdivision is limited to employer payments required to be made on behalf of employees of the licensee, as part of the overall compensation of those employees, which the licensee fails to pay.

Old Text

B&P 7071.10

The qualifying individual's bond required by this article shall be executed by an admitted surety insurer in favor of the State of California, in a form acceptable to the registrar and filed with the registrar by the qualifying individual. The qualifying individual's bond shall not be required in addition to the contractor's bond when, as set forth under paragraph (1) of subdivision (b) of Section 7068, the individual proprietor has qualified for the license by his or her personal appearance, or the qualifier is a general partner as set forth under paragraph (2) of subdivision (b) of Section 7068. The qualifying individual's bond shall be for the benefit of the following persons:

(a) A homeowner contracting for home improvement upon the homeowner's personal family residence damaged as a result of a violation of this chapter by the licensee.

(b) A property owner contracting for the construction of a single-family dwelling who is damaged as a result of a violation of this chapter by the licensee. That property owner shall only recover under this subdivision if the single-family dwelling is not intended for sale or offered for sale at the time the damages were incurred.

(c) A person damaged as a result of a willful and deliberate violation of this chapter by the licensee, or by the fraud of the licensee in the execution or performance of a construction contract.

(d) An employee of the licensee damaged by the licensee's failure to pay wages.

(e) A person or entity, including an express trust fund described in Section 3111 of the Civil Code, to whom a portion of the compensation of an employee of a licensee is paid by agreement with that employee or the collective bargaining agent of that employee, that is damaged as the result of the licensee's failure to pay fringe benefits for its employees including, but not limited to, employer payments described in Section 1773.1 of the Labor Code and regulations adopted thereunder (without regard to whether the work was performed on a public or private work). Damage to an express trust fund is limited to employer payments required to be made on behalf of employees of the licensee, as part of the overall compensation of those employees, which the licensee fails to pay.

Revised to include new terminology and reference to new Section 8000 et seq.

New Text (Operative July 1, 2012)

B&P 7159

(a) (1) This section identifies the projects for which a home improvement contract is required, outlines the contract requirements, and lists the items that shall be included in the contract, or may be provided as an attachment.

(2) This section does not apply to service and repair contracts that are subject to Section 7159.10, if the contract for the applicable services complies with Sections 7159.10 to 7159.14, inclusive.

(3) This section does not apply to the sale, installation, and servicing of a fire alarm sold in conjunction with an alarm system, as defined in subdivision (n) of Section 7590.1, if all costs attributable to making the fire alarm system operable, including sale and installation costs, do not exceed five hundred dollars ($500), and the licensee complies with the requirements set forth in Section 7159.9.

(4) This section does not apply to any costs associated with monitoring a burglar or fire alarm system.

(5) Failure by the licensee, his or her agent or salesperson, or by a person subject to be licensed under this chapter, to provide the specified information, notices, and disclosures in the contract, or to otherwise fail to comply with any provision of this section, is cause for discipline.

(b) For purposes of this section, "home improvement contract" means an agreement, whether oral or written, or contained in one or more documents, between a contractor and an owner or between a contractor and a tenant, regardless of the number of residence or dwelling units contained in the building in which the tenant resides, if the work is to be performed in, to, or upon the residence or dwelling unit of the tenant, for the performance of a home improvement, as defined in Section 7151, and includes all labor, services, and materials to be furnished and performed thereunder, if the aggregate contract price specified in one or more improvement contracts, including all labor, services, and materials to be furnished by the contractor, exceeds five hundred dollars ($500). "Home improvement contract" also means an agreement, whether oral or written, or contained in one or more documents, between a salesperson, whether or not he or she is a home improvement salesperson, and an owner or a tenant, regardless of the number of residence or dwelling units contained in the building in which

Old Text

B&P 7159

(a)(1) This section identifies the projects for which a home improvement contract is required, outlines the contract requirements, and lists the items that shall be included in the contract, or may be provided as an attachment.

(2) This section does not apply to service and repair contracts that are subject to Section 7159.10, provided the contract for the applicable services complies with Sections 7159.10 to 7159.14, inclusive.

(3) This section does not apply to the sale, installation, and servicing of a fire alarm sold in conjunction with an alarm system, as defined in subdivision (n) of Section 7590.1, provided all costs attributable to making the fire alarm system operable, including sale and installation costs, do not exceed five hundred dollars ($500), and the licensee complies with the requirements set forth in Section 7159.9.

(4) This section does not apply to any costs associated with monitoring a burglar or fire alarm system.

(5) Failure by the licensee, his or her agent or salesperson, or by a person subject to be licensed under this chapter, to provide the specified information, notices, and disclosures in the contract, or to otherwise fail to comply with any provision of this section, is cause for discipline.

(b) For purposes of this section, "home improvement contract" means an agreement, whether oral or written, or contained in one or more documents, between a contractor and an owner or between a contractor and a tenant, regardless of the number of residence or dwelling units contained in the building in which the tenant resides, if the work is to be performed in, to, or upon the residence or dwelling unit of the tenant, for the performance of a home improvement, as defined in Section 7151, and includes all labor, services, and materials to be furnished and performed thereunder, if the aggregate contract price specified in one or more improvement contracts, including all labor, services, and materials to be furnished by the contractor, exceeds five hundred dollars ($500). "Home improvement contract" also means an agreement, whether oral or written, or contained in one or more documents, between a salesperson, whether or not he or she is a home improvement salesperson, and an owner or a tenant, regardless of the number of residence or dwelling units contained in the building in which the tenant resides, which provides for the sale, installation, or furnishing of home improvement goods or services.

(c) In addition to the specific requirements listed under this section, every home improvement contract and any

New Text (Operative July 1, 2012)	Old Text

the tenant resides, which provides for the sale, installation, or furnishing of home improvement goods or services.

(c) In addition to the specific requirements listed under this section, every home improvement contract and any person subject to licensure under this chapter or his or her agent or salesperson shall comply with all of the following:

(1) The writing shall be legible.

(2) Any printed form shall be readable. Unless a larger typeface is specified in this article, text in any printed form shall be in at least 10-point typeface and the headings shall be in at least 10-point boldface type.

(3) (A) Before any work is started, the contractor shall give the buyer a copy of the contract signed and dated by both the contractor and the buyer. The buyer's receipt of the copy of the contract initiates the buyer's rights to cancel the contract pursuant to Sections 1689.5 to 1689.14, inclusive, of the Civil Code.

(B) The contract shall contain on the first page, in a typeface no smaller than that generally used in the body of the document, both of the following:

(i) The date the buyer signed the contract.

(ii) The name and address of the contractor to which the applicable "Notice of Cancellation" is to be mailed, immediately preceded by a statement advising the buyer that the "Notice of Cancellation" may be sent to the contractor at the address noted on the contract.

(4) The contract shall include a statement that, upon satisfactory payment being made for any portion of the work performed, the contractor, prior to any further payment being made, shall furnish to the person contracting for the home improvement or swimming pool work a full and unconditional release from any potential lien claimant claim or mechanics lien authorized pursuant to Sections 8400 and 8404 of the Civil Code for that portion of the work for which payment has been made.

(5) A change-order form for changes or extra work shall be incorporated into the contract and shall become part of the contract only if it is in writing and signed by the parties prior to the commencement of any work covered by a change order.

(6) The contract shall contain, in close proximity

person subject to licensure under this chapter or his or her agent or salesperson shall comply with all of the following:

(1) The writing shall be legible.

(2) Any printed form shall be readable. Unless a larger typeface is specified in this article, text in any printed form shall be in at least 10-point typeface and the headings shall be in at least 10-point boldface type.

(3) (A) Before any work is started, the contractor shall give the buyer a copy of the contract signed and dated by both the contractor and the buyer. The buyer's receipt of the copy of the contract initiates the buyer's rights to cancel the contract pursuant to Sections 1689.5 to 1689.14, inclusive, of the Civil Code.

(B) The contract shall contain on the first page, in a typeface no smaller than that generally used in the body of the document, both of the following:

(i) The date the buyer signed the contract.

(ii) The name and address of the contractor to which the applicable "Notice of Cancellation" is to be mailed, immediately preceded by a statement advising the buyer that the "Notice of Cancellation" may be sent to the contractor at the address noted on the contract.

(4) A statement that, upon satisfactory payment being made for any portion of the work performed, the contractor shall, prior to any further payment being made, furnish to the person contracting for the home improvement or swimming pool work a full and unconditional release from any claim or Mechanic's lien pursuant to Section 3114 of the Civil Code for that portion of the work for which payment has been made.

(5) A change-order form for changes or extra work shall be incorporated into the contract and shall become part of the contract only if it is in writing and signed by the parties prior to the commencement of any work covered by a change order.

(6) The contract shall contain, in close proximity to the signatures of the owner and contractor, a notice stating that the owner or tenant has the right to require the contractor to have a performance and payment bond.

(7) If the contract provides for a contractor to furnish joint control, the contractor shall not have any financial or other interest in the joint control.

(8) The provisions of this section are not exclusive and do not relieve the contractor from compliance with any other applicable provision of law.

to the signatures of the owner and contractor, a notice stating that the owner or tenant has the right to require the contractor to have a performance and payment bond.

(7) If the contract provides for a contractor to furnish joint control, the contractor shall not have any financial or other interest in the joint control.

(8) The provisions of this section are not exclusive and do not relieve the contractor from compliance with any other applicable provision of law.

(d) A home improvement contract and any changes to the contract shall be in writing and signed by the parties to the contract prior to the commencement of work covered by the contract or an applicable change order and, except as provided in paragraph (8) of subdivision (a) of Section 7159.5, shall include or comply with all of the following:

(1) The name, business address, and license number of the contractor.

(2) If applicable, the name and registration number of the home improvement salesperson that solicited or negotiated the contract.

(3) The following heading on the contract form that identifies the type of contract in at least 10-point boldface type: "Home Improvement."

(4) The following statement in at least 12-point boldface type: "You are entitled to a completely filled in copy of this agreement, signed by both you and the contractor, before any work may be started."

(5) The heading: "Contract Price," followed by the amount of the contract in dollars and cents.

(6) If a finance charge will be charged, the heading: "Finance Charge," followed by the amount in dollars and cents. The finance charge is to be set out separately from the contract amount.

(7) The heading: "Description of the Project and Description of the Significant Materials to be Used and Equipment to be Installed," followed by a description of the project and a description of the significant materials to be used and equipment to be installed. For swimming pools, the project description required under this paragraph also shall include a plan and scale drawing showing the shape, size, dimensions, and the construction and equipment specifications.

(8) If a downpayment will be charged, the details of the downpayment shall be expressed in substantially the following form, and shall include

(d) A home improvement contract and any changes to the contract shall be in writing and signed by the parties to the contract prior to the commencement of any work covered by the contract or applicable change order and, except as provided in paragraph (8) of subdivision (a) of Section 7159.5, shall include or comply with all of the following:

(1) The name, business address, and license number of the contractor.

(2) If applicable, the name and registration number of the home improvement salesperson that solicited or negotiated the contract.

(3) The following heading on the contract form that identifies the type of contract in at least 10-point boldface type: "Home Improvement."

(4) The following statement in at least 12-point boldface type: "You are entitled to a completely filled in copy of this agreement, signed by both you and the contractor, before any work may be started."

(5) The heading: "Contract Price," followed by the amount of the contract in dollars and cents.

(6) If a finance charge will be charged, the heading: "Finance Charge," followed by the amount in dollars and cents. The finance charge is to be set out separately from the contract amount.

(7) The heading: "Description of the Project and Description of the Significant Materials to be Used and Equipment to be Installed," followed by a description of the project and a description of the significant materials to be used and equipment to be installed. For swimming pools, the project description required under this paragraph also shall include a plan and scale drawing showing the shape, size, dimensions, and the construction and equipment specifications.

(8) If a downpayment will be charged, the details of the downpayment shall be expressed in substantially the following form, and shall include the text of the notice as specified in subparagraph (C):

(A) The heading: "Down Payment."

(B) A space where the actual downpayment appears.

(C) The following statement in at least 12-point boldface type:

"THE DOWN PAYMENT MAY NOT EXCEED $1,000 OR 10 PERCENT OF THE CONTRACT PRICE, WHICHEVER IS LESS."

(9) If any payments, other than the downpayment, are to be made before the project is completed, the details of these payments, known as progress payments, shall be expressed in substantially the following form, and

New Text (Operative July 1, 2012)

the text of the notice as specified in subparagraph (C):

(A) The heading: "Downpayment."

(B) A space where the actual downpayment appears.

(C) The following statement in at least 12-point boldface type:

"THE DOWNPAYMENT MAY NOT EXCEED $1,000 OR 10 PERCENT OF THE CONTRACT PRICE, WHICHEVER IS LESS."

(9) If payments, other than the downpayment, are to be made before the project is completed, the details of these payments, known as progress payments, shall be expressed in substantially the following form, and shall include the text of the statement as specified in subparagraph (C):

(A) A schedule of progress payments shall be preceded by the heading: "Schedule of Progress Payments."

(B) Each progress payment shall be stated in dollars and cents and specifically reference the amount of work or services to be performed and materials and equipment to be supplied.

(C) The section of the contract reserved for the progress payments shall include the following statement in at least 12-point boldface type:

"The schedule of progress payments must specifically describe each phase of work, including the type and amount of work or services scheduled to be supplied in each phase, along with the amount of each proposed progress payment. IT IS AGAINST THE LAW FOR A CONTRACTOR TO COLLECT PAYMENT FOR WORK NOT YET COMPLETED, OR FOR MATERIALS NOT YET DELIVERED. HOWEVER, A CONTRACTOR MAY REQUIRE A DOWNPAYMENT."

(10) The contract shall address the commencement of work to be performed in substantially the following form:

(A) A statement that describes what constitutes substantial commencement of work under the contract.

(B) The heading: "Approximate Start Date."

(C) The approximate date on which work will be commenced.

(11) The estimated completion date of the work

Old Text

shall include the text of the statement as specified in subparagraph (C):

(A) A schedule of progress payments shall be preceded by the heading: "Schedule of Progress Payments."

(B) Each progress payment shall be stated in dollars and cents and specifically reference the amount of work or services to be performed and any materials and equipment to be supplied.

(C) The section of the contract reserved for the progress payments shall include the following statement in at least 12-point boldface type: "The schedule of progress payments must specifically describe each phase of work, including the type and amount of work or services scheduled to be supplied in each phase, along with the amount of each proposed progress payment. IT IS AGAINST THE LAW FOR A CONTRACTOR TO COLLECT PAYMENT FOR WORK NOT YET COMPLETED, OR FOR MATERIALS NOT YET DELIVERED. HOWEVER, A CONTRACTOR MAY REQUIRE A DOWNPAYMENT."

(10) The contract shall address the commencement of work to be performed in substantially the following form:

(A) A statement that describes what constitutes substantial commencement of work under the contract.

(B) The heading: "Approximate Start Date."

(C) The approximate date on which work will be commenced.

(11) The estimated completion date of the work shall be referenced in the contract in substantially the following form:

(A) The heading: "Approximate Completion Date."

(B) The approximate date of completion.

(12) If applicable, the heading: "List of Documents to be Incorporated into the Contract," followed by the list of documents incorporated into the contract.

(13) The heading: "Note about Extra Work and Change Orders," followed by the following statement: "Extra Work and Change Orders become part of the contract once the order is prepared in writing and signed by the parties prior to the commencement of any work covered by the new change order. The order must describe the scope of the extra work or change, the cost to be added or subtracted from the contract, and the effect the order will have on the schedule of progress payments."

New Text (Operative July 1, 2012)

shall be referenced in the contract in substantially the following form:

(A) The heading: "Approximate Completion Date."

(B) The approximate date of completion.

(12) If applicable, the heading: "List of Documents to be Incorporated into the Contract," followed by the list of documents incorporated into the contract.

(13) The heading: "Note About Extra Work and Change Orders," followed by the following statement:

"Extra Work and Change Orders become part of the contract once the order is prepared in writing and signed by the parties prior to the commencement of work covered by the new change order. The order must describe the scope of the extra work or change, the cost to be added or subtracted from the contract, and the effect the order will have on the schedule of progress payments."

(e) Except as provided in paragraph (8) of subdivision (a) of Section 7159.5, all of the following notices shall be provided to the owner as part of the contract form as specified or, if otherwise authorized under this subdivision, may be provided as an attachment to the contract:

(1) A notice concerning commercial general liability insurance. This notice may be provided as an attachment to the contract if the contract includes the following statement: "A notice concerning commercial general liability insurance is attached to this contract." The notice shall include the heading "Commercial General Liability Insurance (CGL)," followed by whichever of the following statements is both relevant and correct:

(A) "(The name on the license or "This contractor') does not carry commercial general liability insurance."

(B) "(The name on the license or "This contractor') carries commercial general liability insurance written by (the insurance company). You may call (the insurance company) at __________ to check the contractor's insurance coverage."

(C) "(The name on the license or "This contractor') is self-insured."

(D) "(The name on the license or 'This contractor') is a limited liability company that carries liability insurance or maintains other security as required by law. You may call

Old Text

(e) Except as provided in paragraph (8) of subdivision (a) of Section 7159.5, all of the following notices shall be provided to the owner as part of the contract form as specified or, if otherwise authorized under this subdivision, may be provided as an attachment to the contract:

(1) A notice concerning commercial general liability insurance. This notice may be provided as an attachment to the contract if the contract includes the following statement: "A notice concerning commercial general liability insurance is attached to this contract." The notice shall include the heading "Commercial General Liability Insurance (CGL)," followed by whichever of the following statements is both relevant and correct:

(A) "(The name on the license or 'This contractor') does not carry commercial general liability insurance."

(B) "(The name on the license or 'This contractor') carries commercial general liability insurance written by (the insurance company). You may call the (insurance company) at __________ to check the contractor's insurance coverage."

(C) "(The name on the license or 'This contractor') is self-insured."

(2) A notice concerning workers' compensation insurance. This notice may be provided as an attachment to the contract if the contract includes the statement: "A notice concerning workers' compensation insurance is attached to this contract." The notice shall include the heading "Workers' Compensation Insurance" followed by whichever of the following statements is correct:

(A) "(The name on the license or 'This contractor') has no employees and is exempt from workers' compensation requirements."

(B) "(The name on the license or 'This contractor') carries workers' compensation insurance for all employees."

(3) A notice that provides the buyer with the following information about the performance of extra or change-order work:

(A) A statement that the buyer may not require a contractor to perform extra or change-order work without providing written authorization prior to the commencement of any work covered by the new change order.

(B) A statement informing the buyer that extra work or a change order is not enforceable against a buyer unless the change order also identifies all of the following in writing prior to the

New Text (Operative July 1, 2012)

(the insurance company or trust company or bank) at ____ to check on the contractor's insurance coverage or security."

(2) A notice concerning workers' compensation insurance. This notice may be provided as an attachment to the contract if the contract includes the statement: "A notice concerning workers' compensation insurance is attached to this contract." The notice shall include the heading "Workers' Compensation Insurance" followed by whichever of the following statements is correct:

(A) "(The name on the license or "This contractor') has no employees and is exempt from workers' compensation requirements."

(B) "(The name on the license or "This contractor') carries workers' compensation insurance for all employees."

(3) A notice that provides the buyer with the following information about the performance of extra or change-order work:

(A) A statement that the buyer may not require a contractor to perform extra or change-order work without providing written authorization prior to the commencement of work covered by the new change order.

(B) A statement informing the buyer that extra work or a change order is not enforceable against a buyer unless the change order also identifies all of the following in writing prior to the commencement of work covered by the new change order:

(i) The scope of work encompassed by the order.

(ii) The amount to be added or subtracted from the contract.

(iii) The effect the order will make in the progress payments or the completion date.

(C) A statement informing the buyer that the contractor's failure to comply with the requirements of this paragraph does not preclude the recovery of compensation for work performed based upon legal or equitable remedies designed to prevent unjust enrichment.

(4) A notice with the heading "Mechanics Lien Warning" written as follows:

"MECHANICS LIEN WARNING:

Anyone who helps improve your property, but who is not paid, may record what is called mechanics lien on your property. A mechanics lien is a claim, like a mortgage or home equity loan, made against your property and

Old Text

commencement of any work covered by the new change order:

(i) The scope of work encompassed by the order.

(ii) The amount to be added or subtracted from the contract.

(iii) The effect the order will make in the progress payments or the completion date.

(C) A statement informing the buyer that the contractor's failure to comply with the requirements of this paragraph does not preclude the recovery of compensation for work performed based upon legal or equitable remedies designed to prevent unjust enrichment.

(4) A notice with the heading "Mechanics' Lien Warning" written as follows: "MECHANICS LIEN WARNING: Anyone who helps improve your property, but who is not paid, may record what is called a mechanics' lien on your property. A mechanics' lien is a claim, like a mortgage or home equity loan, made against your property and recorded with the county recorder. Even if you pay your contractor in full, unpaid subcontractors, suppliers, and laborers who helped to improve your property may record mechanics' liens and sue you in court to foreclose the lien. If a court finds the lien is valid, you could be forced to pay twice or have a court officer sell your home to pay the lien. Liens can also affect your credit. To preserve their right to record a lien, each subcontractor and material supplier must provide you with a document called a '20-day Preliminary Notice.' This notice is not a lien. The purpose of the notice is to let you know that the person who sends you the notice has the right to record a lien on your property if he or she is not paid. BE CAREFUL. The Preliminary Notice can be sent up to 20 days after the subcontractor starts work or the supplier provides material. This can be a big problem if you pay your contractor before you have received the Preliminary Notices. You will not get Preliminary Notices from your prime contractor or from laborers who work on your project. The law assumes that you already know they are improving your property. PROTECT YOURSELF FROM LIENS. You can protect yourself from liens by getting a list from your contractor of all the subcontractors and material suppliers that work on your project. Find out from your contractor when these subcontractors started work and when these suppliers delivered goods or materials. Then wait 20 days, paying attention to the Preliminary Notices you receive. PAY WITH JOINT CHECKS. One way to protect yourself is to pay with

New Text (Operative July 1, 2012)	Old Text

recorded with the county recorder.
Even if you pay your contractor in full, unpaid subcontractors, suppliers, and laborers who helped to improve your property may record mechanics liens and sue you in court to foreclose the lien. If a court finds the lien is valid, you could be forced to pay twice or have a court officer sell your home to pay the lien. Liens can also affect your credit.
To preserve their right to record a lien, each subcontractor and material supplier must provide you with a document called a 'Preliminary Notice.' This notice is not a lien. The purpose of the notice is to let you know that the person who sends you the notice has the right to record a lien on your property if he or she is not paid.
BE CAREFUL. The Preliminary Notice can be sent up to 20 days after the subcontractor starts work or the supplier provides material. This can be a big problem if you pay your contractor before you have received the Preliminary Notices.
You will not get Preliminary Notices from your prime contractor or from laborers who work on your project. The law assumes that you already know they are improving your property.
PROTECT YOURSELF FROM LIENS. You can protect yourself from liens by getting a list from your contractor of all the subcontractors and material suppliers that work on your project. Find out from your contractor when these subcontractors started work and when these suppliers delivered goods or materials. Then wait 20 days, paying attention to the Preliminary Notices you receive.
PAY WITH JOINT CHECKS. One way to protect yourself is to pay with a joint check. When your contractor tells you it is time to pay for the work of a subcontractor or supplier who has provided you with a Preliminary Notice, write a joint check payable to both the contractor and the subcontractor or material supplier.
For other ways to prevent liens, visit CSLB's Internet Web site at www.cslb.ca.gov or call CSLB at 800-321-CSLB (2752).
REMEMBER, IF YOU DO NOTHING, YOU RISK HAVING A LIEN PLACED ON YOUR HOME. This can mean that you may have to pay twice, or face the forced sale of your home to pay what you owe."

(5) The following notice shall be provided in at least 12-point typeface:

"Information about the Contractors' State License Board (CSLB):
CSLB is the state consumer protection agency that licenses and regulates construction contractors.
Contact CSLB for information about the licensed

a joint check. When your contractor tells you it is time to pay for the work of a subcontractor or supplier who has provided you with a Preliminary Notice, write a joint check payable to both the contractor and the subcontractor or material supplier. For other ways to prevent liens, visit CSLB's Web site at www.cslb.ca.gov or call CSLB at 800-321-CSLB (2752). REMEMBER, IF YOU DO NOTHING, YOU RISK HAVING A LIEN PLACED ON YOUR HOME. This can mean that you may have to pay twice, or face the forced sale of your home to pay what you owe."

(5) The following notice shall be provided in at least 12-point typeface: "Information about the Contractors' State License Board (CSLB): CSLB is the state consumer protection agency that licenses and regulates construction contractors. Contact CSLB for information about the licensed contractor you are considering, including information about disclosable complaints, disciplinary actions and civil judgments that are reported to CSLB. Use only licensed contractors. If you file a complaint against a licensed contractor within the legal deadline (usually four years), CSLB has authority to investigate the complaint. If you use an unlicensed contractor, CSLB may not be able to help you resolve your complaint. Your only remedy may be in civil court, and you may be liable for damages arising out of any injuries to the unlicensed contractor or the unlicensed contractor's employees. For more information: Visit CSLB's Web site at www.cslb.ca.gov Call CSLB at 800-321-CSLB (2752) Write CSLB at P.O. Box 26000, Sacramento, CA 95826."

(6) (A) The notice set forth in subparagraph (B) and entitled "Three-Day Right to Cancel," shall be provided to the buyer unless the contract is:

(i) Negotiated at the contractor's place of business.

(ii) Subject to the "Seven-Day Right to Cancel," as set forth in paragraph (8).

(iii) Subject to licensure under the Alarm Company Act (Chapter 11.6 (commencing with Section 7590)), provided the alarm company licensee complies with Sections 1689.5, 1689.6, and 1689.7 of the Civil Code, as applicable.

(B) "Three-Day Right to Cancel "You, the buyer, have the right to cancel this contract within three business days. You may cancel by e-mailing, mailing, faxing, or delivering a written notice to the contractor at the contractor's place of business by midnight of the third business day after you received a signed and dated copy of the

New Text (Operative July 1, 2012)

contractor you are considering, including information about disclosable complaints, disciplinary actions, and civil judgments that are reported to CSLB.
Use only licensed contractors. If you file a complaint against a licensed contractor within the legal deadline (usually four years), CSLB has authority to investigate the complaint. If you use an unlicensed contractor, CSLB may not be able to help you resolve your complaint. Your only remedy may be in civil court, and you may be liable for damages arising out of any injuries to the unlicensed contractor or the unlicensed contractor's employees.
For more information:
Visit CSLB's Internet Web site at www.cslb.ca.gov
Call CSLB at 800-321-CSLB (2752)
Write CSLB at P.O. Box 26000, Sacramento, CA 95826."

(6) (A) The notice set forth in subparagraph (B) and entitled "Three-Day Right to Cancel," shall be provided to the buyer unless the contract is:
(i) Negotiated at the contractor's place of business.
(ii) Subject to the "Seven-Day Right to Cancel," as set forth in paragraph (7).
(iii) Subject to licensure under the Alarm Company Act (Chapter 11.6 (commencing with Section 7590)), provided the alarm company licensee complies with Sections 1689.5, 1689.6, and 1689.7 of the Civil Code, as applicable.
(B):

"Three-Day Right to Cancel

You, the buyer, have the right to cancel this contract within three business days. You may cancel by e-mailing, mailing, faxing, or delivering a written notice to the contractor at the contractor's place of business by midnight of the third business day after you received a signed and dated copy of the contract that includes this notice. Include your name, your address, and the date you received the signed copy of the contract and this notice.
If you cancel, the contractor must return to you anything you paid within 10 days of receiving the notice of cancellation. For your part, you must make available to the contractor at your residence, in substantially as good condition as you received them, goods delivered to you under this contract or sale. Or, you may, if you wish, comply with the contractor's instructions on how to return the goods at the contractor's expense and risk. If you do make the goods available to the contractor and the contractor does not pick them up within 20 days of the date of your notice of cancellation, you may keep them without any further obligation. If you fail to make the goods

Old Text

contract that includes this notice. Include your name, your address, and the date you received the signed copy of the contract and this notice. If you cancel, the contractor must return to you anything you paid within 10 days of receiving the notice of cancellation. For your part, you must make available to the contractor at your residence, in substantially as good condition as you received it, any goods delivered to you under this contract or sale. Or, you may, if you wish, comply with the contractor's instructions on how to return the goods at the contractor's expense and risk. If you do make the goods available to the contractor and the contractor does not pick them up within 20 days of the date of your notice of cancellation, you may keep them without any further obligation. If you fail to make the goods available to the contractor, or if you agree to return the goods to the contractor and fail to do so, then you remain liable for performance of all obligations under the contract."

(C) The "Three-Day Right to Cancel" notice required by this paragraph shall comply with all of the following:

(i) The text of the notice is at least 12-point boldface type.

(ii) The notice is in immediate proximity to a space reserved for the owner's signature.

(iii) The owner acknowledges receipt of the notice by signing and dating the notice form in the signature space.

(iv) The notice is written in the same language, e.g., Spanish, as that principally used in any oral sales presentation.

(v) The notice may be attached to the contract if the contract includes, in at least 12-point boldface type, a checkbox with the following statement:

"The law requires that the contractor give you a notice explaining your right to cancel. Initial the checkbox if the contractor has given you a 'Notice of the Three-Day Right to Cancel.'"

(vi) The notice shall be accompanied by a completed form in duplicate, captioned "Notice of Cancellation," which shall also be attached to the agreement or offer to purchase and be easily detachable, and which shall contain the following statement written in the same language, e.g., Spanish, as used in the contract: "Notice of Cancellation" /enter date of transaction/

______________________.

New Text (Operative July 1, 2012)

available to the contractor, or if you agree to return the goods to the contractor and fail to do so, then you remain liable for performance of all obligations under the contract."

(C) The "Three-Day Right to Cancel" notice required by this paragraph shall comply with all of the following:
(i) The text of the notice is at least 12-point boldface type.
(ii) The notice is in immediate proximity to a space reserved for the owner's signature.
(iii) The owner acknowledges receipt of the notice by signing and dating the notice form in the signature space.
(iv) The notice is written in the same language, e.g., Spanish, as that principally used in any oral sales presentation.
(v) The notice may be attached to the contract if the contract includes, in at least 12-point boldface type, a checkbox with the following statement: "The law requires that the contractor give you a notice explaining your right to cancel. Initial the checkbox if the contractor has given you a "Notice of the Three-Day Right to Cancel.' "
(vi) The notice shall be accompanied by a completed form in duplicate, captioned "Notice of Cancellation," which also shall be attached to the agreement or offer to purchase and be easily detachable, and which shall contain the following statement written in the same language, e.g., Spanish, as used in the contract:

""Notice of Cancellation"
/enter date of transaction/

____
(Date)

"You may cancel this transaction, without any penalty or obligation, within three business days from the above date.

If you cancel, any property traded in, any payments made by you under the contract or sale, and any negotiable instrument executed by you will be returned within 10 days following receipt by the seller of your cancellation notice, and any security interest arising out of the transaction will be canceled.

If you cancel, you must make available to the seller at your residence, in substantially as good condition as when received, any goods delivered to you under this contract or sale, or you may, if you wish, comply with the instructions of the seller regarding the return shipment of the goods at

Old Text

(Date)

"You may cancel this transaction, without any penalty or obligation, within three business days from the above date. If you cancel, any property traded in, any payments made by you under the contract or sale, and any negotiable instrument executed by you will be returned within 10 days following receipt by the seller of your cancellation notice, and any security interest arising out of the transaction will be canceled. If you cancel, you must make available to the seller at your residence, in substantially as good condition as when received, any goods delivered to you under this contract or sale, or you may, if you wish, comply with the instructions of the seller regarding the return shipment of the goods at the seller's expense and risk. If you do make the goods available to the seller and the seller does not pick them up within 20 days of the date of your notice of cancellation, you may retain or dispose of the goods without any further obligation. If you fail to make the goods available to the seller, or if you agree to return the goods to the seller and fail to do so, then you remain liable for performance of all obligations under the contract." To cancel this transaction, mail or deliver a signed and dated copy of this cancellation notice, or any other written notice, or send a telegram to______________________________,

(name of seller)

at ______________________________

(address of seller's place of business)

not later than midnight of__________.

(Date)

I hereby cancel this transaction .

____

Buyer's Signature

____

Date

(7) (A) The following notice entitled "Seven-Day Right to Cancel" shall be provided to the buyer for any contract that is written for the repair or restoration of residential premises damaged by any sudden or catastrophic event for which a state of emergency has been declared by the President of the United States or the Governor, or for which a local emergency has been declared by the executive officer or governing body of any city, county, or city and county: "Seven-Day Right to Cancel You, the buyer, have the right to

New Text (Operative July 1, 2012)

the seller's expense and risk.

If you do make the goods available to the seller and the seller does not pick them up within 20 days of the date of your notice of cancellation, you may retain or dispose of the goods without any further obligation. If you fail to make the goods available to the seller, or if you agree to return the goods to the seller and fail to do so, then you remain liable for performance of all obligations under the contract."

To cancel this transaction, mail or deliver a signed and dated copy of this cancellation notice, or any other written notice, or send a telegram

*to*__________________________________,

(name of seller)

*at*__________________________________

/address of seller's place of business/

not later than midnight of:

____________________________________.

(Date)

I hereby cancel this transaction.

____

(Date)

____

(Buyer's signature)

(7) (A) The following notice entitled "Seven-Day Right to Cancel" shall be provided to the buyer for any contract that is written for the repair or restoration of residential premises damaged by any sudden or catastrophic event for which a state of emergency has been declared by the President of the United States or the Governor, or for which a local emergency has been declared by the executive officer or governing body of any city, county, or city and county:

"Seven-Day Right to Cancel

You, the buyer, have the right to cancel this contract within seven business days. You may cancel by e-mailing, mailing, faxing, or delivering a written notice to the contractor at the contractor's place of business by midnight of the seventh business day after you received a signed and dated copy of the contract that includes this notice. Include your name, your address, and the date you received the signed copy of the contract and this notice.

If you cancel, the contractor must return to you anything you paid within 10 days of receiving the notice of cancellation. For your part, you must make available to the contractor at your residence, in substantially as good condition as you received them, goods delivered to you under this contract or sale. Or, you may, if you wish,

Old Text

cancel this contract within seven business days. You may cancel by e-mailing, mailing, faxing, or delivering a written notice to the contractor at the contractor's place of business by midnight of the seventh business day after you received a signed and dated copy of the contract that includes this notice. Include your name, your address, and the date you received the signed copy of the contract and this notice. If you cancel, the contractor must return to you anything you paid within 10 days of receiving the notice of cancellation. For your part, you must make available to the contractor at your residence, in substantially as good condition as you received it, any goods delivered to you under this contract or sale. Or, you may, if you wish, comply with the contractor's instructions on how to return the goods at the contractor's expense and risk. If you do make the goods available to the contractor and the contractor does not pick them up within 20 days of the date of your notice of cancellation, you may keep them without any further obligation. If you fail to make the goods available to the contractor, or if you agree to return the goods to the contractor and fail to do so, then you remain liable for performance of all obligations under the contract."

(B) The "Seven-Day Right to Cancel" notice required by this subdivision shall comply with all of the following:

(i) The text of the notice is at least 12-point boldface type.

(ii) The notice is in immediate proximity to a space reserved for the owner's signature.

(iii) The owner acknowledges receipt of the notice by signing and dating the notice form in the signature space.

(iv) The notice is written in the same language, e.g., Spanish, as that principally used in any oral sales presentation.

(v) The notice may be attached to the contract if the contract includes, in at least 12-point boldface type, a checkbox with the following statement: "The law requires that the contractor give you a notice explaining your right to cancel. Initial the checkbox if the contractor has given you a 'Notice of the Seven-Day Right to Cancel.'"

(vi) The notice shall be accompanied by a completed form in duplicate, captioned "Notice of Cancellation," which shall also be attached to the agreement or offer to purchase and be easily detachable, and which shall contain the following statement written in the same language, e.g., Spanish, as used in the contract: "Notice of Cancellation" /enter date of transaction/

New Text (Operative July 1, 2012)

comply with the contractor's instructions on how to return the goods at the contractor's expense and risk. If you do make the goods available to the contractor and the contractor does not pick them up within 20 days of the date of your notice of cancellation, you may keep them without any further obligation. If you fail to make the goods available to the contractor, or if you agree to return the goods to the contractor and fail to do so, then you remain liable for performance of all obligations under the contract."

(B) The "Seven-Day Right to Cancel" notice required by this subdivision shall comply with all of the following:

(i) The text of the notice is at least 12-point boldface type.

(ii) The notice is in immediate proximity to a space reserved for the owner's signature.

(iii) The owner acknowledges receipt of the notice by signing and dating the notice form in the signature space.

(iv) The notice is written in the same language, e.g., Spanish, as that principally used in any oral sales presentation.

(v) The notice may be attached to the contract if the contract includes, in at least 12-point boldface type, a checkbox with the following statement: "The law requires that the contractor give you a notice explaining your right to cancel. Initial the checkbox if the contractor has given you a "Notice of the Seven-Day Right to Cancel.' "

(vi) The notice shall be accompanied by a completed form in duplicate, captioned "Notice of Cancellation," which shall also be attached to the agreement or offer to purchase and be easily detachable, and which shall contain the following statement written in the same language, e.g., Spanish, as used in the contract:

""Notice of Cancellation"
/enter date of transaction/

____
(Date)

"You may cancel this transaction, without any penalty or obligation, within seven business days from the above date. If you cancel, any property traded in, any payments made by you under the contract or sale, and any negotiable instrument executed by you will be returned within 10 days following receipt by the seller of your cancellation notice,

Old Text

____________________________.
(Date)

"You may cancel this transaction, without any penalty or obligation, within seven business days from the above date. If you cancel, any property traded in, any payments made by you under the contract or sale, and any negotiable instrument executed by you will be returned within 10 days following receipt by the seller of your cancellation notice, and any security interest arising out of the transaction will be canceled. If you cancel, you must make available to the seller at your residence, in substantially as good condition as when received, any goods delivered to you under this contract or sale, or you may, if you wish, comply with the instructions of the seller regarding the return shipment of the goods at the seller's expense and risk. If you do make the goods available to the seller and the seller does not pick them up within 20 days of the date of your notice of cancellation, you may retain or dispose of the goods without any further obligation. If you fail to make the goods available to the seller, or if you agree to return the goods to the seller and fail to do so, then you remain liable for performance of all obligations under the contract." To cancel this transaction, mail or deliver a signed and dated copy of this cancellation notice, or any other written notice, or send a telegram to__________________________,
(name of seller)

at ____________________________
(address of seller's place of business)

not later than midnight of__________.
(Date)

I hereby cancel this transaction .

____
Buyer's Signature

____
Date

____
(Buyer's signature)

New Text (Operative July 1, 2012)	Old Text

and any security interest arising out of the transaction will be canceled.

If you cancel, you must make available to the seller at your residence, in substantially as good condition as when received, any goods delivered to you under this contract or sale, or you may, if you wish, comply with the instructions of the seller regarding the return shipment of the goods at the seller's expense and risk.

If you do make the goods available to the seller and the seller does not pick them up within 20 days of the date of your notice of cancellation, you may retain or dispose of the goods without any further obligation. If you fail to make the goods available to the seller, or if you agree to return the goods to the seller and fail to do so, then you remain liable for performance of all obligations under the contract."

To cancel this transaction, mail or deliver a signed and dated copy of this cancellation notice, or any other written notice, or send a telegram to

____________________________________,

/name of seller/

at ____________________________________

/address of seller's place of business/

not later than midnight of

____________________________________.

(Date)

I hereby cancel this transaction.

____

(Date)

____

(Buyer's signature)

Amended by Senate Bill 190
(Approved by Governor June 29, 2011 and filed with Secretary of State July 1, 2011)
Revised to include new terminology and reference to new Section 8000 et seq.

New Text (Operative July 1, 2012)

B&P 7159.1

(a) In any contract for the sale of home improvement goods or services offered by door-to-door sale that contains or is secured by a lien on real property, the contract shall be accompanied by the following notice in 18-point boldfaced type:

"WARNING TO BUYER: IF YOU SIGN THE CONTRACT WHICH ACCOMPANIES THIS NOTICE, YOU WILL BE PUTTING UP YOUR HOME AS SECURITY. THIS MEANS THAT YOUR HOME COULD BE SOLD WITHOUT YOUR PERMISSION AND WITHOUT ANY COURT ACTION IF YOU MISS ANY PAYMENT REQUIRED BY THIS CONTRACT."

This notice shall be written in the same language as the rest of the contract. It shall be on a separate piece of paper from the rest of the contract and shall be signed and dated by the buyer. The home improvement contractor or home improvement salesperson shall deliver to the buyer at the time of the buyer's signing and dating of the notice a legible copy of the signed and dated notice. A security interest created in any contract described in this section that does not provide the notice as required by this section shall be void and unenforceable.

(b) This section shall not apply to any of the following:

(1) Any contract that is subject to Chapter 1 (commencing with Section 1801) of Title 2 of Part 4 of Division 3 of the Civil Code.

(2) A mechanics lien established pursuant to Chapter 4 (commencing with Section 8400) of Title 2 of Part 6 of Division 4 of the Civil Code.

(3) Any contract that is subject to subdivision (a) of Section 7159.2.

Old Text

B&P 7159.1

In any contract for the sale of home improvement goods or services offered by door-to-door sale that contains or is secured by a lien on real property, the contract shall be accompanied by the following notice in 18-point boldfaced type:

"WARNING TO BUYER: IF YOU SIGN THE CONTRACT WHICH ACCOMPANIES THIS NOTICE, YOU WILL BE PUTTING UP YOUR HOME AS SECURITY. THIS MEANS THAT YOUR HOME COULD BE SOLD WITHOUT YOUR PERMISSION AND WITHOUT ANY COURT ACTION IF YOU MISS ANY PAYMENT REQUIRED BY THIS CONTRACT."

This notice shall be written in the same language as the rest of the contract. It shall be on a separate piece of paper from the rest of the contract and shall be signed and dated by the buyer. The home improvement contractor or home improvement salesperson shall deliver to the buyer at the time of the buyer's signing and dating of the notice a legible copy of the signed and dated notice. A security interest created in any contract described in this section that does not provide the notice as required by this section shall be void and unenforceable.

This section shall not apply to any of the following:

(a) Any contract that is subject to Chapter 1 (commencing with Section 1801) of Title 2 of Part 4 of Division 3 of the Civil Code.

(b) A mechanic's lien established pursuant to Chapter 2 (commencing with Section 3109) of Title 15 of Part 4 of Division 3 of the Civil Code.

(c) Any contract that is subject to subdivision (a) of Section 7159.2.

Revised to include new terminology and reference to new Section 8000 et seq.

New Text (Operative July 1, 2012)

B&P 7159.5

This section applies to all home improvement contracts, as defined in Section 7151.2, between an owner or tenant and a contractor, whether a general contractor or a specialty contractor, that is licensed or subject to be licensed pursuant to this chapter with regard to the transaction.

(a) Failure by the licensee or a person subject to be licensed under this chapter, or by his or her agent or salesperson, to comply with the following provisions is cause for discipline:

(1) The contract shall be in writing and shall include the agreed contract amount in dollars and cents. The contract amount shall include the entire cost of the contract, including profit, labor, and materials, but excluding finance charges.

(2) If there is a separate finance charge between the contractor and the person contracting for home improvement, the finance charge shall be set out separately from the contract amount.

(3) If a downpayment will be charged, the downpayment may not exceed one thousand dollars ($1,000) or 10 percent of the contract amount, whichever is less.

(4) If, in addition to a downpayment, the contract provides for payments to be made prior to completion of the work, the contract shall include a schedule of payments in dollars and cents specifically referencing the amount of work or services to be performed and any materials and equipment to be supplied.

(5) Except for a downpayment, the contractor may neither request nor accept payment that exceeds the value of the work performed or material delivered.

(6) Upon any payment by the person contracting for home improvement, and prior to any further payment being made, the contractor shall, if requested, obtain and furnish to the person a full and unconditional release from any potential lien claimant claim or mechanics lien authorized pursuant to Sections 8400 and 8404 of the Civil Code for any portion of the work for which payment has been made. The person contracting for home improvement may withhold all further payments until these releases are furnished.

(7) If the contract provides for a payment of a salesperson's commission out of the contract price, that payment shall be made on a pro rata basis in proportion to the schedule of payments made to the contractor by the disbursing party in accordance with paragraph (4).

(8) A contractor furnishing a performance and payment

Old Text

B&P 7159.5

This section applies to all home improvement contracts, as defined in Section 7151.2, between an owner or tenant and a contractor, whether a general contractor or a specialty contractor, who is licensed or subject to be licensed pursuant to this chapter with regard to the transaction.

(a) Failure by the licensee or a person subject to be licensed under this chapter, or by his or her agent or salesperson, to comply with the following provisions is cause for discipline:

(1) The contract shall be in writing and shall include the agreed contract amount in dollars and cents.

The contract amount shall include the entire cost of the contract, including profit, labor, and materials, but excluding finance charges.

(2) If there is a separate finance charge between the contractor and the person contracting for home improvement, the finance charge shall be set out separately from the contract amount.

(3) If a downpayment will be charged, the downpayment may not exceed one thousand dollars ($1,000) or 10 percent of the contract amount, whichever is less.

(4) If, in addition to a downpayment, the contract provides for payments to be made prior to completion of the work, the contract shall include a schedule of payments in dollars and cents specifically referencing the amount of work or services to be performed and any materials and equipment to be supplied.

(5) Except for a downpayment, the contractor may neither request nor accept payment that exceeds the value of the work performed or material delivered.

(6) Upon any payment by the person contracting for home improvement, and prior to any further payment being made, the contractor shall, if requested, obtain and furnish to the person a full and unconditional release from any potential lien claimant claim or mechanic's lien pursuant to Section 3114 of the Civil Code for any portion of the work for which payment has been made. The person contracting for home improvement may withhold all further payments until these releases are furnished.

(7) If the contract provides for a payment of a salesperson's commission out of the contract price, that payment shall be made on a pro rata basis in proportion to the schedule of payments made to the contractor by the disbursing party in accordance with paragraph (4).

New Text (Operative July 1, 2012)

bond, lien and completion bond, or a bond equivalent or joint control approved by the registrar covering full performance and payment is exempt from paragraphs (3), (4), and (5), and need not include, as part of the contract, the statement regarding the down payment specified in subparagraph (C) of paragraph (8) of subdivision (d) of Section 7159, the details and statement regarding progress payments specified in paragraph (9) of subdivision (d) of Section 7159, or the Mechanics Lien Warning specified in paragraph (4) of subdivision (e) of Section 7159. A contractor furnishing these bonds, bond equivalents, or a joint control approved by the registrar may accept payment prior to completion. If the contract provides for a contractor to furnish joint control, the contractor shall not have any financial or other interest in the joint control.

(b) A violation of paragraph (1), (3), or (5) of subdivision (a) by a licensee or a person subject to be licensed under this chapter, or by his or her agent or salesperson, is a misdemeanor punishable by a fine of not less than one hundred dollars ($100) nor more than five thousand dollars ($5,000), or by imprisonment in a county jail not exceeding one year, or by both that fine and imprisonment.

(1) An indictment or information against a person who is not licensed but who is required to be licensed under this chapter shall be brought, or a criminal complaint filed, for a violation of this section, in accordance with paragraph (4) of subdivision (d) of Section 802 of the Penal Code, within four years from the date of the contract or, if the contract is not reduced to writing, from the date the buyer makes the first payment to the contractor.

(2) An indictment or information against a person who is licensed under this chapter shall be brought, or a criminal complaint filed, for a violation of this section, in accordance with paragraph (2) of subdivision (d) of Section 802 of the Penal Code, within two years from the date of the contract or, if the contract is not reduced to writing, from the date the buyer makes the first payment to the contractor.

(3) The limitations on actions in this subdivision shall not apply to any administrative action filed against a licensed contractor.

(c) Any person who violates this section as part of a plan or scheme to defraud an owner or tenant of a residential or nonresidential structure, including a mobilehome or manufactured home, in connection

Old Text

(8) A contractor furnishing a performance and payment bond, lien and completion bond, or a bond equivalent or joint control approved by the registrar covering full performance and payment is exempt from paragraphs (3), (4), and (5), and need not include, as part of the contract, the statement regarding the downpayment specified in subparagraph (C) of paragraph (8) of subdivision (d) of Section 7159, the details and statement regarding progress payments specified in paragraph (9) of subdivision (d) of Section 7159, or the Mechanics' Lien Warning specified in paragraph (4) of subdivision (e) of Section 7159. A contractor furnishing these bonds, bond equivalents, or a joint control approved by the registrar may accept payment prior to completion. If the contract provides for a contractor to furnish joint control, the contractor shall not have any financial or other interest in the joint control.

(b) A violation of paragraph (1), (3), or (5) of subdivision (a) by a licensee or a person subject to be licensed under this chapter, or by his or her agent or salesperson, is a misdemeanor punishable by a fine of not less than one hundred dollars ($100) nor more than five thousand dollars ($5,000), or by imprisonment in a county jail not exceeding one year, or by both that fine and imprisonment.

(1) An indictment or information against a person who is not licensed but who is required to be licensed criminal complaint filed, for a violation of this section, in accordance with paragraph (4) of subdivision (d) of Section 802 of the Penal Code, within four years from the date of the contract or, if the contract is not reduced to writing, from the date the buyer makes the first payment to the contractor.

(2) An indictment or information against a person who is licensed under this chapter shall be brought, or a criminal complaint filed, for a violation of this section, in accordance with paragraph (2) of subdivision (d) of Section 802 of the Penal Code, within two years from the date of the contract or, if the contract is not reduced to writing, from the date the buyer makes the first payment to the contractor.

(3) The under this chapter shall be brought, or a limitations on actions in this subdivision shall not apply to any administrative action filed against a licensed contractor.

(c) Any person who violates this section as part of a plan or scheme to defraud an owner or tenant of a residential or nonresidential structure, including a mobile home or

New Text (Operative July 1, 2012)

with the offer or performance of repairs to the structure for damage caused by a natural disaster, shall be ordered by the court to make full restitution to the victim based on the person's ability to pay, as defined in subdivision (e) of Section 1203.1b of the Penal Code. In addition to full restitution, and imprisonment authorized by this section, the court may impose a fine of not less than five hundred dollars ($500) nor more than twenty-five thousand dollars ($25,000), based upon the defendant's ability to pay. This subdivision applies to natural disasters for which a state of emergency is proclaimed by the Governor pursuant to Section 8625 of the Government Code, or for which an emergency or major disaster is declared by the President of the United States.

Old Text

manufactured home, in connection with the offer or performance of repairs to the structure for damage caused by a natural disaster, shall be ordered by the court to make full restitution to the victim based on the person's ability to pay, as defined in subdivision (e) of Section 1203.1b of the Penal Code. In addition to full restitution, and imprisonment authorized by this section, the court may impose a fine of not less than five hundred dollars ($500) nor more than twenty-five thousand dollars ($25,000), based upon the defendant's ability to pay. This subdivision applies to natural disasters for which a state of emergency is proclaimed by the Governor pursuant to Section 8625 of the Government Code, or for which an emergency or major disaster is declared by the President of the United States.

NOTE: Amended by Senate Bill 190
(Approved by Governor June 29, 2011 and filed with Secretary of State July 1, 2011)
Revised to include new terminology and reference to new Section 8000 et seq.

New Text

B&P 7159.14

(a) This section applies to a service and repair contract as defined in Section 7159.10. A violation of this section by a licensee or a person subject to be licensed under this chapter, or by his or her agent or salesperson, is cause for discipline.

(1) The contract may not exceed seven hundred fifty dollars ($750).

(2) The contract shall be in writing and shall state the agreed contract amount, which may be stated as either a fixed contract amount in dollars and cents or, if a time and materials formula is used, as an estimated contract amount in dollars and cents.

(3) The contract amount shall include the entire cost of the contract including profit, labor, and materials, but excluding finance charges.

(4) The actual contract amount of a time and materials contract may not exceed the estimated contract amount without written authorization from the buyer.

(5) The prospective buyer must have initiated contact with the contractor to request work.

(6) The contractor may not sell the buyer goods or services beyond those reasonably necessary to take care of the particular problem that caused the buyer to contact the contractor.

Old Text

B&P 7159.14

(a) This section applies to a service and repair contract as defined in Section 7159.10. A violation of this section by a licensee or a person subject to be licensed under this chapter, or by his or her agent or salesperson, is cause for discipline.

(1) The contract may not exceed seven hundred fifty dollars ($750).

(2) The contract shall be in writing and shall state the agreed contract amount, which may be stated as either a fixed contract amount in dollars and cents or, if a time and materials formula is used, as an estimated contract amount in dollars and cents.

(3) The contract amount shall include the entire cost of the contract including profit, labor, and materials, but excluding finance charges.

(4) The actual contract amount of a time and materials contract may not exceed the estimated contract amount without written authorization from the buyer.

(5) The prospective buyer must have initiated contact with the contractor to request work.

(6) The contractor may not sell the buyer goods or services beyond those reasonably necessary to take care of the particular problem that caused the buyer to contact the contractor.

(7) No payment may be due before the project is completed.

(8) A service and repair contractor may charge only

New Text (Operative July 1, 2012)

(7) No payment may be due before the project is completed.

(8) A service and repair contractor may charge only one service charge. For purposes of this chapter, a service charge includes such charges as a service or trip charge, or an inspection fee.

(9) A service and repair contractor charging a service charge must disclose in all advertisements that there is a service charge and, when the customer initiates the call for service, must disclose the amount of the service charge.

(10) The service and repair contractor must offer to the customer any parts that were replaced.

(11) Upon any payment by the buyer, the contractor shall, if requested, obtain and furnish to the buyer a full and unconditional release from any potential lien claimant claim or mechanics lien authorized pursuant to Sections 8400 and 8404 of the Civil Code for any portion of the work for which payment has been made.

(b) A violation of paragraph (1), (2), (3), (4), (5), (6), or (8) of subdivision (a) by a licensee or a person subject to be licensed under this chapter, or by his or her agent or salesperson, is a misdemeanor punishable by a fine of not less than one hundred dollars ($100) nor more than five thousand dollars ($5,000), or by imprisonment in a county jail not exceeding one year, or by both that fine and imprisonment.

(1) An indictment or information against a person who is not licensed but who is required to be licensed under this chapter shall be brought, or a criminal complaint filed, for a violation of this section, in accordance with paragraph (4) of subdivision (d) of Section 802 of the Penal Code, within four years from the date of the contract or, if the contract is not reduced to writing, from the date the buyer makes the first payment to the contractor.

(2) An indictment or information against a person who is licensed under this chapter shall be brought, or a criminal complaint filed, for a violation of this section, in accordance with paragraph (2) of subdivision (d) of Section 802 of the Penal Code, within two years from the date of the contract or, if the contract is not reduced to writing, from the date the buyer makes the first payment to the contractor.

(3) The limitations on actions in this subdivision shall not apply to any administrative action filed against a licensed contractor. *(c) Any person who violates this section as part of a plan or scheme to defraud an owner or tenant of a*

Old Text

one service charge. For purposes of this chapter, a service charge includes such charges as a service or trip charge, or an inspection fee.

(9) A service and repair contractor charging a service charge must disclose in all advertisements that there is a service charge and, when the customer initiates the call for service, must disclose the amount of the service charge.

(10) The service and repair contractor must offer to the customer any parts that were replaced.

(11) Upon any payment by the buyer, the contractor shall, if requested, obtain and furnish to the buyer a full and unconditional release from any potential lien claimant claim or mechanic's lien pursuant to Section 3114 of the Civil Code for any portion of the work for which payment has been made.

(b) A violation of paragraph (1), (2), (3), (4), (5), (6), or (8) of subdivision (a) by a licensee or a person subject to be licensed under this chapter, or by his or her agent or salesperson, is a misdemeanor punishable by a fine of not less than one hundred dollars ($100) nor more than five thousand dollars ($5,000), or by imprisonment in a county jail not exceeding one year, or by both that fine and imprisonment.

(1) An indictment or information against a person who is not licensed but who is required to be licensed under this chapter shall be brought, or a criminal complaint filed, for a violation of this section, in accordance with paragraph (4) of subdivision (d) of Section 802 of the Penal Code, within four years from the date of the contract or, if the contract is not reduced to writing, from the date the buyer makes the first payment to the contractor.

(2) An indictment or information against a person who is licensed under this chapter shall be brought, or a criminal complaint filed, for a violation of this section, in accordance with paragraph (2) of subdivision (d) of Section 802 of the Penal Code, within two years from the date of the contract or, if the contract is not reduced to writing, from the date the buyer makes the first payment to the contractor.

(3) The limitations on actions in this subdivision shall not apply to any administrative action filed against a licensed contractor.

(c) Any person who violates this section as part of a plan or scheme to defraud an owner or tenant of a residential or nonresidential structure, including a mobile home or manufactured home, in connection with the offer or performance of repairs to the structure for damage caused by a natural disaster, shall be ordered by the court to make full restitution to the victim based on the person's ability to pay, as

New Text (Operative July 1, 2012) | **Old Text**

residential or nonresidential structure, including a mobilehome or manufactured home, in connection with the offer or performance of repairs to the structure for damage caused by a natural disaster, shall be ordered by the court to make full restitution to the victim based on the person's ability to pay, as defined in subdivision (e) of Section 1203.1b of the Penal Code. In addition to full restitution, and imprisonment authorized by this section, the court may impose a fine of not less than five hundred dollars ($500) nor more than twenty-five thousand dollars ($25,000), based upon the defendant's ability to pay. This subdivision applies to natural disasters for which a state of emergency is proclaimed by the Governor pursuant to Section 8625 of the Government Code, or for which an emergency or major disaster is declared by the President of the United States.

defined in subdivision (e) of Section 1203.1b of the Penal Code. In addition to full restitution, and imprisonment authorized by this section, the court may impose a fine of not less than five hundred dollars ($500) nor more than twenty-five thousand dollars ($25,000), based upon the defendant's ability to pay. This subdivision applies to natural disasters for which a state of emergency is proclaimed by the Governor pursuant to Section 8625 of the Government Code, or for which an emergency or major disaster is declared by the President of the United States.

NOTE: Amended by Senate Bill 190
(Approved by Governor June 29, 2011 and filed with Secretary of State July 1, 2011)
Revised to include new terminology and reference to new Section 8000 et seq.

•••

B&P 7164

(a) Notwithstanding Section 7044, every contract and any changes in a contract, between an owner and a contractor, for the construction of a single-family dwelling to be retained by the owner for at least one year shall be evidenced in writing signed by both parties.

(b) The writing shall contain the following:

(1) The name, address, and license number of the contractor.

(2) The approximate dates when the work will begin and be substantially completed.

(3) A legal description of the location where the work will be done.

(4) A statement with the heading "Mechanics Lien Warning" as follows:

"MECHANICS LIEN WARNING:

Anyone who helps improve your property, but who is not paid, may record what is called a mechanics lien on your property. A mechanics lien is a claim, like a mortgage or home equity loan, made against your property and recorded with the county recorder.

Even if you pay your contractor in full, unpaid subcontractors, suppliers, and laborers who helped to

B&P 7164

(a) Notwithstanding Section 7044, every contract and any changes in a contract, between an owner and a contractor, for the construction of a single-family dwelling to be retained by the owner for at least one year shall be evidenced in writing signed by both parties.

(b) The writing shall contain the following:

(1) The name, address, and license number of the contractor.

(2) The approximate dates when the work will begin and be substantially completed.

(3) A legal description of the location where the work will be done.

(4) A statement with the heading "Mechanics' Lien Warning" as follows:

"MECHANICS LIEN WARNING:

Anyone who helps improve your property, but who is not paid, may record what is called a mechanics' lien on your property. A mechanics' lien is a claim, like a mortgage or home equity loan, made against your property and recorded with the county recorder.

Even if you pay your contractor in full, unpaid subcontractors,

New Text (Operative July 1, 2012)

improve your property may record mechanics liens and sue you in court to foreclose the lien. If a court finds the lien is valid, you could be forced to pay twice or have a court officer sell your home to pay the lien. Liens can also affect your credit.

To preserve their right to record a lien, each subcontractor and material supplier must provide you with a document called a 'Preliminary Notice.' This notice is not a lien. The purpose of the notice is to let you know that the person who sends you the notice has the right to record a lien on your property if he or she is not paid.

BE CAREFUL. The Preliminary Notice can be sent up to 20 days after the subcontractor starts work or the supplier provides material. This can be a big problem if you pay your contractor before you have received the Preliminary Notices.

You will not get Preliminary Notices from your prime contractor or other persons you contract with directly or from laborers who work on your project. The law assumes that you already know they are improving your property.

PROTECT YOURSELF FROM LIENS. You can protect yourself from liens by getting a list from your contractor of all the subcontractors and material suppliers that work on your project. Find out from your contractor when these subcontractors started work and when these suppliers delivered goods or materials. Then wait 20 days, paying attention to the Preliminary Notices you receive.

PAY WITH JOINT CHECKS. One way to protect yourself is to pay with a joint check. When your contractor tells you it is time to pay for the work of a subcontractor or supplier who has provided you with a Preliminary Notice, write a joint check payable to both the contractor and the subcontractor or material supplier.

For other ways to prevent liens, visit CSLB's Web site at www.cslb.ca.gov or call CSLB at 800-321-CSLB (2752).

REMEMBER, IF YOU DO NOTHING, YOU RISK HAVING A LIEN PLACED ON YOUR HOME. This can mean that you may have to pay twice, or face the forced sale of your home to pay what you owe."

(5) (A) A statement prepared by the board through regulation that emphasizes the value of commercial general liability insurance and encourages the owner to verify the contractor's insurance coverage and status.

(B) A check box indicating whether or not the contractor carries commercial general liability insurance, and if that is the case, the name and the telephone number of the insurer.

(c) The writing may also contain other matters agreed to by the parties to the contract. The writing shall

Old Text

suppliers, and laborers who helped to improve your property may record mechanics' liens and sue you in court to foreclose the lien. If a court finds the lien is valid, you could be forced to pay twice or have a court officer sell your home to pay the lien. Liens can also affect your credit.

To preserve their right to record a lien, each subcontractor and material supplier must provide you with a document called a '20-day Preliminary Notice.' This notice is not a lien. The purpose of the notice is to let you know that the person who sends you the notice has the right to record a lien on your property if he or she is not paid.

BE CAREFUL. The Preliminary Notice can be sent up to 20 days after the subcontractor starts work or the supplier provides material. This can be a big problem if you pay your contractor before you have received the Preliminary Notices.

You will not get Preliminary Notices from your prime contractor or from laborers who work on your project. The law assumes that you already know they are improving your property.

PROTECT YOURSELF FROM LIENS. You can protect yourself from liens by getting a list from your contractor of all the subcontractors and material suppliers that work on your project. Find out from your contractor when these subcontractors started work and when these suppliers delivered goods or materials. Then wait 20 days, paying attention to the Preliminary Notices you receive.

PAY WITH JOINT CHECKS. One way to protect yourself is to pay with a joint check. When your contractor tells you it is time to pay for the work of a subcontractor or supplier who has provided you with a Preliminary Notice, write a joint check payable to both the contractor and the subcontractor or material supplier.

For other ways to prevent liens, visit CSLB's Web site at www.cslb.ca.gov or call CSLB at 800-321-CSLB (2752).

REMEMBER, IF YOU DO NOTHING, YOU RISK HAVING A LIEN PLACED ON YOUR HOME. This can mean that you may have to pay twice, or face the forced sale of your home to pay what you owe."

(5) (A) A statement prepared by the board through regulation that emphasizes the value of commercial general liability insurance and encourages the owner to verify the contractor's insurance coverage and status.

(B) A check box indicating whether or not the contractor carries commercial general liability insurance, and if that is the case, the name and the telephone number of the insurer.

(c) The writing may also contain other matters agreed to by the parties to the contract. The writing shall be legible and shall clearly describe any other document

New Text (Operative July 1, 2012)

be legible and shall clearly describe any other document which is to be incorporated into the contract. Prior to commencement of any work, the owner shall be furnished a copy of the written agreement, signed by the contractor. The provisions of this section are not exclusive and do not relieve the contractor from compliance with all other applicable provisions of law.

(d) Every contract subject to the provisions of this section shall contain, in close proximity to the signatures of the owner and contractor, a notice in at least 10-point boldface type or in all capital letters, stating that the owner has the right to require the contractor to have a performance and payment bond and that the expense of the bond may be borne by the owner.

(e) The requirements in paragraph (5) of subdivision (b) shall become operative three months after the board adopts the regulations referenced in subparagraph (A) of paragraph (5) of subdivision (b).

(f) This section shall become operative on January 1, 2006.

Old Text

which is to be incorporated into the contract. Prior to commencement of any work, the owner shall be furnished a copy of the written agreement, signed by the contractor. The provisions of this section are not exclusive and do not relieve the contractor from compliance with all other applicable provisions of law.

(d) Every contract subject to the provisions of this section shall contain, in close proximity to the signatures of the owner and contractor, a notice in at least 10-point bold type or in all capital letters, stating that the owner has the right to require the contractor to have a performance and payment bond and that the expense of the bond may be borne by the owner.

(e) The requirements in paragraph (5) of subdivision (b) shall become operative three months after the board adopts the regulations referenced in subparagraph (A) of paragraph (5) of subdivision (b).

(f) This section shall become operative on January 1, 2006.

Revised to include new terminology.

B&P 8513

(a) The board shall prescribe a form entitled "Notice to Owner" that shall describe, in nontechnical language and in a clear and coherent manner using words with common and everyday meaning, the pertinent provisions of this state's mechanics lien laws and the rights and responsibilities of an owner of property and a registered pest control company thereunder. Each company registered under this chapter, prior to entering into a contract with an owner for work for which a company registration is required, shall give a copy of this "Notice to Owner" to the owner, his or her agent, or the payer.

(b) No company that is required to be registered under this chapter shall require or request a waiver of lien rights from any subcontractor, employee, or supplier.

(c) Each company registered under this chapter that acts as a subcontractor for another company registered under this chapter shall, within 20 days of commencement of any work for which a company registration is required, give the preliminary notice in accordance with Chapter 2 (commencing with Section 8200) of Title 2 of Part

B&P 8513

(a) The board shall prescribe a form entitled "Notice to Owner" that shall describe, in nontechnical language and in a clear and coherent manner using words with common and everyday meaning, the pertinent provisions of this state's mechanics' lien laws and the rights and responsibilities of an owner of property and a registered pest control company thereunder. Each company registered under this chapter, prior to entering into a contract with an owner for work for which a company registration is required, shall give a copy of this "Notice to Owner" to the owner, his or her agent, or the payer.

(b) No company that is required to be registered under this chapter shall require or request a waiver of lien rights from any subcontractor, employee, or supplier.

(c) Each company registered under this chapter that acts as a subcontractor for another company registered under this chapter shall, within 20 days of commencement of any work for which a company registration is required, give the preliminary 20-day notice (private work) in accordance with the provisions of Section 3097 of the Civil Code, to the owner, his or her agent, or the payer.

(d) Each company registered under this chapter that acts as

New Text (Operative July 1, 2012)

6 of Division 4 of the Civil Code, to the owner, his or her agent, or the payer.

(d) Each company registered under this chapter that acts as a prime contractor for work for which a company registration is required shall, prior to accepting payment for the work, furnish to the owner, his or her agent, or the payer a full and unconditional release from any claim of mechanics lien by any subcontractor entitled to enforce a mechanics lien pursuant to Section 8410 of the Civil Code.

(e) Each company registered under this chapter that subcontracts to another company registered under this chapter work for which a company registration is required shall furnish to the subcontractor the name of the owner, his or her agent, or the payer.

(f) The provisions of this section shall be applicable only to those registered companies, as defined in Section 8506.1, operating pursuant to a Branch 1 or Branch 3 registration.

(g) A violation of the provisions of this section is a ground for disciplinary action.

Old Text

a prime contractor for work for which a company registration is required shall, prior to accepting payment for the work, furnish to the owner, his or her agent, or the payer a full and unconditional release from any claim of mechanics' lien by any subcontractor entitled to enforce a mechanics' lien pursuant to Section 3114 of the Civil Code.

(e) Each company registered under this chapter that subcontracts to another company registered under this chapter work for which a company registration is required shall furnish to the subcontractor the name of the owner, his or her agent, or the payer. (f) The provisions of this section shall be applicable only to those registered companies, as defined in Section 8506.1, operating pursuant to a Branch 1 or Branch 3 registration.

(g) A violation of the provisions of this section is a ground for disciplinary action.

NOTE: Amended by Senate Bill 190
(Approved by Governor June 29, 2011 and filed with Secretary of State July 1, 2011)
Revised to include new terminology and reference to new Section 8000 et seq.

B&P 17577.5

(a) No contract or offer for the sale, lease, or rental of a home water treatment device and no purchase money loan, as defined in subdivision (b), shall provide for a lien on real property. Any lien taken in violation of this section is void and unenforceable.

(b) For the purpose of this section, "purchase money loan" means a loan or an advance under an open-end credit account if both of the following occur:

(1) The primary purpose of the loan or the primary purpose of establishing the open-end credit account is to finance all or a portion of the purchase price or any of the lease or rental payments for a water treatment device.

(2) The creditor knows the primary purpose of the loan or the primary purpose of establishing the open-end credit account when the loan is initially made or the open-end credit account is established.

(c) The creditor shall be deemed to know that the

B&P 17577.5

(a) No contract or offer for the sale, lease, or rental of a home water treatment device and no purchase money loan, as defined in subdivision (b), shall provide for a lien on real property. Any lien taken in violation of this section is void and unenforceable.

(b) For the purpose of this section, "purchase money loan" means a loan or an advance under an open-end credit account if both of the following occur:

(1) The primary purpose of the loan or the primary purpose of establishing the open-end credit account is to finance all or a portion of the purchase price or any of the lease or rental payments for a water treatment device.

(2) The creditor knows the primary purpose of the loan or the primary purpose of establishing the open-end credit account when the loan is initially made or the open-end credit account is established.

(c) The creditor shall be deemed to know that the primary purpose of the loan or the primary purpose of establishing the open-end credit account is the primary purpose described in paragraph (1) of

New Text (Operative July 1, 2012)

primary purpose of the loan or the primary purpose of establishing the open-end credit account is the primary purpose described in paragraph (1) of subdivision (b) if any of the following occur:

(1) The consumer's application for credit or any other document in the creditor's possession before the loan is made or the open-end account is established indicates the primary purpose of the loan or the open-end credit account.

(2) The seller, lessor, or renter arranges or guarantees the loan or open-end account, or participates in the preparation of the consumer's application for credit or other loan documents, or receives from the creditor a loan commission, brokerage, or referral fee.

(d) For the purpose of this section, "open-end credit" has the same meaning as used in Section 226.2 of Title 12 of the Code of Federal Regulations.

(e) This section does not apply to mechanics liens established pursuant to Chapter 4 (commencing with Section 8400) of Title 2 of Part 6 of Division 4 of the Civil Code.

Old Text

subdivision (b) if any of the following occur:

(1) The consumer's application for credit or any other document in the creditor's possession before the loan is made or the open-end account is established indicates the primary purpose of the loan or the open-end credit account.

(2) The seller, lessor, or renter arranges or guarantees the loan or open-end account, or participates in the preparation of the consumer's application for credit or other loan documents, or receives from the creditor a loan commission, brokerage, or referral fee.

(d) For the purpose of this section, "open-end credit" has the same meaning as used in Section 226.2 of Title 12 of the Code of Federal Regulations.

(e) This section does not apply to mechanics' liens established pursuant to Chapter 2 (commencing with Section 3109) of Title 15 of Part 4 of Division 3 of the Civil Code.

Revised to include new terminology and reference to new Section 8000 et seq.

CODE OF CIVIL PROCEDURE SECTIONS ("CCP")

CCP 86

(a) The following civil cases and proceedings are limited civil cases:

(1) A case at law in which the demand, exclusive of interest, or the value of the property in controversy amounts to twenty-five thousand dollars ($25,000) or less. This paragraph does not apply to a case that involves the legality of any tax, impost, assessment, toll, or municipal fine, except an action to enforce payment of delinquent unsecured personal property taxes if the legality of the tax is not contested by the defendant.

(2) An action for dissolution of partnership where the total assets of the partnership do not exceed twenty-five thousand dollars ($25,000); an action of interpleader where the amount of money or the value of the property involved does not exceed twenty-five thousand dollars ($25,000).

(3) An action to cancel or rescind a contract when the relief is sought in connection with an action to recover money not exceeding twenty-five thousand dollars ($25,000) or property of a value not exceeding twenty-five thousand dollars ($25,000), paid or delivered under, or in consideration of, the contract; an action to revise a contract where the relief is sought in an action upon the contract if the action otherwise is a limited civil case.

(4) A proceeding in forcible entry or forcible or unlawful detainer where the whole amount of damages claimed is twenty-five thousand dollars ($25,000) or less.

(5) An action to enforce and foreclose a lien on personal property where the amount of the lien is twenty-five thousand dollars ($25,000) or less.

(6) An action to enforce and foreclose, or a petition to release, a lien arising under the provisions of Chapter 4 (commencing with Section 8400) of Title 2 of Part 6 of Division 4 of the Civil Code, or to enforce and foreclose an assessment lien on a common interest development as defined in Section 1351 of the Civil Code, where the amount of the liens is twenty-five thousand dollars ($25,000) or less. However, if an action to enforce the lien affects property that is also affected by a similar pending action that is not a limited civil case, or if the total amount of liens sought to be foreclosed against the same property aggregates an amount in excess of twenty-five thousand dollars

CCP 86

(a) The following civil cases and proceedings are limited civil cases:

(1) Cases at law in which the demand, exclusive of interest, or the value of the property in controversy amounts to twenty- five thousand dollars ($25,000) or less. This paragraph does not apply to cases that involve the legality of any tax, impost, assessment, toll, or municipal fine, except actions to enforce payment of delinquent unsecured personal property taxes if the legality of the tax is not contested by the defendant.

(2) Actions for dissolution of partnership where the total assets of the partnership do not exceed twenty-five thousand dollars ($25,000); actions of interpleader where the amount of money or the value of the property involved does not exceed twenty- five thousand dollars ($25,000).

(3) Actions to cancel or rescind a contract when the relief is sought in connection with an action to recover money not exceeding twenty-five thousand dollars ($25,000) or property of a value not exceeding twenty-five thousand dollars ($25,000), paid or delivered under, or in consideration of, the contract; actions to revise a contract where the relief is sought in an action upon the contract if the action otherwise is a limited civil case.

(4) Proceedings in forcible entry or forcible or unlawful detainer where the whole amount of damages claimed is twenty-five thousand dollars ($25,000) or less.

(5) Actions to enforce and foreclose liens on personal property where the amount of the liens is twenty-five thousand dollars ($25,000) or less.

(6) Actions to enforce and foreclose, or petitions to release, liens of mechanics, materialmen, artisans, laborers, and of all other persons to whom liens are given under the provisions of Chapter 2 (commencing with Section 3109) of Title 15 of Part 4 of Division 3 of the Civil Code, or to enforce and foreclose an assessment lien on a common interest development as defined in Section 1351 of the Civil Code, where the amount of the liens is twenty-five thousand dollars ($25,000) or less. However, where an action to enforce the lien affects property that is also affected by a similar pending action that is not a limited civil case, or where the total amount of the liens sought to be foreclosed against the same property aggregates an amount in

New Text (Operative July 1, 2012)

($25,000), the action is not a limited civil case.

(7) An action for declaratory relief when brought pursuant to either of the following:

(A) By way of cross-complaint as to a right of indemnity with respect to the relief demanded in the complaint or a cross-complaint in an action or proceeding that is otherwise a limited civil case.

(B) To conduct a trial after a nonbinding fee arbitration between an attorney and client, pursuant to Article 13 (commencing with Section 6200) of Chapter 4 of Division 3 of the Business and Professions Code, where the amount in controversy is twenty-five thousand dollars ($25,000) or less.

(8) An action to issue a temporary restraining order or preliminary injunction; to take an account, where necessary to preserve the property or rights of any party to a limited civil case; to make any order or perform any act, pursuant to Title 9 (commencing with Section 680.010) of Part 2 (enforcement of judgments) in a limited civil case; to appoint a receiver pursuant to Section 564 in a limited civil case; to determine title to personal property seized in a limited civil case.

(9) An action under Article 3 (commencing with Section 708.210) of Chapter 6 of Division 2 of Title 9 of Part 2 for the recovery of an interest in personal property or to enforce the liability of the debtor of a judgment debtor where the interest claimed adversely is of a value not exceeding twenty-five thousand dollars ($25,000) or the debt denied does not exceed twenty-five thousand dollars ($25,000).

(10) An arbitration-related petition filed pursuant to either of the following:

(A) Article 2 (commencing with Section 1292) of Chapter 5 of Title 9 of Part 3, except for uninsured motorist arbitration proceedings in accordance with Section 11580.2 of the Insurance Code, if the petition is filed before the arbitration award becomes final and the matter to be resolved by arbitration is a limited civil case under paragraphs (1) to (9), inclusive, of subdivision (a) or if the petition is filed after the arbitration award becomes final and the amount of the award and all other rulings, pronouncements, and decisions made in the award are within paragraphs (1) to (9), inclusive, of subdivision (a).

(B) To confirm, correct, or vacate a fee arbitration award between an attorney and client that is binding or has become binding, pursuant to Article 13 (commencing with Section 6200) of Chapter 4 of

Old Text

excess of twenty-five thousand dollars ($25,000), the action is not a limited civil case.

(7) Actions for declaratory relief when brought pursuant to either of the following:

(A) By way of cross-complaint as to a right of indemnity with respect to the relief demanded in the complaint or a cross- complaint in an action or proceeding that is otherwise a limited civil case.

(B) To conduct a trial after a nonbinding fee arbitration between an attorney and client, pursuant to Article 13 (commencing with Section 6200) of Chapter 4 of Division 3 of the Business and Professions Code, where the amount in controversy is twenty- five thousand dollars ($25,000) or less.

(8) Actions to issue temporary restraining orders and preliminary injunctions, and to take accounts, where necessary to preserve the property or rights of any party to a limited civil case; to make any order or perform any act, pursuant to Title 9 (commencing with Section 680.010) of Part 2 (enforcement of judgments) in a limited civil case; to appoint a receiver pursuant to Section 564 in a limited civil case; to determine title to personal property seized in a limited civil case.

(9) Actions under Article 3 (commencing with Section 708.210) of Chapter 6 of Division 2 of Title 9 of Part 2 for the recovery of an interest in personal property or to enforce the liability of the debtor of a judgment debtor where the interest claimed adversely is of a value not exceeding twenty-five thousand dollars ($25,000) or the debt denied does not exceed twenty-five thousand dollars ($25,000).

(10) Arbitration-related petitions filed pursuant to either of the following:

(A) Article 2 (commencing with Section 1292) of Chapter 5 of Title 9 of Part 3, except for uninsured motorist arbitration proceedings in accordance with Section 11580.2 of the Insurance Code, if the petition is filed before the arbitration award becomes final and the matter to be resolved by arbitration is a limited civil case under paragraphs (1) to (9), inclusive, of subdivision (a) or if the petition is filed after the arbitration award becomes final and the amount of the award and all other rulings, pronouncements, and decisions made in the award are within paragraphs (1) to (9),

New Text (Operative July 1, 2012)

Division 3 of the Business and Professions Code, where the arbitration award is twenty-five thousand dollars ($25,000) or less.

(b) The following cases in equity are limited civil cases:

(1) A case to try title to personal property when the amount involved is not more than twenty-five thousand dollars ($25,000).

(2) A case when equity is pleaded as a defensive matter in any case that is otherwise a limited civil case.

(3) A case to vacate a judgment or order of the court obtained in a limited civil case through extrinsic fraud, mistake, inadvertence, or excusable neglect.

Old Text

inclusive, of subdivision (a).

(B) To confirm, correct, or vacate a fee arbitration award between an attorney and client that is binding or has become binding, pursuant to Article 13 (commencing with Section 6200) of Chapter 4 of Division 3 of the Business and Professions Code, where the arbitration award is twenty-five thousand dollars ($25,000) or less.

(b) The following cases in equity are limited civil cases:

(1) Cases to try title to personal property when the amount involved is not more than twenty-five thousand dollars ($25,000).

(2) Cases when equity is pleaded as a defensive matter in any case that is otherwise a limited civil case.

(3) Cases to vacate a judgment or order of the court obtained in a limited civil case through extrinsic fraud, mistake, inadvertence, or excusable neglect.

Clarified wording; Revised to include new terminology and reference to new Section 8000 et seq.

CCP 410.42

(a) The following provisions of a contract between the contractor and a subcontractor with principal offices in this state, for the construction of a public or private work of improvement in this state, shall be void and unenforceable:

(1) A provision which purports to require any dispute between the parties to be litigated, arbitrated, or otherwise determined outside this state.

(2) A provision which purports to preclude a party from commencing such a proceeding or obtaining a judgment or other resolution in this state or the courts of this state.

(b) For purposes of this section, "construction" means any work or services performed on, or materials provided for, a work of improvement, as defined in Section 8050 of the Civil Code, and for which a lien may be claimed pursuant to Section 8400 of the Civil Code (whether or not a lien is in fact claimed) or for which such a lien could be claimed but for Section 8160 of the Civil Code.

CCP 410.42

The following provisions of a contract between the contractor and a subcontractor with principal offices in this state, for the construction of a public or private work of improvement in this state, shall be void and unenforceable:

(a) A provision which purports to require any dispute between the parties to be litigated, arbitrated, or otherwise determined outside this state.

(b) A provision which purports to preclude a party from commencing such a proceeding or obtaining a judgment or other resolution in this state or the courts of this state.

For purposes of this section, "construction" means any work or services performed on, or materials provided for, a work of improvement, as defined in Section 3106 of the Civil Code, and for which a lien may be claimed pursuant to Section 3110 of the Civil Code (whether or not a lien is in fact claimed) or for which such a lien could be claimed but for Section 3109.

Revised reference to new Section 8000 et seq.

New Text (Operative July 1, 2012)

CCP 708.760

(a) If the judgment debtor named in the abstract or certified copy of the judgment filed pursuant to this article is a contractor upon a public work, the cost of which is to be paid out of public moneys voted, appropriated, or otherwise set apart for such purpose, only so much of the contract price shall be deemed owing and unpaid within the meaning of Section 708.740 or 708.750 as may remain payable under the terms of the contractor's contract, upon the completion thereof, after deducting sums due and to become due to persons described in Section 9100 of the Civil Code. In ascertaining the sums due or to become due to such persons, only claims which are filed against the moneys due or to become due to the judgment debtor in accordance with Chapter 4 (commencing with Section 9350) of Title 3 of Part 6 of Division 4 of the Civil Code shall be considered.

(b) The Controller, auditor, or other public disbursing officer whose duty it is to make payments under the provisions of the contract may not deposit an amount with the court pursuant to this article until the contract is completed, but may deposit an amount with the court to satisfy the claim of the judgment debtor before the payments specified in subdivision (a) are made so long as a sufficient amount is retained for the satisfaction of the claims of persons described in Section 9100 of the Civil Code.

Old Text

CCP 708.760

(a) If the judgment debtor named in the abstract or certified copy of the judgment filed pursuant to this article is a contractor upon a public work, the cost of which is to be paid out of public moneys voted, appropriated, or otherwise set apart for such purpose, only so much of the contract price shall be deemed owing and unpaid within the meaning of Section 708.740 or 708.750 as may remain payable under the terms of the contractor's contract, upon the completion thereof, after deducting sums due and to become due to persons described in Section 3181 of the Civil Code. In ascertaining the sums due or to become due to such persons, only claims which are filed against the moneys due or to become due to the judgment debtor in accordance with the provisions of Chapter 4 (commencing with Section 3179) of Title 15 of Part 4 of Division 3 of the Civil Code shall be considered.

(b) The Controller, auditor, or other public disbursing officer whose duty it is to make payments under the provisions of the contract may not deposit an amount with the court pursuant to this article until the contract is completed, but may deposit an amount with the court to satisfy the claim of the judgment debtor before the payments specified in subdivision (a) are made so long as a sufficient amount is retained for the satisfaction of the claims of persons described in Section 3181 of the Civil Code.

Revised reference to new Section 8000 et seq.

•••

CCP 1203.61

(a) Any lien provided for by this chapter shall be enforced in the same manner as provided in Chapter 4 (commencing with Section 8400) of Title 2 of Part 6 of Division 4 of the Civil Code. The action shall be filed within 180 days from the time of the recording of the lien. If a credit is given and notice of the fact and terms of the credit is filed in the office of the county recorder subsequent to the filing of the lien and prior to the expiration of the 180-day period, then the lien continues in force until 180 days after the expiration of the credit, but no lien continues in force by reason of any agreement to give credit for a longer time than

CCP 1203.61

(a) Any lien provided for by this chapter shall be enforced in the same manner as provided in Title 15 (commencing with Section 3082), Part 4, Division 3, of the Civil Code. Such action shall be filed within 180 days from the time of the recording of the lien provided for herein. If a credit be given and notice of the fact and terms of such credit be filed in the office of the county recorder subsequent to the filing of such lien and prior to the expiration of said 180-day period, then such lien continues in force until 180 days after the expiration of such credit, but no lien continues in force by reason of any agreement to give credit for a

New Text (Operative July 1, 2012)

one year from the time the work is completed. If the proceedings to enforce the lien are not prosecuted to trial within two years after commencement, the court may in its discretion dismiss the action for want of prosecution, and in all cases the dismissal of the action (unless it is expressly stated that it is without prejudice) or a judgment in the action that no lien exists is equivalent to the cancellation and removal from the record of the lien.

(b) As against any purchaser or encumbrancer for value and in good faith whose rights are acquired subsequent to the expiration of the 180-day period following the filing of the lien, no giving of credit or extension of the lien or time to enforce the lien shall be effective unless evidenced by a notice or agreement filed for record in the office of the county recorder prior to the acquisition of the rights of the purchaser or encumbrancer.

Old Text

longer time than one year from the time the work is completed. If the proceedings to enforce the lien be not prosecuted to trial within two years after the commencement thereof, the court may in its discretion dismiss the same for want of prosecution, and in all cases the dismissal of such action (unless it be expressly stated that the same is without prejudice) or a judgment rendered therein that no lien exists shall be equivalent to the cancellation and removal from the record of such lien.

(b) As against any purchaser or encumbrancer for value and in good faith whose rights are acquired subsequent to the expiration of the 180-day period following the filing of such lien, no giving of credit or extension of the lien or time to enforce the same shall be effective unless evidenced by a notice or agreement filed for record in the office of the county recorder prior to the acquisition of the rights of such purchaser or encumbrancer.

Clarified and revised to include reference to new Section 8000 et seq.

••

CCP 1281.5

(a) Any person who proceeds to record and enforce a claim of lien by commencement of an action pursuant to Chapter 4 (commencing with Section 8400) of Title 2 of Part 6 of Division 4 of the Civil Code, does not thereby waive any right of arbitration the person may have pursuant to a written agreement to arbitrate, if, in filing an action to enforce the claim of lien, the claimant does either of the following:

(1) Includes an allegation in the complaint that the claimant does not intend to waive any right of arbitration, and intends to move the court, within 30 days after service of the summons and complaint, for an order to stay further proceedings in the action.

(2) At the same time that the complaint is filed, the claimant files an application that the action be stayed pending the arbitration of any issue, question, or dispute that is claimed to be arbitrable under the agreement and that is relevant to the action to enforce the claim of lien.

(b) Within 30 days after service of the summons and complaint, the claimant shall file and serve a motion and notice of motion pursuant to Section 1281.4 to stay the action pending the arbitration of any issue, question, or dispute that is claimed to be arbitrable

CCP 1281.5

(a) Any person who proceeds to record and enforce a claim of lien by commencement of an action pursuant to Title 15 (commencing with Section 3082) of Part 4 of Division 3 of the Civil Code, does not thereby waive any right of arbitration the person may have pursuant to a written agreement to arbitrate, if, in filing an action to enforce the claim of lien, the claimant does either of the following:

(1) Includes an allegation in the complaint that the claimant does not intend to waive any right of arbitration, and intends to move the court, within 30 days after service of the summons and complaint, for an order to stay further proceedings in the action.

(2) At the same time that the complaint is filed, the claimant files an application that the action be stayed pending the arbitration of any issue, question, or dispute that is claimed to be arbitrable under the agreement and that is relevant to the action to enforce the claim of lien.

(b) Within 30 days after service of the summons and complaint, the claimant shall file and serve a motion and notice of motion pursuant to Section 1281.4 to stay the action pending the arbitration of any issue, question, or dispute that is claimed to be arbitrable

New Text (Operative July 1, 2012) | **Old Text**

under the agreement and that is relevant to the action to enforce the claim of lien. The failure of a claimant to comply with this subdivision is a waiver of the claimant's right to compel arbitration.

(c) The failure of a defendant to file a petition pursuant to Section 1281.2 at or before the time the defendant answers the complaint filed pursuant to subdivision (a) is a waiver of the defendant's right to compel arbitration.

under the agreement and that is relevant to the action to enforce the claim of lien. The failure of a claimant to comply with this subdivision is a waiver of the claimant's right to compel arbitration.

(c) The failure of a defendant to file a petition pursuant to Section 1281.2 at or before the time the defendant answers the complaint filed pursuant to subdivision (a) is a waiver of the defendant's right to compel arbitration.

Revised to include reference to new Section 8000 et seq.

CCP 1800

(a) As used in this section, the following terms have the following meanings:

(1) "Insolvent" means:

(A) With reference to a person other than a partnership, a financial condition such that the sum of the person's debts is greater than all of the person's property, at a fair valuation, exclusive of both of the following:

(i) Property transferred, concealed, or removed with intent to hinder, delay, or defraud the person's creditors.

(ii) Property that is exempt from property of the estate pursuant to the election of the person made pursuant to Section 1801.

(B) With reference to a partnership, financial condition such that the sum of the partnership's debts are greater than the aggregate of, at a fair valuation, both of the following:

(i) All of the partnership's property, exclusive of property of the kind specified in clause (i) of subparagraph (A).

(ii) The sum of the excess of the value of each general partner's separate property, exclusive of property of the kind specified in clause (ii) of subparagraph (A), over the partner's separate debts.

(2) "Inventory" means personal property leased or furnished, held for sale or lease, or to be furnished under a contract for service, raw materials, work in process, or materials used or consumed in a business, including farm products such as crops or livestock, held for sale or lease.

(3) "Insider" means:

CCP 1800

(a) In this section:

(1) The term "insolvent" means:

(A) With reference to a person other than a partnership, a financial condition such that the sum of the person's debts is greater than all of the person's property, at a fair valuation, exclusive of both of the following:

(i) Property transferred, concealed, or removed with intent to hinder, delay, or defraud the person's creditors.

(ii) Property that is exempt from property of the estate pursuant to the election of the person made pursuant to Section 1801.

(B) With reference to a partnership, financial condition such that the sum of the partnership's debts are greater than the aggregate of, at a fair valuation, both of the following:

(i) All of the partnership's property, exclusive of property of the kind specified in clause (i) subparagraph (A).

(ii) The sum of the excess of the value of each general partner's separate property, exclusive of property of the kind specified in clause (ii) of subparagraph (A), over the partner's separate debts.

(2) The term "inventory" means personal property leased or furnished, held for sale or lease, or to be furnished under a contract for service, raw materials, work in process, or materials used or consumed in a business, including farm products such as crops or livestock, held for sale or lease.

(3) The term "insider" means:

(A) If the assignor is an individual, any of the following:

New Text (Operative July 1, 2012)

(A) If the assignor is an individual, any of the following:
(i) A relative of the assignor or of a general partner of the assignor.
(ii) A partnership in which the assignor is a general partner.
(iii) A general partner of the assignor.
(iv) A corporation of which the assignor is a director, officer, or person in control.
(B) If the assignor is a corporation, any of the following:
(i) A director of the assignor.
(ii) An officer of the assignor.
(iii) A person in control of the assignor.
(iv) A partnership in which the assignor is a general partner.
(v) A general partner of the assignor.
(vi) A relative of a general partner, director, officer, or person in control of the assignor.
(C) If the assignor is a partnership, any of the following:
(i) A general partner in the assignor.
(ii) A relative of a general partner in, general partner of, or person in control of the assignor.
(iii) A partnership in which the assignor is a general partner.
(iv) A general partner of the assignor.
(v) A person in control of the assignor.
(D) An affiliate of the assignor or an insider of an affiliate as if the affiliate were the assignor.
(E) A managing agent of the assignor.
As used in this paragraph, the following terms have the following meanings:
"Relative" means an individual related by affinity or consanguinity within the third degree as determined by the common law, or an individual in a step or adoptive relationship within the third degree.
An "affiliate" means a person that directly or indirectly owns, controls, or holds, with power to vote, 20 percent or more of the outstanding voting securities of the assignor, or 20 percent or more of whose outstanding voting securities are directly or indirectly owned, controlled, or held with power to vote by the assignor, excluding securities held in a fiduciary or agency capacity without sole discretionary power to vote, or held solely to secure a debt if the holder has not in fact

Old Text

(i) A relative of the assignor or of a general partner of the assignor.
(ii) A partnership in which the assignor is a general partner.
(iii) A general partner of the assignor.
(iv) A corporation of which the assignor is a director, officer, or person in control.
(B) If the assignor is a corporation, any of the following:
(i) A director of the assignor.
(ii) An officer of the assignor.
(iii) A person in control of the assignor.
(iv) A partnership in which the assignor is a general partner.
(v) A general partner of the assignor.
(vi) A relative of a general partner, director, officer, or person in control of the assignor.
(C) If the assignor is a partnership, any of the following:
(i) A general partner in the assignor.
(ii) A relative of a general partner in, general partner of, or person in control of the assignor.
(iii) A partnership in which the assignor is a general partner.
(iv) A general partner of the assignor.
(v) A person in control of the assignor.
(D) An affiliate of the assignor or an insider of an affiliate as if the affiliate were the assignor.
(E) A managing agent of the assignor.

As used in this paragraph, "relative" means an individual related by affinity or consanguinity with the third degree as determined by the common law, or an individual in a step or adoptive relationship within the third degree; and an "affiliate" means a person that directly or indirectly owns, controls or holds with power to vote 20 percent or more of the outstanding voting securities of the assignor or 20 percent or more of whose outstanding voting securities are directly or indirectly owned, controlled or held with power to vote by the assignor (excluding securities held in a fiduciary or agency capacity without sole discretionary power to vote, or held solely to secure a debt if the holder has not in fact exercised the power to vote), or a person who operates the business of the assignor under a lease or operating agreement or whose business is operated by the assignor under a lease or operating agreement.

(4) The term "judicial lien" means a lien obtained by

New Text (Operative July 1, 2012)

exercised the power to vote, or a person who operates the business of the assignor under a lease or operating agreement or whose business is operated by the assignor under a lease or operating agreement.

(4) "Judicial lien" means a lien obtained by judgment, levy, sequestration, or other legal or equitable process or proceeding.

(5) "New value" means money or money's worth in goods, services, or new credit, or release by a transferee of property previously transferred to the transferee in a transaction that is neither void nor voidable by the assignor or the assignee under any applicable law, but does not include an obligation substituted for an existing obligation.

(6) "Receivable" means a right to payment, whether or not the right has been earned by performance.

(7) "Security agreement" means an agreement that creates or provides for a security interest.

(8) "Security interest" means a lien created by an agreement.

(9) "Statutory lien" means a lien arising solely by force of a statute on specified circumstances or conditions, or lien of distress for rent, whether or not statutory, but does not include a security interest or judicial lien, whether or not the interest or lien is provided by or is dependent on a statute and whether or not the interest or lien is made fully effective by statute.

(10) "Transfer" means every mode, direct or indirect, absolute or conditional, voluntary or involuntary, or disposing of or parting with property or with an interest in property, including retention of title as a security interest.

(b) Except as provided in subdivision (c), the assignee of any general assignment for the benefit of creditors, as defined in Section 493.010, may recover any transfer of property of the assignor that is all of the following:

(1) To or for the benefit of a creditor.

(2) For or on account of an antecedent debt owed by the assignor before the transfer was made.

(3) Made while the assignor was insolvent.

(4) Made on or within 90 days before the date of the making of the assignment or made between 90 days and one year before the date of making the assignment if the creditor, at the time of the transfer, was an insider and had reasonable cause to believe the debtor was insolvent at the

Old Text

judgment, levy, sequestration, or other legal or equitable process or proceeding.

(5) The term "new value" means money or money's worth in goods, services, or new credit, or release by a transferee of property previously transferred to the transferee in a transaction that is neither void nor voidable by the assignor or the assignee under any applicable law, but does not include an obligation substituted for an existing obligation.

(6) The term "receivable" means a right to payment, whether or not the right has been earned by performance.

(7) The term "security agreement" means an agreement that creates or provides for a security interest.

(8) The term "security interest" means a lien created by an agreement.

(9) The term "statutory lien" means a lien arising solely by force of a statute on specified circumstances or conditions, or lien of distress for rent, whether or not statutory, but does not include security interest or judicial lien, whether or not the interest or lien is provided by or is dependent on a statute and whether or not the interest or lien is made fully effective by statute.

(10) The term "transfer" means every mode, direct or indirect, absolute or conditional, voluntary or involuntary, or disposing of or parting with property or with an interest in property, including retention of title as a security interest.

(b) Except as provided in subdivision (c), the assignee of any general assignment for the benefit of creditors (as defined in Section 493.010) may recover any transfer of property of the assignor:

(1) To or for the benefit of a creditor;

(2) For or on account of an antecedent debt owed by the assignor before the transfer was made;

(3) Made while the assignor was insolvent;

(4) Made on or within 90 days before the date of the making of the assignment or made between 90 days and one year before the date of making the assignment if the creditor, at the time of the transfer, was an insider and had reasonable cause to believe the debtor was insolvent at the time of the transfer; and

(5) That enables the creditor to receive more than another creditor of the same class.

(c) The assignee may not recover under this section a transfer:

New Text (Operative July 1, 2012)

time of the transfer.

(5) Enables the creditor to receive more than another creditor of the same class.

(c) The assignee may not recover under this section a transfer as follows:

(1) To the extent that the transfer was both of the following:

(A) Intended by the assignor and the creditor to or for whose benefit the transfer was made to be a contemporaneous exchange for new value given to the assignor.

(B) In fact a substantially contemporaneous exchange.

(2) To the extent that the transfer was all of the following:

(A) In payment of a debt incurred in the ordinary course of business or financial affairs of the assignor and the transferee.

(B) Made in the ordinary course of business or financial affairs of the assignor and the transferee.

(C) Made according to ordinary business terms.

(3) Of a security interest in property acquired by the assignor that meets both of the following:

(A) To the extent the security interest secures new value that was all of the following:

(i) Given at or after the signing of a security agreement that contains a description of the property as collateral.

(ii) Given by or on behalf of the secured party under the agreement.

(iii) Given to enable the assignor to acquire the property.

(iv) In fact used by the assignor to acquire the property.

(B) That is perfected within 20 days after the security interest attaches.

(4) To or for the benefit of a creditor, to the extent that, after the transfer, the creditor gave new value to or for the benefit of the assignor that meets both of the following:

(A) Not secured by an otherwise unavoidable security interest.

(B) On account of which new value the assignor did not make an otherwise unavoidable transfer to or for the benefit of the creditor.

(5) Of a perfected security interest in inventory or a receivable or the proceeds of either, except to the extent that the aggregate of all the transfers to the transferee caused a reduction, as of the date of

Old Text

(1) To the extent that the transfer was:

(A) Intended by the assignor and the creditor to or for whose benefit the transfer was made to be a contemporaneous exchange for new value given to the assignor; and

(B) In fact a substantially contemporaneous exchange;

(2) To the extent that the transfer was:

(A) In payment of a debt incurred in the ordinary course of business or financial affairs of the assignor and the transferee;

(B) Made in the ordinary course of business or financial affairs of the assignor and the transferee; and

(C) Made according to ordinary business terms;

(3) Of a security interest in property acquired by the assignor:

(A) To the extent the security interest secures new value that was:

(i) Given at or after the signing of a security agreement that contains a description of the property as collateral;

(ii) Given by or on behalf of the secured party under the agreement;

(iii) Given to enable the assignor to acquire the property; and

(iv) In fact used by the assignor to acquire the property; and

(B) That is perfected within 20 days after the security interest attaches;

(4) To or for the benefit of a creditor, to the extent that, after the transfer, the creditor gave new value to or for the benefit of the assignor:

(A) Not secured by an otherwise unavoidable security interest; and

(B) On account of which new value the assignor did not make an otherwise unavoidable transfer to or for the benefit of the creditor;

(5) Of a perfected security interest in inventory or a receivable or the proceeds of either, except to the extent that the aggregate of all the transfers to the transferee caused a reduction, as of the date of the making of the assignment and to the prejudice of other creditors holding unsecured claims, of any amount by which the debt secured by the security interest exceeded the value of all security interest for the debt on the later of:

New Text (Operative July 1, 2012)

the making of the assignment and to the prejudice of other creditors holding unsecured claims, of any amount by which the debt secured by the security interest exceeded the value of all security interest for the debt on the later of the following:

(A) Ninety days before the date of the making of the assignment.

(B) The date on which new value was first given under the security agreement creating the security interest.

(6) That is the fixing of a statutory lien.

(7) That is payment to a claimant, as defined in Section 8004 of the Civil Code, in exchange for the claimant's waiver or release of any potential or asserted claim of lien, stop payment notice, or right to recover on a payment bond, or any combination thereof.

(8) To the extent that the transfer was a bona fide payment of a debt to a spouse, former spouse, or child of the debtor, for alimony to, maintenance for, or support of, the spouse or child, in connection with a separation agreement, divorce decree, or other order of a court of record, or a determination made in accordance with state or territorial law by a governmental unit, or property settlement agreement; but not to the extent that either of the following occurs:

(A) The debt is assigned to another entity voluntarily, by operation of law or otherwise, in which case the assignee may not recover that portion of the transfer that is assigned to the state or any political subdivision of the state pursuant to Part D of Title IV of the Social Security Act (42 U.S.C. Sec. 601 et seq.) and passed on to the spouse, former spouse, or child of the debtor.

(B) The debt includes a liability designated as alimony, maintenance, or support, unless the liability is actually in the nature of alimony, maintenance, or support.

(d) An assignee of any general assignment for the benefit of creditors, as defined in Section 493.010, may avoid a transfer of property of the assignor transferred to secure reimbursement of a surety that furnished a bond or other obligation to dissolve a judicial lien that would have been avoidable by the assignee under subdivision (b). The liability of the surety under the bond or obligation shall be discharged to the extent of the value of the property recovered by the assignee or

Old Text

(A) Ninety days before the date of the making of the assignment.

(B) The date on which new value was first given under the security agreement creating the security interest; or

(6) That is the fixing of a statutory lien.

(7) That is payment to a claimant, as defined in Section 3085 of the Civil Code, in exchange for the claimant's waiver or release of any potential or asserted claim of lien, stop notice, or right to recover on a payment bond, or any combination thereof.

(8) To the extent that the transfer was a bona fide payment of a debt to a spouse, former spouse, or child of the debtor, for alimony to, maintenance for, or support of, the spouse or child, in connection with a separation agreement, divorce decree, or other order of a court of record, or a determination made in accordance with state or territorial law by a governmental unit, or property settlement agreement; but not to the extent that either of the following occurs:

(A) The debt is assigned to another entity voluntarily, by operation of law or otherwise, in which case, the assignee may not recover that portion of the transfer that is assigned to the state or any political subdivision of the state pursuant to Part D of Title IV of the Social Security Act (42 U.S.C. Sec. 601, et. seq.) and passed on to the spouse, former spouse, or child of the debtor.

(B) The debt includes a liability designated as alimony, maintenance, or support, unless the liability is actually in the nature of alimony, maintenance, or support.

(d) An assignee of any general assignment for the benefit of creditors (as defined in Section 493.010), may avoid a transfer of property of the assignor transferred to secure reimbursement of a surety that furnished a bond or other obligation to dissolve a judicial lien that would have been avoidable by the assignee under subdivision (b) of this section. The liability of the surety under the bond or obligation shall be discharged to the extent of the value of the property recovered by the assignee or the amount paid to the assignee.

(e)(1) For the purposes of this section:

(A) A transfer of real property other than fixtures, but including the interest of a seller or purchaser under a contract for the sale of real property, is

New Text (Operative July 1, 2012)

the amount paid to the assignee.

(e) (1) For the purposes of this section:

(A) A transfer of real property other than fixtures, but including the interest of a seller or purchaser under a contract for the sale of real property, is perfected when a bona fide purchaser of the property from the debtor, against whom applicable law permits the transfer to be perfected, cannot acquire an interest that is superior to the interest of the transferee.

(B) A transfer of a fixture or property other than real property is perfected when a creditor on a simple contract cannot acquire a judicial lien that is superior to the interest of the transferee.

(2) For the purposes of this section, except as provided in paragraph (3), a transfer is made at any of the following times:

(A) At the time the transfer takes effect between the transferor and the transferee, if the transfer is perfected at, or within 10 days after, the time, except as provided in subparagraph (B) of paragraph (3) of subdivision (c).

(B) At the time the transfer is perfected, if the transfer is perfected after the 10 days.

(C) Immediately before the date of making the assignment if the transfer is not perfected at the later of:

(i) The making of the assignment.

(ii) Ten days after the transfer takes effect between the transferor and the transferee.

(3) For the purposes of this section, a transfer is not made until the assignor has acquired rights in the property transferred.

(f) For the purposes of this section, the assignor is presumed to have been insolvent on and during the 90 days immediately preceding the date of making the assignment.

(g) An action by an assignee under this section must be commenced within one year after making the assignment.

Old Text

perfected when a bona fide purchaser of the property from the debtor against whom applicable law permits the transfer to be perfected cannot acquire an interest that is superior to the interest of the transferee.

(B) A transfer of a fixture or property other than real property is perfected when a creditor on a simple contract cannot acquire a judicial lien that is superior to the interest of the transferee.

(2) For the purposes of this section, except as provided in paragraph (3), a transfer is made at any of the following times:

(A) At the time the transfer takes effect between the transferor and the transferee, if the transfer is perfected at, or within 10 days after, the time, except as provided in subparagraph (B) of paragraph (3) of subdivision (c).

(B) At the time the transfer is perfected, if the transfer is perfected after the 10 days.

(C) Immediately before the date of the making of the assignment if the transfer is not perfected at the later of:

(i) The making of the assignment.

(ii) Ten days after the transfer takes effect between the transferor and the transferee.

(3) For the purposes of this section, a transfer is not made until the assignor has acquired rights in the property transferred.

(f) For the purposes of this section, the assignor is presumed to have been insolvent on and during the 90 days immediately preceding the date of the making of the assignment.

(g) An action by an assignee under this section must be commenced within one year after the making of the assignment.

Revised to include new terminology and reference to new Section 8000 et seq.

New Text (Operative July 1, 2012) **Old Text**

EDUCATION CODE SECTIONS ("EC")

<u>EC 17307.5</u>

(a) Notwithstanding any provision of law to the contrary, including, but not limited to, Title 3 (commencing with Section 9000) of Part 6 of Division 4 of the Civil Code, the Department of General Services may issue a stop work order when construction work on a public school is not being performed in accordance with existing law and would compromise the structural integrity of the building, thereby endangering the public safety. The Department of General Services shall allow construction of incidental and minor nonstructural additions or nonstructural alterations without invoking its stop work authority.

(b) A school district, county superintendent of schools, county board of education, or other public board, body, or officer whose construction work on a public school is subject to a stop work order issued pursuant to subdivision (a) shall not be held liable in any action filed against the public board, body, or officer for stopping work as required by the stop work order, or for any delays caused by compliance with the stop work order, except to the extent that an error or omission by the public board, body, or officer is the basis for the issuance of the stop work order.

EC 17307.5

(a) Notwithstanding any provision of law to the contrary, including, but not limited to, Title 15 (commencing with Section 3082) of Part 4 of the Civil Code, the Department of General Services may issue a stop work order when construction work on a public school is not being performed in accordance with existing law and would compromise the structural integrity of the building, thereby endangering the public safety. The Department of General Services shall allow construction of incidental and minor nonstructural additions or nonstructural alterations without invoking its stop work authority.

(b) A school district, county superintendent of schools, county board of education, or other public board, body, or officer whose construction work on a public school is subject to a stop work order issued pursuant to subdivision (a) shall not be held liable in any action filed against the public board, body, or officer for stopping work as required by the stop work order, or for any delays caused by compliance with the stop work order, except to the extent that an error or omission by the public board, body, or officer is the basis for the issuance of the stop work order.

Revised to include reference to new Section 9000 et seq.

New Text (Operative July 1, 2012)

EC 81133.5

(a) Notwithstanding any provision of law to the contrary, including, but not limited to, Title 3 (commencing with Section 9000) of Part 6 of Division 4 of the Civil Code, the Department of General Services may issue a stop work order when construction work on a community college is not being performed in accordance with existing law and would compromise the structural integrity of the building, thereby endangering the public safety. The Department of General Services shall allow construction of incidental and minor nonstructural additions or nonstructural alterations without invoking its stop work authority.

(b) A community college district or other public board, body, or officer whose construction work on a community college is subject to a stop work order issued pursuant to subdivision (a) shall not be held liable in any action filed against the public board, body, or officer for stopping work as required by the stop work order, or for any delays caused by compliance with the stop work order, except to the extent that an error or omission by the public board, body, or officer is that basis for the issuance of the stop work order.

Old Text

EC 81133.5

(a) Notwithstanding any provision of law to the contrary, including, but not limited to, Title 15 (commencing with Section 3082) of Part 4 of the Civil Code, the Department of General Services may issue a stop work order when construction work on a community college is not being performed in accordance with existing law and would compromise the structural integrity of the building, thereby endangering the public safety. The Department of General Services shall allow construction of incidental and minor nonstructural additions or nonstructural alterations without invoking its stop work authority.

(b) A community college district or other public board, body, or officer whose construction work on a community college is subject to a stop work order issued pursuant to subdivision (a) shall not be held liable in any action filed against the public board, body, or officer for stopping work as required by the stop work order, or for any delays caused by compliance with the stop work order, except to the extent that an error or omission by the public board, body, or officer is that basis for the issuance of the stop work order.

GOVERNMENT CODE SECTIONS ("GC")

__GC 7480__

Nothing in this chapter shall prohibit any of the following:

(a) The dissemination of any financial information that is not identified with, or identifiable as being derived from, the financial records of a particular customer.

(b) When any police or sheriff's department or district attorney in this state certifies to a bank, credit union, or savings association in writing that a crime report has been filed that involves the alleged fraudulent use of drafts, checks, access cards, or other orders drawn upon any bank, credit union, or savings association in this state, the police or sheriff's department or district attorney, a county adult protective services office when investigating the financial abuse of an elder or dependent adult, or a long-term care ombudsman when investigating the financial abuse of an elder or dependent adult, may request a bank, credit union, or savings association to furnish, and a bank, credit union, or savings association shall furnish, a statement setting forth the following information with respect to a customer account specified by the requesting party for a period 30 days prior to, and up to 30 days following, the date of occurrence of the alleged illegal act involving the account:

(1) The number of items dishonored.

(2) The number of items paid that created overdrafts.

(3) The dollar volume of the dishonored items and items paid which created overdrafts and a statement explaining any credit arrangement between the bank, credit union, or savings association and customer to pay overdrafts.

(4) The dates and amounts of deposits and debits and the account balance on these dates.

(5) A copy of the signature card, including the signature and any addresses appearing on a customer's signature card.

(6) The date the account opened and, if applicable, the date the account closed.

(7) Surveillance photographs and video recordings of persons accessing the crime victim's financial account via an automated

GC 7480

Nothing in this chapter shall prohibit any of the following:

(a) The dissemination of any financial information that is not identified with, or identifiable as being derived from, the financial records of a particular customer.

(b) When any police or sheriff's department or district attorney in this state certifies to a bank, credit union, or savings association in writing that a crime report has been filed that involves the alleged fraudulent use of drafts, checks, access cards, or other orders drawn upon any bank, credit union, or savings association in this state, the police or sheriff's department or district attorney, a county adult protective services office when investigating the financial abuse of an elder or dependent adult, or a long-term care ombudsman when investigating the financial abuse of an elder or dependent adult, may request a bank, credit union, or savings association to furnish, and a bank, credit union, or savings association shall furnish, a statement setting forth the following information with respect to a customer account specified by the requesting party for a period 30 days prior to, and up to 30 days following, the date of occurrence of the alleged illegal act involving the account:

(1) The number of items dishonored.

(2) The number of items paid that created overdrafts.

(3) The dollar volume of the dishonored items and items paid which created overdrafts and a statement explaining any credit arrangement between the bank, credit union, or savings association and customer to pay overdrafts.

(4) The dates and amounts of deposits and debits and the account balance on these dates.

(5) A copy of the signature card, including the signature and any addresses appearing on a customer's signature card.

(6) The date the account opened and, if applicable, the date the account closed.

(7) Surveillance photographs and video recordings of persons accessing the crime victim's financial account via an automated teller machine (ATM) or from within the financial institution for

New Text (Operative July 1, 2012)

teller machine (ATM) or from within the financial institution for dates on which illegal acts involving the account were alleged to have occurred. Nothing in this paragraph does any of the following:

(A) Requires a financial institution to produce a photograph or video recording if it does not possess the photograph or video recording.

(B) Affects any existing civil immunities as provided in Section 47 of the Civil Code or any other provision of law.

(8) A bank, credit union, or savings association that provides the requesting party with copies of one or more complete account statements prepared in the regular course of business shall be deemed to be in compliance with paragraphs (1), (2), (3), and (4).

(c) When any police or sheriff's department or district attorney in this state certifies to a bank, credit union, or savings association in writing that a crime report has been filed that involves the alleged fraudulent use of drafts, checks, access cards, or other orders drawn upon any bank, credit union, or savings association doing business in this state, the police or sheriff's department or district attorney, a county adult protective services office when investigating the financial abuse of an elder or dependent adult, or a long-term care ombudsman when investigating the financial abuse of an elder or dependent adult, may request, with the consent of the accountholder, the bank, credit union, or savings association to furnish, and the bank, credit union, or savings association shall furnish, a statement setting forth the following information with respect to a customer account specified by the requesting party for a period 30 days prior to, and up to 30 days following, the date of occurrence of the alleged illegal act involving the account:

(1) The number of items dishonored.

(2) The number of items paid that created overdrafts.

(3) The dollar volume of the dishonored items and items paid which created overdrafts and a statement explaining any credit arrangement between the bank, credit union, or savings association and customer to pay overdrafts.

Old Text

dates on which illegal acts involving the account were alleged to have occurred. Nothing in this paragraph does any of the following:

(A) Requires a financial institution to produce a photograph or video recording if it does not possess the photograph or video recording.

(B) Affects any existing civil immunities as provided in Section 47 of the Civil Code or any other provision of law.

(8) A bank, credit union, or savings association that provides the requesting party with copies of one or more complete account statements prepared in the regular course of business shall be deemed to be in compliance with paragraphs (1), (2), (3), and (4).

(c) When any police or sheriff's department or district attorney in this state certifies to a bank, credit union, or savings association in writing that a crime report has been filed that involves the alleged fraudulent use of drafts, checks, access cards, or other orders drawn upon any bank, credit union, or savings association doing business in this state, the police or sheriff's department or district attorney, a county adult protective services office when investigating the financial abuse of an elder or dependent adult, or a long-term care ombudsman when investigating the financial abuse of an elder or dependent adult, may request, with the consent of the accountholder, the bank, credit union, or savings association to furnish, and the bank, credit union, or savings association shall furnish, a statement setting forth the following information with respect to a customer account specified by the requesting party for a period 30 days prior to, and up to 30 days following, the date of occurrence of the alleged illegal act involving the account:

(1) The number of items dishonored.

(2) The number of items paid that created overdrafts.

(3) The dollar volume of the dishonored items and items paid which created overdrafts and a statement explaining any credit arrangement between the bank, credit union, or savings association and customer to pay overdrafts.

(4) The dates and amounts of deposits and debits and the account balance on these dates.

(5) A copy of the signature card, including the

New Text (Operative July 1, 2012) | **Old Text**

(4) The dates and amounts of deposits and debits and the account balance on these dates.
(5) A copy of the signature card, including the signature and any addresses appearing on a customer's signature card.
(6) The date the account opened and, if applicable, the date the account closed.
(7) Surveillance photographs and video recordings of persons accessing the crime victim's financial account via an automated teller machine (ATM) or from within the financial institution for dates on which illegal acts involving this account were alleged to have occurred. Nothing in this paragraph does any of the following:
(A) Requires a financial institution to produce a photograph or video recording if it does not possess the photograph or video recording.
(B) Affects any existing civil immunities as provided in Section 47 of the Civil Code or any other provision of law.
(8) A bank, credit union, or savings association doing business in this state that provides the requesting party with copies of one or more complete account statements prepared in the regular course of business shall be deemed to be in compliance with paragraphs (1), (2), (3), and (4).
(d) For purposes of subdivision (c), consent of the accountholder shall be satisfied if an accountholder provides to the financial institution and the person or entity seeking disclosure, a signed and dated statement containing all of the following:
(1) Authorization of the disclosure for the period specified in subdivision (c).
(2) The name of the agency or department to which disclosure is authorized and, if applicable, the statutory purpose for which the information is to be obtained.
(3) A description of the financial records that are authorized to be disclosed.
(e)(1) The Attorney General, a supervisory agency, the Franchise Tax Board, the State Board of Equalization, the Employment Development Department, the Controller or an inheritance tax referee when administering the Prohibition of Gift and Death Taxes (Part

signature and any addresses appearing on a customer's signature card.
(6) The date the account opened and, if applicable, the date the account closed.
(7) Surveillance photographs and video recordings of persons accessing the crime victim's financial account via an automated teller machine (ATM) or from within the financial institution for dates on which illegal acts involving this account were alleged to have occurred. Nothing in this paragraph does any of the following:
(A) Requires a financial institution to produce a photograph or video recording if it does not possess the photograph or video recording.
(B) Affects any existing civil immunities as provided in Section 47 of the Civil Code or any other provision of law.
(8) A bank, credit union, or savings association doing business in this state that provides the requesting party with copies of one or more complete account statements prepared in the regular course of business shall be deemed to be in compliance with paragraphs (1), (2), (3), and (4).
(d) For purposes of subdivision (c), consent of the accountholder shall be satisfied if an accountholder provides to the financial institution and the person or entity seeking disclosure, a signed and dated statement containing all of the following:
(1) Authorization of the disclosure for the period specified in subdivision (c).
(2) The name of the agency or department to which disclosure is authorized and, if applicable, the statutory purpose for which the information is to be obtained.
(3) A description of the financial records that are authorized to be disclosed.
(e)(1) The Attorney General, a supervisory agency, the Franchise Tax Board, the State Board of Equalization, the Employment Development Department, the Controller or an inheritance tax referee when administering the Prohibition of Gift and Death Taxes (Part 8 (commencing with Section 13301) of Division 2 of the Revenue and Taxation Code), a police or sheriff's department or district attorney, a county adult protective services office when

New Text (Operative July 1, 2012)

8 (commencing with Section 13301) of Division 2 of the Revenue and Taxation Code), a police or sheriff's department or district attorney, a county adult protective services office when investigating the financial abuse of an elder or dependent adult, a long-term care ombudsman when investigating the financial abuse of an elder or dependent adult, a county welfare department when investigating welfare fraud, a county auditor-controller or director of finance when investigating fraud against the county, or the Department of Corporations when conducting investigations in connection with the enforcement of laws administered by the Commissioner of Corporations, from requesting of an office or branch of a financial institution, and the office or branch from responding to a request, as to whether a person has an account or accounts at that office or branch and, if so, any identifying numbers of the account or accounts.

(2) No additional information beyond that specified in this section shall be released to a county welfare department without either the accountholder's written consent or a judicial writ, search warrant, subpoena, or other judicial order.

(3) A county auditor-controller or director of finance who unlawfully discloses information he or she is authorized to request under this subdivision is guilty of the unlawful disclosure of confidential data, a misdemeanor, which shall be punishable as set forth in Section 7485.

(f) The examination by, or disclosure to, any supervisory agency of financial records that relate solely to the exercise of its supervisory function. The scope of an agency's supervisory function shall be determined by reference to statutes that grant authority to examine, audit, or require reports of financial records or financial institutions as follows:

(1) With respect to the Commissioner of Financial Institutions by reference to Division 1 (commencing with Section 99), Division 1.5 (commencing with Section 4800), Division 2 (commencing with Section 5000), Division 5

Old Text

investigating the financial abuse of an elder or dependent adult, a long-term care ombudsman when investigating the financial abuse of an elder or dependent adult, a county welfare department when investigating welfare fraud, a county auditor-controller or director of finance when investigating fraud against the county, or the Department of Corporations when conducting investigations in connection with the enforcement of laws administered by the Commissioner of Corporations, from requesting of an office or branch of a financial institution, and the office or branch from responding to a request, as to whether a person has an account or accounts at that office or branch and, if so, any identifying numbers of the account or accounts.

(2) No additional information beyond that specified in this section shall be released to a county welfare department without either the accountholder's written consent or a judicial writ, search warrant, subpoena, or other judicial order.

(3) A county auditor-controller or director of finance who unlawfully discloses information he or she is authorized to request under this subdivision is guilty of the unlawful disclosure of confidential data, a misdemeanor, which shall be punishable as set forth in Section 7485.

(f) The examination by, or disclosure to, any supervisory agency of financial records that relate solely to the exercise of its supervisory function. The scope of an agency's supervisory function shall be determined by reference to statutes that grant authority to examine, audit, or require reports of financial records or financial institutions as follows:

(1) With respect to the Commissioner of Financial Institutions by reference to Division 1 (commencing with Section 99), Division 1.5 (commencing with Section 4800), Division 2 (commencing with Section 5000), Division 5 (commencing with Section 14000), Division 7 (commencing with Section 18000), Division 15 (commencing with Section 31000), and Division 16 (commencing with Section 33000), of the Financial Code.

(2) With respect to the Controller by reference

New Text (Operative July 1, 2012)

(commencing with Section 14000), Division 7 (commencing with Section 18000), Division 15 (commencing with Section 31000), and Division 16 (commencing with Section 33000), of the Financial Code.

(2) With respect to the Controller by reference to Title 10 (commencing with Section 1300) of Part 3 of the Code of Civil Procedure.

(3) With respect to the Administrator of Local Agency Security by reference to Article 2 (commencing with Section 53630) of Chapter 4 of Part 1 of Division 2 of Title 5 of the Government Code.

(g) The disclosure to the Franchise Tax Board of (1) the amount of any security interest that a financial institution has in a specified asset of a customer or (2) financial records in connection with the filing or audit of a tax return or tax information return that are required to be filed by the financial institution pursuant to Part 10 (commencing with Section 17001), Part 11 (commencing with Section 23001), or Part 18 (commencing with Section 38001), of the Revenue and Taxation Code.

(h) The disclosure to the State Board of Equalization of any of the following:

(1) The information required by Sections 6702, 6703, 8954, 8957, 30313, 30315, 32383, 32387, 38502, 38503, 40153, 40155, 41122, 41123.5, 43443, 43444.2, 44144, 45603, 45605, 46404, 46406, 50134, 50136, 55203, 55205, 60404, and 60407 of the Revenue and Taxation Code.

(2) The financial records in connection with the filing or audit of a tax return required to be filed by the financial institution pursuant to Part 1 (commencing with Section 6001), Part 2 (commencing with Section 7301), Part 3 (commencing with Section 8601), Part 13 (commencing with Section 30001), Part 14 (commencing with Section 32001), and Part 17 (commencing with Section 37001), of Division 2 of the Revenue and Taxation Code.

(3) The amount of any security interest a financial institution has in a specified asset of a customer, if the inquiry is directed to the

Old Text

to Title 10 (commencing with Section 1300) of Part 3 of the Code of Civil Procedure.

(3) With respect to the Administrator of Local Agency Security by reference to Article 2 (commencing with Section 53630) of Chapter 4 of Part 1 of Division 2 of Title 5 of the Government Code.

(g) The disclosure to the Franchise Tax Board of (1) the amount of any security interest that a financial institution has in a specified asset of a customer or (2) financial records in connection with the filing or audit of a tax return or tax information return that are required to be filed by the financial institution pursuant to Part 10 (commencing with Section 17001), Part 11 (commencing with Section 23001), or Part 18 (commencing with Section 38001), of the Revenue and Taxation Code.

(h) The disclosure to the State Board of Equalization of any of the following:

(1) The information required by Sections 6702, 6703, 8954, 8957, 30313, 30315, 32383, 32387, 38502, 38503, 40153, 40155, 41122, 41123.5, 43443, 43444.2, 44144, 45603, 45605, 46404, 46406, 50134, 50136, 55203, 55205, 60404, and 60407 of the Revenue and Taxation Code.

(2) The financial records in connection with the filing or audit of a tax return required to be filed by the financial institution pursuant to Part 1 (commencing with Section 6001), Part 2 (commencing with Section 7301), Part 3 (commencing with Section 8601), Part 13 (commencing with Section 30001), Part 14 (commencing with Section 32001), and Part 17 (commencing with Section 37001), of Division 2 of the Revenue and Taxation Code.

(3) The amount of any security interest a financial institution has in a specified asset of a customer, if the inquiry is directed to the branch or office where the interest is held.

(i) The disclosure to the Controller of the information required by Section 7853 of the Revenue and Taxation Code.

(j) The disclosure to the Employment Development Department of the amount of any security interest a financial institution has in a specified asset of a customer, if the inquiry is directed to the branch or

New Text (Operative July 1, 2012)

branch or office where the interest is held.

(i) The disclosure to the Controller of the information required by Section 7853 of the Revenue and Taxation Code.

(j) The disclosure to the Employment Development Department of the amount of any security interest a financial institution has in a specified asset of a customer, if the inquiry is directed to the branch or office where the interest is held.

(k) The disclosure by a construction lender, as defined in Section 8006 of the Civil Code, to the Registrar of Contractors, of information concerning the making of progress payments to a prime contractor requested by the registrar in connection with an investigation under Section 7108.5 of the Business and Professions Code.

(l) Upon receipt of a written request from a local child support agency referring to a support order pursuant to Section 17400 of the Family Code, a financial institution shall disclose the following information concerning the account or the person named in the request, whom the local child support agency shall identify, whenever possible, by social security number:

(1) If the request states the identifying number of an account at a financial institution, the name of each owner of the account.

(2) Each account maintained by the person at the branch to which the request is delivered, and, if the branch is able to make a computerized search, each account maintained by the person at any other branch of the financial institution located in this state.

(3) For each account disclosed pursuant to paragraphs (1) and (2), the account number, current balance, street address of the branch where the account is maintained, and, to the extent available through the branch's computerized search, the name and address of any other person listed as an owner.

(4) Whenever the request prohibits the disclosure, a financial institution shall not disclose either the request or its response, to an owner of the account or to any other person, except the officers and employees of the financial institution who are involved in responding to the request and to attorneys, employees of the local child support agencies, auditors, and regulatory authorities who

Old Text

office where the interest is held.

(k) The disclosure by a construction lender, as defined in Section 3087 of the Civil Code, to the Registrar of Contractors, of information concerning the making of progress payments to a prime contractor requested by the registrar in connection with an investigation under Section 7108.5 of the Business and Professions Code.

(l) Upon receipt of a written request from a local child support agency referring to a support order pursuant to Section 17400 of the Family Code, a financial institution shall disclose the following information concerning the account or the person named in the request, whom the local child support agency shall identify, whenever possible, by social security number:

(1) If the request states the identifying number of an account at a financial institution, the name of each owner of the account.

(2) Each account maintained by the person at the branch to which the request is delivered, and, if the branch is able to make a computerized search, each account maintained by the person at any other branch of the financial institution located in this state.

(3) For each account disclosed pursuant to paragraphs (1) and (2), the account number, current balance, street address of the branch where the account is maintained, and, to the extent available through the branch's computerized search, the name and address of any other person listed as an owner.

(4) Whenever the request prohibits the disclosure, a financial institution shall not disclose either the request or its response, to an owner of the account or to any other person, except the officers and employees of the financial institution who are involved in responding to the request and to attorneys, employees of the local child support agencies, auditors, and regulatory authorities who have a need to know in order to perform their duties, and except as disclosure may be required by legal process.

(5) No financial institution, or any officer, employee, or agent thereof, shall be liable to any person for (A) disclosing information in response to a request pursuant to this subdivision, (B) failing to notify the owner of an account, or complying with a request under this paragraph not

New Text (Operative July 1, 2012)

have a need to know in order to perform their duties, and except as disclosure may be required by legal process.

(5) No financial institution, or any officer, employee, or agent thereof, shall be liable to any person for (A) disclosing information in response to a request pursuant to this subdivision, (B) failing to notify the owner of an account, or complying with a request under this paragraph not to disclose to the owner, the request or disclosure under this subdivision, or (C) failing to discover any account owned by the person named in the request pursuant to a computerized search of the records of the financial institution.

(6) The local child support agency may request information pursuant to this subdivision only when the local child support agency has received at least one of the following types of physical evidence:

(A) Any of the following, dated within the last three years:

(i) Form 599.

(ii) Form 1099.

(iii) A bank statement.

(iv) A check.

(v) A bank passbook.

(vi) A deposit slip.

(viii) A copy of a federal or state income tax return.

(viii) A debit or credit advice.

(ix) Correspondence that identifies the child support obligor by name, the bank, and the account number.

(x) Correspondence that identifies the child support obligor by name, the bank, and the banking services related to the account of the obligor.

(xi) An asset identification report from a federal agency.

(B) A sworn declaration of the custodial parent during the 12 months immediately preceding the request that the person named in the request has had or may have had an account at an office or branch of the financial institution to which the request is made.

(7) Information obtained by a local child support agency pursuant to this subdivision shall be used only for purposes that are

Old Text

to disclose to the owner, the request or disclosure under this subdivision, or (C) failing to discover any account owned by the person named in the request pursuant to a computerized search of the records of the financial institution.

(6) The local child support agency may request information pursuant to this subdivision only when the local child support agency has received at least one of the following types of physical evidence:

(A) Any of the following, dated within the last three years:

(i) Form 599.

(ii) Form 1099.

(iii) A bank statement.

(iv) A check.

(v) A bank passbook.

(vi) A deposit slip.

(viii) A copy of a federal or state income tax return.

(viii) A debit or credit advice.

(ix) Correspondence that identifies the child support obligor by name, the bank, and the account number.

(x) Correspondence that identifies the child support obligor by name, the bank, and the banking services related to the account of the obligor.

(xi) An asset identification report from a federal agency.

(B) A sworn declaration of the custodial parent during the 12 months immediately preceding the request that the person named in the request has had or may have had an account at an office or branch of the financial institution to which the request is made.

(7) Information obtained by a local child support agency pursuant to this subdivision shall be used only for purposes that are directly connected with the administration of the duties of the local child support agency pursuant to Section 17400 of the Family Code.

(m)(1) As provided in paragraph (1) of subdivision (c) of Section 666 of Title 42 of the United States Code, upon receipt of an administrative subpoena on the current federally approved interstate child support enforcement form, as

New Text (Operative July 1, 2012)

directly connected with the administration of the duties of the local child support agency pursuant to Section 17400 of the Family Code.

(m)(1) As provided in paragraph (1) of subdivision (c) of Section 666 of Title 42 of the United States Code, upon receipt of an administrative subpoena on the current federally approved interstate child support enforcement form, as approved by the federal Office of Management and Budget, a financial institution shall provide the information or documents requested by the administrative subpoena.

(2) The administrative subpoena shall refer to the current federal Office of Management and Budget control number and be signed by a person who states that he or she is an authorized agent of a state or county agency responsible for implementing the child support enforcement program set forth in Part D (commencing with Section 651) of Subchapter IV of Chapter 7 of Title 42 of the United States Code. A financial institution may rely on the statements made in the subpoena and has no duty to inquire into the truth of any statement in the subpoena.

(3) If the person who signs the administrative subpoena directs a financial institution in writing not to disclose either the subpoena or its response to any owner of an account covered by the subpoena, the financial institution shall not disclose the subpoena or its response to the owner.

(4) No financial institution, or any officer, employee, or agent thereof, shall be liable to any person for (A) disclosing information or providing documents in response to a subpoena pursuant to this subdivision, (B) failing to notify any owner of an account covered by the subpoena or complying with a request not to disclose to the owner, the subpoena or disclosure under this subdivision, or (C) failing to discover any account owned by the person named in the subpoena pursuant to a computerized search of the records of the financial institution.

(n) The dissemination of financial information and records pursuant to any of the following:

Old Text

approved by the federal Office of Management and Budget, a financial institution shall provide the information or documents requested by the administrative subpoena.

(2) The administrative subpoena shall refer to the current federal Office of Management and Budget control number and be signed by a person who states that he or she is an authorized agent of a state or county agency responsible for implementing the child support enforcement program set forth in Part D (commencing with Section 651) of Subchapter IV of Chapter 7 of Title 42 of the United States Code. A financial institution may rely on the statements made in the subpoena and has no duty to inquire into the truth of any statement in the subpoena.

(3) If the person who signs the administrative subpoena directs a financial institution in writing not to disclose either the subpoena or its response to any owner of an account covered by the subpoena, the financial institution shall not disclose the subpoena or its response to the owner.

(4) No financial institution, or any officer, employee, or agent thereof, shall be liable to any person for (A) disclosing information or providing documents in response to a subpoena pursuant to this subdivision, (B) failing to notify any owner of an account covered by the subpoena or complying with a request not to disclose to the owner, the subpoena or disclosure under this subdivision, or (C) failing to discover any account owned by the person named in the subpoena pursuant to a computerized search of the records of the financial institution.

(n) The dissemination of financial information and records pursuant to any of the following:

(1) Compliance by a financial institution with the requirements of Section 2892 of the Probate Code.

(2) Compliance by a financial institution with the requirements of Section 2893 of the Probate Code.

(3) An order by a judge upon a written ex parte application by a peace officer showing specific and articulable facts that there are reasonable

New Text (Operative July 1, 2012)

(1) Compliance by a financial institution with the requirements of Section 2892 of the Probate Code.
(2) Compliance by a financial institution with the requirements of Section 2893 of the Probate Code.
(3) An order by a judge upon a written ex parte application by a peace officer showing specific and articulable facts that there are reasonable grounds to believe that the records or information sought are relevant and material to an ongoing investigation of a felony violation of Section 186.10 or of any felony subject to the enhancement set forth in Section 186.11.
(A) The ex parte application shall specify with particularity the records to be produced, which shall be only those of the individual or individuals who are the subject of the criminal investigation.
(B) The ex parte application and any subsequent judicial order shall be open to the public as a judicial record unless ordered sealed by the court, for a period of 60 days. The sealing of these records may be extended for 60-day periods upon a showing to the court that it is necessary for the continuance of the investigation. Sixty-day extensions may continue for up to one year or until termination of the investigation of the individual or individuals, whichever is sooner.
(C) The records ordered to be produced shall be returned to the peace officer applicant or his or her designee within a reasonable time period after service of the order upon the financial institution.
(D) Nothing in this subdivision shall preclude the financial institution from notifying a customer of the receipt of the order for production of records unless a court orders the financial institution to withhold notification to the customer upon a finding that the notice would impede the investigation.
(E) Where a court has made an order pursuant to this paragraph to withhold notification to the customer under this paragraph, the peace officer or law enforcement agency who obtained the

Old Text

grounds to believe that the records or information sought are relevant and material to an ongoing investigation of a felony violation of Section 186.10 or of any felony subject to the enhancement set forth in Section 186.11.
(A) The ex parte application shall specify with particularity the records to be produced, which shall be only those of the individual or individuals who are the subject of the criminal investigation.
(B) The ex parte application and any subsequent judicial order shall be open to the public as a judicial record unless ordered sealed by the court, for a period of 60 days. The sealing of these records may be extended for 60-day periods upon a showing to the court that it is necessary for the continuance of the investigation. Sixty-day extensions may continue for up to one year or until termination of the investigation of the individual or individuals, whichever is sooner.
(C) The records ordered to be produced shall be returned to the peace officer applicant or his or her designee within a reasonable time period after service of the order upon the financial institution.
(D) Nothing in this subdivision shall preclude the financial institution from notifying a customer of the receipt of the order for production of records unless a court orders the financial institution to withhold notification to the customer upon a finding that the notice would impede the investigation.
(E) Where a court has made an order pursuant to this paragraph to withhold notification to the customer under this paragraph, the peace officer or law enforcement agency who obtained the financial information shall notify the customer by delivering a copy of the ex parte order to the customer within 10 days of the termination of the investigation.
(4) No financial institution, or any officer, employee, or agent thereof, shall be liable to any person for any of the following:
(A) Disclosing information to a probate court pursuant to Sections 2892 and 2893.
(B) Disclosing information in response to a

New Text (Operative July 1, 2012)

financial information shall notify the customer by delivering a copy of the ex parte order to the customer within 10 days of the termination of the investigation.

(4) No financial institution, or any officer, employee, or agent thereof, shall be liable to any person for any of the following:

(A) Disclosing information to a probate court pursuant to Sections 2892 and 2893.

(B) Disclosing information in response to a court order pursuant to paragraph (3).

(C) Complying with a court order under this subdivision not to disclose to the customer, the order, or the dissemination of information pursuant to the court order.

(o) Disclosure by a financial institution to a peace officer, as defined in Section 830.1 of the Penal Code, pursuant to the following:

(1) Paragraph (1) of subdivision (a) of Section 1748.95 of the Civil Code, provided that the financial institution has first complied with the requirements of paragraph (2) of subdivision (a) and subdivision (b) of Section 1748.95 of the Civil Code.

(2) Paragraph (1) of subdivision (a) of Section 4002 of the Financial Code, provided that the financial institution has first complied with the requirements of paragraph (2) of subdivision (a) and subdivision (b) of Section 4002 of the Financial Code.

(3) Paragraph (1) of subdivision (a) of Section 22470 of the Financial Code, provided that any financial institution that is a finance lender has first complied with the requirements of paragraph (2) of subdivision (a) and subdivision (b) of Section 22470 of the Financial Code.

(p) When the governing board of the Public Employees' Retirement System or the State Teachers' Retirement System certifies in writing to a financial institution that a benefit recipient has died and that transfers to the benefit recipient's account at the financial institution from the retirement system occurred after the benefit recipient's date of death, the financial institution shall furnish the retirement system with the name and address of any coowner,

Old Text

court order pursuant to paragraph (3).

(C) Complying with a court order under this subdivision not to disclose to the customer, the order, or the dissemination of information pursuant to the court order.

(o) Disclosure by a financial institution to a peace officer, as defined in Section 830.1 of the Penal Code, pursuant to the following:

(1) Paragraph (1) of subdivision (a) of Section 1748.95 of the Civil Code, provided that the financial institution has first complied with the requirements of paragraph (2) of subdivision (a) and subdivision (b) of Section 1748.95 of the Civil Code.

(2) Paragraph (1) of subdivision (a) of Section 4002 of the Financial Code, provided that the financial institution has first complied with the requirements of paragraph (2) of subdivision (a) and subdivision (b) of Section 4002 of the Financial Code.

(3) Paragraph (1) of subdivision (a) of Section 22470 of the Financial Code, provided that any financial institution that is a finance lender has first complied with the requirements of paragraph (2) of subdivision (a) and subdivision (b) of Section 22470 of the Financial Code.

(p) When the governing board of the Public Employees' Retirement System or the State Teachers' Retirement System certifies in writing to a financial institution that a benefit recipient has died and that transfers to the benefit recipient's account at the financial institution from the retirement system occurred after the benefit recipient's date of death, the financial institution shall furnish the retirement system with the name and address of any coowner, cosigner, or any other person who had access to the funds in the account following the date of the benefit recipient's death, or if the account has been closed, the name and address of the person who closed the account.

(q) When the retirement board of a retirement system established under the County Employees Retirement Law of 1937 certifies in writing to a financial institution that a retired member or the beneficiary of a retired member has died and that transfers to the account of the retired member or beneficiary of a retired member at the financial

New Text (Operative July 1, 2012)	Old Text
cosigner, or any other person who had access to the funds in the account following the date of the benefit recipient's death, or if the account has been closed, the name and address of the person who closed the account. *(q) When the retirement board of a retirement system established under the County Employees Retirement Law of 1937 certifies in writing to a financial institution that a retired member or the beneficiary of a retired member has died and that transfers to the account of the retired member or beneficiary of a retired member at the financial institution from the retirement system occurred after the date of death of the retired member or beneficiary of a retired member, the financial institution shall furnish the retirement system with the name and address of any coowner, cosigner, or any other person who had access to the funds in the account following the date of death of the retired member or beneficiary of a retired member, or if the account has been closed, the name and address of the person who closed the account.* *(r) When the Franchise Tax Board certifies in writing to a financial institution that (1) a taxpayer filed a tax return that authorized a direct deposit refund with an incorrect financial institution account or routing number that resulted in all or a portion of the refund not being received, directly or indirectly, by the taxpayer; (2) the direct deposit refund was not returned to the Franchise Tax Board; and (3) the refund was deposited directly on a specified date into the account of an accountholder of the financial institution who was not entitled to receive the refund, then the financial institution shall furnish to the Franchise Tax Board the name and address of any coowner, cosigner, or any other person who had access to the funds in the account following the date of direct deposit refund, or if the account has been closed, the name and address of the person who closed the account.*	institution from the retirement system occurred after the date of death of the retired member or beneficiary of a retired member, the financial institution shall furnish the retirement system with the name and address of any coowner, cosigner, or any other person who had access to the funds in the account following the date of death of the retired member or beneficiary of a retired member, or if the account has been closed, the name and address of the person who closed the account. (r) When the Franchise Tax Board certifies in writing to a financial institution that (1) a taxpayer filed a tax return that authorized a direct deposit refund with an incorrect financial institution account or routing number that resulted in all or a portion of the refund not being received, directly or indirectly, by the taxpayer; (2) the direct deposit refund was not returned to the Franchise Tax Board; and (3) the refund was deposited directly on a specified date into the account of an accountholder of the financial institution who was not entitled to receive the refund, then the financial institution shall furnish to the Franchise Tax Board the name and address of any coowner, cosigner, or any other person who had access to the funds in the account following the date of direct deposit refund, or if the account has been closed, the name and address of the person who closed the account.

Revised to include reference to new Section 8000 et seq.

New Text (Operative July 1, 2012)

GC 14975

Notwithstanding the provisions of Section 9550 of the Civil Code, the contractor under any contract made under this chapter need not provide a payment bond before the commencement of the work but must provide a payment bond as otherwise required by law prior to payment under the contract.

Old Text

GC 14975

Notwithstanding the provisions of Section 3247 of the Civil Code, the contractor under any contract made under this chapter need not provide a payment bond before the commencement of the work but must provide a payment bond as otherwise required by law prior to payment under the contract.

Revised to include reference to new Section 9000 et seq.

New Text (Operative July 1, 2012)

GC 15820.105

(a) Plans and specifications for the project shall comply with applicable building codes.

(b) The project is hereby deemed to be governed by Title 3 (commencing with Section 9000) of Part 6 of Division 4 of the Civil Code.

(c) The provisions of Chapter 1 (commencing with Section 1720) of Part 7 of Division 2 of the Labor Code shall apply to all public works contracts entered into for the project.

(d) Other than as provided in this section and Sections 15820.101 to 15820.104, inclusive, private sector methods may be used to deliver the project. Specifically, the procurement and contracting for the delivery of the project is not subject to the State Contract Act (Part 2 (commencing with Section 10100) of Division 2 of the Public Contract Code) or any other provision of California law governing public procurement or public works projects.

Old Text

GC 15820.105

(a) Plans and specifications for the project shall comply with applicable building codes.

(b) The project is hereby deemed a "public work" project for purposes of Title 15 (commencing with Section 3082) of Part 4 of Division 3 of the Civil Code.

(c) The provisions of Chapter 1 (commencing with Section 1720) of Part 7 of Division 2 of the Labor Code shall apply to all public works contracts entered into for the project.

(d) Other than as provided in this section and Sections 15820.101 to 15820.104, inclusive, private sector methods may be used to deliver the project. Specifically, the procurement and contracting for the delivery of the project is not subject to the State Contract Act (Part 2 (commencing with Section 10100) of Division 2 of the Public Contract Code) or any other provision of California law governing public procurement or public works projects.

Clarified and revised to include reference to new Section 9000 et seq.

New Text (Operative July 1, 2012) | **Old Text**

<u>GC 27287</u>
Unless it belongs to the class provided for in either Sections 27282 to 27286, inclusive, or Section 1202 or 1203, of the Civil Code, or is a fictitious mortgage or deed of trust as provided
in Section 2952 or 2963 of the Civil Code, or is a fictitious oil and gas lease as provided in Section 1219 of the Civil Code, or is a claim of lien under Section 8416 of the Civil Code or a notice of completion under Section 8182 or 9204 of the Civil Code, before an instrument can be recorded its execution shall be acknowledged by the person executing it, or if executed by a corporation, by its president or secretary or other person executing it on behalf of the corporation, or, except for any quitclaim deed or grant deed other than a trustee's deed or a deed of reconveyance, mortgage, deed of trust, or security agreement, proved by subscribing witness or as provided in Sections 1198 and 1199 of the Civil Code, and the acknowledgment or proof certified as prescribed by law.

GC 27287
Unless it belongs to the class provided for in either Sections 27282 to 27286, inclusive, or Sections 1202 or 1203, of the Civil Code, or is a fictitious mortgage or deed of trust as provided in Sections 2952, or 2963, of the Civil Code, or is a fictitious oil and gas lease as provided in Section 1219 of the Civil Code, or is a claim of lien, as provided in Section 3084 of the Civil Code, or a notice of completion, as provided in Section 3093 of the Civil Code, before an instrument can be recorded its execution shall be acknowledged by the person executing it, or if executed by a corporation, by its president or secretary or other person executing it on behalf of the corporation, or, except for any quitclaim deed or grant deed other than a trustee's deed or a deed of reconveyance, mortgage, deed of trust, or security agreement, proved by subscribing witness or as provided in Sections 1198 and 1199 of the Civil Code, and the acknowledgment or proof certified as prescribed by law.

Revised to include reference to new Section 8000 et seq.

••

<u>GC 27361.9</u>
The board of supervisors of any county may provide for an additional fee for filing every preliminary notice pursuant to subdivision (a) of Section 8214 of the Civil Code for the exclusive purpose of defraying the cost of implementing and maintaining a system to facilitate compliance with subdivision (b) of Section 8214 of the Civil Code.

GC 27361.9
The board of supervisors of any county may provide for an additional fee for filing every preliminary 20-day notice pursuant to paragraph (1) of subdivision (o) of Section 3097 of the Civil Code for the exclusive purpose of defraying the cost of implementing and maintaining a system to facilitate compliance with paragraph (2) of subdivision (o) of Section 3097 of the Civil Code.

Revised to include new terminology and reference to new Section 8000 et seq.

••

New Text (Operative July 1, 2012)

<u>*GC 66499.2*</u>

A bond or bonds by one or more duly authorized corporate sureties for the security of laborers and material suppliers shall be in substantially the following form:

Whereas, The Board of Supervisors of the County of ______________ (or City Council of the City of ___________), State of California, and ________________________ (hereinafter designated as "the principal") have entered into an agreement whereby the principal agrees to install and complete certain designated public improvements, which agreement, dated _________, 20____, and identified as project ____________________, is hereby referred to and made a part hereof; and

Whereas, Under the terms of the agreement, the principal is required before entering upon the performance of the work, to file a good and sufficient payment bond with the County of _______________ (or the City of _______________) to secure the claims to which reference is made in Title 3 (commencing with Section 9000) of Part 6 of Division 4 of the Civil Code.

Now, therefore, the principal and the undersigned as corporate surety, are held firmly bound unto the County of ____________ (or the City of ____________) and all contractors, subcontractors, laborers, material suppliers, and other persons employed in the performance of the agreement and referred to in Title 3 (commencing with Section 9000) of Part 6 of Division 4 of the Civil Code in the sum of ____________ dollars ($____), for materials furnished or labor thereon of any kind, or for amounts due under the Unemployment Insurance Act with respect to this work or labor, that the surety will pay the same in an amount not exceeding the amount hereinabove set forth, and also in case suit is brought upon this bond, will pay, in addition to the face amount thereof, costs and reasonable expenses and fees, including reasonable attorney's fees, incurred by county (or city) in successfully enforcing this obligation, to be awarded and fixed by the court, and to be taxed as costs and to be included in the judgment therein rendered.

It is hereby expressly stipulated and agreed that this bond shall inure to the benefit of any and all persons, companies, and corporations entitled to file claims under Title 3 (commencing with Section 9000) of Part 6 of Division 4 of the Civil Code, so as to give a right of action to them or their assigns in any suit brought upon this bond.

Old Text

GC 66499.2

A bond or bonds by one or more duly authorized corporate sureties for the security of laborers and materialmen shall be in substantially the following form:

Whereas, The Board of Supervisors of the County of ______________ (or City Council of the City of ______________), State of California, and ____________ (hereinafter designated as "the principal") have entered into an agreement whereby the principal agrees to install and complete certain designated public improvements, which agreement, dated ___________, 20 ______, and identified as project ______________, is hereby referred to and made a part hereof; and

Whereas, Under the terms of the agreement, the principal is required before entering upon the performance of the work, to file a good and sufficient payment bond with the County of _______________ (or the City of _________) to secure the claims to which reference is made in Title 15 (commencing with Section 3082) of Part 4 of Division 3 of the Civil Code of the State of California.

Now, therefore, the principal and the undersigned as corporate surety, are held firmly bound unto the County of _______________ (or the City of _______________) and all contractors, subcontractors, laborers, materialmen, and other persons employed in the performance of the agreement and referred to in Title 15 (commencing with Section 3082) of Part 4 of Division 3 of the Civil Code in the sum of ______________ dollars ($_________), for materials furnished or labor thereon of any kind, or for amounts due under the Unemployment Insurance Act with respect to this work or labor, that the surety will pay the same in an amount not exceeding the amount hereinabove set forth, and also in case suit is brought upon this bond, will pay, in addition to the face amount thereof, costs and reasonable expenses and fees, including reasonable attorney's fees, incurred by county (or city) in successfully enforcing this obligation, to be awarded and fixed by the court, and to be taxed as costs and to be included in the judgment therein rendered.

It is hereby expressly stipulated and agreed that this bond shall inure to the benefit of any and all persons, companies, and corporations entitled to file claims under Title 15 (commencing with Section 3082) of Part 4 of Division 3 of the Civil Code, so as to give a right of action to them or their assigns in any suit brought upon this bond.

New Text (Operative July 1, 2012)

Should the condition of this bond be fully performed, then this obligation shall become null and void, otherwise it shall be and remain in full force and effect.

The surety hereby stipulates and agrees that no change, extension of time, alteration, or addition to the terms of the agreement or the specifications accompanying the same shall in any manner affect its obligations on this bond, and it does hereby waive notice of any such change, extension, alteration, or addition.

In witness whereof, this instrument has been duly executed by the principal and surety above named, on ____________, 20____.

Old Text

Should the condition of this bond be fully performed, then this obligation shall become null and void, otherwise it shall be and remain in full force and effect.

The surety hereby stipulates and agrees that no change, extension of time, alteration, or addition to the terms of the agreement or the specifications accompanying the same shall in any manner affect its obligations on this bond, and it does hereby waive notice of any such change, extension, alteration, or addition.

In witness whereof, this instrument has been duly executed by the principal and surety above named, on ______________, 20________.

Revised to include new terminology and reference to new Section 9000 et seq.

New Text (Operative July 1, 2012)

GC 66499.7

The security furnished by the subdivider shall be released in whole or in part in the following manner:

(a) Security given for faithful performance of any act or agreement shall be released upon the performance of the act or final completion and acceptance of the required work. The legislative body may provide for the partial release of the security upon the partial performance of the act or the acceptance of the work as it progresses, consistent with the provisions of this section. The security may be a surety bond, a cash deposit, a letter of credit, escrow account, or other form of performance guarantee required as security by the legislative body that meets the requirements as acceptable security pursuant to law. If the security furnished by the subdivider is a documentary evidence of security such as a surety bond or a letter of credit, the legislative body shall release the documentary evidence and return the original to the issuer upon performance of the act or final completion and acceptance of the required work. In the event that the legislative body is unable to return the original documentary evidence to the issuer, the security shall be released by written notice sent by certified mail to the subdivider and issuer of the documentary evidence within 30 days of the acceptance of the work. The written notice shall contain a statement that the work for which the security was furnished

Old Text

GC 66499.7

The security furnished by the subdivider shall be released in whole or in part in the following manner:

(a) Security given for faithful performance of any act or agreement shall be released upon the performance of the act or final completion and acceptance of the required work. The legislative body may provide for the partial release of the security upon the partial performance of the act or the acceptance of the work as it progresses, consistent with the provisions of this section. The security may be a surety bond, a cash deposit, a letter of credit, escrow account, or other form of performance guarantee required as security by the legislative body that meets the requirements as acceptable security pursuant to law. If the security furnished by the subdivider is a documentary evidence of security such as a surety bond or a letter of credit, the legislative body shall release the documentary evidence and return the original to the issuer upon performance of the act or final completion and acceptance of the required work. In the event that the legislative body is unable to return the original documentary evidence to the issuer, the security shall be released by written notice sent by certified mail to the subdivider and issuer of the documentary evidence within 30 days of the acceptance of the work. The written notice shall contain a statement that the work for which the security was furnished has been performed or completed and accepted by the legislative body, a description of the project subject to the

New Text (Operative July 1, 2012)	Old Text
has been performed or completed and accepted by the legislative body, a description of the project subject to the documentary evidence and the notarized signature of the authorized representative of the legislative body.	documentary evidence and the notarized signature of the authorized representative of the legislative body.
(b) At the time that the subdivider believes that the obligation to perform the work for which security was required is complete, the subdivider may notify the local agency in writing of the completed work, including a list of work completed. Upon receipt of the written notice, the local agency shall have 45 days to review and comment or approve the completion of the required work. If the local agency does not agree that all work has been completed in accordance with the plans and specifications for the improvements, it shall supply a list of all remaining work to be completed.	(b) At the time that the subdivider believes that the obligation to perform the work for which security was required is complete, the subdivider may notify the local agency in writing of the completed work, including a list of work completed. Upon receipt of the written notice, the local agency shall have 45 days to review and comment or approve the completion of the required work. If the local agency does not agree that all work has been completed in accordance with the plans and specifications for the improvements, it shall supply a list of all remaining work to be completed.
(c) Within 45 days of receipt of the list of remaining work from the local agency, the subdivider may then provide cost estimates for all remaining work for review and approval by the local agency. Upon receipt of the cost estimates, the local agency shall then have 45 days to review, comment, and approve, modify, or disapprove those cost estimates. No local agency shall be required to engage in this process of partial release more than once between the start of work and completion and acceptance of all work; however, nothing in this section prohibits a local agency from allowing for a partial release as it otherwise deems appropriate.	(c) Within 45 days of receipt of the list of remaining work from the local agency, the subdivider may then provide cost estimates for all remaining work for review and approval by the local agency. Upon receipt of the cost estimates, the local agency shall then have 45 days to review, comment, and approve, modify, or disapprove those cost estimates. No local agency shall be required to engage in this process of partial release more than once between the start of work and completion and acceptance of all work; however, nothing in this section prohibits a local agency from allowing for a partial release as it otherwise deems appropriate.
(d) If the local agency approves the cost estimate, the local agency shall release all performance security except for security in an amount up to 200 percent of the cost estimate of the remaining work. The process allowing for a partial release of performance security shall occur when the cost estimate of the remaining work does not exceed 20 percent of the total original performance security unless the local agency allows for a release at an earlier time. Substitute bonds or other security may be used as a replacement for the performance security, subject to the approval of the local agency. If substitute bonds or other security is used as a replacement for the performance security released, the release shall not be	(d) If the local agency approves the cost estimate, the local agency shall release all performance security except for security in an amount up to 200 percent of the cost estimate of the remaining work. The process allowing for a partial release of performance security shall occur when the cost estimate of the remaining work does not exceed 20 percent of the total original performance security unless the local agency allows for a release at an earlier time. Substitute bonds or other security may be used as a replacement for the performance security, subject to the approval of the local agency. If substitute bonds or other security is used as a replacement for the performance security released, the release shall not be effective unless and until the local agency receives and approves that form of replacement security. A reduction in the performance security, authorized under this section, is not, and shall not be deemed to be, an acceptance by the local agency of the

New Text (Operative July 1, 2012)	Old Text

effective unless and until the local agency receives and approves that form of replacement security. A reduction in the performance security, authorized under this section, is not, and shall not be deemed to be, an acceptance by the local agency of the completed improvements, and the risk of loss or damage to the improvements and the obligation to maintain the improvements shall remain the sole responsibility of the subdivider until all required public improvements have been accepted by the local agency and all other required improvements have been fully completed in accordance with the plans and specifications for the improvements.

(e) The subdivider shall complete the works of improvement until all remaining items are accepted by the local agency.

(f) Upon the completion of the improvements, the subdivider, or his or her assigns, shall be notified in writing by the local agency within 45 days.

(g) Within 45 days of the issuance of the notification by the local agency, the release of any remaining performance security shall be placed upon the agenda of the legislative body of the local agency for approval of the release of any remaining performance security. If the local agency delegates authority for the release of performance security to a public official or other employee, any remaining performance security shall be released within 60 days of the issuance of the written statement of completion.

(h) Security securing the payment to the contractor, his or her subcontractors and to persons furnishing labor, materials or equipment shall, after passage of the time within which claims of lien are required to be recorded pursuant to Article 2 (commencing with Section 8410) of Chapter 4 of Title 2 of Part 6 of Division 4 of the Civil Code and after acceptance of the work, be reduced to an amount equal to the total claimed by all claimants for whom claims of lien have been recorded and notice thereof given in writing to the legislative body, and if no claims have been recorded, the security shall be released in full.

(i) The release shall not apply to any required guarantee and warranty period required by Section 66499.9 for the guarantee or warranty

completed improvements, and the risk of loss or damage to the improvements and the obligation to maintain the improvements shall remain the sole responsibility of the subdivider until all required public improvements have been accepted by the local agency and all other required improvements have been fully completed in accordance with the plans and specifications for the improvements.

(e) The subdivider shall complete the works of improvement until all remaining items are accepted by the local agency.

(f) Upon the completion of the improvements, the subdivider, or his or her assigns, shall be notified in writing by the local agency within 45 days.

(g) Within 45 days of the issuance of the notification by the local agency, the release of any remaining performance security shall be placed upon the agenda of the legislative body of the local agency for approval of the release of any remaining performance security. If the local agency delegates authority for the release of performance security to a public official or other employee, any remaining performance security shall be released within 60 days of the issuance of the written statement of completion.

(h) Security securing the payment to the contractor, his or her subcontractors and to persons furnishing labor, materials or equipment shall, after passage of the time within which claims of lien are required to be recorded pursuant to Article 3 (commencing with Section 3114) of Chapter 2 of Title 15 of Part 4 of Division 3 of the Civil Code and after acceptance of the work, be reduced to an amount equal to the total claimed by all claimants for whom claims of lien have been recorded and notice thereof given in writing to the legislative body, and if no claims have been recorded, the security shall be released in full.

(i) The release shall not apply to any required guarantee and warranty period required by Section 66499.9 for the guarantee or warranty nor to the amount of the security deemed necessary by the local agency for the guarantee and warranty period nor to costs and reasonable expenses and fees, including reasonable attorneys' fees.

(j) The legislative body may authorize any of its public officers or employees to authorize release or reduction of the security in accordance with

New Text (Operative July 1, 2012)

nor to the amount of the security deemed necessary by the local agency for the guarantee and warranty period nor to costs and reasonable expenses and fees, including reasonable attorneys' fees.

(j) The legislative body may authorize any of its public officers or employees to authorize release or reduction of the security in accordance with the conditions hereinabove set forth and in accordance with any rules that it may prescribe.

(k) This section shall remain in effect only until January 1, 2016, and as of that date is repealed, unless a later enacted statute, that is enacted before January 1, 2016, deletes or extends that date.

Old Text

the conditions hereinabove set forth and in accordance with any rules that it may prescribe.

(k) This section shall remain in effect only until January 1, 2016, and as of that date is repealed, unless a later enacted statute, that is enacted before January 1, 2016, deletes or extends that date.

NOTE: Amended by Senate Bill 190
(Approved by Governor June 29, 2011 and filed with Secretary of State July 1, 2011)
Revised to include reference to new Section 8000 et seq.

HEALTH AND SAFETY CODE SECTIONS ("H&S")

H&S 5463

Any health officer or governing board of any city, county, sanitary district, or other district having the power to operate and maintain a sewerage system, having served written notice upon the owner or reputed owner of land upon which there is a dwelling house, and the owner or reputed owner, after 30 days, having refused, neglected, or failed to connect the dwelling house, together with all toilets, sinks, and other plumbing therein, properly vented, and in a sanitary manner, with the adjoining street sewer, may construct the same at a reasonable cost, and the person doing that work at the request of the health officer or governing board has a lien upon that real estate for his or her work done and materials furnished, and the work done and materials furnished shall be held to have been done and furnished at the instance of the owner or reputed owner, or person claiming or having any interest therein. The governing board may pay all or any part of the cost or price of such connection to the person or persons who furnished labor, materials, or equipment for the same, and, to the extent the governing board pays the cost or price of the connection, it shall succeed to and have all the rights, including the lien provided for above, of the person or persons against the real estate and against the owner or reputed owner thereof.

As an alternative power to the enforcement of the lien provided for in this section, the governing body of the public agency performing the work of connection to the public sewer may, by order entered upon its minutes, declare that the amount of the costs of the work and the administrative expenses incurred by the governing body incident to the proceedings, together with other charges uniformly applicable within the jurisdiction of the governing body for the connection of the premises to the public sewer, shall be transmitted to the assessor and tax collector of the public agency, whereupon it shall be the duty of those officers to add the amount of the assessment to the next regular bill for taxes levied against the lot or parcel of land.

The liens provided for by this section shall be enforced in the same manner as those provided for by Part 6 (commencing with Section 8000) of Division 4, of the Civil Code.

The governing board may also use the procedures in Section 5474 for levying the costs incurred for the construction of the improvements for the connection of the premises to the public sewer.

H&S 5463

Any health officer or governing board of any city, county, sanitary district, or other district having the power to operate and maintain a sewerage system, having served written notice upon the owner or reputed owner of land upon which there is a dwelling house, and such owner or reputed owner, after 30 days, having refused, neglected, or failed to connect such dwelling house, together with all toilets, sinks, and other plumbing therein, properly vented, and in a sanitary manner, with the adjoining street sewer, may construct the same at a reasonable cost, and the person doing said work at the request of such health officer or governing board has a lien upon said real estate for his work done and materials furnished, and such work done and materials furnished shall be held to have been done and furnished at the instance of such owner or reputed owner, or person claiming or having any interest therein. Such governing board may pay all or any part of the cost or price of such connection to the person or persons who furnished labor, materials, or equipment for the same, and, to the extent such governing board pays the cost or price of said connection, it shall succeed to and have all the rights, including the lien provided for above, of such person or persons against the real estate and against the owner or reputed owner thereof.

As an alternative power to the enforcement of the lien provided for in this section, the governing body of the public agency performing the work of connection to the public sewer may, by order entered upon its minutes, declare that the amount of the costs of such work and the administrative expenses incurred by the governing body incident to the proceedings, together with other charges uniformly applicable within the jurisdiction of the governing body for the connection of the premises to the public sewer, shall be transmitted to the assessor and tax collector of the public agency, whereupon it shall be the duty of those officers to add the amount of the assessment to the next regular bill for taxes levied against the lot or parcel of land.

The liens provided for by this section shall be enforced in the same manner as those provided for by Title 15 (commencing with Section 3082), Part 4, Division 3, of the Civil Code.

The governing board may also use the procedures in Section 5474 for levying the costs incurred for the construction of the improvements for the connection of the premises to the public sewer.

Clarified and revised to include reference to new Section 8000 et seq.

New Text (Operative July 1, 2012) | **Old Text**

H&S 16017.5

(a) Notwithstanding any provision of law to the contrary, including, but not limited to, Part 6 (commencing with Section 8000) of Division 4 of the Civil Code, the Department of General Services may issue a stop work order when construction work on an essential services facility is not being performed in accordance with existing law and would compromise the structural integrity of the building, thereby endangering the public safety. The Department of General Services shall allow construction of incidental and minor nonstructural additions or nonstructural alterations without invoking its stop work authority.

(b) A public board, body, or officer whose construction work on an essential services facility is subject to a stop work order issued pursuant to subdivision (a) shall not be held liable in any action filed against the public board, body, or officer for stopping work as required by the stop work order, or for any delays caused by compliance with the stop work order, except to the extent that an error or omission by the public board, body, or officer is the basis for the issuance of the stop work order.

H&S 16017.5

(a) Notwithstanding any provision of law to the contrary, including, but not limited to, Title 15 (commencing with Section 3082) of Part 4 of the Civil Code, the Department of General Services may issue a stop work order when construction work on an essential services facility is not being performed in accordance with existing law and would compromise the structural integrity of the building, thereby endangering the public safety. The Department of General Services shall allow construction of incidental and minor nonstructural additions or nonstructural alterations without invoking its stop work authority.

(b) A public board, body, or officer whose construction work on an essential services facility is subject to a stop work order issued pursuant to subdivision (a) shall not be held liable in any action filed against the public board, body, or officer for stopping work as required by the stop work order, or for any delays caused by compliance with the stop work order, except to the extent that an error or omission by the public board, body, or officer is the basis for the issuance of the stop work order.

Revised to include reference to new Section 8000 et seq.

New Text (Operative July 1, 2012)

H&S 19825

(a) Every city, county, or city and county, whether general law or chartered, that requires the issuance of a permit as a condition precedent to the construction, alteration, improvement, demolition, or repair of any building or structure, shall require the execution of a permit application, in substantially the same form set forth under this subdivision, and require any individual who executes the Owner-Builder Declaration to present documentation sufficient to identify the property owner and, as necessary, verify the signature of the property owner. A city, county, or city and county may require additional information on the permit application.

PERMIT APPLICATION
BUILDING PROJECT IDENTIFICATION

Applicant's Mailing Address

____

____

____

Property Location or Address

____

____

Property Owner's Name

____

Property Owner's Telephone No.

____

Licensed Design Professional (Architect or Engineer) in charge of the project

____

Mailing Address of Licensed Design Professional

____

____

*License No.*____________________________

LICENSED CONTRACTOR'S DECLARATION

I hereby affirm under penalty of perjury that I am licensed under provisions of Chapter 9 (commencing with Section 7000) of Division 3 of the Business and Professions Code, and my license is in full force and effect.

Old Text

H&S 19825

(a) Every city, county, or city and county, whether general law or chartered, that requires the issuance of a permit as a condition precedent to the construction, alteration, improvement, demolition, or repair of any building or structure, shall require the execution of a permit application, in substantially the same form set forth under this subdivision, and require any individual who executes the Owner-Builder Declaration to present documentation sufficient to identify the property owner and, as necessary, verify the signature of the property owner. A city, county, or city and county may require additional information on the permit application.

PERMIT APPLICATION
BUILDING PROJECT IDENTIFICATION

Applicant's Mailing Address

____

____

____

Property Location or Address

____

____

Property Owner's Name

____

Property Owner's Telephone No.

____

Licensed Design Professional (Architect or Engineer) in charge of the project

____

Mailing Address of Licensed Design Professional

____

____

License No.____________________________

LICENSED CONTRACTOR'S DECLARATION

I hereby affirm under penalty of perjury that I am licensed under provisions of Chapter 9 (commencing with Section 7000) of Division 3 of the Business and Professions Code, and my license is in full force and effect.

New Text (Operative July 1, 2012)

License Class: ____________________
License No. ____________________
Date ____________________
Contractor Signature:

____

OWNER-BUILDER DECLARATION

I hereby affirm under penalty of perjury that I am exempt from the Contractors' State License Law for the reason(s) indicated below by the checkmark(s) I have placed next to the applicable item(s) (Section 7031.5, Business and Professions Code: Any city or county that requires a permit to construct, alter, improve, demolish, or repair any structure, prior to its issuance, also requires the applicant for the permit to file a signed statement that he or she is licensed pursuant to the provisions of the Contractors' State License Law (Chapter 9 (commencing with Section 7000) of Division 3 of the Business and Professions Code) or that he or she is exempt from licensure and the basis for the alleged exemption. Any violation of Section 7031.5 by any applicant for a permit subjects the applicant to a civil penalty of not more than five hundred dollars ($500).):

(_) I, as owner of the property, or my employees with wages as their sole compensation, will do (_) all of or (_) portions of the work, and the structure is not intended or offered for sale (Section 7044, Business and Professions Code: The Contractors' State License Law does not apply to an owner of property who, through employees' or personal effort, builds or improves the property, provided that the improvements are not intended or offered for sale. If, however, the building or improvement is sold within one year of completion, the Owner-Builder will have the burden of proving that it was not built or improved for the purpose of sale.).

(_) I, as owner of the property, am exclusively contracting with licensed Contractors to construct the project (Section 7044, Business and Professions Code: The Contractors' State License Law does not apply to an owner of property who builds or improves thereon, and who contracts for the projects with a licensed Contractor pursuant to the Contractors' State License Law.).

(_) I am exempt from licensure under the Contractors' State License Law for the following reason:

____
____
____

By my signature below I acknowledge that, except for my

Old Text

License Class ____________________
License No. ____________________
Date ____________________
Contractor Signature:

____

OWNER-BUILDER DECLARATION

I hereby affirm under penalty of perjury that I am exempt from the Contractors' State License Law for the reason(s) indicated below by the checkmark(s) I have placed next to the applicable item(s) (Section 7031.5, Business and Professions Code: Any city or county that requires a permit to construct, alter, improve, demolish, or repair any structure, prior to its issuance, also requires the applicant for the permit to file a signed statement that he or she is licensed pursuant to the provisions of the Contractors' State License Law (Chapter 9 (commencing with Section 7000) of Division 3 of the Business and Professions Code) or that he or she is exempt from licensure and the basis for the alleged exemption. Any violation of Section 7031.5 by any applicant for a permit subjects the applicant to a civil penalty of not more than five hundred dollars ($500).):

(__) I, as owner of the property, or my employees with wages as their sole compensation, will do (_) all of or (_) portions of the work, and the structure is not intended or offered for sale (Section 7044, Business and Professions Code: The Contractors' State License Law does not apply to an owner of property who, through employees' or personal effort, builds or improves the property, provided that the improvements are not intended or offered for sale. If, however, the building or improvement is sold within one year of completion, the Owner-Builder will have the burden of proving that it was not built or improved for the purpose of sale.).

(__) I, as owner of the property, am exclusively contracting with licensed Contractors to construct the project (Section 7044, Business and Professions Code: The Contractors' State License Law does not apply to an owner of property who builds or improves thereon, and who contracts for the projects with a licensed Contractor pursuant to the Contractors' State License Law.).

(__) I am exempt from licensure under the Contractors' State License Law for the following reason:

____
____
____

New Text (Operative July 1, 2012)

personal residence in which I must have resided for at least one year prior to completion of the improvements covered by this permit, I cannot legally sell a structure that I have built as an owner-builder if it has not been constructed in its entirety by licensed contractors. I understand that a copy of the applicable law, Section 7044 of the Business and Professions Code, is available upon request when this application is submitted or at the following Web site: http://www.leginfo.ca.gov/calaw.html.

Date ______________________________

Signature of Property Owner or Authorized Agent:
____

WORKERS' COMPENSATION DECLARATION

WARNING: FAILURE TO SECURE WORKERS' COMPENSATION COVERAGE IS UNLAWFUL, AND SHALL SUBJECT AN EMPLOYER TO CRIMINAL PENALTIES AND CIVIL FINES UP TO ONE HUNDRED THOUSAND DOLLARS ($100,000), IN ADDITION TO THE COST OF COMPENSATION, DAMAGES AS PROVIDED FOR IN SECTION 3706 OF THE LABOR CODE, INTEREST, AND ATTORNEY'S FEES.

I hereby affirm under penalty of perjury one of the following declarations:
____ I have and will maintain a certificate of consent to self-insure for workers' compensation, issued by the Director of Industrial Relations as provided for by Section 3700 of the Labor Code, for the performance of the work for which this permit is issued.
Policy No. __________________________

____ I have and will maintain workers' compensation insurance, as required by Section 3700 of the Labor Code, for the performance of the work for which this permit is issued. My workers' compensation insurance carrier and policy number are:

Carrier ____________________________
Policy Number ______________________
Expiration Date ______________________
Name of Agent ______________________
Phone # ______________________

____ I certify that, in the performance of the work for which this permit is issued, I shall not employ any person in any manner so as to become subject to the workers' compensation laws of California, and agree that, if I should

Old Text

By my signature below I acknowledge that, except for my personal residence in which I must have resided for at least one year prior to completion of the improvements covered by this permit, I cannot legally sell a structure that I have built as an owner-builder if it has not been constructed in its entirety by licensed contractors. I understand that a copy of the applicable law, Section 7044 of the Business and Professions Code, is available upon request when this application is submitted or at the following Web site: http://www.leginfo.ca.gov/calaw.html.

Date ______________________________

Signature of Property Owner or Authorized Agent:
____

WORKERS' COMPENSATION DECLARATION

WARNING: FAILURE TO SECURE WORKERS' COMPENSATION COVERAGE IS UNLAWFUL, AND SHALL SUBJECT AN EMPLOYER TO CRIMINAL PENALTIES AND CIVIL FINES UP TO ONE HUNDRED THOUSAND DOLLARS ($100,000), IN ADDITION TO THE COST OF COMPENSATION, DAMAGES AS PROVIDED FOR IN SECTION 3706 OF THE LABOR CODE, INTEREST, AND ATTORNEY'S FEES.

I hereby affirm under penalty of perjury one of the following declarations:
_____ I have and will maintain a certificate of consent to self-insure for workers' compensation, issued by the Director of Industrial Relations as provided for by Section 3700 of the Labor Code, for the performance of the work for which this permit is issued.
Policy No. __________________________

_____ I have and will maintain workers' compensation insurance, as required by Section 3700 of the Labor Code, for the performance of the work for which this permit is issued. My workers' compensation insurance carrier and policy number are:

Carrier ____________________________
Policy Number ______________________
Expiration Date ______________________
Name of Agent ______________________
Phone # ______________________

_____ I certify that, in the performance of the work for which this permit is issued, I shall not employ any person in any manner so as to become subject to the workers'

New Text (Operative July 1, 2012)

become subject to the workers' compensation provisions of Section 3700 of the Labor Code, I shall forthwith comply with those provisions.

____
Signature of Applicant

____
Date

DECLARATION REGARDING CONSTRUCTION LENDING AGENCY

I hereby affirm under penalty of perjury that there is a construction lending agency for the performance of the work for which this permit is issued (Section 8172, Civil Code).

Lender's Name ______________________________
Branch Designation ______________________________
Lender's Address ______________________________

By my signature below, I certify to each of the following:

- *I am the property owner or authorized to act on the property owner's behalf.*
- *I have read this application and the information I have provided is correct.*
- *I agree to comply with all applicable city and county ordinances and state laws relating to building construction.*
- *I authorize representatives of this city or county to enter the above-identified property for inspection purposes.*

Signature of Property Owner or Authorized Agent:

____
Date ______________________________

(b) When the Permit Application and the Owner-Builder Declaration have been executed by a person other than the property owner, prior to issuing the permit, the following shall be completed by the property owner and returned to the agency responsible for issuing the permit:

AUTHORIZATION OF AGENT TO ACT ON PROPERTY OWNER'S BEHALF

Excluding the Notice to Property Owner, the execution of which I understand is my personal responsibility, I hereby authorize the following person(s) to act as my agent(s) to apply for, sign, and file the documents necessary to obtain

Old Text

compensation laws of California, and agree that, if I should become subject to the workers' compensation provisions of Section 3700 of the Labor Code, I shall forthwith comply with those provisions.

____
Signature of Applicant

____
Date

DECLARATION REGARDING CONSTRUCTION LENDING AGENCY

I hereby affirm under penalty of perjury that there is a construction lending agency for the performance of the work for which this permit is issued (Section 3097, Civil Code).

Lender's Name

____
Lender's Address

____

By my signature below, I certify to each of the following:

- I am the property owner or authorized to act on the property owner's behalf.
- I have read this application and the information I have provided is correct.
- I agree to comply with all applicable city and county ordinances and state laws relating to building construction.
- I authorize representatives of this city or county to enter the above-identified property for inspection purposes.

Signature of Property Owner or Authorized Agent:

____
Date ______________________________

(b) When the Permit Application and the Owner-Builder Declaration have been executed by a person other than the property owner, prior to issuing the permit, the following shall be completed by the property owner and returned to the agency responsible for issuing the permit:

AUTHORIZATION OF AGENT TO ACT ON PROPERTY OWNER'S BEHALF

Excluding the Notice to Property Owner, the execution of which I understand is my personal responsibility, I hereby authorize the following person(s) to act as my agent(s) to apply for, sign, and file the documents necessary to obtain

New Text (Operative July 1, 2012)

an Owner-Builder Permit for my project.

Scope of Construction Project (or Description of Work):

____

Project Location or Address:

____

Name of Authorized Agent:

____

Address of Authorized Agent:

____

Phone Number of Authorized Agent:

____

I declare under penalty of perjury that I am the property owner for the address listed above and I personally filled out the above information and certify its accuracy.
Property Owner's Signature:

____

Date: ___________________________

Note: A copy of the owner's driver's license, form notarization, or other verification acceptable to the agency is required to be presented when the permit is issued to verify the property owner's signature.

(c) When the Owner-Builder Declaration required under subdivision (a) is executed, a Notice to Property Owner also shall be executed by the property owner in substantially the same form set forth under this section. The Notice to Property Owner shall appear on the official letterhead of the issuer and shall be provided to the applicant by one of the following methods chosen by the permitting authority: regular mail, electronic format, or given directly to the applicant at the time the application for the permit is made. Except as otherwise provided, the Notice to Property Owner pursuant to this section shall be completed and signed by the property owner and returned prior to issuance of the permit. An agent of the owner shall not execute this notice unless the property owner obtains the prior approval of the permitting authority. A permit shall not be issued unless the property owner complies with this section.

Old Text

an Owner-Builder Permit for my project.

Scope of Construction Project (or Description of Work):

____

Project Location or Address:

____

Name of Authorized Agent:

____

Address of Authorized Agent:

____

Phone Number of Authorized Agent:

____

I declare under penalty of perjury that I am the property owner for the address listed above and I personally filled out the above information and certify its accuracy.
Property Owner's Signature:

____

Date: ___________________________

Note: A copy of the owner's driver's license, form notarization, or other verification acceptable to the agency is required to be presented when the permit is issued to verify the property owner's signature.

(c) When the Owner-Builder Declaration required under subdivision (a) is executed, a Notice to Property Owner also shall be executed by the property owner in substantially the same form set forth under this section. The Notice to Property Owner shall appear on the official letterhead of the issuer and shall be provided to the applicant by one of the following methods chosen by the permitting authority: regular mail, electronic format, or given directly to the applicant at the time the application for the permit is made. Except as otherwise provided, the Notice to Property Owner pursuant to this section shall be completed and signed by the property owner and returned prior to issuance of the permit. An agent of the owner shall not execute this notice unless the property owner obtains the prior approval of the permitting authority. A permit shall not be issued unless the property owner complies with this section.

New Text (Operative July 1, 2012)

NOTICE TO PROPERTY OWNER

Dear Property Owner:

An application for a building permit has been submitted in your name listing yourself as the builder of the property improvements specified at ________________________________. We are providing you with an Owner-Builder Acknowledgment and Information Verification Form to make you aware of your responsibilities and possible risk you may incur by having this permit issued in your name as the Owner-Builder. We will not issue a building permit until you have read, initialed your understanding of each provision, signed, and returned this form to us at our official address indicated. An agent of the owner cannot execute this notice unless you, the property owner, obtain the prior approval of the permitting authority.

OWNER'S ACKNOWLEDGMENT AND VERIFICATION OF INFORMATION

***DIRECTIONS**: Read and initial each statement below to signify you understand or verify this information.*

____1. I understand a frequent practice of unlicensed persons is to have the property owner obtain an "Owner-Builder" building permit that erroneously implies that the property owner is providing his or her own labor and material personally. I, as an Owner-Builder, may be held liable and subject to serious financial risk for any injuries sustained by an unlicensed person and his or her employees while working on my property. My homeowner's insurance may not provide coverage for those injuries. I am willfully acting as an Owner-Builder and am aware of the limits of my insurance coverage for injuries to workers on my property.

____2. I understand building permits are not required to be signed by property owners unless they are responsible for the construction and are not hiring a licensed Contractor to assume this responsibility.

____3. I understand as an "Owner-Builder" I am the responsible party of record on the permit. I understand that I may protect myself from potential financial risk by hiring a licensed Contractor and having the permit filed in his or her name instead of my own.

____4. I understand Contractors are required by law to be licensed and bonded in California and to list their license numbers on permits and contracts.

____5. I understand if I employ or otherwise engage any persons, other than California licensed Contractors, and the total value of my construction is at least five hundred dollars ($500), including labor and materials, I may be

Old Text

NOTICE TO PROPERTY OWNER

Dear Property Owner:

An application for a building permit has been submitted in your name listing yourself as the builder of the property improvements specified at ________________________________. We are providing you with an Owner-Builder Acknowledgment and Information Verification Form to make you aware of your responsibilities and possible risk you may incur by having this permit issued in your name as the Owner-Builder. We will not issue a building permit until you have read, initialed your understanding of each provision, signed, and returned this form to us at our official address indicated. An agent of the owner cannot execute this notice unless you, the property owner, obtain the prior approval of the permitting authority.

OWNER'S ACKNOWLEDGMENT AND VERIFICATION OF INFORMATION

DIRECTIONS: Read and initial each statement below to signify you understand or verify this information.

_____1. I understand a frequent practice of unlicensed persons is to have the property owner obtain an "Owner-Builder" building permit that erroneously implies that the property owner is providing his or her own labor and material personally. I, as an Owner-Builder, may be held liable and subject to serious financial risk for any injuries sustained by an unlicensed person and his or her employees while working on my property. My homeowner's insurance may not provide coverage for those injuries. I am willfully acting as an Owner-Builder and am aware of the limits of my insurance coverage for injuries to workers on my property.

_____2. I understand building permits are not required to be signed by property owners unless they are responsible for the construction and are not hiring a licensed Contractor to assume this responsibility.

_____3. I understand as an "Owner-Builder" I am the responsible party of record on the permit. I understand that I may protect myself from potential financial risk by hiring a licensed Contractor and having the permit filed in his or her name instead of my own.

_____4. I understand Contractors are required by law to be licensed and bonded in California and to list their license numbers on permits and contracts.

_____5. I understand if I employ or otherwise engage any persons, other than California licensed Contractors, and the total value of my construction is at least five hundred dollars ($500), including labor and materials, I may be considered

New Text (Operative July 1, 2012)

considered an "employer" under state and federal law.

____6. I understand if I am considered an "employer" under state and federal law, I must register with the state and federal government, withhold payroll taxes, provide workers' compensation disability insurance, and contribute to unemployment compensation for each "employee." I also understand my failure to abide by these laws may subject me to serious financial risk.

____7. I understand under California Contractors' State License Law, an Owner- Builder who builds single-family residential structures cannot legally build them with the intent to offer them for sale, unless all work is performed by licensed subcontractors and the number of structures does not exceed four within any calendar year, or all of the work is performed under contract with a licensed general building Contractor.

____8. I understand as an Owner-Builder if I sell the property for which this permit is issued, I may be held liable for any financial or personal injuries sustained by any subsequent owner(s) that result from any latent construction defects in the workmanship or materials.

____9. I understand I may obtain more information regarding my obligations as an "employer" from the Internal Revenue Service, the United States Small Business Administration, the California Department of Benefit Payments, and the California Division of Industrial Accidents. I also understand I may contact the California Contractors' State License Board (CSLB) at 1-800-321-CSLB (2752) or www.cslb.ca.gov for more information about licensed contractors.

____10. I am aware of and consent to an Owner-Builder building permit applied for in my name, and understand that I am the party legally and financially responsible for proposed construction activity at the following address:

____

____

____11. I agree that, as the party legally and financially responsible for this proposed construction activity, I will abide by all applicable laws and requirements that govern Owner-Builders as well as employers.

____ 12. I agree to notify the issuer of this form immediately of any additions, deletions, or changes to any of the information I have provided on this form.

Licensed contractors are regulated by laws designed to protect the public. If you contract with someone who does not have a license, the Contractors' State License Board may be unable to assist you with any financial loss you may sustain as a result of a complaint. Your only remedy against unlicensed Contractors may be in civil court. It is also important for you to understand that if an unlicensed Contractor or employee of that individual or firm is injured

Old Text

an "employer" under state and federal law.

_____6. I understand if I am considered an "employer" under state and federal law, I must register with the state and federal government, withhold payroll taxes, provide workers' compensation disability insurance, and contribute to unemployment compensation for each "employee." I also understand my failure to abide by these laws may subject me to serious financial risk.

_____7. I understand under California Contractors' State License Law, an Owner-Builder who builds single-family residential structures cannot legally build them with the intent to offer them for sale, unless all work is performed by licensed subcontractors and the number of structures does not exceed four within any calendar year, or all of the work is performed under contract with a licensed general building Contractor.

_____8. I understand as an Owner-Builder if I sell the property for which this permit is issued, I may be held liable for any financial or personal injuries sustained by any subsequent owner(s) that result from any latent construction defects in the workmanship or materials.

_____9. I understand I may obtain more information regarding my obligations as an "employer" from the Internal Revenue Service, the United States Small Business Administration, the California Department of Benefit Payments, and the California Division of Industrial Accidents. I also understand I may contact the California Contractors' State License Board (CSLB) at 1-800-321-CSLB (2752) or www.cslb.ca.gov for more information about licensed contractors.

_____ 10. I am aware of and consent to an Owner-Builder building permit applied for in my name, and understand that I am the party legally and financially responsible for proposed construction activity at the following address:

____

____

_____11. I agree that, as the party legally and financially responsible for this proposed construction activity, I will abide by all applicable laws and requirements that govern Owner-Builders as well as employers.

_____12. I agree to notify the issuer of this form immediately of any additions, deletions, or changes to any of the information I have provided on this form.

Licensed contractors are regulated by laws designed to protect the public. If you contract with someone who does not have a license, the Contractors' State License Board may be unable to assist you with any financial loss you may sustain as a result of a complaint. Your only remedy against unlicensed Contractors may be in civil court. It is also important for you to understand that if an unlicensed Contractor or employee of that individual or firm is injured

New Text (Operative July 1, 2012)

while working on your property, you may be held liable for damages. If you obtain a permit as Owner- Builder and wish to hire Contractors, you will be responsible for verifying whether or not those Contractors are properly licensed and the status of their workers' compensation insurance coverage.
Before a building permit can be issued, this form must be completed and signed by the property owner and returned to the agency responsible for issuing the permit.

Note: A copy of the property owner's driver's license, form notarization, or other verification acceptable to the agency is required to be presented when the permit is issued to verify the property owner's signature.

Signature of Property Owner:

____

Date: ______________________________

Old Text

while working on your property, you may be held liable for damages. If you obtain a permit as Owner-Builder and wish to hire Contractors, you will be responsible for verifying whether or not those Contractors are properly licensed and the status of their workers' compensation insurance coverage.
Before a building permit can be issued, this form must be completed and signed by the property owner and returned to the agency responsible for issuing the permit.

Note: A copy of the property owner's driver's license, form notarization, or other verification acceptable to the agency is required to be presented when the permit is issued to verify the property owner's signature.

Signature of Property Owner:

____

Date: ______________________________

Revised to include reference to new Section 8000 et seq.

••

New Text (Operative July 1, 2012)

H&S 34218

Chapter 5 (commencing with Section 9550) of Title 3 of Part 6 of Division 4 of the Civil Code applies to any housing project constructed under this chapter. Notwithstanding the provisions of this section, a housing authority may require a 20 percent cash escrow or a 25 percent irrevocable letter of credit or the payment bond required by this section if the contract is for work undertaken pursuant to the Comprehensive Improvement Assistance Program established by Section 14 of the United States Housing Act of 1937, as amended (42 U.S.C.A. Secs. 1437d and 1437l), or the Public Housing Modernization Act established by Section 5(c)(3)(C) of the United States Housing Act of 1937, as amended (42 U.S.C.A. Secs. 1437d and 1437l).

Old Text

H&S 34218

Chapter 7 (commencing with Section 3247) of Title 15 of Part 4 of Division 3 of the Civil Code applies to any housing project constructed under this chapter. Notwithstanding the provisions of this section, a housing authority may require a 20 percent cash escrow or a 25 percent irrevocable letter of credit or the payment bond required by this section if the contract is for work undertaken pursuant to the Comprehensive Improvement Assistance Program established by Section 14 of the United States Housing Act of 1937, as amended (42 U.S.C.A. Secs. 1437d and 1437l), or the Public Housing Modernization Act established by Section 5(c)(3)(C) of the United States Housing Act of 1937, as amended (42 U.S.C.A. Secs. 1437d and 1437 l).

Revised to include reference to new Section 9000 et seq.

••

New Text (Operative July 1, 2012) | **Old Text**

INSURANCE CODE SECTIONS ("INS")

INS 11751.82

(a) An insurer under a wrap-up insurance policy shall report workers' compensation losses and payroll information for each contractor and subcontractor to its rating organization on a timely basis and in accordance with the uniform statistical plan. Within 10 days, upon request, the insurer shall provide to each contractor and subcontractor copies of the report covering workers' compensation losses and payroll information for that contractor or subcontractor.

(b) For the purposes of this section, a "wrap-up insurance policy" is an insurance policy, or series of policies, written to cover risks associated with a work of improvement, as defined in Section 8050 of the Civil Code, and covering two or more of the contractors or subcontractors that work on that work of improvement.

INS 11751.82

(a) An insurer under a wrap-up insurance policy shall report workers' compensation losses and payroll information for each contractor and subcontractor to its rating organization on a timely basis and in accordance with the uniform statistical plan. Within 10 days, upon request, the insurer shall provide to each contractor and subcontractor copies of the report covering workers' compensation losses and payroll information for that contractor or subcontractor.

(b) For the purposes of this section, a "wrap-up insurance policy" is an insurance policy, or series of policies, written to cover risks associated with a work of improvement, as defined in Section 3106 of the Civil Code, and covering two or more of the contractors or subcontractors that work on that work of improvement.

Revised to include reference to new Section 8000 et seq.

New Text (Operative July 1, 2012) **Old Text**

LABOR CODE SECTION ("LABOR")

LABOR 218.5

In any action brought for the nonpayment of wages, fringe benefits, or health and welfare or pension fund contributions, the court shall award reasonable attorney's fees and costs to the prevailing party if any party to the action requests attorney's fees and costs upon the initiation of the action. This section shall not apply to an action brought by the Labor Commissioner. This section shall not apply to a surety issuing a bond pursuant to Chapter 9 (commencing with Section 7000) of Division 3 of the Business and Professions Code or to an action to enforce a mechanics lien brought under Chapter 4 (commencing with Section 8400) of Title 2 of Part 6 of Division 2 of the Civil Code. This section does not apply to any action for which attorney's fees are recoverable under Section 1194.

LABOR 218.5

In any action brought for the nonpayment of wages, fringe benefits, or health and welfare or pension fund contributions, the court shall award reasonable attorney's fees and costs to the prevailing party if any party to the action requests attorney's fees and costs upon the initiation of the action. This section shall not apply to an action brought by the Labor Commissioner. This section shall not apply to a surety issuing a bond pursuant to Chapter 9 (commencing with Section 7000) of Division 3 of the Business and Professions Code or to an action to enforce a mechanics lien brought under Chapter 2 (commencing with Section 3109) of Title 15 of Part 4 of Division 3 of the Civil Code. This section does not apply to any action for which attorney's fees are recoverable under Section 1194.

Revised to include reference to new Section 8000 et seq.

New Text (Operative July 1, 2012) | **Old Text**

PUBLIC CONTRACT CODE SECTION ("PCC")

PCC 4107.7

If a contractor who enters into a contract with a public entity for investigation, removal or remedial action, or disposal relative to the release or presence of a hazardous material or hazardous waste fails to pay a subcontractor registered as a hazardous waste hauler pursuant to Section 25163 of the Health and Safety Code within 10 days after the investigation, removal or remedial action, or disposal is completed, the subcontractor may serve a stop notice upon the public entity in accordance with Chapter 4 (commencing with Section 9350) of Title 3 of Part 6 of Division 4 of the Civil Code.

PCC 4107.7

If a contractor who enters into a contract with a public entity for investigation, removal or remedial action, or disposal relative to the release or presence of a hazardous material or hazardous waste fails to pay a subcontractor registered as a hazardous waste hauler pursuant to Section 25163 of the Health and Safety Code within 10 days after the investigation, removal or remedial action, or disposal is completed, the subcontractor may serve a stop notice upon the public entity in accordance with Chapter 4 (commencing with Section 3179) of Title 15 of Part 4 of Division 3 of the Civil Code.

Revised to include reference to new Section 9000 et seq.

PCC 7103

(a) (1) Every original contractor that is awarded a contract by a state entity, as defined in subdivision (d), involving an expenditure in excess of twenty-five thousand dollars ($25,000) for any public work shall, before entering upon the performance of the work, file a payment bond with and approved by the officer or state entity that awarded the contract. The bond shall be in a sum not less than 100 percent of the total amount payable by the terms of the contract.

(2) The state entity shall state in its call for bids for any contract that a payment bond is required in the case of such an expenditure.

(b) A payment bond filed and approved in accordance with this section shall be sufficient to enter upon the performance of work under a duly authorized contract that supplements the contract for which the payment bond was filed if the requirement of a new bond is waived by the state entity.

(c) For purposes of this section, providers of architectural, engineering, and land surveying services pursuant to a contract with a state entity for a public work shall not be deemed an original contractor and shall not be required to post or file the payment bond required in subdivisions (a) and (b).

(d) For purposes of this section, "state entity" means every state office, department, division, bureau,

PCC 7103

(a)(1) Every original contractor to who is awarded a contract by a state entity, as defined in subdivision (d), involving an expenditure in excess of twenty-five thousand dollars ($25,000) for any public work shall, before entering upon the performance of the work, file a payment bond with and approved by the officer or state entity by who the contract was awarded. The bond shall be in a sum not less than 100 percent of the total amount payable by the terms of the contract.

(2) The state entity shall state in its call for bids for any contract that a payment bond is required in the case of such an expenditure.

(b) A payment bond filed and approved in accordance with this section shall be sufficient to enter upon the performance of work under a duly authorized contract that supplements the contract for which the payment bond was filed if the requirement of a new bond is waived by the state entity.

(c) For purposes of this section, providers of architectural, engineering, and land surveying services pursuant to a contract with a state entity for a public work shall not be deemed an original contractor and shall not be required to post or file the payment bond required in subdivisions (a) and (b).

(d) For purposes of this section, "state entity" means every state office, department, division, bureau, board, or commission, but does not include the Legislature, the courts, any agency in the judicial branch of

New Text (Operative July 1, 2012)

board, or commission, but does not include the Legislature, the courts, any agency in the judicial branch of government, or the University of California. All other public entities shall be governed by Section 9550 of the Civil Code.

(e) For purposes of this section, "public work" includes the erection, construction, alteration, repair, or improvement of any state structure, building, road, or other state improvement of any kind.

Old Text

government, or the University of California. All other public entities shall be governed by Section 3247 of the Civil Code.

(e) For purposes of this section, "public work" includes the erection, construction, alteration, repair, or improvement of any state structure, building, road, or other state improvement of any kind.

Clarified and revised to include reference to new Section 9000 et seq.

PCC 7201

(a) (1) This section shall apply with respect to all contracts entered into on or after January 1, 2012, between a public entity and an original contractor, between an original contractor and a subcontractor, and between all subcontractors thereunder, relating to the construction of any public work of improvement.

(2) Under no circumstances shall any provision of this section be construed to limit the ability of any public entity to withhold 150 percent of the value of any disputed amount of work from the final payment, as provided for in subdivision (c) of Section 7107. In the event of a good faith dispute, nothing in this section shall be construed to require a public entity to pay for work that is not approved or accepted in accordance with the proper plans or specifications.

(3) For purposes of this section, "public entity" means the state, including every state agency, office, department, division, bureau, board, or commission, the California State University, the University of California, a city, county, city and county, including charter cities and charter counties, district, special district, public authority, political subdivision, public corporation, or nonprofit transit corporation wholly owned by a public agency and formed to carry out the purposes of the public agency.

(b) (1) The retention proceeds withheld from any payment by a public entity from the original contractor, by the original contractor from any subcontractor, and by a subcontractor from any subcontractor thereunder shall not exceed 5 percent of the payment. In no event shall the total retention proceeds withheld exceed 5 percent of the contract

No previous text

New Text (Operative July 1, 2012) **Old Text**

price. In a contract between the original contractor and a subcontractor, and in a contract between a subcontractor and any subcontractor thereunder, the percentage of the retention proceeds withheld shall not exceed the percentage specified in the contract between the public entity and the original contractor.

(2) This subdivision shall not apply if the contractor provides written notice to the subcontractor, pursuant to subdivision (c) of Section 4108, prior to, or at, the time that the bid is requested, that bonds shall be required, and the subcontractor subsequently is unable or refuses to furnish to the contractor a performance and payment bond issued by an admitted surety insurer.

(3) Notwithstanding any other provision of this subdivision, the retention proceeds withheld from any payment by an awarding entity set forth in paragraphs (1) to (5), inclusive, of subdivision (a) of Section 10106, from the original contractor, by the original contractor from any subcontractor, and by a subcontractor from any subcontractor thereunder, may exceed 5 percent on specific projects where the director of the department has made a finding prior to the bid that the project is substantially complex and therefore requires a higher retention amount than 5 percent and the department includes both this finding and the actual retention amount in the bid documents. In a contract between the original contractor and a subcontractor, and in a contract between a subcontractor and any subcontractor thereunder, the percentage of the retention proceeds withheld shall not exceed the percentage specified in the contract between the department and the original contractor.

(4) Notwithstanding any other provision of this subdivision, the retention proceeds withheld from any payment by the awarding entity of a city, county, city and county, including charter cities and charter counties, district, special district, public authority, political subdivision, public corporation, or nonprofit transit corporation wholly owned by a public agency and formed to carry out the purposes of the public agency, from the original contractor, by the original contractor from any subcontractor, and by a subcontractor from any subcontractor thereunder, may exceed 5 percent on specific projects where the governing body of the public entity or designee, including, but not limited to, a general manager or other director of an appropriate department, has

New Text (Operative July 1, 2012) | **Old Text**

approved a finding during a properly noticed and normally scheduled public hearing and prior to bid that the project is substantially complex and therefore requires a higher retention amount than 5 percent and the awarding entity includes both this finding and the actual retention amount in the bid documents. In a contract between the original contractor and a subcontractor, and in a contract between a subcontractor and any subcontractor thereunder, the percentage of the retention proceeds withheld shall not exceed the percentage specified in the contract between the department and the original contractor.

(c) A party identified in subdivision (a) shall not require any other party to waive any provision of this section.

(d) This section shall remain in effect only until January 1, 2016, and as of that date is repealed, unless a later enacted statute, that is enacted before January 1, 2016, deletes or extends that date.

NOTE: Added through Senate Bill 293 (Approved by Governor on October 9, 2011)

PCC 10222

(a) Each bond shall equal at least one-half of the contract price, except as otherwise provided in Section 9554 of the Civil Code, in the California Toll Bridge Authority Act (Chapter 1 (commencing with Section 30000) of Division 7 of the Streets and Highways Code), or in subdivision (b).

(b) Notwithstanding subdivision (a), for projects with a contract price greater than two hundred fifty million dollars ($250,000,000), the Department of Transportation shall have the discretion to specify that the payment bond shall equal not less than one-half of the contract price or five hundred million dollars ($500,000,000), whichever is less.

PCC 10222

(a) Each bond shall equal at least one-half of the contract price, except as otherwise provided in Section 3248 of the Civil Code, in the California Toll Bridge Authority Act (Chapter 1 (commencing with Section 30000) of Division 7 of the Streets and Highways Code), or in subdivision (b).

(b) Notwithstanding subdivision (a), for projects with a contract price greater than two hundred fifty million dollars ($250,000,000), the Department of Transportation shall have the discretion to specify that the payment bond shall equal not less than one-half of the contract price or five hundred million dollars ($500,000,000), whichever is less.

Revised to include reference to new Section 9000 et seq.

PCC 10822

Each bond shall be in a sum equal to at least one-half of the contract price, except as otherwise provided in Section 9554 of the Civil Code.

PCC 10822

Each bond shall be in a sum equal to at least one-half of the contract price, except as otherwise provided in Section 3248 of the Civil Code.

Revised to include reference to new Section 9000 et seq.

New Text (Operative July 1, 2012)

PCC 20104

(a) (1) This article applies to all public works claims of three hundred seventy-five thousand dollars ($375,000) or less which arise between a contractor and a local agency.

(2) This article shall not apply to any claims resulting from a contract between a contractor and a public agency when the public agency has elected to resolve any disputes pursuant to Article 7.1 (commencing with Section 10240) of Chapter 1 of Part 2.

(b) (1) "Public work" means "public works contract" as defined in Section 1101 but does not include any work or improvement contracted for by the state or the Regents of the University of California.

(2) "Claim" means a separate demand by the contractor for (A) a time extension, (B) payment of money or damages arising from work done by, or on behalf of, the contractor pursuant to the contract for a public work and payment of which is not otherwise expressly provided for or the claimant is not otherwise entitled to, or (C) an amount the payment of which is disputed by the local agency.

(c) The provisions of this article or a summary thereof shall be set forth in the plans or specifications for any work which may give rise to a claim under this article.

(d) This article applies only to contracts entered into on or after January 1, 1991.

Old Text

PCC 20104

(a) (1) This article applies to all public works claims of three hundred seventy-five thousand dollars ($375,000) or less which arise between a contractor and a local agency.

(2) This article shall not apply to any claims resulting from a contract between a contractor and a public agency when the public agency has elected to resolve any disputes pursuant to Article 7.1 (commencing with Section 10240) of Chapter 1 of Part 2.

(b) (1) "Public work" has the same meaning as in Sections 3100 and 3106 of the Civil Code, except that "public work" does not include any work or improvement contracted for by the state or the Regents of the University of California.

(2) "Claim" means a separate demand by the contractor for (A) a time extension, (B) payment of money or damages arising from work done by, or on behalf of, the contractor pursuant to the contract for a public work and payment of which is not otherwise expressly provided for or the claimant is not otherwise entitled to, or (C) an amount the payment of which is disputed by the local agency.

(c) The provisions of this article or a summary thereof shall be set forth in the plans or specifications for any work which may give rise to a claim under this article.

(d) This article applies only to contracts entered into on or after January 1, 1991.

Revised to include new terminology and reference to new Section 9000 et seq.

••

PCC 20134

(a) In cases of emergency, when repair or replacements are necessary to permit the continued conduct of county operations or services, the board of supervisors, by majority consent, may proceed at once to replace or repair any and all structures without adopting the plans, specifications, strain sheets, or working details or, subject to Chapter 2.5 (commencing with Section 22050), giving notice for bids to let contracts. If notice for bids to let contracts will not be given, the board shall comply with Chapter 2.5 (commencing with Section 22050). The work may

PCC 20134

(a) In cases of emergency, when repair or replacements are necessary to permit the continued conduct of county operations or services, the board of supervisors, by majority consent, may proceed at once to replace or repair any and all structures without adopting the plans, specifications, strain sheets, or working details or, subject to Chapter 2.5 (commencing with Section 22050), giving notice for bids to let contracts. If notice for bids to let contracts will not be given, the board shall comply with Chapter 2.5 (commencing with Section 22050). The work may be done by day labor under the direction of the board, *be done by day labor under the direction of the board, by contract, or by a combination of the two. If the work is done wholly or in part by contract, the contractor shall be paid the actual cost of the use of machinery and tools and of material, and labor and of workers' compensation insurance expended by him or her in doing the work, plus not more than 15 percent to cover all profits and administration. No more than the lowest current market prices shall be paid for materials whenever possible.*

(b) In a county of the first, second, third, or fourth class, which is under court order to relieve jail overcrowding or in which the sheriff certifies that the inmate capacity of the county jail system is exceeded by more than 20 percent and that the overpopulation is likely to continue and poses a threat to public safety, health, and welfare, the board of supervisors may contract for the construction or expansion of jail facilities without the formality of obtaining bids, adopting plans and specifications, or complying with other requirements of this article, except as required by this subdivision. The person to whom the contract is awarded shall execute a bond for faithful performance in accordance with Section 20129. Any plans and specifications adopted by the board may only be altered or changed in accordance with Section 20135 and all contracts awarded pursuant to this subdivision may only be altered or changed in accordance with Sections 20136, 20137, and 20138. The award of the contract shall be made after a public hearing on the basis of a request for proposals advertised in accordance with Section 6062 or 6062a of the Government Code. The contract may be awarded only to a contractor who has responded to the request for proposals and who is licensed to do the work in accordance with Chapter 9 (commencing with Section 7000) of Division 3 of the Business and Professions Code. The contract shall be upon terms which the board determines are necessary for the expeditious completion of the work. A contract shall not be entered into unless at least three proposals to do the work have been evaluated by a competitive process established by the board. If the board does not select the lowest bid, it shall make a finding stating the reasons that the lowest bid was not selected.

(c) In any county that has agreed to permit the transfer of prisoners or parole violators under Section 2910 or 2910.5 of the Penal Code or of wards under Section 1753.3 of the Welfare and Institutions Code, the board

by contract, or by a combination of the two. If the work is done wholly or in part by contract, the contractor shall be paid the actual cost of the use of machinery and tools and of material, and labor and of workers' compensation insurance expended by him or her in doing the work, plus not more than 15 percent to cover all profits and administration. No more than the lowest current market prices shall be paid for materials whenever possible.

(b) In a county of the first, second, third, or fourth class, which is under court order to relieve jail overcrowding or in which the sheriff certifies that the inmate capacity of the county jail system is exceeded by more than 20 percent and that the overpopulation is likely to continue and poses a threat to public safety, health, and welfare, the board of supervisors may contract for the construction or expansion of jail facilities without the formality of obtaining bids, adopting plans and specifications, or complying with other requirements of this article, except as required by this subdivision. The person to whom the contract is awarded shall execute a bond for faithful performance in accordance with Section 20129. Any plans and specifications adopted by the board may only be altered or changed in accordance with Section 20135 and all contracts awarded pursuant to this subdivision may only be altered or changed in accordance with Sections 20136, 20137, and 20138. The award of the contract shall be made after a public hearing on the basis of a request for proposals advertised in accordance with Section 6062 or 6062a of the Government Code. The contract may be awarded only to a contractor who has responded to the request for proposals and who is licensed to do the work in accordance with Chapter 9 (commencing with Section 7000) of Division 3 of the Business and Professions Code. The contract shall be upon terms which the board determines are necessary for the expeditious completion of the work. A contract shall not be entered into unless at least three proposals to do the work have been evaluated by a competitive process established by the board. If the board does not select the lowest bid, it shall make a finding stating the reasons that the lowest bid was not selected.

(c) In any county that has agreed to permit the transfer of prisoners or parole violators under Section 2910 or 2910.5 of the Penal Code or of wards under Section 1753.3 of the Welfare and Institutions Code, the board of supervisors may contract for the construction or expansion of the facilities to be used for that purpose without the formality of obtaining bids, adopting plans and specifications, or

New Text (Operative July 1, 2012)

of supervisors may contract for the construction or expansion of the facilities to be used for that purpose without the formality of obtaining bids, adopting plans and specifications, or complying with other requirements of this article, except as required by this subdivision. The person to whom the contract is awarded shall execute a bond for faithful performance in accordance with Section 20129. Any plans and specifications adopted by the board may only be altered or changed in accordance with Section 20135 and all contracts awarded pursuant to this subdivision may only be altered or changed in accordance with Sections 20136, 20137, and 20138. The award of the contract shall be made after a public hearing on the basis of a request for proposals advertised in accordance with Section 6062 or 6062a of the Government Code.

The contract may be awarded only to a contractor who has responded to the request for proposals and who is licensed to do the work in accordance with Chapter 9 (commencing with Section 7000) of Division 3 of the Business and Professions Code. The contract shall be upon terms which the board determines are necessary for the expeditious completion of the work. A contract shall not be entered into unless at least three proposals to do the work have been evaluated by a competitive process established by the board and the lowest bid is selected.

(d) Proposed construction or expansion of jail or return-to-custody facilities as authorized under subdivision (b) or (c) shall not commence in a county of the third class without the affirmative vote of a majority of the city council of the incorporated city within which the construction or expansion is proposed.

(e) The board of supervisors may waive the requirements of Title 3 (commencing with Section 9000) of Part 6 of Division 4 of the Civil Code for work performed pursuant to subdivision (b) or (c).

(f) If any county that is under court order to relieve overcrowding in a county juvenile facility, as defined by subdivision (c) of Section 4481 of the Penal Code or in which the chief probation officer certifies that the juvenile detention capacity of the county juvenile facilities is exceeded by more than 20 percent and that the overpopulation is likely to continue and poses a threat to public safety, health, and welfare, the board of supervisors may contract for the construction or

Old Text

complying with other requirements of this article, except as required by this subdivision. The person to whom the contract is awarded shall execute a bond for faithful performance in accordance with Section 20129. Any plans and specifications adopted by the board may only be altered or changed in accordance with Section 20135 and all contracts awarded pursuant to this subdivision may only be altered or changed in accordance with Sections 20136, 20137, and 20138. The award of the contract shall be made after a public hearing on the basis of a request for proposals advertised in accordance with Section 6062 or 6062a of the Government Code.

The contract may be awarded only to a contractor who has responded to the request for proposals and who is licensed to do the work in accordance with Chapter 9 (commencing with Section 7000) of Division 3 of the Business and Professions Code. The contract shall be upon terms which the board determines are necessary for the expeditious completion of the work. A contract shall not be entered into unless at least three proposals to do the work have been evaluated by a competitive process established by the board and the lowest bid is selected.

(d) Proposed construction or expansion of jail or return-to-custody facilities as authorized under subdivision (b) or (c) shall not commence in a county of the third class without the affirmative vote of a majority of the city council of the incorporated city within which the construction or expansion is proposed.

(e) The board of supervisors may waive the requirements of Title 15 (commencing with Section 3082) of Part 4 of Division 3 of the Civil Code for work performed pursuant to subdivision (b) or (c).

(f) If any county that is under court order to relieve overcrowding in a county juvenile facility, as defined by subdivision (c) of Section 4481 of the Penal Code or in which the chief probation officer certifies that the juvenile detention capacity of the county juvenile facilities is exceeded by more than 20 percent and that the overpopulation is likely to continue and poses a threat to public safety, health, and welfare, the board of supervisors may contract for the construction or expansion of county juvenile facilities without the formality of obtaining bids, adopting plans and specifications, or complying with other requirements of this article, except as required by this subdivision. The person to whom the contract is awarded shall execute a bond for faithful performance in accordance with Section 20129. Any plans and

New Text (Operative July 1, 2012)

expansion of county juvenile facilities without the formality of obtaining bids, adopting plans and specifications, or complying with other requirements of this article, except as required by this subdivision. The person to whom the contract is awarded shall execute a bond for faithful performance in accordance with Section 20129. Any plans and specifications adopted by the board may only be altered or changed in accordance with Section 20135 and all contracts awarded pursuant to this subdivision may only be altered or changed in accordance with Sections 20136, 20137, and 20138. The award of the contract shall be made after a public hearing on the basis of a request for proposals advertised in accordance with Section 6062 or 6062a of the Government Code. The contract may be awarded only to a contractor who has responded to the request for proposals and who is licensed to do the work in accordance with Chapter 9 (commencing with Section 7000) of Division 3 of the Business and Professions Code. The contract shall be upon terms which the board determines are necessary for the expeditious completion of the work. A contract shall not be entered into unless at least three proposals to do the work have been evaluated by a competitive process established by the board. If the board does not select the lowest bidder, it shall make a finding stating the reasons that the lowest bidder was not selected.

(g) In a county of the third class in which there are no available courtrooms to accommodate all authorized judicial positions or in which the board of supervisors certifies that there is a significant need to expeditiously construct new court and court support facilities, the board of supervisors may contract for the construction or expansion of court and court support facilities without the formality of obtaining bids, adopting plans and specifications, or complying with other requirements of this article, except as required by this subdivision. The person to whom the contract is awarded shall execute a bond for faithful performance in accordance with Section 20129. Any plans and specifications adopted by the board may only be altered or changed in accordance with Section 20135 and all contracts awarded pursuant to this subdivision may only be altered or changed in accordance with Sections 20136, 20137, and 20138.

The award of the contract shall be made after a public hearing on the basis of a request for proposals

Old Text

specifications adopted by the board may only be altered or changed in accordance with Section 20135 and all contracts awarded pursuant to this subdivision may only be altered or changed in accordance with Sections 20136, 20137, and 20138. The award of the contract shall be made after a public hearing on the basis of a request for proposals advertised in accordance with Section 6062 or 6062a of the Government Code. The contract may be awarded only to a contractor who has responded to the request for proposals and who is licensed to do the work in accordance with Chapter 9 (commencing with Section 7000) of Division 3 of the Business and Professions Code. The contract shall be upon terms which the board determines are necessary for the expeditious completion of the work. A contract shall not be entered into unless at least three proposals to do the work have been evaluated by a competitive process established by the board. If the board does not select the lowest bidder, it shall make a finding stating the reasons that the lowest bidder was not selected.

(g) In a county of the third class in which there are no available courtrooms to accommodate all authorized judicial positions or in which the board of supervisors certifies that there is a significant need to expeditiously construct new court and court support facilities, the board of supervisors may contract for the construction or expansion of court and court support facilities without the formality of obtaining bids, adopting plans and specifications, or complying with other requirements of this article, except as required by this subdivision. The person to whom the contract is awarded shall execute a bond for faithful performance in accordance with Section 20129. Any plans and specifications adopted by the board may only be altered or changed in accordance with Section 20135 and all contracts awarded pursuant to this subdivision may only be altered or changed in accordance with Sections 20136, 20137, and 20138.

The award of the contract shall be made after a public hearing on the basis of a request for proposals advertised in accordance with Section 6062 or 6062a of the Government Code. The contract may be awarded only to a contractor who has responded to the request for proposals and who is licensed to do the work in accordance with Chapter 9 (commencing with Section 7000) of Division 3 of the Business and Professions Code. The contract shall be upon terms which the board determines are necessary for the expeditious completion of

New Text (Operative July 1, 2012)

advertised in accordance with Section 6062 or 6062a of the Government Code. The contract may be awarded only to a contractor who has responded to the request for proposals and who is licensed to do the work in accordance with Chapter 9 (commencing with Section 7000) of Division 3 of the Business and Professions Code. The contract shall be upon terms which the board determines are necessary for the expeditious completion of the work. A contract shall not be entered into unless at least three proposals to do the work have been evaluated by a competitive process established by the board and the lowest bid is selected. This subdivision shall remain in effect until December 31, 1994.

Old Text

the work. A contract shall not be entered into unless at least three proposals to do the work have been evaluated by a competitive process established by the board and the lowest bid is selected. This subdivision shall remain in effect until December 31, 1994.

Revised to include reference to new Section 9000 et seq.

PCC 20461

No assignment by the contractor of the whole or any part of the money, assessment, partial assessment, any reassessment and any bonds which may be issued to represent any assessment or reassessment, due or to be due under the contract, or for "extras" in connection therewith, whether made before or after a verified claim is filed pursuant to this chapter, shall take priority over the claims, and the assignment shall have no binding force insofar as the rights of the claimants, or their assigns, are concerned. None of the provisions of Title 3 (commencing with Section 9000) of Part 6 of Division 4 of the Civil Code shall be applicable to any assessment, partial assessment, reassessment, bonds, moneys or funds payable to the contractor or assignee under this division or to any matter contained in this chapter.

PCC 20461

No assignment by the contractor of the whole or any part of the money, assessment, partial assessment, any reassessment and any bonds which may be issued to represent any assessment or reassessment, due him or to be due him under the contract, or for "extras" in connection therewith, whether made before or after a verified claim is filed pursuant to this chapter, shall take priority over such claims, and such assignment shall have no binding force insofar as the rights of the claimants, or their assigns, are concerned. None of the provisions of Title 15 (commencing with Section 3082), Part 4, Division 3, of the Civil Code, shall be applicable to any assessment, partial assessment, reassessment, bonds, moneys or funds payable to the contractor or his assignee under this division or to any matter contained in this chapter.

Revised to include reference to new Section 9000 et seq.

PCC 20496

The provisions of Title 3 (commencing with Section 9000) of Part 6 of Division 4 of the Civil Code are hereby expressly made applicable to the construction of works and improvements under this article.

PCC 20496

The provisions of Title 15 (commencing with Section 3082), Part 4, Division 3, of the Civil Code are hereby expressly made applicable to the construction of works and improvements under this article.

Revised to include reference to new Section 9000 et seq.

New Text (Operative July 1, 2012)

<u>*PCC 20682.5*</u>

(a) A district may construct or complete any building, structure, or improvement with its own forces or by contract without bidding when the cost does not exceed twenty-five thousand dollars ($25,000).

(b) All contracts for the construction or completion of any building, structure, or improvement, when the cost exceeds twenty-five thousand dollars ($25,000), shall be contracted for and let to the lowest responsible bidder after notice. If two or more bids are the same and the lowest, the district board may accept the one it chooses.

(c) The district shall publish a notice inviting bids for any contract for which competitive bidding is required at least one time in a newspaper of general circulation in the district at least 10 days before the time specified for receiving bids. The notice inviting bids shall set a date for opening the bids and distinctly state the work to be done.

(d) If the general manager recommends and the board of directors determines that the publication of advertisements of the notice in trade journals and papers in lieu of publication pursuant to subdivision (c) will increase the number of business enterprises receiving that notice, the board of directors may by resolution declare that those notices shall be published in trade journals and papers at least 10 days prior to the time specified for receiving bids.

(e) If plans and specifications are prepared describing the work, all bidders shall be afforded an opportunity to examine the plans and specifications, and the plans and specifications shall be attached to and become part of the contract, if one is awarded.

(f) At its discretion, the board of directors may reject any bids presented and readvertise.

(g) In the case of an emergency, the board of directors may act pursuant to Chapter 2.5 (commencing with Section 22050).

(h) The board of directors may, subject to Chapter 5 (commencing with Section 9550) of Title 3 of Part 6 of Division 4 of the Civil Code, require the posting of those bonds it deems desirable as a condition to the filing of a bid or the letting of a contract."

(i) The district shall keep cost records of the work in the manner provided in Chapter 1 (commencing

Old Text

PCC 20682.5

(a) A district may construct or complete any building, structure, or improvement with its own forces or by contract without bidding when the cost does not exceed twenty-five thousand dollars ($25,000).

(b) All contracts for the construction or completion of any building, structure, or improvement, when the cost exceeds twenty-five thousand dollars ($25,000), shall be contracted for and let to the lowest responsible bidder after notice. If two or more bids are the same and the lowest, the district board may accept the one it chooses.

(c) The district shall publish a notice inviting bids for any contract for which competitive bidding is required at least one time in a newspaper of general circulation in the district at least 10 days before the time specified for receiving bids. The notice inviting bids shall set a date for opening the bids and distinctly state the work to be done.

(d) If the general manager recommends and the board of directors determines that the publication of advertisements of the notice in trade journals and papers in lieu of publication pursuant to subdivision (c) will increase the number of business enterprises receiving that notice, the board of directors may by resolution declare that those notices shall be published in trade journals and papers at least 10 days prior to the time specified for receiving bids.

(e) If plans and specifications are prepared describing the work, all bidders shall be afforded an opportunity to examine the plans and specifications, and the plans and specifications shall be attached to and become part of the contract, if one is awarded.

(f) At its discretion, the board of directors may reject any bids presented and readvertise.

(g) In the case of an emergency, the board of directors may act pursuant to Chapter 2.5 (commencing with Section 22050).

(h) The board of directors may, subject to Chapter 7 (commencing with Section 3247) of Title 15 of Part 4 of Division 3 of the Civil Code, require the posting of those bonds it deems desirable as a condition to the filing of a bid or the letting of a contract.

(i) The district shall keep cost records of the work in the manner provided in Chapter 1 (commencing with Section 4000) of Division 5 of Title 1 of the Government Code.

(j) As an alternate to the procedures required by this

New Text (Operative July 1, 2012) | **Old Text**

with Section 4000) of Division 5 of Title 1 of the Government Code.

(j) As an alternate to the procedures required by this section, a district may rely on the Uniform Public Construction Cost Accounting Act, Chapter 2 (commencing with Section 22000) of Part 3 of Division 2.

section, a district may rely on the Uniform Public Construction Cost Accounting Act, Chapter 2 (commencing with Section 22000) of Part 3 of Division 2.

Revised to include reference to new Section 9000 et seq.

PCC 20688.4

An agency shall require each successful bidder to file with it good and sufficient bonds, to be approved by it. The bonds shall be conditioned upon the faithful performance of the contract and upon the payment of all claims for labor and material in connection with the contract. The bonds shall contain the terms and conditions set forth in Chapter 5 (commencing with Section 9550) of Title 3 of Part 6 of Division 4 of the Civil Code and are subject to the provisions of that chapter.

PCC 20688.4

An agency shall require each successful bidder to file with it good and sufficient bonds, to be approved by it. The bonds shall be conditioned upon the faithful performance of the contract and upon the payment of all claims for labor and material in connection with the contract. The bonds shall contain the terms and conditions set forth in Chapter 7 (commencing with Section 3247) of Title 15 of Part 4 of Division 3 of the Civil Code and are subject to the provisions of that chapter.

Revised to include reference to new Section 9000 et seq.

PCC 20813

(a) All contracts for the construction or completion of any building, structure, or improvement, when the expenditure required for the work exceeds ten thousand dollars ($10,000), shall be contracted for and let to the lowest responsible bidder after notice. If two or more bids are the same and the lowest, the district board may accept the one it chooses.

(b) The notice inviting bids shall set a date for the opening of bids. The first publication or posting of the notice shall be at least 10 days before the date of opening the bids. Notice shall be published at least twice, not less than five days apart, in a newspaper of general circulation in the district, or if there is none, it shall be posted in at least three public places in the district. The notice shall distinctly state the work to be done.

(c) In its discretion, the district board may reject any bids presented and readvertise.

(d) In the case of an emergency, the district board may act pursuant to Chapter 2.5 (commencing with Section 22050).

(e) The district board may, subject to the provisions of

PCC 20813

(a) All contracts for the construction or completion of any building, structure, or improvement, when the expenditure required for the work exceeds ten thousand dollars ($10,000), shall be contracted for and let to the lowest responsible bidder after notice. If two or more bids are the same and the lowest, the district board may accept the one it chooses.

(b) The notice inviting bids shall set a date for the opening of bids. The first publication or posting of the notice shall be at least 10 days before the date of opening the bids. Notice shall be published at least twice, not less than five days apart, in a newspaper of general circulation in the district, or if there is none, it shall be posted in at least three public places in the district. The notice shall distinctly state the work to be done.

(c) In its discretion, the district board may reject any bids presented and readvertise.

(d) In the case of an emergency, the district board may act pursuant to Chapter 2.5 (commencing with Section 22050).

(e) The district board may, subject to the provisions of

New Text (Operative July 1, 2012)

Chapter 5 (commencing with Section 9550) of Title 3 of Part 6 of Division 4 of the Civil Code, require the posting of those bonds it deems desirable as a condition to the filing of a bid or the letting of a contract."

(f) Cost records of the work shall be kept in the manner provided in Chapter 1 (commencing with Section 4000) of Division 5 of Title 1 of the Government Code.

Old Text

Chapter 7 (commencing with Section 3247) of Title 15 of Part 4 of Division 3 of the Civil Code, require the posting of those bonds it deems desirable as a condition to the filing of a bid or the letting of a contract.

(f) Cost records of the work shall be kept in the manner provided in Chapter 1 (commencing with Section 4000) of Division 5 of Title 1 of the Government Code.

Revised to include reference to new Section 9000 et seq.

••

PCC 20815.3

(a) A district shall publish notice inviting bids for any contract for which competitive bidding is required at least one time in a newspaper of general circulation in the district at least one week before the time specified for receiving bids. The notice shall distinctly state the work to be done.

(b) In its discretion, the board of directors may do any of the following:

(1) Reject all bids and readvertise.

(2) By a four-fifths vote, elect to purchase the materials or supplies in the open market.

(3) By a four-fifths vote, elect to construct the building, structure, or improvement by force account.

(c) In the case of an emergency, the board of directors may act pursuant to Chapter 2.5 (commencing with Section 22050).

(d) The board of directors may, subject to the provisions of Chapter 5 (commencing with Section 9550) of Title 3 of Part 6 of Division 4 of the Civil Code, require the posting of those bonds it deems as a condition to the filing of a bid or the letting of a contract.

(e) The district shall keep cost records of the work pursuant to Chapter 1 (commencing with Section 4000) of Division 5 of Title 1 of the Government Code.

PCC 20815.3

(a) A district shall publish notice inviting bids for any contract for which competitive bidding is required at least one time in a newspaper of general circulation in the district at least one week before the time specified for receiving bids. The notice shall distinctly state the work to be done.

(b) In its discretion, the board of directors may do any of the following:

(1) Reject all bids and readvertise.

(2) By a four-fifths vote, elect to purchase the materials or supplies in the open market.

(3) By a four-fifths vote, elect to construct the building, structure, or improvement by force account.

(c) In the case of an emergency, the board of directors may act pursuant to Chapter 2.5 (commencing with Section 22050).

(d) The board of directors may, subject to the provisions of Chapter 7 (commencing with Section 3247) of Title 15 of Part 4 of Division 3 of the Civil Code, require the posting of those bonds it deems as a condition to the filing of a bid or the letting of a contract.

(e) The district shall keep cost records of the work pursuant to Chapter 1 (commencing with Section 4000) of Division 5 of Title 1 of the Government Code.

Revised to include reference to new Section 9000 et seq.

••

New Text (Operative July 1, 2012)

PCC 20991

All contracts for any improvement or unit of work, except as provided in this article, estimated to cost in excess of twenty-five thousand dollars ($25,000), shall be let to the lowest responsible bidder in the manner provided in this article. The board of supervisors of the district shall advertise by five or more insertions in a daily newspaper of general circulation, or by two or more insertions in a weekly newspaper of general circulation, printed and published in the district, inviting sealed proposals for the construction of the improvement or work. The board shall require the successful bidder or bidders to file with the board good and sufficient bonds, to be approved by the board, conditioned upon the faithful performance of the contract and upon the payment of all claims for labor and material. The bonds shall contain the terms and conditions set forth in Chapter 5 (commencing with Section 9550) of Title 3 of Part 6 of Division 4 of the Civil Code and shall be subject to the provisions of that chapter. The board shall have the right to reject any bid not suitable to the best interests of the district. In the event all proposals are rejected or no proposals are received pursuant to advertisement, or the estimated cost of the work does not exceed ten thousand dollars ($10,000), or the work consists of channel protection, dam protection, temporary work, maintenance work, or emergency work, the board of supervisors may, without advertising for bids, have the work done by force account. Emergency work may also be done by negotiated contract without advertising for bids. In case of an emergency, if notice for bids to let contracts will not be given, the board shall comply with Chapter 2.5 (commencing with Section 22050).

Old Text

PCC 20991

All contracts for any improvement or unit of work, except as provided in this article, estimated to cost in excess of twenty-five thousand dollars ($25,000), shall be let to the lowest responsible bidder in the manner provided in this article. The board of supervisors of the district shall advertise by five or more insertions in a daily newspaper of general circulation, or by two or more insertions in a weekly newspaper of general circulation, printed and published in the district, inviting sealed proposals for the construction of the improvement or work. The board shall require the successful bidder or bidders to file with the board good and sufficient bonds, to be approved by the board, conditioned upon the faithful performance of the contract and upon the payment of all claims for labor and material. The bonds shall contain the terms and conditions set forth in Chapter 7 (commencing with Section 3247) of Title 15 of Part 4 of Division 3 of the Civil Code and shall be subject to the provisions of that chapter. The board shall have the right to reject any bid not suitable to the best interests of the district. In the event all proposals are rejected or no proposals are received pursuant to advertisement, or the estimated cost of the work does not exceed ten thousand dollars ($10,000), or the work consists of channel protection, dam protection, temporary work, maintenance work, or emergency work, the board of supervisors may, without advertising for bids, have the work done by force account. Emergency work may also be done by negotiated contract without advertising for bids. In case of an emergency, if notice for bids to let contracts will not be given, the board shall comply with Chapter 2.5 (commencing with Section 22050).

Revised to include reference to new Section 9000 et seq.

New Text

PCC 21061

(a) All contracts for any improvement or unit of work, except as provided in this article, estimated to cost in excess of twenty-five thousand dollars ($25,000), shall be let to the lowest responsible bidder in the manner provided in this article.

(b) The board of supervisors of the district shall advertise by five or more insertions in a daily newspaper of general circulation, or by two or more insertions in a weekly newspaper of general circulation, printed and published in the district, inviting sealed proposals for

Old Text

PCC 21061

(a) All contracts for any improvement or unit of work, except as provided in this article, estimated to cost in excess of twenty-five thousand dollars ($25,000), shall be let to the lowest responsible bidder in the manner provided in this article.

(b) The board of supervisors of the district shall advertise by five or more insertions in a daily newspaper of general circulation, or by two or more insertions in a weekly newspaper of general circulation, printed and published in the district, inviting sealed proposals for the construction of

New Text (Operative July 1, 2012)

the construction of the improvement or work. The board shall require the successful bidder or bidders to file with the board good and sufficient bonds, to be approved by the board, conditioned upon the faithful performance of the contract and upon the payment of all claims for labor and material, the bonds to contain the terms and conditions set forth in Chapter 5 (commencing with Section 9550) of Title 3 of Part 6 of Division 4 of the Civil Code and to be subject to that chapter.

(c) The board may also reject any bid not suitable to the best interests of the district. If all proposals are rejected or no proposals are received pursuant to advertisement therefor, or the work consists of channel protection, dam protection, temporary work, maintenance work, or of emergency work, the board of supervisors may, without advertising for bids, have the work done by force account. Emergency work may also be done by negotiated contract without advertising for bids or requiring bonds. In case of an emergency, if notice for bids to let contracts will not be given, the board shall comply with Chapter 2.5 (commencing with Section 22050).

(d) The board of supervisors, acting as the board of the district, may, by ordinance, resolution, or board order, authorize the flood control engineer or other county officer to order changes or additions in work being performed under a construction contract. When so authorized, any change or addition in the work shall be ordered in writing by the flood control engineer, or other designated officer, and the extra cost for any change or addition to the work so ordered shall not exceed five thousand dollars ($5,000) when the total amount of the original contract does not exceed fifty thousand dollars ($50,000), nor 10 percent of the amount of any original contract that exceeds fifty thousand dollars ($50,000), but does not exceed two hundred fifty thousand dollars ($250,000). For contracts whose original cost exceeds two hundred fifty thousand dollars ($250,000), the extra cost for any change or addition to the work so ordered shall not exceed twenty-five thousand dollars ($25,000), plus 5 percent of the amount of the original contract costs in excess of two hundred fifty thousand dollars ($250,000). In no event shall any such change or alteration exceed one hundred fifty thousand dollars ($150,000).

Old Text

the improvement or work. The board shall require the successful bidder or bidders to file with the board good and sufficient bonds, to be approved by the board, conditioned upon the faithful performance of the contract and upon the payment of all claims for labor and material, the bonds to contain the terms and conditions set forth in Chapter 7 (commencing with Section 3247) of Title 15 of Part 4 of Division 3 of the Civil Code and to be subject to that chapter.

(c) The board may also reject any bid not suitable to the best interests of the district. If all proposals are rejected or no proposals are received pursuant to advertisement therefor, or the work consists of channel protection, dam protection, temporary work, maintenance work, or of emergency work, the board of supervisors may, without advertising for bids, have the work done by force account. Emergency work may also be done by negotiated contract without advertising for bids or requiring bonds. In case of an emergency, if notice for bids to let contracts will not be given, the board shall comply with Chapter 2.5 (commencing with Section 22050).

(d) The board of supervisors, acting as the board of the district, may, by ordinance, resolution, or board order, authorize the flood control engineer or other county officer to order changes or additions in work being performed under a construction contract. When so authorized, any change or addition in the work shall be ordered in writing by the flood control engineer, or other designated officer, and the extra cost for any change or addition to the work so ordered shall not exceed five thousand dollars ($5,000) when the total amount of the original contract does not exceed fifty thousand dollars ($50,000), nor 10 percent of the amount of any original contract that exceeds fifty thousand dollars ($50,000), but does not exceed two hundred fifty thousand dollars ($250,000). For contracts whose original cost exceeds two hundred fifty thousand dollars ($250,000), the extra cost for any change or addition to the work so ordered shall not exceed twenty-five thousand dollars ($25,000), plus 5 percent of the amount of the original contract costs in excess of two hundred fifty thousand dollars ($250,000). In no event shall any such change or alteration exceed one hundred fifty thousand dollars ($150,000).

Revised to include reference to new Section 9000 et seq.

New Text (Operative July 1, 2012)

PCC 21071

(a) All contracts for any improvement or unit of work except as provided in this article estimated to cost in excess of ten thousand dollars ($10,000) shall be let to the lowest responsible bidder in the manner provided in this article. The board of supervisors of the district shall advertise by three insertions in a daily newspaper of general circulation or two insertions in a weekly newspaper of general circulation printed and published in the district inviting sealed proposals for the construction of, the improvement or work before any contract shall be made for the improvement or work, and may let by contract separately any part of the work or improvement. The board shall require the successful bidder to file with the board good and sufficient bonds to be approved by the board conditioned upon the faithful performance of the contract and upon the payment of their claims for labor and material in connection with the contract. The bonds shall contain the terms and conditions set forth in Chapter 5 (commencing with Section 9550) of Title 3 of Part 6 of Division 4 of the Civil Code and be subject to the provisions of that chapter. The board shall also have the right to reject any and all bids. If all proposals are rejected or no proposals are received pursuant to the advertisement, the estimated cost of the work does not exceed the sum of ten thousand dollars ($10,000), or the work consists of channel protection, maintenance work, or emergency work when necessary in order to protect life and property from impending flood damage, the board of supervisors may, without advertising for bids, have the work done by force account or negotiated contract.

(b) The district shall have the power to purchase in the open market without advertising for bids, materials, supplies, equipment, and other personal property for use in any work either under contract or by force account if the costs do not exceed ten thousand dollars ($10,000). It shall be the duty of the purchasing agent of Ventura County, as the ex officio purchasing agent of the Ventura County Watershed Protection District, unless otherwise ordered by the board of supervisors, to purchase for the district all materials, supplies, equipment, and other personal property necessary to carry out the purposes of this article, and to engage independent contractors to perform sundry services for the district, if the aggregate cost of such work, exclusive of materials to be furnished by the district, does not exceed ten thousand dollars

Old Text

PCC 21071

(a) All contracts for any improvement or unit of work except as provided in this article estimated to cost in excess of ten thousand dollars ($10,000) shall be let to the lowest responsible bidder in the manner provided in this article. The board of supervisors of the district shall advertise by three insertions in a daily newspaper of general circulation or two insertions in a weekly newspaper of general circulation printed and published in the district inviting sealed proposals for the construction of, the improvement or work before any contract shall be made for the improvement or work, and may let by contract separately any part of the work or improvement. The board shall require the successful bidder to file with the board good and sufficient bonds to be approved by the board conditioned upon the faithful performance of the contract and upon the payment of their claims for labor and material in connection with the contract. The bonds shall contain the terms and conditions set forth in Chapter 7 (commencing with Section 3247) of Title 15 of Part 4 of the Civil Code and be subject to the provisions of that chapter. The board shall also have the right to reject any and all bids. If all proposals are rejected or no proposals are received pursuant to the advertisement, the estimated cost of the work does not exceed the sum of ten thousand dollars ($10,000), or the work consists of channel protection, maintenance work, or emergency work when necessary in order to protect life and property from impending flood damage, the board of supervisors may, without advertising for bids, have the work done by force account or negotiated contract.

(b) The district shall have the power to purchase in the open market without advertising for bids, materials, supplies, equipment, and other personal property for use in any work either under contract or by force account if the costs do not exceed ten thousand dollars ($10,000). It shall be the duty of the purchasing agent of Ventura County, as the ex officio purchasing agent of the Ventura County Watershed Protection District, unless otherwise ordered by the board of supervisors, to purchase for the district all materials, supplies, equipment, and other personal property necessary to carry out the purposes of this article, and to engage independent contractors to perform sundry services for the district, if the aggregate cost of such work, exclusive of materials to be furnished by the district, does not exceed ten thousand dollars ($10,000).

New Text (Operative July 1, 2012) | **Old Text**

($10,000).

(c) The purchasing agent shall make all purchases and contracts upon proper requisition, signed by the engineer-manager of the district, or his or her authorized representative.

(d) If the work consists of the maintenance or alteration of existing facilities, including electrical, painting, and roofing if the cost of labor and materials for the work according to the engineer's estimate will exceed five thousand dollars ($5,000), and if the work is not of the type of work referred to in this section, the maintenance and alteration work shall be performed under a contract or contracts that shall be let to the lowest responsible bidder or bidders in the manner described in this section.

(c) The purchasing agent shall make all purchases and contracts upon proper requisition, signed by the engineer-manager of the district, or his or her authorized representative.

(d) If the work consists of the maintenance or alteration of existing facilities, including electrical, painting, and roofing if the cost of labor and materials for the work according to the engineer's estimate will exceed five thousand dollars ($5,000), and if the work is not of the type of work referred to in this section, the maintenance and alteration work shall be performed under a contract or contracts that shall be let to the lowest responsible bidder or bidders in the manner described in this section.

Revised to include reference to new Section 9000 et seq.

••

PCC 21081

All contracts for any improvement or unit of work, when the cost, according to the estimate of the engineer, will exceed five thousand dollars ($5,000), shall be let to the lowest responsible bidder or bidders in the manner provided in this article. The board shall first determine whether the contract shall be let as a single unit for the whole of the work, or shall be divided into severable parts, or both, according to the best interests of the district. The board shall call for bids and advertise the call by three insertions in a daily newspaper of general circulation or by two insertions in a weekly newspaper of general circulation printed and published in the district inviting sealed proposals for the construction or performance of the improvement or work before any contract is made. The call for bids shall state whether the work is to be performed as a unit or divided into severable specific parts, or both, as stated in the call. The board may let the work by single contract for the whole or it may divide such work into severable parts by separate contracts, as stated in such call, according to the best interests of the district. The board shall require the successful bidder or bidders to file with the board good and sufficient bonds to be approved by the board conditioned upon the faithful performance of the contract and upon the payment of their claims for labor and material, the bonds to contain the terms and conditions set forth in Title 3 (commencing with Section 9000) of Part 6 of Division 4 of the Civil Code and to be subject to the provisions of that title. The board shall also have the right to reject any bid. In the event all proposals are rejected or no proposals are received pursuant to advertisement, or the

PCC 21081

All contracts for any improvement or unit of work, when the cost, according to the estimate of the engineer, will exceed five thousand dollars ($5,000), shall be let to the lowest responsible bidder or bidders in the manner provided in this article. The board shall first determine whether the contract shall be let as a single unit for the whole of the work, or shall be divided into severable parts, or both, according to the best interests of the district. The board shall call for bids and advertise the call by three insertions in a daily newspaper of general circulation or by two insertions in a weekly newspaper of general circulation printed and published in the district inviting sealed proposals for the construction or performance of the improvement or work before any contract is made. The call for bids shall state whether the work is to be performed as a unit or divided into severable specific parts, or both, as stated in the call. The board may let the work by single contract for the whole or it may divide such work into severable parts by separate contracts, as stated in such call, according to the best interests of the district. The board shall require the successful bidder or bidders to file with the board good and sufficient bonds to be approved by the board conditioned upon the faithful performance of the contract and upon the payment of their claims for labor and material, the bonds to contain the terms and conditions set forth in Title 15 (commencing with Section 3082) of Part 4 of Division 3 of the Civil Code and to be subject to the provisions of that title. The board shall also have the right to reject any bid. In the event all proposals are rejected or no proposals are received pursuant to advertisement, or the estimated cost of such work

New Text (Operative July 1, 2012)

estimated cost of such work does not exceed five thousand dollars ($5,000), or the work consists of channel protection, maintenance work, or emergency work, the board of supervisors may, without advertising for bids, have the work done by force account. The district may purchase in the open market, without advertising for bids, materials and supplies for use in any work either under contract or by force account.

Old Text

does not exceed five thousand dollars ($5,000), or the work consists of channel protection, maintenance work, or emergency work, the board of supervisors may, without advertising for bids, have the work done by force account. The district may purchase in the open market, without advertising for bids, materials and supplies for use in any work either under contract or by force account.

Revised to include reference to new Section 9000 et seq.

••

New Text (Operative July 1, 2012)

PCC 21091

All contracts for any improvement or unit of work, except as otherwise provided in this act, estimated to cost in excess of fifteen thousand dollars ($15,000) shall be let to the lowest responsible bidder in the manner provided in this article. The board of supervisors of the district shall advertise by three insertions in a daily newspaper of general circulation or two insertions in a weekly newspaper of general circulation printed and published in the district inviting sealed proposals for the construction of the improvement or work before any contract is made, and may let by contract separately any part of the work or improvement. The board shall require the successful bidder to file with the board good and sufficient bonds to be approved by the board conditioned upon the faithful performance of the contract and upon the payment of their claims for labor and material. The bonds shall contain the terms and conditions set forth in Sections 10223 and 10224, and Section 9554 of the Civil Code and be subject to those sections. The board shall also have the right to reject any bid. If all proposals are rejected or no proposals are received pursuant to advertisement, or where the estimated cost of the work does not exceed fifteen thousand dollars ($15,000), or the work consists of channel protection, maintenance work, or emergency work, the board of supervisors may, without advertising for bids, have the work done by force account. In case of an emergency, if notice for bids to let contracts will not be given, the board shall comply with Chapter 2.5 (commencing with Section 22050). The district may purchase in the open market, without advertising for bids, materials and supplies for use in any improvement or unit of work either under contract or by force account.

Old Text

PCC 21091

All contracts for any improvement or unit of work, except as otherwise provided in this act, estimated to cost in excess of fifteen thousand dollars ($15,000) shall be let to the lowest responsible bidder in the manner provided in this article. The board of supervisors of the district shall advertise by three insertions in a daily newspaper of general circulation or two insertions in a weekly newspaper of general circulation printed and published in the district inviting sealed proposals for the construction of the improvement or work before any contract is made, and may let by contract separately any part of the work or improvement. The board shall require the successful bidder to file with the board good and sufficient bonds to be approved by the board conditioned upon the faithful performance of the contract and upon the payment of their claims for labor and material. The bonds shall contain the terms and conditions set forth in Sections 10223 and 10224 of the Public Contract Code and Section 3248 of the Civil Code and be subject to those sections. The board shall also have the right to reject any bid. If all proposals are rejected or no proposals are received pursuant to advertisement, or where the estimated cost of the work does not exceed fifteen thousand dollars ($15,000), or the work consists of channel protection, maintenance work, or emergency work, the board of supervisors may, without advertising for bids, have the work done by force account. In case of an emergency, if notice for bids to let contracts will not be given, the board shall comply with Chapter 2.5 (commencing with Section 22050). The district may purchase in the open market, without advertising for bids, materials and supplies for use in any improvement or unit of work either under contract or by force account.

Revised to include reference to new Section 9000 et seq.

••

New Text (Operative July 1, 2012)

PCC 21101

All contracts for any improvement or unit of work, when the cost, according to the estimate of the engineer, will exceed five thousand dollars ($5,000), shall be let to the lowest responsible bidder or bidders in the manner provided in this article. The board shall first determine whether the contract shall be let as a single unit for the whole of the work, or shall be divided into parts, or both, according to the best interests of the district. The board shall call for bids and advertise the call by three insertions in a daily newspaper of general circulation or two insertions in a weekly newspaper of general circulation printed and published in the district inviting sealed proposals for the construction or performance of the improvement or work before any contract shall be made. The call for bids shall state whether the work is to be performed as a unit or is to be divided into severable specific parts, or both, as stated in the call. The board may let the work by single contract for the whole as a unit or it may divide the work into severable parts by separate contracts, as stated in the call, according to the best interests of the district. The board shall require the successful bidder or bidders to file with the board good and sufficient bonds to be approved by the board conditioned upon the faithful performance of the contract and upon the payment of their claims for labor and material, the bonds to contain the terms and conditions set forth in Title 3 (commencing with Section 9000) of Part 6 of Division 4 of the Civil Code and to be subject to the provisions of that title. The board shall also have the right to reject any bid. In the event all proposals are rejected or no proposals are received pursuant to advertisement, or the estimated cost of the work does not exceed five thousand dollars ($5,000), or the work consists of channel protection, maintenance work, or emergency work, the board of supervisors may, without advertising for bids, have the work done by force account. In case of an emergency, if notice for bids to let contracts will not be given, the board shall comply with Chapter 2.5 (commencing with Section 22050). The district shall have the power to purchase in the open market without advertising for bids, materials and supplies for use in any work either under contract or by force account.

Old Text

PCC 21101

All contracts for any improvement or unit of work, when the cost, according to the estimate of the engineer, will exceed five thousand dollars ($5,000), shall be let to the lowest responsible bidder or bidders in the manner provided in this article. The board shall first determine whether the contract shall be let as a single unit for the whole of the work, or shall be divided into parts, or both, according to the best interests of the district. The board shall call for bids and advertise the call by three insertions in a daily newspaper of general circulation or two insertions in a weekly newspaper of general circulation printed and published in the district inviting sealed proposals for the construction or performance of the improvement or work before any contract shall be made. The call for bids shall state whether the work is to be performed as a unit or is to be divided into severable specific parts, or both, as stated in the call. The board may let the work by single contract for the whole as a unit or it may divide the work into severable parts by separate contracts, as stated in the call, according to the best interests of the district. The board shall require the successful bidder or bidders to file with the board good and sufficient bonds to be approved by the board conditioned upon the faithful performance of the contract and upon the payment of their claims for labor and material, the bonds to contain the terms and conditions set forth in Title 15 (commencing with Section 3082) of Part 4 of Division 3 of the Civil Code and to be subject to the provisions of that title. The board shall also have the right to reject any bid. In the event all proposals are rejected or no proposals are received pursuant to advertisement, or the estimated cost of the work does not exceed five thousand dollars ($5,000), or the work consists of channel protection, maintenance work, or emergency work, the board of supervisors may, without advertising for bids, have the work done by force account. In case of an emergency, if notice for bids to let contracts will not be given, the board shall comply with Chapter 2.5 (commencing with Section 22050). The district shall have the power to purchase in the open market without advertising for bids, materials and supplies for use in any work either under contract or by force account.

Revised to include reference to new Section 9000 et seq.

New Text (Operative July 1, 2012)

PCC 21111

(a) All contracts for the construction of any unit of work, except as provided in this article, estimated to cost in excess of ten thousand dollars ($10,000) shall be let to the lowest responsible bidder in the manner provided in this article. The board of directors of the agency shall advertise by three insertions in a daily newspaper of general circulation or two insertions in a weekly newspaper of general circulation published in the agency's jurisdiction inviting sealed proposals for the construction of the work before any contract shall be made, and may let by contract separately any part of the work. The board shall require the successful bidder to file with the board good and sufficient bonds to be approved by the board conditioned upon the faithful performance of the contract and upon the payment of the claims for labor and material. The faithful performance bond shall contain terms and conditions as the board may specify, and the payment bond shall be subject to the provisions of, and shall contain the terms and conditions set forth in Title 3 (commencing with Section 9000) of Part 6 of Division 4 of the Civil Code, as applicable. The board shall also have the right to reject any bid, in which case the board may advertise for new bids. In the event no proposals are received pursuant to advertisement, or where the estimated cost of the work does not exceed ten thousand dollars ($10,000), or the work consists of emergency work, the board of directors by unanimous vote of all members present may, without advertising for bids, have the work done by force account. In case of an emergency, if notice for bids to let contracts will not be given, the board shall comply with Chapter 2.5 (commencing with Section 22050). The agency may purchase in the open market, and may authorize the Purchasing Agent of the County of Santa Barbara to purchase, without advertisement for bids, materials and supplies for use in any work either under contract or by force account.

(b) If the work to be performed by or on behalf of the agency does not involve an expenditure of ten thousand dollars ($10,000) or more, or if the work consists of emergency work, the agency may require a faithful performance bond. The agency may require a payment bond on work performed on behalf of the agency which does not involve an expenditure of more than ten thousand dollars ($10,000).

Old Text

PCC 21111

(a) All contracts for the construction of any unit of work, except as provided in this article, estimated to cost in excess of ten thousand dollars ($10,000) shall be let to the lowest responsible bidder in the manner provided in this article. The board of directors of the agency shall advertise by three insertions in a daily newspaper of general circulation or two insertions in a weekly newspaper of general circulation published in the agency's jurisdiction inviting sealed proposals for the construction of the work before any contract shall be made, and may let by contract separately any part of the work. The board shall require the successful bidder to file with the board good and sufficient bonds to be approved by the board conditioned upon the faithful performance of the contract and upon the payment of the claims for labor and material. The faithful performance bond shall contain terms and conditions as the board may specify, and the payment bond shall be subject to the provisions of, and shall contain the terms and conditions set forth in Title 15 (commencing with Section 3082) of Part 4 of Division 3 of the Civil Code, as applicable. The board shall also have the right to reject any bid, in which case the board may advertise for new bids. In the event no proposals are received pursuant to advertisement, or where the estimated cost of the work does not exceed ten thousand dollars ($10,000), or the work consists of emergency work, the board of directors by unanimous vote of all members present may, without advertising for bids, have the work done by force account. In case of an emergency, if notice for bids to let contracts will not be given, the board shall comply with Chapter 2.5 (commencing with Section 22050). The agency may purchase in the open market, and may authorize the Purchasing Agent of the County of Santa Barbara to purchase, without advertisement for bids, materials and supplies for use in any work either under contract or by force account.

(b) If the work to be performed by or on behalf of the agency does not involve an expenditure of ten thousand dollars ($10,000) or more, or if the work consists of emergency work, the agency may require a faithful performance bond. The agency may require a payment bond on work performed on behalf of the agency which does not involve an expenditure of more than ten thousand dollars ($10,000).

Revised to include reference to new Section 9000 et seq.

New Text (Operative July 1, 2012)

PCC 21121

(a) All contracts for any improvement or unit of work, if the cost according to the estimate of the engineer, exceeds five thousand dollars ($5,000), shall be let to the lowest responsible bidder or bidders.

(b) The board shall first determine whether the contract shall be let as a single unit for the whole of the work, or shall be divided into severable parts, or both, according to the best interests of the agency.

(c) The board shall call for bids and advertise the call by three insertions in a daily newspaper of general circulation or by two insertions in a weekly newspaper of general circulation printed and published in the territory of the agency inviting sealed proposals for the construction or performance of the improvement or work before any contract is entered into. The call for bids shall state whether the work is to be performed as a unit or shall be divided into severable specific parts, or both, as stated in the call. The board may let the work by single contract or it may divide the work into severable parts by separate contracts, as stated in the call, according to the best interests of the agency.

(d) The board shall require the successful bidder or bidders to file with the board good and sufficient bonds to be approved by the board conditioned upon the faithful performance of the contract and upon the payment of their claims for labor and material in connection with the contract. The bonds shall contain the terms and conditions set forth in Title 3 (commencing with Section 9000) of Part 6 of Division 4 of the Civil Code and are subject to the provisions of that title.

(e) The board may reject any bid. The board of supervisors may, without advertising for bids, have the work done by force account if any of the following requirements are met:

(1) All the projects are rejected.

(2) No proposals are received in response to the advertisement.

(3) The estimated cost of the work does not exceed five thousand dollars ($5,000).

(4) The work consists of channel protection, maintenance work, or emergency work. In case of an emergency, if notice for bids to let contracts will

Old Text

PCC 21121

(a) All contracts for any improvement or unit of work, if the cost according to the estimate of the engineer, exceeds five thousand dollars ($5,000), shall be let to the lowest responsible bidder or bidders.

(b) The board shall first determine whether the contract shall be let as a single unit for the whole of the work, or shall be divided into severable parts, or both, according to the best interests of the agency.

(c) The board shall call for bids and advertise the call by three insertions in a daily newspaper of general circulation or by two insertions in a weekly newspaper of general circulation printed and published in the territory of the agency inviting sealed proposals for the construction or performance of the improvement or work before any contract is entered into. The call for bids shall state whether the work is to be performed as a unit or shall be divided into severable specific parts, or both, as stated in the call. The board may let the work by single contract or it may divide the work into severable parts by separate contracts, as stated in the call, according to the best interests of the agency.

(d) The board shall require the successful bidder or bidders to file with the board good and sufficient bonds to be approved by the board conditioned upon the faithful performance of the contract and upon the payment of their claims for labor and material in connection with the contract. The bonds shall contain the terms and conditions set forth in Title 15 (commencing with Section 3082) of Part 4 of Division 3 of the Civil Code and are subject to the provisions of that title.

(e) The board may reject any bid. The board of supervisors may, without advertising for bids, have the work done by force account if any of the following requirements are met:

(1) All the projects are rejected.

(2) No proposals are received in response to the advertisement.

(3) The estimated cost of the work does not exceed five thousand dollars ($5,000).

(4) The work consists of channel protection, maintenance work, or emergency work. In case of an emergency, if notice for bids to let contracts will not be given, the board shall comply with Chapter 2.5 (commencing with Section 22050).

New Text (Operative July 1, 2012)

not be given, the board shall comply with Chapter 2.5 (commencing with Section 22050).

(f) The agency may purchase in the open market, without advertising for bids, materials and supplies for use in any work either under contract or by force account.

(g) The Monterey County Board of Supervisors may grant to the board of directors, appointed pursuant to Section 49 of the Monterey County Water Resources Agency Act (Chapter 1159 of the Statutes of 1990), any of the powers or duties granted to the Monterey County Board of Supervisors by this section.

Old Text

(f) The agency may purchase in the open market, without advertising for bids, materials and supplies for use in any work either under contract or by force account.

(g) The Monterey County Board of Supervisors may grant to the board of directors, appointed pursuant to Section 49 of the Monterey County Water Resources Agency Act (Chapter 1159 of the Statutes of 1990), any of the powers or duties granted to the Monterey County Board of Supervisors by this section.

Revised to include reference to new Section 9000 et seq.

•••

PCC 21131

(a) All contracts for the construction of any unit of work, except as provided in this article, estimated to cost in excess of two thousand five hundred dollars ($2,500) shall be let to the lowest responsible bidder in the manner provided in this article. The board shall advertise by three placements in a daily newspaper of general circulation or two insertions in a weekly newspaper of general circulation published in the district inviting sealed proposals for the construction of the work before any contract is made, and may let by contract separately any part of the work. The board shall require the successful bidder to file with the board good and sufficient bonds to be approved by the board conditioned upon the faithful performance of the contract and upon the payment of the claims for labor and material in connection therewith, the bonds to contain the terms and conditions set forth in Title 3 (commencing with Section 9000) of Part 6 of Division 4 of the Civil Code, and to be subject to the provisions of that title. The board may reject any bid, in which case the board may advertise for new bids.

(b) In the event no proposals are received pursuant to advertisement therefor, or where the work consists of emergency work, the board of directors, by unanimous vote of all members present, may, without advertising for bids, have the work done by

PCC 21131

(a) All contracts for the construction of any unit of work, except as provided in this article, estimated to cost in excess of two thousand five hundred dollars ($2,500) shall be let to the lowest responsible bidder in the manner provided in this article. The board shall advertise by three placements in a daily newspaper of general circulation or two insertions in a weekly newspaper of general circulation published in the district inviting sealed proposals for the construction of the work before any contract is made, and may let by contract separately any part of the work. The board shall require the successful bidder to file with the board good and sufficient bonds to be approved by the board conditioned upon the faithful performance of the contract and upon the payment of the claims for labor and material in connection therewith, the bonds to contain the terms and conditions set forth in Title 15 (commencing with Section 3082) of Part 4 of Division 3 of the Civil Code, and to be subject to the provisions of that title. The board may reject any bid, in which case the board may advertise for new bids.

(b) In the event no proposals are received pursuant to advertisement therefor, or where the work consists of emergency work, the board of directors, by unanimous vote of all members present, may, without advertising for bids, have the work done by force account. In case of an emergency, if notice for bids to

New Text (Operative July 1, 2012)

force account. In case of an emergency, if notice for bids to let contracts will not be given, the board shall comply with Chapter 2.5 (commencing with Section 22050).

(c) The district may purchase in the open market without advertisement for bids, materials and supplies for use in any work either under contract or by force account; provided, however, that materials and supplies for use in any new construction work or improvement, except work authorized and required under circumstances referred to in subdivision (b), may not be purchased if the cost exceeds two thousand five hundred dollars ($2,500), without advertising for bids and awarding the contract to the lowest responsible bidder.

(d) This section does not apply to a contract entered into with the United States or the State of California or other governmental agency under the authority of Section 3 of Chapter 2126 of the Statutes of 1959, or to a contract authorized by a vote of the electorate of the district.

(e) The district may rent or otherwise contract for equipment with or without an operator and use it on works of the district, if the contract is approved by the board.

Old Text

let contracts will not be given, the board shall comply with Chapter 2.5 (commencing with Section 22050).

(c) The district may purchase in the open market without advertisement for bids, materials and supplies for use in any work either under contract or by force account; provided, however, that materials and supplies for use in any new construction work or improvement, except work authorized and required under circumstances referred to in subdivision (b), may not be purchased if the cost exceeds two thousand five hundred dollars ($2,500), without advertising for bids and awarding the contract to the lowest responsible bidder.

(d) This section does not apply to a contract entered into with the United States or the State of California or other governmental agency under the authority of Section 3 of Chapter 2126 of the Statutes of 1959, or to a contract authorized by a vote of the electorate of the district.

(e) The district may rent or otherwise contract for equipment with or without an operator and use it on works of the district, if the contract is approved by the board.

Revised to include reference to new Section 9000 et seq.

New Text (Operative July 1, 2012)

PCC 21141

(a) All contracts for the construction of any unit of work, except as provided in this article, estimated to cost in excess of two thousand dollars ($2,000) shall be let to the lowest responsible bidder in the manner provided in this article. The board shall advertise by three insertions in a daily newspaper of general circulation or two insertions in a weekly newspaper of general circulation published in the district inviting sealed proposals for the construction of the work before any contract shall be made, and may let by contract separately any part of the work. The board shall require the successful bidder to file with the board good and sufficient bonds to be approved by the board conditioned upon the faithful performance of the contract and upon the payment of the claims for labor and material, the bonds to contain the terms and conditions set forth in Title 3 (commencing with Section 9000) of Part 6 of Division 4 of the Civil Code, and to be subject to the provisions of that title. The board shall also have the right to reject any bid, in which case the board may advertise for new bids.

(b) In the event no proposals are received pursuant to advertisement, where the estimated cost of the work does not exceed the sum of two thousand dollars ($2,000), or where the work consists of emergency work, the board of directors, by unanimous vote of all members present, may, without advertising for bids, have the work done by force account. In case of an emergency, if notice for bids to let contracts will not be given, the board shall comply with Chapter 2.5 (commencing with Section 22050).

(c) The district may purchase in the open market, without advertisement for bids, materials and supplies for use in any work either under contract or by force account; provided, however, that materials and supplies for use in any new construction work or improvement, except work referred to in subdivision (b), may not be purchased if the cost exceeds two thousand five hundred dollars ($2,500), without advertising for bids and awarding the contract therefor to the lowest responsible bidder.

(d) The provisions of this section have no application to a contract entered into with the United States under the authority of Section 3, or to a contract authorized by a vote of the electorate of the district.

Old Text

PCC 21141

(a) All contracts for the construction of any unit of work, except as provided in this article, estimated to cost in excess of two thousand dollars ($2,000) shall be let to the lowest responsible bidder in the manner provided in this article. The board shall advertise by three insertions in a daily newspaper of general circulation or two insertions in a weekly newspaper of general circulation published in the district inviting sealed proposals for the construction of the work before any contract shall be made, and may let by contract separately any part of the work. The board shall require the successful bidder to file with the board good and sufficient bonds to be approved by the board conditioned upon the faithful performance of the contract and upon the payment of the claims for labor and material, the bonds to contain the terms and conditions set forth in Title 15 (commencing with Section 3082) of Part 4 of Division 3 of the Civil Code, and to be subject to the provisions of that title. The board shall also have the right to reject any bid, in which case the board may advertise for new bids.

(b) In the event no proposals are received pursuant to advertisement, where the estimated cost of the work does not exceed the sum of two thousand dollars ($2,000), or where the work consists of emergency work, the board of directors, by unanimous vote of all members present, may, without advertising for bids, have the work done by force account. In case of an emergency, if notice for bids to let contracts will not be given, the board shall comply with Chapter 2.5 (commencing with Section 22050).

(c) The district may purchase in the open market, without advertisement for bids, materials and supplies for use in any work either under contract or by force account; provided, however, that materials and supplies for use in any new construction work or improvement, except work referred to in subdivision (b), may not be purchased if the cost exceeds two thousand five hundred dollars ($2,500), without advertising for bids and awarding the contract therefor to the lowest responsible bidder.

(d) The provisions of this section have no application to a contract entered into with the United States under the authority of Section 3, or to a contract authorized by a vote of the electorate of the district.

Revised to include reference to new Section 9000 et seq.

New Text (Operative July 1, 2012)

PCC 21151

All contracts for any improvement or unit of work when the cost according to the estimate of the engineer will exceed twenty-five thousand dollars ($25,000), with or without the furnishing of materials or supplies, shall be let to the lowest responsible bidder or bidders in the manner provided in this article.

Construction of improvements or works shall not be staged to avoid the bidding process. The board shall first determine whether the contract shall be let as a single unit for the whole of the work, or shall be divided into severable parts, or both, according to the best interests of the district. The board shall call for bids and advertise the call by inviting sealed proposals for the construction or performance of the improvement or work before any contract is made. The board shall invite the bids by publishing a notice of the call for bids pursuant to Section 6062 or 6066 of the Government Code in a newspaper of general circulation in the county. The call for bids shall state whether the work is to be performed as a unit or shall be divided into severable specific parts, or both, as stated in the call. The board may let the work by single contract or it may divide the work into severable parts by separate contracts, as stated in the call, according to the best interests of the district. The board shall require the successful bidder or bidders to file with the board good and sufficient bonds to be approved by the board conditioned upon the faithful performance of the contract and upon the payment of their claims for labor and material, the bonds to contain the terms and conditions set forth in Title 3 (commencing with Section 9000) of Part 6 of Division 4 of the Civil Code and to be subject to the provisions of that title. The board shall also have the right to reject any bid. In the event the engineer's estimate is twenty-five thousand dollars ($25,000) or less, or in the event no proposals are received pursuant to advertisement therefor, or in the event the work consists of channel protection or maintenance work, or emergency work, the board of supervisors may, without advertising for bids, have the work done by day labor under the direction of the board, by contract, or by a combination of the two. In

Old Text

PCC 21151

All contracts for any improvement or unit of work when the cost according to the estimate of the engineer will exceed twenty-five thousand dollars ($25,000), with or without the furnishing of materials or supplies, shall be let to the lowest responsible bidder or bidders in the manner provided in this article.

Construction of improvements or works shall not be staged to avoid the bidding process. The board shall first determine whether the contract shall be let as a single unit for the whole of the work, or shall be divided into severable parts, or both, according to the best interests of the district. The board shall call for bids and advertise the call by inviting sealed proposals for the construction or performance of the improvement or work before any contract is made. The board shall invite the bids by publishing a notice of the call for bids pursuant to Section 6062 or 6066 of the Government Code in a newspaper of general circulation in the county. The call for bids shall state whether the work is to be performed as a unit or shall be divided into severable specific parts, or both, as stated in the call. The board may let the work by single contract or it may divide the work into severable parts by separate contracts, as stated in the call, according to the best interests of the district. The board shall require the successful bidder or bidders to file with the board good and sufficient bonds to be approved by the board conditioned upon the faithful performance of the contract and upon the payment of their claims for labor and material, the bonds to contain the terms and conditions set forth in Title 15 (commencing with Section 3082) of Part 4 of Division 3 of the Civil Code and to be subject to the provisions of that title. The board shall also have the right to reject any bid. In the event the engineer's estimate is twenty-five thousand dollars ($25,000) or less, or in the event no proposals are received pursuant to advertisement therefor, or in the event the work consists of channel protection or maintenance work, or emergency work, the board of supervisors may, without advertising for bids, have the work done by day labor under the direction of the board, by contract, or by a combination of the two. In case of an emergency, if notice for bids to let contracts will not be given, the board shall comply with Chapter 2.5

New Text (Operative July 1, 2012) | **Old Text**

case of an emergency, if notice for bids to let contracts will not be given, the board shall comply with Chapter 2.5 (commencing with Section 22050). The district may acquire in the open market without advertising for bids, materials, equipment, and supplies for use in any work or for any other purpose.

(commencing with Section 22050). The district may acquire in the open market without advertising for bids, materials, equipment, and supplies for use in any work or for any other purpose.

Revised to include reference to new Section 9000 et seq.

••

PCC 21171

(a) All contracts for any improvement or unit of work when the cost, according to the estimate of the engineer, will exceed two thousand dollars ($2,000), shall be let to the lowest responsible bidder or bidders in the manner provided in this article. The board shall first determine whether the contract shall be let as a single unit for the whole of the work, or shall be divided into severable parts, or both, according to the best interests of the district. The board shall call for bids and advertise the call by three insertions in a daily newspaper of general circulation or by two insertions in a weekly newspaper of general circulation printed and published in the district inviting sealed proposals for the construction or performance of the improvement or work before any contract is made. The call for bids shall state whether the work is to be performed as a unit for the whole thereof or shall be divided into severable specific parts, or both, as stated in the call. The board may let the work by single contract as a unit or it may divide the work into severable parts by separate contracts, as stated in the call, according to the best interests of the district. The board shall require the successful bidder or bidders to file with the board good and sufficient bonds to be approved by the board conditioned upon the faithful performance of the contract and upon the payment of their claims for labor and material, the bonds to contain the terms and conditions set forth in Title 3 (commencing with Section 9000) of Part 6 of Division 4 of the Civil Code and to be subject to the provisions of that title. The board shall also have the right to reject any bid.

PCC 21171

(a) All contracts for any improvement or unit of work when the cost, according to the estimate of the engineer, will exceed two thousand dollars ($2,000), shall be let to the lowest responsible bidder or bidders in the manner provided in this article. The board shall first determine whether the contract shall be let as a single unit for the whole of the work, or shall be divided into severable parts, or both, according to the best interests of the district. The board shall call for bids and advertise the call by three insertions in a daily newspaper of general circulation or by two insertions in a weekly newspaper of general circulation printed and published in the district inviting sealed proposals for the construction or performance of the improvement or work before any contract is made. The call for bids shall state whether the work is to be performed as a unit for the whole thereof or shall be divided into severable specific parts, or both, as stated in the call. The board may let the work by single contract as a unit or it may divide the work into severable parts by separate contracts, as stated in the call, according to the best interests of the district. The board shall require the successful bidder or bidders to file with the board good and sufficient bonds to be approved by the board conditioned upon the faithful performance of the contract and upon the payment of their claims for labor and material, the bonds to contain the terms and conditions set forth in Title 15 (commencing with Section 3082) of Part 4 of Division 3 of the Civil Code and to be subject to the provisions of that title. The board shall also have the right to reject any bid.

(b) In the event all proposals are rejected or no proposals are received pursuant to advertisement, or the

New Text (Operative July 1, 2012)

(b) In the event all proposals are rejected or no proposals are received pursuant to advertisement, or the estimated cost of the work does not exceed two thousand dollars ($2,000), or the work consists of channel protection, maintenance work, or emergency work, the board of supervisors may, without advertising for bids, have the work done by force account. In case of an emergency, if notice for bids to let contracts will not be given, the board shall comply with Chapter 2.5 (commencing with Section 22050).

(c) The district may purchase in the open market, without advertising for bids, materials and supplies for use in any work either under contract or by force account; provided, however, that materials and supplies for use in any new construction work or improvements, except work referred to in subdivision (b), may not be purchased if the cost exceeds two thousand five hundred dollars ($2,500), without advertising for bids and awarding the contract to the lowest responsible bidder.

Old Text

estimated cost of the work does not exceed two thousand dollars ($2,000), or the work consists of channel protection, maintenance work, or emergency work, the board of supervisors may, without advertising for bids, have the work done by force account. In case of an emergency, if notice for bids to let contracts will not be given, the board shall comply with Chapter 2.5 (commencing with Section 22050).

(c) The district may purchase in the open market, without advertising for bids, materials and supplies for use in any work either under contract or by force account; provided, however, that materials and supplies for use in any new construction work or improvements, except work referred to in subdivision (b), may not be purchased if the cost exceeds two thousand five hundred dollars ($2,500), without advertising for bids and awarding the contract to the lowest responsible bidder.

Revised to include reference to new Section 9000 et seq.

PCC 21181

(a)All contracts for any improvement or unit of work when the cost according to the estimate of the engineer, will exceed four thousand dollars ($4,000), shall be let to the lowest responsible bidder or bidders in the manner provided in this article. The board shall first determine whether the contract shall be let as a single unit or shall be divided into severable parts, or both, according to the best interests of the district. The board shall call for bids and advertise the call in the district pursuant to Section 6066 of the Government Code inviting sealed proposals for the construction or performance of the improvement or before any contract is made. The call for bids shall state whether the work is to be performed as a unit or shall be divided into severable specific parts, or both, as stated in the call. The board may let the work by single contract or it may divide the work into severable parts by separate contracts, as stated

PCC 21181

(a)All contracts for any improvement or unit of work when the cost according to the estimate of the engineer, will exceed four thousand dollars ($4,000), shall be let to the lowest responsible bidder or bidders in the manner provided in this article. The board shall first determine whether the contract shall be let as a single unit or shall be divided into severable parts, or both, according to the best interests of the district. The board shall call for bids and advertise the call in the district pursuant to Section 6066 of the Government Code inviting sealed proposals for the construction or performance of the improvement or before any contract is made. The call for bids shall state whether the work is to be performed as a unit or shall be divided into severable specific parts, or both, as stated in the call. The board may let the work by single contract or it may divide the work into severable parts by separate contracts, as stated in the call, according to the best interests of the district. The

New Text (Operative July 1, 2012)

in the call, according to the best interests of the district. The board shall require the successful bidder or bidders to file with the board good and sufficient bonds to be approved by the board conditioned upon the faithful performance of the contract and upon the payment of their claims for labor and material, the bonds to contain the terms and conditions set forth in Title 3 (commencing with Section 9000) of Part 6 of Division 4 of the Civil Code and to be subject to the provisions of that title. The board shall also have the right to reject any bid.

(b) In the event no proposals are received pursuant to advertisement or the estimated cost of the work does not exceed four thousand dollars ($4,000), or the work consists of channel protection, maintenance work, or emergency work, the board of supervisors may, without advertising for bids, have the work done by day labor, under the direction of the board, by contract, or by the combination of the two. In case of an emergency, if notice for bids to let contracts will not be given, the board shall comply with Chapter 2.5 (commencing with Section 22050).

(c) The district may acquire in the open market, without advertising for bids, materials, equipment, and supplies for use in any work or for any other purpose; provided, however, that materials and supplies for use in any new construction work or improvement, except work referred to in subdivision (b), may not be purchased if the cost exceeds two thousand five hundred dollars ($2,500), without advertising for bids and awarding the contract to the lowest responsible bidder.

Old Text

board shall require the successful bidder or bidders to file with the board good and sufficient bonds to be approved by the board conditioned upon the faithful performance of the contract and upon the payment of their claims for labor and material, the bonds to contain the terms and conditions set forth in Title 15 (commencing with Section 3082) of Part 4 of Division 3 of the Civil Code and to be subject to the provisions of that title. The board shall also have the right to reject any bid.

(b) In the event no proposals are received pursuant to advertisement or the estimated cost of the work does not exceed four thousand dollars ($4,000), or the work consists of channel protection, maintenance work, or emergency work, the board of supervisors may, without advertising for bids, have the work done by day labor, under the direction of the board, by contract, or by the combination of the two. In case of an emergency, if notice for bids to let contracts will not be given, the board shall comply with Chapter 2.5 (commencing with Section 22050).

(c) The district may acquire in the open market, without advertising for bids, materials, equipment, and supplies for use in any work or for any other purpose; provided, however, that materials and supplies for use in any new construction work or improvement, except work referred to in subdivision (b), may not be purchased if the cost exceeds two thousand five hundred dollars ($2,500), without advertising for bids and awarding the contract to the lowest responsible bidder.

Revised to include reference to new Section 9000 et seq.

New Text (Operative July 1, 2012)

PCC 21196

(a) All contracts for the construction of any unit of work, except as provided in this article, estimated to cost in excess of two thousand five hundred dollars ($2,500) shall be let to the lowest responsible bidder in the manner provided in this article. The board of directors of the district shall call for bids and advertise the call by three insertions in a daily newspaper of general circulation or two insertions in a weekly newspaper of general circulation published in the district inviting sealed proposals for the construction of the work before any contract is made, and may let by contract separately any part of the work. The board shall require the successful bidder to file with the board good and sufficient bonds to be approved by the board conditioned upon the faithful performance of the contract and upon the payment of the claims for labor and material, the bonds to contain the terms and conditions set forth in Title 3 (commencing with Section 9000) of Part 6 of Division 4 of the Civil Code and to be subject to the provisions of that title The board shall also have the right to reject any bid, in which case the board may advertise for new bids.

(b) In the event no proposals are received pursuant to advertisement, or where the estimated cost of the work does not exceed two thousand five hundred dollars ($2,500), or the work consists of emergency work, the board of directors by unanimous vote of all members present, may, without advertising for bids, have the work done by force account. In case of an emergency, if notice for bids to let contracts will not be given, the board shall comply with Chapter 2.5 (commencing with Section 22050). The district may purchase in the open market, without advertisement for bids, materials and supplies for use in any work either under contract or by force account.

(c) The provisions of this section have no application to a contract entered into with the United States under the authority of the Solano County Flood Control and Water Conservation District Act, or to a contract authorized by a vote of the electorate of the district.. ."

Old Text

PCC 21196

(a) All contracts for the construction of any unit of work, except as provided in this article, estimated to cost in excess of two thousand five hundred dollars ($2,500) shall be let to the lowest responsible bidder in the manner provided in this article. The board of directors of the district shall call for bids and advertise the call by three insertions in a daily newspaper of general circulation or two insertions in a weekly newspaper of general circulation published in the district inviting sealed proposals for the construction of the work before any contract is made, and may let by contract separately any part of the work. The board shall require the successful bidder to file with the board good and sufficient bonds to be approved by the board conditioned upon the faithful performance of the contract and upon the payment of the claims for labor and material, the bonds to contain the terms and conditions set forth in Title 15 (commencing with Section 3082) of Part 4 of Division 3 of the Civil Code and to be subject to the provisions of this title. The board shall also have the right to reject any bid, in which case the board may advertise for new bids.

(b) In the event no proposals are received pursuant to advertisement, or where the estimated cost of the work does not exceed two thousand five hundred dollars ($2,500), or the work consists of emergency work, the board of directors by unanimous vote of all members present, may, without advertising for bids, have the work done by force account. In case of an emergency, if notice for bids to let contracts will not be given, the board shall comply with Chapter 2.5 (commencing with Section 22050). The district may purchase in the open market, without advertisement for bids, materials and supplies for use in any work either under contract or by force account.

(c) The provisions of this section have no application to a contract entered into with the United States under the authority of the Solano County Flood Control and Water Conservation District Act, or to a contract authorized by a vote of the electorate of the district.

Revised to include reference to new Section 9000 et seq.

PCC 21212

PCC 21212

New Text (Operative July 1, 2012)

(a) All contracts for the construction of any unit of work, except as provided in this article, estimated to cost in excess of three thousand dollars ($3,000), shall be let to the lowest responsible bidder in the manner provided in this article. The board of directors of the agency shall advertise pursuant to Section 6066 of the Government Code in a newspaper of general circulation published in the agency's jurisdiction inviting sealed proposals for the construction of the work before any contract is made, and may let by contract separately any part of the work. The board shall require the successful bidder to file with the board good and sufficient bonds to be approved by the board conditioned upon the faithful performance of the contract and upon the payment of any claims for labor and material and containing the terms and conditions set forth in Title 3 (commencing with Section 9000) of Part 6 of Division 4 of the Civil Code and to be subject to the provisions of that title. The board shall also have the right to reject any bid, in which case the board may advertise for new bids.

(b) In the event no proposals are received pursuant to advertisement, or where the estimated cost of the work does not exceed three thousand dollars ($3,000), or the work consists of emergency work, the board of directors, by unanimous vote of all members present, may, without advertising for bids, have the work done by force account. In case of an emergency, if notice for bids to let contracts will not be given, the board shall comply with Chapter 2.5 (commencing with Section 22050).

(c) The agency may purchase in the open market without advertisement for bids, materials and supplies for use in any work either under contract or by force account.

(d) The provisions of this section have no application to a contract entered into with the United States under the authority of Section 6 of Chapter 10 of the Statutes of the 1952 First Extraordinary Session, or to a contract authorized by a vote of the electorate of the agency.

Old Text

(a) All contracts for the construction of any unit of work, except as provided in this article, estimated to cost in excess of three thousand dollars ($3,000), shall be let to the lowest responsible bidder in the manner provided in this article. The board of directors of the agency shall advertise pursuant to Section 6066 of the Government Code in a newspaper of general circulation published in the agency's jurisdiction inviting sealed proposals for the construction of the work before any contract is made, and may let by contract separately any part of the work. The board shall require the successful bidder to file with the board good and sufficient bonds to be approved by the board conditioned upon the faithful performance of the contract and upon the payment of any claims for labor and material and containing the terms and conditions set forth in Title 15 (commencing with Section 3082) of Part 4 of Division 3 of the Civil Code and to be subject to the provisions of that title. The board shall also have the right to reject any bid, in which case the board may advertise for new bids.

(b) In the event no proposals are received pursuant to advertisement, or where the estimated cost of the work does not exceed three thousand dollars ($3,000), or the work consists of emergency work, the board of directors, by unanimous vote of all members present, may, without advertising for bids, have the work done by force account. In case of an emergency, if notice for bids to let contracts will not be given, the board shall comply with Chapter 2.5 (commencing with Section 22050).

(c) The agency may purchase in the open market without advertisement for bids, materials and supplies for use in any work either under contract or by force account.

(d) The provisions of this section have no application to a contract entered into with the United States under the authority of Section 6 of Chapter 10 of the Statutes of the 1952 First Extraordinary Session, or to a contract authorized by a vote of the electorate of the agency.

Revised to include reference to new Section 9000 et seq.

New Text (Operative July 1, 2012)

PCC 21231

Any improvement or unit of work when the cost, according to the estimate of the engineer, will exceed five thousand dollars ($5,000), shall be done by contract let to the lowest responsible bidder or bidders in the manner provided in this article. The board shall first determine whether the contract will be let as a single unit, or will be divided into severable parts, or both, according to the best interests of the district. The board shall call for bids and advertise the call pursuant to Section 6066 of the Government Code in the district, inviting sealed proposals for the construction or performance of the improvement or before any contract is made. The call for bids shall state whether the work is to be performed as a unit or shall be divided into separate specific parts, or both, as stated in the call. The board may let the work by single contract or it may divide the work into severable parts by separate contracts, as stated in the call, according to the best interests of the district. The board shall require the successful bidder or bidders to file with the board good and sufficient bonds to be approved by the board conditioned upon the faithful performance of the contract and upon the payment of their claims for labor and material, the bonds to contain the terms and conditions set forth in Title 3 (commencing with Section 9000) of Part 6 of Division 4 of the Civil Code and to be subject to the provisions of that title. The board shall also have the right to reject any bid. In the event no proposals are received pursuant to advertisement, or the estimated cost of the work does not exceed five thousand dollars ($5,000), or the work consists of channel protection, maintenance work, or emergency work, the board of supervisors may, without advertising for bids, have the work done by day labor, under the direction of the board, by contract, or by a combination of the two. In case of an emergency, if notice for bids to let contracts will not be given, the board shall comply with Chapter 2.5 (commencing with Section 22050).

The district may acquire in the open market without advertising for bids, materials, equipment and supplies for use in any work or for any other purpose; provided, however, that materials and

Old Text

PCC 21231

Any improvement or unit of work when the cost, according to the estimate of the engineer, will exceed five thousand dollars ($5,000), shall be done by contract let to the lowest responsible bidder or bidders in the manner provided in this article. The board shall first determine whether the contract will be let as a single unit, or will be divided into severable parts, or both, according to the best interests of the district. The board shall call for bids and advertise the call pursuant to Section 6066 of the Government Code in the district, inviting sealed proposals for the construction or performance of the improvement or before any contract is made. The call for bids shall state whether the work is to be performed as a unit or shall be divided into separate specific parts, or both, as stated in the call. The board may let the work by single contract or it may divide the work into severable parts by separate contracts, as stated in the call, according to the best interests of the district. The board shall require the successful bidder or bidders to file with the board good and sufficient bonds to be approved by the board conditioned upon the faithful performance of the contract and upon the payment of their claims for labor and material, the bonds to contain the terms and conditions set forth in Title 15 (commencing with Section 3082) of Part 4 of Division 3 of the Civil Code and to be subject to the provisions of that title. The board shall also have the right to reject any bid. In the event no proposals are received pursuant to advertisement, or the estimated cost of the work does not exceed five thousand dollars ($5,000), or the work consists of channel protection, maintenance work, or emergency work, the board of supervisors may, without advertising for bids, have the work done by day labor, under the direction of the board, by contract, or by a combination of the two. In case of an emergency, if notice for bids to let contracts will not be given, the board shall comply with Chapter 2.5 (commencing with Section 22050).

The district may acquire in the open market without advertising for bids, materials, equipment and supplies for use in any work or for any other purpose; provided, however, that materials and supplies for use in any new construction work or improvement, except work referred to in the preceding sentence,

New Text (Operative July 1, 2012)

supplies for use in any new construction work or improvement, except work referred to in the preceding sentence, may not be purchased if the cost exceeds five thousand dollars ($5,000), without advertising for bids and awarding the contract to the lowest responsible bidder.

Old Text

may not be purchased if the cost exceeds five thousand dollars ($5,000), without advertising for bids and awarding the contract to the lowest responsible bidder.

Revised to include reference to new Section 9000 et seq.

••

PCC 21241

All contracts for any improvement or unit of work when the cost, according to the estimate of the engineer, will exceed two thousand dollars ($2,000), shall be let to the lowest responsible bidder or bidders in the manner provided in this article. The board shall first determine whether the contract shall be let as a single unit or shall be divided into severable parts, or both, according to the best interests of the zone. The board shall call for bids and advertise the call pursuant to Section 6066 of the Government Code in the district inviting sealed proposals for the construction or performance of the improvement or work before any contract is made. The call for bids shall state whether the work is to be performed as a unit or shall be divided into severable specific parts, or both, as stated in the call. The board may let the work by single contract or it may divide the work into severable parts by separate contracts, as stated in the call, according to the best interests of the district. The board shall require the successful bidder or bidders to file with the board good and sufficient bonds to be approved by the board conditioned upon the faithful performance of the contract and upon the payment of their claims for labor and material, the bonds to contain the terms and conditions set forth in Title 3 (commencing with Section 9000) of Part 6 of Division 4 of the Civil Code and to be subject to the provisions of that title. The board shall also have the right to reject any bid. In the event no proposals are received pursuant to advertisement, or the estimated cost of the work does not exceed two thousand dollars ($2,000), or the work consists of emergency work, the board of supervisors may,

PCC 21241

All contracts for any improvement or unit of work when the cost, according to the estimate of the engineer, will exceed two thousand dollars ($2,000), shall be let to the lowest responsible bidder or bidders in the manner provided in this article. The board shall first determine whether the contract shall be let as a single unit or shall be divided into severable parts, or both, according to the best interests of the zone. The board shall call for bids and advertise the call pursuant to Section 6066 of the Government Code in the district inviting sealed proposals for the construction or performance of the improvement or work before any contract is made. The call for bids shall state whether the work is to be performed as a unit or shall be divided into severable specific parts, or both, as stated in the call. The board may let the work by single contract or it may divide the work into severable parts by separate contracts, as stated in the call, according to the best interests of the district. The board shall require the successful bidder or bidders to file with the board good and sufficient bonds to be approved by the board conditioned upon the faithful performance of the contract and upon the payment of their claims for labor and material, the bonds to contain the terms and conditions set forth in Title 15 (commencing with Section 3082) of Part 4 of Division 3 of the Civil Code and to be subject to the provisions of that title. The board shall also have the right to reject any bid. In the event no proposals are received pursuant to advertisement, or the estimated cost of the work does not exceed two thousand dollars ($2,000), or the work consists of emergency work, the board of supervisors may, without advertising for bids, have the work done by day labor, under the direction of the board, by contract, or

New Text (Operative July 1, 2012) | **Old Text**

without advertising for bids, have the work done by day labor, under the direction of the board, by contract, or by a combination of the two. In case of an emergency, if notice for bids to let contracts will not be given, the board shall comply with Chapter 2.5 (commencing with Section 22050). The board may acquire in the open market, without advertising for bids, materials, equipment, and supplies for use in any work or for any other purpose; provided, however, that materials and supplies for use in any new construction work or improvement, except work referred to in the preceding sentence, may not be purchased if the cost exceeds two thousand five hundred dollars ($2,500), without advertising for bids and awarding the contract to the lowest responsible bidder.

by a combination of the two. In case of an emergency, if notice for bids to let contracts will not be given, the board shall comply with Chapter 2.5 (commencing with Section 22050). The board may acquire in the open market, without advertising for bids, materials, equipment, and supplies for use in any work or for any other purpose; provided, however, that materials and supplies for use in any new construction work or improvement, except work referred to in the preceding sentence, may not be purchased if the cost exceeds two thousand five hundred dollars ($2,500), without advertising for bids and awarding the contract to the lowest responsible bidder.

Revised to include reference to new Section 9000 et seq.

PCC 21251

(a) (1) All contracts for any improvement or unit of work, if the cost according to the estimate of the engineer will exceed thirty thousand dollars ($30,000), shall be let to the lowest responsible bidder or bidders as provided in this article. The board shall first determine whether the contract shall be let as a single unit or divided into severable parts, or both.

(2) All contracts for any improvement or unit of work, if the cost according to the estimate of the engineer is thirty thousand dollars ($30,000) or less, may be let without advertising for bids in accordance with procedures adopted by the board.

(b) The board shall call for bids and advertise the call pursuant to Section 6063 of the Government Code in the district, inviting sealed proposals for the construction or performance of the improvement or work before any contract is made. The call for bids shall state whether the work is to be performed as one unit or divided into severable specific parts.

(c) The work may be let under a single contract or several contracts, or both, as stated in the call. The board shall require the successful bidder or bidders

PCC 21251

(a) (1) All contracts for any improvement or unit of work, if the cost according to the estimate of the engineer will exceed thirty thousand dollars ($30,000), shall be let to the lowest responsible bidder or bidders as provided in this article. The board shall first determine whether the contract shall be let as a single unit or divided into severable parts, or both.

(2) All contracts for any improvement or unit of work, if the cost according to the estimate of the engineer is thirty thousand dollars ($30,000) or less, may be let without advertising for bids in accordance with procedures adopted by the board.

(b) The board shall call for bids and advertise the call pursuant to Section 6063 of the Government Code in the district, inviting sealed proposals for the construction or performance of the improvement or work before any contract is made. The call for bids shall state whether the work is to be performed as one unit or divided into severable specific parts.

(c) The work may be let under a single contract or several contracts, or both, as stated in the call. The board shall require the successful bidder or bidders to file with the board good and sufficient bonds to be approved by the board conditioned upon the faithful

New Text (Operative July 1, 2012)

to file with the board good and sufficient bonds to be approved by the board conditioned upon the faithful performance of the contract and upon the payment of their claims for labor and material. The bonds comply with Title 3 (commencing with Section 9000) of Part 6 of Division 4 of the Civil Code. The board may reject any bid.

(d) If all proposals are rejected or no proposals are received, or the estimated cost of the work does not exceed five thousand dollars ($5,000), or the work consists of channel protection, maintenance work, or emergency work, the board may have the work done by force account without advertising for bids. In case of an emergency, if notice for bids to let contracts will not be given, the board shall comply with Chapter 2.5 (commencing with Section 22050).

(e) The district may purchase in the open market, without advertising for bids, materials and supplies for use in any work either under contract or by force account.

Old Text

performance of the contract and upon the payment of their claims for labor and material. The bonds shall comply with Title 15 (commencing with Section 3082) of Part 4 of Division 3 of the Civil Code. The board may reject any bid.

(d) If all proposals are rejected or no proposals are received, or the estimated cost of the work does not exceed five thousand dollars ($5,000), or the work consists of channel protection, maintenance work, or emergency work, the board may have the work done by force account without advertising for bids. In case of an emergency, if notice for bids to let contracts will not be given, the board shall comply with Chapter 2.5 (commencing with Section 22050).

(e) The district may purchase in the open market, without advertising for bids, materials and supplies for use in any work either under contract or by force account.

Revised to include reference to new Section 9000 et seq.

••

PCC 21261

All contracts for any improvement or unit of work when the cost, according to the estimate of the engineer, will exceed two thousand dollars ($2,000), shall be let to the lowest responsible bidder or bidders in the manner provided in this article. The board shall first determine whether the contract shall be let as a single unit for the work, or shall be divided into severable parts, or both, according to the best interests of the district. The board shall call for bids and advertise the call pursuant to Section 6066 of the Government Code in the district inviting sealed proposals for the construction or performance of the improvement or work before any contract is made. The call for bids shall state whether the work is to be performed as a unit or shall be divided into severable specific parts, or both, as stated in the call. The board may let the work by single contract or it may divide the work into severable parts by separate contracts, as stated in the call, according to the best interests of the district. The board shall require the successful bidder or bidders to file with the board good and sufficient bonds to be approved by the board conditioned

PCC 21261

All contracts for any improvement or unit of work when the cost, according to the estimate of the engineer, will exceed two thousand dollars ($2,000), shall be let to the lowest responsible bidder or bidders in the manner provided in this article. The board shall first determine whether the contract shall be let as a single unit for the work, or shall be divided into severable parts, or both, according to the best interests of the district. The board shall call for bids and advertise the call pursuant to Section 6066 of the Government Code in the district inviting sealed proposals for the construction or performance of the improvement or work before any contract is made. The call for bids shall state whether the work is to be performed as a unit or shall be divided into severable specific parts, or both, as stated in the call. The board may let the work by single contract or it may divide the work into severable parts by separate contracts, as stated in the call, according to the best interests of the district. The board shall require the successful bidder or bidders to file with the board good and sufficient bonds to be approved by the board conditioned upon the faithful performance of the contract and

New Text (Operative July 1, 2012)

upon the faithful performance of the contract and upon the payment of their claims for labor and material, the bonds to contain the terms and conditions set forth in Title 3 (commencing with Section 9000) of Part 6 of Division 4 of the Civil Code and to be subject to the provisions of that title. The board shall also have the right to reject any bid. In the event all proposals are rejected or no proposals are received pursuant to advertisement, or the estimated cost of the work does not exceed two thousand dollars ($2,000), or the work consists of channel protection, maintenance work, or emergency work, the board of supervisors may, without advertising for bids, have the work done by force account. In case of an emergency, if notice for bids to let contracts will not be given, the board shall comply with Chapter 2.5 (commencing with Section 22050). The district may purchase in the open market, without advertising for bids, materials and supplies for use in any work either under contract or by force account.

Old Text

upon the payment of their claims for labor and material, the bonds to contain the terms and conditions set forth in Title 15 (commencing with Section 3082) of Part 4 of Division 3 of the Civil Code and to be subject to the provisions of that title. The board shall also have the right to reject any bid. In the event all proposals are rejected or no proposals are received pursuant to advertisement, or the estimated cost of the work does not exceed two thousand dollars ($2,000), or the work consists of channel protection, maintenance work, or emergency work, the board of supervisors may, without advertising for bids, have the work done by force account. In case of an emergency, if notice for bids to let contracts will not be given, the board shall comply with Chapter 2.5 (commencing with Section 22050). The district may purchase in the open market, without advertising for bids, materials and supplies for use in any work either under contract or by force account.

Revised to include reference to new Section 9000 et seq.

•••

PCC 21271

All improvement and units of work to be performed by or for the district shall be performed in accordance with the following procedures and requirements:

(a) If the work consists of the protection or maintenance of channels, storm drains, dams or other flood control works, or emergency work, the board of directors may, without advertising for bids therefor, have the work done by day labor under the direction of the board, by contract, or by a combination of the two. In case of an emergency, if notice for bids to let contracts will not be given, the board shall comply with Chapter 2.5 (commencing with Section 22050).

(b) If the work consists of the construction of new flood control channels, storm drains, dams, or other unit or units of work, and if the cost of the work, according to the estimate of the engineer, will exceed ten thousand dollars ($10,000), and if the work is not the type of work referred to in subdivision (a) or (c) of this section, the new construction shall be performed under a contract or contracts which shall be let to the lowest responsible bidder or bidders in the manner

PCC 21271

All improvement and units of work to be performed by or for the district shall be performed in accordance with the following procedures and requirements:

(a) If the work consists of the protection or maintenance of channels, storm drains, dams or other flood control works, or emergency work, the board of directors may, without advertising for bids therefor, have the work done by day labor under the direction of the board, by contract, or by a combination of the two. In case of an emergency, if notice for bids to let contracts will not be given, the board shall comply with Chapter 2.5 (commencing with Section 22050).

(b) If the work consists of the construction of new flood control channels, storm drains, dams, or other unit or units of work, and if the cost of the work, according to the estimate of the engineer, will exceed ten thousand dollars ($10,000), and if the work is not the type of work referred to in subdivision (a) or (c) of this section, the new construction shall be performed under a contract or contracts which shall be let to the lowest responsible bidder or bidders in the manner provided in subdivision (d) of this section.

(c) If the work consists of the maintenance or alteration of *provided in subdivision (d) of this section.*

(c) If the work consists of the maintenance or alteration of existing facilities, including electrical, painting, and roofing work, and if the cost of labor and materials for the work according to the engineer's estimate, will exceed three thousand five hundred dollars ($3,500), and if the work is not the type of work referred to in subdivision (a) or (b) of this section, the maintenance and alteration work shall be performed under a contract or contracts which shall be let to the lowest responsible bidder or bidders in the manner provided in subdivision (d) of this section.

(d) The board shall first determine whether the work shall be let as a single unit or shall be divided into severable parts, or both, according to the best interests of the district. The board shall call for bids and advertise the call pursuant to Section 6066 of the Government Code in the district inviting sealed proposals for the construction or performance of the work before any contract is made. The call for bids shall state whether the work is to be performed as a unit or shall be divided into severable, specific parts, or both, as stated in the call. The board may let the work by single contract or it may divide the work into severable parts by separate contracts, as stated in the call, according to the best interests of the district. The board shall require the successful bidder or bidders to file with the board good and sufficient bond to be approved by the board conditioned upon the faithful performance of the contract and upon the payment of the claims for labor and material. The faithful performance bond shall contain the terms and conditions as the board may specify, and the payment bond shall contain the terms and conditions set forth in, and shall be subject to, the provisions of Title 3 (commencing with Section 9000) of Part 6 of Division 4 of the Civil Code. If the work to be performed on behalf of the district does not involve an expenditure of fifteen thousand dollars ($15,000) or more, the district may require a faithful performance bond or a payment bond. The board shall also have the right to reject any bid.

(e) If no proposals are received pursuant to advertisement, or if the estimated cost of work of

existing facilities, including electrical, painting, and roofing work, and if the cost of labor and materials for the work according to the engineer's estimate, will exceed three thousand five hundred dollars ($3,500), and if the work is not the type of work referred to in subdivision (a) or (b) of this section, the maintenance and alteration work shall be performed under a contract or contracts which shall be let to the lowest responsible bidder or bidders in the manner provided in subdivision (d) of this section.

(d) The board shall first determine whether the work shall be let as a single unit or shall be divided into severable parts, or both, according to the best interests of the district. The board shall call for bids and advertise the call pursuant to Section 6066 of the Government Code in the district inviting sealed proposals for the construction or performance of the work before any contract is made. The call for bids shall state whether the work is to be performed as a unit or shall be divided into severable, specific parts, or both, as stated in the call. The board may let the work by single contract or it may divide the work into severable parts by separate contracts, as stated in the call, according to the best interests of the district. The board shall require the successful bidder or bidders to file with the board good and sufficient bond to be approved by the board conditioned upon the faithful performance of the contract and upon the payment of the claims for labor and material. The faithful performance bond shall contain the terms and conditions as the board may specify, and the payment bond shall contain the terms and conditions set forth in, and shall be subject to, the provisions of Title 15 (commencing with Section 3082) of Part 4 of Division 3 of the Civil Code. If the work to be performed on behalf of the district does not involve an expenditure of fifteen thousand dollars ($15,000) or more, the district may require a faithful performance bond or a payment bond. The board shall also have the right to reject any bid.

(e) If no proposals are received pursuant to advertisement, or if the estimated cost of work of the type referred to in subdivision (b) of this section does not exceed ten thousand dollars ($10,000), or if the estimated cost of work of the type referred to in subdivision (c) of this section does not exceed three thousand five hundred dollars ($3,500), the board of directors may, without

New Text (Operative July 1, 2012) **Old Text**

the type referred to in subdivision (b) of this section does not exceed ten thousand dollars ($10,000), or if the estimated cost of work of the type referred to in subdivision (c) of this section does not exceed three thousand five hundred dollars ($3,500), the board of directors may, without advertising for bids, have the work done by day labor, under the direction of the board, by contract, or by combination of the two. If any change or alteration in a contract awarded under the provisions of this section for work of the type referred to in subdivision (b) or (c) is deemed necessary and the cost does not exceed 10 percent of the original contract price, the board may authorize the contractor to proceed with the change or alteration without the formality of obtaining bids.

(f) Notwithstanding the foregoing provisions, the district shall have the power to acquire in the open market, and may authorize the Purchasing Agents of the County of Santa Barbara to acquire in the open market, without advertising for bids, materials, equipment and supplies for use in any work or for any other purpose; provided, however, that materials and supplies for use in any new construction work or improvement, except work referred to in subdivision (a) of this section, may not be purchased without advertising for bids and awarding the contract to the lowest responsible bidder if the cost exceeds two thousand five hundred dollars ($2,500), unless the purchase is made by the county purchasing agent at the request of the district, in which case the cost shall not exceed six thousand five hundred dollars ($6,500).

advertising for bids, have the work done by day labor, under the direction of the board, by contract, or by combination of the two. If any change or alteration in a contract awarded under the provisions of this section for work of the type referred to in subdivision (b) or (c) is deemed necessary and the cost does not exceed 10 percent of the original contract price, the board may authorize the contractor to proceed with the change or alteration without the formality of obtaining bids.

(f) Notwithstanding the foregoing provisions, the district shall have the power to acquire in the open market, and may authorize the Purchasing Agents of the County of Santa Barbara to acquire in the open market, without advertising for bids, materials, equipment and supplies for use in any work or for any other purpose; provided, however, that materials and supplies for use in any new construction work or improvement, except work referred to in subdivision (a) of this section, may not be purchased without advertising for bids and awarding the contract to the lowest responsible bidder if the cost exceeds two thousand five hundred dollars ($2,500), unless the purchase is made by the county purchasing agent at the request of the district, in which case the cost shall not exceed six thousand five hundred dollars ($6,500).

Revised to include reference to new Section 9000 et seq.

<u>***PCC 21311***</u>

(a) All contracts for any improvement or unit of work when the cost, according to the estimate of the engineer, will exceed two thousand dollars ($2,000), shall be let to the lowest responsible bidder or bidders in the manner provided in this article. The board shall first determine whether the contract shall be let as a single unit, or shall be divided into severable parts, or both, according to the best interests of the district. The board shall call for bids and advertise the call by three

PCC 21311

(a) All contracts for any improvement or unit of work when the cost, according to the estimate of the engineer, will exceed two thousand dollars ($2,000), shall be let to the lowest responsible bidder or bidders in the manner provided in this article. The board shall first determine whether the contract shall be let as a single unit, or shall be divided into severable parts, or both, according to the best interests of the district. The board shall call for bids and advertise the call by

New Text (Operative July 1, 2012)	Old Text
insertions in a daily newspaper of general circulation or by two insertions in a weekly newspaper of general circulation printed and published in the district inviting sealed proposals for the construction or performance of the improvement or work before any contract is made. The call for bids shall state whether the work is to be performed as a unit or shall be divided into severable specific parts, or both, as stated in the call. The board may let the work by single contract for the whole as a unit or it may divide the work into severable parts by separate contracts, as stated in the call, according to the best interests of the district. The board shall require the successful bidder or bidders to file with the board good and sufficient bonds to be approved by the board conditioned upon the faithful performance of the contract and upon the payment of their claims for labor and material, the bonds to contain the terms and conditions set forth in Title 3 (commencing with Section 9000) of Part 6 of Division 4 of the Civil Code and to be subject to the provisions of that title. The board shall also have the right to reject any bid.	three insertions in a daily newspaper of general circulation or by two insertions in a weekly newspaper of general circulation printed and published in the district inviting sealed proposals for the construction or performance of the improvement or work before any contract is made. The call for bids shall state whether the work is to be performed as a unit or shall be divided into severable specific parts, or both, as stated in the call. The board may let the work by single contract for the whole as a unit or it may divide the work into severable parts by separate contracts, as stated in the call, according to the best interests of the district. The board shall require the successful bidder or bidders to file with the board good and sufficient bonds to be approved by the board conditioned upon the faithful performance of the contract and upon the payment of their claims for labor and material, the bonds to contain the terms and conditions set forth in Title 15 (commencing with Section 3082) of Part 4 of Division 3 of the Civil Code and to be subject to the provisions of that title. The board shall also have the right to reject any bid.
(b) In the event no proposals are received pursuant to advertisement, or the estimated cost of the work does not exceed two thousand dollars ($2,000), or the work consists of channel protection, maintenance work, or emergency work, the board of supervisors may, without advertising for bids, have the work done by day labor, under the direction of the board, by contract, or by a combination of the two. In case of an emergency, if notice for bids to let contracts will not be given, the board shall comply with Chapter 2.5 (commencing with Section 22050).	(b) In the event no proposals are received pursuant to advertisement, or the estimated cost of the work does not exceed two thousand dollars ($2,000), or the work consists of channel protection, maintenance work, or emergency work, the board of supervisors may, without advertising for bids, have the work done by day labor, under the direction of the board, by contract, or by a combination of the two. In case of an emergency, if notice for bids to let contracts will not be given, the board shall comply with Chapter 2.5 (commencing with Section 22050).
(c) The district may acquire in the open market, without advertising for bids, materials, equipment, and supplies for use in any work or for any other purpose; provided, however, that materials and supplies for use in any new construction work or improvement, except work referred to in subdivision (b), shall not be purchased if the cost exceeds two thousand five hundred dollars ($2,500), without advertising for bids and awarding the contract to the lowest responsible bidder.	(c) The district may acquire in the open market, without advertising for bids, materials, equipment, and supplies for use in any work or for any other purpose; provided, however, that materials and supplies for use in any new construction work or improvement, except work referred to in subdivision (b), shall not be purchased if the cost exceeds two thousand five hundred dollars ($2,500), without advertising for bids and awarding the contract to the lowest responsible bidder.

Revised to include reference to new Section 9000 et seq.

New Text (Operative July 1, 2012)

PCC 21321

(a) All contracts for any improvement or unit of work, when the cost according to the estimate of the engineer will exceed thirty thousand dollars ($30,000), shall be let to the lowest responsible bidder or bidders as provided in this article. The board shall first determine whether the contract shall be let as a single unit, or divided into severable parts. The board shall advertise for bids by three insertions in a daily newspaper of general circulation or by two insertions in a weekly newspaper of general circulation printed and published in the agency's jurisdiction, inviting sealed proposals for the construction or performance of the improvement or work. The call for bids shall state whether the work shall be performed in one unit or divided into parts. The work may be let under a single contract or several contracts, as stated in the call.

The board shall require the successful bidders to file with the board good and sufficient bonds to be approved by the board conditioned upon the faithful performance of the contract and upon the payment of their claims for labor and material. The bonds shall comply with Title 3 (commencing with Section 9000) of Part 6 of Division 4 of the Civil Code.

(b) The board may reject any bid. In the event all proposals are rejected or no proposals are received, or the estimated cost of the work does not exceed five thousand dollars ($5,000), or the work consists of channel protection, maintenance, or emergency work, the board may have the work done by force account without advertising for bids. In case of an emergency, if notice for bids to let contracts will not be given, the board shall comply with Chapter 2.5 (commencing with Section 22050). In the event that no proposals are received, or if only one responsive proposal is received, the board may negotiate a contract for construction or performance of the work or improvement or substantially similar work or improvement. However, if only one responsive proposal is received, the contract must be negotiated with the bidder.

(c) The agency may purchase in the open market without advertising for bids, materials and supplies

Old Text

PCC 21321

(a) All contracts for any improvement or unit of work, when the cost according to the estimate of the engineer will exceed thirty thousand dollars ($30,000), shall be let to the lowest responsible bidder or bidders as provided in this article. The board shall first determine whether the contract shall be let as a single unit, or divided into severable parts. The board shall advertise for bids by three insertions in a daily newspaper of general circulation or by two insertions in a weekly newspaper of general circulation printed and published in the agency's jurisdiction, inviting sealed proposals for the construction or performance of the improvement or work. The call for bids shall state whether the work shall be performed in one unit or divided into parts. The work may be let under a single contract or several contracts, as stated in the call.

The board shall require the successful bidders to file with the board good and sufficient bonds to be approved by the board conditioned upon the faithful performance of the contract and upon the payment of their claims for labor and material. The bonds shall comply with Title 15 (commencing with Section 3082) of Part 4 of Division 3 of the Civil Code.

(b) The board may reject any bid. In the event all proposals are rejected or no proposals are received, or the estimated cost of the work does not exceed five thousand dollars ($5,000), or the work consists of channel protection, maintenance, or emergency work, the board may have the work done by force account without advertising for bids. In case of an emergency, if notice for bids to let contracts will not be given, the board shall comply with Chapter 2.5 (commencing with Section 22050). In the event that no proposals are received, or if only one responsive proposal is received, the board may negotiate a contract for construction or performance of the work or improvement or substantially similar work or improvement. However, if only one responsive proposal is received, the contract must be negotiated with the bidder.

(c) The agency may purchase in the open market without advertising for bids, materials and supplies for use in any work, either under contract or by force account.

(d) Sections 4300 to 4305, inclusive, of the Government Code do not apply to the agency's Middle Fork

New Text (Operative July 1, 2012) | **Old Text**

for use in any work, either under contract or by force account.

(d) Sections 4300 to 4305, inclusive, of the Government Code do not apply to the agency's Middle Fork American River Project.

(e) This section applies to all proposals or contracts whether or not received or entered into prior to the effective date of the amendment of this provision made at the 1963 Regular Session of the Legislature.

American River Project.

(e) This section applies to all proposals or contracts whether or not received or entered into prior to the effective date of the amendment of this provision made at the 1963 Regular Session of the Legislature.

Revised to include reference to new Section 9000 et seq.

PCC 21331

(a) All contracts for the construction of any unit of work, except as provided in this article, estimated to cost in excess of three thousand five hundred dollars ($3,500) shall be let to the lowest responsible bidder in the manner provided in this article. The board shall advertise by three insertions in a daily newspaper of general circulation or two insertions in a weekly newspaper of general circulation published in the district inviting sealed proposals for the construction of the work before any contract shall be made, and may let by contract separately any part of the work. The board shall require the successful bidder to file with the board good and sufficient bonds to be approved by the board conditioned upon the faithful performance of the contract and upon the payment of all claims for labor and material, the bonds to contain the terms and conditions set forth in Title 3 (commencing with Section 9000) of Part 6 of Division 4 of the Civil Code, and to be subject to the provisions of that title. The board shall also have the right to reject any bid, in which case the board may advertise for new bids.

(b) In the event no proposals are received pursuant to advertisement, where the estimated cost of the work does not exceed five thousand dollars ($5,000), or where the work consists of emergency work, the board of directors, by unanimous vote of all members present, may, without advertising for bids, have the work done by force account. In case of an emergency, if notice for bids to let contracts will not be given, the board shall comply with Chapter 2.5 (commencing with Section 22050).

(c) The district may purchase in the open market, without

PCC 21331

(a) All contracts for the construction of any unit of work, except as provided in this article, estimated to cost in excess of three thousand five hundred dollars ($3,500) shall be let to the lowest responsible bidder in the manner provided in this article. The board shall advertise by three insertions in a daily newspaper of general circulation or two insertions in a weekly newspaper of general circulation published in the district inviting sealed proposals for the construction of the work before any contract shall be made, and may let by contract separately any part of the work. The board shall require the successful bidder to file with the board good and sufficient bonds to be approved by the board conditioned upon the faithful performance of the contract and upon the payment of all claims for labor and material, the bonds to contain the terms and conditions set forth in Title 15 (commencing with Section 3082) of Part 4 of Division 3 of the Civil Code, and to be subject to the provisions of that title. The board shall also have the right to reject any bid, in which case the board may advertise for new bids.

(b) In the event no proposals are received pursuant to advertisement, where the estimated cost of the work does not exceed five thousand dollars ($5,000), or where the work consists of emergency work, the board of directors, by unanimous vote of all members present, may, without advertising for bids, have the work done by force account. In case of an emergency, if notice for bids to let contracts will not be given, the board shall comply with Chapter 2.5 (commencing with Section 22050).

(c) The district may purchase in the open market, without

New Text (Operative July 1, 2012)

advertisement for bids, materials and supplies for use in any work either under contract or by force account; provided, however, that materials and supplies for use in any new construction work or improvement, except work referred to in subdivision (b), may not be purchased if the cost exceeds five thousand dollars ($5,000), without advertising for bids and awarding the contract to the lowest responsible bidder.

(d) The provisions of this section have no application to a contract entered into with the United States under the authority of Section 3 of Chapter 1280 of the Statutes of 1957, or to a contract authorized by a vote of the electorate of the district.

Old Text

advertisement for bids, materials and supplies for use in any work either under contract or by force account; provided, however, that materials and supplies for use in any new construction work or improvement, except work referred to in subdivision (b), may not be purchased if the cost exceeds five thousand dollars ($5,000), without advertising for bids and awarding the contract to the lowest responsible bidder.

(d) The provisions of this section have no application to a contract entered into with the United States under the authority of Section 3 of Chapter 1280 of the Statutes of 1957, or to a contract authorized by a vote of the electorate of the district.

Revised to include reference to new Section 9000 et seq.

PCC 21341

(a) All contracts for the construction of any unit of work, except as provided in this article, estimated to cost in excess of five thousand dollars ($5,000) shall be let to the lowest responsible bidder. The board shall advertise by three insertions in a daily newspaper of general circulation or two insertions in a weekly newspaper of general circulation published by the agency inviting sealed proposals for the construction of the work before any contract is made, and may let by contract separately any part of the work. The board shall require the successful bidder to file with the board good and sufficient bonds to be approved by the board conditioned upon the faithful performance of the contract and upon the payment of the claims for labor and material, the bonds to contain the terms and conditions set forth in Title 3 (commencing with Section 9000) of Part 6 of Division 4 of the Civil Code, and to be subject to the provisions of that title. The board shall also have the right to reject any bid, in which case the board may advertise for new bids. In the event no proposals are received pursuant to advertisement or where the estimated cost of the work does not exceed five thousand dollars ($5,000), or where the work consists of emergency work, the board, by unanimous vote of all members present, may, without advertising for bids, have the work done by force account. In case of an emergency, if notice for bids to let contracts will not be given, the board shall

PCC 21341

(a) All contracts for the construction of any unit of work, except as provided in this article, estimated to cost in excess of five thousand dollars ($5,000) shall be let to the lowest responsible bidder. The board shall advertise by three insertions in a daily newspaper of general circulation or two insertions in a weekly newspaper of general circulation published by the agency inviting sealed proposals for the construction of the work before any contract is made, and may let by contract separately any part of the work. The board shall require the successful bidder to file with the board good and sufficient bonds to be approved by the board conditioned upon the faithful performance of the contract and upon the payment of the claims for labor and material, the bonds to contain the terms and conditions set forth in Title 15 (commencing with Section 3082) of Part 4 of Division 3 of the Civil Code, and to be subject to the provisions of that title. The board shall also have the right to reject any bid, in which case the board may advertise for new bids. In the event no proposals are received pursuant to advertisement or where the estimated cost of the work does not exceed five thousand dollars ($5,000), or where the work consists of emergency work, the board, by unanimous vote of all members present, may, without advertising for bids, have the work done by force account. In case of an emergency, if notice for bids to let contracts will not be given, the board shall comply with Chapter 2.5

New Text (Operative July 1, 2012) | Old Text

comply with Chapter 2.5 (commencing with Section 22050). The agency may purchase in the open market, without advertisement for bids, materials and supplies for use in any work either under contract or by force account.

(b) The provisions of this section have no application to a contract entered into with the United States under the authority of Section 59 of Chapter 1512 of the Statutes of 1957, or to a contract authorized by a vote of the electorate of the agency.

(commencing with Section 22050). The agency may purchase in the open market, without advertisement for bids, materials and supplies for use in any work either under contract or by force account.

(b) The provisions of this section have no application to a contract entered into with the United States under the authority of Section 59 of Chapter 1512 of the Statutes of 1957, or to a contract authorized by a vote of the electorate of the agency.

Revised to include reference to new Section 9000 et seq.

••

PCC 21351

All contracts for any improvement or unit of work, when the cost according to the estimate of the engineer will exceed five thousand dollars ($5,000), shall be let to the lowest responsible bidder or bidders as provided in this article. The board shall first determine whether the contract shall be let as a single unit, or divided into severable parts. The board shall advertise for bids by three insertions in a daily newspaper of general circulation or by two insertions in a weekly newspaper of general circulation printed and published by the agency, inviting sealed proposals for the construction or performance of the improvement or work. The call for bids shall state whether the work shall be performed in one unit or divided into parts. The work may be let under a single contract or several contracts, as stated in the call. The board shall require the successful bidders to file with the board good and sufficient bonds to be approved by the board conditioned upon the faithful performance of the contract and upon the payment of their claims for labor and material. The bonds shall comply with Title 3 (commencing with Section 9000) of Part 6 of Division 4 of the Civil Code. The board may reject any bid. In the event all proposals are rejected or no proposals are received, or the estimated cost of the work does not exceed five thousand dollars ($5,000), or the work consists of channel protection, maintenance work, or emergency work, the board may have the work done by force account without advertising for bids.

In case of an emergency, if notice for bids to let contracts will not be given, the board shall comply with

PCC 21351

All contracts for any improvement or unit of work, when the cost according to the estimate of the engineer will exceed five thousand dollars ($5,000), shall be let to the lowest responsible bidder or bidders as provided in this article. The board shall first determine whether the contract shall be let as a single unit, or divided into severable parts. The board shall advertise for bids by three insertions in a daily newspaper of general circulation or by two insertions in a weekly newspaper of general circulation printed and published by the agency, inviting sealed proposals for the construction or performance of the improvement or work. The call for bids shall state whether the work shall be performed in one unit or divided into parts. The work may be let under a single contract or several contracts, as stated in the call. The board shall require the successful bidders to file with the board good and sufficient bonds to be approved by the board conditioned upon the faithful performance of the contract and upon the payment of their claims for labor and material. The bonds shall comply with Title 15 (commencing with Section 3082) of Part 4 of Division 3 of the Civil Code. The board may reject any bid. In the event all proposals are rejected or no proposals are received, or the estimated cost of the work does not exceed five thousand dollars ($5,000), or the work consists of channel protection, maintenance work, or emergency work, the board may have the work done by force account without advertising for bids.

In case of an emergency, if notice for bids to let contracts will not be given, the board shall comply with Chapter 2.5

Chapter 2.5 (commencing with Section 22050). The board may purchase in the open market without advertising for bids, materials and supplies for use in any work, either under contract or by force account. In awarding any contract or authorizing any work, the board shall comply with the provisions of Article 2 (commencing with Section 1770) of Chapter 1 of Part 7 of Division 2 of the Labor Code.

(commencing with Section 22050). The board may purchase in the open market without advertising for bids, materials and supplies for use in any work, either under contract or by force account. In awarding any contract or authorizing any work, the board shall comply with the provisions of Article 2 (commencing with Section 1770) of Chapter 1 of Part 7 of Division 2 of the Labor Code.

Revised to include reference to new Section 9000 et seq.

PCC 21361

All contracts for any improvement or unit of work, when the cost according to the estimate of the engineer will exceed five thousand dollars ($5,000), shall be let to the lowest responsible bidder or bidders as provided in this article. The board shall first determine whether the contract shall be let as a single unit, or divided into severable parts. The board shall advertise for bids by three insertions in a daily newspaper of general circulation or by two insertions in a weekly newspaper of general circulation printed and published in the agency's jurisdiction, inviting sealed proposals for the construction or performance of the improvement or work. The call for bids shall state whether the work shall be performed in one unit or divided into parts. The work may be let under a single contract or several contracts, as stated in the call. The board shall require the successful bidders to file with the board good and sufficient bonds to be approved by the board conditioned upon the faithful performance of the contract and upon the payment of their claims for labor and material. The bonds shall comply with Title 3 (commencing with Section 9000) of Part 6 of Division 4 of the Civil Code. The board may reject any bid. In the event all proposals are rejected or no proposals are received, or the estimated cost of the work does not exceed five thousand dollars ($5,000), or the work consists of channel protection, maintenance work, or emergency work, the board of supervisors may have the work done by force account without advertising for bids. In case of an emergency, if notice for bids to let contracts will not be given, the board shall comply with Chapter 2.5 (commencing with Section 22050). The district may

PCC 21361

All contracts for any improvement or unit of work, when the cost according to the estimate of the engineer will exceed five thousand dollars ($5,000), shall be let to the lowest responsible bidder or bidders as provided in this article. The board shall first determine whether the contract shall be let as a single unit, or divided into severable parts. The board shall advertise for bids by three insertions in a daily newspaper of general circulation or by two insertions in a weekly newspaper of general circulation printed and published in the agency's jurisdiction, inviting sealed proposals for the construction or performance of the improvement or work. The call for bids shall state whether the work shall be performed in one unit or divided into parts. The work may be let under a single contract or several contracts, as stated in the call. The board shall require the successful bidders to file with the board good and sufficient bonds to be approved by the board conditioned upon the faithful performance of the contract and upon the payment of their claims for labor and material. The bonds shall comply with Title 15 (commencing with Section 3082) of Part 4 of Division 3 of the Civil Code. The board may reject any bid. In the event all proposals are rejected or no proposals are received, or the estimated cost of the work does not exceed five thousand dollars ($5,000), or the work consists of channel protection, maintenance work, or emergency work, the board of supervisors may have the work done by force account without advertising for bids. In case of an emergency, if notice for bids to let contracts will not be given, the board shall comply with Chapter 2.5 (commencing with Section 22050). The district may purchase in the open market without advertising for bids, materials and supplies for use in any work, either under contract or by force account.

New Text (Operative July 1, 2012) | **Old Text**

purchase in the open market without advertising for bids, materials and supplies for use in any work, either under contract or by force account.

Revised to include reference to new Section 9000 et seq.

••

PCC 21371

All contracts for any improvement or unit of work, when the cost according to the estimate of the engineer will exceed five thousand dollars ($5,000), shall be let to the lowest responsible bidder or bidders as provided in this article. The board shall first determine whether the contract shall be let as a single unit, or divided into severable parts. The board shall advertise for bids by three insertions in a daily newspaper of general circulation or by two insertions in a weekly newspaper of general circulation printed and published in the agency's jurisdiction, inviting sealed proposals for the construction or performance of the improvement or work. The call for bids shall state whether the work shall be performed in one unit or divided into parts. The work may be let under a single contract or several contracts, as stated in the call. The board shall require the successful bidders to file with the board good and sufficient bonds to be approved by the board conditioned upon the faithful performance of the contract and upon the payment of their claims for labor and material. The bonds shall comply with Title 3 (commencing with Section 9000) of Part 6 of Division 4 of the Civil Code. The board may reject any bid. In the event all proposals are rejected or no proposals are received, or the estimated cost of the work does not exceed five thousand dollars ($5,000), or the work consists of emergency work, the board may have the work done by force account without advertising for bids. In case of an emergency, if notice for bids to let contracts will not be given, the board shall comply with Chapter 2.5 (commencing with Section 22050). The district may purchase in the open market without advertising for bids, materials and supplies for use in any work, either under contract or by force account.

PCC 21371

All contracts for any improvement or unit of work, when the cost according to the estimate of the engineer will exceed five thousand dollars ($5,000), shall be let to the lowest responsible bidder or bidders as provided in this article. The board shall first determine whether the contract shall be let as a single unit, or divided into severable parts. The board shall advertise for bids by three insertions in a daily newspaper of general circulation or by two insertions in a weekly newspaper of general circulation printed and published in the agency's jurisdiction, inviting sealed proposals for the construction or performance of the improvement or work. The call for bids shall state whether the work shall be performed in one unit or divided into parts. The work may be let under a single contract or several contracts, as stated in the call. The board shall require the successful bidders to file with the board good and sufficient bonds to be approved by the board conditioned upon the faithful performance of the contract and upon the payment of their claims for labor and material. The bonds shall comply with Title 15 (commencing with Section 3082) of Part 4 of Division 3 of the Civil Code. The board may reject any bid. In the event all proposals are rejected or no proposals are received, or the estimated cost of the work does not exceed five thousand dollars ($5,000), or the work consists of emergency work, the board may have the work done by force account without advertising for bids. In case of an emergency, if notice for bids to let contracts will not be given, the board shall comply with Chapter 2.5 (commencing with Section 22050). The district may purchase in the open market without advertising for bids, materials and supplies for use in any work, either under contract or by force account.

Revised to include reference to new Section 9000 et seq.

••

New Text (Operative July 1, 2012) | **Old Text**

PCC 21381

All contracts for any improvement or unit of work, except as provided in this article, estimated to cost in excess of five thousand dollars ($5,000) shall be let to the lowest responsible bidder in the manner provided in this article. The board of supervisors of the district shall advertise by three insertions in a daily newspaper of general circulation or two insertions in a weekly newspaper of general circulation printed and published in the district inviting sealed proposals for the construction of the improvement or work before any contract shall be made, and may let by contract separately any part of said work or improvement. The board shall require the successful bidder to file with the board good and sufficient bonds to be approved by the board conditioned upon the faithful performance of the contract and upon the payment of their claims for labor and material, the bonds contain the terms and conditions set forth in Title 3 (commencing with Section 9000) of Part 6 of Division 4 of the Civil Code and to be subject to the provisions of that part. The board shall also have the right to reject any bid. In the event all proposals are rejected or no proposals are received pursuant to advertisement, or where the estimated cost of the work does not exceed five thousand dollars ($5,000), or the work consists of channel protection, maintenance work, or emergency work, the board of supervisors may, without advertising for bids, have the work done by force account. In case of an emergency, if notice for bids to let contracts will not be given, the board shall comply with Chapter 2.5 (commencing with Section 22050). The district may purchase in the open market without advertising for bids, materials and supplies for use in any work either under contract or by force account.

PCC 21381

All contracts for any improvement or unit of work, except as provided in this article, estimated to cost in excess of five thousand dollars ($5,000) shall be let to the lowest responsible bidder in the manner provided in this article. The board of supervisors of the district shall advertise by three insertions in a daily newspaper of general circulation or two insertions in a weekly newspaper of general circulation printed and published in the district inviting sealed proposals for the construction of the improvement or work before any contract shall be made, and may let by contract separately any part of said work or improvement. The board shall require the successful bidder to file with the board good and sufficient bonds to be approved by the board conditioned upon the faithful performance of the contract and upon the payment of their claims for labor and material, the bonds to contain the terms and conditions set forth in Title 15 (commencing with Section 3082) of Part 4 of Division 3 of the Civil Code and to be subject to the provisions of that title. The board shall also have the right to reject any bid. In the event all proposals are rejected or no proposals are received pursuant to advertisement, or where the estimated cost of the work does not exceed five thousand dollars ($5,000), or the work consists of channel protection, maintenance work, or emergency work, the board of supervisors may, without advertising for bids, have the work done by force account. In case of an emergency, if notice for bids to let contracts will not be given, the board shall comply with Chapter 2.5 (commencing with Section 22050). The district may purchase in the open market without advertising for bids, materials and supplies for use in any work either under contract or by force account.

Revised to include reference to new Section 9000 et seq.

PCC 21391

(a) All contracts for the construction of any unit of work, except as provided in this article, estimated to cost in excess of two thousand dollars ($2,000) shall be let to the lowest responsible bidder in the manner provided in this article. The board shall advertise by three insertions in a daily newspaper of general circulation or two insertions in a weekly

PCC 21391

(a) All contracts for the construction of any unit of work, except as provided in this article, estimated to cost in excess of two thousand dollars ($2,000) shall be let to the lowest responsible bidder in the manner provided in this article. The board shall advertise by three insertions in a daily newspaper of general circulation or two insertions in a weekly newspaper of general

New Text (Operative July 1, 2012)

newspaper of general circulation published in the district, inviting sealed proposals for the construction of the work before any contract shall be made, and may let by contract separately any part of the work. The board shall require the successful bidder to file with the board good and sufficient bonds to be approved by the board conditioned upon the faithful performance of the contract and upon the payment of all claims for labor and material, the bonds to contain the terms and conditions set forth in Title 3 (commencing with Section 9000) of Part 6 of Division 4 of the Civil Code, and to be subject to the provisions of that title. The board shall also have the right to reject any and all bids, in which case the board may advertise for new bids.

(b) In the event no proposals are received pursuant to advertisement therefor, where the estimated cost of the work does not exceed two thousand dollars ($2,000), or where the work consists of emergency work necessary in order to protect life and property, the board of directors, by unanimous vote of all members present, may, without advertising for bids, have the work done by force account. In case of an emergency, if notice for bids to let contracts will not be given, the board shall comply with Chapter 2.5 (commencing with Section 22050).

(c) The district may purchase in the open market without advertisement for bids, materials and supplies for use in any work either under contract or by force account; provided, however, that materials and supplies for use in any new construction work or improvement, except work referred to in subdivision (b), may not be purchased if the cost exceeds two thousand five hundred dollars ($2,500), without advertising for bids and awarding the contract to the lowest responsible bidder.

(d) The provisions of this section have no application to a contract entered into with the United States under the authority of Section 3 of Chapter 2114 of the Statutes of 1959, or to a contract authorized by a vote of the electorate of the district.

Old Text

circulation published in the district, inviting sealed proposals for the construction of the work before any contract shall be made, and may let by contract separately any part of the work. The board shall require the successful bidder to file with the board good and sufficient bonds to be approved by the board conditioned upon the faithful performance of the contract and upon the payment of all claims for labor and material, the bonds to contain the terms and conditions set forth in Title 15 (commencing with Section 3082) of Part 4 of Division 3 of the Civil Code, and to be subject to the provisions of that title. The board shall also have the right to reject any and all bids, in which case the board may advertise for new bids.

(b) In the event no proposals are received pursuant to advertisement therefor, where the estimated cost of the work does not exceed two thousand dollars ($2,000), or where the work consists of emergency work necessary in order to protect life and property, the board of directors, by unanimous vote of all members present, may, without advertising for bids, have the work done by force account. In case of an emergency, if notice for bids to let contracts will not be given, the board shall comply with Chapter 2.5 (commencing with Section 22050).

(c) The district may purchase in the open market without advertisement for bids, materials and supplies for use in any work either under contract or by force account; provided, however, that materials and supplies for use in any new construction work or improvement, except work referred to in subdivision (b), may not be purchased if the cost exceeds two thousand five hundred dollars ($2,500), without advertising for bids and awarding the contract to the lowest responsible bidder.

(d) The provisions of this section have no application to a contract entered into with the United States under the authority of Section 3 of Chapter 2114 of the Statutes of 1959, or to a contract authorized by a vote of the electorate of the district.

Revised to include reference to new Section 9000 et seq.

New Text (Operative July 1, 2012)

PCC 21401

(a) All contracts for the construction of any unit of work, except as provided in this article, estimated to cost in excess of two thousand dollars ($2,000) shall be let to the lowest responsible bidder in the manner provided in this article. The board shall advertise by three insertions in a daily newspaper of general circulation or two insertions in a weekly newspaper of general circulation published in the district inviting sealed proposals for the construction of the work before any contract shall be made, and may let by contract separately any part of the work. The board shall require the successful bidder to file with the board good and sufficient bonds to be approved by the board conditioned upon the faithful performance of the contract and upon the payment of all claims for labor and material, the bonds to contain the terms and conditions set forth in Title 3 (commencing with Section 9000) of Part 6 of Division 4 of the Civil Code, and to be subject to the provisions of that title. The board shall also have the right to reject any bids, in which case the board may advertise for new bids.

(b) In the event no proposals are received pursuant to advertisement, where the estimated cost of the work does not exceed two thousand dollars ($2,000), or where work consists of emergency work, the board of directors, by unanimous vote of all members present, may, without advertising for bids, have the work done by force account. In case of an emergency, if notice for bids to let contracts will not be given, the board shall comply with Chapter 2.5 (commencing with Section 22050).

(c) The district may purchase in the open market without advertisement for bids, materials and supplies for use in any work either under contract or by force account; provided, however, that materials and supplies for use in any new construction work or improvement, except work referred to in subdivision (b), may not be purchased if the cost exceeds two thousand five hundred dollars ($2,500), without advertising for bids and awarding the contract to the lowest responsible bidder.

Old Text

PCC 21401

(a) All contracts for the construction of any unit of work, except as provided in this article, estimated to cost in excess of two thousand dollars ($2,000) shall be let to the lowest responsible bidder in the manner provided in this article. The board shall advertise by three insertions in a daily newspaper of general circulation or two insertions in a weekly newspaper of general circulation published in the district inviting sealed proposals for the construction of the work before any contract shall be made, and may let by contract separately any part of the work. The board shall require the successful bidder to file with the board good and sufficient bonds to be approved by the board conditioned upon the faithful performance of the contract and upon the payment of all claims for labor and material, the bonds to contain the terms and conditions set forth in Title 15 (commencing with Section 3082) of Part 4 of Division 3 of the Civil Code, and to be subject to the provisions of that title. The board shall also have the right to reject any bids, in which case the board may advertise for new bids.

(b) In the event no proposals are received pursuant to advertisement, where the estimated cost of the work does not exceed two thousand dollars ($2,000), or where work consists of emergency work, the board of directors, by unanimous vote of all members present, may, without advertising for bids, have the work done by force account. In case of an emergency, if notice for bids to let contracts will not be given, the board shall comply with Chapter 2.5 (commencing with Section 22050).

(c) The district may purchase in the open market without advertisement for bids, materials and supplies for use in any work either under contract or by force account; provided, however, that materials and supplies for use in any new construction work or improvement, except work referred to in subdivision (b), may not be purchased if the cost exceeds two thousand five hundred dollars ($2,500), without advertising for bids and awarding the contract to the lowest responsible bidder.

New Text (Operative July 1, 2012) | **Old Text**

(d) The provisions of this section have no application to a contract entered into with the United States under the authority of Section 3 of Chapter 2121 of the Statutes of 1959, or to a contract authorized by a vote of the electorate of the district.

(d) The provisions of this section have no application to a contract entered into with the United States under the authority of Section 3 of Chapter 2121 of the Statutes of 1959, or to a contract authorized by a vote of the electorate of the district.

Revised to include reference to new Section 9000 et seq.

••

PCC 21411

All contracts for any improvement or unit of work, when the cost according to the estimate of the engineer will exceed five thousand dollars ($5,000) shall be let to the lowest responsible bidder or bidders as provided in this article. The board shall first determine whether the contract shall be let as a single unit, or divided into severable parts. The board shall advertise for bids by three insertions in a daily newspaper of general circulation or by two insertions in a weekly newspaper of general circulation printed and published in the agency's jurisdiction, inviting sealed proposals for the construction or performance of the improvement or work. The call for bids shall state whether the work shall be performed in one unit or divided into parts. The work may be let under a single contract or several contracts, as stated in the call. The board shall require the successful bidders to file with the board good and sufficient bonds to be approved by the board conditioned upon the faithful performance of the contract and upon the payment of their claims for labor and material. The bonds shall comply with Title 3 (commencing with Section 9000) of Part 6 of Division 4 of the Civil Code. The board may reject any bid. In the event all proposals are rejected or no proposals are received, or the estimated cost of the work does not exceed five thousand dollars ($5,000), or the work consists of channel protection, maintenance work, or emergency work, the board may have the work done by force account without advertising for bids. In case of an emergency, if notice for bids to let contracts will not be given, the board shall comply with Chapter 2.5 (commencing with Section 22050). In that event a majority vote of all board

PCC 21411

All contracts for any improvement or unit of work, when the cost according to the estimate of the engineer will exceed five thousand dollars ($5,000) shall be let to the lowest responsible bidder or bidders as provided in this article. The board shall first determine whether the contract shall be let as a single unit, or divided into severable parts. The board shall advertise for bids by three insertions in a daily newspaper of general circulation or by two insertions in a weekly newspaper of general circulation printed and published in the agency's jurisdiction, inviting sealed proposals for the construction or performance of the improvement or work. The call for bids shall state whether the work shall be performed in one unit or divided into parts. The work may be let under a single contract or several contracts, as stated in the call. The board shall require the successful bidders to file with the board good and sufficient bonds to be approved by the board conditioned upon the faithful performance of the contract and upon the payment of their claims for labor and material. The bonds shall comply with Title 15 (commencing with Section 3082) of Part 4 of Division 3 of the Civil Code. The board may reject any bid. In the event all proposals are rejected or no proposals are received, or the estimated cost of the work does not exceed five thousand dollars ($5,000), or the work consists of channel protection, maintenance work, or emergency work, the board may have the work done by force account without advertising for bids. In case of an emergency, if notice for bids to let contracts will not be given, the board shall comply with Chapter 2.5 (commencing with Section 22050). In that event a majority vote of all board members shall be required. The board may purchase in the open market, without *members shall be required. The board may purchase in the open market, without advertising for bids, materials and supplies for use in any work, either under contract or by force account.*

advertising for bids, materials and supplies for use in any work, either under contract or by force account.

Revised to include reference to new Section 9000 et seq.

••

PCC 21421

(a) All contracts for the construction of any unit of work, except as provided in this article, estimated to cost in excess of two thousand dollars ($2,000), shall be let to the lowest responsible bidder in the manner provided in this article. The board shall advertise by three insertions in a daily newspaper of general circulation or two insertions in a weekly newspaper of general circulation published in the district inviting sealed proposals for the construction of the work before any contract shall be made, and may let by contract separately any part of the work. The board shall require the successful bidder to file with the board good and sufficient bonds to be approved by the board conditioned upon the faithful performance of the contract and upon the payment of all claims for labor and material, the bonds to contain the terms and conditions set forth in Title 3 (commencing with Section 9000) of Part 6 of Division 4 of the Civil Code, and to be subject to the provisions of that title. The board shall also have the right to reject any bid, in which case the board may advertise for new bids.

(b) In the event no proposals are received pursuant to advertisement, where the estimated cost of the work does not exceed two thousand dollars ($2,000), or where the work consists of emergency work, the board of directors, by unanimous vote of all members present, may, without advertising for bids, have the work done by force account. In case of an emergency, if notice for bids to let contracts will not be given, the board shall comply with Chapter 2.5 (commencing with Section 22050).

(c) The district may purchase in the open market without advertisement for bids, materials and supplies for use in any work either under contract or by force account; provided, however, that materials and supplies for use in any new construction work or improvement, except work referred to in subdivision (b), may not be

PCC 21421

(a) All contracts for the construction of any unit of work, except as provided in this article, estimated to cost in excess of two thousand dollars ($2,000), shall be let to the lowest responsible bidder in the manner provided in this article. The board shall advertise by three insertions in a daily newspaper of general circulation or two insertions in a weekly newspaper of general circulation published in the district inviting sealed proposals for the construction of the work before any contract shall be made, and may let by contract separately any part of the work. The board shall require the successful bidder to file with the board good and sufficient bonds to be approved by the board conditioned upon the faithful performance of the contract and upon the payment of all claims for labor and material, the bonds to contain the terms and conditions set forth in Title 15 (commencing with Section 3082) of Part 4 of Division 3 of the Civil Code, and to be subject to the provisions of that title. The board shall also have the right to reject any bid, in which case the board may advertise for new bids.

(b) In the event no proposals are received pursuant to advertisement, where the estimated cost of the work does not exceed two thousand dollars ($2,000), or where the work consists of emergency work, the board of directors, by unanimous vote of all members present, may, without advertising for bids, have the work done by force account. In case of an emergency, if notice for bids to let contracts will not be given, the board shall comply with Chapter 2.5 (commencing with Section 22050).

(c) The district may purchase in the open market without advertisement for bids, materials and supplies for use in any work either under contract or by force account; provided, however, that materials and supplies for use in any new construction work or improvement, except work referred to in subdivision (b), may not be purchased if the cost exceeds two thousand five hundred dollars ($2,500), without advertising for bids *purchased if the cost exceeds two thousand five hundred dollars ($2,500), without advertising for bids and awarding the contract to the lowest responsible bidder.*

(d) The provisions of this section have no application to a contract entered into with the United States under the authority of Section 3 of Chapter 2123 of the Statutes of 1959, or to a contract authorized by a vote of the electorate of the district.

and awarding the contract to the lowest responsible bidder.

(d) The provisions of this section have no application to a contract entered into with the United States under the authority of Section 3 of Chapter 2123 of the Statutes of 1959, or to a contract authorized by a vote of the electorate of the district.

Revised to include reference to new Section 9000 et seq.

••

PCC 21431

(a) All contracts for the construction of any unit of work, except as provided in this article, estimated to cost in excess of two thousand dollars ($2,000), shall be let to the lowest responsible bidder in the manner provided in this article. The board shall advertise by three insertions in a daily newspaper of general circulation or two insertions in a weekly newspaper of general circulation published in the district inviting sealed proposals for the construction of the work before any contract shall be made, and may let by contract separately any part of the work. The board shall require the successful bidder to file with the board good and sufficient bonds to be approved by the board conditioned upon the faithful performance of the contract and upon the payment of all claims for labor and material, the bonds to contain the terms and conditions set forth in Title 3 (commencing with Section 9000) of Part 6 of Division 4 of the Civil Code, and to be subject to the provisions of that title. The board shall also have the right to reject any bid, in which case the board may advertise for new bids.

(b) In the event no proposals are received pursuant to advertisement, where the estimated cost of the work does not exceed two thousand dollars ($2,000), the board of directors, by unanimous vote of all members present, may without advertising for bids, have the work done by force account. In case of an emergency, if notice for bids to let contracts will not be given, the board shall comply with Chapter 2.5 (commencing with Section 22050).

(c) The district may purchase in the open market without advertisement for bids, materials and supplies for use in any work either under contract or by force account; provided, however, that materials and supplies for use in any new

PCC 21431

(a) All contracts for the construction of any unit of work, except as provided in this article, estimated to cost in excess of two thousand dollars ($2,000), shall be let to the lowest responsible bidder in the manner provided in this article. The board shall advertise by three insertions in a daily newspaper of general circulation or two insertions in a weekly newspaper of general circulation published in the district inviting sealed proposals for the construction of the work before any contract shall be made, and may let by contract separately any part of the work. The board shall require the successful bidder to file with the board good and sufficient bonds to be approved by the board conditioned upon the faithful performance of the contract and upon the payment of all claims for labor and material, the bonds to contain the terms and conditions set forth in Title 15 (commencing with Section 3082) of Part 4 of Division 3 of the Civil Code, and to be subject to the provisions of that title. The board shall also have the right to reject any bid, in which case the board may advertise for new bids.

(b) In the event no proposals are received pursuant to advertisement, where the estimated cost of the work does not exceed two thousand dollars ($2,000), the board of directors, by unanimous vote of all members present, may without advertising for bids, have the work done by force account. In case of an emergency, if notice for bids to let contracts will not be given, the board shall comply with Chapter 2.5 (commencing with Section 22050).

(c) The district may purchase in the open market without advertisement for bids, materials and supplies for use in any work either under contract or by force account; provided, however, that materials and supplies for use in any new construction work or improvement, except work referred to in subdivision (b), may not be

New Text (Operative July 1, 2012)

construction work or improvement, except work referred to in subdivision (b), may not be purchased if the cost exceeds two thousand five hundred dollars ($2,500), without advertising for bids and awarding the contract to the lowest responsible bidder.

(d) The provisions of this section have no application to a contract entered into with the United States under the authority of Section 3 of Chapter 2127 of the Statutes of 1959, or to a contract authorized by a vote of the electorate of the district.

Old Text

purchased if the cost exceeds two thousand five hundred dollars ($2,500), without advertising for bids and awarding the contract to the lowest responsible bidder.

(d) The provisions of this section have no application to a contract entered into with the United States under the authority of Section 3 of Chapter 2127 of the Statutes of 1959, or to a contract authorized by a vote of the electorate of the district.

Revised to include reference to new Section 9000 et seq.

••

__PCC 21441__

(a) All contracts for any improvement or unit of work, when the cost according to the estimate of the engineer will exceed five thousand dollars ($5,000) shall be let to the lowest responsible bidder or bidders as provided in this article. The board shall first determine whether the contract shall be let as a single unit, or divided into severable parts. The board shall advertise for bids by three insertions in a daily newspaper of general circulation or by two insertions in a weekly newspaper of general circulation printed and published in the authority, inviting sealed proposals for the construction or performance of the improvement work. The call for bids shall state whether the work shall be performed in one unit or divided into parts. The work may be let under a single contract or several contracts, as stated in the call. The board shall require the successful bidders to file with the board good and sufficient bonds to be approved by the board conditioned upon the faithful performance of the contract and upon the payment of their claims for labor and material. The bonds shall comply with Title 3 (commencing with Section 9000) of Part 6 of Division 4 of the Civil Code. The board may reject any bid. In the event all proposals are rejected or no proposals are received, or the estimated cost of the work does not exceed five thousand dollars ($5,000), or the work consists of channel protection, maintenance work, or

PCC 21441

All contracts for any improvement or unit of work, when the cost according to the estimate of the engineer will exceed five thousand dollars ($5,000) shall be let to the lowest responsible bidder or bidders as provided in this article. The board shall first determine whether the contract shall be let as a single unit, or divided into severable parts. The board shall advertise for bids by three insertions in a daily newspaper of general circulation or by two insertions in a weekly newspaper of general circulation printed and published in the authority, inviting sealed proposals for the construction or performance of the improvement work. The call for bids shall state whether the work shall be performed in one unit or divided into parts. The work may be let under a single contract or several contracts, as stated in the call. The board shall require the successful bidders to file with the board good and sufficient bonds to be approved by the board conditioned upon the faithful performance of the contract and upon the payment of their claims for labor and material. The bonds shall comply with Title 15 (commencing with Section 3082) of Part 4 of Division 3 of the Civil Code. The board may reject any bid. In the event all proposals are rejected or no proposals are received, or the estimated cost of the work does not exceed five thousand dollars ($5,000), or the work consists of channel protection, maintenance work, or emergency work, the board may have the work done by force account without advertising for bids. In case of an emergency, if notice for bids to let contracts will not be given, the board shall comply with Chapter 2.5 (commencing with Section 22050). The authority may purchase in the open market

New Text (Operative July 1, 2012) | **Old Text**

emergency work, the board may have the work done by force account without advertising for bids.

(b) In case of an emergency, if notice for bids to let contracts will not be given, the board shall comply with Chapter 2.5 (commencing with Section 22050). The authority may purchase in the open market without advertising for bids, materials, and supplies for use in any work, either under contract or by force account.

without advertising for bids, materials and supplies for use in any work, either under contract or by force account.

Revised to include reference to new Section 9000 et seq.

PCC 21451

All contracts for any improvement or unit of work, when the cost according to the estimate of the engineer will exceed twelve thousand five hundred dollars ($12,500), shall be let to the lowest responsible bidder or bidders as provided in this article. The board shall first determine whether the contract shall be let as a single unit or divided into severable parts. The board shall advertise for bids by three insertions in a daily newspaper of general circulation or by two insertions in a weekly newspaper of general circulation printed and published in the agency, inviting sealed proposals for the construction or performance of the improvement or work. The call for bids shall state whether the work shall be performed in one unit or divided into parts. The work may be let under a single contract or several contracts, as stated in the call. The board shall require the successful bidders to file with the board good and sufficient bonds to be approved by the board conditioned upon the faithful performance of the contract and upon the payment of their claims for labor and material. The payment bonds shall comply with Chapter 5 (commencing with Section 9550) of Title 3 of Part6 of Division 4 of the Civil Code. The board may reject any bid. If all proposals are rejected or no proposals are received, or the estimated cost of the work does not exceed twelve thousand five hundred dollars ($12,500), or the work consists of channel protection, maintenance

PCC 21451

All contracts for any improvement or unit of work, when the cost according to the estimate of the engineer will exceed twelve thousand five hundred dollars ($12,500), shall be let to the lowest responsible bidder or bidders as provided in this article. The board shall first determine whether the contract shall be let as a single unit or divided into severable parts. The board shall advertise for bids by three insertions in a daily newspaper of general circulation or by two insertions in a weekly newspaper of general circulation printed and published in the agency, inviting sealed proposals for the construction or performance of the improvement or work. The call for bids shall state whether the work shall be performed in one unit or divided into parts. The work may be let under a single contract or several contracts, as stated in the call. The board shall require the successful bidders to file with the board good and sufficient bonds to be approved by the board conditioned upon the faithful performance of the contract and upon the payment of their claims for labor and material. The payment bonds shall comply with Chapter 7 (commencing with Section 3247) of Division 3 of Title 15 of the Civil Code. The board may reject any bid. If all proposals are rejected or no proposals are received, or the estimated cost of the work does not exceed twelve thousand five hundred dollars ($12,500), or the work consists of channel protection, maintenance work, or emergency work, the board may have the work done

New Text (Operative July 1, 2012)

work, or emergency work, the board may have the work done by force account without advertising for bids. In case of an emergency, if notice for bids to let contracts will not be given, the board shall comply with Chapter 2.5 (commencing with Section 22050). The agency may purchase in the open market without advertising for bids, materials and supplies for use in any work, either under contract or by force account.

Old Text

by force account without advertising for bids. In case of an emergency, if notice for bids to let contracts will not be given, the board shall comply with Chapter 2.5 (commencing with Section 22050). The agency may purchase in the open market without advertising for bids, materials and supplies for use in any work, either under contract or by force account.

Revised to include reference to new Section 9000 et seq.

PCC 21461

All contracts for any improvement or unit of work, when the cost according to the estimate of the engineer will exceed five thousand dollars ($5,000), shall be let to the lowest responsible bidder or bidders as provided in this article. The board shall first determine whether the contract shall be let as a single unit, or divided into severable parts. The board shall advertise for bids by three insertions in a daily newspaper of general circulation or by two insertions in a weekly newspaper of general circulation printed and published in the agency, inviting sealed proposals for the construction or performance of the improvement or work. The call for bids shall state whether the work shall be performed in one unit or divided into parts. The work may be let under a single contract or several contracts, as stated in such call. The board shall require the successful bidders to file with the board good and sufficient bonds to be approved by the board conditioned upon the faithful performance of the contract and upon payment of their claims for labor and material. The bonds shall comply with Title 3 (commencing with Section 9000) of Part 6 of Division 4 of the Civil Code. The board may reject any and all bids. In the event all proposals are rejected or no proposals are received, or the estimated cost of the work does not exceed five thousand dollars ($5,000), or the work consists of channel protection, maintenance work, or emergency work, the board of supervisors may

PCC 21461

All contracts for any improvement or unit of work, when the cost according to the estimate of the engineer will exceed five thousand dollars ($5,000), shall be let to the lowest responsible bidder or bidders as provided in this article. The board shall first determine whether the contract shall be let as a single unit, or divided into severable parts. The board shall advertise for bids by three insertions in a daily newspaper of general circulation or by two insertions in a weekly newspaper of general circulation printed and published in the agency, inviting sealed proposals for the construction or performance of the improvement or work. The call for bids shall state whether the work shall be performed in one unit or divided into parts. The work may be let under a single contract or several contracts, as stated in such call. The board shall require the successful bidders to file with the board good and sufficient bonds to be approved by the board conditioned upon the faithful performance of the contract and upon payment of their claims for labor and material. The bonds shall comply with Title 15 (commencing with Section 3082) of Part 4 of Division 3 of the Civil Code. The board may reject any and all bids. In the event all proposals are rejected or no proposals are received, or the estimated cost of the work does not exceed five thousand dollars ($5,000), or the work consists of channel protection, maintenance work, or emergency work, the board of supervisors may have the work done by force account without advertising for bids. In case of an emergency, if notice for bids to let

New Text (Operative July 1, 2012)

have the work done by force account without advertising for bids. In case of an emergency, if notice for bids to let contracts will not be given, the board shall comply with Chapter 2.5 (commencing with Section 22050). The district may purchase in the open market without advertising for bids, materials and supplies for use in any work, either under contract or by force account.

Old Text

contracts will not be given, the board shall comply with Chapter 2.5 (commencing with Section 22050). The district may purchase in the open market without advertising for bids, materials and supplies for use in any work, either under contract or by force account.

Revised to include reference to new Section 9000 et seq.

••

PCC 21491

(a) All contracts for any improvement or unit of work, when the cost according to the estimate of the engineer will exceed ten thousand dollars ($10,000), shall be let to the lowest responsible bidder or bidders as provided in this article. The board shall first determine whether the contract shall be let as a single unit, or divided into severable parts. The board shall advertise for bids by three insertions in a daily newspaper of general circulation or by two insertions in a weekly newspaper of general circulation printed and published in the agency, inviting sealed proposals for the construction or performance of the improvement or work. The call for bids shall state whether the work shall be performed in one unit or divided into parts. The work may be let under a single contract or several contracts, as stated in such call. The board shall require the successful bidders to file with the board good and sufficient bonds to be approved by the board conditioned upon the faithful performance of the contract and upon the payment of their claims for labor and material. The bonds comply with Title 3 (commencing with Section 9000) of Part 6 of Division 4 of the Civil Code. The board may reject any bid.

(b) In the event all proposals are rejected or no proposals are received, or the estimated cost of the work does not exceed ten thousand dollars ($10,000), or the work consists of channel protection, maintenance work, or emergency work, the board may have the work done by force account without advertising for bids. In case of an emergency, if notice for bids to let contracts will not be given, the board shall comply with Chapter 2.5 (commencing with Section 22050).

PCC 21491

(a) All contracts for any improvement or unit of work, when the cost according to the estimate of the engineer will exceed ten thousand dollars ($10,000), shall be let to the lowest responsible bidder or bidders as provided in this article. The board shall first determine whether the contract shall be let as a single unit, or divided into severable parts. The board shall advertise for bids by three insertions in a daily newspaper of general circulation or by two insertions in a weekly newspaper of general circulation printed and published in the agency, inviting sealed proposals for the construction or performance of the improvement or work. The call for bids shall state whether the work shall be performed in one unit or divided into parts. The work may be let under a single contract or several contracts, as stated in such call. The board shall require the successful bidders to file with the board good and sufficient bonds to be approved by the board conditioned upon the faithful performance of the contract and upon the payment of their claims for labor and material. The bonds shall comply with Title 15 (commencing with Section 3082) of Part 4 of Division 3 of the Civil Code. The board may reject any bid.

(b) In the event all proposals are rejected or no proposals are received, or the estimated cost of the work does not exceed ten thousand dollars ($10,000), or the work consists of channel protection, maintenance work, or emergency work, the board may have the work done by force account without advertising for bids. In case of an emergency, if notice for bids to let contracts will not be given, the board shall comply with Chapter 2.5 (commencing with Section 22050).

(c) The agency may purchase in the open market without advertising for bids, materials and supplies for use in any

New Text (Operative July 1, 2012) | **Old Text**

(c) The agency may purchase in the open market without advertising for bids, materials and supplies for use in any work, either under contract or by force account; provided, however, that materials and supplies for use in any new construction work or improvement, except work referred to in subdivision (b), may not be purchased if the cost exceeds ten thousand dollars ($10,000), without advertising for bids and awarding the contract to the lowest responsible bidder.

work, either under contract or by force account; provided, however, that materials and supplies for use in any new construction work or improvement, except work referred to in subdivision (b), may not be purchased if the cost exceeds ten thousand dollars ($10,000), without advertising for bids and awarding the contract to the lowest responsible bidder.

Revised to include reference to new Section 9000 et seq.

<u>PCC 21501</u>

(a) All contracts for any improvement or unit of work, when the cost according to the estimate of the engineer will exceed fifteen thousand dollars ($15,000), shall be let to the lowest responsible bidder or bidders as provided in this article. The board shall first determine whether the contract shall be let as a single unit, or divided into severable parts. The board shall advertise for bids by three insertions in a daily newspaper of general circulation or by two insertions in a weekly newspaper of general circulation printed and published in the agency, inviting sealed proposals for the construction or performance of the improvement or work. The call for bids shall state whether the work shall be performed in one unit or divided into parts. The work may be let under a single contract or several contracts, as stated in such call. The board shall require the successful bidders to file with the board good and sufficient bonds to be approved by the board conditioned upon the faithful performance of the contract and upon the payment of their claims for labor and material. The bonds shall comply with Chapter 5 (commencing with Section 9550) of Title 3 of Part 6 of Division 4 of the Civil Code. The board may reject any and all bids.

(b) The board may have work done by force account without advertising for bids or by informal bidding procedures in any of the following situations:

(1) All proposals are rejected.

(2) No proposals are received.

PCC 21501

(a) All contracts for any improvement or unit of work, when the cost according to the estimate of the engineer will exceed fifteen thousand dollars ($15,000), shall be let to the lowest responsible bidder or bidders as provided in this article. The board shall first determine whether the contract shall be let as a single unit, or divided into severable parts. The board shall advertise for bids by three insertions in a daily newspaper of general circulation or by two insertions in a weekly newspaper of general circulation printed and published in the agency, inviting sealed proposals for the construction or performance of the improvement or work. The call for bids shall state whether the work shall be performed in one unit or divided into parts. The work may be let under a single contract or several contracts, as stated in such call. The board shall require the successful bidders to file with the board good and sufficient bonds to be approved by the board conditioned upon the faithful performance of the contract and upon the payment of their claims for labor and material. The bonds shall comply with Chapter 7 (commencing with Section 3247) of Title 15 of Part 4 of Division 3 of the Civil Code. The board may reject any and all bids.

(b) The board may have work done by force account without advertising for bids or by informal bidding procedures in any of the following situations:

(1) All proposals are rejected.

(2) No proposals are received.

(3) The estimated cost of the work does not exceed fifteen thousand dollars ($15,000) until January 1,

New Text (Operative July 1, 2012)

(3) The estimated cost of the work does not exceed fifteen thousand dollars ($15,000) until January 1, 1989. After January 1, 1989, the estimated cost of the work shall not exceed ten thousand dollars ($10,000).

(4) The work consists of channel protection.

(5) The work consists of maintenance work, except that informal bidding procedures may be used only where the estimated cost does not exceed twenty-five thousand dollars ($25,000).

(6) The work consists of emergency work. In case of an emergency, if notice for bids to let contracts will not be given, the board shall comply with Chapter 2.5 (commencing with Section 22050).

(c) The agency may purchase in the open market without advertising for bids, materials and supplies for use in any work, either under contract or by force account, except that, materials and supplies for use in any new construction work or improvement, except work referred to in subdivision (b), may not be purchased, if the cost exceeds fifteen thousand dollars ($15,000), without advertising for bids and awarding the contract to the lowest responsible bidder.

(d) As used in this section, "informal bidding procedures" means that the board shall, at a minimum, award a contract to the lowest responsible bidder after publishing a notice which generally describes the work to be performed and invites written bids in a newspaper of general circulation in the agency once a week for two successive weeks. The board shall obtain a minimum of three written bids.

Old Text

1989. After January 1, 1989, the estimated cost of the work shall not exceed ten thousand dollars ($10,000).

(4) The work consists of channel protection.

(5) The work consists of maintenance work, except that informal bidding procedures may be used only where the estimated cost does not exceed twenty-five thousand dollars ($25,000).

(6) The work consists of emergency work. In case of an emergency, if notice for bids to let contracts will not be given, the board shall comply with Chapter 2.5 (commencing with Section 22050).

(c) The agency may purchase in the open market without advertising for bids, materials and supplies for use in any work, either under contract or by force account, except that, materials and supplies for use in any new construction work or improvement, except work referred to in subdivision (b), may not be purchased, if the cost exceeds fifteen thousand dollars ($15,000), without advertising for bids and awarding the contract to the lowest responsible bidder.

(d) As used in this section, "informal bidding procedures" means that the board shall, at a minimum, award a contract to the lowest responsible bidder after publishing a notice which generally describes the work to be performed and invites written bids in a newspaper of general circulation in the agency once a week for two successive weeks. The board shall obtain a minimum of three written bids.

Revised to include reference to new Section 9000 et seq.

<u>PCC 21511</u>

(a) All contracts for any improvement or unit of work, when the cost according to the estimate of the engineer will exceed fifty thousand dollars ($50,000), shall be let to the lowest responsible bidder or bidders as provided in this article. The board shall first determine whether the contract shall be let as a single unit or divided into severable

PCC 21511

(a) All contracts for any improvement or unit of work, when the cost according to the estimate of the engineer will exceed fifty thousand dollars ($50,000), shall be let to the lowest responsible bidder or bidders as provided in this article. The board shall first determine whether the contract shall be let as a single unit or divided into severable parts. The board shall

New Text (Operative July 1, 2012)

parts. The board shall advertise for bids by three insertions in a daily newspaper of general circulation or by two insertions in a weekly newspaper of general circulation printed and published in the agency, inviting sealed proposals for the construction or performance of the improvement or work. The call for bids shall state whether the work shall be performed in one unit or divided into parts. The work may be let under a single contract or several contracts, as stated in the call. The board shall require the successful bidders to file with the board good and sufficient bonds to be approved by the board conditioned upon the faithful performance of the contract and upon the payment of their claims for labor and material. The bonds shall comply with Title 3 (commencing with Section 9000) of Part 6 of Division 4 of the Civil Code. The board may reject any and all bids.

(b) In the event all proposals are rejected or no proposals are received, or the estimated cost of the work does not exceed ten thousand dollars ($10,000), or the work consists of channel protection, maintenance work, or emergency work, the board may have the work done by force account without advertising for bids. In case of an emergency, if notice for bids to let contracts will not be given, the board shall comply with Chapter 2.5 (commencing with Section 22050).

(c) The agency may purchase in the open market without advertising for bids, materials and supplies for use in any work, either under contract or by force account. However, materials and supplies for use in any new construction work or improvement, except work referred to in subdivision (b), may not be purchased, if the cost exceeds thousand dollars ($50,000), without advertising for bids and awarding the contract to the lowest responsible bidder.

Old Text

advertise for bids by three insertions in a daily newspaper of general circulation or by two insertions in a weekly newspaper of general circulation printed and published in the agency, inviting sealed proposals for the construction or performance of the improvement or work. The call for bids shall state whether the work shall be performed in one unit or divided into parts. The work may be let under a single contract or several contracts, as stated in the call. The board shall require the successful bidders to file with the board good and sufficient bonds to be approved by the board conditioned upon the faithful performance of the contract and upon the payment of their claims for labor and material. The bonds shall comply with Title 15 (commencing with Section 3082) of Part 4 of Division 3 of the Civil Code. The board may reject any and all bids.

(b) In the event all proposals are rejected or no proposals are received, or the estimated cost of the work does not exceed ten thousand dollars ($10,000), or the work consists of channel protection, maintenance work, or emergency work, the board may have the work done by force account without advertising for bids. In case of an emergency, if notice for bids to let contracts will not be given, the board shall comply with Chapter 2.5 (commencing with Section 22050).

(c) The agency may purchase in the open market without advertising for bids, materials and supplies for use in any work, either under contract or by force account. However, materials and supplies for use in any new construction work or improvement, except work referred to in subdivision (b), may not be purchased, if the cost exceeds thousand dollars ($50,000), without advertising for bids and awarding the contract to the lowest responsible bidder.

Revised to include reference to new Section 9000 et seq.

New Text (Operative July 1, 2012)

PCC 21521

All contracts for any improvement or unit of work, when the cost according to the estimate of the engineer will exceed five thousand dollars ($5,000) shall be let to the lowest responsible bidder or bidders as provided in this article. The board shall first determine whether the contract shall be let as a single unit, or divided into severable parts. The board shall advertise for bids by three insertions in a daily newspaper of general circulation or by two insertions in a weekly newspaper of general circulation printed and published in the agency, inviting sealed proposals for the construction or performance of the improvement or work. The call for bids shall state whether the work shall be performed in one unit or divided into parts. The work may be let under a single contract or several contracts, as stated in the call. The board shall require the successful bidders to file with the board good and sufficient bonds to be approved by the board conditioned upon the faithful performance of the contract and upon the payment of their claims for labor and material. The bonds shall comply with Title 3 (commencing with Section 9000) of Part 6 of Division 4 of the Civil Code. The board may reject any bid. In the event all proposals are rejected or no proposals are received, or the estimated cost of the work does not exceed five thousand dollars ($5,000), or the work consists of channel protection, maintenance work, or emergency work, the board may have the work done by force account without advertising for bids. In case of an emergency, if notice for bids to let contracts will not be given, the board shall comply with Chapter 2.5 (commencing with Section 22050). In that event a majority vote of all board members shall be required. The board may purchase in the open market without advertising for bids, materials and supplies for use in any work, either under contract or by force account.

Old Text

PCC 21521

All contracts for any improvement or unit of work, when the cost according to the estimate of the engineer will exceed five thousand dollars ($5,000) shall be let to the lowest responsible bidder or bidders as provided in this article. The board shall first determine whether the contract shall be let as a single unit, or divided into severable parts. The board shall advertise for bids by three insertions in a daily newspaper of general circulation or by two insertions in a weekly newspaper of general circulation printed and published in the agency, inviting sealed proposals for the construction or performance of the improvement or work. The call for bids shall state whether the work shall be performed in one unit or divided into parts. The work may be let under a single contract or several contracts, as stated in the call. The board shall require the successful bidders to file with the board good and sufficient bonds to be approved by the board conditioned upon the faithful performance of the contract and upon the payment of their claims for labor and material. The bonds shall comply with Title 15 (commencing with Section 3082) of Part 4 of Division 3 of the Civil Code. The board may reject any bid. In the event all proposals are rejected or no proposals are received, or the estimated cost of the work does not exceed five thousand dollars ($5,000), or the work consists of channel protection, maintenance work, or emergency work, the board may have the work done by force account without advertising for bids. In case of an emergency, if notice for bids to let contracts will not be given, the board shall comply with Chapter 2.5 (commencing with Section 22050). In that event a majority vote of all board members shall be required. The board may purchase in the open market without advertising for bids, materials and supplies for use in any work, either under contract or by force account.

Revised to include reference to new Section 9000 et seq.

New Text (Operative July 1, 2012)

PCC 21531

(a) The Castaic Lake Water Agency shall have power to prescribe methods for the construction of works and for the letting of contracts for the construction of works, structures, or equipment, or the performance or furnishing of labor, materials, or supplies, necessary or convenient for carrying out any of the purposes of this act or for the acquisition or disposal of any real or personal property; provided, that all contracts for any improvement or unit of work, when the cost according to the estimate of the engineer will exceed five thousand dollars ($5,000), shall be let to the lowest responsible bidder or bidders as provided in this article. The board shall first determine whether the contract shall be let as a single unit or divided into severable parts. The board shall advertise for bids by three insertions in a daily newspaper of general circulation published in the agency or by two insertions in a nondaily newspaper of general circulation published in the agency or, if no newspaper is published in the agency, in any newspaper of general circulation distributed in the agency, inviting sealed proposals for the construction or performance of the improvement or work. The call for bids shall state whether the work shall be performed in one unit or divided into parts. The work may be let under a single contract or several contracts, as stated in the call. The board shall require the successful bidders to file with the board good and sufficient bonds to be approved by the board conditioned upon the faithful performance of the contract and upon the payment of their claims for labor and material. The bonds shall comply with Title 3 (commencing with Section 9000) of Part 6 of Division 4 of the Civil Code. The board may reject any bid.

(b) In the event all proposals are rejected or no proposals are received, or the estimated cost of the work does not exceed five thousand dollars ($5,000), or the work consists of channel protection, maintenance work, or emergency work, the board may have the work done by force account without advertising for bids. In case of an emergency, if notice for bids to let contracts will not be given. The board shall comply with Chapter 2.5

Old Text

PCC 21531

(a) The Castaic Lake Water Agency shall have power to prescribe methods for the construction of works and for the letting of contracts for the construction of works, structures, or equipment, or the performance or furnishing of labor, materials, or supplies, necessary or convenient for carrying out any of the purposes of this act or for the acquisition or disposal of any real or personal property; provided, that all contracts for any improvement or unit of work, when the cost according to the estimate of the engineer will exceed five thousand dollars ($5,000), shall be let to the lowest responsible bidder or bidders as provided in this article. The board shall first determine whether the contract shall be let as a single unit or divided into severable parts. The board shall advertise for bids by three insertions in a daily newspaper of general circulation published in the agency or by two insertions in a nondaily newspaper of general circulation published in the agency or, if no newspaper is published in the agency, in any newspaper of general circulation distributed in the agency, inviting sealed proposals for the construction or performance of the improvement or work. The call for bids shall state whether the work shall be performed in one unit or divided into parts. The work may be let under a single contract or several contracts, as stated in the call. The board shall require the successful bidders to file with the board good and sufficient bonds to be approved by the board conditioned upon the faithful performance of the contract and upon the payment of their claims for labor and material. The bonds shall comply with Title 15 (commencing with Section 3082) of Part 4 of Division 3 of the Civil Code. The board may reject any bid.

(b) In the event all proposals are rejected or no proposals are received, or the estimated cost of the work does not exceed five thousand dollars ($5,000), or the work consists of channel protection, maintenance work, or emergency work, the board may have the work done by force account without advertising for bids. In case of an emergency, if notice for bids to let contracts will not be given. The board shall comply with Chapter 2.5 (commencing with Section 22050).

(c) The agency may purchase in the open market without

New Text (Operative July 1, 2012) | **Old Text**

(commencing with Section 22050).

(c) The agency may purchase in the open market without advertising for bids, materials and supplies for use in any work, either under contract or by force account; provided, however, that materials and supplies for use in any new construction work or improvement, except work referred to in subdivision (b), may not be purchased if the cost exceeds five thousand dollars ($5,000), without advertising for bids and awarding the contract to the lowest responsible bidder.

advertising for bids, materials and supplies for use in any work, either under contract or by force account; provided, however, that materials and supplies for use in any new construction work or improvement, except work referred to in subdivision (b), may not be purchased if the cost exceeds five thousand dollars ($5,000), without advertising for bids and awarding the contract to the lowest responsible bidder.

Revised to include reference to new Section 9000 et seq.

••

PCC 21541

(a) The Crestline-Lake Arrowhead Water Agency shall have power to prescribe methods for the construction of works and for the letting of contracts for the construction of works, structures, or equipment, or the performance or furnishing of labor, materials, or supplies, necessary or convenient for carrying out any of the purposes of this act or for the acquisition or disposal of any real or personal property. However, all contracts for the construction of any improvement or unit of work, when the cost, according to the estimate of the engineer, will exceed twenty-five thousand dollars ($25,000), shall be let to the lowest responsible bidder or bidders as provided in this article. The board shall first determine whether the contract shall be let as a single unit or divided into severable parts. The board shall advertise for bids by three insertions in a daily newspaper of general circulation or by two insertions in a weekly newspaper of general circulation printed and published in the agency, inviting sealed proposals for the construction or performance of the improvement or work. The call for bids shall state whether the work shall be performed in one unit or divided into parts. The work may be let under a single contract or several contracts, as stated in the call.

The board shall require the successful bidders to file with the board good and sufficient bonds to be

PCC 21541

(a) The Crestline-Lake Arrowhead Water Agency shall have power to prescribe methods for the construction of works and for the letting of contracts for the construction of works, structures, or equipment, or the performance or furnishing of labor, materials, or supplies, necessary or convenient for carrying out any of the purposes of this act or for the acquisition or disposal of any real or personal property. However, all contracts for the construction of any improvement or unit of work, when the cost, according to the estimate of the engineer, will exceed twenty-five thousand dollars ($25,000), shall be let to the lowest responsible bidder or bidders as provided in this article. The board shall first determine whether the contract shall be let as a single unit or divided into severable parts. The board shall advertise for bids by three insertions in a daily newspaper of general circulation or by two insertions in a weekly newspaper of general circulation printed and published in the agency, inviting sealed proposals for the construction or performance of the improvement or work. The call for bids shall state whether the work shall be performed in one unit or divided into parts. The work may be let under a single contract or several contracts, as stated in the call.

The board shall require the successful bidders to file with the board good and sufficient bonds to be approved by the board conditioned upon the faithful performance of the contract and upon the payment of

New Text (Operative July 1, 2012)	Old Text

approved by the board conditioned upon the faithful performance of the contract and upon the payment of their claims for labor and material. The bonds shall comply with Title 3 (commencing with Section 9000) of Part 6 of Division 4 of the Civil Code. The board may reject any bid.

(b) In the event all proposals are rejected or no proposals are received, or the estimated cost of the work does not exceed five thousand dollars ($5,000), or the work consists of channel protection, maintenance work, or emergency work, the board may have the work done by force account without advertising for bids. In case of an emergency, if notice for bids to let contracts will not be given, the board shall comply with Chapter 2.5 (commencing with Section 22050).

(c) The agency may purchase in the open market without advertising for bids, materials and supplies for use in any work, either under contract or by force account. However, materials and supplies for use in any new construction work or improvement, except work referred to in subdivision (b), may not be purchased if the cost exceeds twenty-five thousand dollars ($25,000), without advertising for bids and awarding the contract to the lowest responsible bidder.

their claims for labor and material. The bonds shall comply with Title 15 (commencing with Section 3082) of Part 4 of Division 3 of the Civil Code. The board may reject any bid.

(b) In the event all proposals are rejected or no proposals are received, or the estimated cost of the work does not exceed five thousand dollars ($5,000), or the work consists of channel protection, maintenance work, or emergency work, the board may have the work done by force account without advertising for bids. In case of an emergency, if notice for bids to let contracts will not be given, the board shall comply with Chapter 2.5 (commencing with Section 22050).

(c) The agency may purchase in the open market without advertising for bids, materials and supplies for use in any work, either under contract or by force account. However, materials and supplies for use in any new construction work or improvement, except work referred to in subdivision (b), may not be purchased if the cost exceeds twenty-five thousand dollars ($25,000), without advertising for bids and awarding the contract to the lowest responsible bidder.

Revised to include reference to new Section 9000 et seq.

PCC 21572

Any improvement or unit of work, except as provided in this article, estimated to cost in excess of five thousand dollars ($5,000), shall be done by contract and let to the lowest responsible bidder in the manner provided in this article. The board of directors of the agency shall advertise by three insertions in a daily newspaper of general circulation or two insertions in a weekly newspaper of general circulation published in the agency, inviting sealed proposals for the construction of the work before any contract shall be made, and may let by contract separately any part of the work. The board shall require the successful bidder to file with the board good and sufficient bonds to be approved by the board, conditioned upon the faithful performance of the contract, and upon the payment

PCC 21572

Any improvement or unit of work, except as provided in this article, estimated to cost in excess of five thousand dollars ($5,000), shall be done by contract and let to the lowest responsible bidder in the manner provided in this article. The board of directors of the agency shall advertise by three insertions in a daily newspaper of general circulation or two insertions in a weekly newspaper of general circulation published in the agency, inviting sealed proposals for the construction of the work before any contract shall be made, and may let by contract separately any part of the work. The board shall require the successful bidder to file with the board good and sufficient bonds to be approved by the board, conditioned upon the faithful performance of the contract, and upon the payment of the claims for labor and material, the

New Text (Operative July 1, 2012)

of the claims for labor and material, the bonds to contain the terms and conditions set forth in Title 3 (commencing with Section 9000) of Part 6 of Division 4 of the Civil Code, and to be subject to the provisions of that title. The board shall also have the right to reject any and all bids, and readvertise for new bids, or by a two-thirds vote may elect to undertake the work by force account. In the event no proposals are received pursuant to advertisement, or where the estimated cost of such work does not exceed five thousand dollars ($5,000), the board of directors by unanimous vote of all members present may without advertising for bids have the work done by force account. In case of an emergency, if notice for bids to let contracts will not be given, the board shall comply with Chapter 2.5 (commencing with Section 22050). The agency may purchase in the open market without advertisement for bids, materials and supplies for use in any work either under contract or by force account.

Old Text

bonds to contain the terms and conditions set forth in Title 15 (commencing with Section 3082) of Part 4 of Division 3 of the Civil Code, and to be subject to the provisions of that title. The board shall also have the right to reject any and all bids, and readvertise for new bids, or by a two-thirds vote may elect to undertake the work by force account. In the event no proposals are received pursuant to advertisement, or where the estimated cost of such work does not exceed five thousand dollars ($5,000), the board of directors by unanimous vote of all members present may without advertising for bids have the work done by force account. In case of an emergency, if notice for bids to let contracts will not be given, the board shall comply with Chapter 2.5 (commencing with Section 22050). The agency may purchase in the open market without advertisement for bids, materials and supplies for use in any work either under contract or by force account.

Revised to include reference to new Section 9000 et seq.

••

PCC 21581

(a) Any improvement or unit of work when the cost according to the estimate of the engineer will exceed five thousand dollars ($5,000), shall be done by contract and shall be let to the lowest responsible bidder or bidders in the manner provided in this article.

The board shall first determine whether the contract shall be let as a single unit or shall be divided into severable parts, or both, according to the best interests of the district. The board shall call for bids and advertise the call by three insertions in a daily newspaper of general circulation or by two insertions in a weekly newspaper of general circulation printed in the district inviting sealed proposals for the construction or performance of the improvement or work before any contract is made. The call for bids shall state whether the work is to be performed as a unit or shall be divided into severable specific parts, or both, as stated in the call. The board may let the work by single contract for the whole or it may divide the work into severable parts by separate contracts, as stated in the call, according to the best interests of the district. The board shall require the successful bidder or bidders to file with

PCC 21581

(a) Any improvement or unit of work when the cost according to the estimate of the engineer will exceed five thousand dollars ($5,000), shall be done by contract and shall be let to the lowest responsible bidder or bidders in the manner provided in this article.

The board shall first determine whether the contract shall be let as a single unit or shall be divided into severable parts, or both, according to the best interests of the district. The board shall call for bids and advertise the call by three insertions in a daily newspaper of general circulation or by two insertions in a weekly newspaper of general circulation printed in the district inviting sealed proposals for the construction or performance of the improvement or work before any contract is made. The call for bids shall state whether the work is to be performed as a unit or shall be divided into severable specific parts, or both, as stated in the call. The board may let the work by single contract for the whole or it may divide the work into severable parts by separate contracts, as stated in the call, according to the best interests of the district. The board shall require the successful bidder or bidders to file with the board a good and sufficient bond to be approved by the board conditioned upon

New Text (Operative July 1, 2012)

the board a good and sufficient bond to be approved by the board conditioned upon the payment of their claims for labor and material, the bond to contain the terms and conditions set forth in Title 3 (commencing with Section 9000) of Part 6 of Division 4 of the Civil Code and to be subject to the provisions of that title. The board shall also have the right to reject any and all bids and readvertise for new bids, or by a two-thirds vote may elect to undertake the work by force account.

(b) In the event no proposals are received pursuant to advertisement, or the estimated cost of the work does not exceed five thousand dollars ($5,000), or the work consists of channel protection, maintenance work, or emergency work, the board of supervisors may, without advertising for bids, have the work done by employees of the district, by day labor, under the direction of the board, by contract, or by any combination of those methods. In case of an emergency, if notice for bids to let contracts will not be given, the board shall comply with Chapter 2.5 (commencing with Section 22050).

(c) The district may acquire in the open market without advertising for bids, materials, equipment, and supplies for use in any work or for any other purpose; provided, however, that materials and supplies for use in any new construction work or improvement, except work referred to in subdivision (b), may not be purchased if the cost exceeds five thousand dollars ($5,000), without advertising for bids and awarding the contract to the lowest responsible bidder.

Old Text

the payment of their claims for labor and material, the bond to contain the terms and conditions set forth in Title 15 (commencing with Section 3082) of Part 4 of Division 3 of the Civil Code and to be subject to the provisions of that title. The board shall also have the right to reject any and all bids and readvertise for new bids, or by a two-thirds vote may elect to undertake the work by force account.

(b) In the event no proposals are received pursuant to advertisement, or the estimated cost of the work does not exceed five thousand dollars ($5,000), or the work consists of channel protection, maintenance work, or emergency work, the board of supervisors may, without advertising for bids, have the work done by employees of the district, by day labor, under the direction of the board, by contract, or by any combination of those methods. In case of an emergency, if notice for bids to let contracts will not be given, the board shall comply with Chapter 2.5 (commencing with Section 22050).

(c) The district may acquire in the open market without advertising for bids, materials, equipment, and supplies for use in any work or for any other purpose; provided, however, that materials and supplies for use in any new construction work or improvement, except work referred to in subdivision (b), may not be purchased if the cost exceeds five thousand dollars ($5,000), without advertising for bids and awarding the contract to the lowest responsible bidder.

Revised to include reference to new Section 9000 et seq.

New Text

__PCC 21591__

(a) Any improvement or unit of work, when the cost, according to the estimate of the engineer, will exceed twenty-five thousand dollars ($25,000), shall be done by contract and shall be let to the lowest responsible bidder or bidders as provided in this article. The board shall first determine whether the contract shall be let as a single unit or divided into severable parts. The board shall advertise for bids by three insertions in a daily newspaper of general circulation or by two insertions in a weekly newspaper of general circulation printed and published in the agency, if there is a newspaper printed and published in the agency, inviting sealed proposals for the construction

Old Text

PCC 21591

(a) Any improvement or unit of work, when the cost, according to the estimate of the engineer, will exceed twenty-five thousand dollars ($25,000), shall be done by contract and shall be let to the lowest responsible bidder or bidders as provided in this article. The board shall first determine whether the contract shall be let as a single unit or divided into severable parts. The board shall advertise for bids by three insertions in a daily newspaper of general circulation or by two insertions in a weekly newspaper of general circulation printed and published in the agency, if there is a newspaper printed and published in the agency, inviting sealed proposals for the construction or performance of the improvement or work. The call for *or performance of the improvement or work. The call for bids shall state whether the work shall be performed in one unit or divided into parts. The work may be let under a single contract or several contracts, as stated in the call. The board shall require the successful bidders to file with the board good and sufficient bonds to be approved by the board conditioned upon the faithful performance of the contract and upon the payment of their claims for labor and material. The bonds shall comply with Title 3 (commencing with Section 9000) of Part 6 of Division 4 of the Civil Code. The board may reject any and all bids and readvertise, or by a two-thirds vote may elect to undertake work by force account.*

(b) If no proposals are received, or the estimated cost of the work does not exceed twenty-five thousand dollars ($25,000), or the work consists of channel protection, maintenance work, or emergency work, the board may have the work done by force account without advertising for bids. In case of an emergency, if notice for bids to let contracts will not be given, the board shall comply with Chapter 2.5 (commencing with Section 22050).

(c) The agency may purchase in the open market without advertising for bids, materials and supplies for use in any work, either under contract or by force account; provided, however, that materials and supplies for use in any new construction work or improvement, except work referred to in subdivision (b), may not be purchased if the cost exceeds twenty-five thousand dollars ($25,000), without advertising for bids and awarding the contract to the lowest responsible bidder.

bids shall state whether the work shall be performed in one unit or divided into parts. The work may be let under a single contract or several contracts, as stated in the call. The board shall require the successful bidders to file with the board good and sufficient bonds to be approved by the board conditioned upon the faithful performance of the contract and upon the payment of their claims for labor and material. The bonds shall comply with Title 15 (commencing with Section 3082) of Part 4 of Division 3 of the Civil Code. The board may reject any and all bids and readvertise, or by a two-thirds vote may elect to undertake work by force account.

(b) If no proposals are received, or the estimated cost of the work does not exceed twenty-five thousand dollars ($25,000), or the work consists of channel protection, maintenance work, or emergency work, the board may have the work done by force account without advertising for bids. In case of an emergency, if notice for bids to let contracts will not be given, the board shall comply with Chapter 2.5 (commencing with Section 22050).

(c) The agency may purchase in the open market without advertising for bids, materials and supplies for use in any work, either under contract or by force account; provided, however, that materials and supplies for use in any new construction work or improvement, except work referred to in subdivision (b), may not be purchased if the cost exceeds twenty-five thousand dollars ($25,000), without advertising for bids and awarding the contract to the lowest responsible bidder.

Revised to include reference to new Section 9000 et seq.

PCC 21601

Any improvement or unit of work, when the cost, according to the estimate of the engineer, will exceed five thousand dollars ($5,000), shall be done by contract and let to the lowest responsible bidder or bidders as provided in this article. The board shall first determine whether the contract shall be let as a single unit or divided into severable parts. The board shall advertise for bids by three insertions in a daily newspaper of general circulation, or by two insertions in a weekly newspaper of general circulation, printed and published in the agency, inviting sealed proposals for the construction or performance of the improvement or work. The call for bids shall state whether the work shall be

PCC 21601

Any improvement or unit of work, when the cost, according to the estimate of the engineer, will exceed five thousand dollars ($5,000), shall be done by contract and let to the lowest responsible bidder or bidders as provided in this article. The board shall first determine whether the contract shall be let as a single unit or divided into severable parts. The board shall advertise for bids by three insertions in a daily newspaper of general circulation, or by two insertions in a weekly newspaper of general circulation, printed and published in the agency, inviting sealed proposals for the construction or performance of the improvement or work. The call for bids shall state whether the work shall be

New Text (Operative July 1, 2012)

performed in one unit or divided into parts. The work may be let under a single contract or several contracts, as stated in the call. The board shall require the successful bidders to file with the board good and sufficient bonds to be approved by the board conditioned upon the faithful performance of the contract and upon payment of their claims for labor and material. The bonds shall comply with Title 3 (commencing with Section 9000) of Part 6 of Division 4 of the Civil Code. The board may reject any and all bids and readvertise, or, by a two-thirds vote, may elect to undertake the work by force account. If no proposals are received, the estimated cost of the work does not exceed five thousand dollars ($5,000), or the work consists of channel protection, maintenance work, or emergency work, the board of supervisors may have the work done by force account without advertising for bids. In case of an emergency, if notice for bids to let contracts will not be given, the board shall comply with Chapter 2.5 (commencing with Section 22050). The district may purchase in the open market without advertising for bids, materials, and supplies for use in any work, either under contract or by force account.

Old Text

performed in one unit or divided into parts. The work may be let under a single contract or several contracts, as stated in the call. The board shall require the successful bidders to file with the board good and sufficient bonds to be approved by the board conditioned upon the faithful performance of the contract and upon payment of their claims for labor and material. The bonds shall comply with Title 15 (commencing with Section 3082) of Part 4 of Division 3 of the Civil Code. The board may reject any and all bids and readvertise, or, by a two-thirds vote, may elect to undertake the work by force account. If no proposals are received, the estimated cost of the work does not exceed five thousand dollars ($5,000), or the work consists of channel protection, maintenance work, or emergency work, the board of supervisors may have the work done by force account without advertising for bids. In case of an emergency, if notice for bids to let contracts will not be given, the board shall comply with Chapter 2.5 (commencing with Section 22050). The district may purchase in the open market without advertising for bids, materials, and supplies for use in any work, either under contract or by force account.

Revised to include reference to new Section 9000 et seq.

PCC 21622

The board shall require the successful bidder or bidders to file with the board, good and sufficient bonds, to be approved by the board conditioned upon the faithful performance of the contract and upon the payment of their claims for labor and material in connection therewith. Such contracts shall be subject to the provisions of Title 3 (commencing with Section 9000) of Part 6 of Division 4 of the Civil Code.

PCC 21622

The board shall require the successful bidder or bidders to file with the board, good and sufficient bonds, to be approved by the board conditioned upon the faithful performance of the contract and upon the payment of their claims for labor and material in connection therewith. Such contracts shall be subject to the provisions of Title 15 (commencing with Section 3200) of Part 4 of Division 3 of the Civil Code.

Revised to include reference to new Section 9000 et seq.

PCC 21631

(a) Any improvement or unit of work when the cost, according to the estimate of the engineer, will exceed six thousand five hundred dollars ($6,500), shall be done by contract and shall be let to the lowest responsible bidder or bidders in the manner provided in this article. The board shall first determine whether the contract shall be let as a single unit, or shall be divided into severable parts, or both, according to the best interests of the

PCC 21631

(a) Any improvement or unit of work when the cost, according to the estimate of the engineer, will exceed six thousand five hundred dollars ($6,500), shall be done by contract and shall be let to the lowest responsible bidder or bidders in the manner provided in this article. The board shall first determine whether the contract shall be let as a single unit, or shall be divided into severable parts, or both, according to the best interests of the district. The board

New Text (Operative July 1, 2012)

district. The board shall call for bids and advertise the call by three insertions in a daily newspaper of general circulation or by two insertions in a weekly newspaper of general circulation printed in the district inviting sealed proposals for the construction or performance of the improvement or work before any contract is made. The call for bids shall state whether the work is to be performed as a unit or shall be divided into severable parts, or both, as stated in the call. The board may let the work by single contract or it may divide the work into severable parts by separate contracts, as stated in the call, according to the best interests of the district. The board shall require the successful bidder or bidders to file with the board a good and sufficient bond, to be approved by the board, conditioned upon the payment of their claims for labor and material. The bond shall contain the terms and conditions set forth in Title 3 (commencing with Section 9000) of Part 6 of Division 4 of the Civil Code and be subject to the provisions of that title. The board may reject any and all bids and readvertise for new bids, or by a two-thirds vote may elect to undertake the work by force account.

(b) If no proposals are received pursuant to advertisement or the estimated cost of the work does not exceed six thousand five hundred dollars ($6,500), or the work consists of channel protection, maintenance work, or emergency work, the board of supervisors may, without advertising for bids, have the work done by employees of the district, by day labor, under the direction of the board, by contract, or by a combination of those methods. In case of an emergency, if notice for bids to let contracts will not be given, the board shall comply with Chapter 2.5 (commencing with Section 22050).

(c) The district may acquire in the open market, without advertising for bids, materials, equipment, and supplies for use in any work or for any other purpose; provided, however, that materials and supplies for use in any new construction work or improvement, except that work referred to in subdivision (b), may not be purchased if the cost exceeds six thousand five hundred dollars ($6,500), without advertising for bids and awarding the contract to the lowest responsible bidder.

Old Text

shall call for bids and advertise the call by three insertions in a daily newspaper of general circulation or by two insertions in a weekly newspaper of general circulation printed in the district inviting sealed proposals for the construction or performance of the improvement or work before any contract is made. The call for bids shall state whether the work is to be performed as a unit or shall be divided into severable parts, or both, as stated in the call. The board may let the work by single contract or it may divide the work into severable parts by separate contracts, as stated in the call, according to the best interests of the district. The board shall require the successful bidder or bidders to file with the board a good and sufficient bond, to be approved by the board, conditioned upon the payment of their claims for labor and material. The bond shall contain the terms and conditions set forth in Title 15 (commencing with Section 3082) of Part 4 of Division 3 of the Civil Code and be subject to the provisions of that title. The board may reject any and all bids and readvertise for new bids, or by a two-thirds vote may elect to undertake the work by force account.

(b) If no proposals are received pursuant to advertisement or the estimated cost of the work does not exceed six thousand five hundred dollars ($6,500), or the work consists of channel protection, maintenance work, or emergency work, the board of supervisors may, without advertising for bids, have the work done by employees of the district, by day labor, under the direction of the board, by contract, or by a combination of those methods. In case of an emergency, if notice for bids to let contracts will not be given, the board shall comply with Chapter 2.5 (commencing with Section 22050).

(c) The district may acquire in the open market, without advertising for bids, materials, equipment, and supplies for use in any work or for any other purpose; provided, however, that materials and supplies for use in any new construction work or improvement, except that work referred to in subdivision (b), may not be purchased if the cost exceeds six thousand five hundred dollars ($6,500), without advertising for bids and awarding the contract to the lowest responsible bidder.

New Text (Operative July 1, 2012) **Old Text**

STREETS AND HIGHWAYS CODE SECTIONS ("S&H")

S&H 136.5

(a) The contracts referred to in Sections 135, 136, and 136.1 are not subject to the State Contract Act (Part 2 (commencing with Section 10100) of Division 2 of the Public Contract Code). Except for emergency work of the type described in subdivision (b), whenever the estimated amount of a contract exceeds two thousand five hundred dollars ($2,500), it shall be awarded to the lowest responsible bidder, after competitive bidding on any reasonable notice that the department may prescribe. Posting of notice for five days in a public place in the district office within which the work is to be done, or the equipment used, is sufficient. Those contracts shall be subject to the applicable payment bond provisions of Chapter 5 (commencing with Section 9550) of Title 3 of Part 6 of Division 4 of the Civil Code. The department may require faithful performance bonds when considered necessary. The advertisement for each contract shall state whether or not a bond shall be required.

(b) In cases of emergency work necessitated by the imminence or occurrence of a landslide, flood, storm damage, accident, or other casualty, tools or equipment may be rented for a period of not to exceed 60 days without competitive bidding, and the department may waive the requirements of Chapter 5 (commencing with Section 9550) of Title 3 of Part 6 of Division 4 of the Civil Code to the extent that a contractor may commence performance of the work under the contract for the rental of tools or equipment prior to filing a payment bond with the department. In that case, no payment shall be made to the contractor until a payment bond covering all work of the contract is filed with the department.

S&H 136.5

(a) The contracts referred to in Sections 135, 136, and 136.1 are not subject to the State Contract Act (Part 2 (commencing with Section 10100) of Division 2 of the Public Contract Code). Except for emergency work of the type described in subdivision (b), whenever the estimated amount of a contract exceeds two thousand five hundred dollars ($2,500), it shall be awarded to the lowest responsible bidder, after competitive bidding on any reasonable notice that the department may prescribe. Posting of notice for five days in a public place in the district office within which the work is to be done, or the equipment used, is sufficient. Those contracts shall be subject to the applicable payment bond provisions of Chapter 7 (commencing with Section 3247) of Part 4 of Division 3 of the Civil Code. The department may require faithful performance bonds when considered necessary. The advertisement for each contract shall state whether or not a bond shall be required.

(b) In cases of emergency work necessitated by the imminence or occurrence of a landslide, flood, storm damage, accident, or other casualty, tools or equipment may be rented for a period of not to exceed 60 days without competitive bidding, and the department may waive the requirements of Chapter 7 (commencing with Section 3247) of Part 4 of Division 3 of the Civil Code to the extent that a contractor may commence performance of the work under the contract for the rental of tools or equipment prior to filing a payment bond with the department. In that case, no payment shall be made to the contractor until a payment bond covering all work of the contract is filed with the department.

Revised to include reference to new Section 9000 et seq.

Section III
Cross Reference Tables

UPDATED SECTION NUMBERS, OLD TO NEW

The following chart shows the changes in ascending order of the previous code and what the corresponding designation number is for the new code.

Old § Nos.	New § Nos.
B&P 17577.5	B&P 17577.5
B&P 7034	B&P 7034
B&P 7071.10	B&P 7071.10
B&P 7071.5	B&P 7071.5
B&P 7159	B&P 7159
B&P 7159.1	B&P 7159.1
B&P 7159.14	B&P 7159.14
B&P 7159.5	B&P 7159.5
B&P 7164	B&P 7164
B&P 8513	B&P 8513
CC 1917.166	CC 1917.166
CC 1917.615	CC 1917.615
CC 3059	CC 3059
CC 3060	CC 3060
CC 3081.1	CC 8014
CC 3081.1	CC 8300
CC 3081.10	CC 8318
CC 3081.2	CC 8302
CC 3081.3	CC 8304
CC 3081.4	CC 8306
CC 3081.5	CC 8308
CC 3081.6	CC 8310
CC 3081.7	CC 8312
CC 3081.8	CC 8314
CC 3081.9	CC 8316
CC 3082	CC 8000
CC 3083	CC 8532
CC 3083 and CC 3103	CC 8506
CC 3084	CC 8416
CC 3085	CC 8004
CC 3086 (except subd (b))	CC 8180
CC 3086 (except subd (b))	CC 9200
CC 3086(b)	*Repealed*
CC 3087	CC 8006
CC 3088	CC 8008
CC 3088	CC 8016
CC 3089 and CC 3111	CC 8024
CC 3090	CC 8028
CC 3092	CC 8188
CC 3092	CC 9202
CC 3093	CC 8182
CC 3093	CC 8184
CC 3093	CC 9204
CC 3093	CC 9208
CC 3094	CC 8444
CC 3095	CC 8018
CC 3096	CC 8606

Old § Nos.	New § Nos.
CC 3096 and CC 3248	CC 9554
CC 3097 and CC 3098	CC 8034
CC 3097(c)	CC 8102
CC 3097(c)	CC 8202
CC 3097(d)	CC 8204
CC 3097(e)	CC 8212
CC 3097(f)	CC 8116
CC 3097(g)	CC 8206
CC 3097(h)	CC 8216
CC 3097(i)	CC 8172
CC 3097(j)	CC 8174
CC 3097(k)	CC 8104
CC 3097(l) and CC3097(m)	CC 8170
CC 3097(l) and CC3097(m)	CC 8208
CC 3097(n)	CC 8210
CC 3097(o)	CC 8214
CC 3097(p)	*Repealed*
CC 3097, CC 3097(a) and (b)	CC 8200
CC 3097.1	CC 8118
CC 3098(a)	CC 9302
CC 3098(a)	CC 9303
CC 3098(a)	CC 9304
CC 3098(b)	CC 9306
CC 3098(d)	CC 9304
CC 3098(e)	*Repealed*
CC 3098, CC 3098(a) and (c)	CC 9300
CC 3099	CC 8036
CC 3100	CC 8038
CC 3101	CC 8040
CC 3102	CC 8042
CC 3103	CC 8044
CC 3103	CC 8502
CC 3103	CC 9352
CC 3103	CC 9354
CC 3104	CC 8046
CC 3105	
CC 3106	CC 8050
CC 3109	CC 8160
CC 3110	CC 8400
CC 3110 and CC 3112	CC 8404
CC 3110, CC 3111, CC 3112 and CC 3181	CC 9100
CC 3110.5(a)(1) and CC 3110.5(a)(2)	CC 8700
CC 3110.5(b)	CC 8710
CC 3110.5(b)	CC 8720
CC 3110.5(b)(1)	CC 8722
CC 3110.5(b)(2)	CC 8724
CC 3110.5(b)(3)	CC 8726

Old § Nos.	New § Nos.
CC 3110.5(b)(3)	CC 8728
CC 3110.5(c)	CC 8712
CC 3110.5(c)	CC 8730
CC 3110.5(d)	CC 8716
CC 3110.5(e)	CC 8702
CC 3110.5(f)	CC 8704
CC 3110.5(g)	CC 8714
CC 3112	CC 8402
CC 3112 and CC 3128	CC 8440
CC 3114	CC 8410
CC 3115	CC 8412
CC 3116	CC 8414
CC 3117	CC 8186
CC 3118 and CC 3261	CC 8422
CC 3123(a) and (b)	CC 8430
CC 3123(c)	*Repealed*
CC 3124	CC 8432
CC 3128 and CC 3129	CC 8442
CC 3130	CC 8446
CC 3131 (first paragraph)	CC 8448
CC 3131 (second paragraph)	*Repealed*
CC 3134	CC 8450
CC 3135	CC 8454
CC 3136	CC 8456
CC 3137 and CC 3139	CC 8458
CC 3138	CC 8452
CC 3140	CC 8434
CC 3143 and CC 3144.5	CC 8424
CC 3144 and CC 3145	CC 8460
CC 3146	CC 8461
CC 3147	CC 8462
CC 3148	CC 8490
CC 3149	*Repealed*
CC 3150	CC 8464
CC 3151	CC 8466
CC 3152	CC 8468
CC 3153	CC 8470
CC 3154(a)	CC 8482
CC 3154(a), (h), and (i)	CC 8480
CC 3154(b)	CC 8484
CC 3154(b), (e), (f) and (g)	CC 8488
CC 3154(c), (d) and (e)	CC 8486
CC 3156	CC 8160
CC 3158	CC 8520
CC 3159	CC 8530
CC 3159(a) and CC 3162(a)	CC 8536
CC 3159(a) and CC 3162(a)	CC 8538
CC 3159(b) and (c), CC 3162 (b) and (c)	CC 8542
CC 3160	CC 8508
CC 3161	CC 8522
CC 3163	CC 8534
CC 3166	CC 8544
CC 3167	CC 8540
CC 3168	CC 8504
CC 3171	CC 8510
CC 3172	CC 8550
CC 3173	CC 8554
CC 3174	CC 8556
CC 3175	CC 8552
CC 3176	CC 8558
CC 3176.5	CC 8560
CC 3179	CC 9000
CC 3183 and CC 3265	CC 9500
CC 3184	CC 9356
CC 3185	CC 9362
CC 3186	CC 9358
CC 3187	CC 9360
CC 3190	CC 9450
CC 3191	CC 9452
CC 3192	CC 9454
CC 3193	CC 9456
CC 3196	CC 9364
CC 3197	CC 9400
CC 3198	CC 9402
CC 3199	CC 9404
CC 3200	CC 9406
CC 3201	CC 9408
CC 3202	CC 9410
CC 3203	CC 9412
CC 3204	*Repealed*
CC 3205	CC 9414
CC 3210	CC 9502
CC 3211	CC 9504
CC 3212	CC 9508
CC 3213	CC 9510
CC 3214	CC 9506
CC 3225	CC 8152
CC 3226	CC 8154
CC 3227	CC 8614
CC 3227	CC 9562
CC 3235 and CC 3236	CC 8600
CC 3236	CC 8602
CC 3237	CC 8604
CC 3239	CC 8609
CC 3240	CC 8610
CC 3242	CC 8612
CC 3247	CC 9550
CC 3249	CC 9558
CC 3250	CC 9564
CC 3251	CC 9552
CC 3252	CC 9560
CC 3258	CC 8060
CC 3259	CC 8056
CC 3259.5	CC 8190
CC 3260(a)	*Repealed*
CC 3260(b)	CC 8810
CC 3260(c)	CC 8812
CC 3260(c)(1)	*Repealed*

Old § Nos.	New § Nos.
CC 3260(c)(2)	*Repealed*
CC 3260(d)	CC 8814
CC 3260(e)	CC 8814
CC 3260(f)	CC 8816
CC 3260(g)	CC 8818
CC 3260.1	CC 8800
CC 3260.2(a)	CC 8830
CC 3260.2(a)	CC 8832
CC 3260.2(a)	CC 8834
CC 3260.2(a)	CC 8836
CC 3260.2(a)	CC 8840
CC 3260.2(b)	CC 8842
CC 3260.2(c)	CC 8838
CC 3260.2(d)	CC 8844
CC 3260.2(e)	CC 8846
CC 3260.2(f)	CC 8848
CC 3260.2(g)	*Repealed*
CC 3262(a)	CC 8122
CC 3262(a)	CC 8124
CC 3262(b)(1)	CC 8126
CC 3262(b)(2)	CC 8128
CC 3262(c)	CC 8130
CC 3262(d)(1)	CC 8132
CC 3262(d)(2)	CC 8134
CC 3262(d)(3)	CC 8136
CC 3262(d)(4)	CC 8138
CC 3262.5	CC 8802
CC 3263	CC 8062
CC 3264	CC 8500
CC 3264	CC 9350
CC 3266	CC 8054
CC 3267	CC 8608
CC 3267	CC 9566
CC 3319	CC 3319
CC 3320	CC 3320
CC 3321	CC 3321
CCP 1203.61	CCP 1203.61
CCP 1281.5	CCP 1281.5
CCP 1800	CCP 1800
CCP 410.42	CCP 410.42
CCP 708.760	CCP 708.760
CCP 86	CCP 86
EC 17307.5	EC 17307.5
EC 81133.5	EC 81133.5
GC 14975	GC 14975
GC 15820.105	GC 15820.105
GC 27287	GC 27287
GC 27361.9	GC 27361.9
GC 66499.2	GC 66499.2
GC 66499.7	GC 66499.7
GC 7480	GC 7480
H&S 16017.5	H&S 16017.5
H&S 19825	H&S 19825
H&S 34218	H&S 34218
H&S 5463	H&S 5463
INS 11751.82	INS 11751.82
LABOR 218.5	LABOR 218.5
NA	CC 8494
None.	CC 8002
None.	CC 8010
None.	CC8012
None.	CC 8020
None.	CC 8022
None.	CC 8026
None.	CC 8030
None.	CC 8032
None.	CC 8048
None.	CC 8052
None.	CC 8058
None.	CC 8064
None.	CC 8066
None.	CC 8100
None.	CC 8106
None.	CC 8108
None.	CC 8110
None.	CC 8114
None.	CC 8120
None.	CC 8150
None.	CC 8319
None.	CC 8820
None.	CC 8822
PCC 10222	PCC 10222
PCC 10822	PCC 10822
PCC 20104	PCC 20104
PCC 20134	PCC 20134
PCC 20461	PCC 20461
PCC 20496	PCC 20496
PCC 20682.5	PCC 20682.5
PCC 20688.4	PCC 20688.4
PCC 20813	PCC 20813
PCC 20815.3	PCC 20815.3
PCC 20991	PCC 20991
PCC 21061	PCC 21061
PCC 21071	PCC 21071
PCC 21081	PCC 21081
PCC 21091	PCC 21091
PCC 21101	PCC 21101
PCC 21111	PCC 21111
PCC 21121	PCC 21121
PCC 21131	PCC 21131
PCC 21141	PCC 21141
PCC 21151	PCC 21151
PCC 21161	PCC 21161
PCC 21171	PCC 21171
PCC 21181	PCC 21181
PCC 21196	PCC 21196
PCC 21212	PCC 21212
PCC 21231	PCC 21231

Old § Nos.	New § Nos.
PCC 21241	PCC 21241
PCC 21251	PCC 21251
PCC 21261	PCC 21261
PCC 21271	PCC 21271
PCC 21311	PCC 21311
PCC 21321	PCC 21321
PCC 21331	PCC 21331
PCC 21341	PCC 21341
PCC 21351	PCC 21351
PCC 21361	PCC 21361
PCC 21371	PCC 21371
PCC 21381	PCC 21381
PCC 21391	PCC 21391
PCC 21401	PCC 21401
PCC 21411	PCC 21411
PCC 21421	PCC 21421
PCC 21431	PCC 21431
PCC 21441	PCC 21441

Old § Nos.	New § Nos.
PCC 21451	PCC 21451
PCC 21461	PCC 21461
PCC 21491	PCC 21491
PCC 21501	PCC 21501
PCC 21511	PCC 21511
PCC 21521	PCC 21521
PCC 21531	PCC 21531
PCC 21541	PCC 21541
PCC 21572	PCC 21572
PCC 21581	PCC 21581
PCC 21591	PCC 21591
PCC 21601	PCC 21601
PCC 21622	PCC 21622
PCC 21631	PCC 21631
PCC 4107.7	PCC 4107.7
PCC 7103	PCC 7103
S&H 136.5	S&H 136.5

UPDATED SECTION NUMBERS, NEW TO OLD

The following chart shows the changes in ascending order of the new code and what the corresponding designation number is for the previous code.

New § Nos.	Old § Nos.
B&P 17577.5	B&P 17577.5
B&P 7034	B&P 7034
B&P 7071.10	B&P 7071.10
B&P 7071.5	B&P 7071.5
B&P 7159	B&P 7159
B&P 7159.1	B&P 7159.1
B&P 7159.14	B&P 7159.14
B&P 7159.5	B&P 7159.5
B&P 7164	B&P 7164
B&P 8513	B&P 8513
CC 1917.166	CC 1917.166
CC 1917.615	CC 1917.615
CC 3059	CC 3059
CC 3060	CC 3060
CC 8014	CC 3081.1
CC 8300	CC 3081.1
CC 8318	CC 3081.10
CC 8302	CC 3081.2
CC 8304	CC 3081.3
CC 8306	CC 3081.4
CC 8308	CC 3081.5
CC 8310	CC 3081.6
CC 8312	CC 3081.7
CC 8314	CC 3081.8
CC 8316	CC 3081.9
CC 8000	CC 3082
CC 8506	CC 3083 and CC 3103
CC 8532	CC 3083
CC 8416	CC 3084
CC 8004	CC 3085
CC 8180	CC 3086 (except subd (b))
CC 9200	CC 3086 (except subd (b))
CC 8006	CC 3087
CC 8008	CC 3088
CC 8016	CC 3088
CC 8024	CC 3089 and CC 3111
CC 8028	CC 3090
CC 8188	CC 3092
CC 9202	CC 3092
CC 8182	CC 3093
CC 8184	CC 3093
CC 9204	CC 3093
CC 9208	CC 3093
CC 8444	CC 3094
CC 8018	CC 3095
CC 8606	CC 3096
CC 9554	CC 3096 and CC 3248
CC 8034	CC 3097 and CC 3098

New § Nos.	Old § Nos.
CC 8102	CC 3097(c)
CC 8202	CC 3097(c)
CC 8204	CC 3097(d)
CC 8212	CC 3097(e)
CC 8116	CC 3097(f)
CC 8206	CC 3097(g)
CC 8216	CC 3097(h)
CC 8172	CC 3097(i)
CC 8174	CC 3097(j)
CC 8104	CC 3097(k)
CC 8170	CC 3097(l) and CC 3097(m)
CC 8208	CC 3097(l) and CC 3097(m)
CC 8210	CC 3097(n)
CC 8214	CC 3097(o)
	CC 3097(p)
CC 8200	CC 3097, CC 3097(a) and CC 3097(b)
CC 8118	CC 3097.1
CC 9302	CC 3098(a)
CC 9303	CC 3098(a)
CC 9304	CC 3098(a)
CC 9306	CC 3098(b)
CC 9304	CC 3098(d)
	CC 3098(e)
CC 9300	CC 3098, CC 3098(a) and CC 3098(c)
CC 8036	CC 3099
CC 8038	CC 3100
CC 8040	CC 3101
CC 8042	CC 3102
CC 8044	CC 3103
CC 8502	CC 3103
CC 9352	CC 3103
CC 9354	CC 3103
CC 8046	CC 3104
	CC 3105
CC 8050	CC 3106
CC 8160	CC 3109
CC 8400	CC 3110
CC 8404	CC 3110 and CC 3112
CC 9100	CC 3110, CC 3111, CC 3112 and CC 3181
CC 8700	CC 3110.5(a)(1) and CC 3110.5(a)(2)
CC 8710	CC 3110.5(b)
CC 8720	CC 3110.5(b)
CC 8722	CC 3110.5(b)(1)
CC 8724	CC 3110.5(b)(2)
CC 8726	CC 3110.5(b)(3)
CC 8728	CC 3110.5(b)(3)
CC 8712	CC 3110.5(c)
CC 8730	CC 3110.5(c)

New § Nos.	Old § Nos.
CC 8716	CC 3110.5(d)
CC 8702	CC 3110.5(e)
CC 8704	CC 3110.5(f)
CC 8714	CC 3110.5(g)
CC 8402	CC 3112
CC 8440	CC 3112 and CC 3128
CC 8410	CC 3114
CC 8412	CC 3115
CC 8414	CC 3116
CC 8186	CC 3117
CC 8422	CC 3118 and CC 3261
	CC 3123(c)
CC 8432	CC 3124
CC 8442	CC 3128 and CC 3129
CC 8446	CC 3130
CC 8448	CC 3131 (first paragraph)
	CC 3131 (second paragraph)
CC 8450	CC 3134
CC 8454	CC 3135
CC 8456	CC 3136
CC 8458	CC 3137 and CC 3139
CC 8452	CC 3138
CC 8434	CC 3140
CC 8424	CC 3143 and CC 3144.5
CC 8460	CC 3144 and CC 3145
CC 8461	CC 3146
CC 8462	CC 3147
CC 8490	CC 3148
	CC 3149
CC 8464	CC 3150
CC 8466	CC 3151
CC 8468	CC 3152
CC 8470	CC 3153
CC 8482	CC 3154(a)
CC 8480	CC 3154(a), CC 3154(h), and CC 3154(i)
CC 8484	CC 3154(b)
CC 8488	CC 3154(b), (e), (f) and (g)
CC 8486	CC 3154(c), CC 3154(d) and CC 3154(e)
CC 8160	CC 3156
CC 8520	CC 3158
CC 8530	CC 3159
CC 8536	CC 3159(a) and CC 3162(a)
CC 8538	CC 3159(a) and CC 3162(a)
CC 8542	CC 3159(b), (c), CC 3162(b) and (c)
CC 8508	CC 3160
CC 8522	CC 3161
CC 8534	CC 3163
CC 8544	CC 3166
CC 8540	CC 3167
CC 8504	CC 3168
CC 8510	CC 3171
CC 8550	CC 3172
CC 8554	CC 3173
CC 8556	CC 3174

New § Nos.	Old § Nos.
CC 8552	CC 3175
CC 8558	CC 3176
CC 8560	CC 3176.5
CC 9000	CC 3179
CC 9500	CC 3183 and CC 3265
CC 9356	CC 3184
CC 9362	CC 3185
CC 9358	CC 3186
CC 9360	CC 3187
CC 9450	CC 3190
CC 9452	CC 3191
CC 9454	CC 3192
CC 9456	CC 3193
CC 9364	CC 3196
CC 9400	CC 3197
CC 9402	CC 3198
CC 9404	CC 3199
CC 9406	CC 3200
CC 9408	CC 3201
CC 9410	CC 3202
CC 9412	CC 3203
	CC 3204
CC 9414	CC 3205
CC 9502	CC 3210
CC 9504	CC 3211
CC 9508	CC 3212
CC 9510	CC 3213
CC 9506	CC 3214
CC 8152	CC 3225
CC 8154	CC 3226
CC 8614	CC 3227
CC 9562	CC 3227
CC 8600	CC 3235 and CC 3236
CC 8602	CC 3236
CC 8604	CC 3237
CC 8609	CC 3239
CC 8610	CC 3240
CC 8612	CC 3242
CC 9550	CC 3247
CC 9558	CC 3249
CC 9564	CC 3250
CC 9552	CC 3251
CC 9560	CC 3252
CC 8060	CC 3258
CC 8056	CC 3259
CC 8190	CC 3259.5
	CC 3260(a)
CC 8810	CC 3260(b)
CC 8812	CC 3260(c)
	CC 3260(c)(1)
	CC 3260(c)(2)
CC 8814	CC 3260(d)
CC 8814	CC 3260(e)
CC 8816	CC 3260(f)

New § Nos.	Old § Nos.
CC 8818	CC 3260(g)
CC 8800	CC 3260.1
CC 8830	CC 3260.2(a)
CC 8832	CC 3260.2(a)
CC 8834	CC 3260.2(a)
CC 8836	CC 3260.2(a)
CC 8840	CC 3260.2(a)
CC 8842	CC 3260.2(b)
CC 8838	CC 3260.2(c)
CC 8844	CC 3260.2(d)
CC 8846	CC 3260.2(e)
CC 8848	CC 3260.2(f)
	CC 3260.2(g)
CC 8122	CC 3262(a)
CC 8124	CC 3262(a)
CC 8126	CC 3262(b)(1)
CC 8128	CC 3262(b)(2)
CC 8130	CC 3262(c)
CC 8132	CC 3262(d)(1)
CC 8134	CC 3262(d)(2)
CC 8136	CC 3262(d)(3)
CC 8138	CC 3262(d)(4)
CC 8802	CC 3262.5
CC 8062	CC 3263
CC 8500	CC 3264
CC 9350	CC 3264
CC 8054	CC 3266
CC 8608	CC 3267
CC 9566	CC 3267
CC 3319	CC 3319
CC 3320	CC 3320
CC 3321	CC 3321
CC 8430	CC 3123(a) and CC 3123(b)
CCP 1203.61	CCP 1203.61
CCP 1281.5	CCP 1281.5
CCP 1800	CCP 1800
CCP 410.42	CCP 410.42
CCP 708.760	CCP 708.760
CCP 86	CCP 86
EC 17307.5	EC 17307.5
EC 81133.5	EC 81133.5
GC 14975	GC 14975
GC 15820.105	GC 15820.105
GC 27287	GC 27287
GC 27361.9	GC 27361.9
GC 66499.2	GC 66499.2
GC 66499.7	GC 66499.7
GC 7480	GC 7480
H&S 16017.5	H&S 16017.5
H&S 19825	H&S 19825
H&S 34218	H&S 34218
H&S 5463	H&S 5463
INS 11751.82	INS 11751.82
LABOR 218.5	LABOR 218.5

New § Nos.	Old § Nos.
CC 8494	NA
CC 8002	None.
CC 8010	None.
CC 8012	None.
CC 8020	None.
CC 8022	None.
CC 8026	None.
CC 8030	None.
CC 8032	None.
CC 8048	None.
CC 8052	None.
CC 8058	None.
CC 8064	None.
CC 8066	None.
CC 8100	None.
CC 8106	None.
CC 8108	None.
CC 8110	None.
CC 8114	None.
CC 8120	None.
CC 8150	None.
CC 8319	None.
CC 8820	None.
CC 8822	None.
PCC 10222	PCC 10222
PCC 10822	PCC 10822
PCC 20104	PCC 20104
PCC 20134	PCC 20134
PCC 20461	PCC 20461
PCC 20496	PCC 20496
PCC 20682.5	PCC 20682.5
PCC 20688.4	PCC 20688.4
PCC 20813	PCC 20813
PCC 20815.3	PCC 20815.3
PCC 20991	PCC 20991
PCC 21061	PCC 21061
PCC 21071	PCC 21071
PCC 21081	PCC 21081
PCC 21091	PCC 21091
PCC 21101	PCC 21101
PCC 21111	PCC 21111
PCC 21121	PCC 21121
PCC 21131	PCC 21131
PCC 21141	PCC 21141
PCC 21151	PCC 21151
PCC 21161	PCC 21161
PCC 21171	PCC 21171
PCC 21181	PCC 21181
PCC 21196	PCC 21196
PCC 21212	PCC 21212
PCC 21231	PCC 21231
PCC 21241	PCC 21241
PCC 21251	PCC 21251
PCC 21261	PCC 21261

New § Nos.	Old § Nos.
PCC 21271	PCC 21271
PCC 21311	PCC 21311
PCC 21321	PCC 21321
PCC 21331	PCC 21331
PCC 21341	PCC 21341
PCC 21351	PCC 21351
PCC 21361	PCC 21361
PCC 21371	PCC 21371
PCC 21381	PCC 21381
PCC 21391	PCC 21391
PCC 21401	PCC 21401
PCC 21411	PCC 21411
PCC 21421	PCC 21421
PCC 21431	PCC 21431
PCC 21441	PCC 21441
PCC 21451	PCC 21451

New § Nos.	Old § Nos.
PCC 21461	PCC 21461
PCC 21491	PCC 21491
PCC 21501	PCC 21501
PCC 21511	PCC 21511
PCC 21521	PCC 21521
PCC 21531	PCC 21531
PCC 21541	PCC 21541
PCC 21572	PCC 21572
PCC 21581	PCC 21581
PCC 21591	PCC 21591
PCC 21601	PCC 21601
PCC 21622	PCC 21622
PCC 21631	PCC 21631
PCC 4107.7	PCC 4107.7
PCC 7103	PCC 7103
S&H 136.5	S&H 136.5

Section IV
Construction Glossary

ABS Pipe. A plastic pipe sold in 10 and 20 foot lengths in different diameters for stacks and main drains and is used only for drain lines.

Acoustical Block. A masonry block used for its sound-absorbing qualities.

Acoustical Tile. Ceiling panels in board form used for its sound absorbing properties. Sometimes used on walls.

Acoustical Treatment. The act or process of applying acoustical materials to walls and ceilings.

Acrylic. A general class of resinous polymers derived from esters, amides or other acrylic aid derivatives. A transparent plastic material used in sheet form for glazing windows and skylights.

Addenda. A revision in the contract document made prior to the execution of the owner-contractor contract.

Adhesion. The state in which two surfaces are held together by interfacial forces which may consist of valence forces or interlocking action, or both.

Admixture. A material other than water, aggregates, and hydraulic cement used as an ingredient of concrete or mortar, and added immediately before or during its mixing. A chemical additive used to alter the normal properties of concrete.

Aggregate. Inert particles such as sand, gravel, crushed stone, or expanded materials, in a concrete or plaster mixture. Granular material, such as sand, gravel, crushed stone, and iron blast-furnace slag, used with a cementing medium to form a hydraulic-cement, concrete or mortar.

Air Change Method. A method of calculating the quantity of infiltration air into a building. This method is used when construction quality cannot be determined and are based on medium quality of construction.

Air Eliminator. A mechanical device that expels excess air.

Air Entraining Agent. A substance added to concrete, mortar or cement that produces air bubbles during mixing, making it easier to work with, and increasing its resistance to frost.

Air Plenum. Any space used to convey air in a building or structure. The space above a suspended ceiling is often used as an air plenum.

Air-Handling System. A system to heat, cool, humidity, dehumidify, filter and transport air. It consists of an air handling unit, fresh air (F.A.) and exhaust air (E.A.) damper at the building exterior, ductwork, supply air (S.A.), diffusers or registers, and return air (R.A.) grills in the conditioned space.

Alkali. A chemical substance which effectively neutralizes acid material so as to form neutral salts. A base. The opposite of acid. Examples are ammonia and caustic soda.

Alternates. A stipulated construction sum, in addition to the base bid, for specific items to be included or excluded from the project.

Ambient Sound. The quiet-state noise level in a room or space, which is a composite of sounds from many external sources, both near and far, over which one individual has no control.

Anchor Bolt. A bolt embedded in concrete for the purpose of fastening a building frame to a concrete or masonry foundation.

Anchorage. An attachment for resistance to movement. The movement can be a result of overturning, sliding or uplift. The most common anchorage for these movements are tie-downs (hold-downs) for overturning and uplift, and anchor bolts for sliding.

Annunciator Panel. A panel mounted on a surface which indicates by lights which circuits have been activated.

Anodized. A metal that has been subjected to electrolytic action in order to coat with a protective or decorative film.

Anti-siphon. A device to prevent the removal of fluid caused by suction produced by fluid flow.

Application for Payment. A written document forwarded by the contractor requesting payment for work completed.

Arch. A curved structure in which compression is the essential cause of internal stresses. A structural member with an upward-curved centerline axis and a relatively small cross section, supported so that the distance between its ends cannot change.

Aseismic Region. A region that is relatively free of earthquakes.

Ashlar. Masonry composed of squared stones; one pattern of masonry construction.

Asphalt. A residue in petroleum or coal-tar refining that is used for pavements and as a waterproofing cement.

Asphalt-Saturated Felt. A moisture-resistant sheet material, available in several different thicknesses, usually consisting of a heavy paper that has been impregnated with asphalt.

ASTM. American Society for Testing and Materials, 1916 Race Street, Philadelphia, PA 19103, (215) 299-5420.

Attenuation Blanket. Material utilized to help in the reduction of the energy or intensity of sound.

Axial. In a direction parallel to the long axis of a structural member. In line with the axis. An axial force causes tension or compression stress over the cross section of a member.

Backfill. Earth or earthen material used to fill the excavation around a foundation; the act of filling around a foundation.

Backflow Preventer. A device which prevents sewage from the building's sewer from flowing backward into the plumbing fixture(s).

Ballast. A device used with a fluorescent and high intensity lamp, to provide the necessary circuit condition for starting and operation.

Baluster. Vertical members that extend from a stair, or floor, to a handrail. A small pillar or column used to support a rail.

Batch Plant. An operating installation of equipment including batchers and mixers as required for batching or for batching and mixing concrete materials; also called mixing plant when equipment is included.

Batter Board. A temporary framework used to assist in locating the corners when laying a foundation. Also used to maintain proper elevations of excavations and trenches in any kind of below ground construction.

Batter Pile. Pile driven at an angle to brace a structure against lateral thrust.

Bay. A rectangular area of a building defined by four adjacent columns; a portion of a building that projects from a facade.

Beam. A straight structural member that acts primarily to resist transverse loads. A structural element which sustains transverse loading and develops internal forces of bending and shear in resisting the loads. An inclusive term for joists, girders, rafters, and purlins.

Beam Chair. A wire seat or support for reinforcing bars designed to maintain their location while concrete for a beam is poured around them.

Beam Hanger. A strap wire or other device used to hang beam forms from another structural member.

Bearing Pad. A block of plastic or synthetic rubber used to cushion the point at which one element rests upon another.

Bearing Wall. A wall which supports any vertical loads in addition to its own weight.

Bellows. An instrument or machine that draws in air through a valve or orifice by expansion and contraction and expels it through a tube.

Bending. The result of a force which tends to cause curvature in a linear element. Internal stresses of tension and compression are a result of this action.

Bending Moment. The sum of moments for all forces that occur above the neutral axis. The moment that causes a beam or other structural member to bend.

Bending Stress. A compressive or tensile stress resulting from the application of a nonaxial force to a structural member.

Bid Bond. A bond, secured by the bidder, which guarantees that the bidder selected by the owner will accept the project, or the owner will have the project for the bid price as noted in the accepted bid.

Bitumen. A tar based mixture, such as asphalt or coal tar.

Bituminous. Resembling, containing, or impregnated with various mixtures of hydrocarbons (like tar) together with their nonmetallic derivatives.

Bloom. A visible exudation or efflorescence on the surface.

Board Foot. A unit of lumber volume, a rectangular solid nominally 12" x 12" x 1". The equivalent of a board 1 foot square and 1 inch thick.

BOCA. Building Officials and Code Administrators International, an organization that publishes a model building code.

Bollard. Short steel post (usually filled with concrete) set to prevent vehicular access or to protect property from damage by vehicular encroachment. Steel or cast iron post to which ships are tied.

Bond. The adherence of one material to another. Effective bonds must be achieved between the mortar and scratch coat, between the tile and mortar, and between the adhesive and backing.

Bond Beam. A horizontal grouted element within masonry in which reinforcement is embedded.

Bond Breaker. A material used to prevent adhesion of newly placed concrete and the substrate.

Bonding Agent. A substance applied to a suitable substrate to create a bond between it and a succeeding layer as between a subsurface and a terrazzo topping or a succeeding plaster application.

Borrow. Excavated material that has been taken from one area to be used as fill at another location.

Box Beam. A bending member of metal or plywood which, in cross section, resembles a closed rectangular box.

Box Culvert. A concrete drainage structure rectangular-shaped, reinforced and cast either in place or precast in sections.

Broom Finish. A finish applied to an uncured concrete surface, to provide skid or slip resistance, made by dragging a broom across the freshly placed concrete surface.

Brown Coat. The second of three coats of a plaster or stucco application.

Building Envelope. Elements of the building, including all external building materials, windows, and walls, that enclose the internal space.

Building Official. The official charged with administration and enforcement of the applicable building code, or his duly authorized representative.

Building Paper. Water repellent paper used to assist in shedding incidental moisture what may penetrate exterior finishes of exterior wall construction. Thick paper, used to insulate a building before the siding or cladding is installed. Occasionally used in flooring between double floors.

Built-Up Roof. A roof covering made of continuous rolls or sheets of saturated or coated felt. They are then cemented together with asphalt and may have a final coating of gravel or slag.

Bull Float. A tool comprising a large, flat, rectangular piece of wood, aluminum, or magnesium usually 8 in. (20 cm) wide and 42 to 60 in. (100 to 150 cm) long, and a handle 4 to 16 ft. (1 to 5 m) in length used to smooth unformed surfaces of freshly placed concrete.

Bullnose. A trim tile with a convex radius on one edge. This tile is used for finishing the top of a wainscot or for turning an outside corner.

Bullnose Corner. A type of bullnose trim with a convex radius on two adjacent edges.

Bullnose Glazed. A trim tile with a convex radius on one edge that has been given a glassy or glossy surface.

Bumper, Dock. Thick rubber units placed under loading dock openings to absorb the shock and prevent damage when trucks back in for loading or unloading.

Buoyant Uplift. The force of water or liquefied soil that tends to raise a building foundation out of the ground.

Bus Bar. A large, flat conductor, usually solid copper, used for carrying very high electrical currents. An uninsulated bar or tube used as an electrical conductor at a circuit junction.

Bus Duct. A prefabricated unit containing one or more electric conductors, often a metal bar, that serves as a common connection for two or more circuits.

Bus Ground. In the main electrical service panel, where the neutral service wire (generally white) attaches and is linked to the earth by the ground wire.

Bush Hammer. A hammer that has a rectangular head with serrated or jagged faces. The bush hammer is used for roughing concrete.

Bushing. A removable cylindrical lining for an opening used to limit the size of an opening, resist abrasion, or serve as a guide. An electrically insulating lining for a hole to protect a through conductor.

Butt Hinge. A hinge consisting of two plates with a removable connecting pin.

Butt Joint. A plain square joint between two members.

Buttering Trowel. The blade of the buttering trowel is approximately 4-1/2" wide and 7" long. It is used in buttering rich mortar to masonry, a method commonly used in the eastern states.

Butyl Caulking. Synthetic rubber caulking dispensed in a tube made by polymerizing isobutylene.

BX Cable. Type of indoor wiring consisting of two or more insulated wires protected by a wound, galvanized steel strip cover. The metal winding forms a flexible tube.

Cable Bus. An assembly of insulated cables.

Cable Tray. Open track support forces heavily insulated cables.

Caisson. A cylindrical, sitecast concrete foundation that penetrates through unsatisfactory soil to rest upon an underlying stratum of rock or satisfactory soil.

Camber. A deflection that is intentionally built into a structural element or form to improve appearance or to nullify the deflection of the element under the effects of loads, shrinkage and creep. A radius built into a given member to compensate for deflection. A light initial curvature in a beam or slab.

Cant Strip. A strip of material, usually treated wood or fiber, with a sloping face used to ease the transition from a horizontal to a vertical surface at the edge of a flat roof.

Cantilever. A beam, truss, or slab that extends beyond its last point of support. A beam which is supported only at one end.

Cantilever Wall. A retaining wall in which the wall and footing resists earth pressure by cantilever effect.

Cantilevered Beam. A beam that is supported at one end only.

Cap, Pile. A structural member usually fastened to, and placed on the top of a slender timber, concrete or structural element. Used to transmit loads into the pile or group of piles and to connect them.

Capacitor. A device which introduces capacitance into an electric circuit.

Casement. A window in which the sash opens upon hinges.

Casement Window. A window that pivots on an axis, along the vertical line of the frame.

Casework. Assembled cabinetry or millwork.

Casing. The wood finish pieces surrounding the frame of a window or door, or the finished lumber around a post or beam. A cylindrical steel tube used to line a drilled or driven hole in foundation work.

Cast Iron Pipe. Pipe that is manufactured with an alloy of iron, carbon and silicon that is cast in a mold and is more easily fusible than steel.

Cast-In-Place. Mortar or concrete which is deposited in the place where it is required to harden as part of the structure, as opposed to precast concrete.

Castellated Beam. A steel, wide-flange section whose web has been cut along a zigzag path and reassembled by welding in such a way as to create a deeper section.

Casting Bed. A form in which precast concrete units are constructed.

Catch Basin. Formed pan, usually constructed of sheet metal to collect moisture and dirt which comes through grating. Basin usually includes drain connected to plumbing system.

Ceiling And Wall. A type of building framing construction.

Ceiling Joist. The vertical members in a building or structure upon which the roof rafters are attached.

Cell. A void space having a gross cross-sectional area greater than 1-1/2 square inches (967 mm2).

Cement Plaster. Plaster used on exterior surfaces or in damp areas. Plaster having Portland Cement as a binder.

Cement, Portland. A hydraulic cement produced by pulverizing clinker consisting essentially of hydraulic calcium silicates, and usually containing one or more of the forms of calcium sulfate as an interground addition.

Cementitious. Having cementing properties; usually used with reference to inorganic substances, such as portland cement and lime.

Center Pole, Steel. Column in enter of spiral stair which supports stair treads.

Centigrade. A scale of temperature which features 0 degree and 100 degree as the freezing and boiling point of water respectively. To convert centigrade to Fahrenheit multiply by 1.8 and add 32 e.g. (100 degree x 1.8)–32=212 degree F.

Certificate For Payment. A written document forwarded to the general contractor by the architect, engineer, or owner approving payment for work completed.

Certificate for Substantial Completion. A written document forwarded to the general contractor by the architect, engineer, or owner indicating that the project is substantially complete. This document initiates the time period for the final payment to the contractor.

Certificate of Insurance. A certificate provided by the general contractor verifying that he has obtained the required insurance for the project.

CFM. Cubic feet per minute.

Chair. A device used to support reinforcing bars.

Chamfer. A beveled surface cut on the edge of a piece of wood. A strip of wood or other substance cut on an angle and placed in concrete formwork to create a beveled finished surface on the corners of the final concrete shape (beam, column, etc.).

Chamfer Strip. An insert that is triangular or curved, placed in an inside corner to produce a rounded or flat beveled edge at the right angle corner of a construction member.

Channel. A steel or aluminum section shaped like a rectangular box with one side removed.

Check Valve. A device which allows fluid or air to pass through in only one direction. A valve which prevents the back-flow of water or other liquid by automatically closing.

Checking. Short shallow cracks on the surface.

Chicken Wire. Thin, woven wire mounted on an exterior wall as a base for stucco plaster to cling to.

Chiller. A piece of equipment that contains a compressor, condenser and evaporator tank. It produces chilled water for circulation through a building.

Chord. One of the main members of a truss, usually horizontal, and braced by web members of the truss. Perimeter member of a building or structure which resists lateral forces.

Circuit Breaker. An overcurrent protection device.

Class A, B, C, Roofing. Roof covering materials classified according to their resistance to fire when tested in accordance with ASTM E108. Class A is the highest, and Class C is the lowest.

Clay Pipe. Pipe used for drainage systems and sanitary sewers made of earthenware and glazed to eliminate porosity.

Clay Tile Floor. (Earthenware) Quarry tile that is fired and used for flooring.

Cleanout. An opening to the bottom of a grout space of sufficient size and spacing to allow the removal of debris.

Clevis Hanger. A U-shaped metal hanger with the ends drilled to receive a pin or bolt used for attaching or suspending parts.

Closer. The last masonry unit laid in a course; a partial masonry unit used at the corner of a course to adjust the joint spacing.

Closure Strip. A resilient strip, used to close openings created by joining metal panels and flashing.

CMU. Concrete Masonry Unit

Coated Roof. A roof usually flat, that has an asphaltic material applied to it to seal against the elements.

Cofferdam. A watertight enclosure from which water is pumped to expose the bottom of a body of water and permit construction.

Cold Joint. Any point in a tile installation when tile and setting bed have terminated and the surface has lost its plasticity before work is continued. The joint formed between hardened concrete and freshly poured concrete.

Collar. A compression ring around a small circular opening.

Collar Joint. The vertical mortar joint between wythes of masonry.

Collar Tie. A piece of wood nailed across two opposing rafters near the ridge to resist wind uplift.

Collector. A force transfer element that collects loads from a diaphragm (horizontal element) and transfers them to the shear walls (vertical element).

Column. A member used primarily to support axial compression loads and with a height of at least three times its least lateral dimension. An upright structural member acting primarily in compression. A member which is subjected primarily to axial forces. A square, rectangular, or cylindrical support for roofs, ceilings, and so forth, composed of base, shaft, and capital.

Column Pier. A foundation member of plain or reinforced concrete to support a column.

Column Tie. A single loop of steel bar, usually bent into a rectangular configuration, used to tie a concrete column.

Compaction. The process whereby the volume of freshly placed mortar or concrete is reduced to the minimum practical space usually by vibration, centrifugation, tamping, or some combination of these; to mold it within forms or molds and around embedded parts and reinforcement, and to eliminate voids other than entrained air.

Composite Beam. A beam that is composed of two different materials; for example, a wood and a steel beam, or a steel beam and concrete slab, in which the two act as one.

Composite Concrete Flexure Members. The concrete flexural members of pre-cast and cast-in-place concrete elements constructed in separate units but so interconnected that all units respond to a load(s) as a unit.

Compression. Force which tends to crush adjacent particles of a material together and cause overall shortening in the direction of its action. Stress which tends to shorten a member.

Concrete. A composite material which consists essentially of a binding medium within which are embedded particles or fragments of aggregate; in portland cement concrete, the binder is a mixture of portland cement and water. A mixture of cement, water, fine aggregate (and), and coarse aggregate (gravel).

Concrete Admixture. A substance added to concrete to aid in imparting color, control workability, help in waterproofing, control setting and to entrain air.

Concrete Filled Pile. A long slender construction element filled with concrete, driven in the ground for the purpose of supporting a load.

Concrete Masonry Unit (CMU). A block of hardened concrete, with or without hollow cores, designed to be laid in the same manner as a brick; a concrete block.

Concrete, Precast. Cast and cured concrete in other than its final form. Examples are, precast concrete slabs, precast reinforced lintels, beams, columns, piles, parts of walls and floors, etc.

Concrete, Prestressed. Concrete in which internal stresses of such magnitude and distribution are introduced so that the tensile stresses resulting from the service loads are counteracted to a desired degree.

Concrete Topping. To provide durability, safety and beauty, a commercial mixture used to top concrete floor surfaces.

Concrete Waterproofing. An act or process of adding a material to concrete to make it impervious to water or dampness.

Concrete, Lightweight. Concrete that has substantially lower weight than that made from gravel or crushed stone.

Concrete, Structural Lightweight. Concrete containing lightweight aggregate, not exceeding 115 P.C.F.

Condensation. Usually refers to liquid drops which form when a vapor is chilled below its boiling point. Also refers to water droplets that deposit on surfaces whose temperature is below the dewpoint. The process of changing from a gaseous to a liquid state, especially as applied to water.

Condenser. A heat exchanger in a refrigeration cycle used to discharge heat to the outside. Three commonly used types of condensers can be classified as water cooled, air cooled, and evaporative. Condenser water is normally circulated through a cooling tower through which heat is distributed to the atmosphere. A heat exchanger in a refrigeration cycle used to discharge heat to the outside.

Conduit. A protective sleeve usually used for individual electrical cables.

Conduit, Flexible. Metallic conduit that is flexible and is put up in coils instead of lengths. May be used in lieu of the rigid type in most dry locations.

Conduit, Galvanized. Rigid or non-flexible conduit plated with zinc by a galvanized process.

Construction Change Directive. A document that directs a change in the work of the project, prepared by the architect and signed by the owner and architect. This change can adjust the contract sum and/or contract time.

This document shall be used in the absence of total agreement on the terms of a change order.

Continuous Footing. A concrete footing that supports a wall or two or more columns. The footing can vary in width and depth.

Contraction Joint. Formed, sawed, or tooled groove in a concrete structure to create a weakened plane and regulate the location or cracking resulting from the dimensional change of different parts of the structure.

Control Joint. An intentional linear discontinuity in a structure or component, designed to form a plane of weakness where cracking can occur in response to various forces so as to minimize or eliminate cracking elsewhere in the structure.

Convection. Heat transferred by fluid motion.

Convector. A heat exchange device that uses the heat in steam, hot water, or an electric resistance element to warm the air in a room; often called, inaccurately, a radiator.

Corbel. A projection from the face of a beam, girder, column, or wall used as a beam seat or a decoration. A spanning device in which masonry units in successive courses are cantilevered slightly over one another; a project bracket of masonry or concrete. A masonry unit such as brick or stone which projects beyond the unit below.

Core Drilling. The process of drilling which extracts a cylindrical sample of concrete, rock or soil.

Corner Bead. A metal or plastic strip used to form a neat, durable edge at an outside corner of two walls of plaster or gypsum board.

Cornice. The exterior detail at the meeting of a wall and a roof overhang; a decorative molding at the intersection of a wall and a ceiling.

Corrosion. The eating and wearing away by chemical action (pitting, rusting).

Corrugated Panel. Metal or fiberglass sheeting formed into alternating ridges and valleys in parallel and applied as siding on a building or structure.

Counterflashing. An inverted L-shaped metal strip built into a wall to overlap flashing and make a roof watertight. A flashing turned down from above to overlap another flashing turned up from below so as to shed water. Strips of metal used to prevent water from entering the top edge of the vertical side of a roof flashing; they also allow expansion and contraction without danger of breaking the flashing.

Course. A horizontal layer of masonry units, one unit high; a horizontal line of shingles.

Cove. A trim tile unit having one edge with a concave radius. A cove is used to form a junction between the bottom wall course and the floor or to form an inside corner.

Coverage. A measure of the amount of material required to cover a given surface.

CPVC. Chlorinated Polyvinyl Chloride

Crack Length Method. A method of calculating the quantity of infiltration air into a building. This method requires specific information about dimensions and construction details of windows, doors, and other openings.

Crawling. A parting and contraction of the glaze on the surface of ceramic ware during drying or firing, resulting in unglazed areas bordered by coalesced glaze.

Crazing. The cracking which occurs in fired glazes or other ceramic coatings due to critical tensile stress.

Creep. Time-dependent deformation due to sustained load.

Creep. A permanent, inelastic, deformation in a material due to changes in the material caused by the prolonged application of structural stress. Plastic deformation that proceeds with time when certain materials, such as concrete, are subjected to constant, long-duration stress.

Creep (Seismic). Very slow periodic or episodic movement along a fault trace unaccompanied by earthquakes.

Cripple Stud. A wood wall-framing member that is shorter than full-length studs because it is interrupted by a header or sill.

Crown Molding. A type of molding used to make ceiling to wall transitions.

CRSI. Concrete Reinforcing Steel Institute, 933 N. Plum Grove Road, Schaumburg, IL 60173-4758, (708) 517-1200.

Culvert. A drain pipe or masonry crossing made of galvanized corrugated metal, aluminum, steel, or concrete constructed under a road or embankment to provide a waterway.

Curing. Maintenance of humidity and temperature of freshly placed concrete during some definite period following placing, casting, or finishing to assure satisfactory hydration of the cementitious materials and proper hardening of the concrete. The hardening of concrete or plaster.

Curing Blanket. A built-up covering of sacks, matting, hessian, straw, waterproof paper, or other suitable material placed over freshly finished concrete.

Curing Compound. A liquid that can be applied as a coating to the surface of newly placed concrete to retard the loss of water or, in the case of pigmented compounds, also to reflect heat so as to provide an opportunity for the concrete to develop its properties in a favorable temperature and moisture environment.

Curling. The distortion of an originally essentially linear or planar member into a curved shape such as the warping of a slab due to creep or to differences in temperature or moisture content in the zones adjacent to its opposite faces.

Curtain Wall. An exterior building wall that is supported, entirely by the frame of the building, rather than being self-supporting or loadbearing.

Cut and Fill. Excavated material removed from one location and used as fill material in another location.

Cylinder Test. A test to determine the compressive strength of concrete.

D-Cracking. The progressive formation on a concrete surface of a series of fine cracks at rather close intervals, often of random patterns, but in slabs on grade paralleling edges, joints, and cracks and usually curving across slab corners. (Also termed D-cracks and D-line cracks.)

D-Load. A constant load that in structures is due to the mass of the members, the supported structure, and permanent attachments or accessories.

Damper. A flap to control or obstruct the flow of gasses; specifically, a metal control flap in the throat of a fireplace, or in an air duct.

Damping. Dissipation of structure-borne noise by conversion to some other form of energy, usually heat. This usually is accomplished by using a material with a high internal energy-absorbing capacity.

Dampproofing. The treatment of concrete or mortar to help prevent the passage or absorption of water. Applied with a suitable coating to exposed surfaces or applied with a suitable admixture of treated cement.

Darby. A hand-manipulated straightedge, usually 3 to 8 ft. (1 to 2.5 m) long, used in the early stage leveling operations of concrete or plaster, preceding supplemental floating and finishing.

Daylighting. Illuminating the interior of a building by natural means.

DB. Decibel

Deadman. A large and/or heavy object buried in the ground as an anchor.

Deck. The form on which concrete for a slab is placed, also the floor or roof slab itself.

Deed Restrictions. Restrictive covenants often are included a deed which may limit future use(s) of the land, and other restrictions such as height, size, aesthetics, etc., as long as they are not against the public interest.

Deeds. A general term which refers to all documents conveying property, from one person to another.

Deflection. A variation in position or shape of a structure or structural element due to effects of loads or volume change, usually measured as a linear deviation from an established plane rather than an angular variation.

Deformation. A change in the shape of a structure or structural element caused by a load, or force, acting on the structure.

Degree Day Method. A method of computing fuel requirements for HVAC systems.

Degree of Saturation. The amount of water present in the air relative to the maximum amount it can hold at a given temperature without causing condensation.

Delamination. Separation of one layer from another.

Determinate. Having defined limits; definite. In structures, the condition of having exact sufficiency of stability, both externally and internally, therefore being determinable by the resolution of force alone. Short for statically determinate, meaning a structural system in which all the forces can be determined by the equations of statics alone.

Dewatering. To remove water from excavations with pumps, wellpoints or drainage systems.

Diaphragm. A thin, usually rectangular or square element of a structure that is capable of resisting lateral forces in its plane, such as a floor or roof.

Diaphragm Action. A bracing action that derives from the stiffness o a thin plane of material when it is loaded in a direction parallel to the plane. Diaphragms in buildings are typically floor, or roof surfaces of plywood, reinforced masonry, steel decking, or reinforced concrete.

Diffuser. A device for reducing the velocity and increasing the static pressure of a fluid passing through a system.

Direct Burial Conduit. Electric conduit suitable for burial in exterior applications with an outer surface that resists moisture, fungus, and corrosion.

Direct Current (DC). An electrical current that has a constant flow rate induced by a constant voltage.

Direct Drive Fan. A fan that is positively connected in line to a motor to operate at the same speed.

Displacement. Movement away from a fixed reference point.

Dock Leveler. A mechanical device that adjusts to accommodate the different heights of truck beds.

Dome. An arch rotated about a vertical axis passing through its crown, or highest point.

Door Solid Core. A door which has a core constructed with solid materials.

Dope Coat. Neat cement applied to the setting bed.

Double Bullnose. A type of trim with the same convex radius on two opposite sides.

Double Hung Window. The most common operable style of window. It has two sashes that slide vertically in parallel tracks.

Double Tee. A precast concrete slab element that resembles the letters "TT" in cross section.

Dovetail Joint. A joint which has a flaring tenon and a mortise into which it fits tightly and interlocks two pieces.

Dowel. A steel bar, which extends into two adjoining portions of a concrete construction, as at a joint in a pavement slab, so as to connect the portions and transfer shear loads. Also, as used in the construction of column and wall sections, a deformed steel reinforcing bar placed so as to transmit tension or compression as well as shear loads.

Dozer. A slang term used for a bulldozer.

Drag Strut. A structural member used to transfer lateral forces from one vertical element to another.

Dragline. A bucket attachment for a crane in a marsh or marine area, that digs soft, wet materials that must be excavated at some distance from the crane, and draws the bucket towards itself using a cable.

Drain Tile. Short-length sections of burned clay, concrete, etc., laid with open joints and surrounded with aggregate and covered with asphaltic paper or straw to drain the water from an area.

Drift. Lateral deflection of a building caused by wind or earthquake loads. The horizontal displacement or movement of structure when subjected to lateral forces. A discontinuity formed into the underside of a window sill or wall component to force adhering drops of water to fall free of the face of the building rather than move farther toward the interior. The projection of a window sill or water table to allow the water to drain clear of the side of the house below it.

Dry Pack. Concrete or mortar mixtures deposited and consolidated by dry packing. A low-slump grout tamped into the space in a connection between pre-cast concrete members, or between a steel column and the column base-plate.

Dry Set Tile. Tile set into an adhesive that seems dry but that adheres on contact.

Dry Well. A well, usually filled with gravel, to receive rain run-off water, in an area where the ground is not very permeable, for example, in areas of clay soil.

Drywall. An interior facing panel consisting of a gypsum core sandwiched between paper faces, also called gypsum board or plasterboard.

Duct Bus. A prefabricated unit containing one or more electric conductors, often a metal bar, that serves as a common connection for two or more circuits.

Ductile. The ability of a material to deform under tensile load.

Ductile Moment Resisting Space Frame. A three dimensional structural system without bearing walls and composed of interconnecting members that resists lateral forces with or without the aid of horizontal diaphragms.

Ductility. The quality of being able to deform considerably under load before fracturing. Contrasted to the quality of brittleness.

Dummy Joint. A joint placed strictly for design, in sidewalks and patios.

Dunting. The cracking that occurs in fired ceramic bodies due to thermally induced stresses.

DWV Pipe, ABS. A rigid plastic pipe manufactured from acrylonitrile butadiene styrene used as a drain, waste, or vent in a plumbing system.

Dynamic. Having to do with bodies in motion. Implying motion or change of state; opposite of Static (i.e.: an earthquake force is a dynamic force).

Dynamic Force. F=ma, or force equals mass times acceleration, a moving force.

Eagle Beak. A 6" x 3/4" outside corner trim shape tile.

Edge Bead. A strip of metal or plastic used to make a neat, durable edge where plaster or gypsum board abuts another material.

Edger. A finishing tool used on the edges of fresh concrete to provide a rounded corner.

Effective Stiffness. The value of the lateral force in the isolation system, or an element thereof, divided by the corresponding lateral displacement.

Efflorescence. A powdery deposit on the face of a structure of masonry or concrete, caused by the leaching of chemical salts by water migrating from within the structure to the surface.

Elastic. Able to return to its original size and shape after removed of stress.

Elasticity. Property of a material to deform under load and return to its original dimensions when load is removed.

Elastomeric Flashing. A rubber-like material used as flashing on a roof system.

Electrolysis. Production of chemical changes by the passage of current through an electrolyte.

Elevated Slab. A roof slab or floor supported by structural members.

EMT. Electrical Metallic Conduit - Thin Wall Conduit.

End Bell. Cast iron pipe with a wide opening at one end.

End Nail. A nail driven through one piece of lumber and into the end of another.

Energy Dissipation. Reduction in intensity of earthquake shock waves with time and distance.

Engineer. A person who uses the science by which the properties of matter and the sources of energy in nature are made useful to man.

English Bond. Brickwork laid with alternating courses, each consisting entirely of headers or stretchers.

Entrained Air. Microscopic air bubbles intentionally incorporated into mortar or concrete during mixing, usually by use of a surface-active agent, typically between 10 and 1,000 um in diameter and spherical or nearly so.

Epicenter. The point on the earth's surface vertically above the focus or hypocenter of an earthquake. The part of the earth's surface directly above the origin of an earthquake.

Epoxy Flooring. A resin spread on flooring to make a hard, tough surface.

Epoxy Grout. A two-part grout system consisting of epoxy resin and epoxy hardener, especially formulated to have impervious qualities, stain, and chemical resistance, used to fill joints between tile units.

Epoxy Mortar. A two-part mortar system consisting of epoxy resin and epoxy hardener used to bond tile to back-up material where chemical resistance of high bond strength is a consideration.

Equalizer. One that equalizes by distributing evenly or uniformly (as of force).

Equilibrium. A state of rest doe to balanced forces. State of being in balance; implies no tendency to change.

Equipment Pad. A thick slab-type stone or precast concrete block placed under mechanical devices to spread the weight and load of the machinery evenly and to prevent excessive vibration.

Equivalent Static Force Analysis. A method by which a dynamic force is translated into an equivalent static force that produces a similar effect.

Ergonomics. Applied science that investigates the impact of people's physical environment on their health and comfort (e.g., determining the proper chair height for computer operators).

Evaporative Condenser. Hot gas discharged from the compressor is piped to the condenser coil within the casing of the outdoor evaporation condenser. Water is sprayed directly onto the coil where it encounters an air stream causing some of the water to evaporate.

Exhaust Fan. An electrical powered device to withdraw fumes, dusts, or odors from an enclosure.

Exit Light. A light assembly over an exit door that is independently powered to remain lit in the event of a catastrophe, to guide persons to safety.

Expansion Joint. A joint through tile, mortar, and reinforcing wire down to the substrate. A discontinuity intended to allow for gross movement due to thermal stress, or material shrinkage.

Exposed Aggregate Finish. A concrete surface in which the coarse aggregate is revealed.

Extrusion. The process of squeezing a material through a shaped orifice to produce a linear element with the desired cross section; an element produced by this process.

Facade. An exterior face of a building.

Face Brick. A brick selected on the basis of appearance and durability for use in the exposed surface of a wall.

Factored Load. The load imposed on a member multiplied by appropriate factors, used to design reinforced concrete members by the strength design method.

Fan Coil Unit (FCU). A packaged unit consisting of a heating/cooling coil, fan, and filter, without ductwork, used to serve a space or a group of small spaced.

Fascia. A flat member or band at the surface of a building or the edge beam of a bridge; exposed eaves of a building; often inappropriately called facia.

Fatigue. A structural failure which occurs as the result of a load being applied and removed, or reversed, repeatedly over a long period of time, or a large number of cycles.

Fault. A break in the continuity of a rock formation which is caused by the shifting of the earth's crust.

Feather Edge. A wood or metal tool having a beveled edge; used to straighten re-entrant angles in finish plaster coat; also edge of a concrete or mortar placement such as a patch or topping that is beveled at an acute angle.

Feeder Duct. An enclosure for a group of electrical conductors that runs power from a central, large source to one or more secondary distribution centers.

Fiberboard. A homogeneous panel made from wood or cane fibers.

Fiberglass. The name for products made of or with glass fibers ranging from 5 to 600 hundred-thousandths inch in diameter. Used for making textile fabrics, and for heat or sound insulation.

Field Tile. An area of tile covering a wall or floor. The field is bordered by tile trim.

Fillet Weld. A weld at the inside intersection of two metal surfaces that meet at right angles.

Finger Joint. A glued end connection between two pieces of wood, using an interlocking pattern of deeply cut "fingers". A finger joint creates a large surface for the glue bond, to allow it to develop the full tensile strength of the wood it connects.

Finish. The final work on a construction job.

Fire Damper. A damper that automatically closes a duct upon detection of fire.

Fire Detection Annunciator. A mechanical device which audibly announces a warning in case of a fire.

Fire Door. A door which has been manufactured with specific materials to help hold back the spread of fire.

Fire Resistance Rating. The time, in hours, or fractions of an hour, that a material or assembly will resist fire exposure as determined by ASTM E119.

Fire Wall. A wall, required under the building code, which divides two parts of a building, to serve as a deterrent to the spread of fire.

Firestop. A wood baffle used to close an opening between studs or joists in a balloon or platform frame in order to retard the spread of fire through the opening.

Flame Spread Rating. A measure of the rapidity with which fire will spread across the surface of a material as determined by ASTM E84.

Flashing. A thin, continuous sheet of metal, plastic, rubber or waterproof paper used to prevent the passage of water through a joint in a wall, roof or chimney. The material used and the process of making watertight the roof intersections and other exposed places on the outside of the house.

Flemish Bond. Brickwork laid with each course consisting of alternating headers and stretchers.

Flexible Conduit. Metallic conduit that is flexible and is put up in coils instead of lengths. May be used in lieu of the rigid type in most dry locations.

Flexural Strength. A property of a material or structural member that indicates its ability to resist failure in bedding.

Float. A tool or apparatus for smoothing a surface.

Float Finish. A finish coat that is rough from aggregate material found in the plaster mortar.

Float Strip. A strip of wood about 1/4" thick and 1-1/4" wide. It is used as a guide to align mortar surfaces.

Floating. A method of using a straightedge to align mortar with the float strips or screeds. This technique also is called dragging, pulling, rodding, or rodding off.

Floor, Access. A raised floor platform with removable panels to provide access to an area below.

Floor Joist. A common support beam.

Flue. A passage for smoke and combustion products from a furnace, stove, water heater or fireplace.

Fluted Column. Columns with decorative, semi-circular channeled shafts.

Footing. The widened part of a foundation that spreads a load from the building across a broader area of soil. An enlargement at the lower end of a wall, pier, or column, to distribute the load.

Force. Energy exerted on an element tending to cause motion. Magnitude, direction and point of application are all used to describe a force.

Form Oil. Oil applied to interior surface of formwork to promote easy release from the concrete when forms are removed.

Form Tie. A steel rod with fasteners on each end, used to hold together the formwork for a concrete wall.

Formboard. A formwork board or sheet of wood.

Foundation Backfill. Earth or earthen material displaced during excavation and replaced around the constructed foundation.

Foundation Investigation (soil report). A geological report from a geological engineer providing information on the subsurface soil conditions.

Fracture. A break, usually resulting in actual separation of the material. In structures, the characteristic result of tension failure.

Frame, Ductile Moment Resisting. A frame which is capable of resisting bending moments in the joints, enabling it to resist lateral forces or unsymmetrical vertical loads through bending action of the frame. Stability is achieved through bending action rather than bracing.

Frame, Moment. A structural frame which is capable of transferring bending moments through connections, enabling it to resist lateral forces or unsymmetrical vertical loads through overall bending action of the frame.

Framing. The rough timber structure of a building, including interior and exterior walls, floor, roof, and ceilings.

Friction Connection. Two or more structural steel members clamped together by high-strength bolts with sufficient force that the loads on the members are transmitted between them by friction along their mating surfaces.

Friction Piling. A load-bearing pile that has its supporting capacity from the skin friction between the soil in contact with the pile.

Front-End Loader. A tractor or bulldozer with a bucket which operates only at the front.

Furring. Stripping used to build out a surface such as a studded wall where strips of suitable size are added to the studs to accommodate vent pipes or other fixtures. Narrow strips of board nailed upon the walls and ceilings to form a straight surface upon which to lay the lath or other finish.

Fuse. An overcurrent protection device.

Fusion. The process of melting; usually the result of interaction of two or more materials.

Gabion. An iron cylinder filled with earth used in mining.

Gable. The triangular wall beneath the end of a gable roof.

Gable. The vertical triangular end of a building from the eaves to the apex of the roof.

Gable Roof. A roof consisting of two opposite sloping planes that intersect at a level ridge.

Gable-End Rafter. The last rafter system installed at the gable end of a building.

Galvanized. Zinc plating for corrosion protection by hot dipping into molten zinc or by electrolysis.

Gang Box. Electrical boxes constructed of metal or hard plastic, manufactured with knockout holes to pull wire through to connect outlets and switches.

Gate Valve. A valve utilizing a wedge-shaped gate, which allows fluid flow when the gate is lifted from the seat.

General Conditions. A written document, supplementing the specifications, which indicates and defines specific areas of the project.

Girt. A beam that supports wall cladding between columns.

Girt (ribband). The horizontal member of the walls of a full or combination frame house which supports the floor joists or is flush with the top of the joists.

Glaze. A ceramic coating matured to the glassy state on a formed ceramic article. The term glaze also refers to the material or mixture from which the coating is made.

Glazing. The act or process of furnishing or fitting with glass. A transparent or translucent color applied to modify the effect of a painted surface.

Globe Valve. A valve with a rounded disc that shuts off the flow when closed, and seats to prevent fluid flow.

Glue Built-up Members. Structural elements, the sections of which are composed of built-up lumber, wood structural panels or wood structural panels in combination with lumber, all parts bonded together with adhesives.

Glue Joint. A joint held together with glue.

Glue-Laminated Beam. An engineered, stress-rated, product assembled of especially selected and prepared wood laminations that are securely bonded together with adhesives.

Glulam. An abbreviation of glue laminated timber.

Graben (rift valley). A long, narrow trough bounded by one or more parallel normal faults.

Grade. The horizontal ground level of a building or structure.

Grade Beam. A reinforced concrete beam that transmits the load from a bearing wall into spaced foundations such as pile caps or caissons.

Granular Insulation. Insulating material made of granular vermiculite or perlite or beaded styrene, placed in hollow (usually masonry) construction.

Gravel. Rock particles retained on a No. 4 sieve that result from natural disintegration or are processed from weakly bound conglomerate.

Gravel Stop. A metal flange or strip with a vertical lip placed around a built-up roof to prevent loose gravel from falling off the roof.

Gravity Wall. A retaining wall which depends solely on its weight to resist lateral forces of retained earth.

Ground Acceleration. Acceleration of the ground due to earthquake forces.

Ground Bus. In the main electrical service panel, where the neutral service wire (generally white) attaches and is linked to the earth by the ground wire.

Ground Fault Circuit Interrupter (GFCI). Supplies power, as any receptacle does, but also monitors the amount of incoming and outgoing current. Whenever the entering current does not equal the leaving current, indicating current leakage, the GFCI instantly opens the circuit.

Grout. A rich or strong cementitious or chemically setting mix used for filling tile joints. A mixture of portland cement, aggregates, and water, which can be poured or pumped into cavities in concrete or masonry.

Gunite. A term used to describe a concrete material applied by pumping through a hose.

Gusset Plate. A flat steel plate to which the chords are connected at a joint in a truss; a stiffener plate.

Guy Cable. Cable anchored at one end and supporting or stabilizing an object at other end.

Guy Rod. A metal rod with a cable or rope attached, leading to an object to support and stabilize it.

Gypsum. Hydrous calcium sulfate.

Gypsum Board. An interior facing panel consisting of a gypsum core sandwiched between paper faces. Also called drywall or plasterboard.

Gypsum Lath. Small sheets of gypsum board manufactured specifically for use as a plaster base.

Hairline Cracking. Small cracks of random pattern in an exposed concrete surface.

Handicapped Plumbing. Plumbing devices and layouts specifically designed for use by disabled persons.

Hanger. Vertical-tension member supporting a load.

Hanger Joist. A metal stirrup that supports the ends of joists so that they are flush with the girder.

Hard Screed. A mortar screed that has become firm.

Hardboard. A very dense panel product, usually with at least one smooth face, made of highly compressed wood fibers.

Hardware. A general term for metal or plastic fittings used in or on a building and its parts

Hatch. A hinged or removable cover in a floor or roof, which permits ventilation or the passage of persons or objects.

Head Joint. The vertical layer of mortar between ends of masonry units.

Header. Lintel; a joist that supports other joists; in steel construction, a beam that spans between girders.

Headwall. A wall, usually constructed of concrete or masonry, that is placed at the outlet side of a drain or culvert to protect fill from scouring, undermining or to divert flow.

Heat Pump. A unit that supplies heating or cooling to an interior space by either absorbing heat from or rejecting heat to the outside; a unit utilizing the vapor compression refrigeration cycle in the same way a Dx unit or chiller does.

Hertz (Hz). A measurement of the frequency of vibration of sound measured in cycles per second. One cycle per seconds equal one Hertz (Hz).

Hex Nut. A six-sided, short metal nut with a threaded hole for receiving a rod or threaded bolt.

High Chair Reinforcing. A slang term describing a chair-shaped device used to hold steel reinforcement off of the slab.

High-lift Grouting. A method of construction in which concrete block units may be laid the entire height of the wall before grouting. This method of construction requires special inspection.

Hip. The diagonal intersection of planes in a hip roof.

Hip Roof. A roof consisting of four sloping planes that intersect to form a pyramidal or elongated pyramid shape. A roof which slopes up toward the center from all sides, necessitating a hip rafter at each corner.

Hod. A portable trough for carrying mortar, bricks, etc., fixed crosswise on top of a pole and carried on the shoulder.

Hollow Core Slab. A precast concrete slab element that has internal longitudinal cavities to reduce its self-weight.

Hose Bibb. An outdoor water faucet, usually at sill height, used as a hose connection.

Hot Mud or Hot Stuff. Mortar mixed with an accelerator.

Humidity. The amount of water vapor in a given space.

Hung Slab. A nonstructural concrete slab having no bearing on walls, being totally supported from above by an overhead structural element.

HVAC. Heating, ventilation, and air-conditioning system.

Hydrant. A connection to a water main used for the dispensation of water.

Hydrate. A chemical combination of water with another compound or an element.

Hydronic Heating System. A system that circulates warm water through convectors to heat a building.

Hydrostatic Pressure. Pressure exerted by standing water.

Hyperbolic Paraboloid. Double curved surface which can be generated by sliding a straight line along two other lines which are skew to each other but lie in parallel planes.

Hyperbolic paraboloid shell. A concrete roof structure with a saddle shape.

Hypocenter. The point below the epicenter at which an earthquake actually begins; the focus.

I. Represents the moment of inertia of a member.

I-Beam. An obsolete term; an American Standard designation for a section of hot-rolled steel.

ICBO. International Conference of Building Officials, 5360 South Workman Mill Road, Whittier, California 90601, (310) 699-0451.

Ice Dam. An obstruction along the eaves of a roof caused by the refreezing of water emanating from melting snow on the roof surface above.

Indirect Luminaire. A lighting fixture that distributes most of its light upward.

Inelastic Behavior. Behavior of an element beyond its elastic limit.

Instruction To Bidders. More informative information given to identified bidders than included in the invitation to bid.

Insulation. Any material used to reduce the effects of heat, cold or sound and to reduce fire hazard. Any material used in the prevention of the transfer of electricity, heat, cold, moisture and sound.

Interceptors. A device that collects foreign matter and prevents it from reaching the public sewer system.

Invert Manhole. The lowest inside surface of a manhole.

Inverted Roof. A membrane roof assembly in which the thermal insulation lies above the membrane.

Isolation Joint. A separation between adjoining parts of a concrete structure, usually a vertical plane, at a designed location such as to interfere least with performance of the structure, yet such as to allow relative movement and avoid formation of cracks elsewhere in the concrete and through which all or part of the bonded reinforcement is interrupted.

Jack Rafter. A short rafter framing between the wall plate; a hip rafter.

Jalousie Window. A window with stationary or adjustable blinds angled to permit air and provide shade, while at the same time preventing rain from entering.

Jamb. The vertical side of a door or window. The side piece or post of an opening; sometimes applied to the door frame.

Jitterbug. A grate tamper for pushing coarse aggregate slightly below the surface of a slab to facilitate finishing.

Job Built Form. A temporary structure or mold constructed on a jobsite, for the support of concrete while it is setting and gaining sufficient strength to be self-supporting.

Joint. The point of connection between structural members.

Joint Clip. A fastener used vertically, sharp edge down, over the joining edges of two pieces, and then hammered down into them.

Joint Expansion. A discontinuity intended to allow for gross movement to thermal stress, or material shrinkage.

Joist Hanger. A metal stirrup that supports the ends of joists so that they are flush with the girder.

Joist Sister. The reinforcement of a joist by nailing or attaching a stronger piece to a weaker one.

Joists. Timbers supporting the floorboards.

Joule. In the international system of units, the amount of energy needed to raise 1 kilogram of water 1 degree Celsius.

Journeyman. An experienced reliable worker who has learned his trade and works for another person.

Junction Box. A metal box in which runs of cable are protectively enclosed.

K Bracing. That form of bracing where a pair of braces located on one side of a column terminates at a single point within the clear column height.

Keene's Cement. A cement composed of finely ground, anhydrous, calcined gypsum, the set of which is accelerated by the addition of other materials.

Kelly Ball Test. A method by which the workability of fresh concrete can be determined.

Key. A slot formed into a concrete surface for the purpose of interlocking with a subsequent pour of concrete; a slot at the edge of a precast member into which grout will be poured to lock it to an adjacent member.

Kick Plate. A metal plate or strip that runs along the bottom edge of a door to protect against the marring of the finish.

Kiln Dried. Lumber that has been heated in a kiln to control amounts of moisture.

King Post Truss. In a roof system, the member placed vertically between the center of the horizontal tie beam at the lower end of the rafters and the ridge, or apex of the inclined rafters.

Kip. A unit of weight or force equal to 1,000 lbs.

Knee Brace. A corner brace, fastened at an angle from wall stud to rafter, stiffening a wood or steel frame to prevent angular movement.

Knee Wall. A short wall under the slope of a roof.

Labor and Material Bond. A bond, secured by the general contractor, which guarantees that the labor and materials for the project will be paid for.

Lag Rod. A large diameter rod with a square or hexagonal head.

Lag Screw. A large diameter wood screw with a square or hexagonal head.

Laitance. A layer of weak and nondurable material containing cement and fines from aggregates, brought by bleeding water to the top of overwet concrete, the amount of which is generally increased by overworking or over manipulating concrete at the surface by improper finishing or by job traffic.

Lateral. From the side - horizontal; wind and earthquake are considered lateral forces.

Lateral Load. The horizontal component of the force produced by an arch, dome, vault, or rigid frame. A horizontal load applied to a structure or member such as wind or earthquake.

Lateral Thrust. The horizontal component of the force produced by an arch, dome, vault, or rigid frame.

Lateral-Force-Resisting System. That portion of the structure composed of members proportioned to resist forces related to earthquake effects.

Lath. A wood strip or metal mesh, which acts as a background or reinforcing agent for the scratch coat or mortar coat.

Lattice. Crossed wood, iron plate, or bars.

Layout Stick. A long strip of wood marked at the appropriate joint intervals for the tile to be used. It is used to check the length, width, or height of the tilework. A common name for this item is idiot stick.

Leaching Pit. A pit that can hold solids put allows liquids to pass through.

Ledgerboard. The support for the second-floor joists of a balloon-frame house, or for similar uses; ribband.

Leveling Plate. A steel plate placed in grout on top of a concrete foundation to crease a level bearing surface for the lower end of a steel column.

LH Joist. Left hand, long-span, high strength bar joist.

Lift-Slab Construction. A method of building multistory sitecast concrete buildings by casting all the slabs in a stack on the ground, then lifting them up the columns with jacks and welding them in place.

Lightning Arrester. A device that protects electrical units from lightning and power surges.

Lintel. The horizontal beam placed over an opening.

Liquefaction. Transformation of a granular material (soil) from a solid state into a liquefied state as a consequence of vibrations induced by an earthquake.

Live Load. The weight of people, furnishings, machines, and goods in or on a building. The vertical load superimposed by the use and occupancy of a building.

Load. A force that is applied to a body. A weight or force acting on a structure. Applied external force, such as gravity and wind.

Load Bearing. Supporting a superimposed weight or force.

Load, Factored. The load, multiplied by appropriate load factors, used to proportion members by the strength design method of this code.

Load-Bearing Wall. A wall designed and built to carry superimposed vertical and shear loads as opposed to nonload-bearing walls.

Lockset. A device installed in a door that has both a deadbolt and doorknob assembly.

Lookout. The end of a rafter, or the construction which projects beyond the sides of a house to support the eaves; also the projecting timbers at the gables which support the verge boards.

Louver. A construction of numerous sloping, closely spaced slats used to prevent the entry of rain or snow into a ventilating opening. A kind of window, generally in peaks of gables and the tops of towers, provided with horizontal slots which exclude rain and snow and allow ventilation.

Low-Lift Grouting. A method of constructing a reinforced masonry wall in which the wall is grouted in increments not higher than 4 feet.

Lumber. Wood members which are manufactured by sawing, resawing, passing lengthwise through standard planing machine, crosscutting to length, and matching, but without further manufacturing.

Lumen. A quantitative unit for the measurement of the flow of light energy.

Make-Up Air. Air brought into a building from outdoors through the ventilation system and that has not been previously circulated through the system.

Malleable Iron. Iron that can be hammered or bent without breaking.

Manhole. A hole through which a person may go to gain access to an underground or enclosed structure.

Manhole Watertight. A cover for a vertical access shaft that prevents the outside elements in.

Mansard. A roof shape consisting of two superimposed levels of hip roofs with the lower level at a steeper pitch.

Mantle. The main bulk of the earth between the crust and core, varying in depth from 40 to 3,480 kilometers.

Masonry. Brickwork, blockwork, and stonework.

Masonry Reinforcing. Lateral steel rods or mesh placed between courses of masonry units.

Mass. The property of an object that causes it to resist changes in its state of motion. This resistance is called inertia.

Mastic. A viscous, dough-like, adhesive substance; can be any of a large number of formulations for different purposes such as sealants, adhesives, glazing compounds, or roofing membranes.

Maximum Capable Earthquake. The maximum level of earthquake ground shaking which may ever be expected at the building site within the known geological framework. (In Seismic Zones 3 and 4), this intensity may be taken as the level of earthquake ground motion that has a 10 percent probability of being exceeded in a 100-year time period.

Mean Radiant Temperature. The weighted average of all radiating surface temperatures within one line of sight.

Mercury Fixture. A light fixture that has an electric discharge lamp that produces a blue-white light by creating an arc in mercury vapor enclosed in a tube or globe.

Mercury Switch. An electrical switch that has mercury enclosed in a vial to make a silent contact.

Mesh Slab. Welded-wire fabric in sheets or rolls to reinforce concrete slabs.

Millwork. All building materials, such as doors and windows, but not including floors, sidings and ceilings, made of wood produced in a planing mill.

Miter. The joint formed by two abutting pieces meeting at an angle.

Mixer, Colloidal. a mixer designed to produce colloidal grout.

Mixing Water. The water in freshly mixed sand-cement grout, mortar, or concrete, exclusive of any previously absorbed by the aggregate (e.g., water considered in the computation of the net water-cement ratio.)

Modulus of Deformation. A concept of modulus of elasticity expressed as a function of two time variables; strain in loaded concrete as a function of the age at which the load is initially applied and of the length of time the load is sustained.

Moisture Barrier. A membrane used to prevent the migration of liquid water through a floor or wall.

Molding. A strip of wood, plastic or plaster with an ornamental profile.

Molding Plaster. A fast-setting gypsum plaster used for the manufacture of cast ornament.

Moment. A force acting at a distance from a point in a structure so as to cause a tendency of the structure to rotate about that point. The act of a force to cause rotation about a given point or axis.

Moment Connection. A connection between two structural members that is highly resistant to rotation between the members, as differentiated from a pin connection, which allow rotation.

Moment Distribution. A method of structural analysis for continuous beams and rigid frames whereby successive converging corrections are made to an assumed set of moments until the desired precision is obtained; also known as the Hardy Cross method.

Moment Resisting Frame. A frame composed of rigid joints in which the members and joints resist both vertical and horizontal forces.

Moment, Positive. By usual sign convention, a beam which is bent downward (sagging), is considered to be subjected to positive bending.

Monolith. A body of plain or reinforced concrete cast or erected as a single integral mass or structure.

Monolithic Concrete. Concrete cast with no joints or as one piece.

Mortar. A mixture of cement paste and fine aggregate; in fresh concrete, the material occupying the interstices among particles of coarse aggregate; in masonry construction, mortar may contain masonry cement, or may contain hydraulic cement with lime (and possibly other admixtures) to afford greater plasticity and workability than are attainable with standard hydraulic cement mortar.

Mortarboard. The mortarboard is used as a table to hold mortar. It is usually 30" square.

Mortise. The hole which is to receive a tenon, or any hole cut into or through a piece by a chisel; generally of rectangular shape.

Mortise-and-Tenon. A join in which a tongue-like protrusion (tenon) on the end of one piece is tightly fitted into a rectangular slot (mortise) in the side of the other piece.

Mortised Joint. A joint made by cutting a hole or mortise, in one piece, and a tenon, or piece to fit the hole, upon the other.

Mud. A slang term for mortar.

Mullion. A vertical or horizontal bar between adjacent window or door units.

Muntin. The vertical member between two panels of the same piece of panel work. The vertical sash-bars separating the different panels of glass.

Natural Convection. Fluid motion of air caused by the temperature difference between the solid surface and the fluid with which it is in contact.

Natural Frequency. The constant frequency of a vibrating system in the state of natural oscillation.

Neat Cement. Hydraulic cement in the unhydrated state.

Needle Beam. A steel or wood beam threaded through a hole in a bearing wall and used to support the wall and its superimposed loads during underpinning of its foundation.

Negative Pressure. Condition that exists when less air is supplied to a space than is exhausted from the space, so the air pressure within that space is less than that in surrounding areas.

Neoprene. A type of synthetic rubber with outstanding oil resistance. Can be used for quick-setting, high strength adhesives.

Neutral Axis. The line on a member cross-section on which the bending moment is zero.

Nominal Size (Lumber). The commercial size designation of width and depth, in standard sawn lumber and glued-laminated lumber grades; larger than the standard net size of dressed lumber.

Nonaxial. In a direction not parallel to the long axis of a structural member.

Nonbearing. Not carrying a load.

Nosing. The projecting forward edge of a stair tread. The part of a stair tread which projects over the riser, or any similar projection; a term applied to the rounded edge of a board.

Notice of Completion. A written document, filed with the county in which the project is located, verifying that the project is complete and ready for occupancy. This document initiates the beginning of the last 30 days of the lien period.

Oil Switch. A switch or protector relay installed in a flue pipe, that will shut off a burner in case the stack does not come up to a predetermined temperature within 45 seconds after the motor starts.

Ornamental Metal. A detail that is added to a building constructed of metal, with the purpose of embellishment.

Outrigger Flagpole. A projecting pole run out from a main structure to provide additional stability or to support an extension.

Overhang Beam. A beam that is supported by two or more supports and has one or both ends projecting beyond the support.

P-Trap. A P-shaped device that prevents sewer air from escaping from a plumbing fixture, such as a sink.

Pad Bearing. A thick slab-type stone or precast concrete block placed under a structural member of a building to spread the load or weight evenly.

Panic Hardware. A mechanical device that opens a door automatically if pressure is exerted against the device from the interior of the building.

Paper and Wire. Tar paper and wire mesh (or metal lath) that are used as a backing for the installation of tile.

Paper Building. A generic term for felts, papers and sheet materials used in building applications.

Parapet. The region of an exterior wall that projects above the level of the roof.

Parging. Portland cement plaster applied over masonry to make it less permeable to water.

Parquet Floor. A floor covering laid out in a geometric design composed of small pieces of wood.

Particle Board. A building panel composed of small particles of wood bonded together under pressure.

Paver. A half-thickness brick used as finish flooring.

Paver, Stone. Blocks of rock processed by shaping, cutting or sizing, used for driveways and patios.

Pea Gravel. Screened gravel particles most of which would pass through a 3/8 inch (9.5mm) sieve.

Pedestal. A short compression member of reinforced concrete that is placed between a column and the footing to distribute the load to the footing.

Performance Bond. A bond, secured by the general contractor, which guarantees that the contract will be performed.

Perlite. Expanded volcanic rock, used as a lightweight aggregate in concrete and plaster, and as an insulating fill.

Photovoltaic. A process of conversion of sunlight into electricity.

Pier. Timber, concrete, or masonry supports for girders, posts, or arches. Intermediate supports for adjacent ends of two bridge spans. Structure extending outward from shore into water used as a dock for ship. Masonry supports, set independently of the main foundation.

Pilaster. A vertical, integral stiffening rib in a masonry or concrete wall.

Pile. A long, slender, piece of material driven into the ground to act as a foundation. A member embedded into the ground that supports vertical loads. Can be made of wood, steel or concrete.

Pile Cap. A thick slab of reinforced concrete poured across the top of a pile group to cause the group to act as a unit in supporting a column.

Pipe Cleanout. A pipe fitting placed in a drain waste (DWV) system in each horizontal section of drain for removing blockages.

Pipe, PVC. Polyvinyl chloride pipe used mainly for drain lines and is particularly resistant to chemicals.

Plaster. A cementitious material, usually based on gypsum or portland cement, which is applied to lath or masonry in paste form, to harden into a finish surface. A mixture of lime, hair, and sand, or of lime, cement, and sand, used to cover outside and inside wall surfaces.

Plaster of Paris. Pure calcined gypsum.

Plasterboard. A board used in large sheets as a backing or as a substitute for plaster in walls and consisting of fiberboard, paper, or felt, bonded to a hardened gypsum plaster core.

Plastic. In stress analysis, refers to stress/strain behavior beyond the elastic range. Plastic deformation usually implies some permanent shape change.

Plastic Laminate. Sheet material manufactured of multiple layers of paper with top layer of plastic usually 1/16 inch (1.59 mm) thick with decorative finish. Used to finish cabinets and casework. Plastic laminate may be used in flat sheets or heat formed bent, and adhered to single curved base material.

Plasticity. Property of a material to deform under load and to retain the deformation after the load is removed; usually implies that stress is not directly proportional to strain.

Plate. The top horizontal piece of the walls of a frame building upon which the roof rests.

Plate, Armor. A metal plate that is mounted usually not less than 36 inches high on the lower part of a door, to protect it from kicks and scratches.

Plate Cut. The cut in a rafter which rests upon the plate; sometimes called the seat cut.

Plate Girder. A large beam made up of steel plates, sometimes in combination with steel angles, welded, bolted or revitted together.

Plate Glass. Glass of high optical quality produced by grinding and polishing both faces of a glass sheet.

Platform. Horizontal surface occurring in stair at end of flight or between flights, either at floor level or between floors.

Plenum. Air compartment connected to a duct or ducts.

Plumb. Vertical, or perfectly straight up and down.

Plumb Cut. Any cut made in a vertical plane; the vertical cut at the top end of a rafter.

Plumbing. The act or process of installing in a building or structure the pipes, fixtures, or other apparatus for bringing in the water supply and removing liquid and water-borne wastes. The installed fixtures and piping of a building or structure.

Ply. A term used to denote a layer or thickness of building or roofing paper as two-ply, three-ply, etc.

Plywood. A wood panel composed of a number of layers of wood veneer bonded and glued together under pressure.

Plywood Shear Wall. Wall constructed of studs and plywood sheathing that in its own plane resists shear forces resulting from applied wind, earthquake or other transverse loads or provides frame stability.

Pneumatic System. Mechanical devices powered by compressed air.

Pointing Masonry. The act or process of applying mortar to a masonry surface joint after masonry has been laid, either as a means of finishing the joint or to repair a defective joint.

Porch. An ornamental entrance way.

Portland Cement. The element used as the binder in concrete, mortar, and stucco.

Post. A timber set on end to support a wall, girder, or other member of the structure.

Pour. To cast concrete; an increment of concrete casting carried out without interruption.

Precast. Concrete slabs, reinforced lintels, beams, columns and parts of walls and floors that are cast and cured in other than their final position.

Precast Concrete. Concrete cast and cured in a position other than its final position in the structure.

Prehung Door. A door that is hinged to its frame in a factory or shop.

Pressure Regulators. Automatic valves located between a compressor and evaporator outlet that is responsive to its own inlet pressure or to the evaporator or refrigerator temperature. It throttles the vapor flow when necessary to prevent the evaporator pressure from falling below a selected value.

Pressure-Treated Lumber. Lumber that has been impregnated with chemicals under pressure, for the purpose of retarding either decay or fire.

Prestressed Concrete. Concrete that has been pretensioned or post-tensioned.

Pretensioning. A method by which the design tensile force is applied to the steel reinforcing before the concrete is set.

Prism. An assemblage of masonry units and mortar with or without grout used as a test specimen for determining properties of the masonry.

Projecting Sash. A window with sashes that swing either inward or outward.

Proposal. The document submitted by the contractor to the owner for construction of the project, sometimes called "the bid".

Psychrometrics. A branch of physics dealing with the study of atmospheric conditions, specifically the relationships between moisture and air.

Pump, Sump. A small capacity pump that empties pits receiving sewage or liquid waste.

Purger, Air. A mechanical device that removes unwanted air by injecting an inert gas into a ductline, pipeline, container, space, or furnace.

Purlin. A timber supporting several rafters at one or more points, or the roof sheeting directly.

PVC Pipe. Polyvinyl chloride pipe used mainly for drain lines and is particularly resistant to chemicals.

Quarry Tile. A large clay floor tile, usually unglazed.

R-value. The number of minutes (seconds) required for 1 Btu (joule) to penetrate one square foot (square meter) of a material for each degree of temperature difference between the two sides of the material. The resistance of a material to the passage of heat. The reciprocal of conductors (1/c).

Rabbet. A corner cut out of an edge of a piece of wood.

Raceway. Any channel supporting and protecting electrical conductors, including conduits, wireways, surface metal raceway, cable trays, floor and ceiling raceways, busways and cable bus.

Rafter. A framing member that runs up and down the slope of a pitched roof. The beams that slope from the ridge of a roof to the eaves and make up the main body of the roof's framework.

Rafters, Common. Those which run square with the plate and extend to the ridge.

Rail. The horizontal members of the balustrade or panel work.

Rake. The sloping edge of a pitched roof. The trim of a building extending in an oblique line, as rake dado or molding.

Ranch Casing. An architectural style of exposed millwork enclosure of cased beams, posts, pipes, etc. and the exposed molding or lining around doors and windows.

Rapid Start Lamp. A lamp operated by a ballast that provides a low-voltage winding to preheat electrodes and initiate the arc without a starting switch or the application of high voltage.

Re-Entrainment. Situation that occurs when the air being exhausted from a building is immediately brought back into the system through the air intake and other openings in the building envelope.

Receptacle, Combination. An electrical fixture with an outlet for plugging in an electric appliance, along with an electric switch for operating another circuit.

Recessed Light Fixture. A light fixture installed in a suspended ceiling or a recess in a plaster ceiling.

Reciprocating Chiller. A compressor (single-acting) using pistons that are driven by a connecting rod from a crankshaft.

Record Drawings (As Built). A set of drawings prepared by the general contractor, which includes any revisions in the working drawings and specifications during construction, indicating how the project was actually constructed.

Recording Voltmeter. A device which records the continuity, power, grounding, voltage and resistance of electrical circuits.

Reducer. A trim unit used to reduce the radius of a bullnose or a cove to another radius or to a square.

Reducer, Copper. A pipe fitting which connects pipes of different sizes, manufactured from copper.

Reducer, Fuse. The act or process of welding a pipe coupling with one larger end than the other to a length of pipe.

Refraction. The bending of a light ray as it passes obliquely through a material.

Refractories. Heat-resistant non-metallic ceramic materials.

Refractory, Concrete. Concrete having refractory properties, and suitable for use at high temperatures (generally about 315 to 1315 C), in which the binding agent is a hydraulic cement.

Register. An opening to a room or space with a grille and a damper that forms the end of ductwork for the passage of conditioned air. The wall upon which the grille and damper are installed that forms the end of ductwork for the passage of conditioned air.

Reglet. A flat, narrow architectural molding.

Reglet Roof. A roof which has a flat, narrow architectural molding.

Reinforced Concrete. Concrete work into which steel bars have been embedded to impart tensile strength to the construction.

Reinforcement, Mesh. Welded-wire fabric and Welded-wire fabric reinforcement. Heavy wires, welded together and used as reinforcing mostly for slabs.

Relative Humidity. The ratio of the quantity of water vapor actually present to amount present in a saturated atmosphere at a given temperature; expressed as a percentage. The ratio of the actual vapor pressure of the air-vapor pressure to the pressure of saturated water vapor at the same dry-bulb temperature times 100..

Relief Valve. A pressure-activated valve which allows air or fluid to escape if its pressure becomes more excessive than the valve setting.

Resilience. The measurement of the absorption of dynamic energy by a structure without permanent deformation or fracture.

Resolving Forces. Replacing a force or forces with two or more other forces that yield the same effect on a structure as the original forces.

Resonance. Movement produced in an element as a result of movement added to its natural period of movement, which is the same.

Resultant. A force that will produce the same effect as two or more forces.

Retaining Wall. A wall that is designed to resist the lateral pressures of retained soil.

Return. The ending of a small splash wall or a wainscot at right angle to the major wall. The continuation of a molding or finish of any kind in a different direction.

Richter Scale. A logarithmic scale that is used to measure the magnitude of earthquakes.

Rigid Frame. Two columns and a beam or beams attached with moment connections; a moment-resisting building frame. The connections between the beam and columns are constructed so as to transmit moments.

Rigidity. Relative stiffness of a structure or element.

Riprap. A foundation or sustaining wall of stones placed together without order (as in deep water or on an embankment slope to prevent erosion).

Rise. The vertical distance through which anything rises, as the rise of a roof or stair.

Riser. A single vertical increment of a stair; the vertical face between two treads in a stair; a vertical run of plumbing, wiring or ductwork.

Riser Hanger. The horizontal member of a stair structure which supports the riser.

Rock Anchor. A post-tensioned rod or cable inserted into a rock formation for the purpose of tying it together.

Rock Caisson. A drilled, cylindrical foundation shaft filled with rock.

Rod Hanger. A rod for connecting pipe, gutters, or ceiling framework to a support.

Roof Bond. A legal guarantee that a roof installed is in accordance with specifications and will be repaired or replaced if it fails in a certain period of time due to normal weathering.

Room Resonance. The resonance of an enclosed space with reflective material, which depends in the relationship between the sound wavelength and the space dimensions.

Rowlock. A brick laid on its long edge, with its end exposed in the face of the wall.

Run. Horizontal dimension in a stair. The length of the horizontal projection of a piece such as a rafter when in position.

Running Bond. Brickwork consisting entirely of stretchers.

Rusticated Concrete. Beveled edges of concrete making the joints conspicuous.

Sabin. The unit of acoustic absorption. One sabin is the absorption of one square foot of perfect sound-absorbing material.

Safety Nosing. Stair nosing with abrasive non-slip surface flush with tread surface.

Safety Tread. Stair tread which is covered on top surface with abrasive or non-slip material.

Safing. Fire-resistant material inserted into a space between a curtain wall and a spandrel beam or column, to retard the passage of fire through the space.

Sag Pond. A pond occupying depression along a fault. The depression is normally due to uneven settling of the ground or other causes.

Salamander. A portable source of heat, customarily oil-burning, used to heat an enclosure around or over newly placed concrete to prevent the concrete from freezing.

Samples. Material samples requested by the architect of the general contractor or materials specified for the project.

Sandblasting. A method of scarifying the surface of concrete or masonry to provide a bondable surface. Compressed air is used to propel a stream of wet or dry sand onto the surface.

Sander-Grinder (Cutting Tool). In addition to sander and grinder attachment both uninstalled and installed tile. The cutting is done dry.

Sandwich Panel. A panel consisting of two outer faces of wood or metal, bonded to a core of insulating foam.

Sash. A frame that holds glass. The framework which holds the glass in a window.

Sash Bead. A strip with one edge molded, against which a sash slides.

Sash, Transom. The framework of a window over a door or window hinged for ventilation, that holds the glass in place.

Saturated Air. Air that contains all of the moisture it an hold. With saturated air, the dry-bulb, wet-bulb, and dew point temperatures are all equal.

Saw Cut. A cut in hardened concrete utilizing diamond or silicone-carbide blades or discs.

Sawed Joints. A joint cut in hardened concrete, generally not to the full depth of the member, by means of special equipment.

Scab. A short piece of lumber used to splice, or to prevent movement of two other pieces.

Scaffolding. A temporary structure for the support of deck forms, cartways, or workmen, or a combination of these such as an elevated platform for supporting workmen, tools, and materials; adjustable metal scaffolding is frequently adapted for shoring in concrete work.

Scantling. Lumber with a cross-section ranging from 2 by 4 inches to 4 by 4 inches.

Scarf Joint. A glued end connection between two pieces of wood, using a sloping cut to create a large surface for the glue bond, to allow it to develop the full tensile strength of the wood it connects.

Scarfing. A joint between two pieces of wood which allows them to be spliced lengthwise.

Scarifier. A piece of thin sheet metal with teeth or serrations cut in the edge. It is used to roughen fresh mortar surfaces to achieve a good bond for the tile. A scarifier also can be used to roughen the surface of concrete.

Scotia. A hollow molding used as a part of a cornice, and often under the nosing of a stair tread.

Scratch Coat. The first coat in a three-coat application of plaster.

Scratcher. Any serrated or sharply tined object that is used to roughen the surface of one coat of mortar to provide a mechanical key for the next coat.

Scratching. The application of a scratch coat and its combing with a scratcher.

Screed. To strike off mortar laying above the desired plane or shape.

Screed. A strip of wood, metal, or plaster that establishes the level to which concrete or plaster will be placed.

Screed Guide. Firmly established grade strips or side forms for unformed concrete which will guide the strikeoff in producing the desired plane or shape.

Scupper. An opening through which water can drain from the edge of a flat roof. An opening cut through a roof system, acting as a waterway so water can be discharged off the roof.

Section. A drawing showing the kind, arrangement, and proportions of the various parts of a structure. It is assumed that the structure is cut by a plane, and the section is the view gained by looking in one direction.

Seiche. A wave on the surface of water in an enclosed or semi-enclosed area (lake, bay or harbor).

Seismic. Relating to earthquakes.

Self-Furring Lath. Metal lath with dimples that space the lath away from the sheathing behind it to allow plaster to penetrate the lath.

Self-Tapping. Creates its own screw threads on the inside of a hole.

Septic Tank. A private sewage system, installed together with a leaching field, that collects sewage and allows the solid waste to settle to the bottom of an area while the liquid particles of the sewage drain into the leaching field area.

Service Disconnect (or, Main Switch). A means of disconnecting an entire building from electrical service.

Set. The condition reached by a cement paste, mortar, or concrete when it has lost plasticity to an arbitrary degree, usually measured in terms of resistance to penetration or deformation; initial set refers to first stiffening; final set refers to attainment of significant rigidity; also, strain remaining after removal of stress.

Setting Bed. The layer of mortar on which the tile is set. The final coat of mortar on a wall or ceiling also may be called a setting bed.

Shaft. An unbroken vertical passage through a multistory building, used for elevators, wiring, plumbing, ductwork, etc.

Shear Connector. Steel stud or strap, embedded within concrete slab, to transfer horizontal shear loads from slab to supporting structure.

Shear Panel. A vertical plane (wall) that resists lateral forces.

Shear Strength. The strength of an element to resist shear.

Shearwall. A wall designed to resist forces. A wall portion of a structural frame intended to resist lateral forces, such as earthquake, wind, and blast, acting in or parallel to the plane of the wall.

Sheathing. The rough covering applied to the outside of the roof, wall, or floor framing of a structure. Wall boards, roofing boards; generally applied to narrow boards laid with a space between them, according to the length of a shingle exposed to weather.

Shed. A building or dormer with a single pitched roof.

Sheet Flashing. A thin piece of treated metal placed in construction to direct the flow of water or to prevent water penetration.

Sheet Piling. Planking or sheeting made of concrete, timber, metal or steel that is driven in, interlocked or are tongue and grooved in close contact to provide a tight wall to resist the lateral pressure of water, adjacent earth or other materials.

Sheetrock. Plasterboard sheets.

Shell (Concrete). Concrete outside the transverse reinforcement confining the concrete.

Shell (Masonry). The outer portion of a hollow masonry unit as placed in masonry.

Shim. A thin piece of material placed between two components of a building to adjust their relative positions as they are assembled; to insert shims.

Shop Drawings. Drawings of specific items of the project provided by subcontractors.

Shop Painted. Coating(s) of paint applied in shop, usually a primer coat to protect metal from corrosion, which may or may not receive additional coats in the field.

Short-Circuiting. Situation that occurs when the supply air flows to exhaust registers before entering the breathing zone. To avoid short-circuiting, the supply air must be delivered at a temperature and velocity the results in mixing throughout the space.

Shotcrete. A low-slump concrete mixture deposited by being blown from a nozzle at high speed with a stream of compressed air.

Shower Pan. Terminology used in some areas for Waterproof membrane.

Shrinkage. The decrease in volume, or contraction, of a material by the escape of any volatile substance, or by a chemical or physical change in the material.

Shrinkage Cracking. Cracking of a structure or member due to failure in tension caused by external or internal restraints as reduction in moisture content develops, or as carbonation occurs, or both.

Sidelight. A tall, narrow window alongside a door.

Siding. The outside finish between the casings.

Sills. The horizontal timbers of a house which either rest upon the masonry foundations or, in the absence of such, form the foundation.

Simple Beam. A beam that is supported on two supports and where no bending is transferred from the beam to the support.

Single-Hung Window. A window with two overlapping sashes, the lower of which can slide vertically in tracks, and the upper of which is fixed.

Sister Joist. The reinforcement of a joist by nailing or attaching a stronger piece to a weaker one.

Sizing. Working material to the desired size; a coating of glue, shellac, or other substance applied to a surface to prepare it for painting or other method of finish.

Sleeper. A timber laid on the ground to support a floor joist.

Slenderness Ratio. The ratio of the unbraced length of the column to the least dimension.

Slip Coating. A ceramic material or mixture other than a glaze, applied to a ceramic body and fired to the maturity required to develop specified characteristics.

Slip Forming. Building multistory sitecast concrete walls with forms that rise up the wall as construction progresses.

Slot, Anchor. A groove in an object into which a fastener or connector is inserted to attach objects together.

Slot Cut. Description of a tile that has been cut to fit around pipes or switch boxes. This tile is usually in the shape of the letter H or the letter L.

Slump. A measure of consistency of freshly mixed concrete, mortar, or stucco equal to the subsidence measured.

Slump Cone. A mold in the form of the lateral surface of the frustum of a cone with a base diameter of 8 in. (203 mm), top diameter 4 in. (102 mm), and height 12 in. (305 mm), used for fabricate a specimen of freshly mixed concrete for the slump test; a cone 6 in. (152 mm) high is used for tests of freshly mixed mortar and stucco.

Slurry. A mixture of water and any finely divided insoluble material, such as portland cement, slag, or clay in suspension.

Sodium Light. An electric lamp that contains sodium vapor and electrodes between which a luminous discharge takes place and that is used for lighting highways.

Soffit. The underside of a part of member of a structure, such as a beam, stairway, or arch. The undersurface of a horizontal element of a building, especially the underside of a stair or a roof overhang.

Softwood Plywood Panel. Plywood manufactured from softwood species (coniferous trees with needlelike or scalelike (eaves) species such as Douglas fir, western larch, western hemlock Sitka spruce, white cedars, or redwood.

Soil and Waste Pipe. Either plastic, copper, cast iron or DWV drainage, water and vent.

Soil Gases. Gases that enter a building from the surrounding ground (e.g., radon, volatile organics, pesticides).

Soil Stack. A vertical pipe used to carry human waste from toilets.

Soldier. A brick laid on its end, with its narrow face toward the outside of the wall.

Sole Plate. The horizontal piece of dimension lumber at the bottom of the studs in a wall in a light frame building.

Sound Absorption Coefficient. The ratio of sound energy absorbed to the sound energy hitting a surface.

Sound Attenuation. A process in which sound is reduced as its energy is converted to motion or heat.

Sound Transmission Loss (STL). The decrease or attenuation in sound energy, in decibels, of airborne sound as it passes through a building material. In general, transmission loss increases with frequency, the higher the frequency, the greater the sound transmission loss.

Space Frame, Space Truss. A truss that spans with two-way action.

Spall. A fragment, usually in the shape of a flake, detached from a larger mass by a blow, by the action of weather, by pressure, or by expansion within the larger mass.

Span. The distance between supports for a beam, girder, truss, vault, arch or other horizontal structural device; to carry a load between supports. The distance between the bearings of a timber or arch.

Spandrel. That part of a wall between the head of a window and the sill of the window above it.

Specific Gravity. The ratio of the weight of any volume of a mass or substance to the weight of an equal volume of water at a given temperature. The specific gravity of a substance times the density of water equals the density of the substance.

Spiral Reinforcing. Continuously wound reinforcing in the form of a cylindrical helix.

Splash Block. A small precast block of concrete or plastic used to divert water at the bottom of a downspout.

Split Jamb. A door frame fabricated in two interlocking halves, to be installed from the opposite sides of an opening.

Split Ring. A connector for timbers consisting of a metal ring set in circular grooves in two pieces. The assembly is held together by bolts.

Spool Insulator. A device designed and used to support a conductor and electrically separate it from other conductors or objects.

Square. A tool used by mechanics to obtain accuracy; a term applied to a surface including 100 square feet.

Stability. The ability to remain unchanged; equilibrium, steady, constant. Ability to restore to original condition after being disturbed by some force.

Stability. Refers to the quality of being stable, or having the capability of remaining in position.

Stack Effect. Pressure-driven airflow produced by convection as heated air rises, creating a positive pressure area at the top of a building and a negative pressure area at the bottom of a building. The tack effect can overpower the mechanical system and disrupt ventilation and circulation in a building.

Stack Vent. A vent (pipe) that connects to a soil or waster stack above the highest fixture in the system.

Staging. Temporary scaffolding with platforms placed in and around a building to create working spaces.

Stainless Reglet. A groove in a wall to receive flashing which is constructed of an alloy of steel and has resistance to corrosion.

Stair Pan. A stair assembly constructed to hold precast or cast-in place masonry or stone in metal sheet pans at the treads.

Stair Tread, Metal-Pan Concrete Filled. Section formed from sheet metal to receive concrete fill which will function as stair tread.

Standing Seam. A sheet metal roofing seam that projects at right angles to the plane of the roof.

Standing-Seam Roof. A sheet metal roof system that has a roofing seam that projects at right angles to the plane of the roof.

Standpipe. A pipe that extends the full height of a building, used to provide water exclusively for the fighting of fires. A dry standpipe does not have water directly connected to it. A wet standpipe is directly connected to a water supply. This pipe is usually located in a stairway.

Staple. Double pointed, U-shaped piece of metal used for same purposes as nails, but providing additional head holding power.

Starter. A device that insures that a motor does not receive too high a current when starting up.

Static. State of being at rest, having no motion.

Steam Curing. Curing of concrete or mortar in water vapor at atmospheric or higher pressures and at temperatures between about 100° and 420° F (40° and 215° C).

Steel Structural. Steel that is rolled in a variety of shapes and manufactured for use as structural load-bearing members.

Steel Tread. The horizontal part of a stair system, manufactured from steel.

Stiffener Plate. A steel plate attached to a structural member to support it against heavy localized loadings or stresses.

Stiffness. The quality of resistance to deformation on the part of a material, a component member of a structure, or the whole structure.

Stile. A vertical framing member in a panel door.

Still Water. A part of a stream where the gradient is so gentle that no current is visible.

Stirrup. A vertical loop of steel bar used to reinforce a concrete beam against diagonal tension forces.

Stirrup-Tie. A stirrup that forms a complete loop, as differentiated from a U-stirrup, which has an open top.

Storm Window. A sash added to the outside of a window in winter to increase its thermal resistance and decrease air infiltration.

Straightedge. A straight piece of lumber that is used to rod mortar and to align tile.

Strain. Change in shape of a material due to stress.

Strap Channel. A U-shaped or L-shaped iron plate for connecting two or more timbers.

Strength Design. A design theory used for most reinforced concrete designs. A design in which members are designed to fail. Safety is not provided by limiting stresses, but by using a factored load that is greater than the actual load.

Strength Reduction Factor. A factor introduced into the calculation of strength design in reinforced concrete, which increases actual loading, providing an added factor of safety.

Stress. The internal force of a body that resists external force.

Stretcher. A brick or masonry unit laid in its most usual position, with the broadest surface of the unit horizontal and the length of the unit parallel to the surface of the wall.

Striking Joints. A process of removing excess grout from the joints by wiping with a sponge or cloth or scraping with a curved instrument.

Stringer. The sloping wood or steel member supporting the treads of a stair. A long horizontal timber in a structure supporting a floor.

Structural - Use Panel Diaphragm. Structural-use panel sheathing on floors, roofs, or walls which provides shear strength to resist wind and earthquake loads.

Structural Bond. The interlocking pattern of masonry units used to tie two or more wythes together in a wall.

Structural Diaphragms. Structural members, such as floor and roof slabs, which transmit internal forces to lateral-force-resisting members.

Structure. That which gives form to something and works to resist changes in the form due to the action of various forces.

Structure Borne Sound. A condition in which the sound waves are carried by a solid material.

Strut. A compression member, a column, usually implying that it can be placed at any angle, not just vertically.

Stucco. A cement plaster used for coating exterior walls and other exterior surfaces of buildings. Portland cement plaster used as an exterior cladding or siding material. A fine plaster used for interior decoration and fine work.

Stud. Vertical member of appropriate size (2x4 to 4x10 in.) (50x100 to 100x250 mm) and spacing 16in to 30 in.) (400 to 750 mm) to support sheathing of concrete forms; also a headed steel device used to anchor steel plates or shapes to concrete members. One of a set of small vertical elements, usually wood, used to produce a frame wall. An upright beam in the framework of a building.

Studding. The framework of a partition or the wall of a house; usually referred to as 2 by 4's.

Sub-Flooring. Certain materials like plywood, that is mounted to the floor joints of a building or structure, onto which the walls and finished floor is attached.

Subdiaphragm. A portion of a larger wood diaphragm designed to anchor and transfer local forces to primary diaphragm struts and the main diaphragm.

Subduction. The sinking of a plate under an overriding plate in a convergence zone.

Subfloor. A wood floor which is laid over the floor joists and on which the finished floor is laid.

Subpurlin. A very small roof framing member that spans between joists and purlins.

Substrate. The underlying support for the ceramic tile installation.

Surveying. A branch of applied mathematics, including geometry and trigonometry, that aids in determining and delineating the form, extent and position of land.

Suspended Ceiling. A finish ceiling that is hung on wires from the structure above.

Suspended Structure. A structure supported principally by tension members or carrying its loads principally in tension.

Swale Excavation. The digging up of low-lying land such as a small meadow, swamp, or marshy depression.

Switchgear (Switchboard). A freestanding assembly including primary (disconnect) switches, secondary (feeder) switches, and overcurrent protection device (fuses and circuit breakers).

T&G Siding. Tongue and groove exterior siding.

Tack Coat. Application of material made from asphalt on old surface to insure its bond to new construction.

Take-Off Man. Someone who can read blueprints and is familiar with the specifications. This person makes details concerning the project after gathering the necessary information and then the estimator estimates the labor, material quantities, and special items needed to complete the job.

Tapping Valve. A device to open or close a duct, pipe, or other passage, or to regulate flow which has been pierced by another device for tapping into the flow.

Tarpaulin. A waterproofed canvas or other material used for protecting athletic fields, goods or other exposed objects or areas.

Tee. A metal or precast concrete member with a cross section resembling the letter "T".

Tendon. A steel strand used for prestressing a concrete member.

Tensile Strength. The pulling force necessary to break a given specimen divided by the cross sectional area. Units given in lbs./in.2 (P.S.I.). It measures the resistance of a material to stretching without rupture. Normally is not used with reference to elastic materials which recover after elongation.

Tension. Stress which tends to elongate a member.

Tension Ring. A structural element, forming a closed curve in plan, which is in tension because of the action of the test of the structure.

Terminal Adapters. Electrical fittings attached to the end of a conductor or to a piece of equipment for taking power from an outlet in a way for which it was not designed.

Terminal Box. A box, usually with a removable cover, that contains leads from electrical equipment ready for connection to a power source.

Terne. An allow of lead and tin, used to coat sheets of carbon steel or stainless steel for use as metal roofing sheet.

Terra Cotta. Hard baked clayware, including tile, of variable color, averaging reddish red-yellow in hue and of high saturation.

Terrazzo. A finish floor material consisting of concrete with an aggregate of marble chips selected for size and color, which is ground and polished smooth after curing.

Test Pile. To measure the deviation of a pile in the horizontal and vertical planes.

Thermal Conductivity. Ability of a material to conduct heat; physical constant for quantity of heat that passes through unit volume of a substance in unit of time when difference in temperature of two opposite faces is one degree.

Thermal Lag Factor. The time interval between the time heat enters a material at one side and exits at the other side.

Thermodynamics. The science dealing with the relationship between heat and other forms of energy.

Thermoplastic. Having the property of softening when heated and rehardening when cooled.

Thermostat. An automatic device for regulating the supply of gas or electricity to a heating apparatus. A device for actuating fire alarms or for controlling automatic sprinklers.

Thin-set. A term used to describe the bonding of tile with suitable materials applied approximately 1/8" thick.

Threshold. The beveled piece over which the door swings; sometimes called a carpet strip.

Thrust. A lateral or inclined force resulting from the structural action of an arch, vault, dome, suspension structure, or rigid frame.

Tie. A device for holding two part of a construction together, a structural device that acts in tension.

Tie Beam. A reinforced concrete beam cast as part of a masonry wall, whose primary purpose is to hold the wall together, especially against seismic loads, or cast between a number of isolated foundation elements to maintain their relative positions.

Tie Rod. A steel rod that acts in tension.

Tie Strap. A metal plate that fastens two parts together as a post, rod or beam.

Tie Wire. The 18-gauge galvanized wire used in construction work.

Tied Column. A square or rectangular reinforced concrete column containing longitudinal reinforcing and lateral ties.

Tile. A fired clay product that is thin in cross section as compared to a brick, either a thin, flat element (ceramic tile or quarry tile), a thin, curved element (roofing tile), or a hollow element with thin walls.

Timber. Lumber with cross-section over 4 by 6 inches, such as posts, sills, and girders.

To the Weather. A term applied to the projecting of shingles or siding beyond the course above.

Toe Plate. A metal bar fastened to the outer edge of a grating, rear of a tread, or bottom rail of a door.

Tongue and Groove. A type of lumber or precast concrete pile having mated projecting and grooved edges to provide a tight fit, abbreviated "T & G".

Top Plate. The horizontal member at the top of a stud wall. Piece of lumber supporting ends of rafters.

Topping, Concrete. Concrete layer placed to form a floor surface on a concrete base.

Torque. Twisting action; moment.

Torsion. The rotation of a diaphragm caused by lateral forces and whose center of mass does not coincide with the center of rigidity.

Tower Cooling. A device usually placed on a roof for cooling water used in air conditioning. A structure through which heated water is circulated.

Trammel Bar. A trammel bar, which is easy to construct, is more accurate than many other layout tools. It is used to erect perpendicular lines and to bisect angles. The tile setter can make a trammel bar from a stick of a size that is suitable for the particular job.

Transfer. That act of transferring stress in prestressing tendons from jacks or pretensioning bed to concrete member.

Transformer. A device that changes, or transforms, alternating current from one voltage to another.

Transit-Mixed Concrete. Concrete mixed in a drum on the back of a truck as it is transported to the building code.

Translate. To move from one place to another, without rotation. Motion of a body along a line without rotation or turning.

Transom. A transverse piece in a structure, lintel. A horizontal crossbar in a window, over a door, or between a door and a window or a fanlight above it. A window above a door or other window built on and commonly hinged to a transom.

Transverse. Across, at right angles to the main axis of a structural member.

Trap. Located at a plumbing fixture, designed to hold a quantity of water that prevents gasses in the sewer system from entering a room.

Tread. One of the horizontal planes of a stair or step.

Tremie. A large funnel with a tube attached, used to deliver concrete into deep forms or beneath water or slurry.

Trench. A long and narrow deep trough in the sea floor; interpreted as marking the line along which a plate bends down into a subduction zone.

Trim. A term sometimes applied to outside or interior finished woodwork and the finish around openings.

Trimmer. The beam or floor joist into which a header is framed.

Troffer. A channel-like enclosure for light sources.

Trowel Finish. The final finish of concrete, plaster, stucco, etc., by the use of a hand trowel.

Truss. A triangular arrangement of structural members that reduces nonaxial forces on the truss to a set of axial forces in the members. Structural framework of triangular units for supporting loads over long spans.

Tsunami. A sea wave produced by a large displacement of the ocean bottom, the result of earthquakes or volcanic activity.

TWA. Time-weighted Average. In air sampling, this refers to the average air concentration of contaminants during a particular sampling period.

Two-Way Action. Bending of a slab or deck in which bending stresses are approximately equal in the two principal directions of the structure.

Two-Way Concrete Joist System. A reinforced concrete framing system in which columns directly support an orthogonal grid of intersecting joists.

U Bolt. A U-shaped, bent iron bar that has bolts and threads at both ends.

UL. Underwriters Laboratories, Inc., 333 Pfingsten Road, Northbrook, Illinois 60062, (708) 272-8800.

Unbonded Construction. Post-tensioned concrete construction in which the tendons are not grouted to the surrounding concrete.

Undercourse. A course of shingles laid beneath an exposed course of shingles at the lower edge of a wall or roof, in order to provide a waterproof layer behind the joints in the exposed course.

Underdrain. Perforated pipe drain installed in a wedge of stone under a slab to intercept ground water and drain it off.

Underlayment. A layer of hardboard, particleboard, plywood, mastic with latex binders, mastic with asphalt binders, mastic with polyvinyl-acetate, etc., placed to cover subfloor irregularities, to absorb the movement of wood subfloors and to provide a smooth surface for the finish material.

Union Brass. A pipe fitting constructed of brass, used to join two pipes without turning either pipe.

Union Hub. A pipe fitting used to join two pipes without turning either pipe, with one end of the fitting enlarged into a bell or socket.

Unit Substation. A freestanding assembly including a transformer, switchgear and meter(s).

Unit-and-Mullion System. A curtain wall system consisting of prefabricated panel units secured with site-applied mullions.

Upside-Down Roof. A membrane roof assembly in which the thermal insulation lies above the membrane.

Utility Pole. A vertical pole with cross arms, where power company service drops its wires to a service switch on a building or structure.

Valley. A trough formed by the intersection of two roof slopes.

Valley Rafter. A diagonal rafter that supports a roof valley.

Vapor Barrier. Waterproof membrane placed under concrete floor slabs that are placed on grade.

Vapor Retarder. A layer of material intended to obstruct the passage of water vapor through a building assembly. Also called, less accurately, vapor barrier. Sealing material place between building components or materials to arrest movement of moisture within building enclosure assembly.

Vault. An arched surface. An arch translated along an axis normal to the plane of its centerline curve.

Veneer, Ashlar. An ornamental or protective facing of masonry composed of squared stones.

Vent, Foundation. Opening in foundation wall to provide natural ventilation to foundation crawl spaces.

Vent Soffit. An opening under the eaves of a roof used to allow air to flow into the attic or the space below the roof sheathing.

Vestibule. An entrance to a house; usually enclosed.

Vinyl Sheet. The rolled form of vinyl.

Vision Panel. Glass placed in an opening of a door.

Vitreous. That degree of vitrification evidence by low water absorption. Note: The term vitreous generally signifies less than 0.5% absorption for fixtures, except for floor and wall tile and low-voltage electrical porcelain which are considered vitreous up to 3.0% water absorption.

Vitreous Tile. Tile with water absorption of more than 0.5%, but not more than 3.0%.

Vitrification. The progressive reduction in porosity of a ceramic composition as a result of heat treatment, or the process involved.

Vitrified Clay Pipe. Pipes used especially for underground drainage, that are made of clay baked hard and then glazed so they are impervious to water.

Void. An unfilled space in a material of trapped air or other gas.

Volt. Electricity is caused by creating a higher pressure electric charge at one point in a conductor than at another. This potential difference is called voltage, or volt.

Waferboard. A building panel made by bonding together large, flat flakes of wood.

Waffle Slab. A two-way concrete joist system. Two-way slab or flat slab made up of a double system of narrow ribs or joists, usually at right angles to each other, forming a pattern of waffle-like coffers.

Wainscoting. A wall facing, usually of wood, cut stone, or ceramic tile, that is carried only part way up a wall. Matched boarding or panel work covering the lower portion of a wall.

Wale. A horizontal beam.

Wall. A member, usually vertical, used to enclose or separate spaces.

Wall Tie. A mechanical metal fastener which connects wythes of masonry to each other or to other materials.

Waste Stack. A vertical pipe that carries liquids other than human waste.

Water Absorption. The ability to take up and retain water.

Water Cooled Condenser. A condenser in which water is normally circulated through a cooling tower through which heat is distributed to the atmosphere.

Water Hammer. Noise, in a water pipe, occurring when air is trapped in the pipe and collides with the pipe wall at a change in the direction of the pipe.

Water Table. The level at which the pressure of water in the soil is equal to atmospheric pressure; effectively, the level to which ground water will fill an excavation. The finish at the bottom of a house which carries water away from the foundation.

Water Table Molding. A projection on the bottom of an exterior wall to prevent rain or water from seeping through to the wall below.

Water Vapor. Water in its gaseous phase.

Waterproofing. The act or process of making something waterproof. A coating capable of imparting waterproofness.

Waterstop. A synthetic rubber strip used to seal joints in concrete foundation walls.

Wearing Course. A topping or surface treatment to increase the resistance of a concrete pavement or slab to abrasion.

Weather Seal. A flanged channel installed on the top of an exterior door.

Weathered Joint. A mortar joint finished in a sloping, planar profile that tends to shed water to the outside of the wall.

Weatherstrip. A ribbon of resilient material used to reduce air infiltration through the crack around a sash or door.

Web. In a roller or built-up steel beam, the vertical plate connecting the top and bottom flanges.

Web (Masonry). An interior solid portion of a hollow-masonry unit as placed in masonry.

Weep Hole. A small opening, the purpose of which is to permit drainage of water that accumulates inside a building component.

Well. A pit or hole sunk into the earth to reach a supply of water. An open space extending vertically through floors of a structure.

Wellpoint. A perforated pipe surrounded by sand to permit the pumping of ground water.

Wellpoint System. A series of vertical pipes in the ground connected to a header and pump to drain marshy areas or to control ground seepage.

Wheel Barrow. A small vehicle with handles and one or more wheels used for carrying small loads.

Wind ("i" Pronounced as in "Kind"). A term used to describe the surface of a board when twisted (winding) or when resting upon two diagonally opposite corners, if laid upon a perfectly flat surface.

Wind Drift. Horizontal deflection of a frame caused by wind forces.

Wind Load. A load on a building caused by wind pressure.

Wind Uplift. Upward forces on a structure caused by negative aerodynamic pressures that result from certain wind conditions.

Winder. A stair tread that is wider at one end than at the other.

Window Well. Recess created in grade outside window located at or below grade to allow for natural light to reach window, often created by use of corrugated metal in half-round shape.

Wireway. A sheet metal trough with hinge or removable cover to carry up to 30 cables.

Wobble Friction. In prestressed concrete, is friction caused by unintended deviation of prestressing sheath or duct from its specified profile.

Wood Base. Wood strip applied to base of wall to protect wall surface and finish intersection of wall and floor.

Wood Fascia. Flat wood member of cornice or other finish, generally board of cornice to which gutter is secured.

Wood Float. The wood float is sometimes used in place of the flat trowel for floating mortar. It is good for smoothing small irregularities left on the mortar bed, working the surface of the mortar before troweling on the pure coat, or compacting floor and deck mortar.

Wood Frame. Floors, roofs, exterior and bearing walls of a building or structure constructed only with wood.

Wood Nailer. Strip of wood attached to steel or concrete to facilitate making nailed connections.

Wood Riser. The vertical wood board under the tread in a stairway system.

Wood Roof Nailer. Wood strip (usually in plane of roof insulation) secured to structural roof deck used for securing roofing membrane.

Wood Structural Panel. A structural panel product composed primarily of wood. Wood structural panels include all-veneer plywood, composite panels containing a combination of veneer and wood-based material, and mat-formed panels such as oriented strand board and waferboard.

Workability. The property of freshly mixed concrete or mortar which determines the ease and homogeneity with which it can be mixed, placed, compacted, and finished.

Working drawings. Drawings of the project used during construction.

Working Stress. The maximum permissible stress used in the design of a member.

Working Stress Design. A design theory that is used in the design of concrete and masonry members. Safety is provided by limiting allowable stresses.

Wye. A pipe fitting which joins three pipes at a 45 degree angle.

Wythe. A vertical layer of masonry one masonry unit thick. (Rhymes with "scythe" and "tithe".)

Yield Point. The point at which a material deforms with no increase in load. The stress at which a material ceases to deform in a fully elastic manner.

Yield Strength. The stress at which a material ceases to deform in a fully elastic manner.

Z-Tie Wall. A Z-shaped bar used as a support bracket.

Zero-Slump Concrete. A concrete mixed with so little water that it has a slump of zero.

A

B

C

D

W